Pan-American Hitchhiker

Joseph Nanko—hiker—age 24.
(Or, El Andarin—"The Walker"—as they called him.)

Pan-American Hitchhiker

El Andarin—Norte Americano
(The Walker—North American)

Joseph Nanko

VANTAGE PRESS
New York

Published by Vantage Press, Inc.
516 West 34th Street, New York, New York 10001

Manufactured in the United States of America
ISBN: 0-533-14402-7

Library of Congress Catalog Card No.: 2002093669

0 9 8 7 6 5 4 3 2 1

After reading what's left of my diary after fifty-two years, I was amazed at the number of times the truckers have paid for my meals. I, therefore, wish to dedicate this book to them, the many seamen who invited me aboard for lodging and meals, and others who shared my company. As they say in Spanish, *muchas gracias!*

I also wish to thank my wife, Marie, and our five children for their support. They are Kenneth, Linda, Colleen, Michael, and Juanita.

"MADE SUPREME"

The author's brothers: John (at left), age 24, and Michael, age 21.

I would also like to dedicate this book in loving memory of my two brothers who died while in the service: my older brothers, John, who was killed by machine gun fire in Cologne, Germany, on either February 26 or 27, 1945, and my other brother, Michael, who died of his wounds and yellow jaundice in New Guinea on July 17, 1945.

Contents

Preface

Hitchhiking is just another American way of life, like it or not.

Most every American boy has hitchhiked a little or a lot, whether to or from school or cross-country to see what kind of country he has to fight for.

Hitchhiking to me is symbolic of the great freedom that we enjoy in these United States.

Probably no book has ever been written as to how hitchhiking came about or why it has become so popular in the States.

Every American and Canadian knows what a hitchhiker is, but the Spanish dictionary has no word for it; neither do the people have a word for it. The only word near it is an *"andarin,"* which means walker.

The three reasons most people hitchhike are: (1) because they haven't got much money, but still must get to their destination, (2) others hitchhike sometimes because it is faster than public buses or trains and don't have to suffer inconvenience of crowded transportation, and (3) still there are those who hitchhike for adventure, of meeting strange people and circumstances.

Hitchhiking is allowed in practically all parts of the U.S., Canada and Alaska, except the Alcan Highway; it is a military highway, but there are exceptions to the rules there also.

In Yukon Territory, Canada:

One is not allowed to stand along the highway, but must catch his ride within the town. When Canadian officials learn there is a hitchhiker in town, they find him and give him six hours to catch a ride or face deportation.

In Alaska, one hitchhikes on all highways freely.

In all Central and South America, hitchhiking is unknown. When one gets a lift, the driver of the vehicle naturally expects to be paid.

Most vehicles stop for people along the road; they seldom pass a man who raises his palm to say Stop. But it is a rare occasion for the driver to give the man a lift, if the man has no money to pay.

I've seen drivers stop many times, and ask the hiker, "How much will you pay?" The hiker offers little or nothing. The driver says, "Sorry" and drives off. It's only on rare occasions I've seen natives or Indians get free rides.

The Latins have a peculiar custom; I'm thankful for it. They call me an *"Andarin Extranjero"* (foreign walker) and say foreign walkers do not have to pay for rides. They spot me at once for a foreigner because of my light features, blond hair, and strange garb.

The difference between an *"Andarin"* and an American hitchhiker is that the Spanish glorify an *"Andarin."*

An *Andarin* is a traveler who has traveled far, had many girls, and dresses in beautiful form-fitting clothes. He often has medals on his chest and carries a book. In this book he has the autographs of important people he has met and the stamps and seals of distant lands. A successful *"Andarin"* has pride and only lets prominent people sign his book. He has only to present his book and medals to receive money, lodging, food or transportation.

Many times old ladies and men said to me, "You do not dress like an *Andarin;* your clothes are too simple and drab."

Only one country in South American doesn't believe in this custom of generosity to the traveler (*Andarin*). It's Bolivia. There the drivers say, "*Andarin* or no *Andarin,* you pay."

Many were the times I offered money to the drivers, sometimes on buses and trains; they refused it. They said, 'You are a foreign walker, you don't pay anything." Yet many times they knew I was an American.

A number of times, prominent or influential people asked to sign my book, including army officials. They sometimes felt rebuked when I said I didn't carry any. They secretly believed that they weren't good or high enough to sign my book and that I kept it secretly hidden.

Many times I wished I'd carried a book to prevent embarrassing situations and I could easily have started a collection of honorable names. Only I could not see bumming food or lodging or money. I pray so I never have to.

In Latin America, the people do not understand the sign of the thumb; there one must use the palm. It's a disagreeable change, but changes must be made to advance in those countries.

Then also one cannot expect a lot of comfort. In 9,186 miles I've hitchhiked in South America, most of it was in trucks.

South America has a lot of new cars, but you seldom see them on the highway. You find them in the hub of the city. So now I can say, "I went trucking down the Andes."

In the thousands of dusty bumpy miles I've traveled by road, till my stomach hurt, I can only say to the American public: "Be grateful for our highways and engineers; we have the best ever. Our highways in the States are like riding clouds in the sky."

Argentina has a macadam road that stretches form Buenos Aires to the Cordilleras on the Chilean border. They are very proud of it, but it's only second class in comparison to the U.S.

Peru likewise has a road along the coast. It stretches from the Ecuadorian border to Arequipa, near the Chilean border. It is approximately 1,500 miles long. They are proud of it also, but still realize it's only second class to the U.S.

El Salvador has a paved road also from the border of Guatemala to San Miguel, a bit south of the capital.

Mexico also had some paved roads chiefly from the capital (Mexico City) to the U.S. border on the north. South of the capital, paved only a few hours drive.

People ask, "Why do I hitchhike?" I hitchhike, not because I haven't got the money, but merely so I can get a thorough understanding of the country, its people and adventure.

After I quit my job as aviation mechanic in Maiquetía, Venezuela, my boss said he could arrange a free trip to Bogotá, Colombia, a distance of 1,185 miles to help me out on my journey. Because of satisfactory services rendered, I was more or less entitled to a free trip.

I refused the free plane ride. I would prefer risking the dangers of the road, of wild animals, and wild Indians that I heard stories about.

Many people ask, "How did I get started in this hitchhiking business?"

It all started after the war's end. I had been laid off, jobs were scarce, and in the long lines waiting to be interviewed at the unemployment offices were thousands of war veterans. I felt I didn't have a chance.

I was no war veteran. I had a chance to stay out, and I took it. Now I regret that I stayed out, for if a fellow is not a veteran, he runs into difficulties.

Specialized aviation engine testers were no longer needed and army mechanics got the civilian jobs.

Also, many of my buddies returned and had stories to tell about distant lands. I could only sit and listen. I have always been a story-teller myself, even in school. I would listen to "Gangbusters" on the radio and give it for public-speaking talks in class. I'd talk the entire one-hour period, while the teacher took a break and left the room.

My savings gone, I had to sell my car for necessities. To top it off, I lost my girl. I was in love with her, but she did not wish to see me any more.

The reason for the breakup is unknown. Some of my buddies had told her stories that I was no good and not her type.

In the six months we had gone together, we were thoroughly happy. We both loved sports, and she followed me well in bowling, skating, dancing, horseback riding, etc.

When I lost her, I had no desire to remain, I would go abroad. I would go to Alaska. That was how I got started. I had a great fear of Alaska; it was assumed to be full of wild Indians. I had never read up on the true facts. Many of the tales I heard were false, but still I found much pleasure and adventure in that distant land of ours.

I returned from Alaska six months later only because my sister was getting married in colorful European custom. There would be friends and relations from many states attending the wedding.

Having lost two brothers in the war, I believed it only human to be present. Why should three be absent? It would cheer my sister, Mom and Dad if I came home.

Ten days after the wedding, I found the country in a mess worse than before. Jobs were scarce, the food shortage no laughing matter. I was actually starving, I believe.

I went to the Frigidaire ten times a day, opened it unconsciously, and found only beer. I complained to Mom. She said, "Son, what can I do? There is no meat in the butcher shop; then how can I buy it if there isn't any?"

I went to Detroit for a week, hopefully called on my love. She talked for about an hour; still she did not wish to see me.

The unemployment lines were as long as ever. Winter wasn't far away. I decided I'd go to Panama or South America for the winter and try my fortunes.

I believed in the Canal Zone, being a territory of the U.S. like Alaska, I'd be able to find lots of work and there would be no food shortage either. Territories of the U.S. seemed to have more of everything than the States.

I did not plan to hitchhike to Panama. It came accidentally. I hitchhiked to Galveston, Texas.

I intended to work my way down aboard a merchant ship, but I didn't have seaman's papers and there were a lot of seamen on the beach waiting for a ship.

I wanted to fly to Panama. The ticket agent with P.A.A. asked what was the purpose of my trip.

I said, "I hope to get a job there."

"Sorry," he replied. "Unless you have permission from the commanding officer there, we cannot sell you a ticket."

I said, "I'll go as a tourist then."

"Sorry," he replied, "we know your reason."

I had to get a job while I waited for my money to come from the Bank of Fairbanks, Alaska.

I succeeded in getting a job as a longshoreman in Texas City.

My money came from Fairbanks, and I now had a choice of hitchhiking to Panama or waiting several weeks for a boat and paying a high fare.

I decided to hitchhike, and many nights I didn't sleep well as I had been told terrible stories about ruthless Mexican cutthroats. I worried a bit.

Weeks later in Panama, I'd been told by several, "Either you have a lot of nerve or you're plain nuts."

I succeeded in getting a job in the Canal Zone, after eight days trying.

Panamanians, Colombians, Ecuardorians said, "You're American, you'll get a job easy." But it wasn't so easy. The U.S. government had an economy drive on and were laying off army and navy personnel.

I finally got a job as a time checker on the lock overhaul at Gatun.

I did not make much money, but the locks are world famous, and I got to explore the tunnels, culverts, chambers, pits, etc. It was exciting and dangerous work going into the culverts. They are as large as subway tunnels in New York.

They are dark, musty, and water comes to the knees and waist from bad leaks. I had to go below to check on the "silver" help (native workers).

I worked four months in the Canal Zone and had a wonderful time. I saved up enough money to go to Venezuela.

I heard terrible stories about wild Indians there also, and I was shown a picture of a white man with an arrow in his back, shot while at work in Venezuela.

I could not go by road to Venezuela. There is none to Colombia from Panama.

I decided to fly. I arrived in Maracaibo. After four days, I was unsuccessful in getting a job with the oil companies. I had come as a tourist.

Venezuela only wants technicians, engineers, or fellows who can do something that Venezuelans can't do.

Venezuela was short of aviation mechanics and I succeeded in getting a job at the airport in Maiquetia, with Taca.

I worked nine months in Venezuela and I saved my money.

I'd tried life in the Venezuelan manner for a couple of months; then I tried life with Americans in Venezuela.

Both have been very interesting.

I worked with mostly Latins from Peru, Colombia, Costa Rica, Nicaragua, Guatemala, and Venezuela. My *Jefe* (bosses) were Americans.

I learned quite a bit of Spanish working with these fellows.

Working with us also were a lot of immigrants from Europe. Polish, Italian, Portuguese, German. Many were war veterans.

Many interesting things happened during my stay. Twice I got into jail and twice I got into fights.

Xmas and New Years are strange.

Some of my latin friends gave me addresses to look up their brothers, sisters, and families when I passed through their countries. These came in handy, nicely on my trip, so that life did not seem too dull.

When I started on the trip around South America, I told Bearnie, a Polish ex-paratrooper with the R.A.F., that I was a bit scared.

He said, "Now you know what a paratrooper feels like, when he has to jump."

I intended to hitchhike to Colombia, Ecuador, Peru, Bolivia, Chile, Argentina, Uruguay, and to Rio de Janeiro, Brazil. After that I would take a steamer home. I'd hitched all the way to Rio, I'd gone over the Pan-American road, that is merely under study and no car can get through.

I'd walked and gone on horseback through places where a white man has seldom been seen in Ecuador.

I carried no gun or knife and I'd been warned by native women and men that I'd be killed if I went through.

As I look back on my journey, I'd never do it alone again or without a gun for protection.

It actually took me seventy-nine days and three nights to make the journey from Caracas, Venezuela, to Rio de Janeiro at a cost of $61. for transportation. This covered about 9,186 miles approximately.

At times I had to pay for guides and mules, and when bitter cold or "dead" highways came my way, I'd have to take a bus or train. Only for this I paid $61.

From Rio de Janeiro, Brazil, I got the notion to go up the Amazon River. I believed it to be very wild also.

I purchased a ticket on the *Pocone,* a Brazilian steamer.

On it I was surprised to find three English-speaking ladies.

Two were American, the third a Canadian.

Margie was from the Canadian Embassy, Elinore from the American, and Janie was a writer traveling third class.

We all felt sorry for Janie, but she was a tough girl from Frisco who hoped to travel around the world as cheap as she could.

Our boat trip lasted three weeks to Manaus, one-thousand miles up the Amazon. We did not see black faces peering out of the jungle and found cities with taxicabs, streetcars, and opera houses. We wanted to demand our money back.

The American Consul and several engineers at Belem suggested I do not return back down the Amazon, but to continue up the Rio Negro, Rio Branco, Rio Itakutu, and Rio Mahu to British Guiana, then by cattle trail to Georgetown.

There were promises of rapids, waterfalls, primitive Indians, and high adventure.

From Manaus, I followed the river in a launch named *Tartaruga* for twelve days, then a motorboat (rowboat) for three more days.

I could not follow the cattle trail; it was flooded from heavy rain. I became lost for hours in the marshes and swamps. Then I came to a ranch, an American's, of all people.

Stayed here for six days, then went twenty-one miles on bicycle and ox-cart through the marshes to the airstrip. Waited another two days for the plane.

Had been sleeping in a hammock for the past three weeks.

Flew into Georgetown, about 250 miles. Stayed there five days then went in a West Indian schooner for four more days to Trinidad.

The food I had been eating for the last three weeks has been pretty grim.

From Trinidad, I was pretty tired of boats, bad food, hammocks. I was anxious to return to Venezuela and visit my friends. So I flew again about 350 miles.

I received a mighty reception from both Latins and Americans. I stayed a week with them.

The cost of entire trip was $236.90 for transportation, from Caracas and return.

Total cost of trip for hotels, food, film, transportation was $1,200.

Yet I've stayed at the best hotels in all the towns. I had been gone exactly seven months and two weeks, traveling approximately 14,452 miles in South America.

I tried again to work my way home on a ship. The American Consul couldn't help me out because of union laws.

I went aboard American ships, talked to captains; they couldn't let me work away or go as a guest because of union laws.

Just what would a destitute American do? He would stow away, no doubt.

But I'm one of those lucky fellows who has a family who can help me out and a Dutchman named Rudolph.

I then flew Pan American to Miami and hitchhiked home to Pennsylvania.

I wish to say that the entire trip had not been just hitchhiking. It also included travel by plane, boat, train, bus, horseback, bicycle, ox-cart, afoot and schooner. Probably *Pan-American Hitchhiker* is not a suitable title, but I've traveled the most miles this way.

The story covers eighteen countries and two territories.

Time spent in Alaska—6 months;
Time spent in Central and South America—23 months;
Returned to the States, September 29, 1948.

Grand Totals

	Hitchhike	Walk	Bus	Train	Plane	Boat	Horse
Alaska and U.S.A.	7,000	30	650	110	2,300	1,100	
U.S.A. and Central America	3,830	40	330	485	100		15
Panama to Venezuela	500				800		
South America	8,148	400	200	313	750	4,516	125
Venezuela and Home	1,120	30	200	150	1,500		
Approx.	20,598	500	1,380	1,058	5,450	5,626	140

Cost of the Trip

	Only Transportation	Total Costs
Alaska and Return	$230.10	$400.00
States to Panama	43.35	360.00
Panama to Venezuela	52.00	200.00
Trip around South America	236.90	1,200.00
Venezuela to States	153.00	163.00
	$715.00	$2,323.00

In Mexico:

They like the Americans but they hate the English. A Canadian or other who carries a British passport will not be permitted to enter. Canadians are liked, but not permitted entrance with a British passport—cause of trouble: oil.

In Guatemala:

A girl put it this way—"I go only with Americans, I like only Americans, take me to the States with you."

In Costa Rica:

A lad put it this way. I'd known him only two days. "You'll go back, you'll forget about me, you promise to write, but you never never will. You will forget about me."

In Panama:

Panamanians envy the high salary of the Americans in the Zone. Americans have a tendency to discriminate. Latins hate this attitude. Treat them fair and you have good friends. Panamanians prefer Democracy to Communism.

In Venezuela:

A waitress put it this way: "You are from the United States of North America, I am of the United States of Venezuela. United States of Venezuela is *mejor* (better)."

In Colombia:

They have pretty well gotten over their gripe about a share of the Canal Zone payment for the territory. The U.S. had paid Panama the money. It did not recognize the joint government of

New Granada (Colombia-Panama). Colombia did not get a share and had been very bitter.

In Ecuador:

Shortage of farm equipment. Very hospitable ranchers. Stayed at several haciendas (ranch houses). One German rancher, who is on the black list because he deserted his country, said "Good-bye, Good Luck, and Saluté Los Estados Unidos." Saluté the United States.

In Peru:

Women believe American men make good husbands.

In Bolivia:

Met a Bolivian doctor on a train. It was cold. He invited me for tea and whiskey in the dining car. After being served, he said, "You pay half."

In Chile:

A well-to-do Chilean driving a new '48 convertible put it this way about present-day situations. "The world needs a master; rather than see the Germans or Russians be master, I rather see Americans be masters." His opinion comes from the fact that U.S. has people from every country and Germany and Russia are only a separate race.

In Argentina:

I've been asked by an Argentine, "Why do Americans hate us?" I gave the only reason I knew of. Because Argentina has so many "Nazis." The Argentine replied "No, we haven't got any here; they're all in Chile."

Likewise Chile claimed Argentina had them all.

Argentina and Chile are proud of the fact that there are no Indians or Negroes in their countries. They have been more or less completely exterminated in revolutions. About the only Negroes or Indians one sees is when they are government officials of Peru, Paraguay, or Brazil. They have told me, "That is something you have in your country and we don't want it."

In Uruguay:

Had dinner at a peasant's home. He was as white as I. His white woman said, "A black man is as good as a white, where's the difference? There is little discrimination or none at all in Uruguay or Brazil.

In Brazil:

I liked this country best of all—only trouble is they speak Portuguese. A Brazilian hates to be called a Portuguese. They do not like the Portuguese. American rates high here. Brazil had a similar struggle for independence as the U.S. They are a generous people, only they can't understand why we should have trouble with Negroes.

In British Guiana:

They like the Americans. Always you can hear them say, "Hello, Joe," as you pass by. They believe "The sun never sets on English soil," but likewise "it never touches the hearts of British subjects."

In Trinidad:

They say, "Be careful." It's a rough place.

PART ONE

1

Across the United States

I awoke at 5:30, the morning of April 4, 1946. Mom had already prepared breakfast for me. She could not understand why I wanted to leave home. She was crying as I kissed her good- bye and took my grip.

It was raining out. I walked the few blocks to the trolley stop. I waited five minutes for the trolley. I rode it to the edge of town. There by the old Log Cabin, I caught my first ride on my long journey to Alaska.

I would hitchhike by day and look for recreation in the evenings. I made good time and at Springfield, Ohio, I took in a movie and had a milkshake afterwards. I marveled at the large number of girls in that town and I couldn't help but whistle.

The next day, a lieutenant of the U.S. Air Corps gave me a lift. He asked if I could drive. I said, "Yes." It was pleasure to drive his car. It was a 1942 Chrysler New Yorker. He told me to keep it at sixty-five or seventy miles per hour. We picked up several girls who were hitchhiking. We had a jolly trip with pleasant company.

Bill, the lieutenant, said as we passed a graveyard, "You know, Joe, how many of those people are dead?" I said, "Sure, all of them. Do you want off here?" He gave me the blankest look and everybody laughed.

The trip lasted all day to St. Louis, Missouri. Only one of the girls went that far. By coincidence, she was going to Beaumont, Texas, the same destination of the soldier. After dinner we parted in St. Louis and beauty threw a kiss.

Next day I rode to Kansas City with a soldier on a motorcycle. He was dressed warmly. I nearly froze. The scenery was beautifully green, the farms were very scenic. We stopped often for coffee to warm up. We arrived late in the afternoon in Kansas City. I went roller-skating that evening.

The following day an Army captain gave me a ride as far as Salina. He had been all over the world as an Army pilot. At first I admired him for his good looks, size and rank. But when he gave me his viewpoints on sex, my opinion changed.

From there a mother and daughter-in-law gave me a ride in a Ford. They had come from Tennessee and were going to the Veterans Hospital in Denver to see their son who had contracted fungi in the ears in the South Pacific. They picked me up because they might need me to fix a flat tire. We stayed overnight in a tourist camp and arrived in Denver without misfortune the next day.

I liked Denver very much and decided to stay a few days. I enjoyed dancing at Elitches and Lakeside. The gardens at Elitches are world-famous. I found that the B-29 outfits stationed nearby had the situation well in hand at the dance.

Swimming wasn't allowed at Washington park, but the fish were biting and I managed to rent a canoe and reel. I met an Austrian fellow skating, and we went to see Buffalo Bill's grave atop Look Out Mountain. The drive was thrilling up the mountain. Next day we went skiing about fifty or sixty miles west of Denver up in the mountains. There were many young couples, and there was a shack to warm up and get coffee and hamburgers. We stayed several hours there. I lingered longer than I should have. We parted in the late afternoon. I continued westward.

I got several rides, roads were under repair. Night fell. Impossible to get a room. I had to keep going. I met another chap in the same predicament. We were told a lady several miles down the road took in roomers. We walked there and the answer again was, "No Vacancies."

We continued walking and a heavy rain fell. We dashed under a bridge. The river was frozen, but the banks had a soft dusty, dry bearing. It got very cold so we proceeded to build a fire. We had it roaring all night.

First our backs would freeze, turn around and our faces and fronts would freeze. We managed to get a little sleep. We could hear coyotes off in the distance. It was a wonderful feeling to camp out.

Daylight came and the rain persisted. We heard a car, dashed up the bank, and hailed the driver. He stopped and took us to Vernal, Utah. We had ham and eggs, and thereafter I succeeded in reaching Salt Lake City by nightfall, but not before we had run into a freak blizzard, which had made the roads dangerous.

After a good night's rest, I walked down the highway out of Salt Lake City. The first car stopped and picked me up and also a merchant seaman a block or two ahead. This ride lasted all day into Carson City, Nevada. The seaman appeared to be a talented comedian and kept us laughing all day. Towards evening we had dinner and a few beers. Then we sang good American songs the rest of the way to Carson City.

Arriving late, we couldn't get a room again. We went to the Carson City Police Station. We got a night's lodging there. We had warm blankets and a very clean cell. We slept well and about 6:00 A.M. we departed from the Carson City Station.

A distinguished-looking gentleman of about fifty-five, in a '42 Buick, gave us a ride as far as Sacramento, California. It was a bright sunny day and the world seemed just right. We drove through forests of fir, spruce, and redwood, and the coolness was grand. The seaman kept his chatter as usual and we laughed.

From Sacramento to Frisco, we caught another ride. The driver picked up a girl of about thirty, also. She got into the front seat, but presently got into the back seat with me. She asked if she could change her clothes. Before we could answer, she already had her dress off and was putting on a tight sweater. Then she laid down in the back seat and put her head on my lap. She was wearing a turban and I could see short hair that looked like a boy's brush haircut. I thought she was an escaped moron. She didn't talk much sense. I thanked the fellow and said so-long to the comedian. How did I get rid of the woman pest? Well, I just walked faster than she did down Market Street.

I visited friends in Alameda for a day and started for Seattle on U.S. No. 101. It took a couple of more days. I got a great thrill out of the Redwoods. The largest was 346 feet high and was marked. We looked very small in comparison. We could feel the immense greatness of them.

One night I was in a logging town in Oregon. I had a drink at the bar, and a big one-eyed Indian walked in. He was drunk and said he could lick any man in the house. Nobody said anything. He shouted again. One of the loggers walked over and threw a straight punch to the Indian's shoulder. We all heard a crack. He had broken the shoulder bone. The Indian was taken to a hospital. That fellow wasn't as big as the Indian, but these loggers are tough and drink heavily too.

There was a stretch of highway in southern Oregon on U.S. 101 that causes many people to get seasick. It's continuous winding, left, right, left, right does cause back-seat riders to feel sick. It goes for about ninety miles. I rode with a milkman in early morning fog. He drove swiftly and surely. It was indeed a thrill. He told me it would be more thrilling in daytime as I could see the cliffs and ravines. Next day an old-timer gave me a ride. We visited the seal caves and live seals along the rough coast. They were an interesting spectacle. From Portland to Seattle was an easy hop.

I heard good and bad stories about Alaska while transiting Oregon and Washington. People exaggerated the prices. An egg costs a dollar and a beer is also a dollar, and so forth. A fellow said he got a letter from his sister that they were starving up north. They blamed it all on the longshoreman's strike, which was in effect on the West Coast.

Another chap said that Alaska was a good country till the people from the dust country came up. Doors were never locked before either. The fellows who told me Alaska is what I make of it, gave me courage.

I was suddenly stopped short by the Canadian customs at the border. They would not permit me to pass unless I had a ticket to catch the boat out of Vancouver for Alaska. They would not permit me to go by road. They said it was too wild and uninhabited and little traffic went by.

I went back to Seattle and tried to work my way up north on a fishing boat. The Swedes and Norwegians have a clannish attitude and I failed again. I also tried Bellingham, Washington.

6

The strike still being on, I purchased a ticket for a Canadian ship. The Canadians were not strike- bound.

Passage being reserved for a week, I went to work on a farm to save expenses. The man I worked for was middle-aged and retired. His wife was a fortune-teller and his son, a butcher in a slaughter house.

I lived in a cabin with an elderly man. We cleared the land, felled huge spruce and fir trees, fed and cared for the cows and horses. Mr. Webster and I bucked several trees. It wasn't long before I became winded. Mr. Webster was an ex-logger and laughed at me. His wife offered to tell my fortune, only I don't believe in having a troubled mind and said, "No, thanks."

In the evening his son Jack and I went to town in his Model "A" Ford. Beer and wine were the only drinks served in Washington. We "raised Cain" as young fellows can in his "powerful" car.

7

2

Aboard the Canadian Ship, *Prince Rupert*

Wednesday came and with my pay in my pocket, I again got a ride to the border. The officials welcomed me and let me pass. Their grins of amusement irked me. I continued merrily on to Vancouver.

Going steerage on the *Prince Rupert* was a lot of fun. I dined first-class topside and then again, second-class below decks. People were interesting and the stories also. Topside we had dancing and entertainment and below decks we had poker games.

The trip lasted three days through the inside passage, making several stops to load and unload cargo. We had a few beers at Ocean Falls, a town situated against an enormous mountain. We passed acres of rich timberland and many fishing craft. The continuous calling of hundreds of sea gulls caused headaches. We passed a lot of canneries and saw mills.

We stopped for twelve hours at Prince Rupert, B.C. It felt good to walk on ground again. I walked about the interesting city. There was a movie house, many Indian curio shops, and a modern post office. The main street was paved. It went for a few blocks.

At the end of it, I found "Johnny's Café" and decided to have coffee. Inside was a beautiful waitress working alone. It was not a busy place. We took turns playing the nickelodeon.

We spent several hours chatting about Canada and the United States. Making a date for 7:00 P.M. I left and got lost in the hills surrounding the town. When I found my way again, I had only time to keep the date. I was still early and found competition with a couple of Canadian soldiers there. I won her choice, I guess, because I helped wash the dishes.

We went bowling and then walking. At eleven I hated to leave, but the *Prince Rupert* was pulling out.

It was an overnight ride to Ketchikan. The water was rough, and it was pitch dark out. Inside men were playing poker, some looked sick. I went below and lay in my sack; it was a bit chilly. Presently I fell asleep.

We arrived in Ketchikan, Alaska, about 10:00 A.M. The sun was shining brightly. The first thing I noticed was the wooden sidewalks and rough, but friendly nature of the people and their dress. From the rows of taverns lining the boardwalks came the music blaring juke boxes and loud voices.

Finding a room was difficult with the large number of people going north. I slept several nights on a cot at the U.S.C. and local police station on a steel bed. A French lady finally made accommodations. Work was plentiful. I got a job with the K.S.M. (Ketchikan Spruce Mills) at once.

3

Ketchikan and Wonderful Juneau

I liked the work and my fellow workmen. One of the fellows was from Chicago and the other a Tlingit Indian from Sitka. The Indian was a good impersonator of Walt Disney's "Donald Duck" and "Gray Rabbit." Always you could hear him say, "What's up, Doc?" in his funny way.

We decided to go hiking one Sunday up Deer Mountain. The dense woods had signs of jungle growth long past and had an eerie look. We followed a narrow trail and went through a lot of mud. Farther on we went through snow knee-deep. We followed red arrows now. We passed a Coast Guard weather observation recorder and finally came to a log cabin. It was a three-mile hike. We could go no farther, the snow was too deep. We already had passed the timberline. The scene below was worth the climb. It was a reward. We could see the town as a miniature along a coast surrounded by mountain and blue sea. It was breathtaking.

A young couple had ventured up to go skiing. There were supplies and warm clothing supplied by the Coast Guard for emergency. We built a fire, had grub, and spent the better part of the afternoon there. Next day we paid the price in aching muscles.

John C. Baryalde, a French boy, whom I spent many happy hours with in his canoe and various bars, worked in the cold-storage plant. I watched him chop fish's heads off. With a hook he lifted a 26-pound halibut and with a machete in one or two strikes, he cleaned the head off. This spectacle attracts tourists. He makes $1.35 an hour and lots of overtime, but he sure smelled.

After a month I was anxious to leave again. Trying to work or catch a ride in a fishing boat proved fruitless. Longshoremen had ships tied up in a strike. It was necessary to fly with Ellis.

The plane was a ten-passenger, two-engine seaplane. We had a nice takeoff and landing, on water that was choppy. The trip lasted one hour and forty-five minutes, about three-hundred miles farther north to Juneau, Alaska.

The same day I got a job at the local sawmill. I lasted three days, then I got fired and got another job at C.A.A. airport a few miles from town. I worked with a Swede named Ed Anderson. We were linemen and did various jobs. He was about sixty years old and strong as a bull. He had been a wrestler and had all broken knuckles. He spent six years in the navy. He called Alaska "God's Country." He made six trips to his home state of Minnesota and said he always missed Alaska and would stay put now. We would lean on a shovel or stop bucking a tree and swap stories. He enjoyed his life and had had many experiences. He also told me drinking was the style in Alaska. Those words are very true.

We had an Aleut Indian working with us. He simply didn't know how to work and was fired.

Besides working for the sawmill and C.A.A., I worked for a pile-driving company. I worked for two weeks repairing the docks at Juneau. I made twenty-five cents an hour more, $1.50. As I look back now, I recall the unnecessary risks I took.

We had once torn up the 4-inch flooring, only the joists remained. They were about 30 inches apart and 18 feet long or better. Many had rotted away at the joists and lay loosely in place. We had to renew them.

Instead of our walking safely to where the flooring was still intact, we would walk these 4-inch joists, just like an artist walks a tight rope.

Underneath was the old flooring, ripped and torn, full of large spikes floating in the water about thirty feet below.

Red, an ex-sailor, remarked, "This isn't safe," as he started walking over the joist to the other side for a tool. I had to go also so I followed over the loose joist.

The danger was not of falling into the water, but of falling on the driftwood that was full of large nails below.

We made it safely across the joist, wobbling a bit.

Later we tore the joists up. I nearly fell in one morning. I was at a precarious position. I had a mere 10-inch footing. I stood straddle-legged with the joist between my spread feet. I was knocking the old joist lose with a pee-wee, a tool that loggers use to move heavy logs or to turn them about.

I had to apply all my strength and force on the batlike handle. Suddenly the joist gave away, breaking in the middle and one end coming up toward my crotch. I could not step backward, for I'd fall into the sea. Instantly I swung my right leg up and over the bad end, to come to my left leg. The heavy beam or joist went crashing into the water below.

Many spectators watch the repairing of the docks. Many saw my close call and my co-workers said, "You nearly got it that time, Joe." How well I knew it, but it couldn't be helped. The job had to be done.

A few days later, a similar incident happened. I let the pee-wee drop into the sea. I could not extract it in time from its grip on the falling joist.

My boss gave me hell, for many tools were lost in the sea by accident. But a life is worth more than a tool. The boss knew that very well.

The story of Alaska is a beautiful romance and adventure. There are five main tribes of Indians; the Tlingits, in the southeastern part of Alaska are the most fierce; the Kolosh, the fighters; the Kenai, Chigueset, and the Alutes are the friendliest and most peaceful as history goes. Baronoff, the hero of Alaska, was a Russian who established the first colonies and fur-trading companies there. He engaged the Indians in many battles. He got revenge on the fierce Tlingits in 1804 after they had burned and pillaged the Russian settlement of Wrangell, two years previous in 1802. This had been his last and most important battle. It secured the land for the Russians.

A fine, modern hotel in Juneau bears his name. It is the best in the territory. In his life he married an Indian as most of the Russian fur traders had. They all wanted to go back to Russia, but the children of their undoing tore at their heartstrings and so they remained in Alaska.

The Indians of today speak English and their native dialect. Many still speak Russian. They are paid good American wages, the same as many white men. Except for the Alutes in the Pribiloff Islands and nearby, they are paid a few dollars for the seal skins they hunt. Their homes and food are free, paid by the U.S. Government. During the war, many were evacuated to southeastern Alaska.

I had a lot of fun with the Indians, I danced, drank, and even fought with a Tlingit. I was told that Indians gang up on a white man. It was good sportsmanship on their part. A couple of the Indian buddies stood by and never batted an eye to help him. He got the worst of it. We became pretty good friends afterwards.

It seemed I had been out bike-riding with his girl, whom he said was his wife, while he was supposedly still out fishing. She had evidently lied to me about being unmarried.

Next day while having dinner, she came to me again and said, "We really had a good time, didn't we, till my husband came." We did have fun. We watched a baseball game, rented bikes, went five or six miles to Douglas, went to the beach, and afterwards had a few beers and danced. We put on a pretty good act. The bartender set up free drinks and another couple there did likewise and played the juke box for us. The bikes should be in at 10:00. It was 1:00 A.M. We rode hastily on the gravel road; we stopped once to rest. The moon was bright. We lingered in the brush and grassy ground. My arms went around her. She didn't resist. It was some time before we remembered to get back to town. For some reason we were full of pep. Maybe it was the cool evening. Arriving in town we met her boyfriend or husband. He was feeling high and unreasonable. He was a foot taller than I. I was glad I was sober, otherwise I might have got the worst of the fray.

Spending most of the evenings dancing at the Dreamland and Occidental was fun. Most of the "cheechakos" (newcomers) go there. The Baronoff was exclusively for white folks, and the cost of entertainment was very high. The Bubble Room had a gorgeous floor for dancing.

A Filipino operated the Dreamland, a couple of Russians, the Occidental, and a Japanese managed the hotel where I stayed. The Japanese was seventy-four-years old and in his second childhood. He always remarked, "Young man needs woman" and tried to arrange to have girls sleep with me. He embarrassed me many times.

I found the Alaskan girls to be good dancers. My buddy from Seattle went with a beautiful native. He liked her very much and talked about marrying her. Her Indian brother had a fishing boat valued at $10,000. He offered it to my buddy as a gift if he married his sister. My buddy is a fisherman and believes it a good deal. With the boat, in a few seasons he could make his fortune fishing. He had been married before and was now thirty-one years old. He believes that the Indians have more money than the average American will ever have. My buddy told me the story of how she came home one night drunk. She said, "I'll betcha you're mad at me." He could only laugh, and said if his wife, a white woman, came in that way, he would kill her, but this Indian—it was just plain funny.

The Indians have funny ways. The women desire to have a child by a white man, and some get married, but when a ship comes in with someone they like better, they leave the husband flat and he can't do a darn thing about it.

On Sundays, a few people work and it's nice to sit on the dock in the warm sun and talk with your friends or maybe fish a little from the dock. There is always a ball game on Sundays and bicycles are available to go riding. There is the Green Bowl, a park with recreation facilities, and a movie theater. Most of the older fellows play poker in some saloon and school kids hang out at the soda fountain. You can go to Mendenhall Glacier or go for a swim and camp out at Taku Lake and there's plenty of hunting ground. The boat arrivals are one of the main attractions.

Going out to Mendenhall Glacier on a bicycle, I got a flat tire about seven miles out. A lady gave me a ride back to town. The gravel roads are hard on tires.

I stayed in Juneau more than two months and on my last night there, I danced at the Occidental. My buddies said I was crazy to leave, and said I would be back. I must have kissed about ten girls good-bye. The Japanese carried my bag to the small passenger boat, the *Estebeth*. He was a most friendly genial chap.

I sat on the rail as the boat moved out over the placid bay

and watched Juneau fade away in the darkness. I felt a lump in my throat. I hated to leave that happy place. I vowed to myself that I would return.

This was the only place where I had many girlfriends. It was not unusual for me to go to bed alone and at various hours of the night, four, five, or six different girls would knock on the door, saying, "Joey, this is Evelyn," or "this is Ruth," or "this is Sophie, open the door, Joey." Sometimes they would kick and bang the door till I thought it would break. Many were the drinking and dancing parties we had, and the girls paid also.

I went below and fell asleep in the bunk. I was poor company for the two sailors there. I didn't say much.

4

The White Pass and Alcan Road

When I awoke we already had docked at Skagway. We had been there for several hours. Only one woman was aboard, she had overslept also. The skipper and crew had gone to town. We were now in the windy city of Skagway, about 110 miles north of Juneau. The sun was bright, and a strong wind was blowing. We had to walk about a half a mile to the town on a wooden sidewalk.

What once had been a city of 10,000 people, now was a mere 600. The men were like something out of a storybook. They all had immense beards, blond, red, and black ones. These were the real sourdoughs. I had to conceal my amusement in a barroom. The bartender was a young chap with a large red beard. The tie and latest, loudest, sport coat that he wore certainly made him look funny. He would be something for the girls at the Grande Ballroom in Detroit. He probably thought I looked silly being clean shaven.

The citizens put on a show for the passengers that afternoon. It was the shooting of "Soapy Smith," the biggest gambler and cheat of the town by a heroic sheriff in the days of the Gold Rush to the Klondike. The sheriff also died of his wounds in the gun battle. It was the Fourth of July celebration. The passengers really liked the show.

We got lodging at the Golden North Hotel. The next morning we rode the White Pass and Yukon Route train. The wind was terrific. We hastened aboard. The first-class car was beautifully modern, designed in a light blue color with soft seats. The conductor looked like a clown. He wore a large black beard and a French cap. His vest was bright purple, with large gold or brass buttons. He wore a black bow tie and a white shirt. He was amusing and sported chains and nuggets of gold on his suit.

The trip was exciting, indeed, along the trail of "89." We

16

could still see signs of a beaten trail leading north over the rough terrain made by the thousands of gold seekers. I had a nice French girl from Dawson City for company. She had never been to the States and asked many questions. I can't sing too well, but when I'm happy I do. I had the girl blushing a lot by singing to her.

We passed over deep ravines and sheer cliffs. We really held our breaths at times. There were several hard climbs over the mountains. We stopped to have dinner high up in the mountains. It was very windy and chilly. We sat at a long table and helped ourselves to the food. It was a nice place and very clean. Inside the building it was warm. An hour later we were riding again and the Canadian Customs okayed us on the train.

We disembarked at White Horse, Yukon Territory, Canada. We were about 110 miles farther north from Skagway, Alaska. We got rooms at the White Horse Inn. Outside it was raining and everywhere was mud. There were no sidewalks of any kind. Still Whitehorse was an interesting place, and I lingered a few days.

The Canadians had a large army camp there. The barracks and quarters were made of logs and looked solid. The private homes were made of logs also. They had the bark peeled off and were varnished to preserve the color. The streets were wide and homes were neatly spaced. The Yukon River and Alcan Highway went by there. The water was very clear and swift. The Yukon River is a water route.

I walked along the highway for a mile or so and noticed a lot of miniature houses atop a small hill. Curious, I scampered up and soon found it to be an Indian graveyard. The houses were beautifully painted in blue, red, white, and green. They had curtains in the windows, and the doors were padlocked. There were white picket fences around most of them. There were no markers. The story goes that neither rain nor snow shall fall upon the body to make it uncomfortable.

I found in Whitehorse, as I had seen before in Windsor, the Canadians have a law that consumers of drinks must be seated. Drinking at a bar is seldom seen.

The following day I started hitchhiking for Fairbanks on the famous Alcan Road. The Mounted Police picked me up. They

17

took me to the commander of the post. I seemed to amuse him so he gave me six hours of liberty to try to catch a ride within the city of Whitehorse.

There were about ten cars that had come up from all parts of the U.S. Some were already loaded down heavy and couldn't make room. Others were going a short distance to camp for an unknown period, to hunt and to fish.

After several hours I gave up hope and purchased a ticket. I was to leave the next morning via O'Harra Bus. I certainly didn't wish to be deported back to Juneau. The bus had a full load; a fellow had come all the way from New York with his wife and three small children. He was going to teach school at Valdez. Traveling in the company of crying babies is not to my taste.

There were several writers who were picking up some material for a story. Also four lady tourists who had come up from the States. They told their woes of how they stayed one night at a hotel in southeastern Alaska. In the morning the bill was twelve dollars for each. They cried and went to the police. Result, they had to pay.

I had an old-timer for a companion. He must have done a lot of prospecting. Every so often he would point to a mountain or hill and say, "There's gold thar" and point out the characteristics.

The gravel road was good. Every so often the bus stopped. Somebody would scamper off into the brush. There are no rest rooms. Everybody took the opportunity to walk and stretch about. The mosquitoes were tiny, and millions of them swarmed about. It was good to move again.

We had chicken dinner in a tent prepared by a fat jovial woman near Haines Cut-off Junction. It was delicious. We all had appetites. We passed a few army camps. The soldiers kept the road in good shape. There were many trucks and road equipment along the road. We passed many quonset huts, which were emergency shelters and well supplied with food, clothing, and medicine.

We stopped at a village to sleep overnight. It was late in the afternoon. It was situated along a beautiful lake. Before dinner I took a hike along the beach. I came to a cabin. Outside a fire was

18

burning. A man and an Indian woman were sitting beside it. A couple of huskies started barking. The man silenced them.

He was a Frenchman and was married to the Indian. He enjoyed his life. He had a full-grown son, who had his mom's features. He loved his dogs and his home made of logs. It took him and his son three days to build it.

He told me of how his wife had been attacked by a bear one day. She had been chopping wood and raised her head to see a bear charging toward her. She had a heavy piece of wood in her hand, she backed up against a tree and shoved the wood down the bear's open mouth. The wood strangled the bear. The man proudly showed me the skin as evidence.

These people live a hard life. There is no doctor in the village. The bus goes by twice a week to Whitehorse, a city of 2,000 people. On the way back, I saw a man digging a grave. Another Indian had died. He had a smudge pot burning to keep the mosquitoes away as he worked. We all slept in log cabins on cots that night; five dollars was the total cost for lodging, supper, and breakfast. The inn was operated by Canadians.

It was another day's ride to Fairbanks. All along the road, we stopped at villages and picked up mail. At Tok Junction, the schoolteacher and his family, who had been the life of the party, took the road south to Valdez in another bus. We cleared customs there. We were now in U.S. territory again. The road became better from there on to Fairbanks. Along the entire stretch, we crossed very few hills.

Arriving about 9:30 P.M., it was still daylight. Finding a room wasn't easy. I paid nine dollars a week at Lacy's. It had a public shower. Fairbanks looked like a tourist or resort town. It was clean and modern. There were many cars, and I found paved streets again, modern soda fountains, restaurants, post office, schools, a miniature golf course, and a swimming pool. The pool had pipes underneath to heat the water. There were movie theaters and barrooms named after many states of the Union.

19

5

A Month on the Mighty Yukon

Somehow, working underground in a gold mine didn't appeal to me. It paid $8.25 a day, room and board free. I decided to work as a pantry-man on a riverboat, a branch of the Alaska Railroad System. I was issued a pass and took the train for sixty miles south to Nenana, the river port. On the trip down to the port, we passed through dense weeds and stalks. Natives kept the rails clear of the vegetation. It reminded me of a jungle.

A pretty Eskimo girl looked back at me on the train. I smiled and all the way to Nenana, she kept looking at me and hoping I would call her over. The white passengers grinned at me and said, "Go ahead. What are you waiting for?" I only grinned back. When I started off the train, she asked if I was coming back to Fairbanks. I said, "Maybe." I never saw her again.

I saw the boat. It was a beauty, painted white and very clean. Mr. Small was the purser. He introduced me to Captain Decoumb and the chief steward. My duties being assigned, I enjoyed my work very much. I experimented with salads, cutting roasts, turkey, and chickens, dishing out the food. I had only one dislike: I had to do the dishes, but even that turned out all right. I started singing. Soon the waiters, Joe Carrol, Pete, Bill, and Mike, and some of the passengers gathered about the pantry and we all harmonized. It turned out to be a lot of fun. Van, the chief steward, called me a character. We got along swell.

There were thirty-three crewmen. They were all Chiqueset Indians. They lived in the villages along the Yukon. They worked on the boat in the summer and went hunting or working on the railroad in the winter. There were eight of us white men employed on the boat.

Going upstream on the Yukon River, we stopped at Tanana, Rampart, Steven's Village, Purgatory, Beaver, Fort Yukon, and

Circle. They are all Indian villages. We bring them supplies of fish, clothing, food, medicine, and mail. The banks are lined up with the folk from the entire village. The boat arrival is an event to them. The trip takes about ten days upstream to Circle and about four days to return downstream to Nenana.

On the first trip up, we have about thirty-five passengers. Their rooms are cleaned and cared for each day by the waiters. Most of them are tourists; the others are natives who live along the Yukon. The natives sat at separate tables.

Every time the pilot or captain spotted a bear, moose, or naked natives swimming, they rang a bell and the passengers took to the rails with field glasses. We passed many fish traps. We all had our fill of salmon caught in the river and prepared by Van, the chief cook. The river washes the banks away continuously and forms various channels and tributaries. A landslide caused us to change our course once.

At Steven's Village, we met two young blond girls and pretty, too. They operated the store and post office. They were the only two white people there and said their husbands were in Fairbanks on business. They liked it because it was peaceful. They saw white people only when the boat came, about once in two weeks.

Coca-Cola sold for fifty cents, and a cantaloupe cost $1.05 each. We stayed at Steven's Village for four hours. The mosquitoes were terrible. When the boat moved out on the river, we had peace again.

Fort Yukon is about fifteen miles north of the Arctic Circle. Joe Carrol, the head waiter, lives there. He is a Creole (half-breed) and a very nice chap. His home is a log cabin, as all the rest of the buildings are in Fort Yukon. His folks have fifty dogs and the dried fish brought up on the boat for the dogs cost 35 cents a pound. It's the dogs' winter food.

I had spent most of my free time reading *Forever Amber*. I hadn't paid much attention to a beautiful Creole from Fort Yukon. She was angry with me, but said she would go to the dance with me on the return run from Circle. The dance hall was in a cabin at Fort Yukon.

There were beautiful moccasins, fur jackets, and mukluks

(shoes) sold cheap by the natives. The natives wore moccasins with beautiful bead work. They make their living fishing and trapping. They keep their dogs tied up, and beat and starve them to make them mean; thus, they become strong and become good sled dogs.

The midnight sun is a memorable sight on the river. It seems to rise and set in the same place. After the day's work is over, it's nice to join the passengers at the rail on deck, watch the sun set, and listen to the native boys on the barge softly playing a guitar and harmonica.

Arriving at Circle, most of the passengers return to Fairbanks by bus on the Steese Highway. It's about a hundred-mile trip south. We lay over a few days and wait for the steamer *Whitehorse* to come up from Whitehorse, Canada, and pick up passengers and cargo. The river had been muddy the entire trip. It was necessary to clean the water filters often.

Bill was an ex-GI. He was lucky with the cards. The natives thought he was a cheat and meant to gang up on him. Bill wanted to quit the boat, but I persuaded him to stay for the trip down again.

There was a dance at the hall in Circle. The music was furnished by the boys from the boat. Some of the natives stowed liquor aboard at Nenana and sold it at a large profit to the natives at Circle. Some of them became almost wild. A woman of forty-five or fifty, whom Van, the Chief Steward from Montana, called "Mom," was drunk and tried to make me dance. Not being successful, she got Van. They put on a merry show. For a woman her age, I didn't believe she could shake her leading edges and landing gear as she did. Van had all he could do to keep up. His legs moved in a crazy, wobbly way, and my stomach hurt from laughing so much.

We played baseball at Circle, and it was comical the way the natives ran bowlegged. To watch them catch a ball was just as funny. They seldom succeeded in catching the ball in mid-air. Joe Carrol had worked on the boat every year for the past four or five years and seemed to have girls waiting for him at every village. It was peculiar the way he always disappeared when we docked. He showed up when we were about to pull away from

22

shore several hours later. He wanted to join the Navy very much and had me fill out an application for him.

Waiting for the other steamer, we got several good nights' rest. The steward department had their quarters in the stern of the boat. The boat had paddles for propulsion. We always had a rough time sleeping. Now being docked, it was swell to sleep without being rocked and pounded.

Pete was a young waiter from Nenana. He always managed to get fresh tomatoes and lettuce from his mom's garden for the captain and the fellows in the Steward Department. The passengers were out of luck; they didn't get any.

Pete, one day for some reason, decided to slip and roll down the steps from the main deck to the galley below. He nearly went overboard, as there was a large open door in the galley. It's the main source of ventilation below. He sure made a lot of noise and looked silly to our inquisitive stares. Poor Pete, he was the victim of a lot of horseplay on the part of Carrol. He got salt in his milk, crackers in his bunk, and a pie in his face.

Sundays we had fire drill. I was always caught in the midst of carving a turkey. We ran to our stations and manned fire hoses and life boats. We hit a sand bar once. The waiters and I were having dinner. We were thrown to the floor. We became stuck for several hours. The force of the river current and maneuvering on the part of the pilot and the engineer got us free.

The natives thereafter plod the river with long poles and felt for sandbars. They were on forward bow of the barge. The steamers are all flat-bottomed and called stern-wheelers.

Mike was a fellow who assisted in the pantry. He was German and had served in the U.S. Army. His brother served in the German Army and was captured and held prisoner in the U.S. When he quit the boat at Nenana, he was replaced by a cowboy from Montana. He told us he was a cook on a chow wagon on a ranch. He was mostly bald and always wore his big ten-gallon hat. We had to wear white jackets and he really was a sight in the pantry. The passengers couldn't help seeing him and wondering how he would arrange the food.

Instead of slicing tomatoes, he would rip them apart and dish them out. He got drunk one day and couldn't perform his duties. The captain ordered him off the boat at Rampart. That's an awful place to be left stranded. There isn't a white person around, only natives. There is no road or plane to take him back to Nenana, only the river and a boat went by once a week or once in two weeks. He wasn't there anymore on the return trip.

In the evenings we played cards and tricks. It wasn't as exciting as the evenings in Juneau. It was peaceful on the boat. Al was a young passenger from Fairbanks. He asked the skipper for a position; he thought we had a lot of fun.

I worked a month on the boat. I made two trips. The trip was about six-hundred miles one way. I got off the ship at 5:00 one morning. A few minutes later, I watched it go downstream, circle around, and head upstream for another trip. I waved to the fellows on deck and watched the beautiful boat disappear around the bend.

The train going to Fairbanks wouldn't be around till late afternoon. I decided to explore Nenana. I saw the shack where they clock the breaking of the ice in the spring. It's the biggest gamble of the year in Alaska. A fellow in a poor house won by guessing the exact minute and day when the ice would break, permitting travel and commerce on the river.

Nenana is about 300 in population. Most of the buildings were log cabins, some were frame. The school was a great big log cabin also. There were many gardens with flowers and vegetables. The roads were deep in dust. I watched them bury an Indian on the hillside. A Catholic priest said the last words.

I had dinner in a tiny restaurant. There were many fox and beaver skins for sale at $15. Afterwards I went to the "Last Chance Bar." The place was nearly deserted. When the boats come in, it's a boom. The boys and natives from the *Yukon* got high together, afterwards they played and sang for the local girls. A boat seems to unite men as a team. The train came about five in the evening. It was several more hours to Fairbanks. They made long stops to load and unload freight.

Arriving in Fairbanks was like arriving in New York. It was wonderful to see lights again, lots of white people, sidewalks, modern buildings and music. Lacy's Hotel was filled to capacity.

24

Leaving my gear there, I tried in vain to find other accommodations, but had no luck.

Taking in a little night life, feeling good but tired afterwards, I slept on the banks of the Chena River nearby. I slept very well and awoke with the bright warm sun in my eyes. The sun looked about 10:00 A.M.

I had breakfast and success in getting quarters at Lacy's and it being Sunday, I met Bill from the *Yukon*. We painted the town. There had been a terrific fire a few years ago and signs of it still remained. There wasn't much to do in Fairbanks, so we stayed in "style" and visited the various bars. Lots of soldiers were in town from nearby Ladd Field. Most of them liked Alaska and talked about coming back after discharge. Liquor, beer, or whiskey cost forty and fifty cents. It had to be shipped up from the States. We found a fellow playing on an accordion at the Silver Dollar Bar. He had been a passenger on the *Yukon*.

6

Hitchhiking in Bear Country

A few days later, I was on my way to Anchorage via the highway. The first ride took me 1,004 miles to Big Delta on the Alcan road. The second was on the Richardson Highway by an elderly woman. She had picked up another hiker returning from Nome after three years work there as a mechanic. We had carburetor trouble along the way, and the woman was glad she had picked us up. We fixed it in short time. We went as far as Santa Claus Lodge. We had dinner together. It was a large tourist camp, made out of logs. There were skins of bears, lynx, fox, deer, and mounted birds. It was owned and operated by several Americans. The kind lady went on to her home in Galkana about four miles distant. My new friend and I stayed overnight at the lodge. The facilities were of the latest and the rooms were immaculately clean.

Having slept well and after a good breakfast, we started hiking again. It was cold and gray. We passed numerous "banks." They are a food storage house built on 10-foot poles so that wild animals couldn't get to it.

We walked to the junction at Galkana. My friend followed the Richardson Road to Valdez, and I followed the Glenn Highway to Anchorage. Anchorage was 213 miles away. I got several lifts from engineers on a line job. Every twenty or thirty miles, they stopped at a settlement and checked details. I'd hike along and presently they would give me another lift. About five in the evening, we had dinner at an inn. I should have stayed overnight there.

Anxious to reach Anchorage, only eighty miles away, I walked several miles. Not a car went by. It started raining and I came to a cabin. The man did not invite me in, but told me another inn was about two miles distant, around the next curve.

Every mile is marked and I passed 1—2—3—4—5—6—7, and still no sign of a building. It was very dark now and still raining. I had no flashlight, but still could see and feel the gravel underfoot. The white road markers were plainly visible. Tired and cussing, I strode on. It was very quiet. Sheep Mountain wasn't far, and this was bear country. It seemed foolish to build a fire when the inn might be around the next turn.

Suddenly I heard a loud noise in the bushes, I stopped, paralyzed in the center of the road. My hair stood on edge. I felt a chill down my spine. I expected an onrushing bear.

Instead I saw a flock of ptarmigan fly out of the bushes. They made a lot of noise. Then there was a loud laugh. It must have been a lynx. This sent another chill down my spine and I cussed again.

I hastened my stride, and before long a twin set of lights pierced the darkness. It was a truck coming my way. I hailed and it stopped. A man's voice boomed and it sounded good. "What the hell are you doing out here? Do you have a gun?" I said no and he said, "God, man, don't you know you're in bear country?" I told him, "Sure." Then I told him about the bum steer I got and that I wanted to return and clean the fellow's "clock" (punch his nose). The elderly prospector said no, that the fellow was probably a "cheechako" and would eventually receive his dire reward.

It was another twelve miles to the inn. I thanked the fellow graciously and went up the path to it. A couple of huskies barked, and a young girl came out with a lantern. She was very pretty and welcomed me.

Inside, there were hunters, trappers, and engineers gathered about the fireplace. The girl led me upstairs, carrying a lantern. I changed into dry clothes, washed a bit in a basin and joined the fellows by the fireside shortly after.

They had many bear stories to tell; some, of course, were fictitious. One was true and happened this very day in the vicinity of the inn. It was about a couple of prospectors.

The two prospectors had been buddies for many years. They had a lot of bad luck. They had worked hard and barely subsisted from their earnings. Long days of isolation helped to increase their bitterness. They quarreled and blamed one another for bad luck. Tempers became short and nasty, finally the urge to kill possessed one of them.

He made an attempt while his partner slept in the cabin; the partner awoke in time to see a gun barrel pointed at him. He fired first with a revolver that he had kept concealed under the covers and killed his would-be assailant.

The girl at the inn didn't feel sorry for the slain man. She said he was a very nasty man. She was the mistress of the inn. Her husband was in Anchorage on business. They both hailed from Denver, Colorado. She liked her new life very much in this wilderness. She liked her sled dogs very much also. The bears come to the inn quite often, and the dogs chase them away.

Ham and eggs cost two dollars. Blondie warned me not to walk far in trying to catch a ride the next morning. I obeyed and I jitterbugged to keep warm. It was very cold and gray. It drizzled a lot. Several hour later, a '42 station wagon pulled to a stop. It was an O'Harra outfit. I decided to ride. The epidemic in Anchorage had traffic at zero on the roads. It started raining hard, we fairly flew around the mountain curves. We stopped for dinner at Palmer. The restaurant was modern and clean; outside the streets and buildings looked a mess. There were large mud puddles everywhere. We rolled on through Matanuska Valley and past rainbow-colored mountains to Anchorage.

7
Life in Anchorage, Alaska

The rooming situation was bad. I spent three nights at the Palace Hotel. I had three roommates. We slept in cots, price, $1.50 per night. Some of the fellows stayed up all night drinking. In the next room a battle raged. Just like back in Juneau.

A week later I was at Daul's. I had a 6 by 10 foot room to myself, small, clean, neat, and quiet, all for only $14 a week.

Anchorage is fourteen thousand in population and the biggest and most modern city in Alaska. It's surprising how people move about that great territory. I met folks here whom I have met in Ketchikan, Juneau, Fairbanks, and on the river boat.

I met my buddy Bill from Seattle again. He showed me letters from his girl in Juneau. He hoped to join his "caluche" in a few weeks. Walter Goodwin bought himself a lot for $400 and built a cabin for himself. He had a native girl to do his cooking and laundry for him for the privilege of sleeping with him. She had no pride and was very outspoken. When I paid a visit, she'd turn her back, lift a leg and (can't put it in writing) said, "Greeting Joe."

Good carpenters made $2.25 to $2.50 an hour. Being fired twice, I succeeded on the third. Bill's friend, Jim, called me a phony. I didn't want to fight with him, I got feeling high on Sunday and wasn't in the mood for any more ribbing. Jim lost two teeth and I nearly lost a finger as it became badly infected from the cut. Jim had served as a gunner on a B-17 and had seen a lot of action. I was warned that he might retaliate with a knife. But Jim was a great sport and a good loser. Next day he came to me and in a laughing way said I should have knocked his two buck teeth out. He agreed that he had it coming, but he didn't believe I could do it.

Bill, Jim, and I would order gallon bottles of beer called

29

"stobies." We spent quite a few evenings that way at the canteen bar. It wasn't unusual to see a dozen of them on a bar at a time. Drinking is the style in Alaska, and it's rugged.

There were plenty of fights in Anchorage. The jail house was always full. Soldiers got into quite a few, the seamen and fishermen tangled, and Cheechakos with Sourdoughs (newcomers with the resident Alaskan).

Another time, one Sunday, I spent the better part of the afternoon with Bill, Jim, and another fellow, named Bob, at his room. We listened to the radio and drank wine. Jim, for some reason, left the room in a hurry. Bill and I followed him across the street to the canteen. It seemed like Jim's experiences over in Germany came over him. We started back to the hotel. The manager started whipping at us with a rubber hose. He was drunk. We thought he was out of his head. We struck at him in self-defense. Someone called the police. We beat it away at the sight of the police car. They gave us a merry chase, but we got away.

I went home and slept awhile; upon returning to the canteen several hours later, I learned that Bill and Jim were in jail and the police were looking for a fellow with a bandaged hand. That was me, and thereafter for a week I kept my hand in my pocket. Jim and Bill spent forty-eight hours in the brig and were fined twenty dollars each. They related how fellows were sleeping on the floors of the cells and stumbling over one another. It seemed fun to them.

Somebody had made a mess in the hallway of the hotel, and the manager thought we were responsible.

Quite a few Eskimos came to the canteen, and they always were good for a laugh. One of them had served in the South Pacific in the U.S. Army. All he could say about it was, "What a one hell of a place to send an Eskimo." The way he said it was humorous.

Another was sleeping at the bar. The bartender threw water on him to wake him up. The Eskimo reached up to wipe his forehead, and on his wrists was a pair of handcuffs. Apparently he had made good his escape from the police.

Some really cute Eskimo girls came in. They dressed shabbily in men's clothes, mostly pants. They had long straight black hair, but the faces of some really were pretty; others were plain dead pans. They really went for blonds, but few fellows took them out. Oh, yeah!

Many people still believe that the Eskimos live in igloos (snow houses) the year around and always in fur clothes.

The Eskimos live in snow houses only when they go hunting far away from their villages. They build a snow house only when a storm may be coming; other wise they live in wooden shacks or log cabins. In their short summer season, they go about in trousers and shirts and dress like people in the States. It's only in the wintertime that they don heavy fur jackets and mukluks (boots).

They speak their native dialect best and English poorly. I worked with one, and he made the same wages as I did. Others had served in the armed forces of the U.S.

I also knew an Eskimo girl who had gone to the States to college and studied medicine. Her village had paid her expenses. The girl became a good doctor, but had no desire to return to her people. She did return, but longed for the life in the States. Life in Eskimo land is pretty dull and miserable.

The Eskimos are good hunters and make beautiful carvings out of ivory fossils and walrus teeth.

There is no jealousy in the Eskimo. When a hunter's wife is sick and cannot join him on a hunting trip, another Eskimo will willingly let his wife go with the hunter. It is the tradition of the Eskimo that a hunter must not go alone, but must have a wife along on the hunting trip.

A WAC came in one evening and said she had spent four years in the Army and was still a virgin. All the fellows looked at her once, and then a roar of laughter all the way down the bar followed. Her face turned red and she ordered a couple of more liquors and flirted with a very light blond fellow afterwards. She was really high. Not even the boy friend believed her.

Aside from the canteen, there were several very nice clubs, the Aleutians, the South Seas, and the Alto. There was a dance floor in each, but few women to dance with. The few who came were married and had their husband along. Gosh, but there was a scarcity of girls all over Alaska (white girls). The few of them there are in their glory. They lead the men around or else.

The Aleutian Lanes is a grand place to bowl. It's up to date and the younger generation can be found there. There are also quite a few soda fountains and confectionaries. There are a variety of restaurants and certainly no shortage of meat or other food is noted. Alaska is the land of plenty, and the restaurants let you know it. Prices on food are very moderate.

The most popular song was "Hey Bob a le Bob." The soldiers whooped it up at the "Village" when they played it. On the streets, a nice or odd Eskimo passed and it was "Hey Bob a le Bob" from some joker. An Eskimo was doing a native dance one evening at a local tavern, and someone shouted "Hey Bob a le Bob" and the Eskimo stopped suddenly in the midst of an exciting step and cried out, "What do you mean 'Hey Bob a le Bob?' " Everybody laughed.

Secretary Krug came to Alaska for a few days. A large crowd gathered to see him at the station in Anchorage. The majority of the people in Alaska do not want the territory to become a state, as Secretary Krug evidently found out. His visit lasted four or five days.

Having stayed in Anchorage six weeks, I'd had an opportunity to fish and hunt with a fellow from Santa Fe, New Mexico. His name was Steve Morocco. He worked for the Alaska railroad and lived in a Quonset hut as most of the railroad employees do. They work forty-six hours a week and pay income tax as they do in the States. Steve was going to send for his wife, as Alaska agreed with him.

I have been invited to have dinner one Sunday at Walt Goodwin's place. His woman fixed us a grand dinner of ham, spuds, peas, and canned pineapples. He lived in a tent while he was constructing a cabin. We had some time building a fire in the old-fashioned coal stove. We used fire wood; coal is scarce and expensive.

Next door lived a Frenchman, named Bill. He was about forty and married to a nice Indian girl of about twenty. He had a lovely little son by her. His young sister-in-law of about sixteen lived there also in the two-room shack. He was an auto mechanic and had his shop a short distance away from the shack. He was a nice chap and invited me to have a few drinks in his house. I was surprised at his supply. He enjoyed his life very much. He went back to work, and I went to Walt's tent. About a half an hour later, I left Walt's tent and went through the wooded patch to the road.

I heard footsteps and a girl's voice calling softly. I stopped and in the darkness I could see Ruth, Bill's wife. She said she wanted to talk to me but never got the chance with Bill around. She liked him and liked me too, and she wanted to know why I didn't come more often to visit. She put her arms around me. I had read books about Captain John Smith and Pocahontas, the pretty Indian maid who saved his life. He was a great man.

Something in the night and being in the woods alone together sent exciting chills down my spine. We slipped to the cool grassy ground full of sticks. The bushes and high grass hid us completely. We could hear the faint sounds of Bill hammering away in his garage. Ruth put her hand to her mouth to stifle a laugh.

When we stood up again, she told me to wait a few minutes. She came back with her younger sister, Leslie. They both put their arms around me and beamed happily. Their white teeth shone in the darkness. I remarked that someone was going to get shot, and they said, "We don't care," but they were worried for Ruth went off soon, thinking that Bill would return to the shack, find neither of them in, and start investigating.

Leslie was really cute, though very tiny and young. She knew what she wanted. She said over and over that she loved me since she first saw me two weeks ago. I told her that she mustn't, I had intentions of traveling to distant lands and did not want anybody to fall for me. She said she would wait for me to come back. We sat and talked. She came from Lake Clark with her sister after she was married. She was in the fourth grade and said she was sixteen. She did not like school. Her conversation was not like a fourth-grader's, more like a twenty-one-year-old. We could see Bill going to the house and she hustled away, but not before kissing me good-night.

I finally came to the gravel road. It was two miles to town. I felt good and decided I could walk to town, before the late bus came around. Telling Bill and Jimmy about two sisters falling for me, they wanted to come with me. I would not give the names or addresses. Even native girls are scarce in Anchorage.

Another time I called on my buddy, Walt. He told me they asked for me continuously. Bill was out hunting moose, so the girls had the opportunity to come to Walt's. Ruth played a guitar well and sang nicely too. A soldier came over, and the girls brought a bottle of whiskey. We had a grand time in the shack, dusty floor, littered pots and pans, and dancing in a six-foot square with lots of singing. I felt like a true "sourdough."

I remember waking up about 6:00 A.M. to go to work. I was sleeping in a bunk with Leslie beside me. The soldier was asleep with Ruth beside him in the bunk below. We were in Bill's home. I dressed in a hurry and was glad to get out. There was only one door out and a small window. I felt surely I would have to fight my way out if Bill ever showed up. Ruth said, "You wouldn't hit Bill, would you?" and I said "The hell I wouldn't, it's the only way to get out."

I hoped that I would never get drunk again, so that I could always know what I'm doing. The soldier woke up, and we both headed towards town. The sun was coming out, and the G.I. headed for camp.

I had time for coffee with Bill and Jimmie. They still called me lucky. Afterwards I went to my room at Daul's, changed to my logger's boots, blue jeans, and leather jacket, and headed for work, as a rough carpenter at $1.75 an hour for Bliss Construction Company. My employer had come from Ohio about fifteen years ago and had done a lot of work in building Anchorage. They were very nice fellows to work for. Don Bliss was a little tired and felt he needed a vacation after so many years.

Gold nuggets can be bought very cheaply an beautiful native carvings in fossil of walrus and ivory made in Nome.

People from every state in the union can be found in Alaska. The Victory Bar was operated by a nice fellow from Idaho. His first name was Al. I've met fellows here who came from the deep wilds of Alaska, places such as Bettles, Kayukuk, or Point Barrow. There are very few white men there, and these fellows are radio operators or engineers of the government. They stay at a six- month stretch and are glad to get back to civilization. Last report on Point Barrow was seventeen white men, Bettles, five men, and Kayukuk three men.

I had intentions of going to Kodiak, Seward, and Cordova. They all were enticing places to visit. Walt showed me pictures that he had taken when he came up on the boat. They were enough to make anyone want to see the places.

8

Flying Home with Husky

At the South Seas Nite Club, I made a reservation to fly back to the States. The plane was a C-47, war surplus. The price was cheaper than by boat. It was a new organization set up by a couple of war veterans.

Many "G.I.s" buy war surplus planes and fly cargo and passengers to the States at reduced rates. The big airlines like P.A.A., Alaska Airways, and Northwestern reduce their rates so low that the "G.I.s" cannot fly and make a profit. They call it the "Old Squeeze Game." Soon the "G.I.s" have to quit, then the big airlines raise the prices again.

I called on Walt again; he gave me a beautiful malamute pup. I called him "Husky," as he really was full of health and pep. Walt hated to see me leave. Ruth and Leslie came over. They walked with me to the road. I had to laugh at them. I said there was a whole camp full of soldiers who would be glad to go out with them, and they said yes, they knew, but they weren't as "pretty" as I was.

I kissed them good-bye and hiked it into town with Husky under my arm. Bringing him to the hotel caused a storm of protest from the management, but a number of roomers started playing with Husky and she cooled off. Later he started barking and I took him to the office of Arnald's Air Freight. The girl on duty was glad to take care of him. She wasn't very busy on night duty.

At 4:00 A.M., I was wakened by a cabbie at Dauls. I had fallen asleep and left the light burning. It was a good thing. It's the way he found my room. We picked Husky up and a couple more passengers and were at the airport at the break of dawn.

We took off from a dirt runway and were soon flying at a high altitude. It really got cold. The plane was really a box car. It

36

still retained its war benches, two long ones, one on either side of the ship. There were a couple of "cheechakos" with long beards. They had spent six months on Kenai Peninsula on a road job and were returning to the States. Another chap took a good length of the bench to go to sleep on. He bundled up in a topcoat and a blanket. He kept calling for coffee. He had the looks of a man "the morning after." A couple of young girls were aboard and a fellow with a war dog that had seen plenty of action. Husky tried to make friends with him, but the "Sergeant" barked and snapped and scared Husky away.

Husky was a lot of fun. He'd run up and down the aisle; passengers would trip him and he'd go rolling. He would get up and bite the Joker's ankles. When the engines were throttled faster and louder, he'd jump on the seat and hide his ears in somebody's coat and arm sleeve.

The co-pilot tripped over him once, and the stewardess spilled coffee that she was serving when Husky bit her ankle. They all loved him, though, and scolded him. Husky was really the life of the party on board the plane.

We spent a good bit of the flying time standing under the warm air vents. When it got rough flying, we sat down again. The hostess was a wonderful conversationalist. Her brother was the pilot, and the plane belonged to them and their family. They permitted me to take pictures from the cockpit, and it was also an opportunity to get warm. We ran into sleet and ice. It became blind flying.

We landed once to gas up and have coffee near Ketchikan. The plane became full after we picked up passengers there.

We took off again and arrived in Seattle about four in the afternoon. The whole trip lasted ten hours. At the airport were a lot of sailors and civilians. Husky was spotted as an Alaskan dog, and all eyes and conversation were turned to him. I hoped that I had him trained a little and he would stay beside me. Instead he scampered off and half a dozen people went chasing after him. An elderly fellow caught him and gave him back to me. He said it would be a shame to lose him after bringing him all that distance. I agreed and thanked him.

I did not go to downtown Seattle. I headed for nearby highway No. 10. I was taking the northern route back to Pennsylvania. I got several rides before nightfall, and riding on paved highways again seemed like a dream, like floating on a cloud. We passed through several towns brightly lit up in neon lights. They were wonderful to see, and so were the hundreds of bobby-soxers and young women, going their way, as carefree as can be.

Arriving in Ellensburg, I decided it was time that Husky and I had supper. I was very disappointed in the dinner brought forth. I didn't believe the meat shortage could be so bad. The cost still was the same as Alaska, but our stomachs were only one-fourth as full.

Finding a room with a dog in tow is no easy matter anywhere. At about the fifth or sixth attempt we got a room. Husky was quiet all night and I slept well. When I left the room for the lavoratory, he let loose with a terrific howling. I raced back to the room and took him with me, then he was quiet again and biting my ankles. I scolded him and I loved him.

When ready to leave the hotel, he followed a waitress; they played a while and Husky didn't want to leave. I had to carry him out. On the streets he followed well for a while, till somebody whistled, then off he went to play again. Sometimes he listened, and sometimes I would have to carry him off. I had some time with a bag in one hand and him under my other arm. A few girls stopped me and asked if he was a real husky, and they all petted him.

On the highway he walked behind me well. I'd stop to rest, and he was fun and nice company. We stopped at restaurants, and the waitresses went out of their way to help feed him milk and bread, and he loved fish. We were near Spokane the next night. It was very cold out. It was so cold that I had to put on long underwear. It also got dark earlier than in Alaska. We could see Northern Lights. It had never been so cold in Alaska that I had to put on long johns. We saw a roadside dance hall and we went in.

There was a large crowd, and the orchestra was playing. They tied Husky inside near the door while I got a lunch and coffee. Some of the dancers untied Husky and he was running all over the place. The management didn't like it, but they cheered up and smiled as Husky got so much attention from the customers.

After we had lunch, we started walking again. Several cars stopped, but when they saw the pup, they said sorry he might get sick and drove off.

Next day I decided it best to send Husky home by railroad express. First I had him inoculated, then crated at a local grocery store with plenty of food for four days. He was howling his head off when I left him at the railway depot. I hated to do it, but hitchhiking with a dog loses a lot of good rides.

Soon I caught a ride with an ex-marine to St. Paul, Minnesota. It was about a thousand-mile ride. We took turns driving day and night. We picked up a young fellow in fancy cowboy clothes. He said he was a wild horse rider at rodeos. The marine kidded him a lot and called him a drugstore cowboy. The fancy clothes attracted a lot of attention every place we went to eat and gas up, and the marine was glad when he got off in North Dakota. From St. Paul, I went day and night again to Chicago, Toledo, and Pittsburgh to reach Johnstown, Pennsylvania, my home and only a day before my sister's wedding.

Husky was already home; he came a day earlier than I. Mom cried again and Pop and my three sisters were glad and surprised to see me home for the wedding. Lots of my relatives had come from New York, Ohio, and Michigan, and Pennsylvania for the wedding. It's one of those Ukrainian church weddings that last several days, and a big time it would be.

My two kid brothers loved Husky and my twenty-one-year-old cousin from Ohio cried because she could not have him. I've never seen another dog get so much attention from folks before. For Mom, I had moccasins and for my sister, a gold nugget, and for my brother-in-law, an ivory watch bracelet from Nome.

9

My Sister's Wedding

My sister was married on a Saturday at nine o'clock in a Russian Catholic Orthodox Church. The church was crowded with well-wishers. My dad walked down the aisle with my sister. They came to the altar and knelt to pray beside the groom.

A half an hour later, they arose; the Catholic priest said a prayer, pronounced them man and wife, and gave them blessings. The groom kissed her then, then he stepped aside and well-wishers formed a long line to kiss the bride and congratulate the groom.

The crowd then heads for the church hall where beer and liquor is on the house. There is only a juke box, and some of the younger set start dancing.

At twelve o'clock noon, the tables are set and dinner is ready. There are three long tables; each has settings for about eighty people. The bride and groom sit at the center of the main table. Prayers are said at dinner; then there is a loud clanging of forks and spoons on the dinner plates. It means the crowd wants the groom to kiss the bride. They seem a bit shy; as the clanging grows louder, they have to kiss several times more.

The best man quiets the crowd, makes a short speech; others give speeches also. It's usually to bring cheer and happiness. Then the invited have dinner of chicken, stuffed cabbage, roasts and breaded pork, salads, fruits, and pastry. Beer, liquor (and soda pop for the younger children) flow freely.

The orchestra comes and dancing begins and continues all day. The musicians get pretty high also. They don't have to rise and go to the bar; friends bring it and place it at their feet or on the music stand.

Supper is held at 6:00. The bride and groom return to the hall after resting. The crowd carries on the same as at dinner.

The priest comes to have dinner and to make a speech and offer blessings. After supper a traditional collection is taken up. One donates what one can afford, and almost everyone donates beyond reason through generosity. The crowd becomes larger in the evening. The music is American and European.

About eleven o'clock, a chair is set up in the center of the hall. The bride sits down, and the old European ladies tie a babushka (scarf) around her head. It is a very colorful one of bright yellow and red. She looks like the farmer's daughter or a peasant. The crowd is circled about her and they laugh and joke about her becoming an old woman and a mother of twenty children.

She is still wearing her white gown and in her lap she holds a tray that looks like a Spanish musical instrument or a tambourine. People, old men, old women, young fellows, and young girls drop 50¢, $1, $5, $10, or $20, whatever they can afford to dance with the bride. Around and around they go, someone cutting in every few seconds. After about an hour, the bride is tired and people still are cutting in; the groom is very worried lest she become very sick; he tries to break through the circle of old ladies, and they push him back. He has tears in his eyes, tears of love; finally he breaks through, lifts the bride in his arms and runs off, the old ladies from behind pounding his back in friendly anger. I got pretty drunk and my relatives and family asked me to show them how they danced in Alaska. I embarrassed my mom for God's sakes.

I did a native dance I had learned from an Indian girl in Juneau. Everybody clapped and asked for more. They really enjoyed it. But, oh, poor Mom! Next day I felt sorry I had done it, but still my friends, relatives, brothers, and sisters thought it was grand. My relatives told my Mom I had a right to get drunk on my sister's wedding. Mom cheered up and said she was happy as long as I was home.

10

Going South for the Winter

It was only two weeks since my return from Alaska. It was grand to be back among my folks. The fun of the wedding was over, and all the friends and relatives returned to their native states. There was peace and quiet again.

I found in two weeks time that the food shortage was no laughing matter. I went to the Frigidare ten to twelve times a day unconsciously, opened it and found it empty except for a dozen bottles of beer. I wished I was back in Alaska, the land of abundant food.

Jobs were scarce and strikes made the situation worse. I felt sorry for my veteran buddies, who went to work in the coal mines for low wages. I wished again I was back in Alaska, the land of plenty of work, good salaries, and steady employment.

I decided I'd travel some more and find living conditions better in South America. When I expressed my intentions to Mom, she cried again and said she had hopes of me marrying, but not any more.

The next morning Mom and Dad wished me a good journey, and I walked again to the trolley stop. From there by trolley to the edge of town. The Log Cabin was located there, and it was the scene of many an enjoyable evening with my brothers and friends. I lingered a while and had a spirit lifter, sad and happy memories crowded in.

Soon a truck came along, and we were rolling along a scenic, winding road amidst autumn-colored leaves and trees. Pennsylvania is very beautiful in the autumn and soon the memories faded away in the thrill of traveling again.

We ran into a little rain and nearly collided with another car, passing on a hill. The truck driver applied the air brakes and we skidded a ways. It was a close call for the automobile.

We rolled nine miles into Pittsburgh, and it was usual gray, smoky, and full of busy people. It's an awful town to drive into and out again. It's plumb full of one-way streets and to get on the wrong street by mistake will give anybody a headache before he finds his way out again. But Pittsburgh is not all smoke and grime. It has its beautiful places also and is an interesting, friendly city.

Several more rides took me clear across the state of Ohio, and I was in Detroit, Michigan, by nightfall. I called on a buddy and stayed a week in Detroit. Having tested aircraft engines during the war, I knew Detroit quite well.

I phoned the girl I loved so well. She threw me overboard. She talked to me, but did not wish to see me. Somebody told her I was not her type. In the six months we had gone together, I'm sure we always were happy. We had the same interests and we both loved sports. She promised to write.

My buddy, Johnny and I went to our favorite dance spots, The Grande and The Vanity. It sure was nice to be back and meet old friends again. Detroit is my second home and hard to beat. I love it.

In Detroit I saw long lines of fellows waiting, several blocks long, to get into the unemployment office.

I'd be one fellow who would not wait, but got out into the world and find living conditions easier.

It was cold when I left Detroit for New Orleans via the highway. Only points of interest were a couple of drunken fellows in Tennessee, a father and a son doing a dance to a juke box in a roadside restaurant. They were funny and amused everybody. The other was an incident that gives me the chills yet.

I was stuck in a little town in Alabama and was about to look for a night's lodging at a hotel when a car came along. The fellow rode out on the highway for about ten miles. He was a type of character you don't read many stories about, but hear plenty about them. When he discovered that I did not like his intentions, he stopped the car, got out, pulled a gun, and ordered me to take my bag and walk.

I did as he said and remarked, "You're pretty tough with a gun." He only got madder and said, "Get going." I did and when I turned my back and started walking, I didn't know if the crazy fool would fire or not. It was enough to put chills down my back. I walked a ways; then he got into the car and drove back to town. I failed to get his license in the excitement. He was plenty big and said he was a vet.

A truck came along, and I spent the night in a town about fifty miles further south and the following night in New Orleans. It sure was nice and warm down South after the northern chill of coming winter. Everywhere were palm trees and rich jungle foliage, including banana trees along the highway.

I'd spent several enjoyable days in New Orleans. I found the trip on the river boat *President* a marvelous "voyage." I was on board early in the evening. When the dancing started, the boat moved graciously out on the river. I discovered that everybody had to dress at least semi-formal in order to be allowed to dance.

Wearing khaki trousers and a light blue shirt, I borrowed a coat from one of the Negro deck- hands. The coat had broad shoulders and came almost to my knees. I felt like a zoot-suiter.

I easily got acquainted with a couple of French jitterbugs. When told that I speak Russian, they thought it marvelous and also that I was born and living in Alaska. I had a (now) useless check book from the bank there to back my story (Bank of Fairbanks). It was amusing; the news went around that a Russian was aboard and a dozen girls wanted me to sing and talk to them in Russian. Yes, it sure was a grand time, dancing, singing, and some kidding, and when the boat docked again, I walked down Canal Street with six gals in tow and the seamen and soldiers did whistle.

Finding that the National Maritime Union and the Seafarers International Union had struck again and had all ships tied up, I waited a few days as there was hope for an ending soon. I hoped to ship out to Panama. My hopes were crushed a few days later. The strike was to be continued indefinitely.

I went out on the highway. It was a pleasant afternoon. Beside the famous Huey Long Bridge, I waited for a ride. It came in the form of a large trailer truck driven by a Negro. He was a happy-go-lucky chap. I rode into Houma with him.

I went to supper there and a movie afterwards. I could not

44

get a room at a hotel, so I walked down the street leading out of town. I sat down on a bench near a nice home and fell asleep. I was awakened by a young fellow and his mom returning from a late show. They invited me in. I hated to intrude but they said I was welcome. They had three or four nice clean extra cots in a room upstairs. I slept very well. The next morning I had coffee and thanked the kind folks. The lady said it was all right, as she had a couple of sons, knew they might be in the some predicament sometime, and hoped they would be treated likewise.

I had to walk just about all day; many cars passed me. I didn't mind very much, I liked to hike. I stopped at interesting little homes, mostly poor people, and asked for water and perhaps a sandwich. It was very hot, and I passed no restaurants. People refused the money offered. Everybody was out on their porches. It was a Sunday. They waved and said hello as I moved along.

It was a late hour when a '36 Ford came along. It nearly ran over me as it came to a stop. There were two sailors and two girls. They were still in their teens. They had come all the way from Virginia. They asked me if I had a dollar I could spare; they didn't have enough gas to get to Beaumont, Texas. I gladly gave it to them. Beaumont was several hundred miles away, and I was tired of walking. They were a cheerful party. We sang songs most of the way.

Arriving about 2:00 A.M., Beaumont had a pleasant aspect all lit up in neon light. We parted company. I decided to have lunch, get a little sleep and start out early again. Sleeping on the promenade of a seed and feed warehouse wasn't bad for several hours.

Then at break of dawn, I gloried in the freedom of walking down the highway again in the early coolness. I had several more rides. Then a young fellow named Johnny came along in a '37 Ford. We rode into Galveston in the late afternoon.

Johnny came from Beaumont, Texas. We went looking for work together; then he showed me the town and all the places of entertainment. Afterwards we went to the beach and slept in the car to save on expenses. In the morning we took a swim in the Gulf. We did so for three or four days. It was fun except for the mosquitoes and getting stuck in the sand one day.

I landed a job at Texas City as a longshoreman, a dozen miles away from Galveston. It was hard work loading 135 pounds of flour per sack all day and other days unloading ore in one-hundred-pound sacks. We worked in teams of six men and stripped to the waist. We were all a sweating, cussing, joking crew, and I was a little soft, but in a few days, I felt grand. I found that the longshoreman consumes about as much liquor as do the rugged fellows of the great Northwest logging camps. We worked whenever a ship came in. Some days we worked long hours, fifteen to twenty-four hours straight or until we finished unloading or loading the ship. Other days we only drank and loafed till a ship came in.

One day in that quiet little town, there was a nasty fight. I had been sitting on the porch of the Texas City Hotel with a couple of other fellows. We hardly noticed a fellow enter a dry-cleaning shop across the street.

A few minutes later, we heard a loud conversation and the fellow came out backwards swinging his fists. Another fellow was clubbing him with a lead pipe. Soon his head was cut open, and he became a bloody mess.

We ran over to stop the fight or the man would have been killed. One of my buddies, a big burly fellow, took the lead pipe away from the attacker.

Soon a police car raced to the scene, siren wailing and coming to a sliding stop. They took the bleeding man to a hospital and left the attacker behind.

Someone remarked, "It's about time we had a little excitement in this town." Little did anyone realize that there would be plenty of excitement, about seven weeks from the date. For about seven weeks later, Texas City had a disastrous explosion that the entire world heard about. I was not at the scene of the disaster; it occurred about six weeks after I left, but it chills my spine to think that I had been unloading the very matter that blew up, only six weeks previous.

What had caused the fight was that this fellow entered the dry-cleaning shop a little drunk, found his suit not ready, and made a vulgar remark to the lady clerk.

46

The manager became enraged, grabbed the lead pipe from under the counter, and went into the attack.

I tried again to ship out. The unions told me that a lot of seniority men were waiting for a ship and were on the beach. Therefore I could not receive a trip card for Panama. I then decided to go by road. It would be most exciting surely.

I had tried purchasing an airplane ticket after failure in trying to ship out. The agents asked why I wanted to go to Panama, Canal Zone.

I answered, "To work."

"Sorry," they said, "unless you have permission from the commanding officer of the Canal Zone, we cannot sell you a ticket."

"I will go as a tourist then," I replied.

"Sorry," they answered, "we know your purpose and cannot sell you a ticket."

Disheartened, I felt I had no alternative but to go by bus, train, or hitchhike.

With my pay in my pocket, I left one morning for Mexico. Having no passport, I wondered how far I would get. Several days later I was at Brownsville, Texas, on the border. I obtained a tourist card for Mexico. It cost twelve dollars. I crossed over to Matamoros via bus over the Rio Grande. We rode over a dry plain for ten minutes and passed many ox carts and burros.

We went along narrow streets to the city. By merely going a few miles over the border, one can notice the difference in costume, clothes, language, buildings, and mode of transportation between U.S. and Mexico.

On getting off the bus, a number of fellows yelled, "Taxi, taxi," and boys say, "Shoe shine, Mister, shoe shine," others offer to guide you about the city. A neatly dressed young lad spoke good English. He and I went to the markets. They are an open-air affair, with canvas roofs to keep the sun and rain off.

They have beautiful Mexican-designed clothes, dresses, blouses, jackets, belts, jackets of leather, and fine trimmings of all colors. There are enormous rugs and blankets, beautiful and inexpensive pottery, jewelry, and household utensils, fruits, tamales, and enchiladas.

We stopped for refreshment and every cabaret had musical maestros. From the street they wandered in and out of the cabarets and offer to play for you. Some went alone and others in groups of three or four with a girl. There was music everywhere.

Afterwards I met a U.S. seaman. We had a Mexican dinner together. There certainly was no food shortage in Mexico. We rested at the city park. We had since paid the guide and now wondered why the girls walked one way around the park and the fellows walked the opposite way around the park. We thought the fellows were bashful.

A number of senoritas looked our way and smiled. After they had made four or five trips around the park and each time we received a pleasant smile, we decided to join them; when we approached, they laughed and dodged away.

We found out later that it is a custom of theirs not to talk to the boys until 9:00 P.M.

By ten or eleven, the park is deserted. We didn't think the custom is so bad, certainly it gives either party a chance to pick from a choice of several hundred. We laughed as we remembered the young woman being pulled out of the walking circle by an angry husband and led home.

On Domingo (Sunday) afternoon, everybody heads for the bullfights as if it were the last they will ever see. So we joined the crowd and paid 7.50 pesos to enter the grandstand encircling the arena.

There are two young fighters, one a Mexican and the other a fighter from Spain. He is supposed to come from wealthy parents. There are also two pretty young girl bull fighters, Elisa Gallardo and Teresita Andaluz. The girls put on a grand performance. They were very graceful and daring.

There were four bulls killed, three of them fought courageously and the last one became frightened and jumped over the rail, only to be forced back into the arena to face the cold steel sword.

As the bull enters the arena, two prongs are stuck into his back at the gate. This makes him very angry, and he charges wildly.

The fighter moves left, right, left, right, left, right, very

48

gracefully, as the bull charges the red cloak again and again. Soon the fighter gets tired, and three or four other helpers take over and keep the bull moving and charging.

The bull gets tired and stops, the fighter, in this case, the girl, walks up slowly with arms outstretched forward with a harpoon in each hand. She stops and wiggles her "landing gear," all for the entertainment of the male crowd and their roars of laughter prove they enjoy her antics. She moves forward gracefully then runs and jams the harpoons into the bull's back. The bull throws his head upward and barely misses the girl's arms.

The crowd cheers wildly and she repeats the performance two more times with success. The bull fights on and on, then a sword stuck near his heart slows him down. Then another thrust and he crumbles to the sand. A team of horses takes the carcass away, and attendants prepare the arena for the next bull.

Jose Luis Caro, the wealthy fighter, got hit once and was raised into the air high above the bull. His attendants saved him from being gored. Another time he slipped and had a close call; he nearly got it into the "landing gear" (rump), and the crowd roared with laughter as he scampered up and away.

It's pretty dark by the time the last bull is killed. It has been a grand show of courage and skill and a lot of humor. We return to Brownsville for the night and it's all American again. You can see and feel the difference.

11

On a Mexican Bus and Train

Next morning I took a local bus to Matamoros. It being Monday, I decided to head for Monterrey. Going second class on their buses is cheaper than walking. Ten pesos was the fare, American money $2.10. Monterrey was some two-hundred miles distant. The road was paved for about fifty miles, then it was a rough dirt road all the way. We passed Mexican villages and the natives sold oranges, sodas, and enchiladas. All the homes were made of sticks and old boards. The highway police checked the passengers and took a copy of my tourist card.

I was the only American on the bus. My light features stood out like a torch. I was the object of many curious stares; some did not look pleasant, others were. The fare collector spoke some English and warned me of what a poor Mex would do for ten American dollars. I only grinned. This wasn't the first story I'd heard.

I was fortunate to have a seat; most of the passengers were low-class peons and had to stand most of the way. We rode all day, and when we stopped for lunch, the fellow helped me order. I couldn't speak a word of Spanish. The folk of the village looked at me curiously as I ate and drank my coffee at the crude restaurant.

We passed so many small villages that had big names on the map, that I expected Monterrey to be only a poor little town with dim lights. I was indeed surprised as we rolled along a beautiful modern boulevard, and brightly illuminated. Monterrey was really a large city and quite modern in the late evening.

I managed to get a room above the bus station. The English-speaking ticket collector and the bus driver offered to show me around town. We rode their big bus around, then parked it and took a "libre." The cab was a very early model touring car and had no windows and only a canvas roof. It was very cold as we breezed along to a private club.

The club had a small bar and place to dance in the next room. Mexican coins placed in the juke box furnished the music. My companions and I secured a table and ordered Mexicali, the Mexican beer. Presently three good-looking senoritas joined us.

We danced to Mexican, American, and Polka records. All of the girls were good dancers. After several beers we sooner or later headed for a rest room. The rest room was an open courtyard with trees growing about. Surrounding it was a high concrete wall. We all ducked behind these trees to do our duty. Some of the girls were bold and drunk. They didn't bother to hide. Grin and bear it, they say.

One of my "Amigos" had done a little bullfighting and to hear him talk, motion, and express himself was something. From their expressions I gathered the meaning of the conversation.

We had a swell time. The girls got high and rowdy. We decided to leave. The check was sixty pesos for sixty bottles of Mexicali. We had spent several hours there. My two amigos had ten pesos each. I was stuck to pay the other forty pesos. They promised to repay me next day at the office before they left on the return trip to Matamoros. We then had a bite to eat; I could not swallow the Mexican soup and was satisfied with coffee and a "ham" sandwich, the American way.

The fellows slept on cots in the office, and I slept in a room upstairs.

When I awoke next afternoon, they had already left with my money. I walked about the streets, and I enjoyed the sights very much. I stopped in at the Greyhound Bus station and inquired about the fare to Mexico City. All vacancies had been taken, and it would be three or four days to make a reservation. I met Marie De Los Angles Floreson there. She was very pretty. She could not speak English well, so we wrote on a sheet of paper. We spent about an hour or so doing that. I believe she was afraid to go out or else needed her mama's permission. She wanted me to write to her.

I then left for the train station, and I had an awful time to tell the clerk that I only wanted a ticket to Mexico City. Nobody

51

of American appearance was around to put the situation over. After a trying time, he understood my intentions. The fare was sixty pesos.

I left next afternoon by train, first class. After a while I decided to move. I walked into and through second-class cars. What greeted me was a carload of burly, rugged-looking men. They were unshaven and wore big straw hats; many wore blankets over their shoulders. They were dark complexioned. A few women were aboard with half a dozen children and belongings. They looked tired and very poor.

Everybody stared and some made remarks in Spanish, good or bad, I didn't know. I only grinned and said, "*No Savvy, Hombre,*" and they laughed again. A few who were standing slapped me on the shoulder in a friendly way as I passed.

I went back to first class. Here I met Oliver Vivernois. He was a captain in the Mexican Navy and had taken some training at San Diego. He was on his way back to Mexico City. He spoke fairly good English, so we traveled together.

The train stopped at every little village. We bought oranges, soda pop, beer, enchiladas, and a dozen other food stuffs, the names I do not know, from the natives.

Most of the people wore sandals with a thong of leather rope. It made the big toe protrude grotesquely; others went barefoot. All of them had something to sell except for a few beggars.

An old man extended his hand, and I thought he wanted money. A fellow traveling first class behind me dropped part of a sandwich into his hat. The old man thanked him kindly. I wondered how often he and many others I've seen on this trip went hungry. The people are very poor.

Every village seemed to have at least one fine building. It is a nice white church with a bell in the tower and a cross. Surrounding it are the one- or two-room homes of the natives and behind can be seen rolling plains and hills full of cacti.

The trip seemed endless; it lasted a whole day and a night. We made only one restaurant that was reminiscent of the U.S. on the trip to Mexico City. Oliver's wife, Marie, met us at the station. I was invited to have dinner at their home, but first I secured a room at the Hotel Buenavista, across from the railroad.

Price, seven pesos per day, and it was a good hotel; I liked the management and servants.

The dinner at Oliver's house was swell. I met his sister China, his sister-in-law Rebecca, his two brothers, and the baby. We had rice, lettuce, tomatoes, celery, tortillas, delicious meat bits, and the famous whiskey, tequíla. They liked me and invited me over several more times.

12

Mexico City and Language Difficulties

Oliver and I went to the train station one evening to see the Argentine Navy come in for Miguel Aleman's oath of office ceremony. There was a large crowd. The band struck up a lively tune of the "La Raspa" and the "Bamba." Then the beautiful senoritas went into a dance with gay caballeros. It was wonderful sight. The Argentines disembarked, fell into formation, and marched off. They received a mighty welcome.

A few days later, on Sunday afternoon, they had a parade. Mexican artillery and soldiers went by. A lot of them had served in the South Pacific. The Canadians had a few outfits marching and the Argentine Navy. A large number of U.S. planes flew overhead. Among them were the Super Fortresses. Then a couple of fighter planes ripped across the sky at a low altitude. They certainly were awe-inspiring. A lot of the Mexicans looked at me, knowing I was an American, and I really felt proud.

Oliver had warned me incessantly to keep my hands in my pockets if I had money or other valuables. I had taken pictures of the ceremony and returning to the hotel, I had my camera stolen from under my arm. I had it stolen while my mind concentrated on not losing it. Therefore, I considered the thieves very clever. There is a saying in Mexico: "They can steal your socks without taking your shoes off," but that's only an expression and has its meaning.

I watched the methods used in digging a large foundation for a building in the heart of Mexico City. I was amazed. There were no cranes. Laborers carry the mud from the foundation in large baskets on their backs. A band leads from the forehead to the basket for support. They carry the heavy load forty to sixty feet, then up steep planks to the street level, then again up another plank to the truck level. There are about fifteen or twenty men,

Author on the steamer
Yukon—**Alaska**

Juneau, Alaska

Rough going in Costa Rica

Street scene near Panama City

Spanish jail, Panama City, Panama

Venezuelan roadside scene

Venezuelan laundry woman

Indian boy traveling to market

Village near Valera, Venezuela

Gathering sugar cane near Valera, Venezuela

Church near Merida, Venezuela

Author and friends at roadside stand

Colombian traffic

Funeral wagon in Bogota, Colombia

Indian boy atop Monserrate Hill, Bogota, Colombia

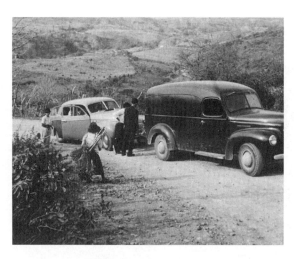

Motor trouble on the Pan-American Highway

Author and friend along road between Santander to Pasto, Colombia

Roadside scene in Panque, Colombia

**Army truck and three Colom-
bian soldiers**

**Three Colombians with whom
author rode for two days**

Mountainside railway, Bogota, Colombia

Railroad tunnel near Bogota, Colombia

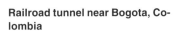

Street scene in Bogota, Colombia

Street scene in Tuquerres, Colombia

Old-time streetcar in Bogota, Colombia

Two of author's "chauffeurs" and their truck

Building under construction in Cali, Colombia

Woman near Cali, Colombia

Sevilla, Colombia

Bullfight in Cucuta, Colombia

Cuenca, Ecuador

Mt. Acero de Awaca, near
Cariamanga, Ecuador

and they work in rotation. They are barefooted, clothes are torn, and trousers come to the knees. It's strenuous work and pays but a few pesos a day.

Along famous Paseo La Reforma Avenue, in the cold night, I've seen mothers and young children freezing in doorways, seemingly homeless and begging for money and food. There were so many.

Oliver and I visited the church of Our Lady of Guadalupe. It was the largest in the Western Hemisphere. We both being Catholic went forward and sat in the front pew. Hundreds of people went up the aisle on their knees, crawling slowly to the altar in a long steady flow, softly praying. Men and boys, young women and old in dark clothes, some with babies, went forward, unashamed, to the altar.

The inside was very beautiful and bedecked with enormous quantities of fresh flowers. There were many blessed statuettes of Jesus, Joseph, Mary, and Virgin Angels. My regrets were that we didn't stay for mass. There were adjoining rooms with many relics and their history. Another room was full of photographs, notes, and names on the great walls of visitors.

Just outside of the church was a great market. They sold pictures and souvenirs of the church, food, clothing, carpets, and blankets. We bought peanuts, then rode a trolley full of dusky Mexicans back to Mexico City.

Every restaurant I went to, I attracted attention. A waiter could not understand English. He would call another, whom he thought spoke English; when he failed to understand me, they called a third and even a fourth, leaving nobody to take care of the long counter. In only a few moments, all eyes were on me. In despair I looked at what the fellow next to me was eating—rice, meat, and milk—so I ordered it.

At the "American Café" where I usually dined, none spoke English. I went to the icebox and pointed out what I wanted. Everybody laughed at me, but when a body gets hungry, it knows no shame. A couple of nice senoritas worked there also. Their eyes told me stories. Gosh, how I wished I could tell them stories, too, in Spanish. Slowly, but surely, I learned a few words—

Chuleta Puerco (pork chops)—and I lived on *Chuleta Puercos* only, for a few days.

I noticed the menu stated $1.50 for the dinner. It seemed odd that the manager should ask a dollar fifty in American money, when he had a business in Mexico, where only Mexican currency was used. I only had Mexican currency; then he charged me $3.35 pesos. It should have been $5.72 in Mexican currency for $1.50 American. He didn't know the rate of exchange.

I met two young Mexicans, who spoke good English at the "Café." They invited me to their apartment for cocktails. It was beautiful. One of them had his work there as an artist for the popular Mexican magazine, *Todo*. One of them had lost a brother in a plane crash in Mexico. He was sad, but cheered up after a while.

We strolled along brightly illuminated, modernistic Paseo La Reforma. Then we went to several clubs, enjoyed the shows, and got high. We stopped to eat at a Chinese place. Coming out of the restaurant, I must have wavered a bit, for I accidentally broke a side window with my elbow.

Feeling cocky, we decided to run. We thought we made good our getaway. We looked back and saw the Chinese manager chasing us. We went up to him and told him to beat it. When we walked off, he kept following us. We went back and he made some remark. My Mexican friend tried to stop me, but I hit him.

A little cop came from somewhere and caught my elbow and said to come along. Certainly I could overpower him and get away, but he only had to blow his whistle and twenty more cops would come in a hurry. I decided to go.

The cop hailed a cab; then the Chinese, the Mexican, the cop, and I went to the station. There the Chinese told the story in Spanish. My Mexican friend said nothing. They only asked how much money I had. I said twenty pesos (about $4.00 U.S.). They took it all and turned my friend and me loose again. I considered myself lucky. If I had had more cash, they would have taken it all.

Outside, we were hep for more adventure and my buddy said, "Let's get a couple of girls to sleep with us. What kind do you want, a rich or a poor one?" I said, "Huh." I had never heard a question put to me that way before.

So we took a cab to a nice section of town. It was late and girls were standing and walking about. They were out for a sole purpose. We talked to several, then my friend suggested another place.

We took a cab again to an apartment house. My buddy knew the girls. We were invited in. We stayed while an organ player and his monkey entertained us on the sidewalks. All operations were a success, and as we left to enter a cab, a drunken Mexican bumped into me on the street and remarked, "You Englishman," in a nasty voice, but before he could start a row, he was roughly put into another cab by his comrades. We then rode merrily on to our hotel. The girls showed us a grand time in Mexican style.

I was successful in acquiring a tourist card for Guatemala at the Guatemalan Consul in Mexico City—good for sixty days and free of charge.

I met Manuel Delgato there. He overheard me saying that I was going to travel by train to the Guatemalan border and then via bus to Guatemala City or via plane from the border if buses weren't traveling, as some folks surmised.

He was a Venezuelan who had spent ten years in the U.S. He spoke English and Spanish perfectly, also Japanese. He said he was traveling via jeep and would enjoy my company. I told him I would gladly go with him, and it would be more fun. He had come all the way from New York by himself. He had also spent four years in the U.S. Merchant Marines.

We lunched together but went to different movies in Mexico City. He saw a picture in Spanish and I one in English. Next day we worked on the jeep. We were told over and over again that there was no road to Guatemala. We laughed and were more determined to find out.

13

Jeeping through Southern Mexico

We left in the late evening. We went through Zocala (downtown). It was still crowded with people celebrating Miguel Aleman's election. Fireworks and rockets went up and lit the sky in lovely colors. A picture of the newly elected president was developed. This was done by fire crackers and colored fuses.

Manuel let me take over driving at night. The jeep fairly squeezed through the maze of traffic. The muffler was broken so the exhaust was thunderous. All eyes were turned our way, and Manuel was anxious to get out of town before we got a ticket. Manuel picked up a fellow who turned out to be dead broke and wanting to go to Guatemala City to visit his father.

Manuel was an interesting person. We had much to talk about. Because he was Venezuelan, he paid two dollars for his tourist card, good for only six days in Guatemala. We had been driving for several hours. It was plenty cold. We stopped and bought fruits from a tiny roadside store. The road was excellent till we came to a small town. Then there just was no more road, only rough cobblestone, dirt streets, and alleys.

We asked a tall fellow, dressed in a large sombrero and the usual blanket wrapped about him, standing conspicuously on a dimly lit corner, for directions. His directions took us into a muddy field. We turned back.

We saw a pair of lights of a truck. We were told by the driver to follow him. We followed him through many fields. Already Manuel and I wondered what the rest of the road would be like. We got on a fine road again all the way to Puebla.

From Puebla we traveled over a gravel road all night. There was a full moon, but we kept the roof and sides up due to the cold.

Morning found us entering a drabby town, lined with white-washed, thatched-roof houses, and cobblestone streets. We went down a steep grade and up another. We stopped on the hill, so we would not have difficulty starting the engine again.

It was a cold morning. We went into a dingy, dark room that served as a restaurant. We had breakfast and hot coffee. Then we started out again. The entire town was gathered about the jeep when we started to leave.

We already were a curiosity.

We rolled along all day, Manuel driving. I didn't mind his running over chickens, but when he ran over a pig, I started worrying. Was he careless or was his eyesight bad?

The pig was stuck under the jeep and squealing its head off. Manuel got out, took a look, and told me to back the jeep up.

I did so and the pig scampered away. Then Manuel jumped in beside me, and I drove off in a hurry. We were in a small village. The natives were coming out of the thatched houses toward us. We didn't want any argument; we only wanted to get away. There were shouts behind us, and we feared someone might shoot.

Soon as we got away, Manual and I breathed a sigh of relief and grinned at one another.

Manuel took over again. Upon our approaching villages, people moved off the road and huddled against fences and houses. Manuel pulled up close and came to a stop, but not before scaring the wits out of an elderly man and woman who were undecided which way to run. From all appearances, it seemed the Natives had a great fear of these newfangled auto machines.

Here we bought oranges, stalks of sugar cane, and an extra supply to last several days. Manuel and Jose jabbered in Spanish to the villagers who curiously walked about the jeep.

When we started again, they gave us plenty of clearance by backing away ten feet or so. We had to laugh at their fears.

Manuel drove all day and towards sundown I offered to take over, not only because I thought he was tired, but because he drove unsteadily and scared me.

He drove along at about twenty miles per hour. The road was bad. It was several inches deep in gravel. There were truck and auto tracks to follow, but Manuel couldn't stay in the tracks to save his life. Each time the wheels went out of the tracks, it had a tendency to throw us into a skid.

Suddenly the jeep went into a terrible skid. It went from one side of the road to the other. On one side was a steep precipice, on the other the mountainside. Luckily, miraculously, we hit the mountainside and turned over.

I was in the middle and smacked my head against the windshield. The force caused it to turn a sparkling white, but it didn't break. Manuel leaped clear as we hit, and Jose was pinned under the jeep, under me, under boxes, sugar cane, and oranges.

He and I were both slightly dazed, only he suffered a nasty cut on his arm.

We were lucky we didn't cause a landslide and doubly lucky that we didn't go over the cliff.

The engine was still running; the jeep was on its side. We hadn't seen a car all day, so we couldn't expect help in righting the jeep. We proceeded to unload the jeep of its heavy load. Then the three of us strained and pushed. After three times we succeeded in righting the jeep.

After reloading the jeep, I got behind the wheel. Manuel said nothing, but seemed to think it only natural that I should take over.

Darkness fell, but it was a clear night. I could see the twin tracks ahead of me, stretching out in the distance, then up and over mountains. Our headlights had been knocked out, and Manuel marveled and asked how I could possibly see and stay in the tracks.

"Better eyes and more driving experience," I answered.

Several hours of this, and I became pretty tired. We came to a wide river. I suggested we camp on the sandy shore. It was a beautiful night for camping, and it wasn't cold here in the valley.

Manuel and Jose disagreed. "It's too dangerous. Bandits may attack and kill." "Okay," I said. They should know best. They said it was safer to sleep in a road camp, even if only twenty people; it was safer than out in the country.

We crossed the wide river. As I started up the steep bank on the other side, the engine stalled. We were stuck in the water above the wheels. "Would it start up again?"

After about five minutes, it did. Then we drove over mountain after mountain, always upward; then it got cold again. Just when I thought I couldn't keep my eyes open any longer, we sighted the road camp.

We drove in. There was a garage with a thatched roof and sticks and boards for walls. A lot of truck parts were littered about.

There were ten men and a few ladies. One of the men was drunk and annoyed Manuel and me. Then the other fellows took him away.

While a lady prepared rice, beans, and meat bits inside a reed hut over a stone stove, Manuel, Jose, and I washed up at a river nearby.

We ate by candlelight. They talked about me, a white man, as I silently ate my rice, beans, meat, then black coffee.

After paying for the food, the three of us slept in the jeep, and cold it was all night. We had a tug of war all night with the only blanket that Manuel had.

At break of dawn, after coffee and bread, we were off again. It was cold. I drove where there was much gravel. About ten o'clock, we came upon a party cutting a road along a mountain. I was surprised to see heavy equipment there. We stopped there to have some welding done on the hold-down plate for the spare tire. It had broken away and sent the tire rolling down a hillside, with Jose after it the day before.

Now we had it welded in place again for a nominal fee.

We then rolled and bounced down the uneven road. We went up and down mountainsides covered with sage and cacti.

Our muffler gave a very loud noise so that villagers in the valley below stood in their doorways, behind fences, and behind trees to watch us come and go.

None of them dared to get in the path, for fear of being struck down.

About noon we came to a large town. I don't recall the name. Manuel pulled up to the *mercado* where there were posted horses. Manuel came very close to them. I expected he would stop, but he evidently was poor-sighted and ran into the horses' legs.

The horses became panic-stricken and tore right through the crowded *mercado*. Old ladies and Indians sitting on the ground lay low flat as the horses charged over them.

The engine stalled and there was no getting away this time. A crowd of surly Indians gathered about the jeep. We feared there would be trouble.

Manuel got out, lifted the hood, and started tinkering with the starter switch. The crowd seemed to forget about the runaway horse and looked in amazement at the engine contraption. When I finally kicked it over, the entire crowd backed away in fright.

We drove away a few blocks and parked it. Jose stood guard while Manuel and I went shopping about the *mercado*.

I was hungry. I bought strange candies, food, meat. None of it looked wholesome.

Manuel felt very much at home at these *mercadoes*. He slowly went here and there, bending low, saying something to the squatting Indians. Peddlers tried to sell us beautiful-colored blankets, but we couldn't afford them.

We drove out of town again. It was bright and sunny. The road was still dirt, full of gravel.

Towards sundown we approached another village and were told a fiesta was going on. Manuel said it would be a good idea to see it. Jose was all for it also, so I said okay.

We found the town pretty well crowded. Manuel said we must get a couple of small boys to watch the jeep and everything in it. I said we could not trust them. Manuel said we could as long as we gave the boys a tip. It's a Spanish custom and they would not run away.

"Okay," I said, "you're Spanish; you know the customs."

We got several boys, gave them handsome tips to watch the jeeps. Then we moved forward into the crowd. We came to a long wooden table. It represented a bar, I guess; unshaven Mexicans were all about it, drinking tequila.

Manuel, Jose, and I came forward, and the fellows made room for us. They inquired, "Who is the light-haired one?"

They were friendly to Americans. They gave us shot after shot of tequila.

Then we heard music. We broke away from the table. We found an orchestra with six fellows playing guitars and marimbas. They played on the porch and the dancing went on inside the adobe house.

Some danced and others sat on long wooden benches along the wall. Old hags tried to get me to dance with young senoritas. I did a few, but I didn't enjoy it much; the girls did not wear clean clothes.

Jose had a big time. He was a show-off, and few people liked him.

Fellows and women asked what songs I liked, and I said the "Bamba." The orchestra played it twice. It is really a lively tune.

Later as Manuel, Jose, and I went to have dinner out on the porch, a member of the orchestra asked me to pay for the songs they played for me. I did. I thought the dinner was only a sign of their hospitality to a couple of travelers. But next morning Manuel told me he had paid for that also.

The music, dancing, drinking, and feasting went on. It was a lively party. At late hours, children were found sprawled and sleeping on the porch.

Because Manuel and Jose were Spanish, they were given a mattress to sleep on. I could sleep in the jeep, because I was a gringo. Manuel told me this next morning to my inquiry.

Early morning found us driving away, waving friendly farewells to the Mexican householders.

We didn't go far before I looked into the glove compartment. I found my second camera missing. Manuel stopped the jeep, looked into his trunk and found his jacket, trousers, and shirt missing. Jose had his old coat and his passport stolen. He claimed he had one; we didn't know if he had one or not.

We decided it senseless to go back. There had been a large crowd, and there was no telling who did the stealing.

As for trusting Mexican kids with a tip, Manuel had to discard that traditional Spanish custom.

We figured Jose would never get into Guatemala without a passport, but he insisted upon trying.

We rode ever southward, then up into mountains so high that we were in the clouds. We had the roof and sides up and still we were cold. We were bundled up, and I had a towel wrapped about my head to keep the cold off.

We passed lonesome solitary Indians along the ridge of the mountain road. It was a sheer cliff in many places. We said "Adios" us we went by and never got an answer. Maybe they didn't speak Spanish.

It was so cold. They were bare legged and bare armed. Only a heavy cloth, like a rug, seemed to be slipped over their shoulders. It had a large V neckline. Their shoulders and thighs were bare. Few seemed to wear white shorts. There was nothing to button the sides. Then they wore a wide straw hat like a Chinese rice picker's. They also carried rifles. They really looked like hearty mountain soldiers.

Coming into Oaxaca, we found the entire village full of these scantily dressed fellows. Even little boys wore the same garb. We could not understand how they withstood the intense cold. They stood about in groups and none seemed to be shivering. We did not bother to stop. If I had had my camera, I'd have gotten some wonderful pictures.

We drove on, on, on. Night fell and we were riding through a forest. Only a narrow trail lay ahead. We asked a lone woodsman, who carried a rifle across his back, if that was the road to Comita. He gave us an affirmative answer.

Manuel and I took turns driving. Jose didn't know how to drive. The road became wavy to our sleepy eyes and rocky at the same time.

What seemed like an endless ride came to an end about 11:00 when we rode into Comita.

The town was much larger than we had expected. It even had paved cobblestoned streets, sidewalks broken in places, a plaza (public square), and several hundred adobe houses with red-and-orange tile roofs. They all had falling plaster or paint.

A crowd of children came running after us. When we stopped, they scampered all over the jeep. Some fellows came toward us to give help or information.

We inquired about a restaurant and were promptly directed to one—a single-room, dirty, plaster falling, a wooden table. We sat on boxes and soon were served eggs, biscuits, beans, rice, and black coffee.

Then we walked two blocks away to a hotel, or should I say a bed, the first since we left Mexico City four days ago.

Manuel and I had separate beds, and Jose slept out in the jeep on guard duty. He had a blanket to keep warm.

We had simple rooms and large locks to lock the immense doors.

We slept very well and awoke very early. We had about sixty kilometers. to the Guatemala border. We hoped to reach it in one day.

While we were packing our things into the jeep, Mexican officials came and wanted to see our documents. They were found in order and stamped.

Then we received the discouraging news that we could drive 60 kilometers and no farther, unless we dismounted the jeep and carried it over the trail to Guatemala.

Other hearty Americans had gone that far and had to return. The Pan-American Highway more or less ended at Comita. There was another route and that was by way of Jalisco and Tapachula.

But at Jalisco the road ended and one had to go by train to Tapachula.

We were disappointed, but there was no other way. We thanked the officials and headed into the forest.

All day we followed the narrow trail. Darkness fell and we were still far from Jalisco. We picked up hitchhikers and they sat on the huge box behind. We had about ten riders.

The road became unbelievably winding, twisting, and bumpy. It was a dizzy downgrade incline, and Manuel decided I'd better take over again. I had all I could do keeping the jeep in low speed going down. This lasted for endless minutes, actually about an hour.

Then we saw the dim lights of Jalisco. I was worn out. When we checked in at the hotel, I went to sleep at once. Manuel and Jose went "Dear" hunting.

I awoke next morning. Manuel said he had no luck "Dear"

hunting, came in early, and found me fast asleep. Jose was on guard duty again because he had no money.

We found the town of Jalisco quite large and the hotel satisfactory—better than expected.

We could still drive a number of miles to Tonala, the freight station. We followed a trail along railroad tracks.

We dived in and out of a couple of creeks, and several times we thought the jeep would tip over sideways, left or right as we went over inclined rain-washed trails. We had to lean one side to the other for leverage.

Tonala seemed farther and farther away. We feared we'd miss the freight train that comes about once a week and was due this very day.

Then we got a blowout on the sharp rocks. It was no wonder. It was our first since leaving Mexico City, and I guess we were fortunate.

We put on the spare in no time; then we continued over the dry, sparse fields to Tonala.

We drove up to a flat car on a side track. There was already a jeep on it. We soon met the party who owned it. Mrs. Catherine Wahler and her daughter, beautiful Trinket; also Mr. Edward Neils and his wife, Ann.

The Wahlers were journalists, and the Neils were photographers and artists. Later we were shown sketches and photos of their trip. They were grand.

We learned that they also had gone as far as Comita and were compelled to backtrack to take the freight. An ex-navy man had been in their party and decided to walk the sixty-kilometer gap to Guatemala or on horseback if necessary and planned to meet them in Guatemala City.

We were called lucky; they had waited a week for the flat car in Tonala. We just came and made arrangements to put our jeep on the same flat car. Three or four natives got long planks, and I drove the jeep up. They then tied down both jeeps and asked for eighty pesos for about a half hour's work.

Right there we had a dilly of an argument. Well, not I, as I could not speak Spanish, nor Mr. Neils either. But Manuel, Mrs. Wahler, and Jose put up a battle royal with the natives.

The Mexicans worked for the railroad but charged their own fee as the company did not pay for their labors. Well, they certainly didn't make eighty pesos in two weeks, and we weren't going to pay that for a half hour's work.

They then threatened to untie the ropes and disconnect the flat car from the freight. One ugly Mexican carried a steel pipe and meant to use it to follow his intentions, but Jose scared him off with a twelve-inch knife. Finally it was settled for forty pesos, still an extravagant price in that country. The fare for each jeep was two-hundred pesos and only one person could ride free of charge per jeep. The rest of us paid 15.60 pesos, ($3.30 U.S.) first class on a freight as passengers.

The train was scheduled to leave at 2:30 P.M. The train master and ticket seller had left to take their two o'clock siesta. We had to chase up dusty streets and broken sidewalks before we found them. When they awoke, they must *first* have dinner and then walk the few blocks to the office. They don't move fast for anything or anybody. Mrs. Wahler had only contempt, for she was, indeed, a very lively woman. We just had to learn to take it and like it.

While we waited we had coconut milk and another native drink that tasted like wine. It was hot and dusty in the little town. Native baskets and clothing sold very cheap.

We rode atop the caboose, and the cool breeze felt grand in the hot sun. It was a wonderful trip as I had beautiful and gorgeous "Trinket" for company. She had curly chestnut hair, blue eyes, and the softest voice. She told me she had spent a number of years in Ecuador and was returning there with her mom to join her dad who was an engineer in the jungles.

We bought ice-cold flavored drinks; also a few hot tamales at some of the village stops.

At night we stood on the edge of the flat car and held on to the jeep. A beautiful full moon was out. The two of us stood alone. We zipped through high brush and this was really adventure. We both started singing. When it got too chilly, we got into Manuel's jeep and chased sleeping Jose into the caboose. We put the roof down. We were riding backwards. We had to hold hands to keep warm. Our faces were black from the soot; only white teeth were visible. "Trinket" remarked that my three-day beard hurt, and she wasn't used to it as I was.

We arrived in Tapachula only too soon. The eighty-mile trip seemed very short. We arrived about midnight. Mrs. Wahler took her daughter and scouted for a hotel. Manuel and Jose went hunting—deer.

I found a lady with a cook stove on a sidewalk. I sat down and again had *chulata percos,* and they were delicious. Mrs. Wahler and Trinket came by and said they had found a nice place for ten pesos and recommended it. Mrs. Wahler was swell and a great help. She had lived in Central and South America and had been around the world. Natives found it hard to cheat her. She had a knowledge of what the regular price should be.

Next morning Trinket and I had breakfast together, and also, Mrs. Wahler. We all looked like different people after taking a shower and a change of clothes.

We then went down to the yards of the station to unload the jeeps. Again the natives wanted fifteen pesos for untying the jeeps and for the use of their planks. Nothing gained by arguing, just pay and forget it. One other American party got on the freight at night. They were driving a new car. The owner was very mad, and said if he never saw Mexico again, he would be happy. We laughed and felt sorry for him. He was overcharged heavily. He was on his way to Costa Rica with his wife and family.

We had to get our passports and tourist cards okayed in Tapachula by the officials there. We all were permitted to leave except Jose, who claimed he had his passport stolen at the dance.

Being broke, Manuel gave him a few dollars and a beautiful jacket he had purchased out of sympathy. Jose wanted us to take him back to Mexico City or give him enough money. That was certainly out of the question. The last we saw of Jose, he was angrily headed for a bar. Thus far the trip from Mexico City had lasted eight days. We had lost two days by going to Comita and backtracking. The train takes four days on the same run.

We left Tapachula in the late afternoon. We were just ahead of the Wahlers and rolling along a good macadam road. Manuel stepped it up, but we hadn't gone far before we noticed the water temperature boiling. We stopped to investigate and found the crankshaft pulley missing.

A truck came along. The driver said that a small boy had found our pulley and was waiting for us to return. The Wahlers passed us. We said we'd meet along the road again. We drove back to town, found the boy, and at a garage obtained additional parts and a fan belt.

We left again. We rolled swiftly toward the border. We reached it at dusk, just as a heavy tropic rain came. The officials made us unpack thoroughly. Manuel was my mouth piece and interpreter when officials asked me questions. They seemed amused. They let us pass.

14

Jeeping through Guatemala

It started raining hard. We picked up a few natives going to Suchate. This was really jungle there. The natives carried big jungle leaves for umbrellas and ran barefooted along the muddy road.

We arrived about ten or eleven o'clock in Suchate, Guatemala. There was a fiesta going on. The rain didn't keep the crowd away. The only light came from candles and lanterns under canvas roofs on the long counters and tables lining the street. We had supper in a restaurant that wasn't much bigger than a ten by ten room, with a kerosene lamp for light. A fellow was working on an automobile motor in the same room. We dined on meat, rice, and fruits. Manuel doesn't like meats and always gave me his share. We had now to pay in quetzales, the Guatemalan dollar. Rate of exchange is a dollar for a quetzal.

We kept the jeep in the light of the doorway. We weren't taking any more chances of suffering losses through carelessness.

We had a policeman direct us through the maze of natives. The exhaust was thunderous. The rain was only a drizzle now; we succeeded in squirming through.

I drove along a muddy road. It was a thrill. We were in deep heavy jungle, but the road was good and mostly level. There didn't seem to be any road signs, so we asked information at isolated houses lining the road. Manuel was nice company and conversation pleasant. I learned all about him, service in the Merchant Marine, life in New York, and love of travel.

We got lost once and had to turn back for fifteen or twenty miles. I became very sleepy, and Manuel took over after we got on the right road again.

I must have slept a few hours; I awoke to find ourselves in a town and Manuel trying to find the right road out. Their were signs about four or five inches square indicating R.T. 1, the International or Pan-American Highway. It directed two ways; one was straight ahead, the other up a steep mountain. We went straight ahead, and after ten miles, we knew we were wrong. We came back and asked a young couple, who were holding hands in a doorway at a very late hour, for directions. We took the steep grade in low, as directed.

I took over again and Manuel went to sleep. Everything was fine for about an hour; then I came to a junction leading three ways. Their was a signpost; the names had no meanings. We had no maps. It was impossible to obtain one. Even the Consulado of Guatemala had none to furnish. I tried two of the roads that looked best. After five or six miles, they looked impassable. I came back to the junction, decided to wait for daylight, and hoped to meet somebody.

Out of the darkness, a woman's voice called. She lived in a house nearby. The noise made by the broken muffler was enough to awaken the dead. Again we were advised to take the third and worst-looking road, up a mountainside.

We were on the right road again. It became nothing more than an ox-cart trail, winding and twisting up and down steep mountains. It became very cold at times. Dawn broke; now we could see what the country looked like. It was mountainous and made me wonder how people could live in a land like that. We could see the road twisting for miles ahead, an orange-red color.

We stopped at villages where roads forked. Very few of the people had ventured far from their villages and knew the road to Guatemala City. They lived and died where they were born. It was a rough bumpy ride all day.

In the late afternoon, the steering gear kept locking. We nearly went over the mountainside. I adjusted it several times, and we continued on. Later we got a jolt as the spring shackle broke. Four suspension bolts worked loose and the spring hit the road. The continuous bumping had worked the nuts loose.

A truck came along, and with a heavy rope, we tied the spring in place temporarily and drove into a town. We had a blacksmith make a suspension plate. I fell asleep sitting on a cushion while he worked.

Later Manuel and I slept overnight at a pension. We had our supper and breakfast and washed at a large concrete water fountain in the courtyard. Everything cost but a few quetzales. About twenty kids gave us a push to get started. The battery had run down overnight. The owner of the pension wanted us to take him into Guatemala City. He wanted the thrill of riding in a jeep.

It was a fine morning. We got a big kick out of seeing a woman running barefooted with a large basket or pot on her head along the road. Others were loaded down with fruits, wares, cloths, and pastry. Their arms swayed in time as they ran, like a pendulum.

The men ran likewise and carried enormous loads of pottery on their backs. They were small, but had a terrific endurance. They were on their way to market. A lot of them came many miles each day, running barefooted.

About noon the fuel pump went bad. We had a spare, but couldn't replace it due to the lack of special wrenches. We succeeded in forcing it to last to within ten miles of the city. In the late afternoon, a highway cop on a motorcycle came by, stopped a truck, and had us towed into Guatemala City.

We parked the jeep in a garage and took a cab to downtown Guatemala City. We stayed at the Inter-American Hotel, across the street from the National Palace (National Capital).

Manuel and I shared the room together. We stayed five days and enjoyed every bit of it. There were a large number of American tourists there, and they were very friendly.

We met the Wahlers and Neils again. It was a pleasure. They said they heard us driving through a village at night where they stopped to sleep. It was terrific in the quiet of the night.

Trinket and I explored the city on bicycles. We visited the parks and a beautiful sculpture of Guatemala in miniature. We stopped and visited the interior of the modern National Capitol and had a guide direct us to various halls and offices. We looked out over the city from the rooftop. It was a splendid view.

We rode along modern streets. The police on duty gave us the dickens for violating some city law. In the evening we dressed in style and went clubbing at the Casablanca and Ciro's. Trinket looked swell in a flowered dress. We danced to American and Spanish music and had a grand time till she became ill and had to return to the hotel.

Manuel and I stopped for refreshments at a modern soda fountain one day. We met two beautiful white Guatemalan girls. We asked them if they cared to join us. They readily did. We walked about town, and the climate was ideal. We sat in the National Plaza and when Manuel said we had a jeep, they were very excited and wanted to go for a ride. Manuel went off to the garage to see if it was ready.

The girls and I waited in the beautiful park. They both had their arms about me and both said they loved me and only go out with Americans. They want only Americans and want to go to America. I said I was going to Panama and other places. They said they would follow me anywhere.

Elderly tourists went by and I bet a lot envied me. They all smiled. A few U.S. G.I.s went by and winked at me.

The girls were sisters, Mary and Margot Apariso. Both had a good knowledge of English. They apparently learned a lot from the Yanks who had been stationed nearby at an airbase.

Manuel finally came, five hours later. The jeep wasn't ready. The girls were really disappointed. We went and had dinner at our pension. Neither wanted to go with Manuel. They told him in a pleasant way that they only went out with Americans. I believe he was hurt a bit by the look in his eyes. He insisted I go out alone with them—so I did.

We met a corporal from the airbase whom Margot knew, we bought some liquor and went to her friend's home. We danced to the radio, had cocktails, and held hands. The friend fixed the drinks and remained. These were nice girls and had to be home by twelve o'clock. The soldier, who had spent a year in Guatemala, said it was a custom of theirs.

I really liked Guatemala City and wanted to stay on and on. The climate was ideal. It was only in the northern part of the country that we encountered hot steaming jungle, cooled by rains.

I succeeded in obtaining a tourist card for El Salvador at the Salvadoran Consul. No charge. Manuel paid a small fee for his visa because he was Venezuelan. We left one bright afternoon and found the road to be dirt, but well graded and excellent. We reached the Salvadoran border in only a few hours' drive.

We had met an American missionary when we stopped for gas at a small town. He was from St. Louis. He had spent six months among the natives. He said how nice the natives were. He couldn't help them out much financially, only spiritually. He gave them morale and eased their misery. Along the road we saw much poverty, but in the hills and beyond, it was ten times worse.

The children had no schools, no clothes, no sanitation or health remedies. We saw many with swollen feet, arms, and necks two to three times the normal size. I was to see much more of this throughout Central America. These poor people deserve help from the U.S. The missionary had his wife there. At first it was unbearable to them, but now they liked it. He had his car and had to learn to be his own mechanic in this country.

We gave a lift to an Amereican hitchhiker as far as the border. He was stopped there because he had no tourist card or passport and wasn't permitted to enter El Salvador. The border gate closed at 6:00 P.M., but for a dollar, they opened it and permitted Manuel and me to pass. We arrived about 10:00 P.M.

Our credentials were okayed. We had our money changed to Salvadoran Colónes, rate 2.25 to one U.S. dollar. We suffered about a 5 pecent loss in changing. The American lad was put up for the night at the border customs house. All these transactions were under kerosene lamps. One of the officials spoke perfect English and had worked in Detroit. We had a nice long chat together while other officials took the numbers of our tires and searched for guns.

15

Christmas Eve in El Salvador

Manuel drove and it was a fine road all the way to the capital. It was black macadam. We stopped once to eat, and three hours later we were looking for a room in San Salvador.

By custom the hotels lock their doors at an early hour. A few opened up when we knocked. No vacancies. We ended up at a pension. There were girls to sleep with. I took one look at them and decided to sleep in the jeep, alone.

I awoke next morning at the sound of voices. The sun was shining brightly, and everybody was laughing at my protruding feet, sticking out of the jeep. I threw the blanket off, grinned back, and said, "Buenos Dias." They all huddled about and jabbered in Spanish.

Finally Manuel came out of the pension, and he looked like the cat who swallowed a canary. He had a grin from ear to ear and looked much better.

We drove around a bit. The city didn't compare to Guatemala City at all. The streets were narrow and crowded, and even the National Capitol seemed crowded. There were markets right in the heart of town, a lot of noise from rowdy bar rooms, and a large gambling place was in full swing. I saw no Americans, only dark-skinned Salvadorans.

One "Palace" Hotel was able to give us quarters, and it was as usual, friendly and courteous.

At night Manuel and I went to the market. We bought some fruit and watched the gambling for a while. We met the manager of the gambling set-up. He spoke English. We talked and drank beer under the canvas roof of the gambling park.

He asked if we cared to go dancing at a nice club. He seemed nice. He was a young chap of twenty-six or twenty-seven. We went out to the country in Manuel's jeep for five or six miles. The club was beautifully concealed from the road. It was a very nice club, and many pretty girls were present to dance with.

They had an orchestra and a baritone singer. We got a table and had a fellow join us who was wearing a fine white suit of clothes. He told us he was a lawyer in town.

In order for the girls to join us in an evening's entertainment elsewhere, we had to pay the bartender five colónes. This sounded strange to me, but in foreign countries, they have different outlooks on life, and Manuel said it was okay. It was the custom.

We went to several other clubs. The lawyer had a girl too. There were eight of us. We had a fine time at the country clubs.

About 2:00 A.M., we started for town again in the jeep. The roof was down and we attracted a lot of attention. There was whoopie here and whoopie there and a lot of singing in Spanish.

We came to a fine restaurant. Everybody ordered a steak dinner. While waiting for the steak, the waiters brought round after round of Mexican tequila. We had vaqueros playing guitars and singing continuously. The dinner was delicious, and everybody had good appetites. After dinner we had more rounds of tequila. When we started to dance, the manager stopped it. It was a swell party.

Every once in a while, Manuel would look at me. We both were wondering who was going to pay for it all. Nine out of ten times, it's the American who pays. Americans are naturally rich.

It was indeed a surprise when the lawyer said he would pay for everything. We wanted to pay our share, but he would have none of it.

We each had a girl. The party broke up about 4:00 A.M. It was still dark when we rode through Salvador with plenty of zest and cheer and to sleep with the girls.

Manuel had intentions to sell his jeep and go back to the States for Xmas. He was a great help to me. We went to the Consulado of Honduras. I was told that they do not issue tourist cards and I must have a U.S. passport to enter Honduras. The regulations were the same for Nicaragua and Costa Rica.

I decided to go via boat. At the office of Grace Lines, I learned I would have to wait a month for passage. I did not wish to fly; I didn't have enough money. An agent advised me that I might be able to obtain a passport at the American Legation if I had enough personal identification.

He was correct. I obtained a U.S. passport within two hours after I showed my birth certificate and Manuel signed as a witness.

It was then an easy matter to get it properly visaed. I told the Consulados of Honduras and Nicaragua that I would continue via road. No charge for visas—$10 for a U.S. passport.

Manuel then sold his jeep. It was a wreck. He had paid $600 and sold it for $880. I felt sorry for him one night. One of his girls had made him sick, but a shot of penicillin fixed him up okay. I went with him to the airport. I sure hated to see him go. He was a grand companion.

I spent Xmas holidays drinking and toasting with the fellows at the hotel. The Mexican football team was staying at this hotel. They were big husky fellows, who came to play against the Salvadoran team. There was also a Costa Rican fellow named Jose. He looked a lot like Caesar Romero. I dined with him quite a few times when Manuel was busy or out. Jose brought a big husky Salvadoran over and we celebrated in Jose's room, drinking tequila. The children celebrated by letting off whistles, firecrackers, and bugles.

It was pretty late in the evening, and I was pretty high. Jose and the Salvadoran suggested we take a walk and find some girls. It sounded like a good idea.

We hadn't walked more than two blocks when I felt the Salvadoran's hand in my pocket. I grabbed it, but he broke loose. I said for him to give me back my money. He said, "No, Joe," and then lashed out with a hard smack to my nose. It started bleeding. I got very angry and plowed into him with all I had. He was much bigger and forty or fifty pounds heavier than I. He tripped me and I fell; then he ran down the street. I started after, but Jose, a cop, and somebody else stopped me. Jose said something in Spanish, and the cop walked off. We then went to the pension. I was very tired and winded.

I awoke with an aching nose, all clogged up, but okay. My eyes had started to get black a little, though I only got hit once.

93

Everybody heard about the fight, and some of the ball players shook my hand, slapped my back, and offered toasts and drinks. I felt as if I were the winner. I was missing fifty or sixty Colónes ($25).

Jose next day asked me to go for a walk to get some refreshment at a corner restaurant. He told me that he did not think his friend took my money and said his friend's father was a police chief. I told him I made no mistake and that a fellow at the pension had seen me being robbed. Jose spoke good English. I said I was willing to forget it.

Jose made a phone call. I was surprised to see his big Salvadoran friend walk to our table a few minutes later. He said hello and extended his big hand. He said he did not take my money. I said, "Forget it," and shook hands.

They wanted to prove to me that they did not steal my money. I said okay after their insistence. They wanted me to celebrate with them. I was curious to see how these Latin neighbors of ours actually played.

They got a cab, then we went to several homes and got four girls. They also got a bottle of tequila. It was about forty miles drive to the beach. It was a nice afternoon. The cab was crowded, and the bottle went around and around. The girls were pretty and no more than eighteen or nineteen years of age. We did not go swimming.

There was a large patio and a number of cabins. We sat, talked and had a few drinks. Presently Jose and the Salvadoran walked off with a girl to individual cabins.

I remained with two pretty señoritas; the cab driver was asleep in the cab. We strolled along the beach, the girls singing Spanish melodies. Then I volunteered and sang a couple in Russian. They liked that and laughed. We stayed on the beach till pretty late in the evening. My mission was a success. A rendezvous with two pretty senoritas on a cool, moonlit tropical beach shall remain in my memory for a long time.

We walked back along the sandy beach to the patio. We found Jose and the Salvadoran in a bad way. Jose was asleep with his head on a table. The girls couldn't wake him up, and the

94

Salvadoran didn't have money to pay for the additional drinks they had.

When I offered to pay, he stubbornly refused. He said he was sorry about last night and wouldn't let me pay. He signed the bill and promised to pay in a few days. We then had to carry Jose to the cab. He finally woke up after a few miles. They sang songs all the way into town.

At the hotel, both were sick. I was glad I took it easy. I hadn't spent a dime. Was the party on my stolen money? It certainly cost more than I had stolen, or was it because they liked my fighting spirit, and felt sorry, or had they mistaken me for a wealthy American? Regardless, they showed much courtesy and respect and could be considered as friends.

When I left the hotel at San Salvador, Jose pleaded for me to stay. The Mexican ballplayer gripped my hand, and he had admiration in his eyes. I'm sure if eyes mean anything, he had a great love and respect for the Americans.

Riding the bus to San Miguel, there were a lot of low-class natives on it. Mostly all of them were barefooted. A few wore sandals. Some carried large *bollas* (knives for cutting cane). I sat beside a chap who looked well to do. He spoke good English. He said he had studied and wanted to go to the U.S. to work, but his hopes were shattered by the U.S. Consul when told he could only go as a visitor. He was a rancher's son and carried a gun under his coat. He said it wasn't safe to trust the natives.

We stopped for lunch at a shack that was in shambles, serving the purpose of a restaurant. There were pigs, dogs, and chickens running in and about. Sitting down on a plank that served as a chair at a roughly hewn table, I ordered the same as my companion who sat next to me. It was chicken. I saw a jar of canned sauerkraut on the table. It looked the same as Mom made.

I put some on my plate, took a large forkful, and swallowed. I then got the worst case of hiccups in my life. The salad was seasoned way beyond my expectations. It was hot. At first the people couldn't figure out what happened and felt a little offended. Sign language worked and they laughed heartily.

It was hot and dry, and at various bus stops the fellow passengers asked me to join them in a bottle of beer. By common belief that the American is rich. I had to say, *"No tengo dinero,"* (No have money). It made no difference and they paid.

The bus did not follow a straight course. It went round about and picked up additional passengers, making it a long trip. The road was good except for inside the various towns. We arrived in San Miguel about 3:00 P.M. The manager of the only hotel spotted me for an American and wanted ten dollars for a room. I couldn't afford and wouldn't pay the cheat anyway. Coke cost 15 cents and he asked 50 cents.

I decided to start walking and maybe catch a ride to Santa Rosa before dark. I walked out of town amidst many curious looks and glances. The dust was inches deep along parts of the road. I stopped for a drink at a public fountain, and the native women giggled at my greetings. I walked on and on, numerous ox carts and peons carrying *bollas* passed me on their way to town and their *fincas* after the day's work. It was always "Adios" on passing. Others carried heavy loads and walked barefooted.

A boy of about fourteen or fifteen years walked alongside of me. He asked where I came from and where I was going. I answered in Spanish. Two or three other elder fellows joined and then mysteriously turned off the road and hurried up a trail. The boy got excited and it seemed like he was trying to warn me of danger. It was getting dark. I had hiked about ten miles from town. We came to a house of sticks and the boy stopped and wouldn't let me continue. I gathered that the three fellows had friends up the road and meant to gang up on me.

A fellow came from the house and invited me over. There was a fire going outside the house and near it were a few naked children, a pig, and a dog. There was also an elderly man, two women, and a young man. They motioned to sit on a crude bench and brought me beans, rice, tortillas, a little cheese, fried pork bits, black coffee, and water in a coconut shell. These folks were poor, but still were willing to feed a hungry person.

A truck came along and I flagged him. He stopped and said he was going only a short distance. I figured I'd be stuck for the night. It was pitch dark and the fire was a welcome sight. I was contemplating I'd be sleeping before long beside it. The folks were nice and tried to keep a conversation going.

Before long, we saw headlights again. We flagged the car. It was a brand new Ford and the fellow said he would be glad to take me to Santa Rosa. I thanked my host for the dinner, and he patted me on the back and wished me luck. The fellow driving was well to do and had a USA .45 beside him on the seat. He spoke good English was young and good looking. He said he was engaged to a girl in Santa Rosa. We made good time over the now rough dirt road. He dropped me off at a hotel. We had a beer together. He wouldn't let me pay and hurried off to his date.

The hotel was fairly decent for that part of the country. Clean sheets and candlelight; no running water and no bathroom. It was a Xmas holiday fiesta, still in progress. I walked about them, and some of the fellows looked as if they had seen a ghost. They neither spoke nor smiled. I didn't feel at ease. I sure wished Manuel was along. We might turn the situation into a lot of fun. I wished also that I could speak Spanish.

I hurried back to my room and fell asleep pronto. I awoke early, had black coffee, rolls, and fried eggs. Everything costs about a dollar.

It was like spring outside. There was a friendly nature to the people as they said "Adios." They were very different from the night. The sun was coming up. I walked down the dusty road toward it. I felt like singing.

About noon I looked back over my shoulder and couldn't believe my eyes. I saw a jeep coming. I waved and it stopped, and in good old American, "What the hell are you doing way out here?" a voice cried out. It was an American on his way to Nicaragua.

He was heavily loaded and pulling a trailer. They made room for me and my gear. His name was Johnny Smith. He was ranching at Boaco, Nicaragua. He had driven all the way from New York, except for a part in Mexico, where he put the jeep on freight. He had his Nicaraguan wife and son along. He was originally from New York and had served in the Revolution of 1931 in Nicaragua. He said it was plenty rough and the U.S. lost about two hundred marines in it. He pointed out the territory that he commanded in Nicaragua next day. His Spanish was perfect, I think.

Before long we were at the Honduras border at Amatillo. There were a lot of soldiers on guard duty. They all were drunk, still celebrating Xmas holidays. They were sensible, though. The officers were high also. We shared a toast with them. They didn't search the jeep and trailer very thoroughly. Passports were okayed and stamped. In going through the other towns in Honduras, we had to have the commandant's permission of each town to leave and his signature. There was a lot of red tape left over from the war. We had to change some money. The roads were ox-cart trails again and rough. We reached Choluteca at dusk the same day. Choluteca was the border town on the south of Honduras. From what we had seen in one day's journey in Honduras, it's a very poor country.

16
Scared Silly in Nicaragua

From the custom house high atop a mountain, we looked down into the valley of Nicaragua. It was a grand view. Johnny Smith took my passport. He made the proper negotiations with the official in charge in the modern white customs house.

Night came. We slowly went down the mountain. A large wooden gate was opened, and we entered Nicaragua. We didn't go far; we were stopped by a soldier with a flashlight. There were many others. Soon they gathered around the jeep. Among them was a captain whom Johnny knew. They had soldiered together during the revolution. I was introduced and we shook hands. We were then directed to the Nicaragua customs house.

The officials in charge really stripped the jeep, trailer, and our gear completely. They were very friendly, but were taking no chances with us. The official in charge showed me maps and the route. He brought out a bottle of liquor. We drank a toast to health. It was easy to see that Americans were liked. The soldiers wore U.S. army uniforms, except for 1918-style hats. They had received their training from Americans.

Several hours later we were checked okay and had everything repacked. It was 89 kilometers to Estelí. It was very dark out. Inside, the jeep was crowded; Johnny Jr. fell asleep on my shoulder. Mrs. Smith chatted in Spanish. I dozed off too. The road was fair; I awoke to see the lights of Estelí ahead. We nearly ran out of gas. Johnny stopped at a village and awakened the gas man. He knew this man well also. The man had gas in hundred-gallon drums. It was necessary to transfer it to the jeep in gallon cans. It was an unearthly hour to get the man up, but he was cheerful. We then rolled into Estelí.

Estelí wasn't very big. It was the lights of the fiesta that we had seen from the distance. After several tries we succeeded in getting lodging at a cheap hotel. I slept well on a cot.

Johnny loved the breakfast brought fourth; I had to pass it up. It looked like corn grits smothered in oil. Coffee and rolls and a few oranges did me good.

This was as far as Johnny intended to go. He meant to look up a relative in Estelí. He changed his mind and we rode through Sebaco, Dario, Maderas, Tipitapa, and into Managua, the capital. We followed the Inter-american Highway. It was well graded, very wide, and ready for the macadam. We made the 150 kilometers in several hours. He pointed out his fine ranch along the Pan- American Highway, then he stopped to chat with his brother-in-law for a few moments. At the city limits of Managua, we had difficulty to enter. It was jammed with ox carts. Managua was a city of about 200,000 people.

Johnny recommended the Colon Pension. He introduced me to the manager, who spoke perfect English. When going to sleep, I had to let the mosquito net down in order to sleep peacefully.

The rate of exchange on money was 5 to 1. On the street or black market, it was 5.32 to 1. Their currency is called Córdobas.

The holiday spirit was still on, and at night all of the people sat in doorways or easy chairs on the sidewalks. At Lago Park, along the banks of the lake, there was a large gambling set-up. It was very crowded. There was a refreshment counter and quiet places to rest. It was full of lovers.

I had hopes of mail at the U.S. Consul. I met an American who was interested in my trip and asked me to pay him a visit at his hotel. I did that very evening. We drank beer and he showed me souvenirs he had picked up from all over the world. He was an ex-merchant seaman, about fifty-four years old.

He kept his door ajar to the sidewalk. Lots of girls passed by and looked in. He would call out, *"Donde Vas."* A few of his girl friends entered, girls of eighteen or nineteen. He told me he had a lot of experience with them, but he was too old to carry on that way now. They sat on his lap, and he seemed contented and understanding. He had spent a lot of time in Nicaragua and had a lot of friends.

When I left, one of his young friends tagged along with me.

100

He advised me not to keep company with her after 12:00. She must be home by twelve or her dad would give her the dickens.

We kept company till 11:00. She was very passionate. She was always laughing. Though we hardly understood one another, we had a lot of fun. In these countries it's the custom to pay the women or girls for an evening's entertainment. They have to live also.

I had no sooner fallen asleep after she left, than I heard a knock on the door. The servant said, "There is a phone call for you." I picked up the receiver. I heard a voice say, "Americano." I said, "Yes." Then he proceeded in Spanish and I couldn't make it out. I hung up angrily.

I fell asleep again. About an hour later, there was a terrible pounding on my door leading from the street. It couldn't be a friend, I only had two American friends. The heavy blows continued. I thought it a band of hoodlums under the influence of liquor. I got out of bed and waited. I was alone and a bit scared, but I wasn't going to open that door. Let it break.

The knocking suddenly stopped and a soft knock came from the door leading to the hallway. I opened and the waiter, the girl's father, husband, and my American friend were there. In English the American said he had called and tried to tell me to get rid of the girl. I told him I did, at eleven o'clock. He said, "Thank God." He then motioned for the father and husband to look for themselves. I grabbed the husband and told him to take a good look. The American stopped me from socking him. I was mad because they had scared me so.

The police held the American and next day released him. The girl still hadn't returned to her home. When I talked to the American again, he said he didn't know she was married and wouldn't have her in his room again.

I had a boy direct me to the Consulados of Costa Rica and Panama. For the service, it's customary and almost a law to tip. It was an easy matter to get visas and only a few questions asked. "Tourist?" "Yes." "How long?" "Two months, maybe, six." "Okay."

The following day I got permission to leave from the police at Managua. I walked through town. A guard checked my permit and passport at the edge of town. I hiked down the highway, and many curious glances came my way. A truck gave me a lift to Casa Colorada and Diriamba. A fellow driving a German mail truck gave me a lift through Jinotepe, Nandaime, Ochomongo, and up to Rivas. The dirt road was excellent. We arrived there at noon, 116 kilometers from Managua.

I met an American minister there. He told me that an American woman journalist, full of spirit, had gone through to Costa Rica. He said I should be able to get through also. The people of the community agreed that the road goes only 36 kilometers to the frontier and then there is no road. Some told me the Negroes were very bad in the Costa Rican jungle and one gave me a crude knife made of steel and sharpened to a keen edge. He said I might need it.

I started hiking down the dusty, gravel road. There was no traffic, only a few horseback riders going in the opposite direction. It was hot and dry. Several hours later I was caught in a tropical storm. There was no place to hide. The jungle foliage offered little protection. I kept going, feeling exhausted and soaked thoroughly. The heavy rain lasted about an hour. I rolled up my trousers to the knee for comfort and to ease the walking effort. The sun came out, and before long, I was dry again.

I came to a village and asked where I might buy some food. A pretty native directed me to her home. Her mom prepared eggs, rice and beans, and a delicious warm drink in a cylindrical wooden container. It tasted like cocoa. The meal cost one Córdoba—about 18¢.

The smiling girl and her brother, who had been chopping wood, helped strap my pack, and off I went. I hiked all day.

Cattle were in the hundreds on the road. It became dark and they bedded down on the road. As I advanced they moved to the edge of the road. It was a cloudy night, and vision of the road was poor. I heard many jungle noises. I startled a couple of horses. They stampeded down the road.

I already had holes in my shoes and was very tired. There were markers to tell the mileage. I had 8-7-6-5 kilometers, yet to go. I heard a shout, and a flashlight played on me. It was the soldiers on duty. They asked for my passport. I presented it, rested a while, and drank four large glasses of water. They said the frontier was three kilometers more and I could get lodging at the barracks there.

Tired, but feeling good, I had two young lads hiking along with me. It was difficult walking in the heavy gravel now. It slowed me down. The lads pointed to a dim light in the distance. That was it.

We reached it. I walked up the dimly lit steps. There were five or six guards on duty. They took my passport, then showed me to an army cot in the barracks. There were many soldiers asleep.

Next morning I awoke at 7:00 A.M. I slept very well. The cook took me into the kitchen, and gave me half a loaf of bread for breakfast. Another thin loaf he wrapped in green leaves and put it into my pack for future use. Then they gave me coffee in a tin can. It was very delicious and sweet. No sugar or malt had been mixed into it. The coffee had been made in a half a drum over an oven made of stones. The soldiers got a big kick out of watching me down several cans of coffee and bread.

About 9:00 A.M., the commanding officer of the camp awoke. I was surprised to hear him address me in perfect English. He invited me to join him at breakfast. He laughed when I said I already had mine. He said, "Have it again." We then had ham and eggs. This was prepared the American way by his mom and wife, who lived at the camp. His name was Jose P. Mena. He held the rank of *Teniente* (Lieutenant).

He was a young chap of thirty-two and had studied aeronautics and soldiering at government expense in the U.S. He liked the U.S. and wished he had money to go back and stay. His wife brought forth a bottle of whiskey, then sewed my trousers. He invited me to stay another day at the camp. I hated to refuse.

He then ordered horses and a soldier to guide me through the jungle to La Cruz, Costa Rica. After four hours of conversation and good liquor, I got on the horse a little unsteadily. They all laughed and I liked them because they were friendly and nice. I promised to write to Teniente Mena.

17

In Jungles of Costa Rica

The "highway" really ended up against a wall of jungle foliage and trees. I waved back and next minute we were beating a path in the jungle. There were many open patches, and even then the weeds and foliage were eight feet high. My guide kept a rapid pace, would get twenty- five or thirty feet ahead, and seem to disappear. We had to keep shouting to keep together. We went straight a short ways; then we turned sharply left and other times right and up a steep incline or down a steep slope.

It was very hot. I kept my field jacket on to ward off the mosquitoes. We then sank into mud up to the horse's belly. Slowly they waddled through. We crossed over fallen trees and debris that was like a trap. I expected the horse to break a leg any minute. We scampered up hills so steep that my head was by the horse's head. Next minute we went down a muddy slope and my head was on the horse's rump. I expected the horse to turn over or slip. I suggested we get off and walk. The soldier only laughed; he spoke fair English. Surely I had never seen the likes of this in Texas or California.

We climbed a mountain. At its peak we changed horses. We got a good view of the valley. All we saw was dense green jungle. We nearly ran the horses down and then through some isolated *fincas*. The vicious dogs there caused our horses to panic and stampede. We brought them under control, but not before we knocked over large trays of beans drying in the sun. Everything crashed to the ground as the horses plowed through. We both suffered minor scratches and bruises going through the brush. We stopped for a rest at a river camp. A partly naked woman was washing clothes in the river and laying the clothes to dry on the rocks. It seemed odd that the mosquitoes were not bothering her. They were killing me.

We rode again and I was wondering if ever this trip would end. I loved it, but my "landing gear" was sore. I hadn't ridden for a long time. I had already contracted severe heat rashes and fungi over the entire body, except face and hands, due to rapid changes in climate. My guide said La Cruz was over the next hill. He pointed to a large wooden cross and said that was it in the distance.

La Cruz was situated atop a high mountain overlooking the Pacific Ocean below. The wind was strong and cold. He took me to the Guanacaste and said he had to hurry back. Teniente Mena had advised me not to pay the guide, but he had been swell. I offered him ten Córdobas. He refused the money, but when I insisted, he grinned and slapped my back. He really appreciated it. We had spent six hours in reaching La Cruz. I wondered how he would fare in the jungle at night on the return trip. There was no path or trail.

Roman Pizarro, the Costa Rican official there, stamped and endorsed my passport. I then rested in a hammock on the porch of the Guanacaste. Alfonzo Pizzaro was the son of Roman, and he became my companion for the time I stayed there. He had a good knowledge of English. He was very proud of his name, as it was after a great Spanish hero.

Next day Alfonzo and I walked down the mountain and stopped at a wealthy rancher's house for refreshments. A young pretty señorita brought us drinks. Alfonzo liked her a lot. Her grandmother looked on and neither smiled nor spoke.

We continued down the rough trail and reached the sandy beach. We enjoyed a swim in the clear water of the ocean. There was a poor man's shack nearby. We went and chatted awhile. The shack was full of smoke. The woman was cooking dinner. A lot of kids ran about in poor ragged clothes. Chickens and dogs walked about the kitchen.

Alfonzo and I started the long climb back up the mountain. It was very hard going, and we perspired a lot. Alfonzo kept saying that before long I would forget that I had ever met him and never write. He wanted to go to the U.S. very much.

By a miracle there was a jeep at La Cruz. It belonged to Don Carlos, a sanitary engineer. He spoke English well and offered to take me into San Jose if we could get through. He assured me the roads were bad, and we might need oxen to get us through. I said I'd go. I'd save money, and it would be more fun.

We left next day at three in the afternoon. Don Carlos had an assistant and two native laborers along. He thought we'd need them. The Pan-American Highway was only an ox cart trail. We had to go very slowly at times so as not to tip over. The trail had been eroded by heavy rains, and large rocks protruded everywhere.

Several hours out we were caught in a heavy rain. It lasted several hours. The four fellows talking softly in continuous Spanish lulled me to sleep. I awoke at night. We appeared to be lost. We were at a *finca* and a lot of cattle were lowing. The laborers opened and closed several gates as we went through. We circled about several times till we found a trail and continued.

We went through fields of hay. The dry hay came up and above the roof of the jeep. With the headlights, Don Carlos tried to follow the faint trail through the ocean of weeds. We all worried lest a spark from the exhaust should set the dry grass afire. We wouldn't stand a chance of getting out alive.

I dozed off and awoke with a jar. The assistant driver had rammed into a large rock. The jeep was stuck on top of it. It was sitting on the flywheel case. With long poles for levers, we got it free again. We came to a river. It was swollen from the rains. It was impossible to get across. We had to lose a number of hours more and go via way of Santa Rosa.

It was uncomfortable riding. We used four-wheel drive to get over obstacles. It didn't seem possible that the jeep would go up sheer rock walls four to eight feet high, but we did and held our breathe going up and over.

We came to streams where mud and water were very deep. There the laborers went to work with shovels, and cut down trees, and laid the logs for foundations to get us through. After all that work, they brought out a box. I thought it was dynamite. They had a roast chicken in it. Boy, we really made a party of it in the cool jungle by the river.

We had rough going for several more hours. Then we reached a rather large town. We had dinner and refreshments. Later we arrived in San Jose. The whole trip had lasted thirty hours.

18

New Year's Eve in Costa Rica

At San Jose, Don Carlos drove about the town trying to find a room for me. A lot of tourists had come to San Jose for the New Year's festival, and all hotels were filled. I succeeded in obtaining a room at Hotel Canada, a fine, respectable, and moderate hotel. It was operated by Canadians. I thanked Don Carlos, then he went home to his wife.

San Jose had much color to display. The Central Plaza was beautifully endraped in streamers and colored lights. Many of the folk were dressed in native, colorful costumes. On New Year's Eve, several good bands played and the girls walked one way and the boys the other way around and around the plaza. They had bags of confetti and showered one another. Others got popped on the head with paper bags. The sidewalks were inches deep in confetti. It looked like snow. A stiff wind blew, and it seemed like winter. Others danced around the gay bandstand. Everybody seemed to be at the Plaza. It was very crowded. The spirit was on and everywhere it was "Feliz Año Nuevo" (Happy New Year) and hugging and kissing. At 12:00 midnight, a great cheer went up.

Every New Year's Eve, someone gets killed. So the people tell us, "It's an awful time to get revenge."

This very evening, about one o'clock, the crowds had gone home, but I lingered and strolled about the streets with two American friends.

We saw a man lying on a park bench with his throat cut and bleeding profusely. We called the police, then they placed him in a car and took him to the hospital. To me, he already looked dead.

Someone evidently had slipped up behind him, while he was sitting on the bench and cut his throat.

My American friends were of German descent. They were big fellows. One of them carried a gun in his waist coast. He said he did not trust the natives in that country. They bragged about the German women. You can beat them; then they love you for it.

They confided in me that they owed two weeks board and rent at the hotel. They were broke. They had plane tickets to the States and planned to steal out of the hotel at 3:00 in the morning, because everyone would be tired and asleep after the celebration.

Two days later the Canadian landlady told me that they stole away without paying. She wouldn't mind it if they told her they were broke, and from where they were going, they could send her the money. She was a kind lady, but she was triumphant. She advised the police. They checked plane flights and wired to Mexico City police to have them picked up when the plane landed.

She received word that the two fellows were in the hands of the Mexican authorities. How they would fare, I don't know.

She told me of a fellow who had come from the States on horseback—came to her broke and admitted he was broke. She put him up with food and lodging. Sometime later she received a letter and money from his father who was a high government official in Washington, D.C. Now the fellow owns a riding stable in Panama.

My friends and I had a great time during the festival. We didn't mind the women hugging and kissing us, but we were not used to the men. We laughed and bore it.

All places of business were closed on New Year's Day. I strolled and explored the city. I stopped to ask a guard for directions. He said, "Momento" and returned with his commanding officer, who spoke English. He was tall and stately looking. I was invited to enter the fortress, which was reminiscent of King Arthur's castle.

The great gates opened and about twenty soldiers on duty snapped to attention. The commander saluted and we walked past. I had no reason to feel like a big shot, but I did.

First we visited the supply room; then the guns and light artillery. Then the galley. There were about ten soldiers sorting beans at a long wooden table. The floor was littered with bad ones. All I could see was soldiers and beans.

We visited sleeping quarters and offices of the officers. Then climbed several stories up a circular winding stairway to the tower. We had a fine view of the city and valley below. The commander got behind a stone block on the wall and demonstrated how easy it would be to shoot an enemy coming up the hill. It was all very interesting. There were about twenty-five soldiers on duty, patrolling the walls in grim silence. The fort would stand little chance against planes.

We then went to his office. He had a very large map of Costa Rica on the wall. I was glad I came. Via the map I could see that the Pan-American Highway was good for one-hundred miles south of the capital, San Jose. The remaining ninety-nine miles to the Panama border was solid jungle, no road.

I observed a fine road to the west to Puntarenas, the seaport. To the east and Atlantic side was a railroad leading to Porta Limon. I was told by the commander that boats do not run on schedule and I might wait several weeks. I decided it was necessary to fly. I did not have enough funds to venture via road and purchase or rent a horse to go through the jungle to Panama.

The commander said he would like very much to go to the U.S. but didn't have money. Although he had a son in the U.S. Navy, he had never crossed the border of his country. When I told him his people and country were more prosperous looking than El Salvador and Honduras, he was pleased.

As he escorted me to the door, the great gates opened again; the soldiers stood at attention. We shook hands. He towered above me. He was about 6 foot 3. He stood straight and clicked his heels as we parted. He made me feel like a great guy. He had a great admiration for Americans.

I was beginning to realize how lucky I was to be an American. I could make $12 a day in the U.S. and consider myself wealthier than a full-fledged commander in the Costa Rican Army.

There were a lot of visitors from the Canal Zone. Among them were two American girls. They stayed at the Hotel Canada. We went to the Plaza and danced to American and Spanish tunes. While we jitterbugged, Costa Ricans rhumbaed. They played the Mexican "Las Raspa." It was a lively tune. Helen and I made the mistake of starting on the wrong foot. We both received hard kicks in the shins. We tried again and the same thing happened. This brought a roar of laughter form the Costa Rican dancers. We gave up and went to several clubs. They were Americanized. American drinks, and American prices. We danced slowly to American and Spanish tunes.

On January 2, I made a reservation to fly to David, Panama, exactly two hundred miles; cost: fifteen dollars.

In the late evening, I walked about the streets, enjoying the sights and the cool breeze. A couple of girls said, "Hello, Joe." I thought they knew me, for Joe is my name. I stopped and we chatted. We then sat in the park awhile. They were pretty, but I wasn't looking for girls and disappointed them by strolling off.

I stopped for refreshments, a coconut cake I purchased turned out to be a rice cake. I walked again and in a doorway were two young girls talking to a Costa Rican. One was as beautiful a girl as I had ever seen. She smiled when I looked at her. I smiled back and passed by. I stopped again for a beer and thought to myself, *Boy, that girl was really pretty.* I decided to walk by again. She was still talking to the fellow and smiled at me as I passed again. I stopped on a corner and glory be, she joined me with her girlfriend in two minutes.

She was lovely. A large chestnut curl fell over her forehead. She was about sixteen or seventeen. Her dress was a lovely pink and her full breast showed faintly from the low-cut dress. Her figure was super, and her hair was long and pretty.

We had a soft drink. Her girlfriend left us alone. We then walked half a dozen blocks to her home. I met her brother and before long, they left us alone. It was easy to see that she and her folks liked Americans. She was warm and pleasant. Half a dozen hours later, I awoke with a start.

Dawn was breaking. I rolled out of bed and put my clothes on. My pretty friend just lay there as pretty as could be, covered with only a linen sheet. She smiled up at me. I smiled back and headed for the door. Suddenly she jumped out of bed, putting on clothes and grabbing me by the lapels. All that loveliness was gone and there was only fire and hate. It seemed like I had done her a mean trick. I hope I never marry a girl who can change so swiftly from lovely to mean and ugly. I realized she wanted money. She said, "Four." I gave her four Colónes; she threw them down angrily. She wanted four American dollars. I said I didn't have that much. She threatened, saying her brother would beat me up. I only laughed. I showed her all the money I had. She took half of what I had, which amounted to about two dollars. I then went past her brother sleeping at the entrance downstairs undisturbed. I returned to Hotel Canada, called a cab, and was at the airport at 7:00.

I was again questioned by Costa Rican Immigration. When asked how I had entered the country, I said, "On horseback." They remarked "On horseback" in disbelief. They checked my passport and saw I came in via La Cruz. Then they believed me. The word went around and the well-dressed air travelers looked at me curiously and asked dozens of questions. They said it must have been quite an adventure. I said it was.

19

On to Panama

The "Taca" plane was a small twelve-passenger ship. I had a Britisher from Honduras and Reynaldo Perez, a Costa Rican for companions.

We could see both the Atlantic and Pacific Oceans. We crossed over some high mountains and green jungles. Then we saw light patches of green. The Britisher said it was a banana plantation of the United Fruit Company, and he worked for them. We saw no highway, only a few trails.

The hostess was a pretty Costa Rican. She was pleasant and courteous. She had me fooled for a while. She only knew the English that was necessary in plane conversation. She had to break down and admit it when other topics were discussed. We all laughed then.

The trip lasted only one hour and fifteen minutes to David, Panama. We landed on a rough grass field. Reynaldo and I were the only two to disembark. It was steaming hot so we peeled off our coats. The stewardess waved as we watched the plane head out for Panama City.

We were about ten miles from town. We waited at the modern customs house for the inspectors to return from town. We waited several hours. Then we took a cab to town in quest of the officials. We found them at a bar drinking.

They took our passports, and left for the airport, and said they would return with our baggage pronto. Reynaldo and I waited six more hours. We finally sent a PAA coach to the airport. It came back in half a hour with baggage stamped and inspected okay.

Reynaldo and I had spent our last $20 for bus fare to Panama City. The Negro manager of the bus gave us a dollar back and Reynaldo and I dined on rice, sauce, meat, and coffee. We laughed about it. I could have hitchhiked it to Panama City, but Reynaldo insisted I could and should stay at his brother-in-law's place in the Canal Zone.

We left in a station wagon; there were fourteen of us crowded into it. I had a cute little Panamanian boy sit on my lap the entire trip. It was a trying time after a while. His mom had put him in the station wagon without a guardian and left it up to the driver to deliver him to his dad. Everybody thought ill of the woman. We rode all night on a gravel road. The driver was reckless and rode fast. We made several stops to load or unload some of the passengers and also for lunch.

We arrived in Panama City about 7:00 A.M. Downtown was not beautiful. We passed ragged houses and narrow streets crowded with naked children and Negroes in undershirts.

Reynaldo and I got off at one of them and took an army bus to Curundu, Canal Zone. Twice the bus stopped at U.S. guard posts and U.S. soldiers looked in. Once they passed us through. The second time they told me to get off the bus. They then checked my passport, made a phone call, then let me pass through. Canal Zone was beautiful, modern, clean, and I gave a sigh of relief.

I met Carl Dishong and Josephine (Reynaldo's sister and brother-in-law). He was very nice and when he learned I was from Johnstown, only thirty miles from Cresson, his hometown, well, it was like meeting a brother. Later he introduced me to Joe Fern, a fellow only a few blocks from my home. With these friends I stayed till I succeeded in getting a job eight days later in the Zone.

113

20
Life in the Canal Zone

I had arrived in the Canal Zone on January 4 and it was necessary to get a permit from Mr. Lee, the quartermaster, in order to stay at Carl Dishong's quarters. The permit was good for ten days as a visitor.

I liked Curundu very much. Everything looked fine clean and modern. The quarters were in neat formations, the lawns were well kept, and all the palm trees had their bases painted white. The roads were paved and even the Negroes and San Blas Indians who worked as servants walked about in neat clean clothes. Curundu is typical of all the other American towns in the Zone.

Carl Dishong had been discharged and continued working as a civilian at P.A.D. He had met his wife Josephine on one of his flights to San Jose, Costa Rica. They both were grand and expecting a junior Dishong soon.

Reynaldo succeeded in getting a job as a sign painter at fifty cents an hour. He was a happy-go-lucky small fellow and very popular at the clubhouse.

The clubhouses are the center of recreation. They have fine bowling alleys and pool tables. They have a swimming pool at some of them. Movies change every few days, and bingo and dances are held quite often. Soda drinks and lunch counters are modern and well managed by "silver" help.

Joe Fern had been discharged in Panama and worked at the U.S. non-profit bar in Corundu. He had married a Colombian girl and had a beautiful girl of three years. He said it was bad enough for one guy to be in Panama from Johnstown, not to have two. We laughed at this.

Carl had bought a war-surplus jeep and a motorcycle, all for less than $500. In those we explored the Zone and Panama City.

We tried the water at Bella Vista Beach, and it was full of gooey snails. We decided the swimming pools were much better.

Because of the terrific changes in climate from Alaska to Panama, I had broken out with heat rashes. It was very annoying because of the itch. I used a lot of heat rash lotion to cure it. Many people suffer from the rash when they change climates. A friend of mine had it so bad he scratched his back with a knife and his bed sheets were always bloody.

Besides the heat rash, I had contacted fungi under my fingernails, on my elbows and palms of the hand. All my nails had fallen off, and new ones grew in. This infection had started in Nicaragua.

Everybody said I'd get a job easy because I was an American. But I had no luck at P.A.D. or P.A.A. The central labor office in Balboa had nothing. The navy had laid off two hundred civilians, and they had seniority. The U.S. Congress was putting an economy drive over also. I had no luck with big shots in the Administration Building. The outlook was bleak. I took a bus to Cristóbal on the Atlantic side. No luck again at the Central Labor office there or at the Navy, French Field, or Mechanical Divisions.

Gold men (Americans) were being laid off and replaced by silver (Colombian, Panamanian, Salvadoran, Jamaican) men. Gold mechanics (carpenters, machinists, truck drivers) made $1.73 to $1.91 an hour. Silver men made 32¢ to 80¢ an hour. Back at the Balboa Labor Office, a gentleman listened to my story and called Mr. Van Sulan at Gatun Locks. He told him that I had hiked, walked, and nearly crawled to Panama. I got the job, as a checker.

I had transportation paid across the Isthmus on the train to Gatun where I was to work. I was issued quarters at Margarita. Gatun had no vacancies. It was necessary to ride a *cheeva* (small bus) or the labor train to work. After a while I got acquainted and rode in cars of fellow workers, to and from work.

Bobby Stiles worked in the office. She was the only girl on the locks. Boy, was she ever popular. She was blonde, pretty, and had a divine figure, and everyone liked the way she wore her skirts.

I was a relief checker for the regular checkers. I took over on their days off. We didn't make much money, but we had more fun than anybody. Most of them were veterans and Canal Zone residents. I worked four days and one night a week. I liked it also.

Bob Budreau, Cushing, Robinson, Hunt, Rathgaber, Bauman, Green, and I were checkers and worked out on the walls, tunnels, chambers, culverts, checking silver and gold men. Herr, Dale, Cox, Rovsh, and Bobby Stiles worked in the office. Out on the "field" was the best.

Being a relief checker, I had different gangs to check each day. I got to know a lot of silver and gold men thus. One day I checked carpenters, next day painters, next day welders, boilermakers, special engineers, and so on. I also had to go to every conceivable part of the locks. I didn't mind. The locks are world famous, and I wondered how they worked. Only a genius could figure out the complicated mass of engineering involved in the operation and functions of the numerous valves, passes, and by-passes that make up the filling and draining of the chambers.

The draining and filling are what bring the ship to sea level. One man alone in the control tower performs the operations. The purpose of the locks is to take care of the difference in the tides on Atlantic and Pacific side. There are three sets of locks in the Canal Zone. One is at Pedro Miguel, the other at Miraflores, and the third at Gatun. The locks at Gatun have three levels and raise the water or lower it as the occasion calls, eighty-seven feet. The other two locks each have one level and about thirty feet rise or fall.

I found it most exciting and dangerous to go to check the men in the culverts. I went down a hole (well) on a ladder for a hundred feet. I had to wear hip boots in the culverts; the water had been drained but the water came up to the hips from bad leaks in the walls. The culvert was immense, dark and musty, and about as big as a subway tunnel in New York. Electric lights were dim and far apart. The whole length was about three-fourths of a mile. There were many holes in the concrete floor, and I had to feel each step. It was easy to step into a dark hole and disappear in the sea beneath. A body would never be found after it once disappeared.

It was necessary to go from one level to another, hand over

hand on a life rope. The water went swishing down the steep incline about my legs.

The men working below reminded me of men in a chain gang. They only wore shorts or trunks and shoes to protect their feet from sharp seashells on the floor. All were sweating, some pulling steel beams in great teams. Others were working at the large valves in cramped positions, cleaning, scraping, painting. I felt like a slave driver as I stopped and took their numbers. Some answered in Spanish, others in English.

The governor of the Canal Zone made a trip through and enjoyed it very much. We got all wet and showered from a few bad leaks and wondered if the roof would give way. After two hours below, it was grand to come up for air and sunshine. Very few people got the opportunity to visit the culverts and tunnels.

I then have Budreau help me check the master sheet. I call out my numbers in Spanish, and he checks them off the sheet. We both are amateurs in Spanish and Herr, the office clerk, remarked, "No wonder there are so many mistakes on the master sheet." Everybody laughed.

Checking the paint gang, it was necessary to go into the gates after a few men. The gates are about 6-foot thick and 80 feet high. They are enormous. The painters use hot mastic and it's dangerous. A few got scalded as they lowered bucket after bucket down the gate via ropes.

I was checking the mechanics one day. I asked a Negro what his number was. He was cleaning a large key, suspended on a crane cable near an open pit. He seemed to be day-dreaming. He answered, "You don't check me." Then he stepped backwards into the open pit of the rising stem valves. He grabbed in vain for the cable and missed. I tried to grab him and was obstructed by the book and pen in my hand. I might have been dragged in also. I watched his body tip and go head first, down the pit. I cried out, "Holy Christ." I then turned my head away as I figured he'd smack the deck head first and be a sure dead one.

I gathered my wits and called, "First Aid for a doc and an ambulance." Then I went into the pit. The Negro had landed on two Salvadorans. That broke his fall and saved his life. He was laid on his back. He had a bad cut over the right eye, and it was at

117

a grotesque angle. The doc came and found him to have his leg broken in several places. The Negro was a husky one and complained he had a couple of teeth missing. The doc and I laughed. That was the least of his worries. We then put him into a stretcher basket and the crane pulled him up and into a waiting ambulance.

The two Salvadorans suffered minor blows. One had a sore thigh and the other a sore neck. It could easily have been broken. They were taken to the hospital for a check-up. Bob Keller a gold mechanic, a fellow I ride to work with, was also working in the pit. He had jumped aside when I cried "Holy Christ" and noticed a shadow. He felt sorry for the Negro. He said that he had been a good worker.

About a week later, the locks suffered its first fatality. Another Salvadoran had been painting on a scaffold on the gates. Nobody saw him fall. A friend of his looked about and then saw him stretched out under the emergency gate in a foot of water. The Doc and safety men went down into the chamber. He had but two minutes to live. He only asked for his "hat." He was but nineteen years old. They brought him up with ropes in a stretcher basket.

Safety was stressed over and over. I had a habit of walking along the chamber walls till one day I stepped in oil and slipped. By a miracle I regained my balance and never walked along the wall again. It was about a 120-foot drop to the chamber bottom when it was drained.

Most of the silver men were a carefree bunch of fellows. When the west side chamber was drained completely to begin overhaul operations, a body of water still remained at the gate stops. The water was about 5 feet deep, 125 feet wide, and 60 feet long. Lots of tarpon from the sea still remained in this body of water. The silver men left their work and went fishing. Some used spears, others a large wire net, and five or six tried to catch them via hand.

They really put on a show. A few were fired, and the fishing continued for several days. The officials decided to let the men catch all the fish. Then they would go to work. From the walls,

118

we few checkers, officials, guards, office workers, mechanics, and a few tourists sat or stood for hours and watched.

About ten men organized and dragged the net from one side of the chamber to the other and forced the three- to seven-foot tarpon into a small space. Then three or four fellows plunged in, and wrestled with the fish, and threw them up onto the dry floor.

A few got away, and a silver man went swimming after it, under water and with his steel helmet still on. This brought a roar of laughter from the watchers. The fellows wrestling with the fish didn't always succeed. With a hard smack of the tail, the fellow was thrown under water for more laughs. With long spears a few were dragged out. The fish were sold at fifteen to twenty cents a pound to restaurants and stores. It was a profit for the silver men. After all the fish were caught from the muddy water, the fellows took a shower in water, which was sprouting from a leak in the center chamber wall. About thirty or forty tarpon were caught, and a lot of cheering and yelling made it more exciting than a football or baseball game.

Working one night a week was a pleasure. It was quiet and peaceful. On Saturday night only a small percentage of personnel worked. I enjoyed the cool night air. It was a bit damp and made the eyelids heavy. I walked along the top level, and only a few "mule" operators were sitting or sleeping in the control tower. Then I walked down the middle level and checked a few welders and boiler makers.

I stop to talk with a fellow interested in Alaska. I tell him it's a good deal. Then I walk down to lower level and check electricians in the caissons. He is nearly asleep and has three silver helpers dozing off in a corner.

We talk awhile about Peru. He spent five years there and liked it a lot. I then walk inside the ventilated, well-illuminated, clean tunnel. I pass signs warning of high voltage. I find nobody in the top level. I awaken a sleeping elevator operator, and he takes me to the chamber floor. I check a few more welders, machinists, and carpenters working on the gate. I have to laugh at the silver men. They are wearing heavy woolen jackets and sweaters. One has a cold and the other seems to be freezing. I only have a T-shirt and feel comfortable.

These silver men had never been out of the tropics, and their blood is thinned out. Just a little air and they feel it. I return to the office, make out my report, and check the master sheet. I've walked twenty-two miles altogether. I have coffee prepared by the night nurse. We talk and wait for dawn for the day shift to start coming in.

I then ride the labor train to Mount Hope. It takes about twenty minutes. The gold men ride in a coach and the silver men ride in box cars. From Mount Hope to Margarita, it is three-tenths of a mile. I can walk or take a cheeva for a nickel. It's a nice walk along well-kept lawns and palm trees, and the road is paved. I have breakfast at the clubhouse; the food is fine, but costly. It's supposed to be a non-profit affair. I think a large profit must be made. Overhead and help are cheap. One pint of milk is twenty cents. Dairies are maintained at low cost. In Alaska one quart is fifteen cents and the cost of maintenance is four and five times as high.

A lot of soldiers eat at the clubhouses. Panama is a paradise for a G.I. A lot of sailors are stationed in the Zone and find it a good deal also. A lot of them are married and have their wives and children living in family quarters. Buying food and clothing at the commissary is also on a non-profit basis. The soldiers are permitted to don civilian clothes on liberty, and they enjoy the privilege.

Working for the Panama Canal, I pay $15.75 a month for bachelor quarters, single room. Fellows working for the army pay $6.00 a month for the same type of quarters. It is necessary to furnish your own pillows and sheets, and light bulbs. The Panama Canal furnishes the bed, a dresser, a chair and a table, and a janitor.

No women are permitted in bachelor quarters, and heavy penalties and fines are imposed. The quarters at Margarita are quiet except after payday or parties. Then the fellows bowl with empty liquor bottles down the hallway, crap games, and singing.

Margarita is a nice quiet community. After the ten or eleven o'clock show lets out, the streets are deserted and the sound of crickets and frogs can be heard.

I often go to town, Colón, with a few of the fellows, Bill

Schraer and Ossie Hardman. They are married and the wives live on opposite side of the canal. They live temporarily at Margarita. They are "loaned" labor for the overhaul at Gatun.

There is a lot of excitement in Colón. The town is full of cabarets, nightclubs and "Blue Mooners," girls who keep company with you and make their livings on commission of drinks you buy them, or if you sleep with them. They can be nice company and dance all night with you, but when you go home, your pocketbook isn't so very big. They can drink an awful lot.

We either go to a few nightclubs and watch a floor show or satisfy by "rolling horses" (dice) for drinks at the Doghouse or Missouri Bar. We like both places. At the Doghouse is a German pianist who had a wonderful knowledge of all American, German, Russian, Spanish, and French tunes. He knows all the army and navy songs, and on certain nights, the navy or army or both gather around him and sing to their heart's content.

A very talented baritone came in one night. He sang opera to the pianist's accompaniment. He was swell and also wonderful. His voice was rich and clear, and it tore at the heart strings. There was absolute silence. Then everybody clapped and made him sing again. He was an ordinary seaman on a U.S. Merchant ship, the S.S. *Christóbal*. He wasn't being paid to sing; he was just a customer who had stopped in for a beer.

A lot of talent is wasted there. The navy is always good and they are born comedians. Then "Jungle Jim" comes in and does cartwheels. He is about fifty-five and has also stopped in for a few beers. He is a veteran of the last war and still wears the remnants of that uniform. He is called "Jungle Jim" because he has a good knowledge of the Panamanian Jungle, and if a plane crashes, he is sent out. I liked to hear him talk under a few beers. He yearns to be in the jungle to hear the sound of the tom-toms. There are a lot of primitive Indians in Panama, and the stories told are weird. Jungle Jim is popular, well-liked, and receives many hand claps on entering the Doghouse and doing his cartwheels.

At the "Missouri Bar" is a beautiful Salvadoran girl named Yolinda. She is very popular and friendly with the army, navy, and civilian alike. She is not a "Blue Mooner," but she does take a sip of your drink. When the house isn't busy, she will keep you company and amaze you with her skill at rolling dice. She really remains true to an American ensign. When he isn't there to take her home, the house man or proprietor does. He's an elderly guardian.

I had met Yolinda at Colon Beach one day. She coaxed me to go swimming. Next day I couldn't hear a thing. I had contracted fungi in the ear. I at once went to the hospital. It took a month to get rid of it. The doctor said, "It only takes once to get it. No more swimming in the tropics for you."

The floor shows in Panama are hard to beat. Among the best was "Beauty and the Beast" and "The Devil and the Virgin." Each had two personalities but performed by one. The girl had her left side as herself and the right draped to represent a devil. One body doing the actions of two made a marvelous performance, and the crowd cheered.

The Argentine Navy came to Panama on a goodwill tour. They stayed thirty-two days. They were a quiet but friendly bunch of sailors. They got drunk and had a good time. Not one landed in jail. If one got rowdy, his buddies took him to the ship. They have no shore patrol. They don't need any. One sailor told me that their captain said, "Go out, have a good time, get drunk, buy things, but no fights." They obeyed and sailed from Panama with a clean record.

The U.S. Navy comes in a few days later, and first night there are fights, drunks, and the jail house is full. The sailors mimic in Spanish and make waiters both angry and make them laugh. They go singing and shouting "Hey Bob a re Bob" and "Open the Door, Richard" down the streets. Shore Patrol was stationed on every corner and every block. They are carefree and have little respect.

The U.S. and Argentines get along swell. It's merely that the languages are different. An American sailor goes drinking with an Argentine. They can't hold a conversation and say "Aw, heck" and each goes his way. But the intentions are good. Both are interested in one another's life, views, and what their country is like. It seems there should be a universal language.

The prices are confusing. A Coke costs a nickel in Cristóbal,

CZ, but cross the street to Colón, Republic of Panama, and it costs fifteen cents. Clothes are very much more expensive in Panama than in the Zone. It is customary for a Panamanian or Columbian or other not employed in the Zone to ask a Zonian or zone employee to purchase food or clothes from the U.S. commissary so as not to pay the high price asked in Panama. Heavy penalties are imposed by the U.S. on violators who are not entitled.

Walking the street alone at night in Colón or Panama City is shunned by Zonians. They have more and more stories to tell of mishaps. However, I suffered one misfortune but still feel at ease, alone in either city. It's advisable to stay on main streets that are well illuminated.

The Panamanian police stop everybody at random, gold or silver alike, and ask for identification. Everybody should have a card and a badge designating the place of employment.

One night a Panamanian cop stopped and asked a young Panamanian lad for identification. The boy was unemployed and didn't have any credentials. The boy decided to run, knowing he would be taken to the police station and held for a couple of days. It was his undoing, for the cop fired and the boy fell, mortally wounded. He died a few days later. The cop stated that he had tripped on the sidewalk and accidentally fired. He was placed in jail. Everybody felt sorry for the boy and hated the cop. He shouldn't have fired.

A few days later, there was a great funeral. It was very impressive. Almost every bus and *cheeva,* full of people, went rolling slowly down Central Avenue. Each bus, car, and *cheeva* had a large flower wreath on the hood or the radiator. Large crowds stood on the sidewalks as if watching a parade. It lasted more than an hour. It seemed to bear ill tidings for the cop in jail. The youth was but nineteen years old.

It was my misfortune one night that I was all alone and feeling blue. I had stopped at a few cabarets. None of my friends were in town. I stayed awhile at the Manhattan Cocktail Lounge preferred by Americans and downed a few. I decided it time to get a *cheeva* and go home. I went down a dark street and stopped to urinate. A colored girl followed, put her arms around my waist from behind, and said, "Sleep with me for three dollars. Sleep with me for three dollars." When I turned around to face her, she gave me a nasty shove and said, "Get away from me or I'll call the police." I said, "Well, get. I didn't call you here."

She went but fifteen feet and I suspected something was wrong. I felt my tiny watch pocket and felt my three twenty-dollar bills gone. I started after her. She ran around the corner. I chased her. There were about ten doorways close together. I lost her there. A light was on in one. I knocked and a voice answered, "Old people live here; go away."

I wasn't going. I didn't make as much money as most Americans, and I couldn't afford to lose two week's savings. If any Negro or Panamanian tried to stop me, I'd ask questions later and sock him in the jaw first.

None did, though quite a few looked on. The Panamanian police came in a hurry. They opened several doors. It was an elderly couple where the light shown. I described the girl, Negro, 5 feet 2 inches, slim, pretty, green dress, upswept hair. In Panama the police make but sixty dollars a month. The Americans feel they are glad when we suffer a loss and even assist the crooked women. These cops really searched every place, in every barroom, alley and street. The secret police came and we rode in the car around the streets, looking closely at all girls wearing green. After what seemed hours, we finally gave up. We were tired and it had been a grand chase. They offered and where nice to drive me several miles to Margarita.

Next day I reported to the Secret Police office and checked photos of Negro, and "moreno" women who had police records. Two of the pictures were close, but on checking records in other files, one was six foot and the other spoke Spanish and was far from slim. Evidently the girl was a new one and had no record yet. The police and I meant to keep our eyes open for the next few days.

Back at work Dale kidded me about what had happened. I could only grin. A Jamaican made us all laugh by telling us of his experiences at the "Red Mill." He then coached us to always look under a bed. There may be a man under it, and if there is a screen, to ask the girl who's behind it, and what way to put your arms around a girl so she won't get into your pockets. This brought a roar of laughter from the fellows as he demonstrated.

Everybody seemed to have suffered a loss at one time or another in Panama. They said I was lucky that I didn't suffer injury.

John Jones of Beaumont, Texas, had been hit with a steel bar, knocked senseless, and robbed in Cristóbal. A Negro jumped out of the bushes and John had a fair glance. John lost all his teeth from the blow. The doc said the same blow on the back of the head would have killed him. John now wears false teeth, and the Negro is serving time. John is an elderly man.

A machinist told me he was ganged up on by five or six Panamanians and Negroes. He was knocked out, and awoke to find his glasses broken, pants cut away, and wallet with seventy dollars stolen. He was about forty years old.

Bill Schraer had been doped in liquor by a girl and had a large sum of money stolen.

Carlos Caspario, a Colombian cab driver in Colón, was robbed, beaten by American soldiers and marines back from the South Pacific, and had his cab stolen and wrecked.

I still like Colón, and in four months I haven't seen a street fight in Colón, though the stories are thick and heavy. I'm inclined to believe what I see and only half of what I hear.

Bob Budreau, Cushing, and I ventured out one evening. We had an early start about 6:00 P.M. We lunched at the popular "Tropics." Then to the "Joe Louis," "Chicago," and "Jimmy's" bars. We saw the floor shows at "Copacabana" and "Saratoga."

We all miss the girl who performed so well in the "Virgin and the Devil." She had taken an overdose of sleeping tablets and was found in critical condition next day. She never regained consciousness and officials were baffled whether it was accidental or suicide.

We got to the "Florida Night Club." We dance with the cabaret girls. We buy them a few drinks. They wear long gowns and make up pretty. Budreau likes his girl and separates to another table. He murmurs sweet words of love into her ears. Cushing and I had long gotten rid of our girls, or should I say they left us when we took it slow on the liquor. Cushing is a very quiet, intel-

125

ligent lad who had seen three year's service on a tanker as a gunner in the U.S. Navy. His innocent looks are deceiving. He is a young man who can stand on his own. We send Budreau and his girl a drink.

He comes back and tells us that he has this girl all figured out, and she is no "Blue Mooner." He says he has a date to go swimming next Wednesday with her. He dances some more till we are ordered to leave, closing time.

Budreau says he spent 20 dollars in two hours. Cushing and I figure he has to learn from experience and only grin. Budreau sports a lot of tattoos and has spent time in the Navy also.

The last bus has left so we head for the "Doghouse." It's open all night. We are issued "certificates of merit" by the manager after we give him sufficient reason for being in the "Doghouse." We are given a membership card, stating that we are now honorary members of the Kommon Kur Klub, and meetings will be held every Friday at 5:30 P.M. Harry Kress signs as the Grand Setter of the Club.

Blackie brings the dice, and we roll for drinks. Rolling for drinks is the style in Panama. Later we roll for small change, and Panamanian police put a stop to it. Second offense and we go off to jail.

Budreau bring out his harmonica and plays the Mexican "La Raspa." Cushing and I break into the dance. We have fun and the few customers at the bar enjoy our show.

About four A.M. we're pretty tired, and Cushing feels it's safe to go home. His dad would be leaving for work. Budreau and I have hot pork sandwich at the "Tropical." He falls asleep waiting for his order, and I awaken him with a glass of ice water down his back. He awakes in a hurry and retaliates with a glass at me. The table cloth and my shirt are ringing wet. We laugh it off, and the sleepy night waitress joins in.

We then go to sit in the grass under the palm trees to wait for the 6:25 labor train. We fall asleep and find ourselves stretched out upon awakening. We awaken to the sound of many voices and open our eyes to see about a hundred silver men gathered about, waiting for the labor train. A lot of them look and laugh at us. The train comes and Budreau and I lie on the benches, head against head, and fall asleep again. Roush and Lucky, a mechanic, awaken us at Gatun. We don't feel much like going to work. Cushing is lucky—it's his day off. We again were told that we were lucky we didn't awaken with our throats cut. We laugh it off and would still do it again.

The Panamanians, Colombians, and others don't make as much as the Americans, but they do want to be treated like humans. They have shown respect and courtesy throughout Central America, and I'm sure Americans cannot repay them likewise. In Panama the cab drivers were my friends. When I appeared alone or with a friend and looking for a nice time with nice people, they knew where to take us and we always had a nice time without fear of getting robbed or getting into fights or trouble. Our fare was always half-price simply because I talked with them, drank and tried a few words in Spanish.

Americans have a tendency to discriminate, and the Canal Zone is the worst I've ever seen. American children born and raised in the zone do not have the slightest interest in learning to speak Spanish, and many will not learn, so to speak. They call all Latins "spicks," and many of the Latins are as white as the next person.

On the job there are two drinking fountains; one is white, the other is brown. A Latin does not dare to drink from the white fountain on penalty of losing his job.

Americans who have married Latins are also looked upon as inferior and have lowered their aristocratic standing in life. Many American soldiers stationed in Panama had flown to Colombia and Costa Rica, married those girls, and brought them to the zone. One of those fellows is a good friend of mine. He had soldiered in Panama, flew to Costa Rica, and married one of the girls. After his discharge he still held a special position at the army airport as a civilian. He would like to stay there for life. He likes the zone, but now he finds life miserable because of the discrimination.

One day we went riding in his car and he said, "Please, Joe, don't make the same mistake I did. Don't marry one of those girls." His wife is very pretty and recently she gave birth to a

127

child. If he were to live anywhere but in the Canal Zone with his pretty Spanish woman, life would be swell.

As we walk along the streets of Colón, little boys of six or seven years of age offer to take us to women. We look amazed, laugh, and keep going. Managers of curio shops call and invite us in. They have wonderful alligator bags, pocketbooks, and belts, Indian clothes, and articles. They ask double and triple the value, but if you're a smart one, you can purchase them at the right price.

The Canal Zone children are healthy and have everything they want. They are spoiled. Their folks have made a lot of money, and during the war, there was a lot of overtime and double pay. There is no income tax to be paid in the zone. It seems odd that Alaska is also a territory of the U.S. and income tax is paid there.

Canal Zone has a lot of recreation facilities. There is skating at the U.S.O. in Ancon and Cristóbal. Also basketball, tennis, baseball, and swimming. Most all zonians swim like fish and play baseball in shorts, due to the hot sun. There is hunting and fishing the year around. A license costs a few dollars. A lot of Americans fish for tarpon and make good profit selling them to restaurants.

Girls are few and spoiled. They go with boys they went to school with or with captains of the Air Corps or ensigns of the Navy. My buddies made no attempts to get me acquainted. If they had a girl, they kept her to themselves. I couldn't blame them.

The Canal Zone Police held a ball at the "Strangers Club." It's the best in Colón. The checkers went as usual. They always managed to have money and were the envy on the locks. We met at the cocktail bar downstairs. It was expensive. We secured a table in the ballroom upstairs and ordered several bottles of American liquor and set-ups. Only Robinson and a friend had brought dates. They were pretty. Everybody was dressed formal or semi-formal. All the girls and women wore beautiful gowns.

Door prizes were chanced off, and soon the dancing started. There were no girls stags, so it was necessary to do as in Alaska clubs if a fellow cared to dance—approach a table and ask the girl if you could have the pleasure of dancing with her. She would smile, ask her boyfriend for permission. Five out of six fellows permit. The sixth can be nasty, a little high, and wants to fight. It's worth the risk. Some of the girls are marvelous dancers and ask for a return dance. They enjoy the checkers' company.

A Latin couple performed a dance so well that everybody cleared the floor. It was an Argentine tango and performed with much ease and grace. Americans applauded loudly, for seldom is seen such marvelous dancing.

The policeman's ball was a success. It was crowded, and people were friendly and having a good time. The two Egger Brothers had eyes half-closed, and Cushing was under the table trying to hold it down.

He is a card. Budreau keeps saying, "Aye, aye." Robinson takes his date home and returns for us checkers. The crowd has left and the checkers are dancing together and still having a party. Robinson has some time driving us all home to Cristóbal, Margarita, and Gatun.

PART TWO

21

On to Venezuela

Monday, April 28, 1947

I had been on a réndezvous all night in Colón, R. de Panama. I only had time to catch a *cheeva* (a bus) to my quarters in Margarita, C.Z.

I took a hasty shower. My gear already being packed, I took a *cheeva* to Mount Hope, the train station and also the cemetery for Canal Zone residents.

The train came. I was taking about my twenty-fifth and last trip across the Isthmus to Balboa on the Pacific side. I always got a big kick out of it.

The train moves along at a terrific rate of speed. The cool wind is soothing. The flat green land and the numerous lagoons and lakes are strangely reminiscent to the wastelands along the mighty Yukon River in Alaska in the summertime.

The Canal Zone firemen continually burn brush and the smoke burns the nostrils as we zip by. We see many native huts made of bamboo and tin roofs. We stop at villages and towns as follows: Gatún, Frioles, Gamboa, Pedro Miguel, Corozal, and Balboa. They are in the Canal Zone and primarily for Americans.

The conductor comes along. I pay for this trip $1.30. I had been terminated from service a week ago and surrendered my pass book. The trip lasts one hour and fifteen minutes. Only the Americans ride first class on this train. Most of them work for the canal. There are quite a few soldiers and sailors. The coaches still retain their kerosene lamps of many years ago, and riding at night they are very dim and evil-looking.

We arrive in Balboa. I only have time to take a cab and catch

133

my plane. It is a big four-engine, P.A.A. plane. The steward checks my passport and tickets. I go aboard.

Soon I fell asleep. There were three or four passengers and none of them spoke English.

The steward awoke me and said to fasten the safety belt. We were going to land at Barranquilla, Colombia. All I could see was flat, dry, barren land below. It had the appearance of a desert in Arizona or New Mexico. The pilot made a nice landing. The trip took only two hours.

At the Immigration and Customs, we had to present health and vaccination documents to the doctors. Everything being in order, we were then directed to a waiting bus, which took us to town free of charge (a service of P.A.A.).

The trip to town brought back memories of deep Mexico. We rolled along a dusty road. There were many peons riding burros and many others riding carts. The men rode the burros with their legs crossed astride the top of the burro's neck. It takes skill to ride that way. It appeared like they were showing off, but I was to see much more of that everywhere in town. It reminded me of young boys riding bicycles with their feet on handlebars and no hands.

I found Barranquilla to be a nice town. Not very big, population about 100,000. There were many fine buildings in Spanish and American architecture. The monuments and cathedrals were wonderful and the bells in the towers of the majestic cathedrals rang with a rich tone on the Hour of Prayer.

We reached the station. A porter carried my gear to Hotel Suiza. It was a very nice hotel and moderately priced. The servants were courteous and everywhere there was a friendly atmosphere.

There was one place where the Americans always went. It was the Bar Victoria, owned and operated by an American. The oil men and construction men who lived in camps always came here. Colombian girls entertained them. Being an American, I was welcomed like a brother and asked to join them. They told me there was plenty of work in Colombia and offered to help me get a job. I thanked them and told them I had my mind set on Venezuela. Some of these fellows marry the Colombian girls.

One old-timer liked a girl named Judy very much. She was young and spirited. She got high and left him at the table.

Next day at noon, he was still waiting for his Judy. He missed a day's work. He would go to sleep for a while, awaken again, and ask if we had seen his Judy. He was more fun; they say "Love is Blind."

I went out in the evening with an American. We went to Chinatown, the American version of Red Mill. I was surprised. We came to a place that had an appearance of a carnival show. Plenty of lights, music, and dust on the ground. Everybody seemed happy, singing, eating, drinking, and walking about. We passed a row of houses. There were girls in every doorway, young, thin, chubby, light- and dark-skinned. The girls called to us, but we kept on walking. We passed many cabarets and watched the dancing. They can really put on a good show, as good as the colored boys and gals in Harlem, only now it's the South American way.

We stopped for a *cerveza* (beer) and street vendors try to sell us chewing gum, eggs, lottery tickets, and what not. Some of them can be very annoying with their persistence, thinking we are American seamen who just got into port and have lots of money to spend.

It's getting very late, so we go back to town. I go to the hotel. As I unlock the door, one of the servants, a pretty one, accosted me and asked me to invite her into my room. It's against the rules of the house, but she works there and the rule applies to outsiders only. She turned out to be nice company, and again I lost sleep.

At 3:30 A.M. the clerk rang as I had directed him. I had made arrangements to fly to Maracaibo, Venezuela, and be at the Station Avianca at 4:20.

Sue Kay, the pretty servant, wanted me to stay another day. I hated to disappoint her. Then she lifted her head, smiled, and left for her room across the hall.

The bus went from one side of the road to the other to avoid the deep ruts. It was still dark out, and we could see men and women coming to market with their burros and carts loaded down with merchandise. There were six people on the bus. One

Venezuelan spoke English. He was going to Caracas, Venezuela, with his aging mother.

Our papers and passports were checked again. We boarded a twin-engine plane of P.A.A. There was a full load. We all had a delicious breakfast of bacon and eggs, coffee, orange juice, and fruit salad at an altitude of about eleven thousand feet, prepared by the Spanish steward.

We crossed over some very rugged mountains. I saw no signs of a road or a trail. I was told the road was bad from Barranquilla to Maracaibo. We ran into a few air pockets, and the elderly women got a little sick. Some of the cloud formations were very impressive. Presently we saw flat dry land again; the trees had no green leaves and looked scorched. The fields looked yellow and dry. We spotted a few camps, with barracks in neat formations. American, probably.

The landing gear went down. We fastened our safety belts again.

The American pilot was a bit cocky. He believed in making quick takeoffs and fast landings. He made a sharp turn left and came in like a P-51 Mustang. We hit a little rough. The elderly woman nearly passed out. Later, I talked with the pilot and his manner was as cocky and self-assured as ever.

There was a large crowd at the airport. It was some time before we cleared Customs and Immigration. The Venezuelan, his mom, and I took a cab to town. We had to pay the fare in Bolivars now and my senses told me we were being sold the "Brooklyn Bridge." We decided not to argue.

I managed to get a moderately priced hotel in downtown Maracaibo. There was a fellow who spoke Russian and assisted me in ordering a dinner. The dinner was splendid American-style. The hotel cost fifteen bolivars per day ($4.50).

I wandered about the streets of Maracaibo. Downtown they were littered with debris. Cabbies and shoe-shine boys hailed. I got a big kick out of being in the city of "Moreno" people (brown). There were quite a few Indians, and their garb was quaint. The Indian women had pretty faces, but the men were fierce looking. Their dresses touched the ground, and some were beautifully

136

decorated. They wore men's hats and sombreros and some looked cute and comical.

The dock was a market place, about a mile long. Some parts had an awful stench. It was interesting and colorful. There were bananas, fruits, clothing, and antiques from all parts of the world. An American ship was in port. The *Santa Monica,* from New York. It was a beautiful clean ship alongside the dock. It reminded me of nice things back home.

I strolled away from the docks and went along Avenida Bella Vista. This was the beautiful section of Maracaibo. The well-to-do lived there. The homes were lovely in Spanish design. They were painted in light colors of blue, green, tan, white, pink, and made of concrete. The entrance walks and patios were made with tile and designed in stars, teardrops, octagons, squares, and figures of all kinds and colors.

Meeting Jose Hernandez on Bella Vista was indeed a pleasure. We had met before in Panama. He had been terminated from Albrook Field and now was seeking work in Venezuela. Together we strolled along, and he pointed out the statue of Simón Bolívar, the hero and liberator of five countries; Bolivia, Venezuela, Colombia, Ecuador, and Peru. There were also four markers to commemorate the four battles he had engaged in. The name of each battle was written with tiny flowers on the ground and the statue of Bolívar on a horse was in the center.

In the cool of the evening, many people came to sit in the park. The fragrance of flowers, for which Venezuela is famous, was intense. There is a rich green all about, and a soft breeze in the palms. It's a relief after the heat of the day.

In Venezuela there is a law concerning labor for Americans. Only 6 percent are American labor. They are skilled technicians, engineers, foremen and Spanish-speaking office workers. It's not advisable to venture and hope for work in Venezuela unless a contract has been made with some company in the States.

American foremen on the job refuse a man work simply because it's irregular and don't want to be held responsible for the hiring.

Going by ferryboat across the gulf, from Maracaibo to Palma Reho lasted approximately forty-five minutes. Trucks, cars, and two jeeps belonging to American engineers were loaded aboard. A large crowd of Venezulians hustled aboard, most of them loaded down with "bags and personal belongings."

From Palma Reho to Cabimas, it was a trip with the Americans. They had two jeeps and two trailers, loaded with gear and equipment for a new experiment in aerial engineering on ground.

It was an hour's drive along a macadam road. The heat was choking. We had the windshield wide open. We passed rows of homes made of mud and thatched roofs. There were numerous pigs, chickens, goats, and dogs running about loose. The children, up to the age of five or six, ran about naked.

The Americans have their own mess hall and quarters at Cabimas. I was invited to dinner and enjoyed the food immensely. There are a lot of oil derricks all about, and the workers dine here. There must have been about two hundred of them.

Being unsuccessful in landing a job with Creole, Medene or Caribbean Oil companies, I tried William Construction Co. And they couldn't break rules. Feeling disappointed I walked down the highway and took some pictures. A truck came along and I got a ride back to Palma Reho and rode the ferry back to Maracaibo. Having dinner at the pension, with a couple of English-speaking Venezuelans, they said they were going to Caracas in the morning and would gladly take me along.

We got an early start and crossed the Gulf of Maracaibo again on the ferry boat to Palma Reho and then Cabimas and Mene Grande over a macadam road.

I managed to get a little sleep and awoke to find ourselves rolling along a dusty, bumpy road to Matatán.

We had dinner at Matatán, consisting of some fried pork, cheese, beans, fruit, and black coffee. It was only a single room with a rough table and chairs. The flies were thick and heavy on the tablecloth. We had washed our faces and hands in a small pan out in the tiny yard. Heavy jungle vegetation was all about. A pretty girl waited on us. She was kind of bashful. Later as her mom chatted with my friends, she leaned on her shoulder and kept looking at me and smiling.

We bought fresh, delicious pineapples for only a few pennies and ate them as we rode along the dusty road. It was difficult to pass at times due to heavy dust raised by vehicles up forward. The driver took many unnecessary chances. Passing on curves and on the hills. He failed to reduce speed on sharp curves. We skidded halfway over a twenty-foot bank and he miraculously worked the car back on the road. When stopping he failed to pull off the road or to the extreme right. Boy, what drivers.

We rolled from green jungle and rolling hills into dry flat country. We enjoyed the mountains best. We stopped late in the afternoon at Trujillo. It seemed odd, the whole town seemed carefree. Men sat in the shade and chatted, some leaned back on chairs, cowboy fashion, and drank beer. A little ways off was another group of young fellows gathered in the shade of a large tree and taking life easy. Nobody seemed to have anything to do. Men sitting under the roof of the local store had a radio and a Victrola for entertainment. As far as the women, they just weren't anywhere to be seen.

We rolled and bumped through numerous more villages; all of the homes were made of grass and mud and some of the locations were very beautiful and picturesque. By eleven at night, we arrived in Barquisimeto. It appeared more like a city with paved streets, lights, and large buildings. We rode rapidly and at every intersection, there was a blast of horns. The first to arrive went through. I expected a crash at most every corner.

We stayed at a pension overnight. The Venezuelans were much older than I, and I felt they wanted to go about town without a young "pup" tagging along. So I went to sleep.

I slept well. We awoke early, had a decent breakfast of eggs, coffee, and *pan* (bread) and hit a good road all the way to Maracay. It felt good to ride on macadam and concrete again. The sun was very hot. We had some Venezuelan soft drinks for refreshment. Maracay was a nice modern town with beautiful parks. They have the largest military school there and it's very modern. On the streets could be seen soldiers in simple olive uniforms courting senoritas.

We gassed up at a modern gas station and rode all afternoon. Some of the highway was lined with trees for many miles. Towards evening we sighted the mountains, and I was told Caracas was up among them. We reached it about eleven. It was already dark.

They recommended a Cuadrico Pension, inexpensive but only half-decent. It was on Primera Avenida (first). They, the three Venezuelans owned and operated a store a few blocks away.

I stayed at the pension six days while I tried to get a job. I had a room to myself, and at night I had to use blankets. It really got cold. I was the only American there.

At breakfast there would be two to ten persons at the table at various hours. Some were friendly and others pretended to be. The elderly woman cook asked me questions, personal and impersonal, but never smiled. What she thought I don't know, but certainly they weren't friendly thoughts.

We had coffee (black), cheese, butter and ham. I waited for my eggs and finally had to ask for them. I received one fried egg and the fellow across from me had four or five.

I missed most of my noon dinners while looking for work. In the evenings we had soup, and I couldn't bear the taste. Sometimes the chicken, fish, and meat were good. We had plenty of rice and beans. The meat becomes spoiled easily in the tropics and the rice had hard seeds that had to be sorted out by tongue. All the food had been prepared over a stove made of stones. Chicken, cats, and dogs roamed through the kitchen, picking at food bits.

We had wash pans and a pitcher of water in our rooms to wash. The walls were tin. Later, I learned that I was paying two Bolivars more than the rest of the tenants and was also underfed (60¢).

Two fellows who spoke some English came to my room at night. We wrote English and Spanish back and forth. Later we strolled the crowded sidewalks to the brightly lit El Silenco Plaza. It was a beautiful modern square. We sat and talked. The air was chilly and I loved it.

Applying for work at Creole and various other companies, it was necessary to furnish photographs with an application. It was difficult to get a job as an American. Americans were hired only when Venezuelans could not qualify for the position.

I decided I could get a job at the airport with my experience on

140

aircraft engines. I took a bus and paid two Bolivars fare (60¢) to the airport. The trip to Maiquetía lasted about an hour and a half. It's actually suicide to ride them. The drivers are incapable. They are uneducated in safety and race and pass one another on the dangerous winding, twisting mountain roads. The guard rails are one continuous example of accidents, which occurred and bear the mark and scars. On one particular sharp "U" turn is a monument: a large pillar with the remains of a Ford on top of it that had gone over the mountainside and into the ravine below. It is a solemn marker, but the natives pay no heed. When I reached Maiguetia, I vowed I would never ride the bus again. I'd feel safer walking or hitchhiking. I did hitchhike, and the driver of the car was just as bad. He drove with elbows near parallel with his shoulders and was on the wrong side of the road most of the time. He missed cars by inches as he swerved back to his side of the road.

I succeeded in getting a job at the airport and went back to Caracas to obtain a *cedula* (permit) to work, and change my tourist visa to one that is for employed. There are several companies, P.A.A., Avensa, Linea Aeropostal, Taca, Cave, and Stubbin Saca. I decided to work for Stubbin Saca. They had three Americans working there. It was funny to hear them say "Savvy, savvy" to the assistant Venezuelan mechanic. They (Venezuelans) always seemed to nod or answer yes.

The work consisted mostly of assembling Piper Cubs and Piper Cruisers. My permit to work is for three months.

Soakie was the chief mechanic. He had flown a war-surplus training plane from California to Venezuela. It had taken him three months to arrange permits and visas from the various countries for the trip.

Upon getting the job, I decided to move to Maiquetía. it was only three miles from work.

Macuto is the best place to live. It is about eight miles from the airport and more expensive living.

Till I got on my feet again, I had to live in Maiquetía, and later I moved to Macuto. I was down to my last fifty dollars.

The ride to and from work is a beating on the dirt roads. The airport at Maiquetía serves Caracas, the capital of Venezuela, 35 miles away.

22
Life in Maiquetía, Venezuela, with Venezuelans

I arise early and look out the window to see the sun shining. Outside people are hustling and bustling, and street vendors are ringing bells. A group of women are gathered at the local water fountain with five-gallon cans and pots for a daily supply of water. Trucks and buses clatter by and raise a cloud of dust. Most of it seems to venture up to my room, which I share with three Venezuelans on the second floor.

The windows have no glass. To look out one side can be seen huge mountains and the streets below. To look out the opposite window can be seen the ocean and the first port of Venezuela, La Guayra, with a few U.S. and Dutch ships anchored out in the stream.

My roommates, Juan Gonzales, Luis Avior, and Alfredo Garerra, have already gone off to work. I go to wash up in the pan we all use. I find about half a pint of water left in the pitcher. That irritates me a little. Hotel servants bring daily supply from the public fountain a block away. I cheer up and look forward to taking a shower at work.

I go downstairs to the dining room, and I know what's for breakfast. It's oatmeal, cheese, butter, bun (bread), and black coffee. It's the same every day, and after a month a body can get used to it (a young body).

I then go off to work in a large public bus. The fare is two luches (8¢) to the airport. Day in and day out, it appears like I'm the only white man on it. I hardly notice the fact now. I get used to the curious glances and looks of the people who know me. The ride lasts about ten minutes. The scenery is old Spanish all the way to work.

142

At the airport, I work for a small American outfit, Saca. In order to take a shower, I have to pump water into a gasoline drum. It's a little work but worth it. The shower at the pension gives me the chills. Roaches can always be seen scampering by. Two weeks ago there was no water to pump because of dry season, and I just went without a bath, like everybody else.

I work with two Americans, Jean Olsen and Soakie, and a Dutchman named Van. Alfredo Garerra is the office secretary and sixteen-year-old Cateria, a Venezuelan, works with us.

The Americans do a lot of flying to Maracaibo and other points and are seldom about. "Cave" is a Venezuelan outfit next to us. Some of the Venezuelans are good workers, but when the bosses are away, they go to sleep at random under the plane wings or sit in easy chairs and talk, talk, and talk. Sometimes their girls or wives come down and they have a session. They are carefree. They have more holidays. If they do show up on a holiday, they don't work, but take it easy. They claim to be very religious but have a habit of forgetting a few commandments.

After four hours work, Dutch and I walked up a dusty path to the Latin Quarters for a Coke. It's a nice restaurant. We wait for the bus. Dutch gets off first at Pariata. He lives with his beloved Venezuelan wife there. I get off at the plaza in Maiquetía.

We have two hours for lunch. Every day we have some kind of soup, rice and beans. Just as often we have green peas and macaroni smothered in white cheese. Meat is served often, and half the time it is spoiled. Meat spoils easily in the tropics. There is a lack of refrigeration. We take it or leave it. On few occasions we are served a slice of Spam. It's delicious to me and only an appetizer.

After dinner I rest; the tropics make everyone lazy and I dislike getting up to go to work again after two hour's break. I take the bus again to the airport. The sun is very strong, and the glare is bad. So we manage to work in the hanger, assembling new Piper Cubs and cruisers. The time goes fast, and Dutch is a good man to work with. He came to Holland eight years ago on an adventure, learned English and Spanish, then got married. He hopes to return soon.

Dutch and I stop for Coke again at the Latin Quarters. Two

girls work there, one pretty, and one not so pretty. They try to teach me Spanish. Learning can be a lot of fun. They are very willing teachers.

I return to the pension for supper. My roommates are swell. They do use my soap, tooth powder, talcum, shaving cream, and stationery. I don't mind that much, but I was irritated when photos of my American girlfriends were stolen from my album. It might have been any of six other fellows in adjoining rooms. There are no locks on the door upstairs, only partitions. Venezuelans love the American girls.

I usually dine with Juan or all three of my roommates. The dining room has 6 tables, and I'm the only American there. They are all friendly, and I feel very much at ease among them. For supper we have soup again, rice and beans, potatoes, meat or fish, *lechosa* (a delicious dessert of tropic fruit), and black coffee in a small cup, about half the U.S. standard size.

Twice I've had fish served to me. It had its insides cleaned, but it still retained its head, tail, and fins. It was fried and breaded. I put it aside gently so as not to offend the others at the table. I also had fish soup served once and I spotted about two inches of fishes' head and eyes in it. That went aside. Whenever I smelled fish in the soup, I never ate it. I still remember the eyes, which gave me goose pimples. Yet these fellows eat it.

I also had macaroni served and as my fork lit into it, I uncovered a dead roach. I put it aside just as the landlady came into the dining room. She noticed the fact and said nothing though she must have felt offended.

Fish soup and macaroni are always put aside. I do enjoy the French-style bread and Yugoslav goulash prepared by the Yugoslav proprietor. A lot of meals and salads are served in European fashion.

The proprietor and his wife are a peculiar couple. She is 6 foot 3, and he is 5 foot 3. He really is a little squirt. They both came from Yugoslavia twenty years ago and seem happily married. The have two beautiful normal children going to Spanish school.

He understands me perfectly in the Czech-Russian lingo I

speak. We are like two brothers in a foreign land. When we talk, the Venezuelans look at us and wonder.

After supper we retire to our room for a short period, then perhaps go to the plaza a few blocks away. In the center is a Guardian Angel and a promenade about it. After the movies are over, the folks come out to promenade about it. There are numerous benches, rich green grass and flowers all about. Off to the end of the Plaza is an enormous Cross with Jesus Christ on it. Underneath is a tomb with Christ laid in it. By peering through iron bars, one can see huge sculptures of the story of The Crucifixion of Jesus Christ. There are fourteen houses with a sculpture in each that tells a marvelous story. They are stations of the cross. It's a lovely sight and gruesome. The Plaza is well lit, with always a crowd sitting or walking about.

There are three movies and a few cantinas with plenty of "Cerveza" and "Ron" that gives everybody a headache next morning. Many beverages are consumed in the tropics and drinking six bottles of Pepsi a day is regular for most everybody. A large modern church chimes the bells on regular hours of prayer.

There is dancing at the Latin Quarter when parties get together and play the Nickelodeon. Cerveza (beer) cost 3.00 Bolivars a bottle ($1.00 U.S.). Night life is expensive in Venezuela, much more than the same in the U.S.

It's nice just to sit in the Plaza and watch folks go by and listen to Spanish music coming over a loudspeaker. On certain nights, the Army Band of Venezuela plays in the Plaza for community entertainment. Life seems peaceful and folks have money to spend, much, much more than the folks throughout Central America and Colombia.

They become well-to-do through American enterprise and yet the people of Venezuela consider themselves *"Mejor"* (better) than Americans and take advantage of them and try their best to make fools of us if we don't savvy Spanish. The average Venezuelan is lucky if he succeeds in obtaining six years of schooling. Education is needed in Venezuela.

They are good ones as far as molesting goes. I was compelled to use violence to hold my dignity at the pension. A young fellow in an adjourning room came to mine in the morning, tickled my feet, and woke me up long before I cared to. Then he would hide so I didn't know who it was. At dinner he rapped the table for my attention and had nothing to say, only a silly laugh. He made remarks and everybody laughed again. I asked him nicely not to molest me anymore.

Then I retired to my room for noon rest, he followed and waved and said, "Hello, Mister" in mocking broken English. I cussed, and told him to get out; when he remained, I got up and he ran out the door and started down the steps. I caught him with a terrific hard smack to the jaw. I was about to follow it with a hard left, when he threw up his hands in front of his face and said, "No mas, Joe." I figured he had enough, and he did, but some of the other roomers must have coached him, for he came back to my room on pretense of seeing the roommates of mine. He said no more to me.

I went to get a bus a half hour later, and he followed me, sat beside me, and kept mumbling about going to the police. I asked him to keep quiet and get away from me. He remained, and I gave him a shove. Immediately he got up and shouted *"Americano Mejor? Extranjero."* (Better, foreigner). He wanted to start a fight, figuring the public was in his favor, and they were, but a half-dozen passengers stopped it and the bus went on till it sighted a policeman. We were both taken to the police station in another public bus. A witness came along to say that I, a foreigner, had shoved a Venezuelan on the bus.

At the police station in Maiquetía, the young fellow from the pension opened his mouth and pointed to where he had two teeth missing in the back of his mouth. The police agreed that I did damage. Even though I explained that it was only to stop him from molesting me, I was a foreigner and an American, so it's my fault, always.

They searched and emptied my pockets, then led me off to a cell. There were about twenty fellows inside, all Venezuelans. Most of them only in shorts. When I entered, a husky fellow ordered me to march forward, then back, then sit down; he closed in on me and also several others. I really expected a beating in retaliation, and said to myself, *Oh, oh, here it comes,* and I was

146

tense and waited, but the husky fellow put his hand on my shoulder, said, "Take it easy," and walked off.

It turned out to be quite a show in the jailhouse. The prisoners weren't in the least feeling blue. They were happy. One young fellow got two empty cans from "Klim" Milk and beat them as drums. He held them between crossed legs. He played well and sang marvelously. A couple of others started dancing in crazy rhythm to the music. They were funny.

They asked me why I was in and I told them. They all appeared to be in for drunkenness, fights, and knifing. All were serving two weeks to three months stretch. They played dominoes and tried to teach me card games. Spanish cards are very different in numbers and figures.

An old fellow was in and they made him take a shower. There were four stalls to take a shower, and they chased him from one to the other. Nobody wanted him to take a shower in his stall. They claimed he had fleas and cooties and they might be contagious. Finally he got into one and while he was taking the shower, they, the prisoners, burned his clothes and battered hat. Boy, was he mad when he found out. He was bare naked for about an hour. The cell was full of smoke. The police finally brought him some fresh clothes, big, but clean.

The cell was really a courtyard, surrounded by high walls; on the opposite side of the wall were women prisoners and they threw notes back and forth over the wall, some nice, and some not so nice. There was plenty of yelling back and forth, also good and bad.

When it rained, we ducked under a large alcove. The tile floor became very slippery and a couple of naked Venezuelans ran, flopped on their stomachs, and slid back and forth on the smooth surface. It was fun to them, and I nearly died laughing. They really acted like three- or four-year-olds.

There were also a couple of mutes, and the prisoners had a lot of fun with them. From above the police officials observed everything, shook their heads, laughed and walked away.

The violent prisoners were kept in tiny cells, and the chief prisoner or trustee wouldn't permit me to observe or view their section.

There were no beds, only the hard concrete benches and table to sleep on, and with magazines and paper for pillows.

About 5:00 P.M., the food was being dished out. The servant said I wasn't to get any. Juan Gonzales and Alfredo Garerra had come to bail me out and said the cost was thirty Bolivars ($10.00). I gave them money to pay it. I then told the servant, "I'm paying 30 Bolivars, and I want my supper." They all laughed and he finally gave it to me. We had beans, a spoonful of rice and bread. The police came to take me out, and I said, "God, give me time to eat." They did and laughed.

Juan and Alfredo walked with me to the pension. I was greeted by several of the roomers and the fellow I had the fight with. They wanted me to shake and forget the incident. I laughed, why should I? It certainly wasn't my fault. I said for the fellow to stay out of my room and I would stay out of his. If I had shaken hands, it would be a sign of weakness and after a few days, it would have been the same story again. Continuous molesting and what not.

I washed in the water pan, had dinner, and joined Juan and Alfredo. The fellow I fought was among them. I said I'd go alone. They sent him off, and the three of us had a few *cervezas* (beer) near the plaza. A couple of friends joined in, including a Venezuelan who spoke good English and had been to the United States. He liked it a lot, but he was still true to Venezuela. He realized it was an uneducated country and in great need of sanitary and health facilities. He preached politics and favored democracy.

We had a few singers and guitar players for added entertainment. Much later we took a bus to the Latin Quarters. We met quite a few fellows we worked with, Venezuelans. We ordered Cerveza at three Bolivars a bottle and played the nickelodeon with reals and Bolivar coins. There were no women, but eight young fellows never had a better time dancing together. The music was congas and rhumbas, and I really learned from the originators how to dance. They were superb. Outside the door could be seen Venezuelan soldiers patrolling the highway. They observed us but never said a word.

Garerra was pretty high and kept ordering drinks. I knew

what he would do. When the check came, he said to me, "You pay, you got money in your pocket." He was the secretary at work and had given me 100 Bolivars for a couple of days' pay. Now he expected me to pay for drinks that he had ordered.

I told him and the management I was broke and turned my pockets inside out. I purposely hid my money. I had already paid $30 to his $10 for the evening. Boy, was he angry, he insisted I had money. In the States I would have loved to clean his clock. But there I was a foreigner and only anxious to see how they treat an American who tried to treat them as people. We left and he promised to pay in a few days. There were no more buses after 12:00 and we hiked to town (about two miles). We did a lot of singing. Juan really liked the tune of "Good-bye, My Lover, Good-bye" and "Oh, My Darling Clementine." Juan could sing well in Spanish. Garerra couldn't and was still burning. Juan and I stopped for coffee and *empanadas* at a street wagon. They had heard us coming down the dark road singing. One of the fellows at the wagon had a bottle of Ron, a strong Venezuelan whiskey. He passed it around. Then we all started singing and Garerra took off alone for the pension.

Juan and I and the other fellows really had fun singing. A truck came along with several men in it. Juan said I was a fine American friend; one of the men laughed in contempt as the truck drove off again, "an American friend, phooey."

Sometime later the fellow who passed the bottle also passed me his beat-up straw hat when I told him I liked it. We shook hands and Juan and I started hiking again. Before we came to the pension, Juan stopped for another bottle of Ron. He still had ten dollars. I was a little surprised. It could have helped to pay that bill, but after all, it wasn't he who did the ordering at the "Latin Quarters."

He suggested we get a couple of girls to sleep with, but we didn't have enough money. When the back room of the *tienda* (store) closed, we went to the front for a soft drink. A big Negro edged me aside roughly and when I remarked, "What's the matter with you?" he shouted, "America foreigner, better than Venezuelan." He didn't try to hit me, but when Juan remarked that I was a good friend, he was mad enough to tear Juan apart and lit-

149

tle Juan wasn't backing away. Only several onlookers broke it up. No blows landed, just a tussle among five or six men.

When we went back to the pension, Juan wanted to still get Blackie. He wanted me to stay at the pension while he went after Blackie. Being unable to make him change his mind, we both went to get Blackie. We looked for him, but he was nowhere to be found. Then we went back to the pension and bed. I really liked Juan; he was ready to fight and argue for me as a swell American. He wasn't very big, but he had no fear. He had many scars of knife wounds and fights on his chest.

I went to the movies several times with Juan and Garerra. Whenever I sat beside a girl, pretty or not, she arose and moved elsewhere. I told Juan that the American doesn't rate beans with the girls; he laughed and said, "It's only their pretense."

In the plaza or elsewhere, I say, "Good morning, Good afternoon, Good evening, and Adios" in Spanish to the senoritas. I get nary a smile nor a word. Gosh, what difference from the beauties of Guatemala, El Salvador, and Costa Rica, who put their arms about you in public and say: "I only want American, I like American."

My American friend, who comes of Puerto Rican descent, says the girls are very religious. For him to take a girl to a movie, he also has to take her mom as a chaperon.

Juan and Alfredo invited me to go to La Guaira to "de dancing and to de girls." La Guaira is the first seaport of Venezuela. It is a very rough place. The girls were drunk and had no shame or respect. American seamen sat at tables in groups of two to six and eight. It was no place for an American to go alone. Juan and Alfredo, I could count on them as friends. Venezuelans danced with the girls, but the Americans only looked on. I talked to them and it was swell to talk to my countrymen.

I'd never seen a pot-bellied Venezuelan and I could easily understand why Juan and Alfredo laughed when a few oldish pot-bellied American seamen came in. Juan blew out his cheeks and stomach in imitation. I had to laugh also.

There was one fight right beside us. Nobody hurt much. Then a soldier, Venezuelan and drunk, asked Juan if I was a bad time. He was a little squirt. Juan said, "No." I was okay. Another

150

drunken civilian kept talking into Alfredo's ear and the management caught him by the seat and tossed him out. La Guaira on Saturday night is one rough *stinking* place. No more to "de dancing and to de girls" for me.

Gosh, but the people are carefree and independent. Their motto seems to be, "Hurray for me and the hell with you."

One truck driver stopped on the highway near Latin Quarters, blocking traffic and deciding to take a nap. He lay on the concrete highway underneath his truck in the shade. Another time a bus driver passed another, one got angry, and pulled in front of the bus I was in, blocking the highway and deciding to have his say to my bus driver, regardless of his passengers and the ones in the bus I was in who were anxious to get home from work. It was funny. Both of these characters would be in jail back in the States. They really argued.

Today is Sunday, June 15, 1947. I usually sleep till noon, but Juan and Alfredo got me up about 10:00. We took some pictures in the plaza and by the Jefatura de Maiquetía (jail). Then we went to the back room of a local *tienda* (store) and they ordered beer to ease their hangover from last night. A couple of the fellows from the pension came in and a few more friends and neighbors of Juan's and Alfredo's.

It was a friendly gathering; they all knew some kind of poem or other. One would rise and everybody clapped when he finished; then another rose and in a strong voice and emphasis, had a better poem to announce. Juan was the smallest, but he seemed to know the best. He got the most cheers. I wish I could understand it all, but I couldn't. It seemed like they were putting a show on just for me.

Juan, for one, really and honestly liked me. He was always doing favors. He spoke of me as one good American, and it was he who got me out of jail. Now he repeated the story, and they all seemed to admire me. About four or five shook my hand and would have hugged and kissed me in Latin style only they must have noticed a reaction.

One of the fellows ordered a fish. It came fried and with its head, tail, and fins on as usual. I did take a nip from the side, but to watch the fellow eat the head gave me goose pimples.

When I offered to pay after about a dozen bottles, they all clamored and pretended to be surprised. They surrounded and patted me. I grinned and paid. It was much less than my share.

All of us were late for dinner at the pension, and the management gave us the dickens. We became noticeably lazy after dinner. We lay down to rest after dinner in our rooms. It was hot and sweaty. I awoke about five and went to a movie. It was cool inside and crowded with little kids and elders.

"Little Abner" was cheered as loudly by these Spanish kids as he was in U.S. Richard Dix played in *The 13th Hour*. The feature was in English, and underneath the words were translated in Spanish.

23

The Fellows I Worked With

I had lived at the Pension Familia for six weeks and decided to move again. Since some of the fellows there realized that they couldn't push me around, they resorted to stealing.

Some of my clothes were stolen and when my reading glasses were stolen, I became furious. I did not know whom to blame. I complained to the management who once had said, "Only good people live here." Who in the world would want to steal personal glasses? The landlady promised to try to locate them.

So I decided to move before I lost everything. I moved to "Quinta San Jose" still in Maiquetía. It was a nicer place and more expensive. It was like a hacienda or a ranch house, with tile floors and red roof. There were large gardens in front of it and behind it. The gardens were full of flowers, palmettos, lemon trees, and palm trees. Underneath some of the trees were tables and chairs to lounge in.

I went out one evening and when I returned, I unlocked the padlock on my door. I could not enter. Something or someone was holding the door closed. I pushed very hard and the door opened about eight inches. I was able to reach in and turn the switch on; then the door was free.

I looked in and saw a huge snake, about three inches diameter and twelve feet long, crawl under my bed and go out a hole in the wall. I found a heavy box in my room and blocked the hole.

There was also a window about two-and-a-half feet square, with no glass or screen, and I worried about bats or snakes coming in. Not long after, I moved to Macuto.

About the same time when I moved, I was being laid off at Saca Stubbins because they were going bankrupt. They gave me a week's notice and an extra week's pay to close my contract sat-

153

isfactorily. I succeeded then in getting a job with Taca (Transports Aereos Central America) de Venezuela. I owe my thanks to an American named Jimmy Hull. He was the boss there and gave me the job. He could only start me out at $250 a month. I'd had a lot of aviation experience, but still I never got my license. I never stayed in one place long enough to get it.

There was good opportunity to raise that to $450 if I worked overtime and Sundays. Income tax was very low, 3 percent, and there were some tempting promises: (1) after six months, one is entitled to two weeks Christmas bonus; (2) after eight months, the company pays two weeks vacation pay; and (3) if fired, the company has to pay an additional thirty days indemption.

I worked for Taca seven and one-half months and this is how things went:

1. On the 24th of December, I had seven and one-half months service in. I received only one week's bonus. The company claimed profits had gone into new airplanes and could not give two weeks.

2. After seven and one-half months, my boss gave me a letter, stating, "Work has been satisfactory; please give him one week vacation pay." The pay master in Caracas refused to recognize it. Said law claimed I must work eight months to receive vacation pay.

3. I asked to be fired; boss couldn't do it. I could be drastic, example: Let air out of all the plane tires, so that they'd be grounded. Decided not to do it. I had enough of the torrid climate. I felt ill in my chest and decided to quit. I just couldn't stand the climate any longer.

The following pages are how things went more or less at work, about Maiquetía, the fellows I worked with, and the holidays.

Mr. Jimmy Hull, our *Jefe* (boss), was an American from the state of Nebraska. He was only twenty-six but looked at least thirty-five. He was chubby, about 5 foot 7 and quite bald. What remained of his hair was blond. He was a likable fellow. He was good-looking and had blue eyes. He had served in the Armed Forces but never overseas. He had married a Peruvian girl when he worked with Panagra at Lima. I thank him for giving me a job. Jimmy liked his liquor and had his hands full at work. The job was too big for the money he got paid. He was my boss for six months, then he quit and got an easier and better job with Creole Oil Company. He believed he would gain experience there then run off to Peru and make good wages. He had lost a brother in the army.

Mr. Jimmy Frew, our new *Jefe* (boss), came after Jimmy Hull quit. He was an American from the state of Oklahoma. Jimmy was a little fellow, lanky and sandy-haired. He usually wore a red baseball cap. He had spent a number of years in Costa Rica as chief of maintenance. He married a Latin girl, from Costa Rica. He wore a small mustache. It's customary to the Latin fellows. The Spanish fellows say the women love mustaches. I never got Jimmy's reason for it. Maybe his wife liked it. Jimmy was a quiet likable fellow. I'd never heard him raise his voice, but I'd seen him angry several times. He was my boss for two months.

Señor Daniel Guiterrez was boss out on the lines. I took orders from him also. He was from Peru. He was brown-complexioned and had dark curly hair and dark eyes. He was more a friend than a boss of mine. He married a pretty white Venezuelan girl. He had worked with Panagra in Peru. Guiterrez was about 5 foot 8 and lanky. He always wanted to box with me. He was about thirty-two, and I gave him a bad time. He gave me jobs, but never hurried me much. He let me taxi the plane once, got hell from Jimmy Hull. Guiterrez gave me his folks' address in Peru. I found his folks come from a very poor family. Guiterrez and I had many pleasant days at work, at dinner, in the plaza drinking rum and Coke. He took my jokes and wisecracks good naturedly.

Mr. David Graham, our radioman, was an American from the state of Kansas. He was thirty-four years old, about 5 foot 10, very thin, curly brown hair, and considered very tight. I didn't work with him, but saw him at work. He lived at Hencoop house with me in Macuto. We got along very well. He loved to travel. He had been there two years already. Had been a foreman in a factory during the war. His mom died and he went home, returned a few weeks later. Lost his girl in the States, engaged to a Costa Rican girl here in Venezuela. He did his work well.

Mr. Layman was an American from California. He was a quiet fellow, speaking Spanish fluently. He was thirty-five, but his gray hair made him look older. He was starter, generator, and electrical engineer for the planes. He was married to a pretty brown-complexioned Venezuelan girl. Rumors had it that when he went to work, she had Latin boyfriends calling at the house. He was tall, lanky, ran around without a shirt and had a deep tan. He had been in South America a number of years and probably would stay there always.

Mr. Herman Welch was an American from the state of Ohio. He was chief inspector of maintenance. I'd worked with him only three months. He had been working in Costa Rica and married a Costa Rican girl. He had her come to Venezuela. Welch was big, husky, blond and about thirty-nine, he liked his drinks and gambling. He was a shyster and a bully. He leased a house for 400 Bolivars a month and rented it out to a fellow at work for 500 Bolivars. He bought watches at a gross and sells them. He was always broke and borrowing money. He liked a lot of girls, made promises and never kept them. I liked him at first, but he pretended to like me. Said he once planned to make the same trip I'm making and the same way—hitchhiking. He never could get nerve enough and was now too old. He and I once got into a fight and in jail.

Mr. George Pigeon was a Latin from Manhattan; he was born American, served with the troops in Africa. He liked to talk of his adventures. He was my size, 5 foot 7, about 145 pounds. He was dark-complexioned, good-looking, with black curly hair. Had a collection of N.Y. wisecracks. Called me a Pennsylvania coal miner. "What's Brooklyn got?" I asked, "We got a tree, eh eh eh." He laughed. George was a likeable kid, but as tight as they come. He would come on the Plaza every night and say in a hefty voice, "I'm broke, fellows, buy me a drink." He did this so often till one night, Tony, our Portuguese friend, said, "Here's twenty Bolivars, God dammit, buy yourself a drink. I'm sick and tired of hearing the same story every night."

George came down several months after I did. He complained a lot about the poor conditions. Was anxious to get Guiterrez's job, as *Jefe,* (boss). That day never came.

They did not get along. One day Guiterrez said, "You're no American, Joey is the only one who is." This made him feel bad.

Mr. Benny Zayas was a Puerto Rican. He had spent much time in N.Y. Had served in the South Pacific. Quit flying when he was discharged and turned mechanic. He was a good joke-teller. Did a lot of swearing in Spanish. He was a good friend to me. He hated Jimmy Hull because he called him a "spick." Benny was 5 foot 7, a bit heavy, and his straight black hair always over his eyes, about twenty-eight years old.

Benny one day said, "The difference between you and me is the color of that skin." He pointed to my arm. This remark was unpredicted. Most Latins have an inferiority complex because of their brown skin. I did not have any feeling of difference toward any of the fellows because of that. I liked the fellows for what they were.

Other Americans were Crutcher—our pilot and chief superintendent; Kitchen, Smith, and Callaway were pilots. All pilots were American, the co-pilots were Venezuelan or Cubans or others. Pilots made approximately $1,000 a month. Co-pilots made $150 dollars a month plus six dollars an hour for every hour over twenty hours. They averaged about $250 per month.

Mr. Arthur Hogg was a Canadian. He was chief of sales and stores department for Taca. He was from Vancouver, B.C. He was short, thin, about forty. He had been in Latin America fifteen years, mostly in Mexico and Costa Rica. He was a bachelor. He hated Herman Welch. He was hard to understand. Sometimes he spoke to me, other times he didn't. He would pass me by and not say a word. After I whipped Welch, he sure liked me. I can see his grinning face still.

Mr. Conners was of English and Spanish descent, born in Honduras, C.A. He was fired and replaced by Mr. Hogg. He was a nice fellow, with good education, good position and salary. He had his wife and children in Miami. He loved Miami but had difficulty getting into the States. He was about thirty-eight, gray-haired, thin and about 5 foot 10. He was a good conversa-

157

tionalist. We spent many evenings on the plaza, drinking rum and Coke. He had no enemies.

From Guatemala we had Flores, Maroquin, and Tom Andredie. Flores was a good-looking kid, with blond wavy hair and blue eyes. He was husky and practiced calisthenics. He was twenty-four years old. Tom Andredie was heavy set, quiet spoken, courteous and helpful. Both he and Flores were related. They were of same height, about 5 foot 6.

Both Tom and Flores had worked for P.A.A. in Guatemala. P.A.A. had sent them to Miami to take a course in aeronautics and to study English; all expenses paid and $25 a week besides for thirteen months. Tom said Flores was very popular with the girls and one used to drive up every day to call for him. After the course, they returned to Guatemala and worked one year for P.A.A. They then quit and came to Venezuela to work. Their wages more than tripled. Neither liked Venezuela much. Both were homesick. They also liked Miami and hoped to return some day. Their salary was $300 a month, with overtime and Sunday brought it to $450 or $500.

Maroquin was an Indian who called me awful names in Spanish. I learned the words and called him likewise. He always wanted to dance with me. For a hat he would wrap a rag like a turban over his head. He looked wilder than ever. He said he was forty, but he didn't look it. He joked like a high school boy. He was a good mechanic though. He only stayed a few months; he became homesick for Guatemala. The other lad I knew was cross-eyed, about twenty-one, and a good hydraulic specialist. He wore a cross on a chain about his neck. Most of the Latin boys did also. Some wore medals and most of them were expensive. Most of the fellows I worked with were very religious. When passing a church or a cross, most of them crossed themselves while riding to or from work in the bus.

From Nicaragua we had only one fellow. His name was Barrios. He was heavy set, about 5 foot 10, had short curly hair. All I remember is that he was kind, polite, joking, and liked me for what I was. We had many long chats and when I returned to Venezuela after completing the trip around S.A., he was at the airport to embrace me and say good-bye as I flew homeward.

From Honduras we had Conners, and two Simon brothers. The brothers looked alike. The younger one was married and had a child; the elder, Edward, was unmarried. They were twenty-one and twenty-six years of age respectively. Edward was much taller and both brothers walked in a strange way, like old men do, very tired. Edward Simon had taken a thirteen-month course in Aeronautics in Miami also. He was in the same class with Flores and Tom Andredie. Edward was a mechanic and inspector. His brother, Roberto, was a mechanic and learned from Edward. Both were courteous and helpful.

From Costa Rica we had a number of fellows. There was Bonilla, Gonzales, Goldoni, Navas, Zapata, Blanco, and two Santa Maria brothers.

Bonilla was a good-looking chap, with a heavy brush haircut. He would wake me up in the morning by putting a cat on my naked chest. I awoke saying "Jesus Christ All Mighty" and Bonilla laughed fit to die. We spent many enjoyable siestas and evenings together over rum and Coke, and canned fish. His wife was in Costa Rica and also his mom. He was very homesick. He worked only three months and went back. On his last night, he got a little drunk. He cried and said to me, pounding on my chest, "I'm going back, I'm going back to my *novia* (sweetheart) and my mamá."

It was hard to believe that a big husky fellow could become so homesick. Bonilla and I had one serious argument. I was sorry it happened. We did not talk for a week or so. He had loaned me some tools and later I thought they belonged to Benny. We argued over that and I was wrong.

Gonzales was a thin lad, about twenty, wore glasses, and talked too much. He used to pull my leg a lot. He was the machinist. He was a very "tight" person. He will be in Venezuela a long time, saving his money. He was always happy.

Goldoni was the hydraulic specialist. He was about thirty-six. Had his wife and children in Costa Rica and got to see them once a year. He went home on his two-week vacations at Christmastime. It's a shame that he should be separated from his family that way. He hoped to save a small fortune and return to Costa Rica. His father was an Italian. Goldoni called me "Pennsylvania."

Navas was a young chap, very quiet, shy, but he had the prettiest girl on the Plaza. As a true nobleman, he courted his girl while her mom and sister chaperoned. Now he walked alone with her and all the fellows sitting on the plaza, wishing they were he.

"Blanco" means white in Spanish, this boy is dark brown, his name does not fit. He had his wife come down from Costa Rica, and she is pretty and white. The baby is white also. Blanco is very proud of them, seems happily married. I've never seen him unhappy yet.

"Zapata" means shoe in Spanish; this fellow has a couple of teeth missing in front. He is skinny, has unruly hair, and is not the least bit handsome, but he is a good lad and a good worker.

The two Santa Maria brothers are very handsome and very religious. The younger one is married, has a child and wife there. He is twenty-one years old. The other brother is single, about twenty-six. He has no desire to get married yet. They kid and pull my leg a lot.

From Colombia we had Marin. He was so small and frail. He looked like an undernourished child. He did not look twenty-five years old. It surprised me more to learn he was married and had a child. He was a quick-tempered, hasty, and talks rapidly in a thin voice. He knew mechanics very well but sometimes I wondered if he had strength enough to work. After coming from a cold climate of Bogota to a hot climate here, he became most uncomfortable. He stayed only two months.

From Peru we had Alfado, Victor Delgado, and Chulito Vargas. Alfado was a tiny fellow, about 5 foot 2. He was inspector out on the line. He kept very busy all the time. Maybe he feared losing his job and the high salary. He could never make the same in Peru. He lived in a cheap hotel in Maiquetía and was able to bank several hundred dollars a month. He was a nice fellow. I visited him sometimes in Maiquetía, and he knew a number of pretty girls there. Probably that was his reason for staying there. Alfado was a decent sort of lad. He would never think of going to

La Guaira. He called the girls there "sons of bitches" who drank and smoked.

I asked if he wanted me to visit his folks when I visited Peru. He smiled for an answer, meaning "Sorry, Joe." He must have had a good reason why I shouldn't. Alfado was a camera fan and liked studying English.

Victor Delgado was a husky fellow, about 5 foot 9. He looked a lot like Turhan Bey, the movie star, only Victor wore a heavy mustache. I asked him to shave it off and boy, did he look funny. He looked better with it. I didn't like him at first. He seemed like a bully. He was always pushing me around or slugging me in the gut. I had trouble pronouncing *estomago* (stomach). I kept saying *estamaga.* He would swear *"Carajo Estomago"* and hit my gut again. Somehow or other he became my best friend. He was not tight like a lot of the fellows. He spent his money foolishly on good times, cameras, rings, and so forth. Victor long ago did speak English, but he forgot most of it and insisted on my speaking Spanish. I learned a lot from his rough treatment.

He gave me a letter of introduction to his brother in Lima, Peru. No wonder he was so carefree, his folks are well to do. I never believed his stories about his car, the athletics club, and his service in the war with Ecuador. But it was true. Victor was my age—twenty-five. I really believe Victor hated to see me leave.

Chulito Vargas. I've never seen a guy more happier than he. He was always laughing about something or pulling wise cracks. George Pigeon said, "He has a bug up his belly." I got to work with this character many times, and I loved his company. One day we had a trying time. He was within the plane, I was outside. We were replacing the tail wheel assembly. There were some fifteen nuts and bolts to tighten on the hold-down plate. We couldn't see one another, and we could likewise hardly hear one another. I hardly understood the Spanish words anyway. We got the job done in time. But put a Latin in the States, in my position, what American would put up with a fellow who didn't savvy the language? Chulito only laughed about it, showing a beautiful set of perfect white teeth. He was a little squirt, 5 foot 2.

From Argentina we had a fellow named Mike. He was a

blond, with curly hair, about thirty-six. The fellows said he was a German Jew. Mike worked in the instrument department. A lot of the fellows didn't like him because he was Jewish. Especially Bernie, the Polish immigrant. I got along with Mike all right. I even felt sorry for him. He had married a Venezuelan girl during my stay. Everybody said he was crazy for getting married. But he seemed to have a nice wife who liked him. Mike was fired unjustly and was able to sue the company and collect indemnity. He did not believe I could accomplish my journey on my planned budget. He was very wrong.

From Portugal we had Silva. I called him "Heigh ho Silva" (Silver) talon, talon, talon, talon, talon. It was funny for a while, then Silva tired of it. Silva had left Portugal eleven years ago. He spent seven years in Brazil and raved how wonderful and cheap everything was there. He hoped to return to Portugal in another year or so. He would have enough savings by then. Silva was a small, thin fellow, about thirty years old. He was sentimental about his folks in Europe. He hasn't seen them in eleven years. He was in the sheet metal department and knew his job very well.

From Portugal we had another kid named Ferdinand. He was about nineteen. He spoke English quite well. He had learned aboard U.S. ships and liked Americans a lot. He was always dreaming and he produced little work. He had skipped a ship in Trinidad, was picked up by the police, and put in jail for fifteen days. The Portuguese consul got him out and sent him to Venezuela. There was a demand for immigrants, and Ferdinand was able to get a job. But it paid very little.

Ferdinand had long hair, covering his eyes. He needed a haircut very badly. His clothes were baggy, and he wore a large zoot-suiter's hat when off work. At work a paper bag served for a hat. Ferdinand spent all his evenings in La Guayra with the girls on "Knob Hill."

From Poland we had Bernie Despot, an ex-paratrooper.

From Italy we had a quiet, intelligent fellow named "Maceo." He was forty years old but looked only twenty-five. He was, without a doubt, of a good family. His politeness and courtesy and well-mannered behavior seemed to indicate his walk of life.

162

Venezuela to him was wilderness, but he seemed to confide in me. He was always sober and serious. He had served in the Italian Air Force. He said he would return to Italy. He could never bring his wife and children here. We had many long talks, and he showed no hatred for the Americans.

The Venezuelans I worked with were Hernandez, Garcia, Moreno, Perez, Pinto and Delgado. Hernandez worked with Conners in the sales office. He spoke Spanish and English fluently. He was well up in his 30s and quite bald. He was a quiet fellow who kept his grudges within himself. When his patience could no longer stand the strain, he really blew up. At the pension he blew up one day. He told the cook over and over he did not like his soup spicy. He banged the table, slammed his chair, swore profoundly, and left the room. We all were amazed at the sudden commotion he had made.

Moreno was from the city of Trujillo, in the state of Trujillo. He was one of few Venezuelan mechanics we had. He was an independent sort of fellow, who preferred working alone.

Garcia worked in the store room. He and I studied English and Spanish together many times. He did extra favors for me in the store room. He always found time to find the right objects I needed. I visited his home several times, and it was mouse poor. Made of mud and adobe. He had a pretty wife and a five-year-old girl. I'd bring her candy on my visits.

Perez worked in the store room also. He was just a boy who perspired continually. I called him Pedro. He taught me some of the words to the song *"Una Vaca Lechera* (One Milk Cow).

Pinto was a colored kid, quite big and husky. Worked on propellers. He used to have a habit of hitting me playfully on the head getting off the bus. This hitting game I didn't like, and one day I smashed him hard. He never hit me again. We seldom talked much after that.

Delgado was a tall, lanky fellow. He was the ugliest fellow working with us. He had huge buck teeth, large glasses. His eyesight and hearing were very bad. He wore baggy overalls. How he got married was a mystery.

Rubio was from Maracaibo, so we called him "Maracucho." He was forty years old and had ten children; he was very active, wore bobby sox, loafers, sport coats with an upturned hat. He looked about twenty-five. He rode the bicycle like a schoolboy, over steps, ruts, and all. His family and wife lived in Maracaibo. He went to see the girls at La Guayra. Rubio spoke English and Spanish well. Everybody liked him because he was fun-loving and doing something crazy all the time.

One day he returned to Maracaibo and got into an auto accident. A co-pilot returned from a flight and said he believed Rubio died. A collection was taken up to get flowers for him. A week later he returned walking and sporting a cut lip and bruised nose. We got our money back. Rubio was a good mechanic, made good wages.

Most of the Venezuelans made less money than the mechanics who were foreigners, and they felt bitter resentment. One could hardly blame them in some ways. In other ways they just didn't have the "know-how." Margarito was a Venezuelan bus driver for Taca. He was tall, lanky, and complaining a lot. The fellows laughed at his complaints. Always he'd say *"Ola, Nanko"* and start dancing. Whenever he saw me, he broke into a dance. It never failed. Margarito forced a car into a ditch one day. Everybody cheered him, but he paid the fine alone 50 Bolivars, his week's pay.

George Fredrick was a colored fellow from British Guiana. He spoke English, French, and Spanish fluently. He was forty, but he did not look it. He was a driver for Taca also. Nobody liked his driving; he made sudden stops and hit heavy bumps. He got into many arguments with the Spanish boys and finally quit.

Holidays and My Work:

Independence day in the United States is July 4. Independence Day is a day later in Venezuela. It is celebrated on July 5.

Venezuela had gained her independence about the same time of our own George Washington. Their hero is Simón Bolívar, a native of Venezuela.

In his battles against the Spanish conquistadores and English pirates, Bolívar and Sucre, another great general, succeeded in gaining freedom for five republics. They are Venezuela, Colombia, Ecuador, Peru and Bolivia. Bolívar and Sucre suffered many hardships and defeats, but in the end they were victorious. All five republics are proud of Simón Bolívar as we in the States are of George Washington. The remains of Bolívar lie in a coffin in a huge Pantheon in Caracas, Venezuela. Only on national holidays, the gates to the pantheon are opened to visitors to view the resting place of the great liberator.

So today, July 5, 1947, a flotilla of Colombian merchant ships (4 in all) arrives in La Guaira, the first seaport of Venezuela, to celebrate the holiday. The ships are flying many gay-colored banners and streamers. They come in as a group and slowly move to dock.

The docks are full of cheering dark-complexioned people and they truly give the Colombians a mighty welcome.

The American vice-consul has his office closed on behalf of the holiday.

I work my way through the dark crowds and return to work in the afternoon. Because of the holiday, few of the fellows come to work, and the few who do, take it very easy.

After work at midnight, I return to the hotel. I look down on the plaza and the feasting, drinking, music, and dancing is still going on. I'd be out of place if I joined in, for I'd be the only blond fellow there.

Three o'clock in the morning, and the band still plays on. The cheers and whoopie go on likewise, and I find it hard going to sleep.

July 24:

It's Simón Bolívar's birthday, the great liberator of South America.

Venezuelan flags of yellow, blue, and red bars and white stars are displayed everywhere. It is a national holiday and few people work.

About noon a heavy rain came. The water came rushing down the mountainsides, bringing mud, rock, and thrash into the streets of Maiquetía, La Guaira, Macuto, and Pariata. The roads soon become blocked with debris. Traffic stalled and became a jam. It seldom rains there in Venezuela, but when it does, it makes up for the time when it doesn't rain.

From the doorway of the Fruente restaurant in Maiquetía, I watched and waited amidst many others for the rain to subside. The muddy waters came rushing down the streets one to two feet deep. It was almost impossible to cross the street. A few bold or foolish ones waded cross the rushing current. They only risked getting their legs cut or bruised from the tin cans, wire hoops, glass and rocks that came tumbling down.

Each time someone ventured out, a shout of boos and cheers followed from watching crowds in doorways of various *tiendas* (stores) and restaurants lining the plaza. The rain soon stopped and the Taca bus came an hour late. The streets were a muddy mess everywhere.

Today I paid double, because of the holiday.

July 29:

From Macuto, I took a bus to La Guaira for one luche ($.04). From there I took a taxi for Caracas, five Bolivars ($1.50). The cab had a full load. The driver turned out to be a bad one. He had everybody scared, passing on curves and driving on the wrong side of the road. A car in front of us went out of control. It zigzagged crazily, then came to a stop. At first we thought the operator was drunk or sick.

Then our driver pulled alongside and stopped on the road, directly in face of approaching traffic at a curve. A high bank of a mountain hid approaching traffic. Any second a car or heavy truck would come bouncing along. Natural instinct made me tell the driver "Pull ahead, dammit, before we get hit." We learned the car had broken its steering axle or tie rods, causing it to sway all over the road.

Upon arriving in Caracas, I immediately went to Ministero de Relationes Interiores. From there I was directed to Jefatura de Sequridad National. I was told there, that to have my tourist visa changed to one of permanent resident and permission to work in Venezuela, I must have written permit (request) from T.A.C.A. main office, and also a stamp for ten Bolivars ($3.00).

I went to T.A.C.A. main office where Señor Cavalera advised me to return the next day. It was late afternoon. A heavy rain fell. Before long water was rushing down the streets 6 to 8 inches deep. It was interesting to watch the cars plowing through. Caracas is located high in the mountains. The rushing water is so clear, so different from the heavy rains of Maiquetía that brings mud, rocks, debris into the city from the mountains.

I waited with fifteen or twenty other unfortunates in a doorway; an hour later it stopped, I checked in at a hotel. The numerous questions asked, identification, where from? where going? I felt like saying, "I'm not a criminal, I only want a room for the night."

I went to a movie, not permitted downstairs in sport shirt, went to the balcony, 60¢ up, 90¢ down. I saw Alan Ladd in *Calcutta*. For some reason the last four pictures I've seen depicted the leading lady as a bad woman. A killer or a narcotic. I keep getting the idea that American women are no good. Surely these kinds of pictures will have an affect on our Latin neighbors.

A very short lunch after the movie, cost the price of a steak in Jersey. Back at the hotel again, had to sleep under blankets. The night was cold but fresh. The bed was clean and most comfortable; tired from walking so much in Caracas. April 2, 1948 I fell asleep pronto; thinking what the boss would say because I didn't come to work on the night shift.

July 30:

Awoke at intervals at 6, 7, 8, and 9 o'clock amidst dreams of incidents back home; my car, Mom, and the gas station.

I seemed bewildered to be in a strange room and far from home upon awakening.

I dressed, washed my face in pan of water, and dried my face in a pillow case; no towels had been furnished.

The air was refreshing. I lunched at a cute Dutch café adjoining the Edificio Bolívar on Calle Cathedral Norte.

A pleasant Dutch woman proprietor took my order. Two fried eggs, coffee and bread. Cost two Bolivars (U.S. 65¢). Many Americans patronized.

I returned to Taca office and Senor Cavalera looked up regulations pertaining to extending my tourist visa to permanent residence in a law book. He then typed out an official document, and we proceeded together to purchase a stamp for it at the local post office (*officina correro*). Cost one Bolivar.

Senor Cavalera was a nice fellow, interested in studying English, and had plans for a trip to Mexico City and U.S. in the near future.

We then went to Ministero Building, and the receptionist took the document and said I would be notified by mail if my request would be granted.

I had no sooner parted with Cavalera than I heard somebody yell, "Hey, Joe."

It was Rene Cuya, a co-pilot for Taca, who lived at the pension with me. I was pleased to see him; meeting a familiar face in the large city of Caracas is wonderful. He is Cuban and also in Caracas to change his passport to one of permanent residence.

We had coffee and took the 11 o'clock bus to Maiquetía airport. It was a Taca bus, and we rode free of charge, being Taca employees. The driver asked for our identification cards.

The ride was very rough, and Rene said it was just like the Taca planes he flies in. We followed a different route part of the way. It was one-way and winding and twisting and narrow. We nearly hit the roof several times. It actually hurt the body on the inside. The driver wasn't the least bit reckless. We passed several trucks with broken springs along the road. The ride lasted one and one-half hours.

We had Cokes at the airport, then took a bus to Maiquetía.

At the pension, we had soup, fish, rice, banana fried, coffee, and a delicious cheese omelet. Some large man passed through the dining room and remarked in English, "I hope you enjoyed your meal."

I soon met him. He told me he would be moving into the pen-

168

sion in a few days. His name was Strause. He was a Chilean of German descent. He was an engineer and a traveler. He had served aboard American ships during the war. He still had American seamen's papers as an engineer.

After lunch I have a drink of *"warapo"* at a tiny restaurant bar. It's very delicious and cold. It's hard to believe it's made of only brown sugar and water. I leave several letters there for a Venezuelan co-pilot to deliver for me on his weekly flight to New York. I have found many faults in the Venezuelan mail system, and I trust my friend to mail the letters in New York personally.

One day in Maiquetía I went to the *officina de Correos* (post office). I had several letters to go to Guatemala. The lady clerk checked the weight of the letter by hand, and asked, "Where's Guatemala, in Europe?"

Holy Hell, I thought, *she's a Latin and doesn't know where Guatemala is. That's probably the reason I never heard from friends in Guatemala; my letters may be in Europe.*

The T.A.C.A. bus comes along. I no sooner go aboard and the motor quits. Flores locates a loose wire in the distributor. We come one-half hour late to work. Had a short service to do on plane A.Z.K. Boy is it hot, wish it were as cool as in Caracas.

Jimmy Hull, our *Jefe* (boss), comes about midnight to check on us. He has his cute little son along.

A week later my request for "permanent resident" visa was granted by the Venezuelan government. Jimmy Hull says to a couple of pilots, "The kid comes here as a tourist, gets a job, and the government lets him stay; that's doing something."

August 2: Getting a Haircut

Today is Saturday. I take the bus to La Guaira. The glare of the sun is hard to bear. Most people wear dark glasses for this reason. No mail today; the U.S. Vice-consul office is closed.

I meet Flores and we go to get a haircut. We wait about an hour and a half. There are three barbers and they start arguing politics. They stop cutting and wave and motion with scissors and comb in hand. Impatiently the customers wait for them to

169

finish their arguments and start work again. One customer remarks, "Less talk, more work." Barbers stop motioning, stare blank, then say *"Carajo"* (dammit) and resume their argument. We finally got our haircut, cost two Bolivars (60¢).

The Horse Races

Flores invited me for dinner at his pension in Macuto. It's called "Think." His landlady is interested in the horse races held Saturday and Sunday in Caracas. She is studying a periodical and names her favorites. The betting is different from the American way. In the States it's Win, Place, and Show, and you bet *individual* races to win or double up. In Venezuela you must pick six or eight horses out of six races in order to win. When you win, it's quite a fortune. Her is how it's done: You buy a sheet for a *real* (15¢), mark your six or eight favorites, and make your bet. The lowest bet is four Bolivars ($1.25). There is no limit. Sometimes two, three, or four fellows place a large sum of money on one sheet. Then they sign it and keep a carbon copy as a receipt. Many Americans try their fortunes.

Flores and I work till midnight, then six hours extra till dawn. The six hours pays double on Sundays.

August 2:

Five of us had worked till morning. There had been a full moon out and when Rubio accidentally knocked out the lights of my extension cord, I asked him to give me the "luna" (moon). He laughed and reached for it. Already I was learning Spanish.

We took the bus to Maiquetía. Rubio and Valera wanted to return at twelve noon. I decided with Flores to return at two o'clock. Valera and I bought nice rosy red apples from a street vendor. Two apples cost 45¢.

170

Misunderstanding

Work was slow in the afternoon. There was a lot of singing and joking as I helped Guatemala and San Jose (Bonilla and Simon) install a gas tank into plane A.Z.K.

At quitting time, I was about to sign the work reports. Flores asked if I had signed them. He must have misunderstood when I said I was on my way to do so. Before I knew it, he threw his report to the ground angrily. He seemed to have tears in his eyes. He said, "I asked you over and over to sign the reports daily." I knew it hopeless to try to explain I was on my way to do so. When angry, he hardly savvied English.

Later I knew he was sorry. I felt sorry for him also. He had embarrassed himself among his friends.

Flores is really a nice fellow, but he sure has a short temper. He has a lot of responsibility and has only been there a month. The *Jefe* (boss) gives him a lot of hell for little reason. Later as I got off the bus at Maiquetía, I said, "See you tomorrow, Flores." "Okay, Joe," he answered as always.

August 6, Catching the Devil:

Landlady give a short nod, but I see her and say, "Okay, I'm up." At work, Jimmy Hull (the boss) gives me hell for being absent yesterday. My buddies have an idea I've been to "Knob Hill" and kid me about it. Assigned to check planes A.Z.J. and A.Z.N.

Received a letter from home; seems like I'm forgotten. Alex has a hard time sneaking into the carnivals.

Washing Clothes:

In the afternoon, I had to wash out my work uniform, in gasoline. Company is short on uniforms. None in store room. Hands burning afterwards. Venezuelan ladies do my laundry; one has to make out an inventory or a shirt, pants, socks, or handkerchief will always be found missing.

171

Sing and Dance:

Had short services to do on A.Z.P. It started raining very hard and continued throughout the day. I got thoroughly wet and got the chills. I like it, though. The wind and rain were driving hard and it reminded me of winters and blizzards back in Pennsylvania and Detroit. Felt like dancing and singing. "Oh, the storm outside is frightful." My Spanish buddies like this tune, and I explain the words to them.

Kilroy Here:

I asked Jimmy Hull if Kilroy had ever been there. He said, "Benny, the Puerto Rican, was the first." We all laughed. We all missed the Kilroy scripture popular in the States.

All Gone:

Worked till 7:00, one hour overtime. There was no water in the tank to take a shower. I was oily, dirty, and plenty mad. I was last and Margarito, the bus driver, was blowing the horn with a dozen fellows hollering to hurry up. The roof of the truck was a sieve, and we got wet again. A short way up the road, we met the T.A.C.A. bus and scrambled off the truck into the bus. *Sorry, you're late!*

I was told supper was served till 8:00 . I came at 7:20. The colored waitress refused to serve me. She said I was late. I met Manuel. He called the landlady, and she politely served me.

Manuel and I talked. He sure missed the States. He spent two years in Kansas City at an engineering school. He is the chief engineer at the control tower at the airport. Manuel has made a tiny radial engine, five cylinders, pistons, crankshaft. It's a hobby and he hopes to have it running some day. It is only about eight inches in circumference. It was truly a masterpiece, and a work of art. Manuel was sent to the States by the Venezuelan government. In case of a change in government, he will lose his

172

job. Because of the change in politics, his dad lost his job and is living out his old age in Barqisimeto, dependent upon Manuel.

August 7, English and Hot Dogs:

Dislike getting up. Landlady gives a short hasty knock. Worked on tail-wheel assembly. More and more my fellow co-workers seem to be interested in learning English. Some have books and catch me with, "I feel sick today," "What's the matter with you?" "What's up, Doc?" or "You are my sweetheart, my love." They all are interested in learning the words to "Hey Bob a re Bob."

We go to Macuto tonight. Flores and I have a few cakes and hot dogs, my first in ten months at "Briza del Mar" (a thatch-roofed restaurant) called "Breeze of the Sea." It's a mere shelter house, with gravel floor and sun chairs all about, and a nickelodeon for music. It's peaceful and quiet in Macuto, except for the pounding of the sea. There is a crowd of people walking on the plaza, in clean dress. Some pretty girls go by. Some laugh at the wolf cry.

I return to La Guaira by bus, then walk to Maiquetía. A lot of people are waiting for a bus, and I believe I can get to Maiquetía sooner walking. If I waited I'd only be pushed and shoved and be last. The crowd there is of the lower class and definitely push a white man around.

August 9, Talk about Shoes:

Came a half hour late to work today. The sun is hot as it usu-ally is, I tried working in the shade of the wing. If there is a job to be done, Flores calls on me. He bothers me too much. Rubio like-wise is bothered by Benny. Had a headache and Venezuelan Cafenole helped. Rubio had loaned me a lot of tools. I'm slow in returning them. Rubio yells, "Joe, I'll wring your neck." I laugh, for he is such a little fellow.

I had bought a pair of Venezuelan factory-made shoes for

five dollars. They lasted about twenty- four hours. It rained a few days ago. I went to Macuto and upon returning, I had to run for a bus over the wet streets. Stepping on the bus, my feet felt cold. Quick observation and I found my soles had fallen out and I was barefooted. Boy, was I mad. The soles were made of paper.

I then had a Polish immigrant make me a pair of sandals by hand. It took eight hours to make them and cost $14. They are made of leather and very cool and handsome and look factory-made. All my buddies like them.

It seldom lightnings and thunders there. I stood under a nacelle, leaned against the oil cooler, and got a terrific shock at the exact second when the lightning struck. I stayed away for a while. It rained a lot. We had about a two-hour break.

Got paid today, $267.80 Bolivars ($80.00) for seven days. Hope I can stick it out for four more months.

August 10, Superstitions:

It is 7:30 Sunday morning. I sit on the low cement wall surrounding the beautiful plaza and statue of an angel. We watch the people go by. They are coming from church and going home. All the ladies, young and old, wear the black veil of Spanish costume.

The sun is as hot as a barber's towel. Soon the TACA bus comes beeping its horn at the intersection. We try to grin and bear the rough ride to the airport. Had a trying time with the tall wheel assembly. All the bush rings and nuts were frozen and rusted. Sunday is a slow day. The *Jefe* (boss) took the day off.

When taking a shower or changing clothes, the fellows call one another "*Nudista*" (a nude). The reason for this is because of some excitement in Caracas a few days ago. A male nudist, draped in only a black cloak and a hood, dropped from a roof into a young girl's room and raped her. Then he ran eight blocks in broad daylight in the business district; police chased and fired at him, but the "nudista" got away.

George Fredrick, a Negro British subject of a Caribbean Island said that it is a spirit. In his island home, this spirit attacks many times. He only rapes, but he does not kill. Police cannot catch or shoot him, so his people are bound to believe it is a spirit. Many Venezuelans believe this also, but the newspaper doesn't claim it's so. It had pictures reenacting the "spirits" entry into the room, how he attacked, and how he ran down the streets. George is forty years old, intelligent, but still believes in this superstition.

August 11, The Egg and I:

Upon arising I found a chicken must have ventured into my room through the open door. I found an egg setting on my work trousers. I told the landlady I'd have it for breakfast. It strikes her as very funny.

I took the 5:30 bus to work. There are only five of us service mechanics on the night shift. Working nights is cool and comfortable. It is very quiet. None of the other airlines are working at night. Avensa, Creole, Linea, Aeropostal, Cave or P.A.A. as I look out over the field and the high mountains and the clear full moon higher yet, I am bound to think of folks back home.

Work is slow and when work is done, we all sit and tell stories, sitting on the ground, under a plane wing. We talk in Spanish and English and as usual ends about girls.

August 12, I said it again!

Up at noon, took a cold shower. Haven't had a hot one in ten months. Only have hot water when the sun heats it. Studied A.B.C. with Martha, the landlady's daughter. She likes English.

I was advised at work that the night shift was being terminated. When Guiterrez, our foreman from Peru told me to be out at 8:00 A.M. next day, I naturally said, "*Nojoda* (damn it)." He just about wrang my neck. Everybody laughed, I again used the wrong word.

August 13, I did it again!

I did not intend and did not go to work at 8:00. Four hours' sleep is not enough. Awoke at noon, stopped for a Coke, and missed my bus. I yelled. I believe some of the fellows saw me, but the bus didn't stop. I decided to take the afternoon off also.

August 16, a night in Macuto:

I went to Macuto this evening and met Flores, Roberto, Simon, Bonilla Gonzales, and a dozen other fellows from the airport. They invited me to drink with them. All of them were in clean summer dress. A few Venezuelan girls were in the crowd also. After a few drinks, we crossed the street to the Miami Hotel. A dance was on.

The orchestra was composed of young boys from ten to twelve years of age. That struck me as very odd. The people danced unconcerned. The boys were good, beating drums, maracas and sticks. Others played flutes and a boy crooned into a microphone.

At the bar I drank brandy and met another Costa Rican lad. He had served in the U.S. Navy as a volunteer in the war. He had served several years and was entitled to U.S. citizenship. He had spent a lot of time in the States, preferred his little country in Central America, and very proud of it, he hoped to settle down in Costa Rica.

When he went to the States, he couldn't speak English. One day on a crowded street car, he stepped on a girl's foot. Instead of saying "Excuse me," he said, "Kiss me." The girl slapped his face. He became very embarrassed and humiliated. Luckily he had a friend along who apologized for him, saying he could not speak English and used the wrong word in his attempt to apologize. The girl then apologized also, and they went out together, and even went to bed.

After midnight the Costa Rican boys roamed the plaza, pushed canoes out to sea, pushed trash cans over, and knocked out an immense beautiful street lamp with rocks. They then ran high-tail up dark streets to their pensions.

August 17, that Guy Rubio:

Sunday again and it feels like blue Monday. The fact that I'm making double pay doesn't cheer me up. Worked all morning greasing four planes.

Rubio's son had lost three hundred Bolivars ($100) somewhere on the field. It was Rubio's entire week's pay. His thirteen-year-old son relayed the news with tears in his eyes. Rubio had let him have the money because he felt it safer to be with him. Nobody would try to rob a young lad. Rubio told him to forget it, lost three hundred Bolivars, so what! No sense in crying about it. Rubio never had a nasty temper or ever got upset.

Rubio and I went to the Paramount Theater in Maiquetía. We saw James Cagney in *Thirteen Rue Madeleine*. Cagney was good as ever and everyone liked him. Rubio said, "I like Cagney because he is always in trouble."

After the movie, we met Schafer, the Chilean, went to a restaurant and had some drinks. Conversation was pleasant. We forgot about going to the dance at Royal Cene (movie), forgot about life back in the States; the doors and shutters closed and we still lingered in this quiet, peaceful haven.

August 22, Seguero Sociale:

Went to the airport in the morning. Told Jimmy I was taken sick and was going to Seguro Social (Social Security) to see a doctor and collect benefits for lost time. Victor, the time keeper, advised me that I could not collect or get free medical care because I made over 800 Bolivars a month. My salary was $834 Bolivars without overtime. It was thirty-four Bolivars over the limit.

We could only try to see what happened. We went to the offices in La Guaira and Maiquetía. Victor tried his best to make them pay. The *Jefe* (boss) at Maiquetía, a big, fat, blubbery fellow who wore large-rim glasses was half-interested and buried his face in a newspaper out of sight. I had a feeling that if I were any other than an American, he would have reconsidered. I've already learned to expect no favors from these people. I have paid Social Security, so I can only expect a refund. In time to come, I never got the refund either.

In La Guaira, at the Seguero Social medical clinic, there were hundreds of patients, all grimy and dark-complexioned, waiting to see the doctor. Some waited all day there. Most of the patients were low-class people. Many were sick and some pretended to be. I'd just as soon go to my own doctor and not have to wait and suffer inconvenience.

I sat on the stone steps the rest of the day and continued reading the *Sea Wolf*. At times I felt like throwing the book away. A pretty neighbor walked by; she stretched her arms gracefully for some tropical fruit. She watched me quietly. I asked what the fruit was. She gave me two; they were green and larger than a crab apple. It tasted sour. She said it was sweet, but it wasn't by a long shot. I ate one and threw the second away. "My name is Carmen; what's yours?" "Joey," I answered. She asked my age and if I were married. I said I was forty and divorced. She doubted the first answer; after the second she disappeared and reappeared no more. (I was twenty-four years old, really.)

I went to see a film from Russia, titled *Girl Number 217*. It was a story about Russian slaves in Germany. It was in Russian, with Spanish words underneath. During one incident the girl slave was locked in a cell, unable to sit, bend or otherwise. She stood upright for many hours. A Nazi poured water on her face to revive her. Some Venezuelans laughed loudly as if it were only a cartoon and not real life. I wondered and hated how ignorant these people were and that a terrible brutal war had just passed.

Mickey, a Dutch lad from Corzal, and I had been to the movies. Afterwards we joined a dozen Polish immigrants in the Plaza. I was surprised to hear them playing "O Susannah" and "Beer Barrel Polka" on a harmonica. They said they learned it from the American troops in Poland. Then they swung into "You Are My Sunshine." Mickey then played Mexican and Dutch tunes. It was entertainment for many Latins seated around the plaza and the illuminated angel.

August 27, Some Names:

After three days rest, I still didn't feel like getting up for work. At work everybody seemed glad to see me, even Flores who for some reason had been acting strange toward me lately. I made visuals and took it sort of easy like.

After dinner I nearly overslept. By sheer force of will power, I got up. The sun was hot and I felt terribly weak and tired. The fellows now call me "Gringito." Bonilla always comes at me with "Hey, Bob, a le Bob." I come back at him with, "Uh, huh, San Jose." We address one another many times from where they come from. Like Lima, San Jose, Tegucigalpa, Guatemala, and Marachucho for fellows from Maracaibo.

The public bus is crowded to Maiquetía. Some passengers voice their thoughts in loud voices. Surely people never get that loud on buses in the States. The driver speeds, double clutches, and races the engine. He has to let everyone know he can drive. How these fellows get through the tight pinches and narrow streets so often is amazing. It's more luck than skill, I'm sure.

August 29, Venezuela on Guard

Up at 8:15, it was too late to go to work. I was angry because the landlady didn't call. I sat on stone steps and studied Spanish. Carmen Rosa Diaz came along and kept up a pleasant chatter. To her questions of what songs I knew, I remarked, "Mumma Yo Quiero" and *"Una Vaca Lechera."* Both are cute ditties in Spanish.

I went to work at noon, everyone acted like I had been away a long time. Jimmy pretended surprise at seeing me. I worked till 7:00 with Vargas on the landing gear.

I went abroad the *Olympic Pioneer* docked in La Guaira. I was late and failed to see Randy, a seaman. Looked for him at the

179

notorious gin mills in La Guaira on "Knob Hill." I felt a little ill at ease being alone. I met familiar faces in each cabaret. At one, I had a highball and talked to several Yanks. Surprised to see Chulito Vargas there. He grinned from ear to ear at the sight of me. Others from the airport were there also. I met a few Canadians and we drank and talked in the more respectable neighborhood of La Guaira. Feeling ill, I only drank Cokes.

It was past midnight as I hiked towards Maiquetía. The streets were dim and dusty. There seemed to be more and more soldiers on guard duty everywhere along the way. Expecting political strife again at the airport, soldiers and sailors are on guard, day and night. At night the guard is tripled.

August 30, High Prices:

Today is clean-up day at work; we wash the floor with disinfectant. Work was slow today. Small pay check. Jimmy was a bit surprised to see me on time. He remarked, "Aren't you up a little early today, Joe?"

Martha at the pension asks for an additional ten Bolivars ($3.00) a month because I had placed a 100-watt bulb in my room. I complained that I couldn't possibly run up a bill like that on one bulb and the little time I used the light. No use being angry, just forget it and pay. As I write, a big bat flies into the room through an open window, swoops up a few mosquitoes, and flies out again. I wish they would eat up the inch and a half roaches that run about my room.

At the Royal Theater in Maiquetía, Bud Abbott and Lou Costello were playing in *Buck Privates Come Home*. I'd never heard such loud cheering and laughing in all my life in a movie. They didn't sound like people. It's impossible to describe. It was amusing the way Costello drove the racing car through impossible obstacles and traffic. When I was a child, I used to laugh loudly at these comedy pictures, but there tonight, to hear mature people shrieking and laughing fit to die, I could only assume thoughts that the people were not very intelligent.

After the movie, I met Juan Gonzales. We stopped at a crude

restaurant that smelled foul of urine. He had a beer and I a Coke. He played a guitar a little while. Soon another joined in with another guitar. A third fellow tried to come to our table to pick a fight with me. His friends stopped him. He was half-tight and evidently had some grudge against the Americans. No words were spoken to me, but one of my companions warned me to be careful.

This was the first incident in my four months there. I didn't take it seriously. I knew so many people there now that Maiquetía seemed like a recluse to me, and Juan would fight anybody for me. He once got me out of jail, and I'm still grateful to him. I left him then at the dim, smelly, rough restaurant amidst many low-class laborers. Juan is a first-class carpenter, with many faults, but still a good fellow to know.

Latin people are very temperamental, especially in hot climates. A few weeks ago, a man was stabbed in the back one evening there in Maiquetía while casually walking about the plaza. Another time a man went berserk and tried to kill his family with a machete. Police had to battle and subdue him. In Maracaibo, where it was recorded as the hottest place in the world in 1946, a very old man stabbed and killed a young girl because she refuse his love affections, and another killed a restaurant proprietor because he refused to give him a glass of water. In Venezuela it is customary for people to walk into any restaurant to only ask for water and buy nothing. Because of the heat, a thirsty man is seldom refused.

August 31, Queer Fellows:

Being Sunday, it is a very slow day at work. I hardly earn the twenty-two dollars today. I worked with good old Chulito Vargas on the flaps.

At noon Bonilla and Jose sure acted odd. Bonilla kissed me on the neck when I wasn't looking. Everybody laughed as my eyes must have opened wide in surprise. Then Jose, (age 40) caressed my chin, and I expected a playful sock to the jaw. Then he puckered his lips, came very close, and almost kissed me smack on the lips. My eyes must have opened wide again, and I said

181

"What the hell's the matter? Are you guys crazy or something?" They all laughed. It was only a joke to tease me. They are such swell characters at times.

The day was hot, a breeze helped cool it, and I went to a movie, with Manuel. Saw *El Huevo y Yo* (*The Egg and I*). It was a nice movie, but I enjoyed the book a lot more. We had Cokes afterwards, and walked to the pension. A full moon is out, so large and clear, a night for romance, peaceful and quiet and no girls, darn it!

October 1, My Last Move:

I decided to move again. My landlady was always broke and kept borrowing money from me. I could no longer sit down to supper without being annoyed. I moved out of Quinta San Jose to Pension Casino in Macuto. It's a nice town and a better class of people live there. I pay one Bolivar a day more (30¢), but the food isn't any better nor is the bed. The bed is a steel-spring cot with a one-inch straw mattress and a linen sheet for covers. The cost is eight Bolivars ($2.50) and 30¢ extra for a quart of milk daily.

Most of the fellows from TACA live there, and we've asked the pretty landlady to change the name of the hotel to TACA. Benny Zayas sure tries his best to date the landlady. She is pretty, slightly heavy, walks erect and graceful, and has a very modulated way of speaking. I like her also.

I enjoyed living at the Pension Casino. Most of the fellows spoke English. Benny was an ex-GI from Puerto Rico. George Pigeon was also an ex-GI, from Manhattan, New York. Rubio had learned English in a private school in Maracaibo, Venezuela, and Victor Delgado, a Peruvian, spoke very little English. These four fellows and I had the upper floor to ourselves.

Conners and Hernandez spoke English fluently also. They were on the main floor along with Gonzales, Bonilla, and Maroquin, who only spoke Spanish. There were other employees and co-pilots also.

We had a special cook, and we all got supplementary orders when we wanted them.

182

First thing upon arising in the morning, Rubio came into my room and turned the radio on as loud as it would go. There was a program on every morning, one that fitted the occasion. It went like this:

"Levanta-se, levanta-se" (rise up, rise up) and then a heavy knocking on the door.

"Levanta-se, levanta-se" (rise up, rise up) and then a heavy knocking on the door again.

Then "Ola, Amigo Emperal, que tal?" (Hello friend, emperor, how are you?)

This loud program got everybody up, and they cussed Rubio and threw shoes at him and at my radio. He seemed to have a lot of fun getting us up every morning and would he ever laugh, until he had us all laughing.

There would be a mad scramble to get into the shower room first, and my Latin buddies on the second floor never bothered to put any clothes on as they raced over the porch to the shower.

If any ladies looked up from the patio or garden below, it was at their own risk of getting embarrassed.

A lot of joking went on at breakfast and "Margaritas," our driver, who kept the bus or truck just outside the pension would sound his horn at 7:30 to let us know it was time to get going. There would be a mad race again to get the best seats. Benny had a German car, and sometimes we rode in it; Benny, George, Victor, Rubio, and I.

It took a half-hour to drive out to the airport at Maiquetía. Most of the fellows by that time, had their eyes closed and were dozing off a bit. The road was paved several miles to La Guaira; after La Guaira, the six extra miles were rough and dusty. Some of the fellows kept handkerchiefs over their noses and mouths continually.

We would race for the time clock, form a line, and start work at 8:00 or a bit later. Our foreman would check pilot reports and assign us our work.

At twelve o'clock, we punched out and rode back to a Macuto. Some of the fellows went to sleep, others wanted to play games. They had a game that drove me crazy. It was a touching game and you are supposed to guess who touched you. It's very childish and annoying.

Sometimes I'd be tapped lightly on the head, the arm, or the shoulders when I was resting with my eyes closed or preoccupied. I complained once, twice, and the third and fourth time, I slugged two fellows; guilty or not, I did not wish to be touched.

The fellows soon learned to leave me out of the game, and it went on for months. They never tired of it. A couple of Americans played the game also. They had been in Venezuela so long I guess that they got used to it.

Arriving in Macuto, we got out at the Colonial Hotel. We would say "only one Cuba libra, (rum and Coke), then to dinner." We always ended up with three or four or five and sometimes came to dinner late, a bit drunk, and still other times we would miss the rest of the day's work. I somehow believe I was the cause many times, for these fellows tried to extend the good neighbor feeling.

We always have a two-hour lunch period (*siesta*); other airlines have three hours' lunch periods. It's a Latin custom and I'm not in favor of it. I'd rather have twenty minutes or a half- hour for lunch and get my day's work over quick.

During these two-hour periods, I've had many a meal of only rum and Coke and sardines or other classes of canned fish with the boys.

After lunch we returned to work again and worked from two to six and overtime if desired. After eight hours we got time and a quarter, Saturdays paid time and a quarter, and Sundays and holidays paid double. Venezuela has many holidays. Twenty-one, I believe.

Returning home, say at 6:30, we would have supper, listen to the radio to Spanish broadcasts and music. Sometimes we danced together. Benny was glad to hear music from Puerto Rico; Victor was happy to hear Peruvian music and whenever English came on, they sneaked into my room and shut it off.

If we didn't listen to the radio, dance, or kid the cook or the landlady, we were sure to be found on the plaza or in the movie.

Everybody loved the plaza. I did also, as did all the Americans. People went strolling up and down the plaza or sat at tables drinking Cuba libras, Cokes, orangeade, Annice (a sweet whiskey), or Monticado (sherbet ice cream).

Usually there was a moon gliding over the palm trees that lined the plaza. It was also cooler in the evening as sea breaks over the sea wall in high white foam.

I had been at the casino several weeks, and the landlady raised the rent by $.60 a day. All the fellows became angry and decided to move out. I tried to advise them that they would not find a cheaper, happier place, so they might just as well stay. They refused to listen and promptly moved out.

The landlady asked me, "Aren't you going to move also?" I answered, "When I move again, it will be on my way to Argentina." I had moved three times, and I was tired of moving.

New tenants came in, old ladies, and some Negroes. I did not feel at ease eating with them. They just seemed to stare at me and say very little.

For this reason, I decided to move again, to the "Hencoop" house, a lot more expensive, but Americans lived there, and it was as modern and comfortable as a home could be. I no longer would sleep on steel springs and straw mattresses.

Some time later I heard that many of the boys moved back to the "Casino" and wanted me to return, but I had already made my last move.

24

The Hencoop House in Macuto

The "Hencoop House" is an affectionate name given to the house of a Dutch proprietor named "Onkoof." We, tenants who lived in this beautiful house, found it easier to call it "Hencoop" rather than Onkoof's house.

It was situated three blocks away from the sea in the beautiful town of Macuto, thirty-five miles from Caracas. It was built of cream stucco and all the floors were tiled so as to keep it cool in the tropical climate. It was of modern design with wide windows and newest bathroom facilities. There were four rooms and a bath upstairs and three rooms, bath, and dining room downstairs for the tenants. There were two of us per room.

Outside was a large tiled porch with comfortable sun and rocker chairs. Still farther out was the garden, with tall shady trees, some bearing lemons.

It was a nice home and comfortable one with a fun-loving group of boarders.

My room was painted a light green. The beds were comfortable. I loved to sit on the windowsill and read, or write, or just listen to the radio or chat with Dave, my roommate. I often would look out the window. The mountain was on this side, and all over it were poor miserable wooden shacks of mud and bamboo. I couldn't tell the pigsty from the native's home. I occasionally borrowed Buck's field glasses and watched the movement of life about or within the shacks.

I'd see young girls in dirty dresses carrying five-gallon water cans atop their heads and gracefully walk up trails that were fit only for mountain goats.

Sometimes I'd see Negro ladies washing and naked babies running about.

These natives surely looked down upon our fine home, and I

186

often wondered what they thought about us. Right there the rich lived beside the poor, as is found all over Central and South America.

Dave is my roommate, so a word about him first. He is the fellow who brought me to this new home.

Dave is thirty-four, slim, dark, and about 5 foot 8. He has been a foreman in an aircraft plant in California during the war and is our radio man with Taca. He pulls down about $500 a month straight salary.

Dave is a kind of fellow who likes to read a lot. He doesn't drink or smoke. His girlfriend in the States has married another fellow. He felt badly about that. But he has another in Caracas. A Venezuelan who is quite a beauty. But Dave seldom goes to see her, and chances are he will lose her also.

Dave is one of the Americans interested in learning to speak Spanish well, and he already has a good knowledge of it. But I've already heard Spanish fellows call him "Codo" and point to their elbows, meaning he is a tight wad. So at the Hencoop House, I heard Americans say so also and I believe he is too.

We have one common interest and that is to visit all of South America, be it by plane, bus, train, boat, or hitchhike. We look forward to our individual trips as an adventure.

Dave had once ridden a bicycle for two months on a journey through the Southwest U.S. He'd love to hitchhike with me as I plan to do, but he feels he is too old. I am now twenty-five and feel old also, but I give myself allowance because this is foreign territory.

Dave's working hours are a little different, but we do manage to see each other at dinner, supper, and evenings.

Next is Mack, whom I like an awful lot. He is Portuguese. He is twenty-eight, heavy-set, about 170, 5 foot 7, and dark-complexioned with black hair. He is loud and talks a lot, saying what he thinks. He talks too much, but we all like him because he is so much fun and always in good humor. Even his sadness strikes us funny because of the faces he makes.

Mack was born in the States and went to school there. When he was sixteen, his father returned to Portugal, taking Mack and the rest of the family along.

Mack did not want to leave, but he had to go with the family. His youth spent in the States, Portugal was a new world to him and a mighty poor one, as he described it.

He spent three years in the Portuguese Army, waited on German officers and fliers during the war. When asked where he liked it best, Portugal or U.S., he answered, "I like it best where people treat me best, and that is the United States."

For these remarks, he got plenty of K.P.

His Army buddies used to ask: "Don't you feel anything toward your blood brothers?"

Mack replied, "What do I care about blood? My home is where people treat me good."

Regardless of what Mack says, or how senseless it may be, he has a forceful, thoughtful way of talking, so that it grabs everyone's interest. Right or wrong, people listen to his chatter.

Mack had married in Portugal. He picked a girl up from the streets, gave her everything, clothes, good home, and a name. While he worked, she brought in boyfriends, and Mack returned home one day early. His findings ended in a broken home and marriage.

He tried to return to the States, but admission was refused. Mack felt badly about that. He was born and raised to the age of sixteen in the States, and could not enter. His English is perfect; one would never call him European. We Americans at the Hencoop House believed his refusal was due to Portugal's place in the war, on the side of the Germans.

Mack works for a steamship company as an agent. He has a good knowledge of import and export affairs.

Without Mack at the table for dinner, the Hencoop House is very quiet.

Mack saunters into the house and says, "Joe, when Latins meet, how do they greet one another?"

I get up from the table, Mack outstretches his arms and we embrace one another, then hug and pat each other's backs.

This little action bring hilarity at once to all present and many comments are made. Mack and I never tire of this one.

The remarks and jokes pulled off, I'm now at a loss to recall, but there were enough to fill a book.

Next we have Mr. and Mrs. Stone and their son Rothel from California. They are Americans.

Mr. Stone is an engineer on a breakwater construction job. He is a big man, a good solid two hundred pounds. He is a quiet fellow and has a deep Southern drawl. His wife is a very pleasant woman and also has a Southern accent. They originally were from Arkansas. Only Rothel doesn't seem to have that accent.

Rothel is eighteen, a big husky lad, about 6 foot 3 and solid. I'd like to have him on my side in any fight. He has his childish ways and his mom scolds him continuously, for stealing meat bits, fruit, or something or another.

We got along very well. He sometimes works, other times he has off for a month. Mrs. Stone doesn't work. She is only down to keep her husband company.

Mr. and Mrs. Stone have been here about a year and don't care or even try to learn a bit of Spanish. The reason I don't know. Rothel is different; he studies a bit. I wonder why he isn't homesick for his friends, but he seems very happy here.

Mrs. Stone is a serious woman, very broadminded. Her boys are carefree, happy.

There is no need for a woman to fear in Macuto, for it is almost like a tourist town and many Venezuelans come there for their vacations to swim or sit on the plaza under sun umbrellas and while the time away.

But Mrs. Stone has a fear of these people and never goes alone to the movie, to the Plaza, or La Guaira.

In La Guaira, I believe a lady should have a companion. It's a rough seaport four miles away.

Now we have Mr. Wilder from Boston. He is an engineer also and from what I gather, he doesn't do anything and gets the most money.

He is middle-aged, partly bald-headed, about 5 foot 6 and a bit heavy set. He is the fellow who seems to know politics well and has heated discussions with Mr. Stone in that respect. He dresses up to dine with the American Vice-Consul. Mr. Wilder believes, "If you want anything done, never go to an American Consul; go to a British consul."

189

He strongly believes the British are the best diplomats in the world.

Mack doesn't think much of the American consul. Mack thinks he's a jerk.

Mr. Wilder has been here only a short time and already he has an interest in picking up Spanish words.

One day he came into my room, and I asked, "What time is it?"

"Say tea tea," he answered.

"What?" I inquired again.

"Say tea, tea," he answered.

Then I understood that he meant "Siete," "Seven" in Spanish. His mispronunciation was bad.

He complained vociferously, "These goddamn bastards don't try to understand." He meant the Latins.

He went into a tiny restaurant that sold an imitation milkshake. It was powdered chocolate mixed with milk. He asked for it, called "Todie Frio." But he said, "Toe-day Frio." The clerk said "What?"

"Toe-day Frio, goddammit," said Mr. Wilder.

This clerk was helpless and did not understand. Mr. Wilder walked out enraged.

Mr. Wilder had the right word but not the correct pronunciation and he blamed the Latins. Not always was it their fault.

Mr. Wilder was a likeable fellow and he kidded me a lot as I was detained one month to another in advancing on my South American journey.

"You'll never leave here, you have a good job," etc. etc.

Then we had Rudolph, a Dutch fellow who was an agent sent over by the Dutch Steamship Lines.

He was a tall, quiet, blond fellow who spoke English well only when calm; least bit excited and he stuttered.

He had been a prisoner of war under the Germans for several years. He was sent here and every two or three years he got a sixty-day vacation paid home.

Mack used to kid him a lot, and we feared some day Rudolph would really hit him. That never happened.

As a matter of fact, they rode to work together every morning. But first Rudolph had to push the English Ford several blocks to get it started. By that time Rudolph was very winded.

Every morning he got his exercise and Mack would holler, "Push, Rudolph, push!"

Oh, what a car that was. Everywhere we went, we had to push it with Mack laughing like hell, hollering, "Push, fellows, push!"

Mack tried to get it fixed. It came back worse. He'd say, "Those bastards, they charged me thirty Bolivars ($10.00) and still the car don't start. Honest to God, Joe, they are so stupid. They fix the brakes, they are worse than ever."

He said he was no mechanic himself and I promised to work on it when I got time. I did one day on my day off, just to borrow it when I needed it. I drove about without a license.

A driver's license cost one-hundred Bolivars ($30.00) good for life. I didn't intend to stay that long.

On the subject of cars, one odd custom is: whenever a driver is caught speeding, they do not fine the driver, but they lock his car up for ten days or so at a police pound. This happened to my friend, Benny. He had to ride a bus to Caracas every day for ten days. That was misery to him. He'd rather pay a fine.

Besides Rudolph, the Dutch boy, we had another American fellow named Buck. He was always cussing somebody out, usually the cook, the waitress, or Mack. But it was only his friendly way.

Buck was an engineer, with a wife in the States. He was short, about forty, lean and lively.

One day he had a serious accident at work. He tried jumping from one barge to another and fell into the water between them. He was promptly crushed by force of water on the barges.

He had something like eighteen bones crushed, ribs, pelvis, and legs. Doctors feared he would die, but one day, months later, he hobbled back into the Hencoop House with crutches, full of fight and spirit, and a smile on his face.

Then last of all there was the Venezuelan woman who spoke no English at all but dined with us at the same table.

She said several times that she felt like a "Burro" (ass) because she dined with us and did not understand the language.

191

I well knew how she felt, for I had my christening to dine with Latins alone also.

Mack, Dave, and I usually explained remarks to her in Spanish. In other words, we were her interpreters.

Her husband was a Venezuelan Navy officer and only seemed to sleep at this house. He never ate there, but he always gave us a courteous "Hello" as he came in or went out.

The lady had several children to take care of. They would come about the dinner table. They were nice white children. She would scold them, and away they went back to their rooms.

Mrs. Stone did not like her because she made so much racket with the children all day long while she tried to rest or read.

But housing facilities were short and the Venezuelans would have to stay till a place was found.

Mrs. Stone usually ate with her husband at one table while the rest of us, Mr. Wilder, Dave, I, Mack, the Venezuelan lady, Rothel and Buck ate at the larger table.

During my stay at the Hencoop House, we had three different waitresses and always the same cook.

None of them spoke English and a tendency that all had, including the cook, was to serve dinner later and later each day, so that when I came home for lunch, and waited one-half hour, I came close to coming late to work.

Dinner generally served at 1:00 would be at 1:45 and supper generally served at 7:00 would be at 8:00 or later.

This was my job now and everyone gives me credit for it, thanks to my limited knowledge of Spanish.

I return from work to find the entire household sitting on porch or standing, hungry and waiting for their supper.

I know my duty, advance to the kitchen, and spread my hands.

"*Caramba,*" I say. "*Que le Pasa, comida no esta listo. Es despues la siete.*"

"Cripes, what's the matter? Dinner not ready, it's after seven."

The cook and waitress fall into action at once, and food starts going to the set tables. Even the landlady, occasionally takes heed, and it amazes me more than anyone else the quick service we get.

It pays to know some Spanish; the others are quite helpless to speak. Mack, who could, is often afraid because he complains a lot about other matters and fears he may be told to get out.

The first waitress we had, her name was Maria. She was a short stocky girl, five by five, about eighteen years of age. She was a quiet one, I guess, because she could not speak English. But she could speak Spanish. Even so we later decided it's best she speak not-at-all.

One had to be on the alert with her around. If you were momentarily speaking or listening, she would take away your unfinished dinner, coffee, orange, or water glass.

We always would have to call "Hey, come back here." We fellows did anyways, but Mrs. Stone was always being polite and would not call.

If we advised, she would say "Oh, leave her go." Soon Mrs. Stone learned to be wary, on guard.

Marie had a habit of always hitting or slapping someone, including me and Mrs. Stone.

One day Dave was walking down the Plaza (our cement Atlantic City boardwalk). There was a crowd of people walking about, sitting on the sea wall or at umbrella tables.

Dave knew a number of these folks, and he liked to carry himself dignantly. Imagine his embarrassment when this 5 by 5 colored waitress slapped him on the back in front of his many acquaintances—so he told me.

Now one day as I entered the house, going upstairs to wash my black greasy hands after working over a kerosene burner, the maid slapped me on the shoulder. I was in no mood to be touched or slapped. I scolded her and I got slapped again.

I put my greasy hand across her face, she wailed and hit me again. She got another greasy hand across the other side, and her face was a black mess. Then she started crying and ran into the kitchen.

I continued upstairs to wash. I heard the loud voices and laughter of the landlady and the cook. They not only laughed at her condition, but gave her hell.

193

A few days later, I had finished taking a shower, and was coming out of the bathroom. Marie was mopping in the hallway. Rothel Stone was coming up the stairs and going into his room; he had to pass Marie and he got slapped on the arm.

His southern temper arose at being slapped by a colored girl (not black but a dark brown), and he slapped her face.

She slapped him back, and Rothel slapped her harder. She hit him again and Rothel, who is a giant in comparison, slapped her a wicked third time that sent her sprawling over bucket, mop and all. Her dress tore open and her naked breasts came out.

Rothel retreated to his room and closed the door. Marie got up again. Mop in hand and crying, she tried to break into Rothel's room.

Rothel tried to keep her out. By this time the landlady, Mrs. Stone, and Buck came up. Marie stopped her pushing as the landlady grabbed her.

She was ordered to clean up the spilt bucket of water. Then Buck said to Rothel, "Ain't you shamed of yourself, striking a defenseless woman?"

The remark came as a laugh. Rothel said something about, "No Negro is going to hit me and get away with it."

Marie was fired that day, and Rothel was ribbed a lot. It surprised us that the police weren't called. But we all agreed that her habit of slapping was annoying and had to be stopped.

I believe Mr. Stone was the only person who was not a victim of her slappings.

Mrs. Stone said she saw Marie several weeks later, and Marie stuck her nose into the air and said not a word.

Our next waitress was a girl named Josephine. She was about seventeen, rather pretty. The first week or so, she greeted everyone with "Hello" and kept herself neat.

After two weeks, her dress was soiled, apron spattered, hair unkempt, and she stopped saying hello. We believed the landlady had advised her that conversation wasn't necessary, for Mack had ridiculed her and this was the result.

She stayed some time. Then one day the landlady fired both the cook and the waitress because they kept late hours.

The cook promised to be better and stayed. Josephine left.

The last I know is "Rosita." She would be a pretty girl if she had her front teeth. She avoided conversation and when she smiled, she forced her upper lip down to cover the space. It gave her face an ugly appearance.

Many lovely Spanish girls and handsome fellows are disfigured because of bad or missing teeth.

I guess last and not the least, is the landlady and the landlord.

The landlady is a very heavy set, good-looking Venezuelan woman of white skin who would be a honey if she wasn't so fat. She has auburn hair, round, robust cheeks, gets excited very quickly, and has a loud voice when excited.

She is about thirty, I believe, and married to a tall, lanky Dutchman, whose hair is turning gray and looks about thirty-eight. His manner is just the opposite from his wife's. Quiet and unexcited. He has to do the apologizing and reasoning for his wife. His name Harry Onkoof—owner of "Hencoop House." I don't believe he knows we call it that.

Besides being owner, he is a naval engineer for the Venezuelan Navy and has a car, 1937 Plymouth, that isn't worth a dime, worse than Mack's.

The food served is not so good at times, and I have to leave the table and satisfy myself at a restaurant. At a minimum cost of five Bolivars ($1.50).

Breakfast usually consists of:

Grapefruit, orange, or tomato juice
1 or 2 fried eggs
bread and butter or cereal
1 cream and coffee

Because I can't eat eggs often, I have fried Spam every morning.

Dinner usually consists of:

Some kind of soup—rice or vegetable
Slices of beef—almost always
Spanish rice

Lettuce and tomato
Boiled potatoes
Dessert—puddings or bananas, black coffee

Supper usually consists of:

Soup
Beef or hash
Fried bananas, guavas, rice, tomato, pudding or orange
black coffee

The price there is twelve Bolivars a day, paid twice monthly. About $3.60 per day.

Some of the folks think the prices are too high and talk about moving.

I advise them not to. I had experienced the worst and I'm sure they would find nothing cheaper and yet as comfortable as here. The Colonial Hotel, second best in Macuto, charges twenty-five Bolivars per day, rooms are tiny, and food is so-so.

The remarks made about the food at the Hencoop; worse were never heard in the King's or Uncle Sam's Army. But most were jokes and none of us ever got sick on it, even though we were served "mystery" food.

The Venezuelan lady amused us one day. She had told Mack what we Americans do that a Venezuelan would never do.

She was the only woman upstairs. She had seen me sleeping only in my shorts. The door had been wide open to keep the room cool. What amused her was that I had a large yellow patch sewed on them.

A Venezuelan would never lie in bed that way with the door open.

Then she spoke about Mr. Wilder. "He comes out of the bathroom, holding a towel in front of his naked body. He says 'Good morning' (*Buenos dias*) as he passes to go to his room. But from behind, he is uncovered.

"A Venezuelan would never do that," but it's funny as we think of Mr. Wilder.

Then one day she dashes into the bathroom, finds me sitting

on the commode. I look up, unexcited; she backs out, closes the door. She could have knocked. What surprised her was that I looked up so unconcerned.

A Venezuelan would never do that. He'd probably jump off the seat and hide.

One day I went upstairs to find Rudolph and Mack playing dice. I had a *real* (15¢). I joined and broke the games in about an hour's time—won eighty Bolivars ($25).

It was very warm; we were only in our shorts. We got hot Spanish music on the radio.

It was the "*Boaté*." It's a lively dance and a happy one, simply one-step all the way through with a swaying of the hips, shoulders, and entire body. We liked it, but it's not accepted in best social circles. It looks crude and indecent.

Mack and I have fun dancing together. Rudolph only laughs. He doesn't dance much.

Later Mack and I box, barehanded. He is much heavier than I. He hurts my side and I his face.

Rudolph laughs and says, "There's someone for you, Mack," as I give him a bad time.

Rudolph likes to seek revenge on Mack because Mack kids him a lot. But Mack and I could never be enemies; we have too much fun together. We both end the tussle, sweating and tired and flop on the cool tile floor laughing.

25

U.S. Seamen's Fight in La Guaira

La Guaira, first seaport of Venezuela, is a busy, dusty, hot port that is continually unloading cargo and sending it up to Caracas and into the interior. Venezuela is one country that is building itself up. In return for materials, she gives oil. Venezuela now claimed to be about the richest producer of oil in the world.

In the early morning or noon, it is always crowded with copper-colored longshoremen, mostly in straw hats, sleeveless shirts, and torn pants, and many are barefooted. There are hundreds of them, and they crowd the one-way street.

A foreigner is easily spotted in that crowd, and many have to work their way through it to get to place of business.

The majority of foreigners are seamen, either English, American, Swede, Dutch, sometimes Canadian, or Greek, and sometimes Chinese.

Coming out of the one and only dock gates, one confronts this native mob of longshoremen, who loiter about waiting for starting time or having breakfast or refreshment due to heat and dust.

Off to the left is a large parking place for taxis, and as you go by, they call out "Caracas, Caracas, Caracas," meaning they are waiting for passengers to go on the thirty-five mile ride to Caracas at $1.50 per seat (five seats per car).

Beyond the lot is a small park and on either side of it are bars, where the sailors get their first beers while ashore.

Beyond this park, bearing to the right, one follows a street that takes one up a steep set of steps, built into the hillside.

Along there are the tiny cabarets that are said to be among the roughest in the world.

There is where the seamen come after getting "gassed" up a bit and looking for excitement.

There is where I sneak, with some of the "Elite" of Macuto when the peace and quiet of Macuto become a bore. Here is music, noise, women, liquor, drunks, fights, and whatever may be called wild and exciting.

This is the "Mu Chinga" of La Guaira. It is not to be spoken of in polite society. But occasionally at the table, in Hencoop House, we referred to its as "Knob Hill," so as not to be vulgar in the presence of Mrs. Stone.

One night Mack, Rothel (Mrs. Stone's son), Rudolph, Mr. Wilder, and I started out for "Knob Hill."

We kidded Mr. Wilder, "Don't you think your a little too old to go there?"

"Hell, no," he answered. "Aren't you afraid of being dishonored if good people in Macuto hear about us going there?" we asked.

"Hell, I've been around myself, when I was a lad," he answered.

We came into La Guaira in Mack's car. There was a huge public meeting for presidential elections. The crowd blocked traffic, so we parked the car.

We mingled in with the brown people, then stopped to listen for a while.

This was to be the first democratic election in the history of Venezuela.

There were several parties: Blanco (white), Rojo (red), Verde (green), Negro (black). White was Accion Democracia, Democratic. Red was Communists—Communist. Green was socialist. Socialist. Black was—I can only guess, not sure. There were two leading favorites, Galligoes and Copea.

Galligoes was democratic and Copea either communist or socialist, I don't recall which. Galligoes was a well-known writer and politician, aged sixty-nine. Several weeks later, in Grand Elections in Caracas, Galligoes won. Many people were afraid to vote because of fear of terror or riots. The town was heavily guarded with police and soldiers to keep order.

Coming back to that evening, as a lady (colored) was making a loud tear-jerking, pleading speech, the crowd listened intently.

199

When she stopped momentarily, Mr. Wilder started clapping his hands and shouting "Hurrah, Hurrah!"

Many brown men and women, turned and looked at him. We expected trouble, also from the police. But they took one look at big Rothel (6 foot 3 and 189 pounds); they kept quiet.

Mr. Wilder didn't understand a word of Spanish, but he felt like cheering anyway. Imagine a guy his age, fifty-six, intelligence and position. He didn't cheer after that anymore.

We had to push our way through the huge mob of people. This would be an awful spot if a riot should break out.

We got through, then proceeded towards Knob Hill. It wasn't very crowded that night. But still there were interesting sights.

We met seamen whom we knew from the *Florida Sword*. Mack and I had dinner aboard it several times. Now we saw one of the seamen, a tall skinny fellow of about 6 foot 4, dancing with cute little Yolanda, 4 foot 10. They jitterbugged and were very funny.

Yolanda quit several times, but the sailor pulled her back. She was blushing red from embarrassment, but everyone, Latins and Americans, enjoyed the show.

Yolanda joined us for a drink and to talk. I kidded her and Mr. Wilder. I called him my pop.

We had spent an enjoyable evening in the rough spots of La Guaira and were returning home.

We heard the sound of crashing glass. A couple of drunken seamen broke store windows. The cops came and a fight resulted.

More sailors came; they were big husky fellows. They tried to stop the fight. Then Venezuelan soldiers came running and started slugging the sailors with rifle butts.

More sailors came; they tried to stop the fight, only to get mixed up in it.

It ended with three dozen police and soldiers leading the eight or ten seamen to jail. Among them were the husky, burly captain and first mate.

Next day all of them were released. All had been bruised,

and the captain had a couple ribs broken and the first mate had a broken arm.

We could easily have gotten into the fight also, but Rothel and I already had a taste of Venezuelan jails.

We also remembered that we were in a foreign country and had respect for it.

Most American seamen don't respect other countries' way of life, customs, and laws.

26

Why Bearnie Disliked America

Bearnie was a Polish immigrant who had served with the R.A.F. He now worked with me as a mechanic with Taca, in Maiquetía, Venezuela.

Bearnie was thirty-four years old. He did not appear that old. I don't know why I liked him or why we got along as well as we did. We never seemed to agree on any subject or matter.

Bearnie was of Polish and French "extraction," as he put it.

He had a good speaking knowledge of English, Spanish, French, Czech and German, as most of the immigrants likewise have. They have it all over us Americans in that respect.

Bearnie had been a paratrooper, and he always was seen jumping off ladders, planes' wings, or moving busses. He still thought he was in the army.

Bearnie was a husky fellow about 5 foot 7 at the most and not bad looking.

He told me one day that he had spent some time in the States, New York to be exact. He said he had cousins there and had stayed with them. All the time spent there, he did not get to like New York, or the girls.

I did not find out why he disliked the girls or the country till some weeks later.

I was introduced to another Polish fellow named Nick one evening on the Plaza (sea board). I told him I worked with Taca and he asked if I knew Bearnie. I said I did.

Now Nick told me of how he and Bearnie had served together in England. After the war, they found conditions unfavorable in England and decided to stow away into the United States.

They succeeded in stowing away but were caught upon trying to enter into the U.S. at New York.

They immediately were placed at Ellis Island and held for many weeks.

So it happened that all Bearnie got to see of New York or the girls is when a kindly immigration official took them ashore for a glass of beer on good conduct behavior.

They then were given a choice of returning to Europe or South America where there was a demand for immigrants.

Bearnie and Nick decided to try their fortunes in Venezuela.

The U.S. government paid their plane fare and gave each $25 to make their start.

Now as I confronted Bearnie, I said, "Where did you stay in New York?" with a wise tone to my voice.

He looked at me funny like, then said at his cousins.

"Cousins, hell," I answered, "Ellis Island. No?"

He looked surprised, then turning red a little, he sheepishly admitted the truth, that he had stowed away, got caught and put in Ellis Island, and that accounted for his dislike of the U.S.

Coming down on the plane, he had met a Venezuelan woman, a woman about his age, and a divorcée. They became pretty well acquainted and presently got married in Venezuela.

Bearnie and I had become pretty good friends. One day he said to me, "How would you like to go to Caracas with me on a double date?" He assured me his girl had a beautiful daughter of eighteen, and I'd be able to go out with her.

Now in Venezuela it is very difficult to find a nice girl of a good family, especially if you are unacquainted with the higher set.

I said I'd be glad to go, so when Saturday came along we dressed in our best and took a taxi, thirty-five miles to Caracas. Then another taxi to the ladies' home.

I truly expected to be introduced to a young girl, instead it was an old lady of about thirty-eight.

I felt like apologizing and excusing myself and return back to Maiquetía.

Instead I forced myself to stay. Both women spoke good English and especially my date. I decided it would be nice just to speak English again. I'd been in Venezuela several months and hearing and speaking only Spanish. After a while, English sounds like music to the ears, especially if well spoken. My date had spent many years in Brooklyn and had the Brooklyn brogue down pat.

My date was not slim, nor was she fat; she was just solid.

First we had dinner at a ritzy Venezuelan restaurant, including wine. Dinner was fine and prices very high.

Then we took a cab out of town aways to a good night club. It was no cheap joint but well designed and decorated in best of design and decoration.

There we spent the evening over cocktails called *Cuba libras* (rum and Coke, lemon) and dancing.

Cuba libra was the cheapest drink and each cost seven Bolivars, about $2.10. We had four or six rounds as the evening wore away.

Bearnie had a tendency to waltz, no matter what the tune. My date and I received applause after jitterbugging.

There were about a dozen other couples, and most of them were Americans.

It was a pretty late hour when we left, hailed a cab going into town, and then through neighborhoods, my date and I sang "I Got Two Pence" and "Roll Me Over."

Bearnie's date asked us over and over to be quiet, for she feared of what the neighbors would say.

Bearnie and I had other good times. One Sunday I was working at the airport, at twelve o'clock, noontime, quitting time, Bearnie drove up.

He said, "Come on, Joe, I got your girl for you. Don't go home to eat, have dinner with us at the terminal restaurant."

I thought he was kidding. I went over to the car and was introduced to his fiancées daughter, Aura.

His girl and fiancée was in the front seat, and Aura was in the back. I got in behind also.

She was such a lovely girl that I was almost speechless and also later when our dinners came, I could hardly eat because of my excitement.

She wore a flimsy white blouse, that showed a good bit of shoulders and breast, a tiny red ribbon at the sleeves and at the middle of her blouse.

She had a light skirt, dark brown hair that curled at the shoulders, and a light healthy tan.

What surprised me more was that she could speak English quite fluently.

Right after dinner we drove out to a small hacienda nearby where Bearnie stayed in partnership with a Polish engineer.

The wife of the engineer had a birthday party, so there were cocktails being passed around and music.

The engineer's wife was a beauty and spoke English quite well also.

They played English, Spanish, and Polish records, and later Aura and I went to the back yard to a couple of swings suspended from a large tree.

It was a little too warm for dancing now, although we danced a number and Aura is a good jitterbug.

Now in the shade of the tree, we swung back and forth. I was glad that she enjoyed my company.

We have a two-hour break from work for lunch called a siesta. How quickly they passed today.

Bearnie decided to work in the afternoon, for he needed money. I did also and Sunday's paid double. We would return to the party after work at 6:10.

There were plenty of other Polish immigrants at the party to entertain Aura and the other ladies.

Some of these immigrant youths were very handsome.

Bearnie and I worked four hours and some of my co-workers had seen me with Aura and said, "Boy, are you lucky, how do you rate?"

It was too far to return home for dress clothes, so Bearnie loaned me a shirt and trousers and I looked sharp again.

The girl in whose honor the party was, was pretty drunk, had a hard time eating hot dogs and sardines.

Bearnie introduced me to some elderly immigrants. They spoke no English except Polish, German, Spanish, so that with my knowledge of Czech and Spanish, they understood me well enough. Europeans always marvel that I'm born American and still speak Czech, as I learned from my father.

The music was going on and on. Aura and a blond fellow

danced, her mom and another fellow and still two other couples. They danced in and out of the one story adobe house onto the tile porch and back in again.

Aura soon came over to me and asked to dance. We danced quite a few English, Polish, Spanish, and we danced well. She kept her face to mine, and it was pleasantly soft. Then came a reproachful call, "Aura," from her mother, and she moved her cheek away.

After a record, she would change it and I went for another highball or talk to other guests, just so she had an opportunity to dance with others. I feared others may be jealous of me dancing with her.

But when she continuously came back and said, "Come on, Joe, let's dance," I could not refuse her and the elderly immigrant lady said, "Go ahead, Joey, your sweetheart calls you."

Aura and I danced and had a wonderful evening, one I will always cherish and remember.

About 11:00 all the guests had gone or were leaving. They all said courteous good-byes, goodnights, and "Pleased to have met you."

Aura and I sat on separate straw chairs, close together. She was tired from dancing all afternoon and evening. Now she laid her head on my shoulder and closed her eyes. Her mom sat across from us on another chair. Everyone else had retired. Bearnie had returned to work at 8:00 and should be coming home about midnight.

I noticed that Bearnie's fiancée was also sleepy and suggested she retire. She said, "Do you want me to go to sleep?" I answered, "Yes." She said, "No."

Then I asked if I could turn the light out; there was a full moon out.

She said, "No."

Then I said, "I feel sorry for the girls in South America; they become old maids before they get away from their mothers. I really do feel sorry for them."

She asked again, "Do you want me to go to sleep?"

"Yes," I answered.

"No," she replied.

Aura had fallen asleep on my shoulder. Soon Bearnie came and we laid her on a bed in one of the rooms. I slept on a cot, just outside her window.

Next morning Bearnie told me her mom didn't sleep at all, she worried about me. I hardly slept also.

27

Christmas in Venezuela

Civilian airlines do not stop flying because of holiday seasons. But I for one never have believed in working on the Savior's birthday; besides I needed a rest after so much work.

I went to Caracas with Mike, the Argentine fellow, and Victor Delgado of Peru. From Le Guaira we went by taxi.

Once in Caracas, Mike, who was a member of some aristocratic social clubs, was able to take us to dinner there. We were led into a large dining room. It was crowded with holiday guests. Many already were in best of spirits.

There were young fellows and old fellows and many pretty senoritas, from the best of families, no doubt. Everyone was at their best.

We had a cocktail before dinner, at dinner, and after dinner. The dinner was turkey and splendid. We spent several hours there and became pretty high.

Victor is a Latin of Arequipa, Peru. Many times later in Peru, his friends said he is a descendant of the Incas. Victor is my age, twenty-five, carefree and happy-go-lucky.

Mike is of German descent, much older, thoughtful, but today in best of spirits.

Today is the 24th of December. It's late afternoon now and we decide we had better get back to Macuto before the road becomes jammed with traffic, but first we stopped at a liquor store and each of us purchased a large bottle of whiskey.

We succeeded in getting a taxi to Macuto after some waiting. The ride lasted an hour and a half. We were singing and drinking all the way, mostly in espanole. The driver refused a drink and it's just as well.

At Macuto we separated to go to our individual homes or pensions for supper.

Because it's Christmas Eve, supper is much better tonight and there is plenty of whiskey in sight. Mr. Stone, Mr. Wilder, Buck, our landlord, everyone had brought some.

Everyone was excited and there was plenty to talk about. Mostly about Christmas back home in Texas, California, Boston, Nebraska, and Pennsylvania, also Holland, and Portugal.

We had a Christmas tree. Mack got that. How he got it is a story in itself. He stole it when he checked a load coming in by plane from the States. There were no pine trees in Venezuela. Seemed like there was one extra for Mack and he "took" it.

We all helped to decorate it. Mr. & Mrs. Stone and Mr. Wilder who no longer were youngsters got as much excitement out of it as we younger fellows, Mack, Rudolph, and me. Buck, Dave, and even the cook and waitress were loudly chattering.

Mrs. Stone got the colored bulbs; she had difficulty, for bulbs are hard to find in Venezuela. They do not decorate trees like Americans do.

Mr. Wilder got icicles and streamers, and Dave borrowed a set of lights from an American who had an extra set.

I made a large tin star, spraying it with yellow prime paint. This was placed atop of the tree. I also made the base for it. It took several hours on company time. The boss knew about my outing, shook his head and grinned.

He knew he may be coming over to see it and enjoy the treats.

We set the 6 foot tree on a table on the porch, placed a sheet at its base and soon it was covered with favorite brands of American whiskey. P.M., Seagram's, Calverts.

Now we were happy, for though we were far from home, we still carried out our tradition of having a Christmas tree at Christmastime. It would never be like Christmas without one.

The landlady had placed oranges and a few apples about it.

A few days previously, there were remarks that the Venezuelan landlady might object to having a tree littering the porch. We decided, if the tree goes out, we move out also.

Apprehensions were wrong, and she seemed to enjoy sitting with us around the tree and drinking highballs.

I took a nap in the evening, for all the excitement tires one out in the tropics. Several sweet hours later I awoke and decided to go to midnight mass.

On the well-illuminated Plaza I found most of my buddies from work drinking *Cuba libras* (rum and Coke). I knew they were strong Catholic followers, but tonight, of all nights, they preferred to sit and drink on the plaza.

I go to the church alone. It's not a very big church, but tonight there must be several thousand in it. The outside is painted a blue-and-white and within, the walls, ceilings, and altar glisten in white and gold.

The crowd fills the aisles all the way back to the entrance. I can only stand there with the crowd. Among them I see more of my friends from work and I'm pleased to see them there. Among them are our cook and landlady.

The organ plays and the choir of small boys and girls sings "Silent Night, Holy Night" in Spanish.

The words are different, as the world knows, but the tune is international.

Now, what shocks and amazes me is to hear the sound of "maracas" in tune to the song.

I, at once expected the entire congregation to start doing the boogie-woogie. You would say, "No, not really, maracas in church, on Christmas Eve?

But yes, that's the way it is. Another Venezuelan custom, and they do not look down upon it either.

The crowd remains as solemn as ever, and there are no demonstrations of boogie-woogie or other.

I awoke Christmas Day about noon, had dinner late, then joined the crowd on the porch. We had visitors. My boss and Welch. They admired our tree.

We spent the day thus, gathered about the tree and talking about Christmas gone by, and work.

The rest of the day was quiet. I visited Latin friends, at their pension. But nowhere was there a tree in sight to symbolize a happy holiday. There were bottles of liquor, but I hadn't seen anyone high as yet. Maybe later some would get high and find a girl to sleep with. One Latin remarked, "That's how we celebrate Christmas. Wine, women, and sleep. No Xmas presents."

210

George Pigeon, a Latin from Manhattan, came up later to see me. He said, "Wished I lived here, you guys have a lot of fun." But the Hencoop House was already filled up.

28

New Year's in Venezuela

Mack was invited to a New Year's party in Caracas and asked to bring along three male guests.

So Mack chose Rudolph, the Dutch lad; Tony, our Portuguese friend; and me, Joey, American, to go to the party.

We were advised days in advance. I was feeling ill from too much Xmas celebrating to go, but I was very much interested to attend a Latin New Year's Eve party.

Came the 31st day of December 1947, about mid-afternoon. The four of us, dressed in our best Sunday suits, climbed into Mack's little English Ford and started chugging away for distant Caracas in yonder high mountains, thirty-five odd miles away.

Along the sea, it is eternally hot in Venezuela. Be it January or July. We removed our coats and laid them across our laps.

With the little breeze coming in through the open windows, the three of us were able to relax comfortably. Mack, the fourth, driving, was all perspired. Handling the steering wheel of that little English Ford was like handling a ten-ton diesel dump truck.

The main road to Caracas was detoured, and we followed a stream of slow-moving cars over a treacherous side road. The drive must have seemed endless to Mack.

The main road entered Caracas through a slum section of town.

Already there was horns blowing, bugles, rattlers, yelling, and drunks weaving their unsteady way through slow-moving cars to cabarets on opposite sides of the street.

It was now dark, about 8:30, and chilly, as we rolled past *"El Silencio,"* the heart of Caracas.

These pedestrians were more sober and in smart clothes. Many had tuxedos while the women were in gowns and furs.

The Elite went to the Majestic Hotel, Avilla Hotel, or one of several expensive clubs.

But we were going to a house party, the way of the majority. We did stop in at the Majestic for a few highballs, only to have a few more by the good neighbor policy.

Floating about the lounge were lovely ladies, one a golden blonde in white silk satin, others in green and black.

No, we must not linger any longer there, but go on to the promised.

We found ourselves in a maze of heavy traffic after this. One time the car stalled and we had to push again.

We had traffic blocked for about ten minutes. We had pushed up a one-way street, going opposite to the arrows. The horns, shouts, what a demonstration. We lost our way, we were in the neighborhood, we knew that, but the one-way streets foiled us. Mack put in a phone call to the party, and we soon got out of the jam.

We brought along extra liquor, and chasers, but they weren't necessary. Venezuelans are considered tight people, but when they give a party, they give the works and there's no limit. I've gone to several and they give the best—flowers, liquor, food, sweets, everything.

It was bout ten o'clock when we arrived. All of us were introduced accordingly. There were a lot of young fellows and girls and mothers.

Music was furnished by radio and records; one large room had been cleared of all furniture and a polished floor stood bare, inviting dancing.

We lunched on sandwiches, then the elders encouraged us to dance because we were slow in getting started.

Mack got to the cream of the corp, a lovely blonde. He danced with her, and I with a comely brunette.

He remarked, "This is my babe; lay off, Joe!"

"Okay," I said, "I always give a pal a break. But what can I do if she comes to me and says 'Let's jitterbug.' " I'm the only one present who can. I danced with her most all evening. Got her phone number, etc.

I believe we all had a nice evening dancing, lunching and

drinking. The dance floor was always full. Only Tony and Rothel didn't dance much.

It was nearing twelve o'clock and all of us were hep for a big hugging and kissing game for 1948, the biggest ever.

At five minutes to twelve, at the height of our expectations, the girls, all of them, young and old, took leave of us males, and went to various rooms and closed the doors behind themselves.

We foreigners, Dutch, Portuguese, American, looked at one another, and raised our shoulders. We got it quick.

It's a Venezuelan custom for the ladies on New Year's Eve to retire to their rooms at 12 midnight sharp and weep. For sentimental reasons.

We foreigners said, "Holy hell," dropped our shoulders, retired to the large open windows, and looked out into the starry night.

In houses lining the street below there were other parties. A cannon boomed from the hilltop, church bells rang and whistles blew. It was twelve o'clock midnight, January 1, 1948, and we were a sad, melancholy foursome. There was no yelling "Happy New Year" or "Feliz Año Nuevo." No hugging, petting, kissing, or singing.

Out came the red-eyed, sniffing damsels, saying quietly, "Happy New Year" and shaking hands with all as if we were meeting for the first time.

The party by no means breaks up at twelve and folks retire. Instead they go visiting one another's home and extend greetings.

We could have joined our hosts on this traditional round, but all of us seemed a little bored.

We thanked our host and departed.

We then drove out to a club on the edge of town. Just to enter cost ten Bolivars ($3.00).

It was a very nice place. There were quite a few quiet guests sitting at tables in the gardens with orange-colored table lamps throwing light shadows on them.

Inside the club and on the patios were many more guests. All of them in fine dresses.

The four of us were directed to a table. We sat down, ordered drinks, and watched the dancing. The orchestra played Spanish

214

numbers and American boogie-woogie. Most of the guests fumbled on the American pieces and presently left the floor. The center of the hall had been cleared of tables and chairs, and the lassies and laddies danced there. Forming a circle and surrounding them were the onlookers, who cheered and clapped in time with the music.

We felt kind of low, chiefly because we had no one to dance with. We decided to leave again and drove off to a large restaurant. It happened to be owned and operated by an Italian immigrant, and so a large crowd of Italians had come here tonight. Most of them were immigrants. Most of them were young fellows, a bit rowdy or high, and no doubt ex-servicemen. There were young Italian girls also, and they brought a lively dance with them.

The lassies and laddies danced and twirled so agilely and quickly they made semi-circles, stopped and resumed. With hands in the air, partners faced each other, never touching but motions in perfect time. A lassie dropped a handkerchief and a laddie gracefully picked it up with his mouth from the floor, his hands behind him and feet still dancing. This part of the dance brought much applause. The music was furnished by Italian records in the juke box. It was one of the nicest performances I'd ever seen, a beautiful Italian folk dance brought to the New World.

We left the restaurant and started homeward. Mack drove quite rapidly through the deserted streets, then we came to the scene of a bad accident, a jeep and a car. The jeep had run over the curb after demolishing the 1940 model car.

Nothing prevented us from returning home, back to Macuto. Along the way all of us agreed that we did not enjoy the Venezuelan New Year's Eve customs. We arrived in Macuto about 4:30. We went right to bed, very tired.

Next day at work, I discussed the evening proceedings with Velasco, a Venezuelan. I told him the women cried. He said, "*No es nada, yo illoro tambien*" (It's nothing, I cried myself). "*Es costumbre,*" he added (It's a custom).

So thus it is in Venezuela on New Year's Eve. Even the men cry. Instead of gaiety and cheer, they cry for sentimental reasons.

215

29

The Fight with Mr. Herman

I was all set to start on my hitchhiking trip of South America. I had been paid off from my job, I had paid my income tax (3% in Venezuela) and had a visa in my passport good for five days to leave the country. I had my gear packed also and was ready to leave in the morning, bright and early.

I had only one thing more to do and that was to collect my money from Herman. I had loaned him two-hundred Bolivars ($60). He had over a month's time to pay me back, but he kept putting it off.

Herman was a big husky fellow, about thirty-nine, weighing about 180 or better and over six feet. He was one of the bosses at Taca. Herman was quite a bully. Several times at work, he grabbed my arm and said, "And I can whip your hide too." I didn't doubt it. He towered way over me. But why did he have to say that? I never offended him. I could only look up at him and say "Sure."

Herman did a lot of drinking and gambling and owed a number of people money.

So tonight, I waited for him on the plaza. He soon came out of the hotel with his Costa Rican wife. They sat outside the hotel at a table. I walked over. I had been sitting on the sea wall, waiting for him to come out.

His face turned red at the sight of me. He knew I planned to leave in the morning, February 9. He invited me to sit down and have a drink.

I sat down, refused the drink, and said I only wanted my money. I'd need every penny I had for my trip.

He said he didn't have it and would send it to me. I said, "No, I want it tonight."

"Don't you trust me?" he asked.

216

"No," I answered.

Then, he became very angry. He said he would get the money, but before he would give it to me, I would have to drink with him, apologize, and then he would clean my clock (beat me up).

We walked all over the plaza, and I felt ridiculous as one person after another refused him the money. His credit was very bad. Finally he stopped a Venezuelan fellow in a yellow convertible he knew and got the money.

Then he said, "Come on, let's get that drink." I refused to go. He said, "If you want your money, you'll have to drink."

I went to the bar with him. He ordered doubles of whiskey. I refused it again.

He said, "If you want your money, drink that."

My God, I thought, *what do I have to do to get my money back? I loan him money as a friend, to help him out, and this is the thanks I get.*

I drank the double clean, then he ordered another double and still another.

"If you want your money, drink that," he kept insisting. I was disgusted, but I figured "okay" and drank it down the way I used to in Alaska, clean and quick.

Then he said, "Come on now, up this back alley." I didn't want to go, but he kept insisting and grabbing my arm.

So we went up the dark alley and I told him I was sorry. "You don't understand my ways and I don't understand yours."

Still he refused to give me the money, and I then became very angry.

"You're asking for it," I said, and I hit him with my left, into the face as hard as I could. It surprised me to see him stagger backwards five or six feet, then fall on his rump. That blow must have surprised him also, for he got up at once, charging at me, swearing, "You son of a bitch."

I backed around in a semicircle and saw his face in the dim light; then I saw my opening and I sent my right fist into his face again, the force of his body still going forward, and he fell on his face to the ground. He was out.

I felt like putting my foot on his back and letting out a cry of triumph like Tarzan does in the funny papers.

I could have taken my money from him and left him there. Instead, I raised and sat him on a curb. I took my money from his pocket. It was about ten minutes before he came to his senses.

A woman had seen the fight and ran for the cops.

Herman's nose and mouth were bleeding bad, and his face and knuckles were bruised when he hit the concrete alley.

First thing he said was, "What you hit me for? I wouldn't have hit you."

"Oh, yeah, who you kidding?" I said.

"Look at my teeth; they're all busted." They were false ones, and he held them in his blood-spattered palm. That would cost him plenty to get new ones in Venezuela.

A policeman came and said to me, "Is that your friend?" I answered, "He was a friend, now I believe we are enemies."

Herman, at sight of the policeman, said, "No, Joe, you can't do this to me. Please, Joe, I don't want to go to jail."

There wasn't anything I could do. I never called him and anyway the police would settle our misunderstanding.

I went in the lead towards the police station, Herman following behind, pleading, "Please Joe, please." Then in a rage he charged at me again. I wasn't looking and I received a heavy blow on my shoulder from behind. Herman fell to the sidewalk as he was still groggy, drunk or clumsy.

In the police station, the desk sergeant took our names and causes of trouble in Spanish.

Herman kept pleading and wailing, "Please, Joe. You can't do this to me, think of my wife, think of my reputation, think of the bills I have to pay."

Then he said slowly, "Joe, are you a Communist or are you American?"

I was disgusted with his pleading and said, "I'm probably more American than you are."

He probably thought I referred to his marriage to a Costa Rican, for he gave me a hard chip under the chin with the back of his hand.

I felt like hitting him, but restrained myself, pushed him into a chair, and said, "Now sit there, dammit."

The desk sergeant had also jumped up and said, "For that, you will pay double," meaning Herman for striking me in the presence of police in a police station.

A police car was called. It came in the form of an old U.S. Army reconnaissance car.

We were driven to La Guaira, several miles away. Herman kept pleading to me "You can't do this to me, Joe, you can't do it." I pushed him away from me, and said, "There's nothing I can do, I didn't call the police."

One of the cops facing us put a night stick between us to keep us apart.

Herman was taken to a hospital, and I was taken to jail. It was near midnight, and as the cell gates were opened for me, I found the room full of prisoners asleep except for the guard. He asked me the reason for being put in. I told him.

I felt very tired. There were long cement tables and benches alongside. The walls, most of them, were occupied with sleeping prisoners. But there was still room for several more. I lay down on one of these and soon fell asleep.

I awoke before long. I had become very chilly. There were no covers to keep warm with. There was no roof over the prison either except for alcoves, under which the tables were and prisoners slept. Even in the tropics, in the summertime, nights get cold.

I looked over towards the guard at the gate. I was surprised to see Herman there. He was sitting on the steps, his arms fallen on his knees and his head bowed down on his arms, evidently asleep. I didn't want to disturb him and likewise I didn't want him near me.

Somehow I fell asleep again, but not for long. Awaking, I heard these words: "You're pretty proud of yourself, aren't you?"

It was Herman, talking through a swollen tongue, and words came out thick and sticky like.

He repeated the words, and I told him to leave me alone. I couldn't go to sleep again, for I feared he might try to bash my head in as I slept.

I felt chilly again and walked back and forth, within the large cell to keep warm.

I sat down near the guard, on the steps. Herman came over and said, "Someone said I'll have to pay double."

I said, "Yes, because you slapped me in the presence of the desk sergeant."

Herman said, "I never touched you."

I said, "Oh, yeah, who you kidding? From now on, you don't have to talk to me any more."

He cursed and said, "To hell with you then" and left me alone.

He retired to a corner and with his bruised face, turned rosy, his white bandages on the chin, he really looked like Santa Claus. He also looked very old and tired, but I could not feel sympathy towards this man anymore.

He had forced me to fight him, and the old saying goes "Loan a friend money, lose a friend thus."

Dawn broke and it was still chilly. Some of the prisoners, only in shorts, took showers under buckets of water and a water hose. Then they started washing down the benches, the tables, the steps and floor, with bucket after bucket of water.

Breakfast was served about nine. We had black coffee in tin cans and biscuits. Had dinner about one; nobody wanted to eat the soup, they claimed it smelled. The cook, the guard, and police chief smelled it, deciding it was not fit to eat. We then got coffee, bread, and some canned beef and rice.

Herman and I had expected to be released about nine. He missed a day's work, and I was supposed to be on the road to Colombia.

After dinner we were still there. They never keep seamen so long.

Herman was very impatient. He came to me and asked, "How long will they keep us here?"

"I don't know and you don't have to talk to me," I said.

He swore again and walked away.

Among the prisoners was a Venezuelan fellow who had worked in the store room for Taca. I always liked him. He spoke English very well also.

He had gotten into a fight with a Venezuelan sailor, then was ganged up on by five of the sailor's buddies. He really was beat up. His face was a black-and-blue mess. He was given six weeks in jail. He didn't have the money to get out.

After noon it became warm, and I decided I could sleep comfortably while I waited to be released.

At 5:00 o'clock, the guard called Herman and me. He said the fine would be fifty Bolivars each.

I said I was willing to pay and be released. Herman didn't have any money and looked pleadingly at me to pay his fine. I said, "Why should I? You got me into this mess."

What caused me to change my mind was the looks and remarks I got from those brown prisoners.

They said, "He's your countryman, pay his way out."

I then said to Herman, "I'll pay your way out, but do I get this money back?"

"Yes, of course," he answered, "come up to the hotel at 8:30 and I'll give it to you."

We were taken to the chief's office. He returned my traveler's checks and money. There was $800 in checks, and I was surprised we weren't charged more. I paid the fines and we then left. Outside we caught a bus going back to Macuto. I had to pay both fares.

At the "Hencoop" house, everyone worried about what had happened to me and why I didn't come home last night. They had a feeling I was in jail, and they kidded me about it.

I told them what happened, and they said I was a fool to pay to get Herman out of jail.

After dinner I went down on the plaza. I met George and Victor. They were all excited and wanted me to tell what had happened. Everybody at work was curious as to why Herman didn't come to work that day.

I told them what happened, and they seemed more excited about the affair than I.

Said George, "I feel sorry for Herman, but he needed a beating."

They were so excited, Victor said, "Tell us about it in Spanish." George said, "No, tell it in English first."

221

I told them I still had to collect again and asked first George, then Victor, if they cared to come along with me.

"No, no," they said, and I had to laugh at their refusal.

I went alone to the hotel at 8:30. I found Herman lying in bed under cover, his wife at his feet. He had company also. Jimmy, my former boss, his wife, and Art from the service store department.

Herman had told them he got drunk and only remembered getting hit by a car and falling on the street.

Herman told his wife to give me fifty Bolivars, then I shook hands with him. He said, "We'll met again some day."

"I doubt it," I answered and left.

In the plaza again, I met George, Victor, and Conners, Art and Jimmy and wife soon came on the plaza also.

Art, Jimmy, and wife knew Herman wasn't fooling them. They suspected what had happened. Art was jubilant, for he had long waited to see someone beat the devil out of Herman.

He had worked with Herman several years in Costa Rica and now here Art was the object of Herman's abuses many times, but he was too small to fight back.

He remarked, "Boy, it'll cost him plenty to get his teeth fixed. He won't come to work for at least a week. His face is a mess."

I guess I was quite a hero that night. I got free *"Cuba libre"* (rum and Coke), and we spent the evening lounging in chairs at the sidewalk café, facing the sea.

George, who was an ex-GI, had served in Africa, said, "I can't figure Joe out. He leans all the way back to stay out of a fight, then he starts on a wild crazy hitchhiking tour of South America. You'd expect a guy like that to be mean and crooked, but he isn't. He's either got nerve or he's nuts."

This was my last night there. I hated to leave this happy place. George said, "This is it," meaning "so long, Joe, may never see you again." We shook hands as we parted on a dark corner, and I went home and left Macuto in the morning.

30
The Simón Bolívar Highway

The Simón Bolívar Highway is named after the great liberator. It stretches from Caracas, Venezuela, to Bogotá, Colombia, a distance of 1,758 kilometers (1,099 miles). Only 400 kilometers approximately is paved in black macadam ((250 miles). The rest of the road is dirt, but pretty well graded. It is also one of the most interesting and dangerous roads I'd traveled. It goes from one extreme to another. From hot streaming jungles to rocky plains and high freezing altitudes.

I do not believe the Simón Bolívar Highway has been considered as part of the great Pan-American road as yet.

Hitchhiking over this road, it took me exactly eight days to reach Bogotá from Caracas, Venezuela. The following is an account of events along the way:

First Day—February 10, 1947

Awoke about 8:30, had breakfast, and packed my gear. Mrs. Stone, Rothel, Buck and Mr. Wilder took a picture of me. First time in my life I've had four cameras turned on me. They wished me luck and asked me to write. I then waved "So long." I walked several blocks to a bus stop, waiting for the "Avation" bus. I made it to Pariata, then got on the road to Caracas.

It was hot and I started sweating at once as I walked up the cement highway. Several cars passed me by. I had walked about a mile, then a car stopped. An Englishman named Roy gave me the lift. I remarked, "You will probably be the first and last English person to give me a lift on my journey. As fate will have it, he was. All the rest of my lifts were by Latins. We drove on into Caracas. He had some business to do; it would take an hour. Then we would proceed to Valencia.

It's Carnival time in Venezuela, and I take pictures of Indians in war dress marching down the streets, beating drums, and spearing one another. Convertibles drive by with lovely senoritas in white gowns and ribbons, sitting proudly on the doors and rumble seats. The carnival lasts for several days and then, one day for three hours, they permit rough stuff.

One must never wear one's best clothes on this day because, as you pass under windows or doorways, you get showered with ashes, paint, tomatoes, and everything messy. You cannot do anything about it because the law permits this rough sport for only three hours.

There is rough stuff in the street also as fellows push one another around roughly; some fall to the pavement and get bruised badly. Venezuelans try not to offend foreigners, but accidents happen.

Roy is ready to leave, and we continue on to Los Tegues and Valencia. We saw three accidents along the winding road. Sun-glare made driving hazardous. One truck nose-dived into an irrigation ditch. It looked funny because it was a funny truck. Then there were two collisions, not very serious. As we drove through villages full of only mud houses, the natives threw buckets of water at the moving car. The water hits as hard as a brick and scares us. Windows were open and we got soaked. It was their way of celebrating the carnival time.

Passing slowly through a town, we saw a man chasing another with a club, over a woman. Villagers overpowered him before he could kill the fellow. Most of them wore costumes, were drunk, and covered with mud, paint, and flour.

The road from Caracas to Valencia was cement and spotted with macadam, but a good road, a total of 161 kilometers (100 miles). Many South American countries believe Venezuela is very rich and has all her highways paved. It is not so. We arrived in Valencia about 7:00 o'clock and Roy directed me to the "Hotel Caracas," about the best in Valencia. Spanish design, good food, good lodging—cost twelve Bolivars ($3.60).

A big dance was on in the Plaza Bolívar. It was beautifully

decorated with streamers and colored lights. It was a very large plaza and crowded. A band played and in one corner, a Polish immigrant put on a show. He danced quite well with a Venezuelan senorita and the crowd applauded.

Second Day—February 11

Awoke early, had breakfast, started walking out of town. It was a beautiful day. Walked about two miles, then came to an intersection and asked directions to Taborda (near Port Cabello).

"En la pies?" (on foot) they asked in amazement. I said, "Yes," for there is no word in the Spanish dictionary for hitchhiker. The people had no word for it either, so how could I explain that I was hitchhiking? I could explain, but it was a long story. Hitchhiking is something new there, especially long distances.

A half-hour later, a young fellow gave me a lift in a '42 Ford Convertible. He was still covered with ashes and paint from the carnival. He drove very fast and a bit recklessly. The road was still paved and winding. An hour later, I got out at Taborda. It was a dirty, dusty little town. There were ancient busses taking on grimy passengers, chickens, baskets, children, and even small pigs. I'd prefer hitchhiking to that kind of a bus ride.

I left the paved road at Taborda and started walking up a dusty dirt road. It was inches deep in dust and gravel. I found my boots ideal on this road. For an hour I walked in the hot sun, following the wide road through the jungles; then a '48 truck came along and stopped. I rode in back with several peons; the cab was full. The road went up and down, left and right, and very rough. We had all we could do to hang on. Twice the truck skidded, spun on the dirt road, and scared us a bit. This driver also was a bit reckless. I was glad when we came to a stop at San Felipe. Out of San Felipe, I walked again for about forty-five minutes, and another '48 Ford truck came to a stop for me. The chubby driver drove me into Chivacoa, a simple crude little town, hot, dusty, cobblestone streets, broken sidewalks, one-story adobe buildings, plaster falling. Out of doorways people watched as I walked along the cobblestone street out of town. As I said *"Adios or "Buenos Tarde,"* they responded.

I stopped for a Coke and simple donut at a *tienda* (store), then continued walking. Another truck stopped and drove me to Yaritagua, and as I crossed the state line, the police questioned me, checked my *pasaporte* (passport), made a note of it. *"En la pies?"* (on foot) they asked."Si, en la pies," I answered.

"Are you crazy but go ahead," they said. They probably never heard of hitchhiking either, and I didn't wish to waste time explaining. Let them think what they will.

The police dropped the chain to let me pass. I walked in the heavy dust and gravel; soon the police station disappeared out of sight; only a few silent mud huts lined the road and silent dark mountains stood out in the distance. It was hot and I became thirsty. This stillness, stirred my imagination of dark Africa, of men pushing onward without water. It was late afternoon with no traffic going either way.

I started down a steep grade and up another, and suddenly a bus came along. It sped down the grade, then had to change gears to go up the hill. By the time it reached me, it was barely crawling. The ticket collector jumped off the bus, walked along with me, slapped my back, and said, *"Usted es Andarin"* (You are a walker). "Yes," I answered. "Hop on," he said and I did. I found a seat in back. The passengers looked at me curiously.

Boy, what a ride; dust swooped in from open windows and doors, chickens cackled, babies cried, with men and women shouting. The ticket collector was a Cuban; he was covered from head to foot with the dust. He stood in the doorway. He made this two-day trip, three times a week, from Caracas to Maracaibo. He did not like his job. With every passenger he had to argue to collect the fare. The passengers usually tried to pay less.

The bus driver drove swiftly and several times the bus skidded slightly, but enough to worry us all.

This lift had been about 60 kilometers and the Cuban refused my fare. He said, *"Andarin extranjeros* (don't pay anything)." *"Muchas gracias,"* I said.

In Barquisimeto, I found the Hotel Astoria to be the best. Cost sixteen Bolivars ($5.00). I met an American girl there. She was from Cleveland, Ohio. Her name was Vera. She had come down several years ago with a couple of other girls. The others had since returned back to the States, and Vera remained with the doctor to continue working at a chemical laboratory. She was the only American at the hotel, and I felt sorry for her. Life was pretty dull in this town, and Vera said I was the first American she had seen in a long time.

There were also two Greek businessmen there, and later the four of us went for a ride in their 1946 Ford sedan. It was merely to show me around the town. The streets were narrow, some well paved; houses were low and came to the corners of the street. Most of the streets were dimly lit. There were several nightclubs, but never a floor show. The main interest was the movie. It was a paramount theater and a nice one.

Everybody dresses in their best clothes to go to the movies. The movie lets out at 10:30; a half-hour later the streets are deserted and quiet. The four of us had taken in the main interest, had a few nightcaps at the hotel, and retired.

Like most American women abroad, Vera had asked me, "Is the money worth it?" meaning—wasting her youth in a place like this.

Third Day—February 12

Had breakfast with Vera and the Greeks. They wished me luck.

Walked about forty-five minutes until a truck stopped for me. Three fellows were in the cab. The driver tied my pack to the gasoline tank, and I then squeezed into the cab also.

Jose, the driver, was a very happy fellow; always he had to laugh. He had many close calls on the narrow, dusty, dirt road. He would only laugh again. The road was so bumpy at times that I thought my insides would break. It hurt plenty.

We rode all morning, stopping at quaint pueblos only for black coffee, cakes and food. At noon we stopped at his home in Pampam, Grandes. There we washed up a bit, and he changed into better clothes. I met his wife; she offered me a chair, then some food. He lived in one of the better class of adobe houses. Pampam Grande is only a small town situated on a rain-washed hillside. Streets and sidewalks were in bad condition. The houses were of stone, adobe and mud.

Jose had just returned from La Guaira and Caracas, bringing this new truck with him. He seemed to know everyone, and here and there he extended greetings, sent by friends in Caracas to friends there in Pampam, Grandes. Jose was waving continually or saying, "Hola, Jose; Hola, Pedro; Hola, Juan" as we drove past his acquaintances.

An hour later we were in Trujillo the capitol of the state of Trujillo. Jose seemed to know a lot of people there likewise. He stopped at house, I waited a half hour, then he came with a beautiful Indian girl. She was smartly dressed in a rose-colored dress. I would say she was of a higher class of families, but when I saw her put on a man's hat, traditional custom of the lower class to shield her eyes from the sun glare, I knew at once she was not of the higher set of people. She rode along with us, arriving in Valera about 6:00 P.M.

When I got off the truck, a bunch of kids tried to carry my pack to a hotel. There was much yelling and grabbing of my arms. They can be a pain in the neck. A couple of cops chased them away. I was directed to a hotel that was terrible, I asked for the principal one. There were three; I checked in at Hotel Martini—average as in U.S.—cost B. 16 ($5.00).

At this hotel, I met Jorge Grancia, an Ecuadorian businessman. He spoke fair English. He showed me the town and points of interest. In the plaza, there was no statue of Bolívar, only the cement base stood where he should have been. Jorge remarked, "Old Simón must be out wolfing at the Botequins" (*cabarets*).

Jorge and I also went to the cabarets, talked to some of his girlfriends, had a few highballs and spent a pleasant, enjoyable evening with them.

Fourth Day—February 13

Had breakfast with Jorge, started walking at 7:45. An hour

later a beer truck stopped for me. The cab was full, so I rode atop the load of beer, a good place to be as any, and alone. It was an unobstructed view of the scenery. In the sun, I was comfortable; in the shade of a mountain, it was very cold. Now we were passing many streams and climbing steadily.

An Indian woman got out of the cab at Quibar, and I took her seat. We had black coffee here, then entered the state of Merida.

We passed many wheat fields, and the ancient custom of tossing the wheat into the air to separate the shells from the seeds was still used by the farmers. There were endless miles of stone walls, in picturesque patterns. I'd never seen so many stones in my life on a farm. They were set up in many designs to prevent erosion of the rich black soil.

Indian garb had changed to warmer blankets or ponchos, thrown over the shoulders. They were mostly a dark brown, blue or black.

The road was narrow, winding, and dangerous to the mountaintop—5,005 kilometers above sea level. The sight was wonderful; for miles and miles, one could see the winding road. It reminded me of pictures I'd seen of the Burma Road. There were trucks moving and raising a cloud of dust in the distance.

The curves are most dangerous and sharp. A truck has to back up, go forward, back up again before it can make the sharp turns. Driving requires good brakes and a steady nerve on this road. The thought of going over the cliff is sickening on the curves; it's many a thousand-foot drop.

Atop the mountain is a statue of an eagle to Bolívar and a placard saying "Glorioso Libertador, Simón Bolívar. We got out of the truck to take some pictures of it. The wind, cold air, and altitude were biting. We could stand it but a few moments and ran shivering back into the cab. Simón Bolívar had marched his army over these mountains; there was no highway in those days and many of his troops perished. He made his journey in the wintertime when the mountains were snowbound to fight the Spaniards.

From the statue, it was now downgrade and driving more hazardous. I only hoped Enrique, the driver, had good brakes. He was a short, thin fellow, about forty, dark-complexioned as

229

most Venezuelans. He was a careful driver. I did not envy his job. He risked his life a hundred times, every time he went on this road. Halfway down the mountain, we stopped at a tiny village for dinner. We entered a large house, made of round stone. We sat at a crude wooden table. It was still very cold, yet Indians ran about the house barefooted on the cold stone floor.

We were served mostly soup, small potatoes, and stewed beef. This had been prepared over a stove made of stone and in blackened pottery pots. Enrique refused to let me pay.

The ride continued all afternoon, past fields of stone. I fell asleep and awoke to find Enrique laughing at me. It had become warm in the cab and I dozed off.

Arrived in Merida at 5:30; best Hotel is Cordillera—cost ten Bolivars ($3.00). It's a nice, modern hotel, facing the beautiful Plaza Bolívar. This town is much colder, cleaner, better designed than Barquisimeto, Trujillo, or Valencia. Streets are deserted at ten o'clock.

Fifth Day—February 14

Most wonderful bed I'd slept in since I left home. After breakfast, I hit the road about 8:00. I passed a long line of Indians, donkeys, oxen bringing their crops and wares to the market. Little barefoot Indian boys, who should be in school, struggled under heavy loads. Some pretty-faced Indian girls carried 100-pound sacks of coal atop their heads and old barefooted men struggled, leading bulls.

A lady stopped and took me five miles farther. Then I walked for three hours. A truck stopped but wasn't going my way. The driver offered me two Bolivars. I said, "No thanks." He insisted I take it. Another truck stopped and the driver offered me a job, to fix two of his trucks and work on his farm. He thought I was an immigrant.

I told him I was neither a farmer nor an immigrant. He complained as most Venezuelans do, that the immigrants are brought there to farm, instead they go into the cities and go into factories, stores, or business.

We parted at San Juan. Now it's hot in this region again. I walk, sweat, and my eyes start burning from the perspiration. Then a Venezuelan army truck comes along, painted tan with army insignia on the door. It's really a farm truck. His cab was full of army rifles and a girl besides. I climbed aboard and held on to the braces. He drove rapidly and passed cars like nobody's business. He slowed down a bit going through herds of cattle, horses, oxen, or donkeys. He sideswiped a few and missed killing them by inches. Around mountain curves, his horn was a continuous blast. He missed projecting rocks by inches; to loosen them would easily cause a landslide, for the soil seemed loosely packed, as if it was only sand and stones and had been under water once.

About mid-afternoon we arrived at Tovar, the halfway mark between Merida and San Cristobal. Strange, but the most beautiful building in each town is the church; then next is the Plaza Bolívar. I walked upgrade, out of town. Started sweating almost immediately. People stared out of doorways and windows. Work stopped at a sawmill and on a farm to watch me go by.

An hour later, well out in the country, I sat under a tree to rest, wiped my forehead and got out of the hot sun. Trees were sparse and far apart. I was beginning to doubt if I would reach San Cristobal by night. Ten minutes later a huge G.M.C. truck came along; the cab was full and I climbed behind, made myself as comfortable as I could amidst gasoline drums. My T-shirt and field jacket were wet. We headed for the mountain again and it became chilly. The driver gave me a blanket to keep warm. It was very considerate of him to do so. The higher we went, the colder it became, and soon we were in the clouds.

Only the dusty road ahead could be barely seen. We stopped at a lonely Indian hut for coffee to warm up. It was terribly cold. Outside the hut, three barefoot little Indian boys wrestled and played together. They wore few clothes and derby hats pulled down over their ears. They sniffled but seemed unmindful of the cold.

I wrapped up in the blanket, then under the canvas tarpaulin. It was still biting cold. It was 9:30 when the driver awoke me and said, "We are in San Cristobal." He had been very nice, and I offered him money. He refused it, saying, "Foreign walkers don't have to pay."

The wild stories I heard about wild Indians about the country seemed like a lot of nonsense. I walked up several unpaved dark streets. Low-class people watched me pass. I didn't feel too much at ease. I'd be more comfortable if I had a buddy along. No one bothered me. Then along several paved and brightened streets till I came to the Plaza Bolívar, center of town.

The two best hotels had no vacancies, or they didn't like my dress and coming in dusty and with an army pack. I checked in at Hotel America, a simple hotel, no food, only towels, shower, and a bed. Cost five Bolivars ($1.50). It was only ten o'clock, but I had to knock for them to open up. In all Latin America, doors close early.

Sixth Day—February 15

Up at 7:00. As I stepped out of the hotel, a cab stopped for me. The driver said fifty Bolivars to Cucuta, Colombia. "Never," I said, "that's too much." He then said ten Bolivars ($3.00). "Okay," I said, being anxious to reach Colombia and cross over in style, so that the Immigration authorities had no knowledge that I was hitchhiking.

It was $3.00 only for a seat; he would have to get other passengers also. At 7:30 no restaurant was open. I got coffee at a pension. We waited till 9:00 o'clock before we got the passengers. San Cristobal was a very interesting town, and has a lovely Plaza Bolívar, with palm trees; the walks were inlaid mosaic or colored tile. The churches were large and lovely, and there were many interesting stores inviting tourists. The climate in San Cristobal is cool in the morning, hot in the day.

The road now was paved again to the frontier and ten miles farther to Cucuta, Colombia. A few spots were dirt and under repair. The ride lasted about two hours.

At the border, Colombian officials said I would need another visa because I was twelve days late. The Venezuelan officials charged me another five Bolivars ($1.50) when they saw I had a *cedula* (work permit). The government charges five Bolivars each year for the permit, they said. I felt I was being robbed. When I paid my income tax in Caracas, they would not omit this item, when they gave me my clearance papers.

Colombian officials let me go to Cucuta, but they picked up my passport. I could come back Monday, pick it up, go to San Antonio de Táchira, Venezuela, and get another visa from the Colombian consulate there and return.

In Cucuta, I checked in at the Palace Hotel, the best in town. It indeed was very modern and on the same style as hotels in Miami, including a swimming pool. Cost eight pesos per day—room and board ($3.00). Food here was more abundant than in Venezuela and many more courses.

Cucuta is in the department (state) of Santander. Founded in 1734 and rebuilt after the earthquake of 1875. It has considerable commercial importance. Population, about 70,000, altitude 703 feet, average temperature 80 degrees, plenty warm. Near Cucuta are the Catatumbo oil fields, the largest in Colombia and Venezuela.

Columbia seems to have a lot more music than Venezuela. Walking along the Plaza Bolívar, I heard a band playing and found it coming out of a large public restaurant. I entered and found it crowded with people seated in straw and bamboo chairs, drinking beer and fruit drinks; beautiful young senoritas in blue and white uniforms drifted among the tables, taking orders. The girls in Colombia were friendlier than in Venezuela. I would say, "*Hola que tal?*" and always receive a smile. So different from the girls in Venezuela.

It being Sunday, I went to the bull fights.

The bull fights start at 4:00 in the afternoon. I arrived at the arena a little too early. A bunch of kids gathered about me, looking for a handout. They believed I was an American with money to spare.

A little fellow came by and the kids cheered; they said he was "Cantinflas," a funny man. Cantinflas came over to me, pulled up his arm sleeve, and showed me a huge scar on his forearm; that had been done by a bull's horn, he told me. He talked about himself a lot. I believed it to be a lot of malarkey. Little did I realize what a wonderful show he could put on and the daring nerve within that small body of his.

The show started at 4:00 and ended at sundown. I had a ringside seat. There had been a large crowd and a number of police to keep order. There were many, many thrills, laughs, and close calls. Usually four bulls are killed per show.

In the first fight, a big black bull came charging out. Two small prongs placed in the back of its neck had made it very angry.

To make the bull madder, it is the custom to place six more prongs in the bull's neck. The matador (fighter) must face the angry bull three times and each time place two prongs in its neck. This is a dangerous thing to do.

One of the matadors walked out to the center of the arena, facing the angry bull. In each hand he had a prong on a stick, about two feet long. With arms outstretched in customary fashion, he ran toward the bull's head. It is important that he reach over the head and horns and place the prongs at the back of the neck. A large bull, standing erect, is taller than a man and to place the prongs in the neck is quite a feat.

The matador ran, but at the last second, he could not make himself reach over the head and horns, and an upward thrust of the bull's head would send him sprawling, with possibilities of a horn stuck in him. The matador became noticeably scared; the crowd booed. He ran again and again and each time he became scared; he could not do it; at the last moment, he turned away. The crowd booed him each time.

Another matador took the prongs away from him and undertook the dangerous feat. He ran three times, placing all six prongs in the proper place. At the third run, the bull was wise and threw its head upward. It caught the matador and sent him flying through the air, but luckily, not a horn touched him and he was unhurt. The crowd cheered wildly and the "coward" matador walked over and embraced him in praise.

After this feat is over, the matadors tire the bull out. They use their red capes. The bull charges it over and over again. The matador must not dance or move, but must stand still as the bull charges. He keeps the cape outstretched first on his right hand

234

side. As the bull passes by, turns and comes back, the cape is out-stretched on the left-hand side. The matador tries to keep his feet hidden. It takes more than one matador to tire a bull out. The matador gets tired first and another takes over. There is plenty of excitement while this goes on. The twirling of the mata-dor, his calm standing and sometimes a bull gets smart and knocks the matador down. Immediately other matadors come to his rescue and distract the bull with their capes. When the bull is very tired and standing, the matador goes forward with his sword and cape and faces the bull. He keeps the cape low and over to his right side. He is only a few feet away from the bull's head. He levels his sword and looks down its edge, aiming at the vital point in the back of the bull's head. Most bulls know a sword means death and fight on. They run for the matador, charge, then toss their head upwards. It spoils the matador's thrust and he has to try again and again. This makes matadors angry and they swear profoundly.

If the first thrust is good and sends the bull to the ground, they receive a mighty cheer from the crowds.

Three bulls were killed and one little white one that was too scared to fight was spared. It would not go into the center of the arena but tried jumping over the railing to get away.

One bull was killed instantly by a sword thrust; this brought a mighty cheer and the matador took a bow.

Another bull knocked the sword out of the matador's hand. It took four thrusts to bring it to the ground. The matador was very angry. The bull still lived and a half-dozen matadors tried to still the bull's thrashing with a short knife. The crowd laughed and booed because it took so many thrusts and matadors to si-lence the bull.

Then two comedians, dressed as clowns, put on their show. One of them was "Cantinflas." The other dresses as a Mexican "Caballero." He came out first, riding a bucking, angry bull. He held on by a mere rope till the bull came to a standstill. It was a laughing merry show. Then these two comedians acted like mat-adors and got the bull angry again.

"Cantinflas" (the real Cantinflas is a Mexican living in Mex-ico) danced a rhumba atop the bull's back.

Then they played dice, directly in front of the bull's face, not two feet away on hands and knees. They rolled the dice, picked them up and rolled them again and again. "Cantinflas" patted the bull's head. The crowd was tense; a blonde Spanish girl gripped my arm. I didn't know her. The bull, still angry, pawed the ground and sent dirt flying. It was a relief when they got up, then the bull chased them; they ducked behind wooden guards lining the arena for protection.

Cantinflas kicked the bull in the face; the bull ran to the center of the arena, "Cantinflas" after it, doing the rhumba and shadow boxing. He was funny and the crowd cheered.

Cantinflas jumped on its back, riding backwards; the other clown caught the tail and the bull raced along for about thirty yards; the clown was skidding along; at the end of that ride, his feet must have been burning hot.

Cantinflas jumped off and somersaulted a few times, the bull went into circles, still dragging the clown around and around like a dog, trying to get rid of a can tied to its tail.

Cantinflas got a big black umbrella; the other comedian kneeled on hands and knees. Then Cantinflas sat on his back, sitting backwards. He dusted the comedian's rump; everybody laughed. He twirled the open umbrella off to his right side. The comedian started moving backwards on all fours, his rump facing the bull.

The angry bull pawed the ground, then charged at this strange contraption. The crowd was tense. At the last second Cantinflas stuck the umbrella in the bull's face. It immediately diverted its direction. The bull charged again and again, finally ripping the umbrella away from Cantinflas and pawing it to ruins. Cantinflas came at him like a boxer, dancing but never hitting.

Cantinflas turned his rump on the bull purposely; everybody was tense, the girl beside me gripping into my arms. The bull hit him squarely and tossed him into the air. Cantinflas fell back on his head and got tossed again, and he fell a third time and got tossed again. This happened near the high railing, and Cantinflas could only fall backward onto the bull's head. It was only a miracle that he didn't get hurt or fall on the horns.

236

Another time he got hit and the horn actually struck him in the rump. He went sprawling but he managed to cover up by somersaulting at almost the same time he got hit. His baggy trousers were badly torn and showed his "cheeks." He changed to another pair that looked like pajamas with red-and-white stripes.

Cantinflas and the comedian really tired the bull out. It was the end of a marvelous show. The tired bull was left in the arena. The little kids of ten years and up jumped over the rails into the arena and with newspapers, shirts, or whatever they could find, they faced the bull, stamped their feet, said "Uh hun toro, Venga" (come). The tired bull made a few vicious lunges; the kids were lucky and sidestepped; a few twirled like a professional would. Many looks of amazement passed over the faces of the onlookers.

Finally the bull was roped and towed into a corner. The arena was full of kids, future matadors. I felt some of them would get hurt and I wondered if these kids had no parents to care or worry about them.

After the bull fight, I returned to the hotel for dinner. It was wonderful and put American and Venezuelan food to shame. I met two Colombian businessmen. One was named Hoffman, the other Rodrigues. Rodrigues was a lawyer, the other an automobile dealer from Bogotá.

After dinner they wanted to show me a good time, Latin courtesy, and we did have a wonderful evening. Rodrigues called a cab, and we went to a very beautiful night club. It had a large tile floor on which to dance; there were many beautiful paintings on the walls; guests sat in upholstered chairs. It was really a cabaret. There were girls to drink with, talk, dance, and sleep with, only it was a nice place, the better class of people came there and there were no rough or vulgar people.

The Colombian music and dance is a bit different from the Venezuelans. Three of the girls kept us pretty busy. I've got the Venezuelan "Bouté" mastered very well. The girls seemed to like it very much and actually believed me to be a Venezuelan because of that. Most of the girls were chubby. Mr. Rodrigues, the lawyer, was in his fifties and still he danced a lot also. We spent the entire evening there, we all split the bill. Another cab took us back to the hotel.

Next day was spent going to San Antonio de Tachira, Venezuela, for a visa for Colombia, returned in a bus, native-style, like a cattle car, eight people per seat. One gets in a side door and slides eight seats over to the other side of the bus.

Colombian immigration officials had me running around town, to various offices for various stamps, signatures, etc. What a workout. This is what wears a tourist out.

Spent evening talking with Americans from the oil fields at the hotel. Mrs. Cullahan was a schoolteacher at the camp. Her husband worked in the Personnel Office. They were from Houston, Texas, had seen Texas City after the explosion and the Texas City Hotel where I had stayed for three weeks was leveled to the ground. Only four survived as it collapsed. The explosion occurred six weeks after I left.

Seventh Day—February 17

Hated to leave the clean and friendly city of Cucuta. Walked out of town about 8:00 o'clock. Got a fine road map of Colombia. It was made by the Esso Oil Company. At the edge of town, it looked rough; poor homes, etc. A fellow standing beside a bus asked,, "Where you headed for?" "Bogotá," I answered. He said he could take me as far as Duitama. I said I had little money. *"No importa,"* (not important) he said.

Rode in the bus all day. It was really a beating I took. I wondered if these people ever get used to such rough rides in such cheap, makeshift buses. They never seem to complain, but take it as a matter of course. Road as usual was dirt and dusty. We had a bit of rain in the early morning. Was checked three times by the police along the way for my passport (*Documentos*).

Many sheep and herders were seen. We passed many rich green farms. The climate became a lot cooler. Men wore strange capes to the waist with "V" necks, made of heavy cloth. They were called "Ponchos." Women wore long black dresses and shawls and men's hats. Many wore sandals and many went barefoot.

We always seemed to be climbing into the mountains. The road was ever reminiscent of the great "Burma Road." We picked up a few passengers along the way, but never were there more than six or seven passengers. We didn't get to eat all day. We got a flat about 6:30, I helped to fix it. My flashlight came in handy in the dark. The bus did not carry any flashlights or flares. About 10:00 we stopped for a soft drink, bread, and a bit of homemade candy. I made a sandwich of it while fellows laughed. There wasn't anything else to eat at this candy (*tienda*) store. We lunched by kerosene lamp—no electricity there.

It became bitter cold; I couldn't fall asleep in the seat because it kept bouncing out of place. Crawled to the floor, very dusty but warmer. I shoved a map down my back to keep it warmer. Managed to sleep a little as we bounced along.

At 3:00 A.M. we arrived in Duitama. All hotels and pensions were locked up, but I spotted a door slightly ajar and an Indian woman said they had beds. I checked my gear and camera. I couldn't trust my four roommates. I advised her to call me at 7:00.

Eighth Day—February 18

Awoke to the landlady's call, hated to roll out from under the heavy warm covers. It was very cold. I shivered as I ate scrambled eggs. The soup was bad, and I left it alone.

I hiked for quite a while. Felt sleepy and tired. Got a short ride in a milk truck. Near Pipa, Indians were going to market in a steady stream. I was very thirsty. I noticed a small mud hut where they gathered for refreshments. I walked inside the hut; the Indians moved aside respectfully. Hundreds of huge flies buzzed around. A lady gave me a shell full of the liquid. It was brown in color and tasted foul, worse than sour cider. She called it "Chicha." I drank very little of it. Said, "I'm libel to get drunk on it," and handed it back. Seeing all those flies made me believe they set on the liquid. It cost two centavos, less than a penny. I guess it's really an Indian's or peon's drink.

Hiked on a ways and sat on a green grassy bank to rest. It was pleasant in the warm morning sun. I could easily have fallen asleep.

Started walking again, twenty minutes later a large gas truck offered to take me as far as Choconta, ninety kilometers from Bogotá. The ride was fine because of the asphalt road. It started at Duitama. Rode with him till after 1:00 P.M. Got a little sleep in the cab. I no sooner got out of the cab when the truck behind us stopped for me and rode me into Bogotá by 4:00 P.M. Driver was young and nice company. He had come from Barranquilla, the seaport with a load of electrical equipment. Rolling into Bogotá, I saw at once it to be a fine modern city.

Kids in bobby sox, pea caps, and short skirts. A beat-up Model "A" convertible loaded with high school kids, zoomed around a corner. We drove along a four-lane highway, passing fine, modern, colonial-style homes.

Downtown Bogotá, I had a variety of hotels to choose from, but I couldn't find them. I walked block after block, through business sections, looking only for a hotel sign. I walked along the main street, Jimenez de Quesada; most of the crowd were in business suits and fine clothes. I felt ill at ease. I was dusty, in boots and a huge pack on my back. People stopped and stared after me. I certainly don't like to be the object of a scene. I turned off the main street, then up another. I noticed an overhanging arch and asked a fellow in the doorway "Is this a hotel?" "Yes," he said, "Hotel Granada."

I knew it to be the best in Bogotá. I also knew it to be very expensive, but I hated to back away, so I went forward. At the desk, the clerk asked "What are you?" "American," I said. "Okay, sign here," he said. Many well-dressed people were in the lobby and they stared at me. But the clerk, if I had been any other than American, he'd probably say, "Sorry, no rooms."

I took a hot shower, but it was only lukewarm. Room was nice but chilly. No radiators, no heat. I had my suit pressed and clean shirt, had dinner in dining room. It was beautiful, red rugs, white walls, and from the ceiling hung golden chandeliers, and crystals. Waiters were dressed in white jackets and black trousers. Dining capacity for several hundred, but only six or seven people dining. The lounge was full of well-dressed people, but few apparently could afford to dine there. Many lived at the hotel, but ate outside. The food served was wonderfully good.

31

Bogotá, City of Contrasts

Bogotá, capital of Colombia, stands on a plateau, 8,564 feet above sea level, with high mountains surrounding it. The climate is cold, average temperature 14°C.

The city was founded in 1538 by the Spanish invader, Gonzalo Jiménez de Quesada, and is an intellectual and cultural center. It has a population of about 500,000. The business and official life center about the Plaza Bolívar, named after the Colombian liberator, Simón Bolívar. It is a city of contrasts; colonial buildings stand side by side with others of the most modern architecture. Most interesting are the capital, the Catholic Cathedral, President's Residence, museums, University City, and the bull ring.

The people of Bogotá walk hastily, are always reading a book, periodical, or letters. A stranger to the city finds them reading on the busses, streetcars, in restaurants, or walking down the street. They are very studious. The majority of the people are of Spanish origin; the rest are Indians and other nationalities. The people wear a lot of black so that to a visitor it seems like the entire city is in mourning. The city is overloaded, so it is no wonder the people walk in the streets in hordes. I'd never seen such street-walking crowds before, and it astonishes all visitors.

The majority of the crowd are men in dark suits and topcoats. I wondered "Where are the women?" Several days later I thought, "They ought to drop a bomb on this town to get rid of the heavy male population." Little did I realize that in a matter of weeks after my departure, Bogotá would have a riot that appalled the world.

Because it was so cold in Bogotá, I only stayed five days. It was colder inside the hotel than outside. There was no radiator heat. Most of the time, a fog blotted out the sun.

Our pilots in Venezuela never liked the trip to Bogotá because of the high altitude, surrounding mountains, and continuous fog. One day a plane crashed into the mountains, killing fifty-four, the world's record for a single crash. It struck only six feet from the mountaintop in the fog.

Most interesting I found was the trip to Monserrate Mountain, one of two peaks rising sharply to the east. A cab from the hotel took me to the foot of the hill. A funicular station is there. For a peso I can ride the funicular train (incline) to the top and return. The incline takes on only passengers, but no trucks, busses, or cars. There is no need. There is only a new church still under construction. The old one was destroyed in an earthquake in 1917. The church is a popular shrine, and beyond are picnic grounds. There is a large platform, giving a bird's-eye view of the red-roofed city on the plain, and highways to the west. Many people come up on Sundays.

The ride up the incline was slow, and I was amazed at the length of it. I inquired of the agent and operator the length of it. Nobody seemed to know. It went around a curve and the station at the foot of the hill disappeared. We still were climbing. I wondered, "God, when is this going to stop?"

Still climbing steadily, we went through a dark tunnel, then around another curve, seemed as if we were going through a coal mine. At length, we saw daylight again. We climbed a bit more past large trees, then came to a stop. There was a modern station at the top, somewhat different from the one at the foot of the incline.

Leading towards the church, through a grove of trees, along a winding path were fourteen stations of the cross spaced every twenty or thirty feet apart. It was the "Calvary Road." Each statue helped tell the story of the Crucifixion of Christ.

Returning by incline, past the foot hill station, a block or two, is the Quinta De Bolívar. Within the house and garden, souvenirs of the liberator are preserved. A soldier was on guard. The entrance gates were locked, the house was undergoing preparation for the United Nations Conference in March. The soldier took me for an American tourist, kindly opened the gates, and directed me around personally and permitted me to take pictures.

Most of my five days were spent having dinner with an American fellow named Miller. We had long chats and took in French movies together. He was a thin, elderly man, he had crews working in the jungles of Colombia and Panama, surveying and working by stars. He had just come out of the bush, and some of his tales were weird. He and his crew worked only at night. The savage Indians were about but never bothered them. All of them carried guns for protection just the same. Mr. Miller had worked in Sweden, China, and practically all parts of the world.

Also at the hotel I met an American professor. Her name was Annie Laurie. She was on her way from Ecuador to Venezuela to teach school at some oil camp. She believed it a good idea for Americans and Latins to exchange and take courses in one another's country. She believed the universities of Colombia were excellent for American students. We danced at the Cocktail Lounge in the basement of the hotel and for a souvenir, she gave me my first Ecuadorian sucre (coin). Another evening found me with a professor from Alabama at a nightclub. They were quite expressive.

One day I went to the Ecuadorian Consul for a visa to visit Ecuador. This was the kind of racket he had. The consul tells me a tourist visa will cost me one dollar and forty cents American money. I tell him I only have Colombian currency. "It must be American money," he insists. This seems odd to me, being in Colombia, surely only Colombian currency should be accepted. "I have $10 U.S. money," I then say. "That's all right, but I'll have to give you change in Colombian money," he answered. "It's okay," I said.

But the son of a gum gives me the official rate of the bank, and he is within the law. The *Cambio* houses pay $2.50 pesos to a dollar on the street corner and it's legal. The bank pays 1.755 pesos per dollar. On $8.60 American money, (my change), he can clear for himself about 6.50 pesos profit ($2.60).

I cannot complain; getting the visa is the important thing. He is within the law.

Along the street, one sees policemen directing traffic from pedestals, in the center of an intersection. What a drill that must be to stand on it for eight hours a day for about $2.00 in wages. The funeral hearses are another sight. It's a stage coach drawn by one to eight horses, depending upon the wealth of the deceased. A man with six to eight horses is a wealthy man. A man with only one is quite poor. The horses are usually black with white hoofs. Coaches and horses are trim, but sober. The open-air streetcars are a sight also. They are very cold, always crowded, with people hanging on all sides and the rear. The trolley only stops for women, but merely slows down for the men. They have to run, hop on and off, just like hopping on or off a freight train.

32
Into the Unknown

In Bogotá, I inquired about the road to Quito. Nobody could give me a satisfactory outline. No one ever travels that far by road. Few Colombians travel, period. The ones who do, go by plane or boat. The tourists agencies had no knowledge about the road. There is no railroad linking those two great countries. Bogotáins who had some knowledge, referred to the people and natives there as "*atrasado*" (backward), and the region was supposed to be teeming with Indians and bandits. No one could tell me if it were a road or a trail.

Undertaking the journey into the unknown was truly an adventure. The trip lasted thirteen days. Eight of these were spent on the road, the other five were spent in the beautiful and warm city of Cali. The result was that there is a satisfactory road. It dives occasionally into a river. Landslides and tropic rains make it hazardous, but still a road unites these two countries, 1,363 kilometers (852 miles) long, through the heart of the Andes Mountains. The road goes from high plateaus and clouds, farmlands, to banana plantations and amid desert and lofty heights again. It crosses the Equator.

I checked out of the Granada Hotel on February 23. Mr. Miller was on hand to see me off. "Take care and have a good trip," he said. "Thanks," I answered. We shook hands. "Wish I were younger, I'd go with you," he added.

A cab took me to the end of town for sixty centavos (25¢). It's sunny and warm today, that's strange at this altitude. Hiking a short while, I stopped at a *tienda* (store) for coffee and rolls. "*Descanse*," the proprietor says. I do just that and drop my pack for a rest.

Fifteen minutes later found me hiking again; a truck stopped, carried me out aways. Another hour's hike along a dirt road. A pick-up stopped. It was loaded with drug store merchandise. The driver was a young Spanish fellow. It started raining heavily. The road became slippery as we speeded along. We had just passed Fosagasga, about forty kilometers from Bogotá. The road was blocked by a landslide. It was still possible to drive through, but dirt and rocks were slowly tumbling down. It was a steep wall, about 200 feet high and it had all appearances of being ready to collapse at any second. The pouring rain didn't help matters any. A line of cars and trucks had stopped, not daring the risk.

My driver and I got out of the pick-up and looked the situation over. He decided to risk it. He drove alone, I stayed behind, the crowd watched tensely as the pick-up chugged and skidded through the dirt on the road. For a while it looked as if he would be stuck. As soon as he got through, other trucks followed suit. I raced on first, over mud and stones after the pick-up. We then drove on to the fellow's home. An hour later we heard that the slide occurred, and a truck, loaded with soft drinks, was hit and covered by it.

In a neighborhood *tienda,* the driver treated me to *chicha* and rice cakes. I didn't relish either much. We would have to wait a while. Another Buick would join us on a trip to Girardot. A fuel pump had to be replaced on the car first, then we'd go. My driver tried selling some merchandise. This took some more time. The *"Un ratito"* (short time) lasted three hours. The rain had subsided. The Buick took the lead, and we followed in the pick-up. A half- hour later, we heard the Buick backfiring and sputtering. At a top of a hill, it came to a stop. The fuel pump had gone bad again. No replacements. The pick-up must have pushed it a hundred and sixty times. Then a slight accident occurred. The Buick received a slight dent in the trunk from the pick-up's bumper. The boy's father and driver of the Buick threw their hands into the air and moaned and bellowed in traditional Latin style. One would believe they had lost a fortune.

No more pushing, now we stole barbed wire from a farmer's fence and made a tow chain out of it. The pick-up towing the Buick and the Buick receiving a slip stream of mud and gravel from the straining pick-up. The chain broke a dozen times, and we had to steal more barbed wire. The Buick had a load of passengers, and the going was tough. Most hitchhikers would desert a lift at this point, but I decided to stick it out.

We stopped at a mud house, out in the country for lunch. Even the floor was mud; only the ceiling was thatched roof. There were a crude table, chairs, boxes, benches, and a bed. Outside we sat on logs, stones, and boxes, waiting for our supper. We got delicious cocoa, bread, and smoked pork bits. Most of the people there like *arepa* (corn bread). Dusk found us sitting and chatting outside the mud hut.

We later drove our forceful way along a road lined with bush palms and tropical brush into Melgar, 103 kilometers (65 miles) from Bogotá. A bad day for any hitchhiker. There was only one small hotel in that little town. The women passengers from the Buick had first choice to the rooms. They looked at the unclean sheets and beds and said, "We'll sleep in the car. We don't want to catch *chinchas* (lice and bed bugs)."

Everybody laughed, even the policeman who directed us to the hotel. The car and pick-up was full, I did not wish to catch lice either, so I strung up my jungle hammock to the hotel post and a tree. Everyone laughed again. I fell asleep at once, and awoke to a deluge of rain. I placed the rubber top over me and the heavy patter of rain soon lulled me to sleep again. Two times more I was rudely awakened by some culprit who shook the hammock rope roughly. I looked up and down the street, but there was no sign of the culprit. It would be too bad for him if I caught him.

At 6:30, daybreak, I awoke to the rough hands of my friends. They were ready to pull out. At a tiny restaurant nearby, there was neither food nor coffee. So my three male friends insisted upon our drinking three rounds of Colombian whiskey.

We drove into rain again; the barbed-wire chain broke again and again. It was messy getting out into the mud and rain to repair it. The Buick was coated heavily with mud from the slip stream; even the windshield was obscured. A bus was coming toward us, headed for Fosagasga. The women passengers got out of the car, pulling suitcases and clothes. They angrily paid the Buick operator the fare to Girardot, although they never reached it and now the time element forced them to return back to

Fosagasga in the bus. The thirty kilometers (20 miles) from Melgar to Girardot took us four-and-one-half hours. My friends apologized for the long trip, but they did not charge me. We shook hands and parted.

I walked through town as hundreds of people stared at me. Many were sitting at sidewalk cafés. I had to walk through them. Girardot is about 30,000 population, the climate is very warm, about one thousand feet above sea level. I stopped at a café, pulled my pack off, and asked, "What do you have for dinner?" I was ravishingly hungry. "Nothing, no sandwiches or anything, only bread and coffee."

I can't live on that, I thought, *I'm no native.* They had sardines and when I ordered a can, the girl said, "A whole can?" "Yes," I said, "a whole can." *Cripes,* I thought, *I'm so hungry I could eat five cans.*

A few natives of the lower class stood in the doorway and watched as I ate. It seemed like they had never eaten sardines in their lives the way they solemnly watched me. I did not doubt it. Just this little incident made me wonder, how rich we average Americans are and we can always have our bellies full.

There was a *ferro carril* (train station) and when I asked for the road to Ibagué, the people said, "the train goes there." It made me so mad. They never heard of hitchhikers before and couldn't understand why I wanted to go by road. I finally worked my way out of town. Once out of it, the outskirts were dusty, dirty, shabby, and low-class. All the people running about barefooted, others swimming naked or washing clothes in the muddy Magdalena River. All of them stopped to watch me go by. I walked over a long bridge crossing the Magdalena.

A truck passed over and missed me by inches on the tight squeeze. The hike continued for nearly an hour, then two rides, a dump truck and a jeep, took me ten miles farther. Hiking again on a dusty ground road, past mud houses, and women carrying laundry bundles atop their heads, arms swaying freely. Sweat broke through my T-shirt and field jacket. I stopped for a *"limonada"* (lemon soda pop) then moved on. Two trucks went by, a third stopped. It was a huge new G.M. truck. A big Negro was driving and two assistants riding atop a load of beer.

249

I rode in the cab, soon a heavy rain fell. The fellows on the top crawled under canvas cover. We arrived in Ibagué in the late afternoon. I had planned to lay over for the night, browse around and sleep. It was a large town and I at once didn't like it. It was hot, dirty, full of mercados, Indians, and burros. Possibilities were I might have only seen the sad part of Ibagué, but since my driver was headed for Cali, I asked if I could continue with him. He said, *"Muy bien"* (very well.) We got gas and oil then pulled out.

He said, "I average twenty-one pesos for a round trip; (three days for $9.00) a ditch digger makes two pesos ($.75) a day for eight hours work." He stopped to pick up passengers; they wanted to ride cheaper, but he charged them regular bus fare. Some rode in the cab, others atop the load of beer. No free rides. The driver in this way makes extra money for himself.

We all had dinner at a truck stop; actually a pension is what it was in Cajamarca. We had soup, rice, beans, eggs, steak, and black coffee.

We drove on through the night for hours. It became very cold. At a chilly mountaintop, we stopped, again for hot black coffee, served in half-size tea cups. In the crude shack, an old man wrapped in heavy warm poncho (blanket) served us by a high-pressure kerosene lamp. A short chat there in Spanish, then we rode down the slippery, foggy mountain in low gear to Calarcá. The driver found a cheap hotel. There were four hard cots, clean sheets, but no blankets. My three roommates got blankets from the lady on night duty. *"Yo quero uno tambien* (I want one also) I said. They all laughed and I got one. It pays to speak some of the language.

These fellows were friendly, but I still slept on the alert. We had stripped getting into bed and I didn't wish to awake with my possessions gone. At 5:30, when Lewis reached over my bed to turn the light on, I was fully awake. Heavy rain pattered on the tin roof. We dressed and drove out of town. The road was muddy. The plain jungle trees and foliage was the only scene. We came to a river. On its opposite bank was a native house of bamboo. We stopped there for breakfast of sausage, potatoes, steak, *arepa* (corn bread), and hot chocolate. Cost forty centavos (20¢ U.S.).

We couldn't complain about that. Drinking hot water was gathered in pots and pans as it rolled off the thatched roof. About our feet pigs grunted, and chickens, dogs, and dirty children loitered. The air was chilly.

We started up the mountainside, and at times we almost didn't make it. The road was muddy and slippery, and the truck's wheels went spinning and smoking. We had sunshine and then rain again as we rolled through Armenia, Caicedonia, Sevilla, Andalucia. In the market squares of these towns, white roofs of linen glistened and choice slabs of meat hung from hooks under them. In the background, the ever-present Catholic Church stood like a guardian.

At noon, just at the entrance to the city of Tuluá, a truck blocked the road. It wouldn't permit traffic to pass either way. The truck chauffeurs (drivers) were going on strike. The city of Tuluá was doubling the fee for trucks going through the community. The fee affected the truck owners, and the drivers got orders not to drive through and to block the road. A large line of trucks, cars, and buses were stalled. The entire community was at the scene.

Two fellows had an argument in Spanish. One fellow took off his coat and handed it to another, ready to fight. The other was afraid, walked away; loudly shouting, he pulled out a gun. A lot of the crowd scattered. The gunman appeared quite nervous. He didn't shoot, but backed hurriedly away toward a crude restaurant. The challenger and crowd followed. The argument continued within. I expected to hear gunshots, but then only a loud jukebox seemed to drown out the excitement.

The driver of the blockading truck locked the ignition, the doors and windows. A few crazy drivers who did not wish to be delayed drove through a deep creek alongside the road. The strikers then blocked the creek with heavy logs. Even ox carts couldn't get through now. Five hours went by. It was late afternoon. An army truck (U.S. dump truck) came along full of soldiers and police to break up the strike. The strikers then sat in the road around the truck. The officer in charge and the leader of the strike had hot words in Spanish. Then they drove off together

251

in a jeep, the striker shouting back, "If I'm not back in an hour, I'm in jail." Some of the crowd laughed.

While everyone waited for his return, another army truck (dump truck) came by with an officer and two soldiers behind. The officer ordered the road opened. One fellow remarked, "We have no key to the truck." The soldiers leveled their carbines. The officer said, "Remove the logs or we'll fire." There was tension and the crowd scattered again. A lady pleaded, "They only want passage; they do not interfere in the strike." The logs were then removed, the truck went lurching through the creek and sent one soldier sprawling inside the truck. Then the creek was blockaded again.

An elderly fellow made a remark, "Colombia is screwed up and is a son of a bitch." A young fellow with patriotic spirit came at him with fists flaring. The crowd and soldiers broke it up. Then some fellows tossed the old man's hat about in play. The fight seemed to replace the tension. Then someone threw a large dog into the blockaded truck. With sticks and stones, they angered it to God's sake. One fellow got his hand bit and the crowd jeered him. Cows, bulls, donkeys, and horses passing the road sent people and soldiers scattering for more laughs. A couple of drunks started an argument in front of the soldiers, trying to make them nervous. Finally they quit.

At sundown the officer and leader of the strike returned. The road must and would be opened. The fee was still double. The road was opened, nobody hurt. The soldiers and police had quite a job straightening the traffic jam. We rode through Tuluá. There was a beautiful plaza and a wide walk, surrounding it was black-and-white checked designs of mosaic tile. The streets and highway were a muddy mess.

From Tuluá to Buga, the road was very slippery, we moved along at a creeping pace. There was danger of sliding into oncoming traffic or sliding off the road into ten-foot ditches. We stopped for lunch, then drove in evening through heavy rains to Palmira. From Palmira to Cali is about twenty-five miles, the road was good, paved in asphalt and cement. It seemed so funny to be riding on pavement that I felt slightly dizzy and sick. Lewis, the Negro driver, pointed out the governor's homes as we went down one of the fine streets in Cali. It was after midnight when Lewis dropped me off at the American Hotel. A fair and inexpensive hotel. Lewis asked for six pesos for the fare.

Cali is the capital of the Valley Department (state), founded in 1536. It is a center of both culture and commerce. It has 125,000 inhabitants. The Ferro Carrille (railroad) connects Cali with Buenaventura, Popayán, and Armenia. Various airlines, both national and international, land at Cali's airport. Cali is the chief commercial town in western Colombia, located 170 kilometers (111 miles) east from the port of Buenaventura. Cali is 3,300 feet above level, has lovely parks with exotic trees, cool, shady benches, and numerous monuments worth visiting. The tower of San Francisco is unique. The climate is warm, and the city is both colonial and modern. Many new hotels were under construction to accommodate the tourists. The Alfere Real Hotel was the best at present.

My five days in Cali were spent sight-seeing, shopping for film (35 millimeter is very hard to find), lounging in the central park and watching crowds of pretty girls go by. (Usually an American can be spotted; he reads or carries the *Times* in his pocket). Going to the movies and open cafés for an ice cream soda, window shopping, and long walks back to the hotel. Most interesting was a Colombian house party I attended.

I had gone to a movie the night previous at the Colon Theater. It was modern. There I met Ray Williams, a good-looking blond fellow. He thought the movie stunk, I enjoyed it. Betty Grable played in *The Years Past*. He had his father's car, a big '48 Oldsmobile, a demonstration car. We stopped at the fine Bolívar theater and on its rooftop patio we had a beer. His dad is an auto dealer in Cali. Roy spent many years in Colombia, speaking English and Spanish fluently. I told him, "You must rate pretty high with the society girls in Cali."

He laughed contemptuously. "They believe they are pretty high. Would you care to join me at one of their parties tomorrow?" "I'd be glad to," I answered.

Next day Roy and his mom and dad called for me. They were both young, pleasant, and came from England. We drove to a fine restaurant. It was full of ladies and girls in smart American

253

dress. We had a delicious lunch, then we drove out to their home, situated out in the country. It was a mansion, and a beautiful lawn faced it. A dog came barking in friendly recognition as we drove into the driveway.

Ray's mom and dad and I had cocktails at a tiny bar within the lovely home, while Ray went to dress up for the party. Soon as he was ready, his dad drove us to the nearest bus stop. Ray and I then took a bus into town. What a ride. We had to stand and our heads hit the roof. It was jammed with dusty people. I did not envy's Ray's lonely life; it seemed lonely to me because of the color line.

We arrived at the party. Ray introduced me to the hostess. "Pleased to have you with us," she said. A German fellow, named "Mike," married to a Colombian girl, was giving the party. Mike had spent a few years in the U.S. The lovely home was crowded with about forty boys and as many girls. They were of the best families. All the boys had suits and ties; the girls wore mostly black gowns. The music was on, and almost everyone was dancing. Our hostess directed us to the bar where beer, liquor, and sandwiches were being passed around. Ray and I joined in the drinks, lunch, and dancing. I managed to dance quite well to the Colombian music and received courteous compliments. Ray and I must have danced with about fifteen different girls. Some were good, others stiff. Only one was agreed to be bad. She was a girl who had spent three years in the U.S.A. at U.C.L.A. She could jitterbug all night, but neither Ray nor I could lead her. She did the leading; one dance with her was enough; she was a beauty.

About midnight, the crowd started leaving. There was no phone to call a taxi. One of the girls wanted me to walk her home. I would if she were alone, but she had her mom along. I felt I came with Ray, and we should leave together. A cab came and four girls piled in. They wanted Ray and me to join them. Ray said, "no," and we walked along and took a cab together. Ray did not wish to pay the fare for four girls. We both had enjoyed the party. Mike and his wife and everyone else had been very nice and there was none of that "Yankee supremacy talk" that can spoil a party for an American. The high-society party was like any house-warming party in the U.S.

Next day, I was on the road again, headed for Popayán, in the *departamento* (state) of Cauca. I called Ray and said "so long" to him and his father. They said, "You won't forget us, will you?" I said I wouldn't. I took a cab to the end of town. The driver asked for two pesos, I gave him one ($.50). I then hiked past cows grazing in green meadows.

In the background was a small hillside full of native shacks. It reminded me of La Guaira, Venezuela. The road was paved for a few miles, then turned into a rough dirt road. I walked all morning. A truck-bus affair stopped for me. The driver asked, "How much will you pay?" "I have little money," I answered. He took me to Port Tejada. There were coffee beans drying everywhere, on tables, in backyards, on the streets.

Pedestrians walked right over them. There we gathered sacks of coffee beans and corn; at the other stops we gathered crates of soap and stalks of bananas. The sun was hot and the air very dry. I helped load and I was sorry I took that ride. I'd be damned if I had to pay for it. We drove out of town, then turned into a one-lane road. It became a solid, steaming jungle, full of banana trees.

We had no sooner left Cali and entered the Cauca state than the population at once changed from "Mereno" and whites to Negro. Again we stopped at a *finca* and loaded the bus to the roof with bananas. As the colored men worked, Negro women walked gracefully out of the jungle, carrying large water pots atop their heads. They stooped very low and the men took dipper fulls of water out of the pots to quench their thirst. An hour was spent there. We drove on and made a few more stops. Finally when we did start rolling, I took a deep breath and we came to Santander, fifty kilometers (31 miles) from Cali. They had more stops to make, and I decided to part with them. No charge.

I stopped at a *tienda* for a lemonade, walking along paved streets of clean Santander. A truck-bus affair came along. Several doors were missing. The exhaust made our seats hot. I was the only passenger. I rode all afternoon on the bumpy dirt road. The evening was cold. I arrived in Popayán at midnight.

My driver checked in at a pension, his assistant slept on a seat; later I turned in on a load of cement sacks behind the seat.

Next day I awoke to find the boys fixing a flat. They said, "Take a walk," so I did. Stopped at a pension for breakfast. I walked a dozen blocks. The town population is about 25,000, all the buildings are two-story of Andalucian design, the blocks run in squares and a river runs through the town. The countryside is green and air a bit cool. The altitude is 7,500 feet above seal level.

In the vicinity are copper, gold, and platinum mines and Popayan claims to have given seven presidents to the republic and one famous poet. Therefore it is an academic center and because of its many fine churches and monasteries is considered an ecclesiastical center. Yet the primitive mode is still seen. Hundreds of mules come into the city loaded down with bricks for construction.

We got started on the road about ten o'clock. The road was quite narrow. Trucks slowed down to almost a stop when passing. We stopped for dinner at Bordo. It was rough. Simple tables, chairs, dishes of various size, coffee cups on a dinner plate, silverware not quite clean. A pretty girl waited on us. She had a lovely, long set of black hair. It was a pity she had her front teeth missing. This was common in Colombia.

The assistant driver was a beginner. It was a slow, tiring ride with him to La Union. Night fell and we had supper by a dim kerosene lamp. We had no idea of what the food looked like. We felt better after eating the native soup, rice, beans, and meat.

The other driver took over, and by one o'clock in the morning, we arrived in Pasto. A girl was waiting for one of the drivers. She ran to him. She sure was glad to see him. All hotels were locked at that hour; the driver knew the owner of the Hotel Bogotá; they opened up and I slept under heavy covers; some were carpets. The bed, sheet, and pillow were moist from the dampness of the air. They smelled also. I feared catching lice. The night was cold. It should be; Pasto is 8,400 feet above seal level on a plateau. I slept unsettled. A barefoot Indian boy of nine served me breakfast.

Pasto lay to the southeast of Colombia in the state of Nariño. It had a population of about 50,000, mostly Indians. There were gold mines in the vicinity also. Pasto looked grimy, had many ragged beggars. Only the church looked fine.

The countryside is beautiful, laid out in patterns, mostly bright yellow and green squares and rectangles. They are the *fincas* (farms) of the well-to-do. They cover entire valleys and mountainsides. They are most impressive and I've never seen the likeness in forty of the United States. They raise, wheat, corn, potatoes.

I walked along the panoramic view highway for an hour, stopped for a lemonade at a *tienda* to freshen up. Two fair Indian maids worked there. They were curious, we chatted awhile. They shyly asked me to take their pictures. They seemed rebuked when I said I'd send it to them. They wanted the pictures on the spot.

A milk truck came along, and I rode behind amidst milk cans and several husky farmers in dark blue and gray ponchos. We went as far as Tanque. I walked along again for a long time. A truck-bus combination came along, and I rode behind amidst household furniture—mattresses, utensils. Only one fellow was behind with me. To stay under the roof, we suffered a lot of dust. We then stood on the end gate and kept our heads above the canvas cover for fresh air. Some of the precipices ahead of us were deep and breathtaking. Túquerres was the end of the line.

The towns seemed black as mingling men in unshaven faces, dark complexions, dark ponchos of brown or black, crowded the main road. They looked filthy and dirty in battered hats and clothes. They looked curiously as I worked my way through them. I let them know they were a sight to me also by taking their picture. I stopped long enough to lunch on coffee and cottage cheese sandwiches.

I walked out of the grimy town, the open country was rich in beauty, with the same colorful square patterns as near Pasto. Before leaving Bogotá, I had a terrible fear of "dead" highways in that region of Colombia. I did not walk long. A bus came, full of Indians, peons, and farmers. It was crowded, but they made room for me. The driver insisted on it. I squeezed in among them. They asked a lot of questions. "Yes, I'm American," I said. They seemed to like me, even if I was.

257

Ticket collectors annoyed me. First one asked the price of my watch, then my ring, then my camera. I said, "You ask too many questions. Please mind your own affairs." He didn't mind. A Spanish fellow pointed out Ipiales and Tulcan as we neared the border. At Ipiales, the bus driver refused my money. He said, "You are an *andarin* (walker); you don't pay anything." "Thanks," I said and shook his hand.

Ipiales, five kilometers from the border, had a large dirt plaza. Young fellows and children were playing Spanish football. Originally a large statue of Simón Bolívar should be there. Ipiales didn't look like a good place to spend the night. It was 5:00 P.M. I paid two pesos extra to have my passport stamped by the *aduana* (customs). It was after working hours. A *Salida* (leaving) visa was necessary.

I got on a bus, jam-packed full of Indians and dusty natives. Women tried passing clothes and cigarettes onto me to pass the Immigration and then return the same. Little children huddled low, under women's aprons, so they wouldn't have to pay bus fare, twenty centavos ($.08). There was much arguing as to who paid and who didn't. The bus was so loaded that the ticket collector had to walk around the bus and collect the money through the open windows. Finally after what seemed a long time, the bus started moving. Minutes later we were at the frontier. Everybody streamed out for inspection. A receptionist took my passport and made a record of its data on the Colombian side.

A dozen paces forward, Ecuadorians took note and stamped it. Because I was American, they seemed to trust me and merely asked what I had in my pack. We then drove on to Tulcan, stopping a dozen blocks below the plaza, the center of town.

The night was dark, the cobblestoned streets dimly lit. I walked in the center of it. A dozen beggars sidled up and asked for a handout. I chased them away. The best hotel was the Granada. I registered, cleaned up, and went to the local theater. The ticket girl had difficulty changing twenty sucres ($1.40). She had to send a barefooted boy to get change. Entrance fee twenty-one cents. The seats were hard benches, the roof and walls were bare timber. The sounding was terrible. About twenty people were inside the theater. After the movie, the safest place looked like the bed. No sense in roaming these dark streets. No other place of interest to visit.

I had slept well; the bed was wet and chilly from dampness and the room foul-smelling. I called at Immigration for visa and inspection. A pleasant gray-haired ancient war veteran stamped my passport. His office aides tried their best to make me sell some U.S. dollars at thirteen sucres. They insisted I'd get less in Quito. Later in Quito I got fifteen to a dollar.

I started walking out of Tulcan about 10:30 in the morning, cold and gray. The road was cobblestoned and narrow. I walked and walked and walked. I passed Indian boys driving herds of cattle. Not a single bus, car, or truck went by. Perhaps this was the "dead" highway I feared in Bogotá. Still I wasn't down-hearted, the countryside was pleasant and the weather reminded me of springtime.

I stopped for drinks at running streams and walked into Julio Andrade, a small village about thirty kilometers from Tulcan. It was dusty. It was late in the afternoon. Just as I entered the village, a bus-truck combination came rolling down the hill and stopped. The driver was a big and husky Ecuadorian, his helper was an Indian. We rode into San Gabriel, stopping at a *tienda* (store) for tropical beverages and smoked spare ribs. Being very thirsty, I had three glasses. The meat bits were delicious. The surroundings weren't clean.

We hit the road again. A heavy rain fell. The mountain road became dangerous. We feared a landslide more than we feared going over the brink. The windshield was a sheet of water, and it became foggy. My driver was tense. I could feel it. This was an awful place to be driving in a heavy rain storm. A couple of hours later, we rolled into a valley. There was a village of grass huts. It looked like an African village. It was called Bolívar. The heavy rains were still persisting. The driver slowly worked the bus-truck through the muddy lanes.

A call rang out in the night, the truck stopped, a Negro lady wanted passage for her family, neighbors, and herself to Ibarra. They had a heavy load of bananas, coal, chopped wood, and fruits and vegetables to take along. We got this loaded on while the rain still poured. We then moved from hut to hut, gathering more matter and waking up the sleeping natives who wished to go to Ibarra also. Inside the bus I waited, hot and stuffy.

When we got rolling again, there wasn't room for another stick in the bus-truck. Behind me sat a load of the blackest Negros I ever saw. They kept up quite a chatter in Spanish. We went down a narrow slippery incline and dived into a wide river. We all feared we'd get stuck in the middle of it. After numberless tense moments, we made it across.

Several hours more of rain, fog, mountain roads, and thrills we arrived in Ibarra long after midnight. The streets were deserted, and the driver headed for a lone restaurant that stayed open all night. There were several more trucks there. It was a simple and crude restaurant, as one can describe. We had lunch of coffee and sandwiches. There I met a nice-looking Ecuadorian lad, who said he would be going to Quito at 5:30 in the morning in a '41 Ford coupe. He would be glad to take me for the small price of thirty sucres ($2.00) 141 kilometers (88 miles). I said, "Okay" and got four hours sleep at a hotel next door. An Indian woman awoke me on time in the morning.

It was dark when we made our way out of Ibarra and it sure felt nice to sit in an automobile again. The road was cobblestones all the way to Quito. We passed two famous snow-capped mountains and the Equatorial line, twenty kilometers north of Quito. The Indians' garb had changed to bright colors of red, yellow, green, and blue. But red is the most predominant. It is the color of certain tribes.

Among the best hotels in Quito are the Ambassador, the Savoy, and the Gremlins. My driver took me to the Savoy. The cost was twenty surcres for a room. It was a two-room apartment, telephone and very comfortable ($1.00). The meals were supberb of Spanish concoctions (1 U.S. dollar). The meals were six courses.

I called at the U.S. Embassy, had six letters waiting, and the address of Wahler, an American friend living in Quito.

33

Quito and the Headhunters

Quito is the capital of Ecuador, situated in a cool green valley of the Andes, only fifteen miles south of the equatorial line in the northwestern part of South America. Today it can be reached by road, plane, or railroad; the railroad connects it with the seaport of Guayaquil, a full day's journey away. Quito is an old and colorful city. There is little modern architecture. Most of the buildings are of old Spanish design. Most interesting are the Indians and market places, the old-time public busses and the streetcars, the cobblestoned streets.

A few modern playgrounds, parks, and schools have been set up. But only the children of the well-to-do are found playing. There are only two classes of people in Ecuador. The well-to-do of Spanish descendants and the mouse-poor Andean Indian. The population is chiefly Indian or *mestizos* (half-breed).

In 1533 Pizarro conquered Ecuador and it was under Spanish rule until 1822. Ecuador was one of the last of the South American countries to gain its independence. At the battle of Pichincha, led by Simón Bolívar, the patriots defeated the monarch's army. Quito then became a part of the Republic of Colombia. It wasn't until 1830 that Ecuador became a republic in itself.

A period of strife followed, stirred up by power-seeking leaders, revolutions broke out. The church joined the conflict and the clerical party tried to control the affairs of the state. They succeeded for a while only to be dismissed from office or assassinated.

In no other S.A. country has there been more revolutions. The country is only peaceful when some dictator has been strong enough to control all factions. The last constitution was framed in 1927, the thirteenth since 1830. There were liberals holding office at present.

261

In Quito I spent nine days. I had moved from the Hotel Savoy to the Gremlin House, so that I could be with the American crowd there. The Gremlin House was owned and operated by an American woman who had spent many years in Ecuador. She was young, good-looking, and married to a G.I. Joe, who had been stationed in Quito during the war. Now the G.I. was tired of Ecuador. He wanted to go back to a country where "when I speak, they understand me, and when they speak, I understand them." Learning Spanish was laborious to him. His wife could speak Spanish fluently.

The Gremlin House was big, modern, Spanish. I liked it as much as the other Americans did, only because we had a lot of fun at dinner and by the fireplace. The landlady could never say "no" when an American came to the door. The house became terribly overcrowded. I slept in a room with Mr. Wahler and a thirteen-year-old boy for roommates. We slept on couches. To get into the bathroom in the morning sometimes meant a two-hour wait. The food served was a combination of Spanish and American. There was only one course in contrast to six courses served at the Savoy. I was unsatisfied. Yet the price was four dollars a day, present or not for dinner.

A couple of girls who worked at the Embassy and lived there were most unhappy and were striving to find another home. After having two rooms and a phone for a dollar a day, I was most uncomfortable in a small room with two roommates and paying four-dollars-a day.

The landlady asked me one day where I liked it best. Being polite, I said, "Here, because we have a lot of company and fun." But if I ever return to Quito, the Savoy is where I'll go.

Mr. Wahler is the father of "Trinket." I called him up on the phone. He said, "Trinket is not here, but you had better come over to the house and I'll tell you the whole story." So over to his house I went. He was living at the Gremlin House. He told me his beautiful daughter, whom I had met in Mexico, where we rode on a freight train, was now married and living in Guatemala and is running a newspaper. I was really sorry to find her gone. For over a year, I looked forward to surprising her when I came to Ecuador. I was disappointed also at not finding Mrs. Wahler at home either.

She was out gathering material for a story in the Galpagos Islands, about six-hundred miles off the coast of Ecuador. It had once been settled by farmers. They left and the islands were now overrun with wild horses, cattle, dogs, and large turtles. Mrs. Wahler was well up in her years, but she was always looking for adventure and finding it all over the globe.

Mr. Wahler was a mining engineer and had explored many wild parts of Ecuador. He had been in the country many years. He invited me to stay for supper and stay at the Gremlin House. I accepted both. From Mr. Wahler I got information of road conditions and what dangers lay ahead. On a map he pointed out two ways for me to travel to Peru. One was to go to Guayaquil, then by boat to Puerto Bolívar near Tumbes, Peru. The other was overland by bus, mule back, and on foot. I decided to go the hard way, the way of the original Pan-American Highway plan, which at present was under government study. From Cuenca to Loja, then Cariamanga, Macara, and Sullana, Peru.

Besides road information he told me places to visit that tourist agencies don't mention. One of these was the "Colorado" Indians, about a hundred miles inland, east of Quito. So one bright Saturday morning, I went scouting for a truck or bus going to Santo Domingo, the region of the "Los Colorados." I asked a half-dozen half-breeds in the neighborhood of the parting trucks and busses. One said up the street, the other said down. Others said left two blocks or right three blocks. The police gave bum steers also. No one knew which truck or bus was going to Santo Domingo.

Discouraged, I finally asked a fellow standing near a new '48 pick-up. He said he was going there and would take me for fifteen sucres ($1.00). "Okay," I said. Fifteen minutes later we started out. I rode in the cab with Jacomi, the driver and a pretty girl named "Blanca" (white). Behind us rode a load of farmers.

Jacomi had been to New York several times on business. He was white, chubby, and about 4 foot 7 inches tall. He looked and dressed like a Brooklyn boy with an upturned brim on his hat.

He spoke English fairly well. Blanca was a quiet, shy girl of average stature.

The road was cobblestoned and narrow, leading into the interior toward the coast. Conversation flowed freely about New York, differences in conditions, and the Colorado Indians. Suddenly a landslide loomed ahead. It was being cleared of its final debris by barefooted Indians up to their knees in mud. A truck was slowly forging through the mud; then we went sliding slowly through.

Jacomi was so preoccupied, telling Blanca and me about his trip to New York, that he did not see a large rock in the middle of the road. Too late, he ran over it, striking it with the fly wheel case. There was a loud bang, then only a steady loud rattling noise continued. One of the farmers from the back seat crawled under the pick-up, pulled off the flywheel case, and straightened out the dent, replacing the case and there was no more rattling. We drove on, but not for long. We got a flat. He fixed that on short notice. We had a spare.

Heavy jungle trees, foliage, and banana trees crowded the dirt road. Now we passed sawmills, plantations, and rushing rivers, and then a heavy tropical rain burst down upon us.

When we arrived in Santo Domingo, the sun was shining brightly and a strange town it was. There was a large square in the center of the village. The houses surrounding it were old and weatherbeaten, made of boards and black palm. Some of the houses were built on poles, high above the ground. Others were two-story shacks built to the ground. Pots, pans, meats, fruit, clothes, and people seemed to hang from them all.

We spotted a couple of Colorado Indians. When Jacomi stopped, I tried to take their pictures, they turned sulkily away. Jacomi said, "It is better tomorrow; they will come tonight and tomorrow to get drunk. You will see lots of them. They work on their tiny farms and only paint up when they come to town on Saturdays and Sundays."

Jacomi and I went into a crude restaurant, and I was introduced to a Mr. and Mrs. Platanoff, a couple of Russians. Blanca lived in this village and she went home. Mr. and Mrs. Platanoff invited us to have some beer at their table. Both of them had been to the States and spoke perfect English. They had been in Ecuador twelve years and spoke Spanish fluently. They owned and operated a large sugar-cane plantation and a government distillery for making whiskey out of sugar cane. They had trouble at the present.

One of their employees had his arm cut off in the cane-cutting machinery a week ago. He had contacted gangrene, and the doctors amputated up to his shoulder. Now his side had become infected, and it was feared he would die. Mrs. Platanoff felt sorry for the boy, he was a nice fellow, but she believed he purposely stuck his arm into the machinery. If the boy lived, he would be able to sue them for every penny they had. Mr. and Mrs. Platanoff invited us to stop over to visit their plantation on our return to Quito. We would go right by it. Jacomi and I promised them we would.

A few tiny one-room *tiendas* (stores) played radio and records. I had dinner and a half-dozen bottles of soda. Santo Domingo is hot and tropic; Quito is temperate. No American visitors or tourists there. The best hotel atop the restaurant would be poor accommodations for lady tourists. No locks on the doors, walls unpainted, windows had no glass or screen. Mosquitoes, gnats, and flying bugs and bats flew in and out the windows. No lavatory or wash basin, no water. Drunks noisy below.

I placed a chair against the door to keep it closed. I had no sooner fallen asleep when the door flew open with a bang. The light went on, and a big fellow stared at me. "What the Christ is going on here?" I asked. He did not answer and walked out.

I reset the chair, turned out the light, fell asleep. Only the roosters disturbed my sleep. They crowed and crowed for several hours. Finally I gave up and got out of bed. I had breakfast below. Natives usually have only black coffee and bread. I had to ask for a little change in custom and ask for eggs.

Outside there were a few "Colorados." There was a young boy with his father and mother. They were very colorful indeed. The boy and father had their hair cut China-style and caked into shape with a bright red mud. It was dried hard and looked like a helmet with a beak on it. The women do not cake or paste their hair. It is long, black, shiny, combed down the back. They don't paint themselves as much as the men. The men stripe themselves with paint, black and blue, zebra-style. They stripe the body, legs, arms, and face. The women stripe their faces, arms, breasts, and stomachs. They all use a black paste on their teeth. It's ugly, but their teeth are well preserved. The men and women wear only a gay cloth around the waist. It is also striped in red and white. Some men have bright cloaks of yellow or red thrown over their shoulders. A few of the men carry single-shot rifles against leopards and snakes in the jungle.

The women's breast are naked, and they wear beads and ornaments of silver on the arms. When married, the men drill a hole into the wife's nose, and the women do likewise to the husband's nose. The hole, on the tip of the nose, stands out quite well. When the Indian washes down, he is as copper-colored as any other Indian. When they come to Quito, they wear pants and shirts and a coat or a poncho. One would never know one for a "Colorado" Indian.

I asked permission of the young "Colorado" in Spanish to take his picture. He said, "Sure, go ahead." But his father said, "No, how much will you pay?" "How much do you want" I asked. "Five sucres each," he answered. We settled for ten sucres. I took a photo of all three together, then a photo of each individually.

Some more Colorados came to town in single file out of the jungle. The large fellows in the lead, the smaller ones and children followed behind. I took their pictures. They did not ask for money, but feeling it a custom, I gave them ten sucres.

(*Author's note:* I gave my roll of film of Colorados to a friend of mine who worked for Kodak in New York to enlarge my 35 millimeter prints. He never returned them. Boy, was I angry!)

I had cakes at a tiny round *tienda* (store) operated by Blanca and her pretty sister Maria. We talked and presently a dozen or more fellows came by. They all lived in that town. Upon meeting, they shook hands with me and one another. Upon parting, likewise. This is one of the Spanish customs. They see each other every day. Why all the handshaking and hugging? Is it necessary? Seems like a waste of time.

Jacomi came later and had me pose with a young, almost naked girl. Some picture that would be. Through the help of my new friends, I was able to get more shots of bashful or fearful Indians. Jacomi, the farmers, and I started out for Quito at noon. We stopped at the sugar-cane plantation of Mrs. Platanoff. She was surprised and glad that we stopped. Her husband was away on business. It seemed like life was just a little bit lonely there. She guided us past the cane-cutting machinery, past a conveyer, and into a room where eighteen enormous barrels of cane juice were fermenting. This juice passed on to several boilers and came pouring out alcohol 75 percent whiskey. The boilers were old-fashioned, and the apparatus surrounding it was very interesting. An Ecuadorian government agent was on duty continually guarding the supply and operations.

At the end of the tour were hundred-gallon drums full of the good liquid. Mrs. Platanoff procured a tiny horn (gun-powder type) and dipped it into the drums. We all sampled the liquid. The sample was actually three shots per horn. It was the strongest I'd ever tasted. One horn was enough. What a knock on the head that was. I had a headache for three days afterwards.

Later we sat and chatted on the porch of the Platanoff house. It overhung a large babbling brook and was very picturesque. It was a large house, built of heavy timber. It was unpainted and unpolished, but very solid and efficient. We had more highballs of lemonade and 75 percent. We kidded Mrs. Platanoff, "You should be very contended with all this 'happy water.'" But strange, indeed, she didn't drink. We thanked her for a pleasant afternoon and said good-bye. We then drove on. It started to rain heavily.

We had been driving for several hours, darkness fell and it became cold. We decided to stop for coffee to warm up. We stayed only a few minutes, then drove on. We didn't drive long. I had become sleepy and dozed off. Suddenly Jacomi stopped, I awoke and looked out. Just ahead of us in the light of the headlights and driving rain, a little landslide occurred. It seemed possible to get through and in the moment that we stopped to decide, large boulders rolled and bounced down the hillside and into the rushing river below.

We backed up instantly and the whole mountainside slid down at about the same time directly in front of us. If we had tried driving through, the moment Jacomi stopped, I'm sure we would have got hit. We turned the pick-up around and headed back for Chiriboga, the place where we had coffee. We all knew that if we hadn't stopped for coffee, we could have made it to Quito.

At Chiriboga, there was no phone to report the slide to Public Works in Quito. Chiriboga was a village of few houses. At the coffee stop, we asked if they had rooms for the night. They said, "Yes." While waiting for supper, I stretched out on a long bench. I awoke to loud noises. A bus and a truckload of passengers were stuck there for the night because of the slide. After native supper I was directed through the rain and darkness to a shack made of weather-beaten boards. Inside, the walls were interesting; they were plastered with magazine pictures of U.S. Marines in the South Pacific, the P-51 Mustang planes, ships, flowers, and girls. A candle was the only light. The straw mattress, sheets, and pillow smelled from the dampness. I slept in my clothes; at least they were dry.

I awoke to the knocks of Jacomi. It was 5:30. After coffee and pan (bread), we started out again towards the landslide and Quito. At the slide was a busload of passengers. They all looked weary and haggard from the long cold night and sleeping in their seats. Most of them were Indians or half-breeds. A truck loaded with rotting black-and-yellow bananas was also stalled.

Work had already started on clearing the road. I had expected to find a bulldozer at work; instead there were about a hundred men and women from the villages and mud huts. Most of the laborers were women. Most of them were barefooted; a few wore sandals. Mud came above the ankles. How they withstood the cold mud, I'll never know. They attacked the slide with picks, shovels, and machetes. Impending rocks overhead made it dangerous work.

The women were something; they wore men's hats, long skirts rolled up and tied between their legs, and sweaters. Others had towels and rags tied about the waists. They were heavily bundled; the men were scantily dressed. The women worked better and harder than the men. It's a known fact in Ecuador, and Americans agree on that. American Construction Companies have women on the payroll as laborers.

One Indian woman had to do her natural duty; she squatted in the middle of the road, the skirt covering her feet. When she walked off, a large wet spot remained. She smiled faintly at me and Jacomi. She was a girl of about twenty. Jacomi's face turned pink.

Little children were off for school; they had to pass over the slide, barefooted, and with books tied to their backs; they scampered over rocks, sharp debris, and oozy mud like little mountain goats. Everybody watched them go through with a smile on their faces.

About noon we were able to drive through. It took six hours to clear a path. We were lucky it didn't rain to make matters worse. A landslide can tie up traffic for days and weeks in this country. We had fifty kilometers to go, then we got another flat. No more spare tires; we hailed a large truck. We rode behind. It was a very chilly ride. Around sharp mountains, curves, the truck wailed its siren and horn. The speed was terrific, and the rough road bounced us inches off the floor as we held onto overhead braces and sides, till we reached Quito.

Back at the Gremlin House, gathered about the fireplace were tourists, soldiers, wives, and guests. All were American except for one Englishman and his Ecuadorian wife. Mrs. Powers was a good-looking, gray-haired journalist, traveling by plane and writing. She had a pleasant gift of jokes and speech. Stopping over for five days. Then there were a Mrs. Huntsman and a Mrs. Webster, traveling together on a tour of South America by ship. They came from Guayaquil by train, would stay a week, and fly back to the ship. Bill, Tom, and Jim were soldiers here on U.S. Army mission. We had five fellows who drove down in two jeeps from Alaska. They met two girls in Panama who joined them. They were Bob, Paul, George, Nick, and Harry; the girls were Jeanie and Dorothy. The boys took the girls along because they had money to finance their trip to Argentina. About the fire or sitting on a sofa were Mr. Wahler, the landlord, Marge and Helen from the Embassy, a thirteen-year-old boy, and myself.

269

Many tales were told there. I told them about the colorful "Colorado" Indians. Mrs. Powers, Huntsman, Webster, and the Englishman and wife had gone to Otavalo just north of Quito to see Indians making rugs. Mr. Wahler told us about many other tribes of Indians; the most interesting were the Jibaros. These were the head hunters in western Ecuador near the head of the Amazon River. I would not be going through that part of the country on my trip south.

The Jibaros were slowly becoming extinct because of their many tribal wars. A Jibaro may kill a man in his tribe, but tribal law forbids him to cut the man's head off. Belonging to the same tribe, they are blood brothers. A Jibaro only cuts off a man's head when he battles other tribes; if he can get away with it. Neither tribe likes to have the heads cut off their dead warriors. A man who cuts off a head for a victory token will be pursued and hunted by the opposing tribe. The victor, according to superstition, must not return to his village but sleep and dream in the woods for three days till the spirit of the dead man leaves. He then must shrink the head to the size of an orange. This is how it's done:

The victor must have another man to help him. The assistant must be a man who has himself at one time cut a man's head off. Superstition has it that a non-killer's hands are unsteady for the process of shrinking a head. The head has been cut off close to the trunk of the body, as required. A knife cut is made from the back of the neck straight up over the head. The skin is pulled off the skull, just like the skin is pulled from a rabbit. It is around the nose, lips, and eyes that great care must be taken and steady hands are required to cut the skin away. The skull is then thrown away and the knife cut is sewed up again and three red strings hold the lips in place.

Great care is taken with the long black hair. Three small round stones are heated in a fire, then dropped through the neck into the head. They are rolled around, and they burn the raw flesh out. The head then has a tendency to shrink. Later hot sand is dropped into the head to burn out the places that the stones could not reach. All along the eyes, nose, lips, cheeks, forehead, are worked into shape, so that when the head hardens and

270

shrinks to the size of an orange, it still retains its original features. The victor then can return to his tribe triumphant, his momento at his stomach, hanging from a string around the neck.

Lots of people pay big money for shrunken heads, but care must be taken. A lot of shysters cure a monkey's head. It looks almost human. It is also illegal to bring them into the U.S. It is said that the Jibaros are quite friendly to a white man. A number of years ago, a tall blond German went into their country. He said he would come back with the whole story of their cult, beliefs, and so forth.

He never came back, but one day in a market place, a white shrunken head with blond hair was seen for sale. It was the German.

Mr. Wahler explained and demonstrated how two unfriendly chiefs would meet. They would shout in a loud, booming voice, making such an effort to make their voices strong and mighty that they both broke into a sweat. Mr. Wahler started sweating also, and he uttered some of the strangest sounds I've ever heard. He made everybody laugh. He then told about the feasts, superstitions, and methods used in killing a blood brother.

A blood brother might wait all night and when morning breaks, he lies in wait for the heavy wooden doors to open of his prey's house. When his prey comes out, he sends a spear or arrow into him. The prey may also set a trap for his enemy. He may bend a strong branch of a tree backwards. On it he has sharpened protruding branches that look like a dagger in a row of four, five, or six. If the suspected foe comes stealing along his private trail at night, he will trip the cord that will release the branch. It will strike about the chest and face with a terrific force that may kill and if not, it will make the enemy cry out in pain. The trapper can then wake up and come to the scene and kill his foe.

Feasts are held after victorious battles and marriage ceremonies.

The jeepers told of their experiences; they camped out a lot. Being five and with two girls, they never were bothered by anyone at night. They asked how I got over to Costa Rica from Nicaragua. I said on horseback. They had to put their jeeps on a boat. From Panama they went by small boat to Costahena, Colombia. They all got sick except for Bob and Dorothy, on the rough water.

271

All of them were flat on their backs, eating crackers. They told me they saw my name in the registry at Tulcan, Ecuador. The hotel owner told them about my walking and hitchhiking. They were very surprised to find me at the Gremlin House. They had left Fairbanks, Alaska, five months ago. They promised to pick me up if they saw me along the road.

Margie, the girl from the embassy, had just come up from Chile. "The roads in Chile are terrible," she said.

Besides the fireside chats, we managed to dance a bit.

The jeepers and I went nightclubbing one night. We had quite a time. At each club we bought a bottle and setups. Canadian whiskey cost 180 Sucres at one club, at another 230 Sucres ($12 and $15). A shot alone cost $1.50. We drank a lot. Bob and I had worked for Packard Motor Car Company in the testing department only at different times. This was a job that we both loved. It was so interesting. Hundreds of gauges, meters, recordings, pressures, temperatures, weights, speed times, consumption, and calculations. It was exciting when things popped in the cell and we got scared. Our inspectors and girl recorders were interesting characters. The last I remember was leaning my head back, tired and awaking next morning with a headache. I asked Bob, Dot, George, everybody, what had happened. They said, "You didn't bother anyone," and let it go at that.

I wasn't the only one with a hangover. We stayed indoors all day and went bowling in the evening. A dozen bottles of orange soda pop didn't help the hangover. The scores were bad, but we blamed the uneven, beat-up alleys and balls. They were full of cracks and chips. There were only two alleys, the only bowling alley in the country. The place was crowded. Latin fellows liked the sport. They liked the American girls too, and some of the girls liked them. Betty, a heavy-set girl from the embassy, did more damage to the alleys than a dozen teams put together. Every ball of hers dropped heavily on the alley. No one could understand why she wasn't barred. Some of us winced each time the ball dropped. But there in Quito, far from home, bowling was a grand pleasure for all of us.

The following day we spent sightseeing. We take a "colectivo" to town. It's a station wagon and carries only seven

272

passengers. The fare is one Sucre ($.07). It's cleaner and faster than the public busses. The bus fare is twenty centavos, (1 1/2¢). From town to Panecillo Hill was a slippery climb up steep cobblestoned streets, then up steps dug into mud, and finally a foot trail up a green grassy slope. It was a long hard climb, but it was worth it. Quito lay in perfect squares in the valley below. One could not believe it once had been an Inca Empire. It was another red-roofed city. Surrounding the valley were other green mountains with white cascading falls glistening in the sunlight.

Atop the hill was a small monument made of bricks. It looked more like the remains of an old chimney. There were some picnickers who had driven up by car and were enjoying the view. We lingered awhile, then returned down by road and stopped to inspect a small fort halfway down the mountain. At the foot we hailed a cab to take us to the famous Equator Line Monument at San Antonio. It was fifteen miles away and the cabbie asked eighty sucres for the trip ($5.00).

We went through a few dusty, poverty-stricken villages, past green fields, then into a great sandy desert. As far as the eye could see was nothing but sand. This was a strange place to set up a monument. We expected it to be in a lush green steaming jungle. The monument was much larger than we expected. It was at least a hundred feet high. A large sphere, representing the world set on a huge four-sided, tapered pillar similar to the Washington Monument in Washington, D.C. Each side of the monument had a large letter. E for East, N for North, W for West, and S for South. The names of the French engineers who founded the exact 0.00 degrees latitude are on the monument. Tourists spread their feet apart, and each foot will be in a different hemisphere. Many have their pictures taken this way. The equator line has been drawn for their benefit on the monument.

We returned to the city, and I called at the Peruvian consul's office for a visa. He did not ask more than two questions. It was the fastest one I ever received. He did not even inquire how I would be traveling. If he knew, perhaps I wouldn't get the visa. He gave me an excellent tourist guide also. A few days later, I headed into the wilds of Ecuador toward Peru.

34

An Ecuadorian Hacienda

I awoke early on the morning of Monday, March 15. I had breakfast with the tourists and jeepers. Some felt the weight of my
pack, others took pictures, of the *"Andarin"* (walker). I said
good-bye. Mr. Wahler walked several blocks to the bus stop with
me. He sure treated me swell.

From the Plaza de la Independencia, a cab took me out of
Quito for five sucres (42¢). Now I walked for ten minutes, then a
pickup truck took me to Machachi. The second lift was a pickup
also. I rode behind. It moved along at a terrific speed. It fairly
bounded on the cobblestoned highway. I had all I could do to
hang on. The ride was not meant for a softie, or a woman. We
rolled into dry country and the dust fairly rolled into the back.
The ride ended a few miles out of Lazzo.

I continued hiking along the cobbles, the snow-covered
mountain of Chimborazo on my left in the distance. The wind
was cool and the sky gray. A third pick-up stopped after a long
walk. I climbed in back with several Indians, two white fellows,
and an old woman. It was rough sitting on the floor. We rolled
from dusty to plush green country along the "Avenue of Vol-
canoes." The highway went between two volcanic mountain
ranges.

This ride ended at Latacunga, a clean and beautiful town of
about 15,000. The plaza (park), the church, the sidewalks were
most picturesque. I was surprised to hear my driver speak almost perfect English. We stopped at a *tienda* (store) for Cokes
and sandwiches. The driver told the lady about my walking and
where I was headed for. *"No tiene miedo, Si le Matan"* (You will
get killed have you no fear?).

It was noon and my friend suggested I should lay over. The
next town was thirty miles away. "You'll never make it," he said.

"I will by midnight," I said. He nearly fell over. The lady said, "Don't go, stay here."

I walked through town; about one-hundred little kids followed in the street. They were going to school. I felt a little silly. They all asked, "Where do you come from, where do you go? You are German. No, he is French. No, no, Italian, Polish, English." Never once did they say "American." They knew I was a foreigner, that was sure, my clothes, my pack, the light features and blond hair. The whole town seemed to be watching the parade. I stopped and told the whole bunch to stand still. An elderly fellow made them understand that I was going to take their picture. They stopped. I snapped them and everybody laughed.

I walked for several hours, then a bus came along and I flagged it. It was so dusty again, that I didn't feel like talking. The country unfolded like the desert and sage of Arizona. I sat several seats behind, when the ticket collector said, "Come sit up front." I said, "No thanks. I'm comfortable here." I knew he and the curious passengers would pummel me with questions. For my silence, I wasn't surprised when they charged me fare, (four Sucres) upon reaching Ambato ($.28).

The town was not pleasant; it was full of beat-up trucks and busses, a busy crowded market place, and hundreds of dusky Indians in colored ponchos. I had a boy guide me to the best hotel. He said it was the Buena Vista and only six or seven blocks away. It was actually one mile out of town. Then the boy wasn't satisfied with a good-sized tip. The house was full of woman, I started to back out, but the landlady called me back. The room was divine and the bed covered with a rich alpaca fur. After dinner I watched Ecuadoreans play bridge. One pretty girl spoke good English. Her mother kept an eye on us as we talked. We went out for a stroll. As we walked up and down past the hotel, a couple of old women from the hotel joined us. Spanish custom, they call it. Indians respectfully moved into the street as we walked by.

Next morning I took a taxi. The driver tried to dump me out at the foot of a steep hill. I gave him hell, and he drove to the top. The top was the edge of town. I took at least a look at the rooftops of Ambato in the valley, then proceeded walking along the

275

cobblestoned road. The morning was cool and pleasant. Several police guards stopped me along the road, "Are you an *Andarin?*" they asked. I replied, "Yes." "*Buen viaje,*" they said (have a good journey).

Nails started coming up into my boots. The heels were wearing down. I pulled the boot off and placed paper inside till I could get them fixed. I walked along and sweated.

A pick-up gave me a lift. The wind was cold on my sweating back as I rode behind. They left me out a half-hour later, out in the country. As I passed a tiny schoolhouse, two half-breed Indians sauntered alongside of me, carrying machetes. None of them were pleasant-looking. I walked along quietly, expecting trouble. They asked some questions and evidently were surprised that I answered in their own language. The tallest then asked, "How much money do you have?" "That's none of your Goddamned business," I answered. Realizing that I carried no gun, I said, "This is my side of the road, the other is yours." If there was to be trouble, I wouldn't want them to start it with a swift blow of the machetes while I'd be off guard. I'd start it now with my fists. They moved to the other side of the road, but kept the same pace as I did.

I had no gun but I did have a dark-brown leather 35 millimeter Mercury II camera strapped on my right hip. It almost looked like a gun holster. I kept my hand on it as if it were a gun. I'm sure the natives thought it was a gun and stayed clear.

Soon a pick-up came along. The driver ordered the natives behind and me in the cab. He said, "I don't trust the natives, and I always carry a gun." He was surprised that I traveled unarmed. He was going to Cajabamba and beyond to his hacienda (ranch). It was right along the Pan-American Highway. It was a good seventy-kilometers lift. We passed beautiful green farmlands and always the inevitable grass mud houses. Many were round-shaped. We dumped the natives out at one of them. My driver, a Señor Calderon, said, "Many of these people are rich, but it's a custom and they prefer to live in mud houses." There were many villages with only mud huts. The last ten kilometers to his Hacienda was a bad, uneven dirt road. It was full of ruts and ditches.

He invited me in for dinner; a dozen or more Indians raised their hats and bowed as we entered. It was their way of greeting. Lifting their hats revealed long black, unruly hair over copper faces. They looked small and comical and were very courteous. Calderon said, "They lie and steal and drive me mad."

Calderon produced a bottle of sweet-tasting whiskey. We had a few drinks, then sandwiches of cheese, delicious soup with a poached egg in it, then meat, macaroni, and sauce. I became full to the gills; then more whiskey. This Ecuadorian courtesy nearly overcame me. Blast the American who returned to Venezuela and told me, "All Ecuador hates the American's guts and you'll be treated mean." Calderon was swell. He was a civil engineer. He said, "You have eighteen more kilometers to Guamote." "So long and thanks," I said.

My belly full, I strolled easy-like up the dirt road. A half-hour went by, then a pick-up rolled and swayed on the uneven road to a stop. I got into the cab, alongside of two husky ranchers. One was a German, the other an Ecuadorian. They were partners. The German was very tall, heavy, and solid. He was middle aged, had curly gray hair and gray eyes. He spoke Spanish fluently, no English. He came to Ecuador before the days of the Nazis. He refused to go back and claimed to be on the black list in Germany. His name was Otto. The Ecuadorian was good looking, tall and husky but inches shorter than Otto. His parents were Spaniards. His name was Chiriboga.

They invited me to visit their hacienda and stay overnight. It was late afternoon, so I accepted the offer. We turned to the right out of Guamote and up a sandy, windblown hillside. The truck wheels whined and churned in the sand. It became cold and I wondered how these fellows could possibly make a living off of these cold, barren, sandy rolling hills.

Otto, Chiriboga and another partner had one thousand Indian employees on their ranch and farmlands. They raised mostly sheep and farmed potatoes. They owned three tractors and built their own roads. The ranch covered 300,000 acres and had mining possibilities.

Along the road were several wild hogs astray. Otto stopped the truck and pulled out a high-powered Czech rifle. The sand blown by the strong wind was blinding. I fired three times, sand kicked up near the hog's head, then they ran off unhurt. Otto was angry I missed.

We came to the hacienda. It had been built by the Spanish over 400 years ago. It was built of stone and heavy timber and looked solid. It was about 120 feet long and 20 feet wide. In front of it was a courtyard, then high mud walls, sheds, and stables. Only the thatched roofs called for repairing every twelve years or so. The dining room and bedrooms were cold and bare.

Barefooted Indians wearing dirty red ponchos and ugly sheepskin leggings, bowed, curtsied, and lifted beat-up hats in "saludé" or greetings as we entered. Otto ordered an Indian girl to fix up supper, they checked on Indians grinding peculiar beans into powder form. This would be the Indians' main food. The grinder was driven by a gas engine. Many sacks of beans lay about, ready to be ground up. Otto, Chiriboga, and I practiced firing buckshot at a target on a wall. My score was lousy; the sight was off, as Otto said. Some birds flew into a tree near the house, and Otto dropped them.

I was introduced to one of the foremen, and Otto told him to take me on a tour of the ranch. We both got spirited horses. We rode down to a grassy lane to check on the Indians guarding the sheep. We received the same courteous greeting, bowing and lifting of the hat. There were long-horned brown sheep, white sheep, and "Merino" sheep imported from Argentina.

We rode up and up over sand and potato patches for miles. It was a climb that called for strong horses. It was very cold, and my chest burned from the cold rawness. I could easily understand why my guide wore heavy ponchos and leggings. We passed dozens of tiny grass houses. They looked like dog houses. "Natives sleep in them overnight," my guide remarked. "They are dirtier than a dog house inside." (Don't know, I haven't investigated). Some of the potato patches were so steep that I don't see how a tractor could work without rolling over and down the hill. The return was steep and fast. We visited an abandoned church near the hacienda. The Crucifix was broken and faded; red, green, and white tinsel and ribbon still lay about. The wooden altar looked like a bench. The church was over four hundred years old.

For supper we had birds, potato soup, cheese, lemon, rice pudding and black coffee.

Otto gave me his bed to sleep in, with plenty of covers. He said, "I have another house five kilometers from here and will drive out there to sleep." After riding horses, I saw no sign of another house for miles. I honestly believe Otto slept in the truck or in the dining room.

I awoke in the middle of the night; the door opened and someone entered. It was pitch dark. I heard him moving about. It scared me a bit. I reached for my flashlight. Then I heard Chiriboga cough, I asked, "What's the matter?" and he said his stomach was bad. He was my roommate. I didn't hear him go out.

Dawn broke cold and gray. I washed up in a pan of ice-cold rainwater. After breakfast Otto hustled the Indians together and I took a picture of him and his team. Otto then shook hands with me and said "*Saludé Los Estados Unidos*" (Salute the United States). He certainly was nice.

Chiriboga and I drove along at a rapid pace. We came to Palmira along a fine road just completed by the Jones Construction Company. We saw the train just pulling out. We then drove to Alausí, twelve miles away. I had decided to take a ride on an Ecuadorian train to Guayaquil for a few days, then return to Alausí, and continue over the Pan-American Highway to Peru.

35
Aboard an Ecuadorian Train

Chiriboga and I had cakes. We waited a half an hour for the train. I went first-class. I waved farewell to Chiriboga. The coach was very old, had black leather seats, and were they hard. Wow! The men and women used the same toilets. The climate changed steadily from cold to hot, the scenery changed from gray hills to green valleys of lush jungle. We went over the Nariz del Diablo (Devil's Nose). It's one of railroad's greatest accomplishments. The train goes up or down the mountain, making a half-dozen switchbacks.

The train stopped at various little towns. People came to the train selling fruit, pastries, soft drinks, milk and lunches. All the towns were dirty. The streets were full of mud. The houses were two-story, unpainted, weather-beaten, and made of wood. Doors and windows were missing. Clothes, utensils, and whatnot were hanging about. The children ran naked, the men in undershirts.

The end of the line was not at Guayaquil, as I had expected. The train stopped at Duran and from there we had to take a launch across the bay to Guayaquil. The crossing took fifteen minutes, and additional fare had to be paid.

At the dock, native porters, cabbies, reached for my pack. Finally I let a boy carry it to Hotel Guayaquil. It was not high class, but the manager spoke English and was nice. I stayed in Guayaquil two days. It's quite modern, has a number of fine buildings, monuments and parks. They surpass Quito. But Guayaquil has its rundown slum sections also. At the hotel they whisper of the dangers for an American who dares to walk down the dimly lit waterfront district.

I came about there by accident. I had been strolling and became lost. I saw three fellows ahead of me; they stopped to talk and watch me come by. I kept walking casually, they followed me close behind. Then I stopped on a street corner waiting. I was ready for them. They split up as they went by me, but none of them stopped. They rejoined again and proceeded across the street.

At the hotel I met a Venezuelan medical student. We spent the evening together. He introduced me to a lovely Ecuadorian girl. Her name was Blanca. She was quiet, soft-spoken and liked Americans. Blanca and I spent the night together at her home. She is a girl to remember because of her beauty. "When you come to Guayaquil, you will not forget to visit me again." I promised her I would, if I ever came back.

I awoke before dawn, the day I left Guayaquil. The rain was pouring. I stopped at a sidewalk café. A Negro operated it. It was the only one open at that early hour. It looked like a carnival hotdog stand. It was made of planks and boards. To the Ecuadoreans, black coffee, hard buns, and butter is like dough-nuts and coffee to an American. That's all the Negro had.

I went to the pier and boarded a dingy launch. There was a crowd of natives pushing and shoving to get on board. It was very dark and the rain still poured down. The mate was shouting in the darkness for everyone to sit down on the benches lining the gunwales. Everyone was standing, squeezing in with luggage and all. The host was tipsy. No one sat down. Next instant the launch tipped over crazily. I was in the center of the crowd, we went leaning heavily toward the left and down.

Water rushed down from the canvas roof and several fellows jumped ashore. The launch righted itself; the mate shouted again, "Be seated," and the frightened passengers responded, seating themselves on the half-moon bench, lining the rails. The mate shouted again and the lights came on. The engine started up. The boat was still at a dizzy angle, and water came to the gunwales on the port side. The heavy cargo was not balanced properly, and as we moved out over the bay, everyone was tense.

No one dared to stand up for fear of capsizing the boat. Many boats had sunk in the bay because of improper loading. No one talked; the fifteen-minute ride seemed like two hours. Bells clanged as we neared dock of Duran. As usual, a mad rush to get ashore first, everyone stood up, the boat wallowed crazily.

Women, frightened, moaned and wailed. More shouts from the mate for order. We docked and fellows jumped off. "I'm off, the hell with you" was the attitude. The boat rocked crazily in the deep waters each time someone jumped off.

I went up dark, muddy streets to the railway station. First-class tickets were all sold out. I did not wish to return to Guayaquil. I bought a second-class ticket to Alausí. The second-class coaches were jammed full.

The doors were locked and passengers still holding second-class tickets sat or stood in the coach platform. Two fat women sat with babes in arms on the cold platform, the rain still persisting.

A sign overhead said in Spanish "No riding on platform," but the conductor came along and collected our tickets. The sign doesn't mean anything in this country. As the train moved out, black soot rolled down on us. I stood on the steps and held on the bars.

When the train stopped at the next town few passengers got off and the ones on the platform squeezed in. Natives at the next town threw fish and large sacks of foul-smelling produce on the platform.

I managed to get inside the coach to get a seat. They were mere benches lining the walls. Other passengers stood or sat on suitcases in the center aisles.

Young native women opened their breasts and milked the babies. A few fellows started a card game and others went to sleep. As we neared town, passengers bought bananas, sugar cane, fruits, sweets, and food through the windows.

Somewhere along the way, one of the natives entered the coach with the foul-smelling sacks of produce. They contained fish, eggs, and scraps, I believe. The stench was sickening. The conductor came along and asked, "Who does this belong to?" The native lad, a good-looking one, kept quiet. When no one answered the second time, the conductor proceeded to throw the bag out. Only then did the native speak up, and out he went with the bag. I had noticed, when the conductor asked the fare for the cargo, the lad shrugged his shoulders, meaning he had no

282

money. Some folks say it's a custom, if you have no money, you can still ride free. The boy rode free.

The conductor then locked the door. I became sick from the various smells, and an Indian beside me chewing coca, which is a drug, made matters worse. Chewing coca leaves makes the Indian dizzy and the smell is sickening.

I wanted to throw up. I couldn't go out on the platform; the door was locked. There was one toilet at the opposite end of the coach. I went over Indians and suitcases and finally reached it. I threw up a dozen times. I spent the better part of the five-hour trip in the toilet, spitting green. I felt I had been poisoned, but it was only Indian smell that made me sick.

Finally we reached Alausí. I then went to a tiny restaurant. I had bologna sandwiches and ordered a couple of sausages boiled. When served they were so greasy that I couldn't eat them.

36

Into the Jungles of Ecuador

I started hiking up a new road, just completed by the Jones Construction Company, toward Chunchi. Feeling sick, I walked slowly and rested many times. No traffic went by. A heavy rain fell and I became soaked. No place to hide; the countryside was bare of trees. The sun came out, and I soon dried again. Up and up I walked till I was in the clouds. Late afternoon I came upon a gang of young natives clearing a landslide, thirteen kilometers south of Alausí.

They called me "Mister." Most of them worked for the Jones Company. They advised me there was no more traffic for the day. One of the fellows had a horse. He would rent it for forty Sucres to get to Chunchi, twenty-seven kilometers away. "Okay," I said. We then hiked three kilometers to the little village where he lived. While he saddled the horse, I had a lunch of canned fish and bread.

We rode down a perilous rocky mountain path to the road below. Then we spurred the horses to high speed. Darkness soon fell and we slowed down. It started raining again, and soon we were wet and chilly. My guide wore rubber pants and heavy ponchos for riding.

The road became muddy underfoot, the horses sank in the mud and stumbled. The bad stretch was about seven or eight kilometers and certainly would have been unpleasant hiking. I was glad I was on horseback.

Soon we spotted some of Jones's equipment along the foggy road. Trucks, tractors, and scrapers stood out ominously in the darkness. We came to an enormous boulder in the center of the road, nearly twenty feet high; all about it were smaller broken ones. We dismounted. With my flashlight we investigated. It would be dangerous footing for the horses. Slowly we walked and guided the horses over the broken boulders. Again the road was fine, hard-packed, to the American camp at Chunchi. We spurred the horses to a gallop as we raced down the hill. We arrived at nine o'clock after riding four hours.

At the American camp, we were stopped at the gate by an Ecuadorean watchman. I asked for lodging. He went forward with my message while I waited at the gate in the rain. He returned and said, "The superintendent will see you." The camp was small, more or less army-style, with four cots to a house. I entered house number 7. I introduced myself to Superintendent Kimberg, Mr. Frank Eppley, and two others. They said, "Let the Indian guide sleep in the rain."

They assigned me to a cot and said, "Go ahead, spill your story. What are you doing here?" I didn't feel like talking much, but what I did say impressed them a little.

Frank worked on a stone crusher and was nursing a touch of sinus in the nose. He bent over a water pan and breathed medicine through a towel. He cussed and swore and complained about "master minds." He was loud, a bit drunk, and made us all laugh. I took a hot shower and turned in.

I stayed in camp two days and three nights. There were about forty Americans. It was a hard and lonely life in this primitive territory. There were only three American women there. They were the wives of the road builders. They did not seem discouraged. They enjoyed the poor and lowly surroundings all about them. Yet they carried themselves like tourists and travelers and not residents of Chunchi.

I'd awaken early for breakfast, then go back to sleep. A tractor was running outside my window, but I slept through it all. At noon the fellows laughed at how well I could sleep.

I went to the little village of Chunchi, with Frank and the Ecuadorean doctor, trained in the U.S. and who speaks English fluently. We stopped for a couple of beers and talked to the American women. They were cheerful. Frank was fed up. He had quit his job. He had an argument with his boss. Only the night previous I had asked him, "The two years you have spent here; is the money worth your youth?" I didn't believe he would take my remark seriously. He was going back to California on the next plane out of Guayaquil and would be happy.

I went hiking with Superintendent Kimberg. We passed a farmer plowing a field with oxen, with a primitive wooden plow. We watched fellows lay in a huge pipeline for a mountain drain, put in a wall where a side was sinking, and bull dozers and scrapers cutting the new road. Two tractors were sunk in the mud, almost out of sight.

Superintendent Kimberg was fed up with the job. That natives were bastards. They steal everything that shines. Even knobs from truck doors, gasoline caps. They have no possible use for it, yet they steal it. He was homesick for his wife and child.

They would only build the road to kilometer 110, there would only remain eighteen miles to Tambo to connect with the long good road to Cuenca. But the Ecuadorean government did not have enough funds to complete the job.

Pat was one of the Americans working on the road, but because he had married a native girl, he had to live the way the natives did. He was not allowed quarters in the camp, but he could eat his meals in the mess hall if he chose. His wife was not permitted. Pat was 28 and had been out of the U.S. for ten years. He had been all over Africa, Alaska, and South America, building air strips. He said to me, "You pay to travel, but I get paid to travel."

Pat invited me to his two-story, weatherbeaten wooden home for dinner. Pat's wife was very dark-complexioned, a full-blooded Indian with long black hair. She was young and pretty. Pat could hardly speak Spanish, but they got along swell. Pat hoped to bring her to the States as soon as the job was finished. Pat said, "She's a little dark. What's the difference? She's a good girl. She said she's going to have a baby, but I don't know."

The furnishings were very poor, moist and dirty. The bed was sunken and the springs nearly touched the floor. Pat had trouble with his family in the States. Because of his long service abroad, his folks believed him to be quite wealthy. I felt sorry for Pat. He was good-looking and husky. I felt he could do better for himself.

We had dinner of chicken, potatoes, soup and black coffee,

then several rounds of whiskey. Pat's tales of the Oriental Indians and his experiences in the Ecuadorean jungle were very interesting. He ran a bulldozer one day and had a native sit beside him with a gun to watch out for savages. They were attacked once. Several workers had been killed. Pat was scared plenty as he ran to safety.

As I said "Good night," he said, "Be careful out in the street; the natives are bastards here. They'll beat you up if they get a chance and rob you." No one bothered me in the dark street as I walked to camp.

On Sundays, the Indians come to town, filling the public square. They set up white-linen tents to sell hogs heads, chops, hams, and all parts of it. They sold other kinds of meat also.

More Indians sit on the ground and sell pottery, fruits, vegetables, and still others sell clothing, shoes, and cooking utensils. Only on Sunday is the square so crowded.

I tried to rent a horse to take me to Tambo. There was only a rough trail. I offered a hundred Sucres ($7.00) for a horse and guide. They gave me tales that it was very cold, very high mountains, and very bad people. Horses and riders die on the trail and it takes more than twelve hours. Frankly I said, "It's a lot of bull." The native boys went to inquire and returned, saying, "No horses available."

So next day I could plan on walking. A train goes to Tambo once or twice a week, but I did not wish to wait for it. I had risen early. Everyone gave me a cheery "Good morning." Pat gave me a lift to the end of the road, it became slick with mud. I said, "What a hell of a road." Pat answered, "You haven't seen anything yet."

I waved back to the boys; the mud got deeper and deeper. Last night's rain made matters worse. Just where the bulldozer had finished a slim cut, the mud was heaviest. What looked like a solid footing, was not. I sank to my knees in it. I felt the cold mud bathe my legs above the twelve-inch boots I wore. This slim trail and heavy mud continued uphill for a quarter of a mile, then down a steep bank, then uphill again for a half a mile.

A native came alongside, barefooted and wearing a bright-red poncho. He said, "I'll rent you my horse for 250 Sucres" ($25.00). I laughed. "Man, you don't want much, do you?"

"Mister, *es muy lejos, se mata,*" (very far, will kill yourself) he continued.

The pioneer trail (bulldozer) ended and a mule trail ensued. It was really holes or steps, fourteen inches apart at a steep incline. It was wet and slippery, and with wet boots I found walking difficult. I slipped and stumbled many times. It was a cold morning and a high altitude, but I was sweating under my load as I clambered steadily upward, reaching for brush and branches for balance.

The native ahead of me walked along easily. It was very surprising. First time in my life, I'd ever believe shoes to be awkward and incapable of holding the earth. He offered to help, so I let him carry my pack. I still had difficulty keeping up with him. He climbed up like a mountain goat over the slippery trail. He was barefooted, with toes that worked like fingers.

We came to a mud hut and stopped to rest. We were atop a mountain. As I looked about for signs of a trail, there were none. I'd never find my way to Tambo in that interminable jungle of rolling hills and trees. The boy asked, "What will you pay if I carry your pack and guide you to Tambo?"

"Twenty-five Sucres," I said.

"Fifty Sucres," he said and I had to agree or continue and become lost. "Okay," I said ($3.50).

At another hut, his home, he got his boots and cleaner trousers and put them in a burlap bag. He only wore shoes when going to town. We hiked along a stony trail through the dense foliage. I wondered if he wouldn't bust a toe.

We came to burned-out fields, then past sheep pastures, then potato patches, and corn fields. We went through fog that touched the ground and hid my guide out of sight, then again up hill and down hill and over mule trails that made walking difficult. Six times I slipped and fell sidewards, backwards, and on my face. I was a muddy mess.

A thin narrow wet path lay ahead of me; it was sloping. As I neared it, I said to myself, "I bet I'll slip on that," and sure enough I did. I slipped off the bank and fell about six feet into a lot of bushes. Boy, what luck, just underneath was a deep ravine, a hundred feet down. Cold sweat broke out on my forehead. My guide was a hundred paces ahead of me. Silently I pulled myself up on the trail and caught up with him.

The boy's toes clawed into the mud like a hawk's talons. After two-and-one-half hours, we came to the railroad track. It started raining. My guide came to a stop at a tiny station. He wanted to wait for a train. "Look," I said, "if you don't want to walk, return the money." I thought I would have to beat him up. He decided to walk.

An hour later he spotted a shelter house. It was raining heavily. He suggested we stay and wait for the train due at noon next day. While I slept, he'd probably make his getaway. "Nothing doing, come on," I said. He complained of being sore and tired.

We followed the tracks for a while, then the trail went up a steep hill again, along a mule path. After a hard climb and descent, we came to the tracks again. We followed it for several kilometers, then my guide stopped for a soft drink and bread at a tiny village station. We both filled up. My guide knew these people, four men and a woman. My guide stalled and I said, "Let's go." Then the "son of a gun" wanted me to carry my own pack. I sternly said, "Walk or return the money." I would hit him and his four friends if they interfered.

His friends grinned as he put the pack on his back and headed into the rain We followed the tracks, then turned off into the hills again. My guide advised me we could reach Tambo in eight hours, but he was wrong. Ten hours after leaving Chunchi, we found ourselves climbing a hill to the village of Tipacocha.

We were wet and cold; we stopped at a mud hut for hot, black coffee. The hut was cold also and to sit brought on the shivers. I went into the next room and sat beside the fire on the ground. I took off my field jacket and shirt and dried them over the fire. The lady was making stew for us. It was good. It was made of guinea pigs. While I sat by the fire, these little creatures ran all about. I thought they were rats at first.

The rain had stopped, but the coming night was cold. I had decided at this point that perhaps my guide was going in circles. There was no sun and I had no compass. A train was due in in about an hour, so the lady said. I decided to finish the stretch to

Tambo by train. We were both exhausted. I arrived in Tambo late at night after approximately an hour's ride. My guide took leave of me and happy he was to be rid of that 45-pound pack.

I went to the only restaurant open. It was eight foot square and dingy. The landlady was fat; she treated me nicely and served me well. She gave me all the hints possible. She wanted my company for the night. I was too tired after the day's journey. I wanted to sleep alone. I went to my room. It was bare as any shed. I slept on a straw mattress. There were no locks on the door and two fellows slept in the next room.

I slept well and late. I called at the same restaurant for breakfast. The fat landlady wanted to know why I didn't return as I promised, to her room last night. She then insisted I show her some pictures. While I did so, she kept leaning closer and closer to me and touching my knees.

She had married an American. He gave her three beautiful blond children. He went back to California, leaving her and the children behind. She very seldom received a card from him. She liked Americans and offered me a free dinner if I stayed till noon. Then she wanted me to take a picture of her three children. I'd wasted two hours here already, when she went to change the children's clothing in the next room, I took off and headed out of town. I hurried lest she come running after me.

The road was fine and wide, no more mule trails and muddy, rocky slopes. An hour went by, and a truck gave me a lift. He asked for five sucres, but he couldn't change my fifty, so I didn't pay him. Another long walk followed, then a truck drove me to Cuenca.

Cuenca was a lovely clean town with many fine parks. It had fine schools, colleges, and churches. I was surprised to find it so, being so far away from Quito and Guayaquil in the interior. I checked in at the Crespo, the best hotel. I had a private shower, and it felt wonderful to wash the mud from my legs and body after the Chunchi—Tambo trip.

After cleaning up, I went downstairs to the modern living room. The dinner was a surprise—American hamburger, peas, mashed potatoes. The proprietor's English-speaking daughter must have prepared it especially for me. After dinner, I enjoyed the company of the English-speaking guests. According to custom, we retired about ten o'clock. Next day my bill for lodging and food nearly knocked me for a loop. It was seventy-seven sucres ($5.00). This was mighty high for that part of the country.

I walked out of town amidst hundreds of incoming Indians, the women wearing long black dresses and white hats. The hats were designed for men, but all the women wore them.

A milk truck gave me a lift to Cumbe. The driver noticed a truck behind us. He stopped it and said it would take me all the way to Loja. The Loja truck carried cement and ten passengers. We sat on crude benches, and a canvas roof overhead kept sudden showers from wetting us. The country is ever-rolling, just like Pennsylvania except for a lack of timbers. We stopped at a hilltop restaurant called "Buenos Aires" (good air) for dinner, then moved on to Loja, arriving in the late afternoon. It was a nice town of several thousand people. Most picturesque was the central plaza and the church that faced it. Hotel International was recommended, neither expensive nor cheap, but satisfactory for a fellow. I went to church; it was amazingly large, fine, and artistic. I prayed for God's protection on my journey. The next few days would be worst part of the Pan-American road in Ecuador.

I met yesterday's driver at breakfast. He looked dopey, sleepy, or drunk. He was a bit unpleasant. I paid little attention to him. I had coffee, cheese and "pan" (bread), excused myself, and headed out of town. A fellow came running after me. He was nearly out of breath. He showed credentials of investigation. He said I should wait till ten o'clock for a bus going to Gonzanama. I advised him I would continue walking, taking pictures and taking the bus when it came along. He smiled and said, "Fine."

He warned me if I attempted to walk, I would kill myself or be killed. I walked along, stopped and chatted with a policeman. All policemen wear U.S. Army blouses and trousers and brass buttons, war surplus, no doubt. I found that Ecuadoreans hate the Peruvians. Ecuador lost territory to them in the war of 1941. The policeman did not hide his hatred. Seldom had I seen a Latin face express hate.

"*Vaya Bien,*" he said, and I moved on. Presently a truck came along. Yesterday's driver and the same truck. I climbed in beside him and several passengers. Again he was making unpleasant remarks. My answers were few. He kept quiet then. We went over mountainous roads, and I began thinking what would it be like for a lone American to be lost or walking in that vast range of gray mountains.

Little did I suspect that I would be alone for two days in that range of mountains. Suddenly I noticed that the truck began weaving from one side of the road to the other. I took it for granted that the driver was showing off and trying to frighten me. I looked at his eyes; they seemed to be crossed or half-closed. I asked if he were sleepy. He said "No."

A few minutes later, he crashed his right side on a curve, shattering the wooden doors and injuring one of the passengers. The passenger moaned and held his left knee. We expected him to pass out. We pulled up his pant leg. The leg and knee appeared fine except for a black and blue bruise on the left kneecap. After a bit, he felt fine and refused to sit on the right side. He then sat in the middle of the front seat. There were six of us in the front seat. The seat was built even with the running board. The driver laughed. "How could he bruise his left knee when the right touched the door?" I tried to explain that accidents produce peculiarities. He laughed again. It didn't make sense to him.

As we continued, his driving did not improve. I felt sure he was drunk, even though I smelled no alcohol. We almost went over a cliff, and I pushed the wheel over. I could see La Toma, the red roofs glistening in the sun about a mile below. I felt like walking, but I held my breath as we went down. I believe I was overcharged when the fellow said five sucres. But it was worth it, just to get out of the truck. I feared for the safety of the other passengers, but this was the end of the road for me; they were on their own.

About two dozen tiny makeshift houses of tin, boards, and mud made up the town. It was very hot. I stopped for a soft drink at the mercado. Little boys and elders laughed as my soft drink squirted out of the bottle after each gulp. The soda was hot also.

"*Vaya bien,*" they said as I took the road leading to the left, towards a range of mountains in the distance. The road was level, but a mere dusty trail. From 9:30 to 12 o'clock, I walked. I came to a river about twenty-five feet wide. There I took off my boots, socks and trousers, and waded across. Water came to my waist, and the strong current forced me to stumble. I regained my balance, but my camera got wet as it dangled over my shoulder, hoping it hasn't ruined the film.

Once across, the hot sun dried me up pronto. I replaced boots and clothing and continued walking, passed houses made of mud and sticks. Dark-complexioned people said, "Good afternoon" or "Adios." Dogs, pigs, chickens, cattle, goats, and horses were everywhere. Now the road continued on an upgrade and continued so till I neared Gonzanama next day.

As I walked, I was ever mindful of the investigation man's remark. That a truck would be leaving Loja for Gonzanama at ten o'clock. Even so, I doubted if it would be able to cross the river. I walked and inquired about horses for rent. "*No hay*" (no have) was the usual remark. After several hours in the open mountains without seeing a single mud house or life, I became hungry and thirsty.

Finally, far ahead of me, I spotted three mud houses. Two were vacant and at the third, vicious dogs made a rumpus at me. I asked for water and an elderly woman poured a cup of muddy water out a long, peculiar gourd. I decided not to drink it. The lady said, "It's good river water." "No thanks," I said.

I then asked for food; I was very hungry. "*No hay*" the lady said. A young fellow and a woman within the hut grinned in amusement at my predicament. A bunch of bananas was hanging from the rafters. I asked for some and offered to pay for them. "*Dueña no aqui*," (Landlady not here) she said.

"Nuts, you're the landlady," I said. Even so, how would she know a couple of bananas were missing from the large stalk. Finally she broke off two, but because she had no change for the ten sucres, she refused to give them to me. I walked off, really surprised and disgusted. They would let a man wander alone and hungry through the mountains without offering any aid. Grumbling to myself, I hiked ever upward. There were a couple of landslides and I managed to walk over them. I was positive now that no bus from Loja could get through to Gonzanama. I would have to walk it.

I spotted a cow drinking water from a tiny spring. It was so tiny that if I hadn't seen the cow bending low, I would never have seen the spring. I chased the cow away, then bent on hands and knee to gulp up the water from the clear, bubbling stream. It was no more than one inch in diameter. Feeling better I continued walking till dark. I believed I would be sleeping in my hammock between trees in the mountains, when suddenly ahead of me appeared several mud houses.

I walked down a steep embankment and encountered an elderly grizzled fellow in sheep herder's gear. I asked for water. He brought forth a cup full of clear spring water, then another to quench my thirst. He invited me to rest; we sat on a long log outside the mud hut. As we talked, I asked if I could string up my hammock under his porch for the night. He said it would be better inside his mud house. So we strung it to the rafters. It was pitch black.

All his sheep and goats had come home for the night, and the yard was full of them. I entered my hammock and fell asleep; a couple of hours later I was awakened and asked to come into the next room for dinner. The old man, his son-in-law, his daughter, and I sat on boxes. There were no chairs or table. His tiny niece sat on the ground. His quiet wife stooped beside the fire on the floor and dished out tin plates of beans and corn pastry.

I got two helpings of beans and pastry. It did my hungry stomach a lot of good. Eating at a fireside, within a mud hut is heart-warming, just like eating outdoors. I chatted a bit, excused myself, and turned in to the hammock. It was a cold evening. I put on my jacket and trousers. It was still cold. The cold swelled my large toe and the right foot. Ingrown toe-nails hurt terrific. I wrapped a handkerchief around it in the darkness, felt fine thereafter. I slept uneasily, awoke to find the old man moving about the room. I hardly slept at all.

Dawn broke; the old man remarked he had been cold all night and couldn't sleep. His bed clothes and blankets were the same that he walked about in all day. For breakfast, no food offered, only water. I gave the old man ten sucres for kindness. He did not ask for anything. The old man said it was twelve kilometers and downgrade to Gonzanama and I could walk it in three hours.

I walked upgrade for four-and-one-half hours steadily and came to a hacienda on a hilltop. I was very hungry again. At first the lady said *"no hay"* food. Then when I offered to pay, she said *"Okay,"* but I'd have to wait till she made coffee. She asked four sucres and refused a tip of two more. I insisted and she thanked me divinely and said *"Vaya bien"* (good going).

The lady said it was fifteen kilometers to Gonzanama and should take only three hours to reach. She had no horses for rent.

I walked along, quenching my thirst at numerous springs. The sun was hot, road dry, and hard walking because of tracks left by horses and trucks at the last rainfall. I came to another hut. They offered me lemonade and brown sugar candy. They had no horses to rent. I walked along and came to still another hut. The fellow was a "quack" doctor. He had drug store supplies spread on the ground before his hut. The remedies in English he did not savvy. He asked me what they were and carefully laid them aside. These supplies came via mule pack from Peru. There they offered me roast corn on the cob. It was good. The "doctor" only had one horse and could not rent it to me. "It's only two-and-a-half hour walk to Gonzanama," he said.

Uphill and ever uphill I go, feet ache and nails coming up in heels of my boots, to make things worse. I had them repaired twice since leaving Macuto, Venezuela. About four in the afternoon, I reached the summit and was able to see Gonzanama in the valley in the distance. A large hacienda overlooked the valley from the summit. Here were many horses, yet they refused to rent them out.

I didn't mind much. It was only five or six kilometers more and downgrade would be easy. As I neared the town, a group of young fellows with bird rifles walked along with me. Laughing, joking, kidding. One carried my pack. I took their pictures. It was so funny. Some took off their hats, solemnly placing them over their stomachs. One would believe a holy occasion was taking place.

As we entered Gonzanama, a town of about a thousand people, the doorways, porches, and streets held many curious on-lookers. I appeared quite tall in the center of the group. There wasn't a paved street or sidewalk in the town. Most of the houses were simple mud, adobe, or plank buildings. We came to a simple, crude drug store. I was introduced to a gent. He would arrange a night's lodging, and with mule and guide for next day's journey.

I had a supper of fried eggs, rice, pan and black coffee—native style. I retired early on a bed of boards, covered with thin blankets. I had to sleep in clothes again; the night was cold.

At dawn, my guide knocked on the door. No water to wash face or hands. Lodging cost 24¢. It was the only hotel. Gonzanama was one of the towns raided by the Peruvians in the great war. The church burned down in 1937 and now was being rebuilt.

My guide and I rode out on two fine white horses. We followed the "Pan-American road." It was roughly pitted with dried-up mule tracks and holes. Some places were mud and the horses sank belly deep. We took a few shortcuts, and I honestly can say we traveled trails that seemed impossible for a horse to get over.

Steep rocky inclines, downgrades, sheer edges of mountains, over large boulders and sheets of sheer rock and mud, mud, mud, and rivers. When we came to level trail, my guide never ran the horses. The four-hour ride took six-and-one-half hours to Cariamanga.

One interesting sight was along enormous, humpback Mount Awaka. There was a beautiful white waterfall, and at its base was a fancy swimming hole about twenty-five feet in diameter. It was full of native boys and girls. While they swam, mothers washed clothes alongside in the warm afternoon sun. I arrived in Cariamanga about two o'clock. I owed the guide thirty sucres ($2.00) for his services and the mule. I hated to change travelers check at 15 to 1. In Quito they were paying 18 to 1. So that on $20 I lost 60 sucres ($4.00). Businessmen accepted Peruvian checks, but they had never seen American Express checks. They were afraid to accept. That is why I got the low rate of exchange.

Cariamanga was an old town with cobblestone streets. It was full of hills. All the buildings were adobe and old Spanish design.

Another thing that surprised me was the whole town's curiosity when a plane flew high overhead. Children yelled and screamed, and the elderly looked upward. The whole town was attracted. A fellow told me that a plane seldom passed over that part of the country.

I made arrangements to ride mules to Macará for one hundred sucres. I ate supper in a large mud house restaurant by kerosene lamp. Folks sat and listened with interest of tales of the U.S. and outside world. The last traveler who came this way was a Czech, about five years ago. White men and strangers seldom come into this territory. Today, March 26, is my birthday, twenty-six years old. I'm not drunk but somehow contented. A native comes in. He has a large black eye. He is drunk and had been in a fight.

I return to my simple, bare room at a hotel. I use the flashlight walking down the dark streets. Barking dogs have quieted down and I should sleep fine.

I was awakened by the peon knocking on the door. He said to get ready and he'd be back in a few minutes.

I hadn't slept well, thinking of folks and Easter holiday back home, of Easter baskets, hams, sausages, colored eggs, candy, butter, cakes and rolls, of going to church and the priest blessing the baskets and returning home at noon for the grand feast.

A knock came on the door. It was the owner of the mules. He said it would cost me another twenty sucres for the peons' and mules' "*Pasto*" (food). I said, "I'm paying twenty sucres over the regular price, what more do you want?"

He said yesterday he didn't "*entiende*" (understand) and that I didn't savvy the "*idioma*" (language). What he meant was, yesterday he didn't know I was an American and today he did. So he must charge me more. Well, dammit, if he is a miser, I'll give it to him.

I had breakfast at the mud house restaurant. The lady sympathized. A customer said he could get a peon and mule to carry me over for 50 sucres. "It's okay," I said. I was anxious to be on my way. The lady and customers said the man was most unpopular and selfish.

Our mules were loaded down with cargo for Macará. This was unexpected and it would slow them down. My tiny peon guide crossed himself, then mounted the loaded mule. It was so high that he had difficulty mounting.

It was a beautiful morning; we trotted down cobblestone streets, past an ancient church. The bell rang its high tone. It was 7:00 A.M. People tipped their hats and said "Good morning" or *"Vaya Bien."* It was cold as we rode into the shade of enormous Mount Acero de *awaca* (Mount of Steel). It stood over Cariamanga like a giant guardian. Almost at once we were on a rough trail going down over sharp-edged stones and dried-up mud steps, made by hundreds of mules passing over the trail. By ten o'clock we stopped for lunch at a mud house because my guide said there would not be any place to eat till we reached Zororanga late at night.

The cook brought us a plate full of *choclo* (corn beans) and dry meat. I asked for a knife and fork to cut it. She said she had none. "It's okay," I said and tore the meat apart with my fingers. As I chewed on it a bit, it smelled and tasted bad, looked green. Decided not to eat anymore. I ate some *choclo* (corn), washing it down with black coffee.

It was a poor, but interesting picture of the cook, wearing a high straw hat, black dirty dress, her husky, husband coming out of the mud hut, and pigs and dogs running about.

My guide is tiny, thirty-four years old, married only three months. He has a large black pimple, the exact shape of a black bean along the side of his nose and wears a twenty-gallon straw hat. All along the trip, he stopped momentarily at roadside statues and crosses, dismounted, crossed himself, said a prayer, and deposited a coin in a box, before mounting he crossed himself again. I do not laugh. I'm Catholic myself, but that's too much. Anyway, I have a fine, honest guide.

All day the trip was up and down steep mountains, some bare and dry, others full of jungle foliage, along narrow mountain cliffs and deep gorges, but always a rocky trail. The mules had wonderful stamina and stumbled but a few times. At times it looked impossible to get over high rocks or to drop to lower level without falling, but they managed.

At 2:30 within a jungle, it started raining. My guide gave me a rubber poncho. It sure came in handy. He had another for himself. We rode into fog, and the cold was biting. We rode over the Cuchilla, a mountaintop, shaped like a knife's edge. There was a thin trail, and to the left and right were steep slopes. We followed the knife's edge for about a mile, praying that the mules would not stumble. For the fall off the edge would mean certain death. My guide preferred to walk over it.

At 6:00, we could see Zororanga on a mountainside from a hilltop. Dusk was falling and the rain slowed to a fine drizzle. Soon it became dark and the lights of Zororanga looked near. They were deceiving. It was a long ride on tired mules through pitch darkness; the lights disappeared around a mountain curve. I could not see my guide. I barely saw the sharp-pointed ears on my mules head. The road was a dark dizzy blur before my eyes. Only the sound of the mule ahead told me we were close together. My guide remarked, "The mules know the trail well." We rode on the edge of steep embankments, and down rocky slopes, across streams without stumbling.

Soon we passed outskirting farm houses of mud; candles lighted up the darkness as farmers looked out into the night, dogs barked as we rode by. I couldn't help thinking about days of yore (old) when the only mode of travel was on horseback and the traveler seeking lodging for the night at strange places.

So it be there; the only possible way to reach Zororanga is on horseback or afoot. No modern car, boat or plane could reach it. We arrived in Zororanga about eight o'clock. Thirteen hours after leaving Cariamanga. It was dimly lit by lanterns and candles. All the buildings were very low. A large square courtyard made up the center of town. We rode catty-corner across it and stopped under an overhanging roof of a house. We dismounted and my guide inquired about a room. Travelers were rare, especially white foreigners. The man of the house pointed out a bed. I remarked, "It's occupied." There were suits and briefcases about. The man said, "It's mine; you can sleep there tonight." I felt I was intruding, but the man would not listen to my objections. "None of that," he said.

I sat on the bed; the entire crowd that had gathered when we rode into town, entered the room, formed a circle and stared at me in the dim light of the candle. *My gosh,* I thought, *am I a freak or have these folks never seen a white man before?* Soon my host got them out, inquiring about my age. He said I was young to be traveling alone in a place like this.

A kindly looking lady prepared supper of onions, rice, (slightly greasy, but tasty) pork and sweet cakes. This was my Easter dinner that I dreamt about. What a strange way to spend the holiday. Today was Easter Sunday. I turned in early, using my host's poncho for a blanket.

I awoke Easter Monday to ringing church bells. I waited for my guide to knock. He was an hour late. I suspected he might have run off and returned to Cariamanga. I looked out into the courtyard; our mules were tied to a pole in the center of it. A boy told me my guide was in church. I should have known. I felt sorry I thought bad about him.

No water to wash up, breakfast the same as last night's dinner. My guide came, prepared the mules, crossed himself, then mounted. Everyone seemed to know him. They gave him money and messages to carry to friends and relatives in Macará. One would believe he was a "Pony Express rider." We rode out of town, everyone waved, said *"Vaya Bien."* The villagers had talked of dangers along the trail; the principal menace were bandits. It was a beautiful day and I decided not to let the tales worry me.

The trail was level and better except for one long steep trying, mountain climb and descent. It was wide and so steep that we had to walk the mules in a crisscross fashion to gain distance. The mules were a bit lazy and for no reason stumbled a lot on the level. My peon guide laughed. "It's a peculiararity with them, on rough terrain, they hold solid, on level they stumble."

At noon we stopped to lunch on some brown sugar-cane candy in the shade of trees by a cool river. The mules liked the candy also. It cost one sucre a kilo. After eating it we drank a gallon of clear river water.

We followed the Macará River all afternoon. It's the boundary between Peru and Ecuador. On both sides of the river were green forests and mountians. The river was very deep, rough and choppy in places.

It had been cool in the green hills of Zororanga, but it became hot and dry as we entered the sandy, desertlike valley of Macara in the late afternoon. Outskirting houses seemed to be made of sticks and the only reason for shelter was against the hot sun.

The center of town has a cobblestone street running a main line for several blocks. Not a vehicle in sight, but plenty of horses and donkeys. No hotels either, at the *aduana* (immigration) a boy said his mom had rooms. His mom ran a utility store. I ate and waited as her children swept and cleaned up the room. It was mud-plastered and whitewashed and the biggest I have ever seen, twenty-five feet square.

Few strangers come to Macará; as I walk down the sidewalks, past people lounging in hammocks, they all look curiously, all necks turn automatically. I stop for dinner at a tiny restaurant and natives watch the "spectacle" through an open doorway. I return to my room and leave the door ajar for light; natives gather and watch the "spectacle." I'd like to send a boot at them; instead I quietly close the door.

I was wishing Manuel Delgado of New York were there, he is a Latin and probably we could dig up some fun, the native way.

37
Over the Desert to Lima, Peru

Seven weeks after leaving Macuto, Venezuela, I crossed over the Macará River into Peru, the country with four seasons the year around, the country that has much to offer to the traveler. The land of enchantment and mystery, the land of the Incas. Peru is the cradle of the oldest civilization in South America. If we go back only as far as the Inca Empire, a search for its source would take us back into unrecorded time.

It is a land of deserts, jungles, and snow-capped mountains, and a land of contrasts. Standing within walking distance of age-old ruins are ultra-modern hotels that satisfy the most fastidious traveler. Standing also are remains of her Spanish heritage, her power and prestige during the Spanish reign. The history of Peru is magnificent.

In the north, Ecuador and Colombia border her boundaries; to the east, Brazil and Bolivia; the south, Chile. To the west lies the Pacific Ocean. Peru is divided into three parts, La Costa (the coast), La Sierra (the Andes), La Montaña (the jungle region). These account for her climatic change and four seasons. Peru has nearly two-thousand miles of coast line. In each of her three regions, the Peruvian government has erected a strategic network of tourist hotels. They are modern and convenient, but a hitchhiker never knows if he will reach them before nightfall.

On the morning of March 30, I cleared immigration at Macará. The officials kept my tourist *cedula* (permit). This annoyed me. It was a nice souvenir.

I walked towards the river; the road and fields were flooded. I waded in mud and water up to my knees. The river was about three hundred yards wide, the water was deep and swift. It would be a hard crossing with a full pack on my back. Indian boys made the crossing on big mules. Little donkeys couldn't make it.

I succeeded in bribing an Indian boy to rent me his mule. I got into his homemade saddle of wood. There were no stirrups, and the saddle was tipsy. I feared losing balance and dropping into the river, pack, camera, and all. The boy rode on the mule's rump; we waded out to the middle of the stream, the water coming above the horse's belly, we seemed to drift along. Then the Indian boy directed me to turn and head the horse downstream, and we catty-cornered for about three hundred feet to the other side. The boy had a knowledge of the deep and shallow spots. The crossing lasted about twenty minutes. It seemed like two hours. I nearly lost balance several times, as the mule tripped slightly. The boy seemed well satisfied with the fifteen cents I gave him.

On the Peruvian shore, the fields were flooded also. I walked over well-placed logs over mud and water ponds. On a hillside stood the village of Latina, the first town in Peru. Peruvian army officers "okayed" my entry and made a note of the passaport. "No stamp." Several soldiers tested the weight of my pack, grinned, said it was heavy. We shook hands on parting. It's a nice custom. Latins like to shake hands a lot.

The road was dusty and hot. The trees were dry and bare. There was very little green, a flock of goats mingled in the shade of several trees. The army officers had asked me to wait for the truck. I felt like walking.

An hour and a half later, the truck came along. I climbed aboard. The truck was full of Ecuadorean transients, dogs, chickens, beer bottles, etc. We rode along for a while, then the truck stopped at another army outpost. Because I was an American, I got special attention and was taken care of first.

The ride to Sullana lasted three hours. The country was flat and sandy, a real desert. Sparse trees and farms emerged only where there was irrigation. Sullana seemed very big after coming out of Ecuador. There were paved streets, a fine theater, and an interesting plaza. I checked in at the Grand Hotel and a badly needed shave cost me seven cents at a barber's.

The following day I registered again at the Office of Immigration at Sullana, as required by law. Soon after, with the pack on my back, I walked a dozen blocks out of town and started hitchhiking along an asphalt highway. A bus stopped, and for fourteen cents, I rode to Piura, a two and a half-hour ride.

I was surprised at the immenseness and cleanliness of the town. It was as modern as any in the United States. I walked through, and then for several hours, I walked along the black road. The land was flat, hot, and a perfect desert. I could see the heat waves.

A truck stopped and I rode behind with a girl for company to a town called Cincuenta (fifty). These were but a few houses built of sticks and straw. I had refreshment of orange juice and cheese sandwiches, then proceeded walking along the black road into the desert and hot sun.

Presently a truck came along, loaded with peons. I managed to squeeze into the cab beside a fat man, a thin man, a fat woman, and a thin woman. The lift lasted seven hours. The road was unpaved for long stretches. The crescent-shaped sand dunes were most interesting. They ranged from thirty feet to a hundred feet across and as high as fifteen feet. It was a wonderful trip because no one talked.

We arrived in Chiclayo in time for supper. My driver refused to accept the fare. He called me an *"Andarin."* At the Royal Hotel, I met Mr. Bassee of Seattle, Washington, a fellow who was trying to open new fishing industries in Peru. Together we strolled in the cool evening through the streets of Chiclayo. Mr. Bassee had only complains about the Latins.

"They are so backward and it is the fault of the Catholic Church. The church is what keeps them from progressing. They put millions into new churches with gold decorations. Why don't they put the money into schools, roads, and hospitals so the public can benefit by it?

"The businessmen don't trust one another as partners. They put two locks on a door and one cannot enter the office or store in the morning or noon unless the other comes."

I liked Chiclayo and decided to stay an extra day. Mr. Bassee was nice company outside of his complaints. A group of pretty Ecuadorean girls had come up from Lima and stopped at the hotel for dinner. Mr. Bassee and I had opportunity to dance with them in the lobby. We spent several enjoyable hours. They were en route north to Ecuador. Mr. Bassee was en route north also and was fortunate to get on the same bus with them. After they were gone, I was lonesome and sat at a sidewalk café drinking Cuba Libras (rum & Coke). After a movie I started for the hotel, I found the sidewalks lined with sleeping forms, wrapped up in blankets. They were natives waiting for the bus to leave at dawn.

I started the following day by getting up late. Something about breakfast or the previous night's food had made me quite ill.

The black road and wind-blown sand dunes stretched ahead of me as far as the eye could see. I let one or two bad rides (trucks) pass by. I thumbed the third, a clean-looking truck. I climbed aboard a pile of lumber alongside a young native girl. We stopped for dinner at a native café, had native food, then drove into Trujillo. The lift cost me nothing. It lasted all day. The country was an endless beautiful desert, full of cone-shaped sand dunes. The driver was courteous enough to drive me to the home of Daniel Guieterrez.

Daniel Guieterrez was one of my foremen at the airport in Maiguetía, Venezuela. He gave me his mom's address and asked me to extend greetings and say "Hello" when I reached Peru. I was most surprised and disappointed. His mom lived in a poor adobe house with a floor of mud. It seemed very crowded and small and not the least bit clean. His mom was very surprised at my presentation. She accepted and acknowledged her son's regards, but she could hardly ask me to enter because of her poor home.

Coming from a poor home like that, I could only say, "Daniel Guieterrez has done very well for himself."

The truck driver was kind enough to drive me many streets to the fine government tourist hotel.

Trujillo is an ultra-modern city with beautiful churches, parks, theaters, hotels, etc. In Trujillo, I lingered for several days, taking in the points of interest, the church, the museum, the bull fights, and the sea side.

On Saturday I rode a truck twenty-five kilometers north of Trujillo to Chiclin's. It was an enormous hacienda. It was constructed by a Peruvian millionaire. There were many pink colored adobe homes for the workers. There were beautiful parks and statues of angels. Within the hacienda was a fine museum.

I rang a doorbell for admission. A pretty girl answered. She became my interpreter and took me on a tour of the museum's contents. There were about a dozen rooms. Some were about twenty feet square, others were oblong and easily one-hundred feet long. In the square rooms were shelves full of pots, vases, jugs. Each had figures of animals, serpents, and faces. The girl interpreted in Spanish the meaning of the various shapes and forms. In other rooms were ornaments, weapons, and pieces of cloth. All these had been excavated from graves and were no less than five hundred years old.

In the oblong room were glass cases or coffins. There were about eight of them. As we walked along, the girl pulled back the covers and revealed the Indian skeletons. Many of the skeletons were only half-decomposed and still retained burial clothing.

There were several smaller glass cases. These contained skeletons of children. They had been buried sitting up, with the arms folded over the knees. These were demonstrated nicely. The last exhibition consisted of shrunken heads from Ecuador and golden headdresses, earrings, necklaces, bracelets, and rings taken from a guarded safe.

At the end of the tour, a card was presented for a donation. I was surprised when the girl brought me change. The fee was ridiculously low.

Returning to Trujillo, I boarded a gondola (bus) to the beach. It was my first sight of the Pacific Ocean after leaving Macuto, Venezuela, fifty-two days ago. "Buenos Aires" beach was disappointing. Dark gray sand lined the beach, chilly, shabby buildings, and few people were about.

On Sunday I went to church; it was large, beautifully designed, and decorated in gold carvings, especially the picture frames and the altar. It had a large Sunday crowd.

In the late afternoon, I went to a bull fight. The matador (bull fighter) was not good. The crowd yelled at him to stand still and not to dance or move as the bull charged by. (A good bull fighter never moves, no matter how close the bull's horns may come, even if it means injury or death. The matador got knocked down once and a second time got his leg hurt. My stomach was in my mouth many times because he was an amateur and stood facing the bull dead center instead of standing to one side or the other. The crowd noticed his fault and let him know it.

There were several elderly assistant bull fighters, one was heavy set. They were experts, skillful and graceful. They only tired the bull out with their cape, for the sword.

The comedian put on a good show. He was dressed in long underwear. His trousers hung at a crazy degree, six inches below the rump, his face striped with black paint and a comical hat that kept falling off.

Twice he somersaulted over the bull's head, placing prongs in its neck at the same time. The third time the bull got wise and threw its head upward, but the comedian was wiser; he placed his prongs in the bull's neck, but did not somersault over; instead he dropped and rolled under the bull and away. The stunt was marvelous, and the crowd thundered applause. It was one of the greatest stunts I'd ever seen.

He placed an arm affectionately around the bull's neck; the angry bull stood still, dumbfounded. With one hand he patted the bull's head; with the other, he plunged a short knife into its vital spot, behind the head; the bull dropped dead. The crowd laughed and cheered.

The comedian killed two bulls and cut off the ears and tail of one for the benefit of the crowd.

The bulls were pulled out of the arena by an old model Ford. Everyone laughed at this new method of removal. Customarily, they were removed by a team of mules or horses.

I opened up the dining room, the day I left Trujillo for Lima. The sleepy waiter turned on the lights and served me good old ham and eggs. It was gray dawn as I walked out of town into the open desert. I advanced a mile or so. I looked back. I could see the drawn line between the yellow desert and the plush green farms of Trujillo. No traffic moved and I was almost afraid to advance farther into the desert. I carried no water canteen, and Lima was hundreds of miles away.

Nothing lay ahead except the black road and open, endless,

307

windswept sand dunes. Three and a half hours, I walked, then I thumbed the only moving vehicle, a yellow bus.

"Going to Lima?" I asked.

"Yes, sir," the husky driver answered.

He drove terribly fast, almost recklessly, about sixty-five miles per hour. The road was fine but not very wide. On passing cars going the opposite way, he didn't slow down, but stepped it up. Sand blown on the highway made it hazardous, like a snow drift.

We stopped for dinner at Chimbote, a crude, Western-style frontier town. It was a seaport.

We follow the sea coast and what beautiful beaches, and sand dunes, for miles and miles on our right and to our left the foothills of the Andes, covered with sand in colors of white, yellow, tan, brown, and gold.

An hour before Lima, we rode along the lip of sand-covered mountain. We could see the sea crashing against the mountainside below. What a drop, wow!

Night fell, the road drifted with sand. It became a hazard. Now a peculiar custom and a law in Peru is: the driver blinks lights on and off for at least a hundred yards when approaching one another. How they manage to see in the pitch darkness momentarily is beyond me. It's a wonder they don't crash into one another or go off the road. Trucks and buses travel without frame lights.

We arrived in Lima at 7:30. I was dropped off in the center of town and was charged half-fare for the bus ride. There had only been two other passengers. The nearest hotel was the Crillon, the newest in Lima. I entered with pack, boots, and all, and the people in the lobby did look. At the desk I was told, "We have no single rooms. How long do you intend to stay?" "One week," I answered.

"In that case we can give you a double room at the price of a single one," the clerk said. Cost $2.50 per night. Only the Bolívar Hotel was slightly more expensive but not as modern. Imagine me, a hitchhiker, sleeping in the best hotel in the capital of Peru.

I fairly danced around my room. It was so nice, comfortable, luxuriant. It was light green, twin beds, telephone, private bath, and a front room facing the street. I had truly expected to be turned away because of my dress, but the clerk must have taken me for an engineer.

38

Lima, the Garden City of Peru

Lima is the capital and chief city of Peru. It is situated on the River Rimac, eight miles from the Pacific port of Callao. Lima has a population bordering well on a million. It has one of the best airfields in all America, and a seaport visited by ships from all over the world.

Lima is known as Peru's "Garden City." She has flowers everywhere, the year around. It is surrounded by beautiful residential suburbs with board avenues, magnificent parks, and sumptuous old and new buildings. The scenery and climate make it a wonderful haven, and in recent years it has adopted a more cosmopolitan air, a bustling activity that daily has become more noticeable.

Its notable buildings include the historic Palace built by Pizarro in 1535, which served as the residence of the Spanish viceroys. The Roman Catholic Cathedral, San Marcas University, and the National Museum, noted for its relics. Her heroes are San Martín and Simón Bolívar. She gained independence in 1821.

Tradition and legend have led many a traveler to think that Lima is a city of the past, romantic but dull. But the fact is that she has progressed on a level with the most modern cities of our time.

My stay in Lima was limited to eight days. Letters of introduction and addresses to friends in Peru from my friends in Venezuela helped a lot towards making my visit in Lima a pleasant one.

One of these letters was from my buddy Victor Delgado, whom I'd worked with at Taca, to his bother Angel. The Delgados were quite well-to-do. No wonder Victor was so carefree and a spend-thrift. His brother Angel was a prominent lawyer, and his father and another brother owned an auto repair shop.

Angel was a little fellow, quiet and likable. One would never believe he was a successful lawyer. He was only twenty-eight. He called for me at the hotel in a 1930 Plymouth car, dressed in a white linen suit. We drove out to the Athletic Club. Angel drove in the most peculiar manner. He rolled up the windshield a bit, stooped low over the steering wheel, and peered through the opening. He drove about fifty miles an hour and kept his eyes on the road. Traffic was heavy. He surprised me by crossing himself every time we passed a church. I don't believe he saw the church at the speed he was traveling, but he knew it was there. I almost laughed out loud.

The Club Salaverry had been founded by Italians, and I met some of Peru's best athletes here. I never suspected Victor belonged to such a fine club. Only members and guests were permitted entrance. It had a fine indoor gymnasium equipped with basketball, volley balls, bars for exercising, boxing, sword fighting, Ping-Pong tables, and a dining room, a bar and a place for dancing. Girls belonged to the club, and I met the queen of the year.

Outside was a grand football field and bleachers. Two teams played on the green. They were husky fellows, the game is very rough. They only use their head and feet to knock the ball around and try for a goal. Many times a fellow would kick the ball while it was in the air and land hard on his rump or back. They wore only shorts, tee shirts, socks and shoes, and no shoulder, knee, or elbow padding.

I met the players, and they asked many questions about their friend Victor. They could not understand why he had decided to leave his happy home and country for Venezuela.

We all had dinner together, then followed rounds of Peruvian pesco and wine. It was of good quality and I liked it. We drank many toasts to Victor, our countries, one another, and to health.

After goodness knows how many, we drank only to health (saluté) but in a peculiar fashion. Be there only five of us or ten, we waited and got attention of all present before we took a sip or swallow. Before a glass was empty, we gave saluté (health) about twenty times, and we sipped or swallowed simultaneously. The custom did not seem bad. I loved it.

When Angel drove me to the hotel, I believed it to be only twelve o'clock—it was three o'clock in the morning.

I had dinner with the boys three more times at the club, and one night all of us drove to a popular Chinese restaurant that was a favorite of Victor's when he was at home. Victor's father, another brother, Robert, and a dear friend of Victor's named Fernando joined us. We had chop suey with chicken, then fried pigeon and various wines and whiskey. I had to make my own opinions about world affairs, our policies, beliefs. They accepted my opinions with sincerest friendliness and keen interest.

After gosh knows how many bottles, we drove off to a private home, relatives of Victor's dad. One of the relatives had a birthday, wine, music, and dancing flowed freely. It was a happy party. The chap celebrating his birthday seemed offended when I asked his age. His expression seemed to say, "It's not a custom to ask such a question." Everyone laughed and I did not ask again.

Upon meeting and parting, it's a custom to shake hands. Back at the hotel, late again at three in the morning. The night clerk said, "It's getting to be a habit."

Angel, Ferenando, and several other athletes took me on a tour of the city. We spent an entire day sightseeing in Angel's car. We drove out to the seaport of Callao, then to a scenic rock and a beach called Aradura (horseshoe). The Aradura is very scenic at sunset. We visited monuments to Chaves, the first Peruvian pilot killed flying over the Alps in Europe. He was famous for his high-altitude flights.

We drove through the beautiful suburbs and parks outlining Lima. We ended the tour at Fernando's beautiful home. He has a fine collection of silverware and a fantastic collection of excavated Indian pottery. These could never be placed on display in a museum. They were too sexy. It kind of amazed me that the ancient Indian would spend his time doing this type of work. Nevertheless, they must have gotten a big bang out of life.

After a number of cocktails, the boys drove me to the hotel. I had a date with a certain young lady. It was the last time I saw

312

the boys. When I got out of the car, I started to say "Adios." It surprised me when they got out of the car also.

In the Spanish way, we embraced and patted one another's back. It's a custom I almost forgot; thus we parted, wishing one another luck and health. It was no joke. They wanted to be sincere friends. I cannot say anything derogatory about them. They refused to let me pay at all times for dinner, wine, pisco and songs. Putting it mildly, they were swell.

The young lady I had a date with is Mrs. Shubert, the wife of a friend of mine in Macuto, Venezuela. When I left Macuto on my journey, Franc Shubert, an American, gave me his wife's address in Lima, Peru. She would fly to Lima in a month or two, and perhaps we could meet each other if we got to Lima at the same time. It took me thirty days by road. It took her two days by plane. As fortune would have it, we did meet and it was a pleasant surprise.

I called at her home on Bolivia Street, and I must say she had several beautiful sisters. We went to dinner at the Trocaderos (one of the best restaurants in Lima), then to the Embassy Night Club, the best in Lima, just off the Plaza San Martín.

Mrs. Shubert was wearing "the new look." Spanish girls preferred it so. We danced to Spanish and English orchestras. There were two, one for the benefit of the English guests, the other for the benefit of the Spanish guests. Each orchestra played an hour, then was relieved by the other. This went on all evening, a pleasant arrangement.

A famous lady bull fighter was there. She sat right across from us at the next table. She was the center of attraction for many. Mrs. Shubert told me all about her, and I was tempted to ask her to dance. Mrs. Shubert held me in place.

She told me how she had met her husband on a blind date. He was so tall that she refused to go out with him on a second date. She felt like a child beside him. She was about 4 foot 2 and Franc was 6 foot 5. Franc kept calling her up and he really loved her. He had good reason to; she was very pretty, spoke English well. Franc, for all his height, was built nice and very good looking. He trusted his wife; that was why I got the address.

We danced till a very late hour, three in the morning. It was a lovely evening, so fine that I wondered, why in hell I hit the dusty, dirty, muddy road. My time should be spent every night at a place like this.

Mrs. Shubert and I had other dates. I called at her home one morning. We took a cab out to her brother-in-law's home. His name was Otto Vasseur. At one time Otto was engaged to Mrs. Shubert, but when she decided to marry Franc, Otto married her sister. He was very upset at the time. Now he had a child and had gotten over his old love affair.

Otto worked for an American concern and spoke English well. He taught his wife how to make Swiss dinners. It was my first. We went driving out to Miraflores, the beautiful section of town, to the beach and to the airport. I talked to some of the American mechanics with Panagna. They said there were good chances to get a job. They seemed to welcome another American in their midst. "Hell, stay a while, work a week; if you don't like it, quit." The prospects looked good, but I did not wish to stay.

In the evening Mrs. Shubert and I took in the movie, the Trocadero, and the Bolívar Night Club at the Bolívar Hotel. We danced a lot and the Mrs. had to hold me tight. I felt like jitter-bugging and spinning her. "No, no, no," she said, "this is a refined club."

At the hotel one morning, I was surprised and pleased to meet Mr. Bassee again, the American I had met in Chiclayo and who had so many gripes. Today he had another.

While walking down the street, a fellow came up from behind and snatched his hat off his head. Mr. Bassee believed someone was playing a joke at first. The fellow ran pell mell down the street and disappeared into some buildings. Mr. Bassee called them, "Thieving bastards is what they are."

Mr. Delgado, a few days ago, had a fine one to tell. One of his mechanics had been cleaning a crankshaft just outside of the garage doors, near the street. The mechanic walked off for a smoke and returned to find the heavy crankshaft gone. Now, who in hell would steal a crankshaft?

I had a sad experience myself. I had been walking in the business district near Plaza San Martín. A young fellow saun-

314

tered up and said, "Hey, look, mister," and in a sly way, he showed me a beautiful gold ring. I never trusted these street vendors, but I'd been told it was customary and the boys get a commission from the jewelers. The jewelers sent these boys out to hunt the tourists and sell the articles.

The boy said, "I stole this. What will you give me for it?" We moved out of the crowded walks to a curb. "What do you want for it?" I asked. "Two hundred soles," he said. "Go on, you stole it, I'll never give you that, I'll give you fifty, take it or leave it," I said. He refused and I walked off. He came after me and said, "Okay, fifty soles."

I bought the ring. It was beautiful, heavy and had Indian carvings and a twenty-carat gold stamp inside. I really got a bargain for four dollars, I thought. Several days later I realized I had been robbed. My finger became black, the gold came off and the bronze came out. The twenty-carat marking was a phony. Boy, was I mad. If ever I found that boy again, I'd clean his "clock."

In Peru the stock market fluctuated a lot. The dollar might drop from eighteen soles one day to ten, eight, or even six the next day. At the U.S. Consul, one can learn the value of the dollar day to day. It is an honest bet to call there first before buying or selling dollars.

At the present the dollar had been staying at 14 soles or a little better for several days. Mr. Bassee and I called the consulate. It was 14.20 soles to a dollar. We went to a bank. The teller at the window said 14.20 to a dollar. We signed our checks at a counter, another clerk marked, "Pay 14 to 1 dollar." "The fellow at the window said 14.20 to 1," we complained. "The market just dropped this minute," the clerk said. We shrugged and said, "Okay."

After eight days in Lima, I felt it was like Cleveland or Detroit. Streetcars went two (2) together as in all big cities, and modern buses helped to increase the aspect. The smell of burning metal and rattle at streetcars was music to my ears.

I usually ate at the hotel, as much as I liked the sidewalk cafés, or yearned to dine in different atmospheres; there were always peddlers to annoy me. During one meal, it is not unusual to say "No" to ten or fifteen people. This goes on and on every day. At the hotel it was peaceful and peddlers were not allowed. It cost a little more, but the peace was worth it.

In the barroom I met so many Americans who stayed at the hotel. A U.S. Army mission stayed here also. They all liked Peru.

39

The Road to Arequipa

The road to Arequipa is on the coastal region of Peru. It follows the Pacific Ocean 1,100 kilometers from Lima, south to Arequipa. It is built along an expanse of desert.

The day I started, I waited for Angel Delgado. He came at 8:00 in the morning. We called on Mrs. Shubert and said "Adios." Angel was swell. He drove quite slowly. We stopped for breakfast at a little village. He wanted to take me back to Lima and put me on a bus to Arequipa.

"No thanks," I said, "this is where we part." We embraced and said "Good-bye." I walked along the macadam road. Angel returned to Lima. I thought to myself, *Boy, Angel sure is swell.* On my right was the blue sea, on my left the foothills of La Sierra (Andes Mountains) and all about was the hot sandy desert.

Several cars and trucks whisked by; an hour later a truck came to a stop. There was no room in the cab, so I climbed aboard and sat on gasoline drums. At various villages we stopped to pick up or drop off passengers, cargo, chicken, fish, etc.

All day I rode on the hard barrels, my rump hurt. The hot sun dipped in golden splendor into the Pacific as we moved along. Soon darkness fell and with it a cold chill. One of the fellows in the cab gave me a warm poncho. I was very grateful. The lift ended only six kilometers out of Pisco at a junction.

From the junction I walked to Pisco. It was very dark; a crescent moon glided along the sky. An irrigation ditch followed the road, and tropical foliage was abundant. The stench of a dead cow filled the air, and I hurried by. An hour and a half later, I walked into the small, but interesting town of Pisco. My boots sounded loudly on the sidewalks, and folks looked after me curiously. I checked in at Hotel Pisco. In a strange fashion, I had to

317

enter my room from the street. My key must have weighed a half a pound.

The following day I hit the road late. A bus gave me a lift to the junction on the main highway. "No charge to *Andarins*," the driver said. Soon afterwards I caught a truck going to Ica. We arrived at noon and had dinner at a cheap restaurant. I felt out of place among the low-class workers.

The fellows had a cargo of cement to unload. They would be going to Chala, about three-hundred kilometers farther south. I decided to wait. I lay in shade in cool grass near a large church and read events of *Time*. At four o'clock they said, "Let's go." We made a few stops, then they said, "We are only going thirty kilometers more, then we sleep. You are welcome to come along." At the truck stop was another truck. The fellow said he would be going to Chala.

"When?" I asked.

"*Ya mismo,*" (right now) he answered.

As I suspected "*Ya mismo*" lasted two hours. Dusk was falling and I got tried of waiting. I retrieved my pack from the truck and headed for Hotel Colon.

I cleaned up and changed clothes, went out for a walk. Outside the hotel, sitting at a table, was a pleasant looking young fellow. "Hello," I said, "are you the fellow I heard speaking English in the hallway?" "No," he said and offered me a seat and a drink.

He was a Swiss, the second I'd ever met. Strangely enough he knew Otto Vasseur, the Swiss I had dinner with in Lima. We had a drink called "Chilcano." It was fine. My friend came to Peru ten years ago. He lived alone with Latins working in the Sierras (mountains) on a dairy farm.

Later we had dinner at the hotel, then went to a movie. We were two blondes among a theater full of black heads.

I hated to get up the next day. I walked out of the grimy town. It had all the appearances of La Guaira, Venezuela, crowded with truck drivers, farmers, donkey carts, laborers, and commercials. Soon I was out in the open desert and the ten o'clock sun beat down heavily.

A half-hour later, I got a lift in an empty truck except for three or four fellows who had all the appearances of being peons (low class Indian or half-breeds). They asked questions. I didn't feel like talking, kept quiet and read a magazine. They took the hint. As one of them stretched out, he wore shoes, but his ankles and legs were caked with mud. It was evidence enough that he wore shoes and better clothes only when going to town.

For a long while, I rode atop the cab. I had a bird's-eye view of the black road, the desert, the sea, and the sandy mountains. Later in the afternoon, it became cold and windy. I climbed down and sat behind the cab.

We stopped at Chala for a short time, then proceeded. Without the fine government tourist hotel facing the sea, Chala is only another poor native village. Only the sea, crashing on the rocky reefs, was very impressive. It'd been a long drive from Ica to Chala, and the tourist hotel is properly located for motorists. The truck was going a hundred kilometers farther south, and I decided to stay with it. It became cold and miserable in the back of the truck. The sand whipped up, hurt, and filled my eyes. I decided to keep my dark glasses on for protection, even though the sun had sunk into the Pacific several hours ago.

We finally came to a stop. It was Atico, a mere truck stop. It was like an oasis in that vast desert. There were five or six adobe houses on the left side of the road. Two of them were restaurants and lodging houses. It was very dark. I joined the driver and passengers at a crude table by kerosene lamp. All of us were very hungry. It was an awful place to be stuck overnight, but it could be a lot worse on the cold desert. We dined on crude soup, rice, eggs, black coffee, and bananas.

My bed wasn't bad. It had a thin mattress and a spring underneath, no boards. The floor had been washed with gasoline to disinfect it. It was still wet and smelly. Nothing to do but turn in early.

I had slept fine and for breakfast had only black coffee. There seemed to be nothing to eat, no place to wash up. I started up the dirt road. From Atico, south, it was not paved, but good nevertheless. The morning was cool, cloudy, and breezy. The ocean nearby was so inviting. I walked, went swimming, sang, rested and read *Time*. It felt wonderful to be free in that strange land.

I had been advised the night before that little traffic went by on Saturdays. It was no lie. The first truck went by at 10:00 A.M. I had left at 5:00 A.M. The second truck came an hour later, loaded down with furniture. There didn't seem to be room enough for me anywhere, yet the driver was kind enough to stop and make room in the cab along with four other passengers.

Most all these trucks have a holy picture of Christ or angels posted over the windshield. At night a red bulb lights it up. All the drivers are very religious.

The fourth day out of Lima, nothing very exciting happened. It was a drive over mostly flat desert. There were seventeen kilometers of mountain road that was very dangerous and narrow. There was a sheer drop to the ocean below. It was breathtaking enough. That, and when we nearly collided with another truck on a curve. We had to back up a long ways and it was a tight squeeze.

At four o'clock I had my first food. What we had was really mulligan stew and black coffee. It was at a quaint little village of reeds, sticks, and bamboo. There were about a dozen of these simple bamboo houses and one of them displayed a very large sign—Hotel.

We rolled out into the sandy desert and mountains and watched the sun go down; and then the cold settled down on us. We closed the windows to shut it out. The wind-blown sand on the road felt like a soft rug or cushion as we rolled over. We arrived in Camaná in the early evening. The towns of northern Peru are much nicer than the southern towns.

I thanked the driver, he refused to accept the fare. He had asked to sign my legendary book. I told him I didn't carry any. The driver told me I had been robbed at last night's lodging. Cheap as it was, I paid five soles. He said it should only be two soles.

The town looks rough. I know there is a tourist hotel there. After a few brief inquiries, I located it. It is very modern but there is a lack of guests. The clerk says, "fourteen soles per night," but the price list in my room says eleven soles. We'll see what the clerk has to say in the morning.

Yesterday I had been quiet and blue, thinking of home; to-day I was thinking of home also and the merrier days at school. I thought about listening to "Gangbusters" on the radio and giving it for public-speaking talks in class. I recited the first two lines of the poem "Casey Jones was an engineer, tried to go to heaven on a bottle of beer."

My teacher got angry and said, "Sit down." Everyone laughed; thereafter I was called "Casey Jones" for a long time. I got an "E" for that talk. To mom I explained an "E" means "Excellent" on my report card.

"Oh, yeah!" said my kid sister.

As I reminisced, I laughed to myself. I found the passengers watching me, wondering what it was all about. Other thoughts were of the days I played "hookey" (truant) from school with four of my pals, the "Buccaneers," riding bicycles and playing football in the leaves in the woods. Mom would ask at noon or after school, "How in the world do you get so dirty?"

"Playing football in gym, Mom," I answered.

"Oh, yeah!" my sister would chime in.

Another laugh was the day when my buddy Frank started a fire drill. We were in our music class. Frank had a sling shot and staples. He was quietly aiming at the fire alarm on the wall. The class was busy studying and the teacher preoccupied. "Go ahead, Frank," I whispered.

Neither he nor I expected him to hit it. It was at least twenty-five feet away. It was a direct hit. The glass broke and the alarm went on. Everybody jumped up, got in line, and marched out with the entire school body, 1,500 strong.

I slept very little at the tourist hotel. My bill for night's lodging was 16.35 soles, including tax. The night clerk was asleep and the waiters took care of it. I had a notion to have him awakened, but decided not to—the reason—would be a waste of time.

The clean white hotel with becoming terraces and gardens is the only nice thing about the town. Even the central plaza is uncared for. I walked down narrow sidewalks. The natives and Indians moved into the gutter respectfully. A few bolder ones called out some remark or another in broken English. I stopped to take a picture. One native sidled up. "Speak English?" "No," I answered. "Speak Italian?" he asked again. "No," I said. "I speakie Filipino." A white man gets tired of answering and talking to low-class Indians and half-breeds in dirty clothes. So I didn't waste time talking and proceeded walking by donkeys, Indians, mud, and reed houses, till I came to the end of town. Nothing lay ahead except the endless sandy beach, the sea, and the foothills of the Andes.

Some time went by, then a truck came along, always trucks, trucks, trucks. I climbed aboard among a dozen Indians, loose baggage, chickens, and dogs. One Indian woman was drunk. She had her front teeth missing and was filthy. She sang some dizzy ballads. The fellows laughed and cheered her on; actually they were laughing at her and "pulling her leg." She had a lovely daughter, and the child pleaded with her to be quiet. Boy, was I glad when she got off.

At noon we stopped for dinner at a village. It was hot, dry, and an arid place. The natives occupied the tables and benches within the reed restaurant. I sat atop a wine barrel at a lonely table. Bits of pork in my soup still had traces of hair. I could not eat raw fish the way the natives did. I sufficed on vegetables.

The country is a grape region, wherever they have irrigation. The fruit on display had hundreds of flies sitting on them.

We started out again, then the truck stalled. Dirt had entered the fuel lines. I expected that when I watched peon helpers place a dirty, sandy hose into the gasoline tank. I dozed off while the fellows cleaned the lines. I awoke with my cheek burning from the hot sun. It wasn't pleasant sitting with a load of Indians. Soon we got started again over sandy plains, then through a tunnel in mountain, then upwards into the dry, barren mountain.

In the late afternoon, we neared Arequipa. Mount Misti, that lofty and perfectly formed sentinel, the most admired and most noted peak of the Andes, stood majestically over the Cuidad Blanca (White City) of Arequipa, the metropolis of southern Peru.

On the outskirts we stopped at a mud house for dinner. The

driver said, "Meals are more expensive in the city." I entered the restaurant for the sake of curiosity. The floors were of mud. Natives sat at long wooden tables, eating and drinking enormous glasses of homemade beer. They offered me some. It tasted bitter, sour, and alcoholic. The fellows tried persuading me to drink more unsuccessfully. I asked for coffee. *"No hay,"* the lady said.

I asked for Coke. *"Si, Si,"* she said.

Native dinner and Coke cost me ten cents.

I climbed aboard the truck. Several pretty girls stopped and questioned me till the truck pulled us apart.

It was Sunday, sunny and warm. We were on the outskirts of Arequipa. Along the road were picnickers in the shade of trees along rushing irrigation ditches, surrounded by flowers and grassy lawns.

Arequipa is called the White City and the Sunshine City because of its many white homes and year around sunshine. It is 7,500 feet above sea level. The altitude gives a most exhilarating tang to the air without the difficult breathing and other disagreeable sensations felt at higher altitudes. Arequipa has streetcars, buses, taxi cabs, beautiful churches, plazas lined with palm trees, modern hotels, and many other fine buildings.

A truck driver stopped in a lowly part of town. No charge. I walked thirteen blocks to the lovely, pink-colored tourist hotel amidst flower gardens, lawns, lagoons, stepping-stone walks and Western-style corral fences. It was located at the edge of town, at the foot of Mount Misti.

After a shower and change of clothes, I came down to the lobby. What a pleasant surprise to meet by the fireside, Mrs. Huntsman and Mrs. Webster, the two American tourists I had met at the Gremlin House in Quito. We had much to talk about. The low cost of my trip from Ecuadorean border to there had cost me seventeen soles (about $1.50), a distance of approximately 1,400 miles. That was most impressive.

I have come to the conclusion that I break out even. Most hotels and restaurants have a tendency to overcharge Americans. The fact that I don't have to pay for transportation covers my losses at the hotels and restaurants. I only regret that the undeserving get my money.

My stay in Arequipa was very short. Two days to be exact. One day Mrs. Huntsman and Mrs. Webster asked me if I cared to join them in visiting a rug factory.

"I'd be glad to," I said.

We started out after dinner. The ladies had been resting and vacationing there for a week and knew their way about the city. "We get on any old bus or trolley, then try to find our way back," they said. For two ladies in their 40's, they sure get around. We rode a bus to the plaza (center of town), then we rode an old-time streetcar well out of town to the rug factory. The ladies refused to let me pay their fare. They were typical of American tourists abroad. They believed in the Dutch custom—"You pay yours, and I'll pay mine." Tourists travel on a strict budget.

The rug factory didn't look like a rug factory. It was a huge adobe building. There was a brass placard on the wall with a prominent name on it. We rang the door bell for admission.

There was a large, bare patio in the center, and surrounding it were rooms. In each of these rooms, Indians were busy at work on large looms. There was an attempt at machinery in one corner. The majority were spinning by hand with an instrument that looked and twirled like a top.

Mrs. Huntsman got the Indians to sit in the sun in the patio. There they squatted on the stone floor and spun their tops. One lady had a top spinning between her large toe. They all were barefooted. They wore derby hats and bright orange, yellow, or red shawls or blankets about themselves. We then took color pictures of them and gave out tips.

We returned to town and back to the hotel. The ladies would be leaving tonight for Cuzco by night train in a sleeper. I would be leaving in the morning by road.

40

Lodging in Andean Mud Huts

I had slept fine at the tourist hotel. I was plenty excited about hitting the road to Cuzco, the Empire of the Incas. The Pan-American road does not go by Cuzco. It goes east to Puno, then south to La Paz, Bolivia, and Chile. The road to Cuzco goes east, then north for 644 kilometers.

I felt funny going into the dining room of this fine hotel in boots, blue jeans, and field jacket, but it was the only type of clothing suitable for the highway traveler. I had a double order of hot cakes. Boy, do these cooks put on the syrup. Wow!

When I checked out, they gave me a bill that was a double order also: 99.80 soles. I hadn't expected more than 40 soles. I had asked in advance. The clerk said 25 soles per day. I could only complain, period.

I rode a bus into town. I asked a policeman, "How do I get on the road to Cuzco?" He decided to guide me through a maze of Indians and a market place to a lowly, grimy bus station. I became angry. All I wanted was to get on the road and stop a bus or truck as it came along. I couldn't expect him to understand. He had probably never heard of "hitchhiking."

A lady at the dingy bus station said, "A bus will leave at five in the afternoon. Why don't you wait?" It made me mad; they actually wanted me to wait ten hours. The policeman (in U.S. Army clothes) noticed my expressions and finally decided to direct me. I told him I would walk.

I walked a few blocks, then took a bus for twenty centimos to a junction. He went right and I took the left fork. I walked several miles to a place called Jesus. Here was a mineral water plant and a few houses. There the paved road ended. Now it was dirt again. I continued walking upgrade around a mountain curve. The green valleys and snow-covered Mount Misti were very scenic. The hot sun started to give me a headache.

Off in the distance, in the valley I saw a truck moving up the road. I hoped it wouldn't stop at the mineral water plant. It didn't stop. It came around the mountain curve and stopped for me. Inside the cab I met a Senor Herrea and his son, Herman, a handsome looking boy.

We climbed all day. The mountains changed from dry, barren to rich, green, and rocky. We looked on the picturesque winding road below. Soon we passed grazing llamas, alpacas, vicunas. They were the first ones I'd ever seen. They are beautiful, graceful creatures. I loved to watch them run in a semicircle, in a gliding, rocking fashion and heads held high.

Soon we are in the clouds. It gets terribly cold. I put on two extra sweaters under my field jacket. We stop at lonely solitary huts. An Indian comes forward. Mr. Herrea and son measure out potatoes, maize, chuno, quaker and duransno in an old antique scale. These solitary Indians maintain the road. The government, through Mr. Herrea, brings them food supplies.

It starts raining and hailing ice. My feet are cold and I wonder how in H—these Indians go about barefooted. Some of the huts are tents, then others of mud, and still others of stone. More and more stone huts as we go along. There are more and more llamas, alpacas, and vicunas roaming the grassy hills as we move along.

In the late afternoon, shivering cold we reach Paty, a community of three or four houses between kilometer 115 and 116. The houses are made of mud and stone. A number of stone fences surround the place. Dusk is falling. It is cold, gray, misty, damp and dismal. I wonder why anyone should want to live at a dreary place like that.

Peons unload our cargo of grain, potatoes, and so forth into one of the houses. I'm invited to enter the house and offered a seat on a bench. It is very cold, and the owner of the house puts a blanket on it for me. Then the owner, who is an elderly Indian, named Luis Hanon, brings forth hot, black coffee and dry bread biscuits (hard tack). I'm very hungry and the biscuits taste good. Anything does on a hungry gut.

The floor is damp mud and even though I wear boots, two pair of cotton, one pair of heavy woolen socks, my feet are still cold. Senor Luis seems to notice it and puts a heavy sheepskin under my feet. This courtesy overwhelms me and I wonder who am I to deserve such treatment? He also gives me a heavy blanket to put over my shoulders to keep warm.

Soon it becomes dark. Candles and lanterns were lit. We sat on the bench along the mud wall, and I answered their questions about the United States, my trip, and likewise listened to their tales. A few of the fellows had been in the Peruvian navy and had traveled north as far as the Canal Zone. Others had traveled to Peru, Chile, Bolivia, and Argentina. They had dreams of seeing the U.S., but they were a little too old now to try again.

In that room full of barrels, bags, bottles, cans, and boxes, there was a warm atmosphere of friendliness and peace. I was surprised about two hours later. Senor Luis started bringing in hot soup, with large pieces of ham in it, bread, then hot tea from another room. The soup was flat, but the meat was fine. We ate with the forks nature gave us. Not long afterwards, some of us started getting sleepy. Two wooden beds were pulled together and six fellows slept across it in all their clothes, blankets and ponchos.

Somewhere they got a U.S. Army canvas cot. Mr. Luis placed heavy llama skins on it. I lay down on the comfortable fur, then covered myself with a blanket. Another blanket was placed atop me by a fellow. Then Luis topped it off with another llama skin. With my clothes on and all those covers, I felt warm, but I must admit there was a foul odor somewhere in those skins. It was impossible to be warm without them. It was just as cold inside the mud house as outside, except for the wind. My roommates laughed at my chills. I blamed the change in climate. After thirteen months in the tropics of Panama and Venezuela, my blood had thinned out.

At midnight, Senor Luis awoke me. He thought he heard a truck coming. We went outside, climbed over swells of molten lava to the road. It was so cold. I thought I'd freeze to death. I couldn't stop my head from shaking side to side. At the road was another mud hut. It was a simple store and a home. Luis hardly whispered for permission to enter. I never heard the answer. The Andean Indians have very keen ears. We entered and waited. A truck did come, but it was going the opposite way—to Arequipa.

Back we went to Luis's house, my head shaking violently. For a half hour, I shivered under the warm covers. At 2:30, we went back up the road to the hut. According to Luis, he was sure that a truck would come at three o'clock. It was a scheduled truck. We waited till dawn, only one truck went by—the opposite way.

I kept my face and hands warm over a kerosene lamp. My feet were coldest. Luis walked back and forth within the hut, then sat quietly against the wall for a half an hour or so at a time.

The owner of the house was a young fellow. He, his wife, and baby slept on a dry bank of mud several feet above the floor. They slept under many blankets. But on the damp, wet floor slept an elderly woman, wrapped in a single blanket. No doubt the mother of the young man or woman.

Dawn broke, very cold and gray. Herrea and his helper were up, loading the truck and refilling the radiator with water. It had been drained the night before to prevent freezing. The frost had to be scraped off the windows. For breakfast we got hot black coffee and bread (hard tack).

I asked Luis what I owed him. "Nothing," he said. He only wanted a picture of me. I gave him one and he was so happy. Then he embraced me in Spanish style and wished me a good journey. He was kind and generous, but the coca leaves he chewed threw off a sickening smell. Cocaine is a drug made from those leaves. It made the Indians groggy, almost drunk.

The truck was stiff; a half-hour later it moved along rapidly. It was very foggy. The road was covered with snow inches deep; farther on there wasn't any. The fields and road became flooded. We got stuck several times. The peons waded barefooted in the icy water and dug away grass sods and stones. It beats me how they could stand the cold. We got out again. On our left were huge broken stones. They were colorful in shades of pink, purple, and white. They stretched for miles. One boulder was called Mancarequipa. It was at least a hundred feet high and thirty feet in diameter.

328

We came to a village called Imata. It is thirty-three kilometers from Paty. It is a weather-observation station and a train stop. There were several stone houses, a flat boat, several llamas, and three permanent residents. They were the weather man, Enrique Cloca, his wife, Maria, and an assistant. The other residents were temporary railroad workers. There I separated from Senor Herrea and his son. They unloaded cargo and were returning back to Arequipa.

From Enrique Cloca, the big, husky, black-bearded weatherman, I learned last night's temperature. It was 8 cent. or 16 F. below zero. The exact altitude is 4,405 meters above sea level. The exact bearing is—Longitude 71 04 30 Latitude 15 49 00 . It is the second highest meteorological station in South America. The first is at the Christ Statue on the Chilean- Argentine border at Las Cuevas.

All his instruments were German, French, and American. Since Germany lost the war, all new equipment comes from the U.S.A. He said Paty is almost the same height as Imata.

We sat on his flat-bottom boat in the warm sun and chatted, waiting for the train to come in. He used the boat when rains or snow flooded the fields. Enrique's wife prepared delicious chops. Said Enrique, "The best meat in the world is right here." It was good, but coming from a man who has spent twelve years at that lonely outpost, I knew what to think. "The last vehicle that came by here was in January." That was over four months ago. He didn't have to tell me it was senseless to wait for another lift. I would take the train when it came to Juliaca.

The train came at 1:30 and stopped only a minute. Enrique told the conductor, who was a friend of his, not to collect fare from me. I waved farewell to another good Joe (a Peruvian).

The conductor asked a few friendly questions, then left me alone to enjoy the passing scenery. The coach was first class, upholstered in black leather. They were quite uncomfortable and old fashioned. We were climbing steadily, and could hardly notice it. We reached an altitude of 14,566 feet at Crucero Alto (high cross). The highest point reached by railroad.

Soon after crossing the divide at Crucero Alto, we go down grade. We go between two lakes, one on either side of us. The

329

Lagunilla and Saracocha. They are very picturesque. As the descent continues, rivers become more plentiful and farms appear. Cultivating the crops and tending sheep are women with babies on their backs. Occasionally one sees an idle man, but never an idle woman. In their spare moments, they are busy spinning or weaving thread even while walking. Men and little boys run along with heavy loads on their backs many times over their own weight. They have endurance and greater lung capacity than a white man.

Feeling tired after my hard night, I dozed off and awoke on arriving in Juliaca. The ride lasted three hours. It was a free ride. Juliaca is a town of many thousands. It is an old city of Spanish design. There is nothing new or modern. Yet seated all about the Plaza on cold cement curbs are hundreds of Indian women in gaudy, colorful costumes, selling clothing, blankets, fur pieces, and small necessities. About the best hotel is the Barrientos. It is not recommended for American tourists, especially lady tourists. To a fellow, it can serve a purpose. The bed was fine, the lobby covered with furs, but one had to wash one's face in a water pan and the toilets are dirty and have no seats or water. Later I walk around town, not a white person in sight. Americans usually go south thirty miles to Puno or continue north to Cuzco 205 miles. The train I came on went south. In Puno and Cuzco are fine government hotels.

Next day I was undecided whether to take the train to Cuzco. It would be the easiest thing to do or struggle and hope for luck on the road to Cuzco. I wanted to hitchhike north, then return south by train. That way I wouldn't miss anything of interest. I walked out of Juliaca about a mile. It was a sunny but cool, ideal for hiking with a pack. I came to another weather observation post. The clean-cut young fellow answered my inquiries. "The temperature last night—2 Centigrade; the altitude 3,825 meters above sea level.

I continued my hike along a dirt road. A pickup came along, and two young fellows gave me a lift for about twenty miles. The road was very rough and bumpy. We passed rich farmlands. The lift ended at a strange place. A bridge was being built; the boys were employed to work on it. There was a bypass, and now I wondered if a vehicle could get over it. I missed the train. I sat down to a study a map. I looked up to see a happy sight, a truck-bus affair was going over the detour and made it. The driver stopped for me. A policeman on the bus asked what American cops make. "Twelve dollars a day," I said.

"I only make ten soles a day (75¢) and I have a wife and two children. The government gives me ten soles a month extra for each child," he told me. Let American cops think that over.

Over the plains we rode to Bucara, a village of mud houses, hundreds of them. Almost every one with a cross atop it, indicative of the fact that the descendants of the race that once had worshiped the Sun and obeyed the mandates of the "Children of the Sun," are now completely under the domination of the religion of the conquerors.

I stopped at a *tienda* (store) for refreshment. No Cokes, or soda, only Argentine Pilsner beer. It did me good. A beautiful girl named Lola and a sister Alicia operated the store. We chatted for some time, the beer helping me out. Lola showed me a fine map of Peru but refused to sell it. She marveled at my memory of Spanish names. Lola had studied English for six years at the college in Cuzco and Lima, but she could not hold a conversation in English.

I was most surprised to be invited to dinner. They locked the doors of the store. We went up a flight of stairs to the second floor. You could have knocked me over with a feather. Their home was luxuriously furnished. Fine rugs covered the stairs and floors. There were four rooms and a modern bath with facilities. The furniture was of latest design, and the living room had soft, green sofas. The walls had large paintings. Without a doubt, Lola and Alicia were the wealthiest people in Bucara. Lola had a victrola and we danced to some English and Spanish tunes. One of the rooms looked like a sunporch with broad windows and flower boxes. We could look out over the rich farmlands, the hillsides, and railroad. This was where we danced. Dinner was served by an Indian maid. The wine, meats, and fruits were splendid.

Several hours later, they reopened the store for business. They told me that a few miles away were Indian grave excavations. Lola had to work, so I had to go alone. I walked till I came to a tiny village of mud and stones, then past it to foothills of Mount Lion. It was called Mount Lion because it had the features of a lion. I went through fields of green grass that came to my waist, then over seven or eight stone fences (walls). The walls were sunburnt and tarnished and had all the appearances of being age-old ruins. I started climbing the rocky mountain past dozens of grazing llamas. I saw a few ruined mud houses and lots of stone walls, but no excavations. I climbed to the top of the mountain. It was hard going hand over hand over the rocks. It was windy and cold at the top and the sun was beginning to set.

The scene below was worthwhile, but I was disappointed in not finding any excavations. I started back down the rocky slope, not as agile as the grazing llamas, but doing a lot of jumping. By the time I crossed the fields, vaulted the stone fences, and reached the road, it was dark. The moon came out and lit up the prairie. It was a night for romance. I wished Lola was walking with me, but I walked alone. As I neared Bucara, a pack of dogs came after me, barking, growling, snapping fiercely at my feet. It made me shudder, but I did not increase my pace or run, for surely then they would attack. I carried no gun, stick or stones. Voices from the dark mud houses called the dogs off.

When I reached town, all the lights were out. It was no later than seven o'clock. I knocked on the door of Alicia's Store; a peon clerk gave me my pack and said I owed three soles for the beer I had. He then directed me to a rooming house. The owner, wife, and a young Indian girl came forward with a lantern. They had me sit at a table while they brought me flat soup, mashed potatoes, sauce, and a meat bone. While I ate they asked me questions. I hadn't asked for food. It was only their generosity to bring me some.

"Are you an *Andarin?*" "Yes," I answered. "Do you carry a book?" "No," I answered. "You are very young. Are your folks dead?" "No," I answered, "they are alive." "Were you in the war? What will happen with Russia and the U.S.A.? How do you like our country? Which Latin country do you like best?" These are the kinds of questions I answered many times.

The Indian girl was a daughter of an Englishman named

Smith. She was very proud of it. She said, "When you came into the house, I was afraid of you. One time a white man came here, asked for service, and slapped me because I didn't understand English?"

It was chilly, so I drank two cups of hot, black coffee. I regretted it later, as it kept me awake. I lay under heavy blankets and carpets. The landlady promised to awake me at 5:00. I hoped to hop the freight train to Cuzco. I awoke at 6:00 and missed the train. I was charged only for lodging two soles (14 cents). The food was free. The lady refused to take more. I walked out of town at 7:30. Alicia and Lola had not yet opened up for business. I did not get to say good-bye or "Thanks."

The landlord told me it was twenty-two kilometers to Tirapata by road. It was flooded and no trucks could get through. He suggested I follow the railroad tracks to Tirapata and the distance would only be ten kilometers. The grade was easy along the tracks. The morning was sunny, but cold.

Following the tracks, I passed green farmlands, houses of mud, grazing sheep and llamas. Walking along the tracks were Indian women wearing peculiar black square or triangular hats with red-and-yellow frillings. Their dress was gaudy, dirty red, yellow, orange. They went barefooted, spinning thread, carrying babies, or driving pack llamas. They fearfully got off the tracks when nearing me and circled through the field and back to the tracks. I couldn't understand what made them so fearful.

I reached Tirapata before noon, and luckily a truck was just pulling out, headed north for Ayaviri. It was a thirty-mile lift over a rough dirt road. I had dinner there, then proceeded through town. It was quite large. The majority of the houses were mud, the rest adobe. They all had crosses on the roof. There was a central plaza and an effort at making streets of cobblestone. Walking through town, the Indian women fearfully moved to opposite side of the road.

I waited out in the country several hours for a lift. Not a vehicle went by. I did not feel like hiking. I merely sat on a bank and waited. I gave up hope and returned back to Ayaviri. The best hotel was a dump and filled up. "No vacancies." At the second hotel, "Circo," they said, "*No ha.*" Then they said to wait. A room was cleared of women's clothing and a trunk. The floor was swept clean, and the bed sheets and covers were change. Evidently few people ever stopped at that town.

My being very hungry, the landlady gave me some smoked spare ribs and potatoes before supper. I ate with fingers, native-style. She was busy within the kitchen. It was dark and full of smoke. A couple of dirty-looking boys were helping her. All of them seemed to have swollen eyes from the smoke. Very little of it went up the chimney and when it did so, the wind blew it right back into the circular dining room where we ate. Something special we had that I suggest to American woman. Stewed potatoes with a slice of white cheese inside.

I had given up hope of hitchhiking all the way to Cuzco. The trip from Arequipa to Cuzco takes only one day by train. My fifth day I was still 249 kilometers away. I decided not to strain myself any longer but take a train. I spent the morning brousing (strolling) about town. The heavy Indian population stared at me as I walked through the plaza. It felt wonderful to relax, knowing that I would catch a sure ride at noon.

I walked the few blocks to the train station. I noticed the prices of fare on a chart. The fare to Cuzco was 26.80 soles. The clerk said, "32.95 Please." I said, "26.80 is the list price." The clerk repeated 32.95 with emphasis. Take it or leave it. I took it. I started to board the train. The conductor took my arm and said I must have an injection against some disease. He started to guide me to a doctor. I said "Whoa," I have health papers along with my passport. He checked them and said, "Okay, go aboard." The coach was first class, but looked like any old coach in the U.S. Plenty of company, but I preferred being alone and not have to talk about myself.

The train climbed steadily till we again reached an altitude of 14,153 feet at La Raya. It is the divide that separates the basin of Lake Titicaca from the waters that flow into the Amazon and eventually the Atlantic Ocean. After the summit is passed, the descent is rapid on the Cuzco side of the divide. The valley widens, cultivation is more abundant, and what amazes me most are the acres upon acres of farms cultivated in the same primitive fashion as the ancient Incas. Towns are more frequent. Inca ruins occasionally are seen. Every little village has a church; every prominent hilltop has a cross, and every roof is mounted with a small cross.

The train pulled into Cuzco at 6:30. Night had fallen and the first real view of the ancient city, the Mecca of all South America, was reserved for tomorrow. Porters and native boys rushed aboard the train, grabbing passenger's bags. I had mine on my back, so I wasn't annoyed much. One has to be careful as many times the porters or carriers disappear with the bags and all. Outside the station, cabbies clamored, but being a hiker, I decided to walk. One of the hotel employees walked along and guided me to the government tourist hotel. He was interested in foreign *Andarins* (walkers) and gave me the straight dope on hotel rates—35 soles a day.

The hotel was exquisite. I often wondered why they don't turn me away because of my dusty appearance. Going upstairs I noticed several American tourists I had seen before in Arequipa and Hotel Crillon in Lima, Peru. They all waved greeting and seemed pleased to see me again. Later after change of clothes, shave, shower, I joined them by the fireplace. Mrs. Huntsman and Webster were there also, and they listened with interest to my tales of sleeping in Andean mud huts under llama skins and wondered how I had lived through it.

41

Cuzco, Archaeological Capital of South America

Cuzco, the scene of the rise and fall of the ancient Inca Empire, is an inland city situated in a most remote and inaccessible valley far up in the Andes. It was built centuries ago in such a substantial manner that the ruthless attacks of conquerors, invaders, revolutionists, and treasure hunters, have failed to destroy the wonderful handiwork of a civilization that flourished for centuries before the discovery of America.

The glory of the Incas perished with the coming of the white man. As far as is known, the name of the tribe was adapted from the name of the ruler, who was called Inca. There were two brothers, Atahualpa and Huascar. The empire was divided between these two brothers. Atahualpa had his capital in Quito, Ecuador, and Huascar had his in Cuzco, Peru. They quarreled over power and Atahualpa defeated Huascar and came into possession of the empire. Such was the situation when Pizarro, a cruel, despotic Spaniard landed on the shores of Peru with a few courageous troops. The Incas were frightened by the sight of a man on a horse. They had never seen horses before and believed the two (man and horse) to be one indivisible form. Only when one man fell off, did their fright subside. They realized the horse was only a conveyance. The Incas fought bravely but stood no chance against the guns, cannon, cavalry, and armor of the Spaniards.

Pizarro captured Atahualpa. The Indians gathered a ransom in gold to have their ruler released. Pizarro took the gold, murdered the prisoner, and marched forward to the conquest of the Empire for Spain. Pizarro entered Cuzco in November of 1533. He had undertaken the conquest for the fabled gold and silver of the country. What he found was beyond his expectations. The gold was so plentiful that according to a legend, it was used to make shoes for the horses, since iron was lacking.

Pizarro marched back to the sea and built a fort to repel invaders. That settlement has become the present-day city of Lima, the capital of Peru. Pizarro himself met the fate his cruel rule merited. He quarreled with his second in command, Almagro. Almagro was defeated and killed. the followers of Almagro became enraged, fell upon Pizarro, and put him to the sword in 1541.

Only one native revolt that had serious results disturbed the Spanish rule. In 1780 Tupac Amaru gathered a force of Incas with the promise of winning freedom from their oppressors. He was successful at first. In the end he met inglorious defeat. Amaru and his entire family were slain and white supremacy ruled again.

The ancient history of Europe has been well established and today archaeologists, writers of history, and searchers of treasures and adventure are turning to South America. Only recently archaeologists have discovered a secret city of refuge of the Virgins of the Sun God, only three hours out of Cuzco by Buda rail car. There at the secret City of Machu Picchu dwelt the last survivors of the court of the Inca Emperor, Atahualpa, whom Pizarro dispossessed and put to death. Machu Picchu was discovered and cleared of the jungle growth covering it by the Yale Scientific Expedition in early 1900.

Cuzco was declared the Archaeological Capital of South America by the XXV Congress of Americanists, which met at La Plata. Few cities in South America have such an exciting background as Cuzco. Few have clung so persistently to their ancient customs or fought so bravely the advance of civilization.

Having arrived in the famous city of Cuzco in the early evening, what could be more interesting or appropriate than to attend an Inca dance? The desk clerk at the hotel was selling tickets for ten soles (80¢) to see the performance. At the appointed hour, I went to the directed building. I heard strange music. I went up a flight of dark wooden stairs. There was light

337

streaming from a doorway, and standing in it were several tourists. They were watching the show.

American, European, and Spanish tourists were seated on flimsy chairs. When the dance ended, we were able to cross the room and take our seats among them. In all there were about fifty patrons.

Three Inca Indians played flutes and another played a crude piano. The outcome was strangely similar to Chinese music. The musicians played with blank expressions. They all wore the highland red poncho and knitted red-and-green caps that came over the ears and cheeks. The Inca girls and boys danced in strange but pretty customs. The girls wore white "Panama" hats with a black band. They wore them well back on their heads. They wore knee-length white linen shirts with tiny black vests and huge red belts. They were very slender and pretty.

The boys were well developed and husky. They wore a short-sleeve white blouse and short skirt. Like the girls they danced barefooted and the stamping was hard and rhythmic. In war dances the fellows swung heavy wooden clubs. A master of ceremonies explained the different dances that they performed. The war, peace, love, and so forth. The dancing was exceptionally well performed, and it had to be seen to be appreciated.

Sometimes the boys and girls, eight in all, sang in Spanish, then in the dialect of the Incas, used till this day among the highland people of Peru and Bolivia. The dances lasted about two hours and were held only on Saturday and Sundays. Everyone present agreed it was a most unusual dance and well worth the price of admission.

On my first day in Cuzco, I was invited to join the tourists on a thirty-mile trip to a native church. It did not seem very interesting, and I decided to rest up. I stayed about the hotel and chatted with a professor from Exeter, New Hampshire. We sat by the fireplace. It was cold outside. Mr. George ——— * wife joined us presently, and we had wine cocktails.

Mr. George ——— had a wonderful knowledge of Cuzco, it's

*My apologies to readers—I cannot remember George's last name.

history, theories, etc. We went on a walking trip about Cuzco. With him explaining, I found the tour very interesting. I could not ask for a better guide.

Up and down these streets, rulers and monarchs have gone, some to the throne, some to the execution block. Victorious armies have marched in celebration and defeated armies have retreated from destruction. Today there are no more monarchs. The army of today is a handful of peace officers. Gone is the glory, the pomp, and glamor of Cuzco, but always will there remain interest and sentiment as long as the enormous monuments of stone stand to pay mute tribute to a civilization that wrought these structures, which have withstood the attacks of time, elements, and invasion.

Walking along the sidewalk, Mr. George ——— pointed out the remains of Inca or pre-Inca walls, doorways, and arches. Many of the walls are perfect and serve no better purpose than foundations for the crude adobe buildings, which house the successors of a once-mighty race. Many of the stones have snakes, animals, serpents, carved onto them. How were they curved? They did not have knowledge of iron or steel in the days of the Inca. Yet the carvings are perfect. A modern stone mason could not do better with the best of tools.

Mr. George took out a pocket knife. He tried to squeeze it between the joints of the stone blocks. It was impossible. Yet there was no cement or mortar to unite or cement them together. The stones were evenly hewn and placed together perfectly. How were they hewn? One man's guess is as good as the next. The more one tries to reason out the problem, the more complex it becomes. Certain it is that no man knows or ever will know.

The more we walked, the more impressive and perplexing the problem became. We walked down a narrow street. On either side of us were huge Inca walls, several hundred feet long and thirty feet high or more. How in the world were those heavy stones lifted to that height? Yet each stone was evenly hewn, not once could Mr. George ———'s knife enter a joint. A native stopped us. He saw that we were examining the stones. He pointed to one and said it had twelve separate sides or joints. We counted them and sure enough the stone block, approximately

339

five feet long, three feet wide, had twelve sides, yet there wasn't a loose crack or separation between all the joints.

Mr. George pointed out the rounded corners on each stone and the perfect line of inclination toward the center from bottom to top on every wall. This line of inclination has a tendency to withstand earthquakes. To the stone mason, this term is called "battering." Many people believe the secret of the wall's long standing is the rounded corners on each stone.

To know Cuzco well, one must have a guide and an interpreter to visit the ruin of the wall that surrounds the city, the stone aqueduct, and irrigation ditches, and the Temple of the Sun. The Temple of the Sun serves as a foundation for the monastery of Santo Domingo. It stands as the most vivid monument to the skill of its builders.

We returned to the hotel and spent the evening chatting by the fireside. There were writers, students, professors, and tourists.

Next day I awoke early. I took Mr. George's advice, packed a lunch, and started climbing the hill on an all-day tour by myself. It was sunny but cool. I came to the top, and just ahead was a mass of huge stones. They were the ruins of Sacsahuaman Fortress. They encircled the entire hilltop in series of stone walls of flintlike stone. Some of them are twenty-five feet high and twelve feet wide. All of them are accurately cut and fitted perfectly. They are classed as one of the wonders of the world.

As little as I knew about the study of the past, I did not have to be a student of Archaeology to wonder and marvel at this great work. When and by whom was this work done? How many thousands of workers or slaves were required for the construction? By what power were these great stones lifted, brought, and placed into position? I spent several hours going through doorways, over steps, walks, and walls several thousand years old. The more I explored, the more I wondered and the questions became more complex. It was an absorbing problem. I could sit on a wall for hours, pondering the amazing mystery. One man's guess is as good as another's. Some believed fire was used to cut the stones, since metal was unknown three thousand years ago, except for gold and copper. Yet these two metals were too soft to cut stone.

Others believed a civilization as modern as we had once lived and perished with time.

The fortress has a large field in front of it that once must have been a parade ground for the vast armies; now a highway goes through it and sheep and goats graze on it.

I proceeded past the enormous white statue of Jesus overlooking Cuzco from a high point on a hill to the Temple of Worship and Sacrifice called Kcenkco. It was about a half a mile distant over lovely green hills. I came upon what looked like a mass of molten lava. Walking over it was dangerous because of wide gaps, holes, and incisions. Seats were carved into this hard rock. They looked like crude bleachers overlooking Cuzco. From the top of the "bleachers" or "grandstand," I looked the opposite way and down onto an arena. It was formed into a semi-circle by huge stone seats. In the center was a high, perpendicular stone. Surrounding it was a huge platform made of large, fine-fitting stones. It was very impressive and old. Truly the Incas had celebrated some kind of ceremony, sacrifice, or performance there.

Nearby was a mud house. On my passing it, a ragged, cross-eyed Indian woman, accustomed to seeing tourists, asked, "Have you been below the rocks?" I said, "No." Then she directed me to a huge incision between the rocks. A path led into it. Then there was a deep drop. Looking down through the incision, I saw a large opening and stone seats. I risked my neck jumping down six to eight feet. To miss my footing would mean falling thirty or forty feet down the rocky incision.

There were three levels to the rock formation. I was amazed when I dropped to the middle level to find a large room, oblong shape, forty-five feet long, fifteen feet wide, with a slanting roof, from five and a half to eight feet at the highest point. Right in the center was without a doubt some kind of a throne or altar. It was carved out of solid rock. It was approximately eight feet long, two-and-one-half feet wide, and four-and-one-half high at the seat. Built into the throne were two lower seats. They might have been the advisors' seats for the ruler or judge. Hidden out of sight, behind a rock wall were beds in a far corner. I couldn't help wondering what kind of ceremonies or verdicts took place there of life and death.

After going to the lower level and finding only a path going one end to the other behind the throne, I returned to the middle level, sat on the throne, and contemplated in wonder for at least an hour till I got jittery and scared of the mystery, loneliness, darkness, and quiet. I must have come in through the back door, for leading out of the middle level was a safe path and stairway leading to the top level at an opposite end of the cave.

Outside it was bright and sunny. I came upon an Indian woman driving cattle. I asked her how I go about getting to the Inca bath ruins called Zampa Machay. She said, "Over that green hill, it's very close." I came to an ancient road. It was lined on both sides with stone walls three or four feet high. It came from Cuzco and went over the hills for miles and miles. I came upon another Indian woman riding a llama. It was the first time I had seen a woman riding one. She wore one of those curious square hats with frillings. Her dress was crude but colorful.

I asked her directions in Spanish. She answered in Quechua. I did not understand. Many of these highland Indians only speak Quechua and no Spanish. I asked to take her picture, then offered her a few centavos. She became very angry and refused to let me take the picture. I took it anyway, then she started throwing rocks at me and saying her husband was coming down the road.

I followed the seemingly endless road and path over hill and dale, drinking clear, fresh water from numerous springs and irrigation ditches. It was ice cold. I passed many Indian women, carrying babies on their backs, driving llamas, goats, and spinning thread as they walked along. In fear, more than anything else, they moved off the trail as I went by in a wide circle.

Finally I came to the dirt highway used by cars. A little farther on, I came to Puca Pucara. It is supposed to be a lookout tower. The stones were not very big, the largest about two feet thick. It hardly looked like a lookout tower. There was a valley below, but a steep hillside behind it. While walking about, inspecting, etc., a car drove up. It was one of the guides from a popular tourist agency in Cuzco. He had one middle-aged patron for an employer. I was invited to follow and listen to the guide's explanations of the ruins. At one point the guide pointed to a hole

342

in the ground and said, "There is a secret doorway below. Push it and it will open." I was in blue jeans and boots. I was prepared to get dirty and learn the truth. I crawled into the deep pit. With matches I could see no doorway, only rocks and dirt. As I entered the pit, I remarked, "Hope there's no mountain lion in here." The guide and tourist laughed; and one said, "It takes a lot of nerve to go in there." There was no door, only rocks and dirt.

The guide seemed amazed when I had walked up. "The Inca baths are about a mile distant along the highway," he advised me. He did not stay more than five minutes at the ruins. I felt sorry for the American tourist. He was rushed and didn't get to take a single picture with his movie camera. How happy I was for taking Mr. George ———'s advice and walking.

It wasn't long till I came to Zampa Machay, the Inca baths. The road was fine along easy grades. The baths were hidden off the main road. An Indian put me straight. The Inca baths were in fine shape and not in ruins. All the stones were in perfect shape, finely chiseled. They ranged in size from two to six feet in length and thickness. The structure was in itself about twenty-five feet high and sixty feet long. There were simple tubs or stalls for bathing, offering no privacy. There were two water spouts carved out of stone. The water rushing through was ice cold and five inches in diameter. The seats were very comfortable, considering the hardness of the stone.

It was a long walk back to the white statue of Christ, then the ruins of Sacsahuaman. There I found more tourists—American mining engineers from Cerro de Pasco, Peru. They were trying to teach some Spanish kids the American way of playing football. One of the miners bent low on the football, scrimmage position, called off a few numbers, said "Hike," and sent the ball backwards. Instead of the Spanish kids catching the ball, they ran off in fright. We all laughed. When they finally got the idea, tried the "Hike" position, they fell on their faces to our Yankee amusement.

The engineers offered me a ride down the hill in their Buick. When we reached the hotel, the sun was beginning to set. A friendly old lady from Chicago invited me to have dinner with her. She heard about my mode of travel and said her son was looking for someone like me to travel together. At present he was at Huancayo. The evening was spent "shooting the breeze" by a fireplace with contented, satisfied tourists.

On the third day, I was awakened by a knock on the door. It was the servant calling me to get ready for an all-day trip to Machu Picchu, the ruins that had recently been discovered. Expecting rough going, I wore blue jeans and boots. It was very early. There were five guests in the dining room. Two were missing. They were the engineers. They had gone to several cheap night clubs last night and got drunk. Our fares were increased from sixty-five to eighty soles apiece ($5.70) to account for the loss.

The hotel station wagon took us to an auxiliary railway station. There we found a Buda rail car waiting. It made us laugh. It looked like an old model car, mounted on railway wheels and axles. It was painted a bright yellow. It had seats for only eight passengers. It sounded a train whistle, later a funny horn. It bumped, swayed, and rolled along like a roller coaster. It was fun.

In front of me was seated Susanne, a nice-looking blond from the American Embassy in Lima. On my left her mom and dad, and behind me were two English-speaking Dutch fellows. Susanne was only nineteen and we spent most of the day together.

Soon after leaving Cuzco, we were going up the mountains. We made five or six switch-backs on the ascent. It was fun the way the Buda car went backwards, then forwards. It wasn't long before the travelers complained about cold feet. Mine were no exception. We rolled along at terrific speed, now along a swift river with huge mountains on either side. Two hours out, the Buda car stopped; our Spanish guide in broken English pointed out the Inca Fortress Ollantaitampu on a mountainside. It was about a mile distant, and our guide said we could not visit it because we did not have time. An hour later we reached Machu Picchu, a scraggly little railroad town. We passed numerous freight cars, third-class passenger coaches, and exactly one mile beyond lay the ruins.

There we stopped, walked down a bank along a tiny trail,

through the brush, then over the rushing river by bridge, up another bank along a wider trail to a large clearing. There we waited for mules and horses. They came almost at once. We found another party of Spanish tourists from Lima, waiting for horses also. It was fun watching the old men, women, younger fellows and girls who hadn't ridden for a long time mount the horses. I helped assist them by adjusting stirrups. Everyone had difficulty getting their mules and horses started. I planted the heavy reins to my lazy horse's flank smartly. He balked and reared, then took the lead.

It was indeed a rocky steep climb. I was way ahead and looked down on the slow-moving caravan. Slowly but surely they came along. It took us exactly one-and-a-half hours to make the ascent. At the top we found a dandy hotel made of huge Inca stones. It would be any camper's or hunter's delight. It was made by the government for tourists' accommodations. Susanne, her mom, and I had Cokes in the simply furnished lounge by a dead fireplace. It was 11:30. We were told we must see the ruins first for an hour or so, have dinner, then descend to the valley below and return to Cuzco.

Outside we found Susanne's father busy photographing the ruins. He was a grumpy old fellow. He bawled his wife out, bawled the guide out, and when I talked to him, he bawled me out. I laughed. It was only his nature. As I checked light meters with him, watched and looked through his range finder, I became separated from our guide, Susanne, and the party.

I excused myself, then climbed over ancient stone stairs fifty or sixty feet high to rooftops. I went from one side of huge walls to another, from one large room into another. Nowhere could I find my party. I walked down steep smooth stairways. It seemed as if they were designed for barefooted people or worn by time. It was dangerous walking in shoes on the smooth-rounded stones. I was quite tired when I rounded a corner and unexpectedly came upon my party. "Playing truant, eh?" they ribbed me. "No, honest, I only got lost," I said.

Susanne and I separated; she explained what I had missed. Two flat stone bowls, that were no more than eighteen inches in diameter were said to represent the Sun and the Moon. I said,

"No, they are used to grind wheat and corn to a fine powder." Susanne laughed, but I was serious because I had seen likenesses coming down the road in Ecuador with Indian women and girls grinding away.

We joined the party and came to some walls that formed a terrace. Our guide said they were Inca walls. The stones were not finely cut, and not large. There was grass and dirt between the joints. I remarked, "This wall isn't Inca. It was built by the Spaniards." Everyone laughed and Susanne's mom said, "Another remark like that and you will be put out of class."

We went through many very interesting rooms. Some one story, some two story. Some were bathrooms, others were used for killing animals for food. Some were lookout rooms, and others had circular stairs of solid stone. Others had peculiar stone hangers, cylindrical shape, protruding out of a stone block or loops cut through a stone block. How these were carved is forever a mystery.

The entire fortress is on a precipitous point of a high hill. The drop and view below is breathtaking. From one point, it is hundreds of feet straight down. There is a throne of solid rock. From here men were punished and sent to death over the cliff. Not far distant is another steep hill. It is impossible to scale it. Our guide then pointed to the terraces and said, "Beyond them lies a cemetery, only bodies of women were found in it." What would the reason be for that? No one knows.

We returned to the hotel for dinner. We had soup, fish, steak, french fries, lettuce, tomatoes, coffee, pie. I remarked, "Wonder if this fish came up on mule back?" They all laughed, remembering the way we came up. We relaxed for a half-hour after dinner, then mounted the mules and horses for the down grade. Everyone feared the return. It was truly a dangerous descent. The decline was so steep at times that the riders hung on for dear life. We reached the bottom in seventy minutes. Susanne has a blister on her ankle and her mom has one on her hand from hanging onto the back of the saddle. Her dad seemed to enjoy the trip very much. He smiled a few times. He rode quite well. Our Dutch friends had never ridden before. One of them had decided to dismount and walk. At the bottom we sat in the grass, tired, and waited for the Buda car to come. Two of them came in about ten minutes, one for the Spanish party, one for us American and Dutch.

It seemed like a very long ride back to Cuzco. It was dark when we came to the switch-backs. We couldn't see where we were going backwards, but an Indian stood on duty with a red light at the end of each switch-back to guide the operator. The lights of Cuzco came into view. They were very bright, a city three thousand years old lit up. It was a wonderful spectre. At the end of the line, a station wagon was waiting to take us back to the hotel. After a perfect day, no hot water blank, blank, blank.

After dinner we sat by the fireplace, talked with Dutch fellows, and a pleasant bald-headed American. Then Susanne came and sat beside me. We sat and talked till everyone retired.

42
Into the Land of Bolivia

The bell rang at 5:30. I had breakfast alone. I had just time enough to buy a ticket to catch the train for Puno. I sat in the dining car with two Peruvian army officers at a table. There were no Americans on the train. One officer spoke some English, had been to Miami, New York, Canada, and Europe. He said he made 1,300 soles a month ($100). He was a *commandante* (commander) and had been in the army thirty-five years.

When we reached Bucara, he and I got off the train momentarily to say hello to Miss Alicia and Lola at the store. Lola wasn't present. They were the nice girls whom I had dinner with. Alicia was nice and friendly. We talked hurriedly, then had to run to catch the train. At Juliaca the officers disembarked. There the train waited about forty-five minutes for the train from Arequipa to come in.

When it came, it was already dark. We had about thirty miles to Puno. When we reached there, I put my pack on my back and the porters and peons who came rushing aboard just left me alone— thank heavens!

I asked directions to the tourist hotel. I received them. I hadn't expected Puno to be so dark and blacked out. At the hotel I was asked if I had reservations. I said, "No." They told me to wait awhile. To my amazement and surprise, a whole party of American men and women trampled in, about thirty-five in all. They filled the entire lobby. I felt my heart sink and felt like leaving into the unknown dark city of Puno.

I didn't think there were enough rooms to go around, but I waited and finally the line thinned out and I evidently got the last room—number one. They worked from the bottom down. Several Spanish fellows were turned away. I had come first. The managers were French immigrants.

There was hot water, but the rooms, lobbies, dining rooms were very cold. No fire in the fireplace either. Everyone was shivering. Puno is located on the edge of Lake Titicaca, 12,500 feet above sea level, the highest body of water in the world. There was good reason for the place to be cold.

At dinner I met the three engineers form Huancayo. They had driven down from Cuzco by car. It was my misfortune. I didn't hitchhike. I could have ridden along with them. They were eating there, but had arrived too late to get a room. They got a cheap hotel nearby, without water. I tried playing the radio afterwards but got only static. I talked to some of the party. They were on a tour of South America. Everyone retired early because of the cold. I had a nightcap called *"Chilcano,"* with the French manager at the bar, then turned in.

I awoke to the sound of train whistles. It was seven o'clock. The train was taking the entire U.S. party north to Cuzco. As I checked out of the hotel, the French manager, his wife, and another French girl shook hands with me and wished me a fine journey. I went to the Peruvian immigration to check out of the country. They gave me a *"Salida"* (leaving) visa. Puno is called the "Pearl of Lake Titicaca." It may be a pearl to an Indian, but not to a white man. Outside of the tourist hotel, Puno had nothing more modern or comfortable to offer.

I walked out of the Indian town, then bore to the left to take pictures of Lake Titicaca. I came upon an army squad. They were lying about in the sun and grass. They were members of a band. Soon they all arose, surrounded me, felt the weight of my pack, asked questions. They all knew I was an *"andarin"* (walker). They got into formation and I took their picture, promising to send it to them some day. I shook hands with them and hiked along. Soon I met a padre, and Italian priest. He spoke English very well. We talked awhile, then he hobbled past up the road, leaning heavily on a cane.

Not long afterwards a truck came along. It was loaded with Indians, some barefooted, some chewing the drug coca. All about where bundles of personal belongings. I climbed aboard, answered a few questions, then answered no more. All along we

349

dropped Indians and picked others up, some barefooted, others wearing sandals made of automobile tires.

At Juli we stopped for a half-hour. There were two ancient Inca temples. They were falling apart. Both were very large. The Santa Cruz was crumbling into ruins. The other, San Juan, was being repaired and made into a church. The carvings on the pillars, arches, and walls were fascinating. Many of the figures had no present-day meaning. How the carving was done in the hard stone really puzzled me.

Many of the homes had doorways and arches of carved Inca stone. There were many high towers crumbling to ruin. I didn't have time to visit them all. I found the truck ready to drive off. I had to run for it. We followed the banks of Lake Titicana, sometimes in a valley, other times along a mountain. About 4:30 we reached Yungayo, the Peruvian border town. I was charged four soles for the lift (30 cents). I presented myself to the police; they recorded my passport number and wished me luck with a customary handshake.

There was another truck loaded with Indians, baggage, farm produce, and bundles of brooms. They were ready to cross the border into Copacabana, Bolivia. I could barely squeeze in among them. Other Indians just hung on to the outside of the endgate, chewing coca. It gave me the goose pimples. Ten minutes later we came to the Bolivian post. Out we all went, customs checking the baggage. Never opened mine or asked questions. They more or less trust an Englishman or American.

Darkness fell and it became very cold. The ride lasted twenty minutes. To go longer seemed unbearable. Upon disembarking, the money collector asked for my fare, but Luis Queda, a white Spanish fellow who rode besides me, said "No" to the money collector. He told him I was an *andarin*." The fellow grumbled a little and said, "Okay." Actually to me it was nothing. Five Bolivianos is about six cents U.S. Nothing to argue about.

The official rate was fifty-four Bolivian bills for ten Peruvian. The Bolivians offered me only forty-five for each ten Peruvian. Luis was Peruvian and returning to Peru next day. So he gave me fifty for each ten Peruvian. Sixty Peruvian equaled three hundred Bolivian, one U.S. equaled seventy Bolivian.

The town was dark and quiet. We inquired about a hotel. We had to use a flashlight to find it. What a joint! Just a bed, table, and a candle. The manager changed sheets and the wife prepared supper. We ate by candlelight—fried onions, steak, and potatoes. It was good. Later we each had a large bottle of sweet, black beer. We retired early, sleeping in the same room.

I slept regular, a bit chilly, my watch said 6:40. An hour difference in time in Bolivia. We dressed, washed faces and brushed teeth at an outside water faucet in the center of a dirty courtyard. No breakfast served. I paid thirty-eight Bolivianos (52 cents) for supper and lodging. Luis insisted on paying for the beer.

I went to immigration at seven. It was closed. The police said it opened early because the trucks leave town early.

In Copacabana is a most unique, picturesque, modern church. It is very different in design from most churches. It is famous and pilgrims from all over the country and Peru come there to pray. Luis and I went inside. On the first floor were a lot of pews and a lovely altar, surrounded by huge carvings in wood, large paintings in gold frames, and statues of Christ. We followed a flight of stairs to a smaller room. An organ was playing and a padre (priest) was singing by a white altar enframed by tiny electric light bulbs. There were many pews occupied by Spanish folks in fine clothes and a few officers in gray uniforms. Standing or kneeling behind were Indians, some barefooted, others in automobile tire sandals, some in work clothes, other in ponchos, several chewing stinking coca leaves. Indian women knelt in the aisles with babies strapped to their backs. The mass was over at 7:30.

Outside again, all the trucks except one had left. It would be leaving shortly also. The immigration office was still closed. The Police, Luis and I went to the administrator's house. What a dump, a mere mud house. The wife said he left. Back we went to the office and waited. He came at 8:10. He hastily recorded an entry into a large book, then stamped my passport. I hurried out. The truck was just going around the corner. I whistled and it came to a stop.

I climbed aboard among the stinking but well-meaning In-

351

dian men and women. It was packed and I sat on a cold gasoline drum. No other places to sit or stand. A cute Indian girl wearing a black derby hat asked, "Caballero, where do you come from?" I told her. Then she advised me that this was the last truck leaving today for La Paz, and tomorrow being a holiday, there would be none leaving at all. It was cold on that barrel, and the air made my nose and eyes water. I shivered all morning.

I checked my passport. It was stamped *"Salida"* (leaving) instead of *Entrada* (entering). It's a bad mistake. I may be stopped by police along the way and made to return for a proper stamp.

About noon we came to Tequina, a crossing of Lake Titicaca. It was very picturesque, the blue water, the sail boats, and green countryside. There were many trucks at the bank. They unloaded cargo and passengers. One truck drove on a barge, then with cars and hoisted sails made the crossing in about twenty minutes. The water was slightly rough, and there was danger of the barge tipping over. Passengers and cargo were taken in other sail boats for the crossing. It was a thrilling ride. I had paid my driver twenty Bolivianos to the lake crossing and decided to ride in another truck and not have to wait for his turn to go over. There were at least ten trucks ahead of him waiting to cross over.

There weren't many Indians or cargo on this second truck. We made good time over the dirt road. Dust blew up and made breathing hard, and it may have been the altitude also. Soon it started hailing and raining. Luckily we had a canvas tarp. We placed it over the overhead beam and guard rails. It wasn't so cold then. Up in front riding in the cab was a Bolivian fellow and his pretty wife from Chile. She spoke English well and had worked with the U.S. Embassy in La Paz. We stopped for lunch, and the fellow insisted on paying for mine. Near Guaqui he came behind because only two people are allowed to ride in the cab. It is a Bolivian law. In Colombia, Ecuador, Peru, Venezuela, they pack them in four, five, six, and seven into the cab.

At Guaqui is the airport for La Paz. Many soldiers were about and rumors were that political strife was about due to bring trouble. An airport is always a hot spot in those countries. We were stopped and soldiers searched for hidden arms. From Guaqui to La Paz, we rolled over a fine cement highway. Down,

down, we went for several miles till we reached La Paz. It is situated in the bottom of a deep ravine. The driver stopped in the low-class, dirty Indian section of town. Boy, what steep streets. From here my Bolivian friend, wife, and I took a cab. They advised the driver to let me out at the U.S. Embassy. They refused to let me pay my fare. They were swell. I entered the embassy twenty minutes before closing time.

A beautiful American girl had three letters for me. I felt sorry for her, being assigned to such a cold, dismal country. She advised me, "The best hotel is the Sucre Palace." I checked in. Plenty expensive, five dollars a day with meals. A suit pressed cost me fifty Bolivianos (55 cents). It was a modern hotel, servants courteous and fine, dressed in white jackets, black trousers. The food mysterious, but splendid. I met an Argentine fellow named Gus Gershwin. We chatted awhile outside the hotel. Lots of pretty girls walking by, making remarks to us. Shall we or shall we not join them? I do and regret it later.

43
La Paz, the Highest City in the World

La Paz is the capital of Bolivia, a country without a seaport. The city was founded in 1548 and called Pueblo Nuevo de Nuestra Senora da la Paz (the New City of Our Lady of Peace). It was rechristened after an important victory in 1825 to La Paz de Ayacucho (the Peace of Ayacucho). It is located in a gigantic canyon, formed by the La Paz River in the western part of the country. Guarding it like a sentinel is snow-capped Mount Illimani, 21,286 feet high.

Among its notable buildings are the Legislative Palace, Municipal Theater, Public library, National Museum, Roman Catholic Cathedral, University of San Andres, a military college and a seminary. An unusual feature is that the National Supreme Court lies at Sucre, the former capital.

Bolivia was named in honor of the great liberator, Simón Bolívar. Its population is approximately 3,500,000. There are only about 400,000 white persons, descendants of the early Spanish colonists, but they rule the country. One-fourth of the population are *mestizos* (mixed bloods). The principal Indian tribes are the Aymaras and Quechuas.

Bolivia became a republic in 1825 after defeating the Spanish with the aid of General Sucre and an army from Colombia under Simón Bolívar. The Bolivians were very grateful to Bolívar and made him the president for life. He served only two years. He was a good soldier, but a poor administrator. Santa Cruz became president and established a dictatorship. When he died, one dictator followed another. Within a period of ninety years, the country had about seventy dictators.

In the Gran Chaco War, she fought Paraguay for seven years. It was put to an end in 1935 by mediations of the U.S. and other leading South American republics. Both sides lost heavily.

In the war with Chile, she lost her only seaport in 1883 and became landlocked.

Brazil bounds Bolivia on the north and east, Paraguay and Argentina on the south, and Peru and Chile on the west. The Andes cover two-fifths of the country to the southwest, to the east are the low lands and tropics called the Montana.

La Paz is the terminal of four railways. One leads to the south to Buenos Aires, Argentina, and Antofagasta, Chile. One to the west to Arica, Chile, one to the north to Lake Titicaca and Mollendo, Peru, and one to the east, tapping the great fruit and agricultural belt of the lower Montana.

I could easily take the train to Chile or Argentina, but I preferred hitchhiking over the great plateau of the Andes to the southwest. At the Automobile Club in La Paz, I was advised it would be a dangerous undertaking. The road was poor, little traffic, and intense cold and snow, a distance of approximately 1,100 kilometers to Antofagasta, Chile.

In La Paz, I stayed only four days. The climate was a bit too cold for me. One day was a holiday. I went sightseeing alone. The sky was clear and blue. Every office, store, or place of business was closed. It was "Workers Holiday." Not even the cops were on duty. The school kids were having a lot of fun; the schools were closed. They ran about the streets, playing football; others were playing "cops" by entering official traffic boxes the policemen use. Drivers ignored their signals and laughed.

Only the poor Indians work. They have a market day. They sit on the street curbs for many blocks. Their dress is very colorful. They wear blankets or ponchos in screaming colors of light blue, green, yellow or red. All of them wear brown or black derby hats. Beyond them lies a background of the most modern buildings, a strong contrast, the primitive beside the modern. Walking out of town, uphill I came upon a native brick yard. The man places mud into a small frame, pulls a stick over the frame, and removes the excess mud away. He lifts the frame and the mud brick is left to dry. Later it is put into ovens and baked. I said to the man, "Today is Workers Holiday, no? Why do you work?" He answered, "A poor Indian has no holiday, he must work every day to live."

355

La Paz has more steep hills, more beautiful homes and stores than any Andean city I've seen. As I pass along, Americans say "Hello" or "Good morning." I become winded on some of the steep streets. At first I thought I must be getting weak, then I remembered the rare thin air at this high altitude.

I returned to the hotel and listened to the war experiences of an Englishman named Sheppard. He was sent by an English cracker company to see what possibilities were of expanding business to South America. He had served in Africa. He remembered lying on a hillside looking at the beautiful flowers while 200-pound German shells whistled overhead. He never got a scratch. He also remembered a party he attended with Russian officers. They were drinking "Vodka," the famous Russian whiskey. Two of his English buddies passed out. Seven Russian officers passed out also, and he continued to the last with an eight. Sheppard sure as hell wasn't going to let the Russian drink him under the table. It all started with a toast to Stalin by the Russians, and the English then gave a toast to the King. The English felt their king was as good as the Russian premier. In the end the King "won."

Another day was spent writing letters, then strolling along the beautiful mosaic plaza with Gus Gershwin, a German-Argentine. He was fifty-nine years old, with a young man's ideas and vitality. We had tea across the way at a nice place and watched the dancing. Then we went to a night club owned and operated by a young German fellow named Johnny. Johnny joined us for a while; he was born in Argentina and had come to Bolivia to make his fortune. He later introduced us to two Bolivian girls. They were from the tropical region of Bolivia. They were a bit too old for me and too young for Gus. We drank and danced and the amazing thing was— almost at once we were out of breath. A little exertion in the high altitudes of La Paz causes this effect. I waltzed and did the slow pieces, Johnny and Gus danced the tangos. The conversation flowed in German, English, and Spanish. The bill came to 885 Bolivianos, the fellows refusing to let me help pay or buy another round. They were swell. The evening ended at two in the morning.

The last day was spent calling at the U.S. Embassy. The consul called the Bolivian immigration and advised them to be lenient about the mistake in my passport. The matter of an "exit visa" instead of an "entrance visa." The Bolivian officials could easily make me return for a proper stamp back at the border. At the Bolivian immigration, they put me through the ropes. I had two more visas put in, more signatures and thirty Bolivianos for stamps, then to the police several blocks away for more stamps and signatures. Then to the Chilean Consulate for a tourist visa. He was very nice to talk to. The visa cost twenty Bolivianos. Last I went to the tourist agency and auto club.

Many a tourist goes through this routine, they no sooner enter a country and have to worry about getting out. A lot of time is wasted with customs and immigrations. I spent the evening with Gus over cocktails at the hotel lounge. He was so homesick for his wife and children in Argentina. He was there on business and hoped to return in a few weeks. I promised to look him up in Buenos Aires. He then wished me a happy trip, return home, safely etc., and live happily ever after.

I had gone to a movie the previous night, one French, the other Spanish. What annoyed me was after being seated, ushers came around with flashlights, checked my ticket number, and directed me to a seat close to the screen. So thus it be in La Paz, when purchasing a ticket, the clerk pulls out a ticket from a board, designating the location of the seat. The customer reserves the right to choose from the board the location he prefers. I learned the hard way.

I awoke at dawn, the day I checked out of Sucre Palace Hotel. My bill came to 1,275 Bolivianos (nineteen dollars) for four days. I waited almost ten minutes outside the hotel for a cab. It was a bright red '36 Chevrolet. I asked in advance the price to the edge of town. The driver said, "Siete cincuenta" (7.50 Bolivianos). "Okay," I said, "let's go."

Along the way he stopped at a police office for ten minutes on a personal account. Another time he stopped for gas and talked for ten more minutes. I gave him hell and said, "Come on, let's go." We rode out of town up a steep dirt road. The main road was closed due to a landslide. His radiator started boiling and he stopped for water. "This is the end," I said, "Here is where I get out." I gave him 7.50 and he asked for ciento-cincuenta (150). I said, "150.00, like hell!"

He said he would go to the police. I answered, "I'm sorry, if I knew it was 150 instead of 7.50 to the edge of town, I'd walk." I gave him all the loose change I had, thirteen Bolivanos in all. So I left him and walked up the hill. He was mad and I believed he would call the police. I hoped I could catch a ride before they came. Several truckloads of Indians went by, then one stopped. The only place to ride was behind with the coca-chewing Indians. The ride lasted six hours.

It was miserably cold and cloudy. The road was dirt, rough and bumpy over endless plains. The Indians talked in Quechua; some played weird tunes on a handmade instrument. They were wooden tubes of various lengths, ranging from 2 inches to 6 inches in length and one-quarter-inch holes. They were bound together by rawhide. They passed it along and fellows took turns blowing and playing tunes. All of them wore the colorful Inca capes that covered the ears and cheeks. All of them wore ponchos. On passing other truckloads of Indians, they threw oranges, apples, wood, and what-not at each other. There was a lot of shouting. On a narrow stretch of road, two trucks slowed down to pass one another; an Indian near me slapped another Indian's face upon passing. He caught his victim unawares. The victim had the funniest expression, and roars of laughter went up from our truck. I couldn't stop laughing for awhile myself.

We got a flat near a police control station. There I had a cheap dinner prepared by an Indian woman in a large mud house. At the station I met a lone American. He was driving a converted command car and hoped to drive to the States. He came from Seattle, shipped his car to Brazil, drove to Argentina, Chile, and north to Bolivia. He could hardly speak a word of Spanish and preferred traveling alone.

A pickup came along. I left the disabled truck. The driver said I owed seventy Bolivianos (1 dollar). "But I'm an *andarin*," I said. Everyone heard and laughed. He said, "Why didn't you say you were in the first place?" I thought if I let him know, he wouldn't let me ride. He grinned a little and said, "Okay, go ahead." The pickup took me only fifteen miles or so, but I was glad be-

Market in Quito, Ecuador

Author and friends in hut near Chunchi, Ecuador

New road being built near Chunchi, Ecuador

Street scene in Guayaquil, Ecuador

Long trail near La Toma, Ecuador

Ecuadorian workers, pausing from clearing a landslide

Waterfall near Cariamanga,
Ecuador

Guide and church in
Cariamanga, Ecuador

Author's guide

Makeshift rail car

Drainpipe installation

Author and friend

Sunday morning market

Guide crossing river on horseback

Three friends in Northern Ecuador

Spinning thread in Azogues, Ecuador

Street scene in Quito, Ecuador

Indian woman and child tending sheep

Hat makers, Azogues, Ecuador

**My guide, barefooted, on the
Pan-American Highway**

Author on horseback

La Toma, Ecuador

Making bricks in La Paz, Bolivia

Pan-American Highway, Chile

Indian woman weaving a rug

Mountain lake near Portillo, Chile, near the Argentine border

Victory parade route in Santiago, Chile

Pro-Peron marchers in Argentina

Train stop at peak of Mt. Corcovado, author wearing tee shirt and dark glasses

Glorious Liberator Statue,
Valera, Venezuela

Author with Cuban friend in
Venezuela

cause it was warm inside the cab. The driver was a prosperous copper mine owner. We stopped at a little village, we entered a mud hut. It was cold and I shivered visibly. They gave me several large cups of hot black coffee. I refused dinner as I had eaten earlier.

Soon we heard a truck coming. I dashed out of the house and stopped it. I had to ride again with a load of Indians, but not as many this time. I wore two T-shirts, two sweaters, a suit coat, field jacket, two pairs of trousers and still I shivered. An Indian gave me a thin blanket, later a canvas cover when it started hailing ice. As before we rode over endless plains of sagebrush, sand, and now salt. The road was rough, and we bounced inches high. We hung onto bags of potatoes and guard rails. It was ever miserably cold. At the end of a long day, we reached Oruro at dusk. The town was much larger and neater than I had expected. There were paved streets, modern stores and buildings, and a nice plaza.

The driver's wife asked for my *pasaje* (fare). I said, "I'm an *andarin* (walker or hitchhiker)." It made no difference to them. "Andarin or no andarin, you pay forty Bolivianos," the woman said. The man said, "Make it thirty." I gave it to them. The ride was long, the fare cheap (45 cents).

I was tired, cold, and hungry, and had supper at the only restaurant open. It was very poor. Many dark-complexioned people looked my way, and some drunk sat at my table, babbling and asking questions. I ignored him as I ate; then the proprietor called a cop to take him away. The officer was only a young boy, not more than seventeen years of age. The drunk protested, but the little squirt took the big middle-aged fellow away. My waitress was a middle-aged lady, wearing a tall white twenty-gallon hat. A two-inch black band embroidered it. It looked like a puritan's hat. It was very stiff and clean. This is the only town or region in all Latin America where these beautiful white high hats are worn by the women.

I talked with the proprietor and several other fellows. They advised me that very little traffic ever goes over the road to Chile. Why should there be when a train goes by twice a week and very cheaply? Because I felt the terrible cold of the highland

375

plateau and worse ahead and possibly no traffic and face danger of getting sick, I decided to take the train, leaving in just a few hours. It followed the highway and touched the same distant towns I had in mind.

My servant said, "Thirty-two Bolivianos." The proprietor said, "No, it's twenty-two," and remarked to her that I was an *andarin*. He knew I was an American, but he refused to overcharge me. I had only enough Bolivian currency to purchase a ticket second class to the Chilean border and a few miles beyond to Calama. I was advised first and second class were alike. I awaited among a large crowd for the train to come in. Little boys stopped, looked at me, and said one to another, "El es Argentino" ("he is an Argentine") and moved on. Some cute senoritas in twos and threes went by, smiled, returned, and smiled again. It was easy, but why bother? I'd be leaving pronto. The train came in late. What a busy station it was, like any busy city in the U.S., yet strangely different.

I sat in first-class coach and hoped the conductor would leave me alone. I chatted with a Bolivian doctor. He invited me to the dining car for tea. Then he advised the waiter to put in some *pisco* (whiskey). It would be fine for our chills. The drink was good. The bill was fourteen Bolivianos. I was surprised to hear the doctor say, "You pay half." I gave the waiter twenty Bolivianos. It was strange to be invited, then asked to pay. The waiter put my change on the doctor's side of the table. He hurriedly picked up the six Bolivianos and put it in his pocket. I decided to keep quiet. Peruvians I know, would never pull a stunt like this. No wonder they call people of Bolivia "*cohudos* (jerks). We went back to first-class coach; the conductors came along and ordered me into second-class coach and gave me hell for being in the dining car on a second-class ticket. The doctor said previously that they wouldn't bother me because I was a white man and would let me ride first class. He was wrong.

What a car, wooden benches for seats, but not too full of Indians. Most of them were rolled up in blankets or ponchos. One young mother milked her baby, breasts wide open. I sat beside a toothless Spanish fellow. It was freezing cold, and he kindly offered me one of his blankets. The first-class coach was bad, but this second-class coach was really rough. I had been ill-advised. Looking out the window, it was dark, but the white salt flats looked like snow along the tracks. All night I dozed on and off. Occasionally I went to first-class coach when we dropped a car or two at some station. I chatted with a Chilean girl, returning home after five years in cold La Paz. She was young, pretty, and pleasant. When the conductor came along, I scooted back to second class. All morning we rolled along, over flats of sand, salt, and snow. The cold did not subside, and I was continually shivering. My toothless friend had disembarked during the night, taking the blankets with him. Off in the distance to the left and right were the peaks of distant mountains.

About noon we reached the Bolivian frontier. We filled out applications for officials of the contents in our bags. Then they checked our bags, and what was not listed on the application blanks, was considered contraband, more or less. At the Bolivian border, it rained heavily. A few miles farther at the Chilean border town of Ollagüe, it snowed heavily.

The Bolivian customs inspectors had their hands full when fat women passengers objected to having their large bundles opened. They argued loudly, then the inspectors carried the suspicious bundles to a special inspection coach. Ladies returned with receipts. They had to pay duty on something or other.

The Chilean officers wore nice uniforms and were big strapping fellows. They were most courteous. They were thorough, but not as noisy as the Bolivian inspectors. Just for curiosity I wandered from one coach to another. I came to the conductor's and inspector's coach. Officials and conductors had been changed at the respective borders. There I found Chilean conductors drinking coffee. They offered me some. They laughed at my surprise. It was strongly blended with pisco, a strong clear white whiskey made of grapes. I thought it was made of sugar cane. I had several cups, feeling fine. I wandered back to my coach.

I had a waiter bring me a dinner. I wasn't permitted in first class. I felt sorry for the waiter. He had to walk four or five cars in order to reach me. Outside each car, the platform was freezing cold. He made four round trips in the course of serving me one meal. Certainly they gave plenty to eat.

All afternoon we rode over snow-covered flat lands. This would be a hell of a place to be stuck hitchhiking. It would be easy to perish on it from cold and hunger. There was no sign of traffic along the road all the way. I was told Calama is tropic and being so near, I thought it impossible. I dozed off a little.

In the late afternoon, it got a little warmer. I was seated near the rest rooms and now had to leave my seat because of the terrific stench. No other seats available, so I rode on the platform. It became cold and I headed for the conductor's coach. These kind Chilean conductors offered me coffee and pisco again. In a few minutes, the waiter walked in with an enormous leg of lamb roast, fried potatoes, onions, and very hot sauce. We sliced off pieces and ate with our fingers. I had one, two, three, then four slices. It was very good. The conductors, inspectors, and two Chilean soldiers kept handing me wine, whiskey, and food one after the other. Once I said, when another round started, "Elders first." They laughed and said, "No, guests first."

They had previously broken the leg off a frozen lamb and had it prepared. It was more or less stolen. They say stolen food tastes best. They were the first Chileans I had met, and when I got off the train at Calama into the dark night, I already had a warm feeling towards them.

I was informed that an American mining camp was nearby. I didn't even have enough change left to take a bus to it. The bus driver said, "Forget it and come aboard." Surprising to find the most modern coaches there. The bus was full of native employees from the camp. We rode sixteen kilometers to the entrance. The bus stopped at the gate. Police guards, fully armed, entered the bus, checking everyone's pass card and photo. They told me to get off the bus. My passport wasn't good enough. Inside their office I said I only wanted lodging, a visit, and to change some traveler's checks. They were courteous and called a Mr. Adams. He gave me permission to come in. This very day the chief of personnel had been killed in an auto accident, so my reception wasn't very warm. Mr. Adams had seen the mangled body and wasn't feeling well enough to see anybody. At the Chilex Club, a servant gave me a key to quarters—staff—B-14. The quarters were army style, the rooms were well furnished with rugs, dressers, writing table, chairs, a fine bed with plenty of warm covers. Returning to Chilex Club, I met a half a dozen Americans. They were from Pennsylvania, Wisconsin, and Montana. Two of the crowd were ladies, the wives of the miners. They lived at the camp. Over beer we chatted at a large table.

The camp is called Chuquicamata. It is the largest copper mine in South America. Chile ranks second in copper production to the U.S. The copper is mined and processed there to 99 percent pure and sent to the States. In this camp, they claimed, was the world's largest electrical transforming plant, believe it or not.

I stayed at the camp for three days. I had hopes of visiting the mines but was unsuccessful. At the personnel office, they advised me I could enter if I had some American employee to guide me. I met two English-speaking Argentines who spoke English with an accent. They pretended to be Englishmen. They promised to take me on a tour of the mines. They never kept their word. I met an American. He was a big husky fellow. He was one of the bosses at the mine. He promised to send a car for me in the morning and take me on a tour. We had been sitting in the club house drinking beer. He said he had been working here for thirty-five years. I said, "That's a long time. Don't you miss the States?" He answered, "The States," and laughed. "What the hell do I care about it? It's no goddamned good. Why should I go back?"

I didn't like his remark and said, "If you don't like the country, why don't you give up your American citizenship? Why work for an American company and draw American high wages?" I was angry. Two of my brothers had died for the country, and I didn't like agitators like him who benefitted from the country and yet besmirched it.

He got up from the table and mumbled something about seeing us at dinner. In the restaurant he sat alone. He never sent a car for me next day either. The Argentine tried consoling me, saying he had been drunk and didn't know what he was saying.

Besides the American clubs and restaurants, there were schools for the children, recreation and movies. On another part

379

of camp were clubs, restaurants, and facilities for the Chilean employees and their families. Herman Grey, the Argentine, and I went to one of their clubs. We could not enter the second-floor dance because we weren't invited. We spent the evening and all night drinking wine and pisco with the Chileans. The Chilean fellows and women were very friendly, even drunk they were hospitable. I bought a round and they bought five or six. Later on Norman argued politics with some of the fellows. He had some gripes against the Americans, but I found the Chileans were in our favor and all were against him so that he had to shut up before long. If he had been sober, he probably never would have started the argument. He left the place without waiting for me.

The morning was freezing cold on this desert as I returned to my quarters. I was awakened at noon by a violent trembling of the earth. I thought it was an earthquake, but it was only blasting in the copper mines. This is supposed to be very picturesque and exciting. I had to miss it. Later I found a group of Chilean students in the restaurant; they had been more fortunate than I, they had been on a tour of the mines.

On my last evening, I was invited to join several American fellows playing dice. They used cups and beans. At this camp there were employed approximately two hundred Americans. They asked me, "What are you doing here?"

"Just as tourist," I said.

"Where do you get the money?" they asked.

"I work, then move on," I said.

"Do you go by plane?" they asked.

"No, I hitchhike by road," I answered.

"What are you doing? Writing a book?" they asked.

I admitted I had hopes. Then they asked what my opinion of the Spanish girl is.

"The Spanish girl is all right," I answered.

Then they said I should stay a month, talk to a certain chap who had been there thirty-three years and to hear his stories of the girls and prostitutes' houses. Then I could write a fine book. I hardly ventured to be inquisitive. I answered their questions and let them talk. One good-looking Irish fellow from California said, "Do you like friend?" "Sure," I said. "Then the hell with you and your friends," he said.

It was an untimely joke. The fellows had been away so long that their jokes were crude. He apologized at once.

"What college did you go to? Where did you get so educated?" they asked.

I didn't think I was so educated, but the compliment was nice. I excused myself and said, "So long; it's been nice knowing you." I went to the bowling alley, surprised to find one there. Then to Staff B-14 and bed.

44

Hitchhiking Along a "Shoestring"

I had been charged for lodging at the camp. It wasn't much, about thirty cents a night. The meals were quite expensive, ranging about a dollar for each meal. The employees eat on a monthly basis and pay only sixteen dollars a month.

I rode two buses on my way out of a camp to Calama. A train was pulling out for Antofagasta, but I decided to stick to the road. The day was ideal, and I did not suffer from cold. I was no longer in the Andes, but on the flat Atacama Desert. I stopped at a tiny cobbler's to have my boots repaired. He asked for fifteen pesos, but I gave him twenty. He worked long and the work was fine. He deserved the ten-cent tip. For the first time, I saw road signs and arrows, like in the U.S. I followed them till I came out of town. There was only a black road and an open desert ahead of me.

I didn't walk long; a truck came by. It stopped when I "thumbed" it. The only place for me was atop a load of beer bottle cases. He was headed for Antofagasta, 217 kilometers away. The road was macadam, then dirt. It alternated several times till we reached Antofagasta on the Pacific Ocean. The entire trip was badlands, a real desert, yet it is the richest part of the country because of mineral deposits and nitrate. We stopped once at a desert village for lunch, then drove on. When we reached Antofagasta, I was surprised to find a very old, shabby city and horse-drawn carts, carriages, and beat-up cars. The outskirting houses, almost to the main street, were rusted tin, and weatherbeaten boards. Even the hotels had little comfort or cleanliness to offer except for the weather-stained Moury Hotel, but it was filled up. The trip took seven hours.

Antofagasta is not as big as it looks on the map. It was taken by Chile in 1879 from Bolivia. Peru sided with Bolivia in the dispute and in the war of 1879. They were quickly defeated by the Chilean Army. Bolivia lost its only seaport, and the province of Antofagasta. Peru lost Tarapaca and surrendered Arica and Tacna for ten years. A vote was to be taken by the people of those cities to determine their future allegiance at the end of the ten year period. It never took place, and war nearly broke out again. Only through the efforts of the U.S. it was avoided and Arica was given to Chile and Tacna to Peru. The region is all desert, but noted for its wealth in nitrate.

Checked in at Gran Hotel, the next best.

"How long will you stay?" the clerk asked.

"Two or three nights," I answered.

"Okay, seventy-five pesos a day," he said.

In the room, a list price said thirty pesos a day. I informed the clerk. He said the place was under new management and the list was old. *I wonder,* I thought. No shower, only wash basin; afraid to use the dirty tub.

I went to a *carnivale* show. I was surprised to recognize several actors whom I had seen perform in Pariata, Venezuela, one day. One was a Negro midget, the other a red-headed clown. One had a trained dog and put on a show. The laugh came when a stray dog walked into the arena, smelling the trained dog. The trainer smacked its rump with a baton. The intruder yelped and ran off with its tail between its hind legs.

The show was mostly burlesque and in Spanish. Many Chilean sailors and soldiers were present in green, German-style uniforms. One soldier went up to the stage and made a request for a song. He also requested the star actress to join him. There was much applauding. He got the song, but the pretty starlet did not come on the stage. He waited, then walked off the stage. It was disappointing and embarrassing.

After the show, I couldn't find my hotel. There was not only one, but five Gran hotels in the city. The directions people gave me took me to all but to the right one. It took an hour to locate it.

Sunday I went strolling through the park, met two Swedish sailors, three lovely Chilean senoritas, and spent the afternoon together in the park. In the evening, we went to "Banoes," a place out of town for dancing. I was surprised to find the Chileans good at jitterbugging. One sailor and a girl were exceptionally "hot." While strolling about the second floor promenade, I was able to look down on the dancing crowd. On passing a couple seated at a table, they called me and invited me to join them for a drink The surprise came when the waiter said, "Twelve pesos please," and the girl said to me, "You pay twelve pesos." *Fine,* I thought, *I get invited and then asked to pay.* The large bottle of beer sufficed for three.

My Swedish friends showed up and joined us. We had a number of beers together. One Swede had only contempt for Chile. He said he could drink any six Chileans under the table. We danced with Lilian, the wife of our Chilean friend. She was a good jitterbug. But the floor was lousy. It was tile and broken in many spots. One cannot slide on cement. Open sky, but no stars. The orchestra played a lot of American pieces, yet I was the only American there to my knowledge.

We had dinner together, then took a cab to town. We asked Lilian and her husband if they needed cab fare to go home. They said, "No." They refused to stay in the cab unless we went along. But when we walked off, we looked back and saw them walking away from the cab. The cost of the evening fell on Swede's and my shoulders. No complaints; Lillian and husband were nice company. Swede, Perry, and I were pretty high, walking arm in arm like drunken soldiers to the hotel. There we parted and they went back to their ship.

I spent three days in Antofagasta, the last day I enjoyed sleeping late, visiting the U.S. consul and enjoying the sights. In the evening I met Swede. We went to the "Navy" bar.

An elderly Spanish-looking fellow came over to us. He said, "I overheard you fellows speaking English; are you Americans?" We advised him, "American and Swedish." We invited him to join us. His name was Fred Bingle, from Tampa, Florida. He was fifty years old and could hardly speak Spanish despite his dark features. His children were married, so one year he worked, the other he took a vacation. So on his vacation he traveled for adventure. He had a strange way of traveling, considering his age. He had gone by boat to Argentina, then crossed the Argentine pampas (plains) and the Andes Mountains into Chile on bicycle. Then he headed northward for the U.S.

He was stopped by the sand on the desert. He became tired and rode third-class on a train to Antofagasta. I felt sorry for him, traveling third class on a Chilean train is no fun. He asked for a second-class hotel, and I said he was welcome to the extra bed in my room. He carried a tent, cooking utensils, etc. He camped out a lot. We had several more beers. Swede gave me his address in Sweden. Couldn't figure it out, all Greek to me.

How my thoughts and luck went the next day, I give by the hour.

6:00: Night watchman bangs on the door. I hardly slept at all. Paul rises, turns on the light, goes to the bathroom naked. He has got a fine physique, hard muscles, average height.

6:30: Already dressed and packed, say "so long" to Paul. He wanted me to stay another day for company. He was quite lonesome. The fact he couldn't speak Spanish made matters worse. (Days later I was sorry I didn't stay for his sake. There is no misery like loneliness.)

7:00: Have hot chocolate and greasy fried eggs at the Mercado (market). Burn my tongue.

7:30: Walking out of town, past Chilean troops on practice march. Some of the rookies were funny. A company would halt, a rookie would be called. He would run twenty paces, turn about, and face the company. The lieutenant made him call out his name over and over in a loud voice. Some of the lieutenants smiled and saluted as I walked by.

8:00: Passed "Population Militar" (military zone) and cavarly training on horseback.

8:30: Two roads lead out of Antofagasta. I guess I took the wrong one. No traffic, military road.

9:00: Officers pass in jeep, salute and roll on.

9:30: Thinking of red-headed girl in "Sloppy Joes."

10:30: A 1920 roadster pulls up, a tight squeeze between two fat Chileans.

11:30: They let me out at Variallas, a tiny railroad stop. Three mud houses, a tiny coral, a barren desert, sandy road inches deep. Have dinner at one house of Chorroes (oysters) and chopped onions, and tea. It's a poor house, and poor folks, yet they refuse my money. They take me for an andarin.

12:30: Waiting for a ride a mile away at a junction. Sun out, cool wind. Two trucks went by, opposite way. They stopped, I said, "No, thanks, I'm going the other way." They drive on, raising a heavy cloud of sand and dust.

3:30: I waited 3 hours, still nothing. I'm getting hungry and thirsty.

4:30: Still waiting and boy, it's getting cold and windy.

5:20: One truck came and turned off at junction. I can see another vehicle raising dust off in the distance. Will it come this way?

5:30: It does and stops. Only place for me is atop a load of beer bottles. Find it most uncomfortable sitting on the bottle caps. Have a lad for company.

6:30: Riding an hour, gets mighty cold, unpack my hammock, use it as a blanket. It helps wonderfully against the wind and cold. There is a strong odor of fish. It comes from a greasy burlap bag. A huge cloud of dust trails behind us.

9:30: Pitch dark, the truck starts swaying left and right, up and down, we must be going into mountains.

10:30: After five hours of riding, we arrive at Taltal, covered with dust and sand, and I thank the driver. No charge. I walk several blocks to main part of town, population not more than 800. I bang on door of one hotel; a pretty girl answers: "No vacancies." Likewise at another. I find a small restaurant open. Several girls, fellows, and a little boy inside. The kid annoyed me with questions. Had two steak sandwiches and beer. While talking to waitress, fellows in another room stretched their ears out the door to catch every word I said. Guys like that make me so mad.

11:30: The little boy guides me to another hotel along the water front. The night is very quiet. After some banging, the manager opened up. At first he said he had no rooms, then asked if I were alone. I said, "Yes." Then he directed me to a room. The little kid had said, *"Todos los Americanos marinos muy generoso,"* (All American seamen are very generous"). It was his way of asking for a tip. I gave him three pesos (6 cents).

12:00: Turn in, had made 236 kilometers all day (148 miles).

Dawn found me outside. I did not have to leave town to wait for a ride. There was one or two vehicles, and if one came, it would not go by unnoticed. I walked about town and found it to be very tranquil. It had a small park along the water front and another in the center of town. The background was bare, dry, sandy, mountainous. Most of the buildings were old and shabby. Taltal is so small and yet it is a seaport. Out in the bay were two ships, one a Chilean Navy destroyer, the other a foreign cargo ship. Many rowboats were in the bay. Several of them were trudging back and forth, unloading the ship. It was a crude method and hard labor, but the ship could not dock at the pier because of shallow water.

For six hours I waited for a ride; not a single vehicle went through town. I returned to the hotel at noon for dinner. A strange fruit or vegetable they served me was called *Alcachofa*. It is pear-shape in dimension, but one peels off leaves like from a head of cabbage. Then the tip is dipped into oil and vinegar and bitten off. The tips and core is all that's eaten, leaving behind a mess of leaves. It tastes like cooked cabbage. The fruit or vegetable has been cooked. As in Peru, raw fish is served occasionally. I don't like it. The natives do. Raw fish is sometimes cut up and mixed with vegetable salad.

I waited three more hours for a ride, none came. I stopped at a bar for beer. The day was hot and dry. I had one, two, three, then four. I talked to the Yugoslav manager and bartender. We drank together. I understood some of his native language, and he said, "You want to get drunk?" I didn't think it was a bad idea. I changed later to wine and drank till midnight. I don't recall how many gallons I drank. We had long conversations. He had come to this country many years ago. He was a good-looking fellow, about fifty, with wavy gray hair. He married a Chilean girl and had a beautiful daughter of about eighteen. She could only speak Spanish. I don't know what made him go to South America instead of the U.S. in the early 1900s. He seemed quite contented with the peaceful life of Taltal. The bar reminded me of some country bar in the back woods in the U.S. All day, about five or six fellows came in, had one drink and left. It was midnight when I left. He was locking the place up, and I must say, I was really drunk, but I managed to weave my way side to side to the hotel alone. Two trucks had gone north to Antofagasta, but none went south.

I decided to take the train in the morning. The chances of catching a ride on a dead sandy highway were too slim. The train came at 7:00 A.M. It comes twice a week. The only class was second class. Not bad, not good. The rest of the cars were freight cars. I had a terrible hangover. I had tea on the train, avoided conversation, slept on my elbow. I was really sick. Four hours later I was in a makeshift kitchenette in the caboose. I ate a cheese sandwich, but had a hell of a time drinking a soft drink. The caboose fairly bounced and swayed on the tracks. The coaches weren't so rough. I banged my teeth and once got splashed in the eyes, trying to swallow a drink. The cook and another fellow laughed to beat the devil at my efforts. We arrived in Catalina four and a half hours after leaving Taltal. There we had to wait for a train going south.

Catalina is east and north of Taltal, but we had to go that way to catch the train going south. At this little desert village, we waited five-and-one-half hours for the train to come in. I still was sick, and two fair senoritas suggested I try eating lettuce and tomatoes for my hangover. I washed it down with several glasses of wine and felt better. The senoritas were my company for the rest of the day. One of them had a million-dollar figure. She had pretty legs and wore her dress above the knees. I bought a ticket to Copiapó, 325 kilometers farther south and hoped I could hit the road again to catch a ride to Santiago.

There was no first- or second-class train going south today, only third class, but it looked better than second class in Bolivia. There are almost no Indians, so the passengers aren't bad. Chileans claim that they annihilated most of them in the civil wars. After two hours riding, the girls and I had soup for supper. Four hours later, near midnight we stopped at Pueblo Hundido. There I parted with my pleasant company. They would have to lay over for the night and take the train to Chanaral in the morning. They seemed a little surprised when I said I was going on a bit farther to Copiapo. The girl, I believe, wanted me to stay over with her. Instead we only embraced in Spanish style and wished one another "good luck."

The train stayed two long hours. I walked outside. Girls on the "loose" paraded up and down beside the train. Many smiled, but I hurried back on board because the night air was very cold. A little boy of about five years came aboard, got atop a bench, and started singing at the top of his voice. He sang three songs to the tired travelers. He received several tips, then went into another coach. We could hear him singing, and everybody smiled. It was one way of earning a living.

Finally we pulled out. I had a big husky fellow for company. He was one of the oar-pulling boatsmen who unloaded cargo ships. He spoke fair English and bought me hot milk at the next stop. He got off and I rolled up on the floor in my hammock; the night was freezing cold. Several hours later I was awakened by the conductor. We were at Copiapo and it was five in the morning.

Outside the station, it was dark and cold. There were at

least a dozen horse-and-buggy taxi cabs. It reminded me of the gay nineties. I could not find a restaurant that was open to warm up. The night was cold and quiet, only the trotting of horses' hoofs on cement streets (of a passing carriage), or the toot-toot of his horn at an intersection broke the stillness.

A policeman at a dismal quiet street corner asked for my papers. Finding them in order, he said I could get coffee at the *Caballernos* (police station). I knocked on the door; a cop in German uniform opened up, said they had no coffee, only wine. "Okay, fine," I said. After talking to the desk sergeant and several other interested officers, they gave me wine, then the sergeant gave me his lunch, a large steak sandwich. I protested, but he insisted; then he ordered coffee made for me.

I felt like a piker. The coffee came piping hot. The cup held at least a quart. They asked about conditions back home, but never was there any trace of dislike for the Americans. I heard stories that the Chileans hate the Americans' guts, yet all I meet are friendly, courteous, and interesting people. I expected to hear contempt from at least one of that group of stalwart officers, but there was only friendliness. They were really swell. Asked if I carried a gun, I said, "No." Then they shook hands with me and wished me luck.

Two hours later I walked through town. It was modern—a fine, big, white building served as a school; facing it were huge trees and a lovely park. Dawn was breaking and found me walking along a four-lane dirt road. Patches of green were signs that the desert was behind me and I was entering the "middle section" of Chile, the section that is rich in agriculture.

I walked for four hours; a car and a truck passed me by. The highway sure looked "dead," and I feared I would have to take a train again. At twelve noon, a car went by, returning a bit later. The driver said he was going into town and would bring me sandwiches. Then we would go together to Santiago. I waited forty minutes, then

12:40: Still waiting, no traffic.

1:40: Guess my friend is a phoney, or is it a Spanish custom to be always late? Two cars went the opposite way. Boy, what big horse flies here. Not much joy waiting, walking into mountains. Boy, could I go for Mom's Sunday dinner now.

2:40: Oh, dear, what a wonderful way to spend a vacation. One truck went south heavily loaded with household furniture. Stopped to rest on a rock pile.

3:15: Sleepy, dreaming of a blond, blue-eyed girl in Detroit. Such warm, cool wind. No traffic either way.

4:00: No traffic, decided I better return to town and take a train. Hate to think of walking back fifteen miles, but it's mostly downhill.

4:10: Well, what do you know? I walked downhill about three minutes, and saw a cloud of dust ahead. It's a car coming up the road. I make an about-face and when the car reaches me, I flag it. It's the old boy I had seen at eleven o'clock who had promised to bring me a lunch. His '46 Ford-Mercury was loaded down with baggage and passengers. I expected him to say , "Sorry." He didn't and I squeezed in front with three husky fellows. The ride was most uncomfortable.

5:30: We got a flat.

6:30: The sun had set.

7:30: We reached Vallenar. Had flat fixed and dinner at an open-roof pension. The place was ice cold. One of the passengers got out there. Vallenar is not as nice as Copiapo. It is grimy and dingy. Everybody walks in the narrow streets.

11:30: At night, we pulled out. I rode in the back seat, a huge bag of tea for a companion. I dozed off at random. I had nightmares and fights with friends I haven't seen in eight years. Next day my driver said I talked loudly in my sleep.

All night Freddie drove. We arrived in Serena before daylight. He pulled up at the Tourist Hotel. He was surprised when I said I'd check in also. He had expected me to look for a cheap room with his two half-breed employees. Freddie and I had separate rooms. After four days and two nights on the road, it felt fine to take a hot shower and turn into a soft, comfortable bed with lots of warm covers.

We stayed in Serena two days, mostly on my account. It was a beautiful little city, and I felt like staying on and on. Freddie was as nice as could be. He was much taller and older than I. He wanted to see that I enjoyed myself in his country. We dressed in our best suits, had dinner together, met many of his friends, and drank *"Menta Flape,"* a sweet peppermint whiskey. We danced with the girls at the hotel. Two of them, he said, were worth 50 to 70 million pesos.

We went to the movies and drove out to Coquimbo, the seaport. The weather was like spring and on Sundays after dinner, the crowd came to the central park in their best clothes. Many of the girls were very good looking and wore the latest "new look" clothes. The fellows dressed handsomely also. An orchestra played in the park, and the crowd walked about in pairs of twos and threes. There were few cars, and many horse-drawn carriages, circling about the park and made it appear like a wonderful hometown.

There in Serena, they bottle papaya juice. It is a Serena specialty. It is very delicious and a good thirst-quencher. Because it has no gases and is a pure fruit drink, it cannot be shipped anywhere. In only a few days, it ferments. In Serena I heard some of the latest American songs—"Kiss on Route 66" and "Chicago Fire." How new and strange they seemed after being away so long.

We started on the road to Santiago again one cool sunny morning. The road to Santiago was dirt as usual. We didn't drive long when Freddie decided we should have breakfast. We stopped at a tourist hotel in a town called Tambillos. Freddie's half-breed employees ate with us. One of them was always "pulling my leg." I came close to hitting him. He got on my nerves. The other was a nice quiet fellow. Freddie was an auto salesman and tried to do some business in that town. While I waited I dropped into a music shop. The fellows and girls got a bang out of my selections. They were in Spanish—*"Quizas, Quizas," "Frenesie,"* and *"Ultima Noche."*

Three hours we waited, then drove out. The road was full of mud puddles. This was the rainy season and rumors were that it rained every day in this region and Santiago. We skidded and nearly got stuck several times on the muddy road. We got a wonderful reception on the radio, many popular American songs. This surprised me. A large percentage of the broadcasts were in English. Freddie and the fellows whooped it up on the hot boogie woogie pieces. Freddie left the English program on for my benefit. It was a long tiring drive for Freddie, so when he said upon arriving in Ovalle, "We shall stay over here tonight," I said, "Okay."

The best hotel was really a pension with a water jug and basin, etc. It was owned and operated by an ex-Aleman (German). He spoke English well. He had been in South American seventeen years: ten in Bolivia and seven in Chile. He learned English working with Americans in the mines.

Freddie seemed to know people in every town. He introduced me to several civilians and an army captain. We then had drinks together and I believe the captain wanted to drink me under the table. He insisted on "bottoms up." I followed easily. He was pretty high when dinner was served. We ate together.

Freddie and I went strolling about town. It was in a poor muddy shape. One dimly lit street made up the center of town. It was undergoing construction. Returning to the hotel, I felt a little cocky. I asked the maid, "Where is my room?" She directed me to it. I put my arm around her waist and asked her to sleep with me. She half-angrily threw my arms down, laughed, and said, "You don't savvy Spanish." And that was the end of that. She told Freddie and the fellows about it, and next day they kidded me.

Without coffee or breakfast, we pulled out of town before dawn. I was most sleepy and dozed off all day. We had trouble with the fuel lines and stopped several times to clean them. The radio helped make the trip enjoyable. All of us were plenty hungry when at noon we arrived at Combarbala, a fair-sized village

393

in a valley. A policeman directed us to a pension. Here we had *"almuerzo pobre"* (poor man's breakfast). It consists of steak, eggs, onions, and potatoes. It's a hungry man's dinner. Following this it is customary to have wine.

At 1:30 we drive out. The radio and Freddie's horn make up the noise. The road becomes paved. There are signs of autumn. Trees are in color and the leaves are falling. The countryside is green with vegetation and farm produce, a sure sign that the Atacama Desert is far behind us. We make good time on the paved road and before long we arrive at Valparaiso, the principal seaport of Chile.

The best hotel was the "Vina del Mar" (wine of the sea). It got its name because of the many acres of vineyards in the locality. It was the home of the gamblers and rich tourists. It was a bit too high for me, and I stayed only two days. (Cost five dollars a night). The rooms were luxurious. I registered at the desk, then Freddie drove me to the docks. There we separated and Freddie continued on to Santiago, 115 miles southeast. The seaport looked rough. There was good reason for Freddie and his helpers to warn me. "Keep your hands in your pockets and watch your money." The town was full of pick-pockets. People, soldiers, and police looked at my strange outfit peculiarly. I had hoped to find some American companion, but I only saw English and Swedish ships. I stopped at a restaurant for dinner and a pisco sour. I stopped at another principal bar but found none of my countrymen. I talked to the bartender and a Chilean air force officer and said "No" to an artist who wanted to sketch me for a price.

Taxi fare to hotel was 80 pesos, the bus 80 escudos. I took the bus. I took a hot bath, changed clothes, and went to the bar. No one there except a Spanish man and a woman at a lonely table. A drink cost seventeen pesos (35 cents). No one in the lounge. What a dismal quiet hotel. Really beautiful, but no guests. The bartender said, "It's winter season and few people come." The famous Monte Carlo Casino, a few blocks away, is closed for the season. Surrounding the hotel on one side are lovely flower gardens, on the other side is a huge swimming pool and the open sea, and to other sides are the lovely sandy beaches with fascinating coral reefs that make it a swimmer's paradise.

The following day was spent sightseeing about the beautiful residential sections. I took pictures of the "Mexican Park," the Casino, the lagoons, and the Presidential Home, situated on one of the nineteen hills that surround the bay. They range from 300 to 1,000 feet in height. A bus ride into heart of Valparaiso, part of the business section is ultra-modern; the other is colonial Spanish. I stopped for a few Pisco Sours at a principal bar. I met two seamen, one American, the other a Chilean of Swedish parents. I changed dollars there at 55; later at the U.S. Consulate, I could have gotten 59. The American invited me aboard his ship for dinner. he was the second mate. The ship was the Grace Liner *Santa Barbara*.

Five Chilean customs officers had dinner on board. They left much of the food on the plate. Latins don't go in for mashed potatoes and gravy, red beets. They didn't have to tell me that American food didn't agree with them. Like it or not, for my part, U.S. food is too simple and plain.

Coming out through the dock gates, I am stopped by several pretty girls. They are very friendly and hand me a card. I read it and they ask if I will come. I say, "I'll try." Chilean fellows look on and smile in an understanding way. I keep the card for a souvenir. This is what it said in bad spelling:

WELCOME AMERICAN BOYS
This is one of the best houses

in Valparaiso.

MISS MERY

Open day and night

Here you can find wonderful Girls
place for Drinking and Dansing

Towe bloks from the Echaurren Spuare
578 Clave St. Valparaiso (Chile)

That evening I went to a movie, saw *Time, Place, and Girl,* in Spanish it's called *Symphony of Love.* I stopped at restaurants afterwards, the waitresses asked many questions. It was easy to make out, but I decided not to and headed for the hotel.

The phone awakened me to another day. It was cold and dark as I walked to the highway and took a bus into Valparaiso. From there a cab driver said it was thirty pesos to the end of town; the bus fare was 60 pesos to Santiago. I decided to wait a half an hour for the bus. What a ride that was, not a bad contraption, only rough rough and beat up. Gas fumes came in from the engine and made everyone dizzy or sick. The road was paved all the way to Santiago. The ride lasted three hours along beautiful green farmlands. I made acquaintance with a Chilean fellow, his wife and child. In the city of Santiago, the child and mother vomited as soon as they got off the bus. I felt sick from the gas fumes also.

Santiago is a large city. My friends guided me to the American consulate. I had six letters. I read them in the office. The receptionist advised me "The Carreara" was the best hotel, but it was very expensive and most Americans went to the "City" hotel. There were no vacancies, and the "Savoy" was recommended. One of the best at only two dollars a day, including a private bath.

45
Santiago de Chile

Santiago, the capital and largest city, lies in the fertile valley of central Chile. It is noted for its beautiful parks, gardens, modern aspect, and German colony. The city was founded by the Spanish invader Pedro de Valdivia in 1541. Today it has a population bordering well on the million. Among the important buildings are the Cathedral, National Congress, Palace of La Moneda (the official residence of the president), Municipal Palace, National Museum, National Library, and the University of Chile.

Chile is called the "Shoe String Republic" because it stretches from Peru on the north to Tierra del Fuego (Land of Fire) on the south. Its total length is approximately 2,650 miles. About 300 miles of the country lie in the Torrid Zone in the north. Its southern part is Cape Horn, a cold, dreary region where the waters of the Atlantic and Pacific meet. In this region are the remnants of the ancient Araucos and Changos Indians. The central part of the country is the agricultural center and lies in the subtropical section.

Magellan was probably the first white man to reach Chile in 1500. Its settlement began forty years later. The Spaniards found it difficult to conquer the hardy Indian race known as the Araucanians. For nearly three hundred years, they resisted the advance of the white man and not until late in the nineteenth century were they persuaded that further resistance was unwise. Today Chileans are proud that they have no Indians floating about their fair cities. If there are any, they are probably officials of Peru, Bolivia, or Paraguay.

Chile has been a republic since 1818 when it threw off the Spanish yoke. With the aid of Argentine soldiers sent over a mountain pass, the Chilean patriots were able to defeat the

Spanish military authority, but it wasn't until 1844 that Spain finally conceded their independence.

Chile has had its civil revolutions like every other South American country. One nearly led to war with the U.S. when several American sailors on shore leave were attacked and one killed. The Chilean government made full amends in 1891.

Chile remained neutral during the First and Second World Wars, but its nitrate fields were the chief source of munitions material for the Allied nations. One Chilean put it this way: "We helped with the war, not with the *brazos* (arm) but with *materiales*" (materials).

The name "Chile" is derived from the Quechuan Indian word *Tchili* or ITchiri, meaning cold. It refers to the perpetual snow that covers Mercedario and other Andean mountain peaks.

Mine was a seven-day visit to the capital city of Chile. "When in Rome, do as the Romans do; when in Chile, do as the Chileans do." I am one who believes in the proverb. My first night in Santiago, I had lunch at one of the numerous "American Milk Bars." They are modern soda fountains and restaurants but do not sell liquor. A girl named Lucie walked in and sat beside me at the counter. We fell into conversation, then walked out and went to a movie. It was a late hour, so we weren't charged admission. After the movie, I saw no reason to take her home and get lost. I put her on a trolley and walked two blocks to my hotel room.

The next day we were to have dinner at noon. I broke the date. I went to see the Victory Parade. Once each year, on May 21, they celebrate the victory of 1879 when Chile defeated Peru and Bolivia. The president rides in a horse-drawn carriage through the city. Cavalry and foot soldiers in full uniform parade through, all of them wearing German helmets. The streets are roped off and hundreds of police are lined up, thirty or forty feet apart, to keep order. The parade is very impressive and the president rides by smiling, waving, wearing a silk high hat and dark clothes.

I returned to the hotel, found a letter from Lucie, asking, "Why did you break the dinner date?" I went to my room, and the phone rang almost at once. It was Lucie. I did not wish to see her,

398

but I decided I'd better see her than spend the evening alone. We went strolling through the *avenidas* (avenues), then through the parks, Lucie pointing out topics of interest. We worked up an appetite, then I suggested we get some dinner. She said she knew a nice place, so we went there. It turned out to be an expensive night club, from the entrance, one would never know it. The dinner and wine set me back a pretty price.

She asked if I had a tuxedo. I said, "No." Then she gave me an address where I could rent one. She wanted me to take her to another place next day, only there one was not permitted unless he was wearing a tuxedo. I thought to myself, *Who the hell does this girl think she is? Or who does she think I am? Cripes, I meet her in a milk bar and she drags me to the most expensive places. For all I know she is just a cheap street walker who goes crazy for Americans, believing I have a million to spend.* After dinner we took in a movie, then I put her on a trolley for home. Next day she called again and again, and the following days. She left letters at the desk for me, and I advised the desk clerk, "If any woman calls for me, I'm not in." He smiled and kept his word. I wasn't bothered any more.

Every day at twelve o'clock sharp, the sidewalks are very crowded. It's like any big city on Xmas or New Year's Eve. One moves along slowly in the crowds. It seemed unbelievable that I was in a big city again. There were hundreds of pretty girls, blonds, brunettes, and red heads. One really can't tell if they are Chilean, American, English, French, Italian, or German, but from earshot everyone seems to speak Spanish, so I guess the majority are Chileans.

They all wore long skirts; some looked good, others not so good. It was my first vision of the "new look." On Sundays the people really dressed up in their best Sunday suits and dresses. The army cadets dressed in light blue-gray uniforms with colored braids on their shoulders. Others wore long gray capes that touched the heels. One can sit in the Plaza de Armas (park) or second- story window of the American Milk Bar and truly enjoy the passing parade of color along the Avenida de Las Delicias (avenue of the delicious). It is the principal thoroughfare in the city.

One evening I met two young fellows. They were Chileans; one was blond, good-looking. He was the son of an Englishman, the other was Spanish and wore an upturned hat, American style. They lived at the Crillon Hotel, one of the most expensive. There Willie and Herman, my Chilean friends, introduced me to Phillip, an Argentine. Philip spoke perfect American; he was raised and had gone to an American school in Buenos Aires, Argentina. His parents were American. He was my age, the first young fellow I'd met in a long time. He was a steward aboard a Pan American D.C.-6 airplane. He flew from Buenos Aires, Argentina, to Miami, Florida, then to Lima, Peru, then Santiago, Chile, and back to Buenos Aires, Argentina. We had a long chat, but he could not join us on an evening's entertainment; it was quite late and he had to fly next day.

Willie, Herman, and I took a cab, went a few blocks, and the front wheel fell off. It rolled down the street a block, then crashed into a car. It was a laugh. The cab was such an old car, even the cabbie tried to suppress a grin. We took another cab to House 640. It turned out to be a private home with plenty of girls, fellows, and a U.S. Army Air Force mechanic named Dick. He was down there with an Army Mission and came there to satisfy his sexual desires. The practice of these houses has been pretty well accepted by all Central and South American countries or rather no great effort has been made to abolish them.

Herman, Willie, Dick, and I drank, played records, and danced with the girls. We spent about three hours there. The girls were pretty but something to watch as they danced. Dick went off with one to a room, came back a few minutes later and griped, "She wants a thousand pesos. What the hell does she think her ass is worth?" Later the lady of the house got him a girl and he only paid three hundred pesos, but before he came out of the room, we heard loud arguments as the girl demanded more money. I don't know if she got it or not.

We all took a cab back to town about three in the morning. The driver asked for 100 pesos. Everyone more or less expected me to pay the entire fare. I gave the cabbie 25 pesos, and Herman argued with the driver and flashed a press card; he was a newspaper agent. "The fare," he said, "should be only 40 pesos." Dick, the soldier gave him 30, making it 55 pesos and we walked off, leaving a frustrated cab driver behind us. I was disappointed in my Chilean friends; they lived at a better hotel than I, they invited me out, then expected me to pay all expenses. American or not, that's a hell of a way to be treated, but it's typical of Latin ways.

One evening I went to the bar of the Savoy Hotel. The bartender was a German. He could speak English fluently. He said he took me for an American at once. He said I should visit Paraguay and see and learn the native Indian customs. He thought I had flown and knew nothing about Indians. I told him I came by road hitchhiking and had seen all the Indians I cared to see. It was wonderful to be in a modern city again.

He was interested and said he liked my way of traveling and suggested I visit the Lake Region in southern Chile. This region is beautiful in the summer time, but at present heavy rains and cold made it dreary. He had been all over the world alone and with his wife. He hated the German army life. He hated to be shouted at and take orders. He had served in the First World War.

He introduced me to Truman Louis, a young American fellow, who was on his way to work in the oil fields in the southernmost tip of Chile, the cold, dreary Tierra del Fuego, the Cape Horn. Truman was a quiet fellow. He could not speak a word of Spanish, although he had Spanish features. He arrived the same day I did, four days ago, what a pity we did not meet sooner. He said he would have given anything to see an American the first day he arrived. At the hotel, they couldn't understand him and he couldn't understand them. Because of bad weather he was laid over in Santiago for a week. The bartender was the fellow who came to his aid and helped him pass the time away by taking him on a sightseeing tour.

We had dinner together at the hotel, then strolled about the city, stopping at various soda fountains and restaurants for Cokes or *Plantanos con Leche* (a delicious drink of bananas mixed with milk). I asked him if he cared to go dancing and see some girls in the Latin manner. He said, "Sure." I asked a cab driver if he knew of any nice places. He said "sure" and drove us to a very nice home. A woman opened a tiny window in the door; we appeared well dressed and sober, so she let us enter.

It seemed like a big party was going on. Everyone was well dressed, men and girls. Our hostess directed us to a sofa, and I ordered the drinks. Soon five or six girls joined us. Truman was very popular. He could not speak a word of Spanish; the girls thought he was only acting. They asked him question after question. He was most silent and very shy; the girls loved him for it. They made him utter a few words, and everybody laughed. I guess it pays to be unable to speak at times.

All the girls except two left us when they realized that we weren't buying them drinks. They got a commission on it. Truman didn't dance and soon his girl had him cornered and was really pouring all her love onto him. I danced a lot to English and Spanish tunes. To sleep with the girls would cost a pretty penny. I paid for our drinks and said we had only enough left to pay for a room and that was all. But because we had such a nice evening, the girls didn't care. They were really swell. Later they warned us to be careful of what streets we followed on returning to the hotel. At 3:00 in the morning, we rang the bell and woke up the sleepy night clerk to open the large steel gates. In Chile, that is a very late hour to be coming home.

The rest of my time in Santiago was spent going to immigration, police, Argentine consul, shopping for film, developing, writing letters, sightseeing and nightclubbing with Truman Louis. Louis said about all he got a kick out of was going to a movie. I just got a big kick out of mixing with the crowd and seeing lovely white senoritas.

We asked a policeman directions to the Casanova Nite Club. He directed us personally about four blocks. As a police sergeant, he made 2,975 pesos a month (about fifty dollars) and supported his family on it. We found the night club empty, but the band played on. We were the only two sitting at a table drinking Pisco sours at a dollar a throw.

46

Over the Andes to Buenos Aires

It was a dreary rainy morning the day I checked out of the hotel. I rode a *trambeo* (trolley) for a dozen blocks to the bus station. I was a half hour early, so I dodged into a coffee joint to get out of the rain. Soon the bus came. It was an old one. It was warm and had leather seats that kept jumping out of place on hitting a bump. Thank heavens there were no gas fumes to make the three-hour trip miserable. For a while we rode on paved roads, then it became dirt, rough and bumpy. The closer we got to the mountains, the worse the road became. We skidded many times on the wet muddy road. The passing scenery is very picturesque. The mountainsides and the valley are spotted with sagebrush and look like a huge leopard rug.

We arrived in the town of Los Andes and the rain was pouring. We stopped at a tiny bus station just opposite a lovely park. Most amazing and interesting was a block and a half of horse-drawn taxi carriages lined up alongside the park. This alone gave the town a peaceful, colonial aspect. It reminded me of a Quaker town in Pennsylvania. The oak trees surrounding the park were losing their leaves. Some were bright yellow and red. Seemed like autumn and it was in this country. There was not a car moving. It was strictly a horse-and-buggy town, yet there were fine streets and sidewalks. It would make a wonderful tourist resort.

It was only noon. I liked the town and decided to linger in it for a day. I checked in at the Hotel Continental. It was very nice. The low rates surprised me—$1.30 per day including room and board. At the bar I was informed the roads were snow bound and I could only go eighteen kilometers to Rio Colorado and no more. My hopes of hitchhiking over the Andes was crushed. It would be impossible to go in a horse-drawn carriage or on horseback either. There were only two other ways, by train or fly.

There would be a freight train going to the frontier in the morning and the following day a passenger train to Mendoza, Argentina. I decided to hop the freight over the Andes in the morning.

At supper I asked if the cook was a Yugoslav because of the dinner served. The maid answered that the manager was, so that accounted for the European dinner. It was rice and hamburger, rolled and cooked in cabbage leaves. I had a pint of red wine as a washdown. In the evening I talked to the carriage drivers.

Then next day, before dawn I walked about six blocks toward the freight station. At six o'clock it pulled out of the yard, and I hopped into the open doorway of a boxcar. I was surprised to find half a dozen fellows inside already. They wore dark clothes and looked like bums. It was still dark. From 6 o'clock to 7:30, I saw no signs of snow. Then I became sleepy, unraveled my hammock, covered myself, and dozed off.

About an hour later, I was awakened. It was the conductor; he asked for my ticket. I was surprised to see a conductor. I said I had no ticket. Then he asked for 104 pesos ($2.00). I paid only because I saw the other fellows paying and presenting tickets. Boy, that's something, hop a freight, then be charged for riding on it, and what's more, it was regular passenger rates like on a passenger train.

Looking out the open door of the box car, the mountain sides and tracks were covered with snow. The highway was pointed out to me. It was snow bound. Two to six feet of snow covered it. I wondered how I ever imagined I could go over it on horseback or afoot. It became very cold. I was shivering cold. We were climbing steadily, but awfully slow. This was the famous Uspallata Pass. I noticed a triple tractor-type chain in the center of the two tracks. Because of the steep incline over the Andes, the train could not make the ascent on tracks alone; for this reason the tractor chain was used.

Through a small open doorway in the rear of the box car, I could see into the caboose. I saw the conductor and brakemen drinking hot tea. I walked over and asked if I could buy some. They invited me into the caboose. There was a pot-bellied stove, and the caboose was very warm. When they learned I was North American and not an immigrant, they became most friendly and asked many questions, especially about prices of new cars and workers' wages. I had several huge cups of tea and bread. A customs inspector on board didn't bother to check my pack, figuring I was okay. They suggested I lay over at the tourist hotel at Portillo to wait for the passenger train due next day. The train would go only five kilometers more to Las Cuevas, the frontier, and there would be no place to sleep.

Four and a half hours after leaving Los Andes, we were high up in the snow-covered Andes Mountains and pulling into Portillo. There was a big modern hotel, and nearby a lonely railroad station, and two or three houses for railroad employees. Surrounding this were huge, looming snow-covered mountains, hidden out of sight beyond the hotel was a lovely tiny mountain lake, said to be full of fish. I hopped off the freight, walked alongside of it in deep snow to a path leading to the hotel. Some hotel employees came to the freight wearing snow shoes. The freight stayed long enough to unload several carloads of coal for the hotel's furnaces.

I entered the hotel; instead of finding a warm reception room, I found a cold, uncompleted basement with half a dozen fellows busy at work. They told me the hotel was closed. One fellow named Enrique Jones said they would make some kind of arrangement to accommodate me. Enrique was a Chilean, a son of an Englishman. He directed me to navy-type, two-decker bunk; only there was nothing but springs to lie on. I spread my hammock on it and soon fell asleep.

I awoke at noon in time for dinner. I ate with Enrique, five chief of maintenance men, and a pretty governess in a room undergoing construction. There were about a hundred men working on the hotel. Enrique said they had worked six years and hoped to complete the work in another year. There would be room for two-hundred persons. After dinner he took me on a tour of the hotel, from the basement, ultra-modern kitchen, to the sixth floor and the roof. Many of the rooms were already fully completed with bath and bedding. Yet much work still had to be done. Many fine views were to be seen, the beautiful lake, the snow-covered rocky mountains, and the ski lift. Starting the next month in June, the heart of the winter season, famous skiers from United States, Canada, France, Italy, and Switzerland would come here to ski. Portillo already was a famous ski resort, yet there I was in that big famous hotel, the only guest.

Enrique had to go back to work, so I decided to go skiing. I rented a pair of skis from a worker. The ski loft was not in use, therefore I had to walk up the steep hill; the snow was very deep, and I walked with the skiis on and using ski poles for balance. It took over an hour to reach the dizzy height. I was very warm and winded from the laborious climb.

Far below lay the beautiful lake, the hotel, and many rocky boulders. I hoped to clear them all as I raced downhill. I rested awhile, then got set for the big thrill. I moved out on the trail, bend forward, pushing out with the ski poles. Imagine my deep disappointment, when instead of going down like a bat out of hell, all I did was sink into the deep snow, despite the steep incline, all the way down I barely slided. I wished I was back in Pennsylvania where one really goes down hill on skies. Why do people pay thousands of dollars to come to this place, but then I guess the snow wasn't right; they had had a blizzard there the night before.

After supper I was shown to my new room. Nice soft bed, private bath, etc. Then I joined the bosses and pretty governess by the fireplace. We chatted and I showed them some pictures I had taken. I'm sure she wanted to be alone with me, but Enrique had a crush on her himself and stayed around like a noble knight. We retired at 11:00.

I slept wonderfully and awoke at 10:30; the day was sunny and bright. I had tea and bread served by the governess. I went to the station and bought a ticket to Mendoza. The station master was a wise guy, wanted Argentine money, changed my Chilean money to Argentine 11.50 to 1.00 instead of 10.00 to 1.00. The train came at 12:15. I waved farewell to Enrique and the girl. I went first class. The coaches were new; someone said they came from England. Slowly we crawled up the steep grade. Here and there were erected wooden tunnels to keep snowdrifts from blocking the railroad. Everywhere were huge, enormous boulders, snowdrifts, and a strong sun glare. Some of the boulders had inscriptions to "Beware and trust in Jesus and God," others had advertisements painted on them.

At Las Cuevas, the Chilean frontier, the train stopped for inspection and I had my passport stamped. We then went through a tunnel in the mountain. Someone said it was 3,200 meters long; by some coincidence it was 3,200 meters to the mountain peak, straight up. There at the level summit of La Cumbre Pass stands the beautiful peace statue, "Christ of the Andes." We cannot see it from the train. One must go by road and it is snowbound. On the statue is a Scripture in Spanish. I am told, it says, "Sooner shall these mountains crumble into dust than the peoples of Argentina and Chile break the peace which at the feet of Christ the Redeemer they have sworn to maintain." It has been erected to insure permanent peace between these two countries and commemorate the peace settlement of the boundary dispute in 1902.

Ten miles from Las Cuevas is Puente del Inca, the Argentine Inspection Station. All of the officials, soldiers, and civilians seemed to be wearing "gaucho" pants. They looked baggy and like bloomers women wore in the early Nineties. The customs officials were very pleasant, never opened my pack. They gave me a declaration slip for my camera. It came in handy later on. Once past the frontier we started rolling down hill. We see less snow. Seemed like Chile had it all. The homes of Argentine railroaders and farmers are made of hewn stone blocks. Certainly they are far better and warmer than the mud or shack houses I've seen everywhere else in the Andes.

There were many camera fans on the train taking pictures of the scenic rocky, cold mountain top. For company I had a Chilean railroad engineer, his wife and three children. They are going to Buenos Aires, then on to Brazil where he will study railroading. He hopes to go to the U.S. and work for the Pennsylvania Railroad. His English is very good. The day seemed to fly away. About 9:30 we arrived in Mendoza, 200 kilometers (125 miles)

407

east of the Christ Statue. We had to move our watches one hour ahead.

In Mendoza were many neon lights designating hotels. A red one shouted out "New Spain." I checked in there. It seemed okay, but at dinner I found dirty tablecloths and a waitress wearing a dirty apron. It was a poor welcome to a new country. The waitress's first question, as in Chile is "What class of wine will you have, red or white?" "Red," I said. Gosh, in Peru, Chile, Bolivia and now here, I must have drunk several barrels of it.

Mendoza is a large town and a beautiful one at that. Nothing very exciting happened during my two days' visit. I stayed over an extra day chiefly because I don't like to travel on Sundays. The business district has modern stores and a fine hotel. The beautiful residential sections are lined with autumn-colored trees. The restaurants in the evening are full of men drinking coffee or wine; the women I guess are at home. There is a lack of soda fountains. Santiago de Chile must have them all. The park on Sundays is full of men on bicycles. In the States these same fellows would have cars. Most of them looked thirty years old or more.

In town on Sunday, they had a parade. Several thousand strong, all civilians. They sang and carried banners of their leader, their president, the honorable Peron. Leading the parade were several women, following came the men, no band, no music, only singing and marching feet. The days were cool and sunny; there are many private country clubs and at last I stopped for a shoe shine. The manager knew me and said to some friends, "He is North American." They came to me, shook my hand, and patted my shoulder. "Welcome," they said, "few North Americans came to Mendoza, our city." There was no sign of hostility or dislike in any of the Argentines I've met, yet there were many rumors that Argentines were unfriendly toward Americans. My informers were Americans.

On Monday I awoke early and walked out of town. It was a long long walk; the night air was cold and made ideal hiking weather. A few cars and horse-drawn carriages and carts passed both ways. I was surprised. It just stayed dark and dawn refused to break, but when it finally did, it was a lovely sight. Along autumn-colored trees lining the paved highway, the golden-red yellow rays broke through. I really enjoyed the thrill of being free and hiking along. Many trucks and cars went by. I didn't even bother to "thumb" them. It was still cool and after three-and-one-half hours walking, I took my first "lift."

I had walked about fourteen kilometers. The truck took me only eight kilometers farther. The driver suggested I wait till nightfall for the wine trucks going to "B. A.." (Buenos Aires is called "B. A." by most Americans in South America). I decided to keep walking instead. It was another hour-and-a-half tramp before I "caught" a ride. I felt silly walking through little towns with the villagers staring after me curiously. The young fellow driving the pickup said we had about three hundred kilometers to go together. At noon he gave me a leg of a chicken. It was a very big one. His name was Enrique, a farmer and a "gaucho" cowboy. He wore those picturesque "bloomer" trousers. He was married, well-to-do, and showed me a picture of his three-year-old daughter. He was mighty proud of her.

We rolled over the endless, almost treeless pampas (prairie). We got a flat and had it fixed at San Luis. We pulled out again about six o'clock. His brother followed in a '40 Chevrolet automobile. He wore the picturesque "gaucho" pants also. We spotted three foxes alongside the rode. Two ran off and a third stopped to stare at us. Enrique stopped the truck, pulled out a 20-gauge rifle, and shot the fox at better than thirty yards. It fell and squirmed in pain. We ran to it and Enrique finished it off by throwing a rock at its head. He threw the fox into the back of the truck; the pelt would be worth fifteen pesos (3 dollars).

We turned off the main road, which was wide and paved to take a shortcut. It was paved also, but had many soft shoulders and was covered with sand. When passing other vehicles, we got a cloud burst. We had about 97 kilometers of this to Mercedes. We arrived at night. No charge. Enrique wished me a good journey and drove on to his home a few miles away. I checked in at a hotel.

At supper, several fellows at the next table were curious as to where I came from. I told them the U.S.A. Later as the landlady asked five pesos for the room, one of the fellows, the landlord I believe, tried to advise her by shouting "Norte Americano," but he was too late. He came beside us and said, "Five pesos is very cheap." I took a walk around the town's square and turned in. I had made good mileage that day, 195 miles.

I hated to get up in the morning, it was so cold. Then I washed my face under a faucet in the courtyard. The waiter brought me bread and butter for breakfast. I guess Argentina is like all other Latin countries in that respect. Then I started walking on the road to B.A. again. Going through town I passed hundreds of school kids, all dressed in white, the girls in white dresses, the boys in white linen coats. They all watched the strange traveler go by. I walked all morning through town, then in the open country. Luckily it was level and not tiresome hiking. There were many farms, the open cattle range. The road was black macadam. This highway is the pride of Argentina, but it is only two lanes. After four and half hours of walking, I stopped to rest on a road bank. Big flies forced me to get up and move along, blast them.

Several small English Fords passed by, then a '36 Plymouth stops for me. The driver looks English, but is a Spanish Argentine. He has small, stained brown teeth. We roll along, then suddenly he hits a bump and we get a terrible knocking behind. It turns out to be a broken spring shackle. We drive on nevertheless while the bolt or bracket keeps banging away. We got as far as Rio Quarto, but he leaves me out at the beginning of the town. It's a hell of a place to be let out, but still I'm grateful for the seventy-five-mile lift.

At a gas station, I inquired what bus to take to get through town. Luckily I met an Argentine Englishman. We had dinner together. He said I was the first North American andarin he knew of to come through that town. After dinner he waited on a corner with me and put me on the right bus going through the town. It was a twenty-minute ride, and I had to stand all the way. The bus was crowded, and the city was congested also. I was happy I got on the bus instead of walking through the town at that busy supper hour. It was at least forty blocks long. Once outside of it, I started walking. Three girls walked behind me; when I stopped they did likewise and we fell into conversation. They asked to take my picture. "Go ahead," I said. Two were pretty, one fat and otherwise. It was an hour and a half before sundown. I wanted to "catch" another ride, so I left them behind and walked and walked.

Dusk was falling when a car finally stopped. Two fellows in it said they could take me seventy kilometers (45 miles) to a gas station that was open all night at Agua Dulce (Sweet Water). They were cowboys and would be turning off to a ranch near there. It was pitch dark when I got out at the crossroads. I found the station closed and locked up. It became very cold.

I walked along to keep warm. I walked several hours; only two huge trucks went by. I became very sleepy. I put on more clothes, unrolled my hammock, and rolled myself up into it on the sand and sage of the Pampa Grande (Great Prairie). My flashlight was out of order, and I couldn't find wood in the dark. The prairie was treeless. I could no longer walk; my knees kept buckling under as I dozed off walking. I feared falling on the pavement or getting hit in case a car did come by. I decided it safest to lie down. It was a cold night with cold winds, but my hammock helped a lot. All night it was twist and turn from one side to another to keep warm. It seemed as if dawn would never break; when it did, I raised up, then flopped down again on my stomach, several times, till the cold forced me to get up and start walking. There was a heavy dew on the grass.

I walked from seven to eleven before a pickup stopped for me. At least a dozen cars and trucks passed me by. He was an Argentine. He said he could take me about two hundred kilometers (125 miles). I said, "Swell." We didn't talk much, and he drove very fast. Every truck or car that had passed me previously, we passed them all. It was level country and we made good time. Two hours later we were in La Carlota.

At a garage, he introduced me to an English chap named Dreyger. Dreyger said he would be going to "B. A." in about three hours and I could go along with him. I said, "Thanks" and went to a hotel for dinner; as usual I had a 16-ounce bottle of wine to follow. Then I walked about the town, came to a park, and sat under a tree. It was a warm day, and I soon dozed off.

I awoke and found it time to meet Dreyger. They had a sun

chair arranged for me in the back of a deliver truck. So thus I rode for nine hours till we reached Buenos Aires. Dreyger and I talked about the war, politics, movies, Chilean girls, etc. He said Chilean girls were very warm.

A Spanish fellow drove the car, steering wheel on the right-hand side, so when passing vehicles, he had to ask Dreyger who was sitting on his left for directions to pass. The Argentines used to drive on the left side of the road like the English do, but it's only a few years since they changed over to the right. The driver was a boxer, with seventy-two fights, winning by knock-outs. We stopped for coffee and lunched at roadhouses or truck stops. They refused to let me pay.

We arrived in the suburbs of "B. A." They took me to a train line. There we parted and I rode the train to the center of Buenos Aires.

A lady from Vienna kept me company. She could speak French, English, German, and Czech. She had spent many years in Argentina and looked like a typical New Yorker on a subway train. She was surprised when I answered some of her Czech, English, Spanish questions, but on French, I was stuck. She seemed to be of the fine European class of people. She doubted I was an American *andarin*. "If it's true," she said, "how wonderful, oh, how marvelous." *Oh, dear,* I thought.

The train pulled into a huge station, something like the one in Pittsburgh. It was just as busy and crowded. Took a cab to a fine hotel. No single rooms. I went to another. No single rooms. I went to a third. No single rooms. The cab driver complained he could not block the traffic while I inquired for rooms at each hotel. I told him to go ahead. At the fourth hotel, I got a double room and had to pay double. I had given up hope of finding a single room; besides, I felt silly walking through crowded streets with a full pack on my back. The hotel manager said, "Maybe manana have sencillo" (single). As it turned out, manana, nor the next day or the next did anyone move out. The room had no private bath, yet it cost four dollars a night. It wasn't worth it, except for being centrally located on Calle (street) Florida.

Since leaving Macuto, Venezuela, I had averaged my best mileage that day, 537 kilometers (334 miles).

47

My Stay in "B. A."

Buenos Aires means "good airs" in Spanish. It is the chief seaport and capital of Argentina. It is located on the estuary of the Rio de La Plata, about 170 miles from the Atlantic Ocean, in the province of Districto Federal. It is the largest city in the world south of the equator and the world's largest Spanish-speaking city.

It was founded in 1580 by Juan de Garay who named it Santa Maria de Buenos Aires. It is important as an educational center. It has the University of Buenos Aires, a technical college, and several art schools. It manufactures shoes and leather goods, woolen materials, furniture and machinery. The prevailing styles of architecture are classical and Italian and Spanish Renaissance. The principal street is the Avenido de Mayo.

The name "Argentina" is derived from the Latin word *Argentum,* meaning silver. The early explorers discovered silver in the vicinity and named the country "Argentina." Today it is one of the most progressive countries of South America. It was first visited by white men when Juan de Salas, a Spaniard, sailed up the broad Rio de La Plata in search of a direct route to India, the goal of all early explorers. He and a number of his men were killed by Indians; the rest returned home. Eleven years later, Sebastian Cabot, son of John Cabot, sailed up the river and established a fort near the present site of Rosario on the Parana River. This fort established the sovereignty of Spain.

Argentina struggled for independence like all other South American countries after the news of the French Revolution and the dissensions of Europe in the Napoleonic Wars. Argentina achieved practical independence in 1824, but formal recognition was not conceded by Spain until 1842. Like all Latin countries, she had suffered much from domestic revolutions, but her most serious internal complications have been settled peacefully and several boundary disputes have been submitted to international arbitration. The U.S. minister to Argentina and the King of England were prominent figures in those issues.

Argentina ranks next to Brazil in size and population. It is bounded on the north by Bolivia and Paraguay; on the east by Brazil, Uruguay, and the Atlantic Ocean; on the south the Atlantic and tip of Chile, and on the west, the three-thousand-mile long, Andes Mountains form a natural boundary, separating it from Chile.

The population is well over 12 million. They are Spanish, Italian, and German.

During both world wars, Argentina was placed in a delicate position. The German campaign seriously interfered with Argentine commerce. The country contained more than 70,000 settlers and sentiment was seriously divided. The government managed to stay neutral.

The first place I visited on first day in Buenos Aires was the U.S. Consulate. I had six letters, that was fine. Who should I meet there but George Aiken and Bob, the "Jeepers" from Alaska. I had met them before at the Gremlin House in Quito. From their tales they were having a rough time, chiefly financial. Because of this they were compelled to stay at the cheapest hotels, and to camp out. They still had the two jeeps. One of their party quit the trip, flew back to the States, and got married. The two girls, Jeanne and Dot, stayed on with the four fellows. At night they spread a tarpaulin over the two jeeps and camped out. They also made their own dinner by campfire and washed laundry in the river. It was a lot of fun, but one day George confided in me and said, "After traveling eight months, we get tired of seeing the same faces every day. Everybody wishes the trip was over."

Bob had even summed up enough courage to hitchhike with Dot from Santiago, Chile, to B. A. He bought himself a pack one day and surprised everyone by leaving camp. The "Jeepers" had driven south into the beautiful Lake Region of Chile, then crossed over the Andes into Argentina. There was an immigration or customs house at that point to clear them. They drove on north into "B.A." and presented themselves to the police. There they ran into trouble. The authorities delayed them for ten days. They could easily have sold the jeeps without paying customs duty. Now the authorities forbade them to sell the jeeps in the country. They would not be able to sell them in Uruguay or Brazil. They would have to ship the jeeps back to the States c.o.d.

These Jeepers were typical of many who had driven down from the States or Alaska. Upon arriving in "B. A.," they learn that hundreds have driven down before them. The Jeepers tried to sell their story to *Life,* but were told it was a daily occurrence.

George and I have lunch together, then call at a big department store to cash some checks. George gets only 5 pesos to a dollar because he has draft checks. I get 5.20; mine are American Express. We drop into Uruguay tourist agency. It's a fine one and we find the clerk pleasant to talk to. We then go sightseeing by ourselves.

We found that "B.A." was a big modern city. It had a fine bus, trolley, and a subway system. The subway surprised me. The trains were new, perfect to effect of new coaches, full of bobby soxers. Large electric markers designated the stops, and huge arrows pointed out directions.

"B.A." is a clean town, but so terribly overcrowded. Up and down Calle Florida, pedestrians walk to and fro, from one sidewalk to the street, to the opposite sidewalk. It is nothing but a maze of moving populace. One cannot stretch one's arms without socking someone nor can one gain distance in a hurry on this street full of people in various preoccupations of mind. Calle Florida is similar to street-walking pedestrians of Bogotá, Colombia. I imagine one can get used to walking in the street and get to love the customs and the crowds. It reminded me of "V.J. Day" in Detroit.

In contrast to the street-walking crowds of Calle Florida are the steady flow of auto and bus traffic on Avenida De Mayo. There are six or eight lanes, and traffic is heavy at all times.

George and I went to the water front district one night. I had once been warned in Venezuela by American seamen that it was a notorious and dangerous place. It took half an hour by bus to reach it. We went into one cabaret. It was almost empty. Girls grabbed our arms and insisted that we sit down and have a

415

drink. There was no music as yet. It must be early, so we walked out. We went a block or two and entered another. We met a couple of Englishmen and had beer with them. Surrounding the dance floor were tables and wherever a seaman sat, girls came to join them. The orchestra played tangos. It is said the tango was born along this water front and in Argentina they dance the tango at breakfast, dinner, and at supper. It is a nice tricky dance.

We leave this place and go to another cabaret. There we meet Americans and an Irish fellow from Frisco, California. Nowhere have I seen a place as rough as La Guaira, Venezuela. The water front district of B.A. is timid in comparison. We join the Americans in whiskey and beer.

The Irish fellow was singing at the top of his lungs. He had a marvelous voice. He sang to accompaniment of a pianist and a fiddler. He was about forty, had fought in Spain and shipped out as a seaman during the present war. They sang popular songs, the kind good fellows do when they get together. It made me think of my two lost brothers. It made me think about how they used to sing, so young, healthy, carefree, and full of life. Now they were gone. It made me very sad. They would never sing again, and I would never see them again. The gay happy fellows made me so melancholy that tears swelled in my eyes. I dropped my head on my arm and cried. I couldn't help myself. Over and over I said to myself, "I'll never see them again." The Irish fellow said, "I'm sorry, kid," and I felt his comforting hand on my shoulder. Soon I got over the cry and felt ashamed of myself. One of the seamen said, "Go out and get some air, there's a boxing show next door. Show them how to fight." George and I went. The fights were pretty good. We didn't get into any. I regretted I drank so much; otherwise I wouldn't have made a scene. Every time I drink heavy, I feel all alone; losing my two older brothers, I feel as if I lost my left and right arm and have to fight alone. They died heroically to the last minute. When I go, I hope to go down likewise, fighting.

Following a tip from a shoeshine boy, I was able to get a room at the Tandil Hotel on Avenida de Mayo. There I only paid two dollars a day and it included room and board. The Jockey

Club cost me four dollars a day for room alone. For some reason I slept late, till almost noon. I awoke to find my face and neck dirty. I couldn't understand it. On the third day, it dawned on me that smoke and soot from the kitchen goes up four floors to my open window through a chute and I sleep in a smoke screen.

I called my friend Gus Gershwin, the businessman whom I had met in La Paz, Bolivia. We had dinner several times together in the best restaurants of Buenos Aires. We dined at the Richmond Hotel, the Boston Bar, and at Schartiz's, a fine German place. There Gus treated me to a German dish of goose and herring smothered with raw onions and a strong vinegar sauce. He always insisted on paying. He was quite a fellow. He was 59 years old, quite bald, played tennis, and defeated 25- and 30-year-olds in five matches each Sunday. He was married but still had young girlfriends on the side. One of them, he said, was pregnant, and he helped her out financially. He liked to get himself into difficulties; otherwise life wouldn't be interesting. He hated traveling; how many times he told me that—whistle. He was a good friend of President Peron. He was going to arrange a dinner date for us three when business called him off to Belgium. Why he treated me so nice, I'll never know. I guess it's because I'm an American.

With the hotel owner's son and several Argentine friends, I visited the parks and one large private club. This club had three thousand members. My friends were members and could take me in as a guest only after presenting my passport. American tourists can go to almost any club.

It was a fine modern club with five or six floors, reached by elevator and stairway. There were gymnasiums complete with bars basketballs, boxing, mats, tennis, etc. Then there was a large indoor swimming pool, ice- and roller-skating rinks, restaurants and a dance hall. The roller rink was closed and used only on special parties or occasions.

We sat at a table in the ballroom and had tea. The crowd started coming about 5:30. They were mostly young girls and boys. The music started at 6:00, tangos and American pieces. My friends danced with several of the girls. Members come there often and get to know one another. All of them were nicely dressed.

417

I summoned up enough courage to go to a table and ask a girl to dance. Boy, was I surprised when she said, "Sure." But we only danced one song, she said, "Thanks" and sat down.

It was some time before I asked another girl with my friends' encouragement. She accepted also and it only lasted one song. *Dear me,* I thought, *rebuffs like this make me homesick for my own kind of girls.* (U.S.) Sometime later, a third try with a girl in bobby-sox clothes, but certainly not in her teens anymore. I lasted longest with her, about four songs. We danced to American tunes well, and everyone seemed to take notice. I was asked if I were a new member by several. I said, "No, only an invited guest." It was beginning to look like I was going to have a grand time when the band played "Wha Wha Wha," a sleepy tune that designated it as the last tune of the evening. It was 8:30. Time to go home, have dinner, and retire.

Such is the life among *"Gente Decente"* (good people). But by no means is the city "dead." There are enough people of different classes and other countries to keep life going to a later hour, mostly by sitting at sidewalk cafés and drinking coffee, tea, beer or wine, but chiefly coffee till I don't know what hour. The latest I was up was at midnight, that's when the magazine vendor boards up his corner shop to go home.

"B.A." had a fine bowling alley at the bottom of the Richmond Hotel. About six or eight alleys in all. I watched three American seaman bowling, asked to join in; they refused and said, "It's only us guys from the ship." "Okay, sorry," I said.

I spent one day riding the subways to Plaza Italia and nearby Palomar. It is as fine botanical garden, containing a fine zoo with a collection of worldwide animals, some of which I'd never seen likeness of in the States. Then there are beautiful driveways, lawns, lakes and statues, and long-legged pink birds, strange geese, ducks, birds, etc. One can spend an entire day strolling and watching the canoists paddling by in the lagoons.

My last evening in "B.A.," I took in an Argentine floor show with the hotel owner's son. The show was on the burlesque side; a couple of colorful "gauchos" (cowboys) and senoritas put on a singing and comedy show. The night club looked cheap inside, but the doorman had insisted upon our wearing ties. My companion liked my U.S. tie, so I gave it to him. It was my last. I had lost all my others by checking out of a hotel one day and leaving them behind on a hidden hanger. Nowhere in "B. A." can one buy a colorful tie. All are conservative or dark colored. The stores have the remains of what had once been popular in the U.S. twenty years ago. For this reason I gave my companion my tie. I promised to send him more.

In Buenos Aires I've been asked, "Why do Americans hate us?" I gave the only reason I knew of, "Because there are too many Nazis in Argentina." They answered, "We don't have them; Chile has them all." Likewise Chile said Argentina had them all.

As I look back on the people of Argentina, I don't see any reason why we should dislike them. They were swell.

48
Hitchhiking in Uruguay

After eight days, I bade farewell to "B.A.," one cool dark morning. I had walked, then taken a *trambeo* (trolley) to the steamer *Colonia.* The customs officers hardly checked my pack. Guess it was too much trouble. About two hundred passengers were making the two-and-one-half hour crossing to Colonia, Uruguay.

Tugboats pulled us away from the docks into the stream. It seemed quite narrow. Twenty minutes later we were under our own power and pushing across the choppy Rio de La Plata. It became very cold. Most everybody stayed indoors, including myself. The ship had a big saloon and a dining room. Both were very crowded.

I spent the trip alone, with my thoughts. I preferred it so. As a North American, South Americans are only too anxious to hear my story. What part do I come from? Where am I going? Have I been in the war? Will there be a war with Russia? And a hundred other questions.

One chap asked where I came from. "North America," I answered. Strangely enough, he asked no more questions and I was glad. He passed the word around soon enough. Fellows and girls looked my way. It was easy for me to start pleasant conversation, but I got mighty tired talking about myself. To speak to one was to have a curious questioning crowd about me. Most of them were Argentine or Uruguayan and were the better class of people, known as "*gente decente.*" Yet still one gets tired of conversation and wishes to be left alone. So thus I made the crossing of the "Silver River" in utter silence, watching the waves beat up against the sides.

We arrived at Colonia at eleven o'clock. It was another hour clearing Uruguayan customs before I got off the boat. I walked toward town; then two Uruguayan sailors joined me and directed me on a shortcut through fields and barbed-wire fences.

Once in town, it was quiet, peaceful, and clean. The paved streets were littered with fallen leaves. The homes were simple, adobe, Spanish structures. I came to a "Cambio" house. The lady said she changed dollars at 1 peso 30 centésimos, but she refused to accept travelers checks. Later in Montevideo I got 1 peso 86 centésimos on them.

I had no money to buy a dinner, so I told the sailors I could not stay in their fair city without money and I would start hitchhiking for Montevideo at once. They said, "You cannot go hungry, we'll pay for your dinner, and then go."

"Okay," I said, "but I want your address so that I can return the loan."

"No, don't be foolish," they answered.

So I had a free lunch, amidst three dozen dockworkers at a restaurant. Soon afterwards I started walking out of town along a fine cement highway. I was just beginning to enjoy the scenery and landscape of rolling green hills, spotted with a few sparse trees, when a policeman at a guard house interrupted my meditations. I retraced my steps. He asked for my passport, checked it, found it okay, asked a few irrelevant questions, said good luck and good going.

I hiked all afternoon. It was cool and I enjoyed the scenery. An occasional vehicle passed me by. By 5:30 I started looking for wood and a place to camp. At 6:00, when I had succeeded in finding an ideal place, a car sped by. I "thumbed" it. A long ways down the road, it stopped, then returned backwards.

I spotted them as Americans at once. Boy, were they surprised that I was also. They certainly never expected to find an American hitchhiker that far south. In fifteen Latin countries, this was the second time I got a lift from Americans. The first time had been in Nicaragua, Central America.

In the car were two American boys, former ex-GIs. They were Jack Garner and John Wade. They were students in Montevideo, studying Spanish and the import and export business. They had been to Colonia, looking for a side job to cover their social expenses. They had come by boat from the States to Montevideo. They asked if I had met a fellow pushing a bicycle and named Fred Bingle. I told them I had in Antofagasta, Chile. They were surprised. They had come down together on the same boat.

Once in Montevideo, they directed me to a moderate-priced hotel where they had once stayed. The way John explained the features of the room, lights, bath, and water made me laugh, and Jack said, "You'd think he was the owner of the hotel." It was located only one short tiny block away from the Plaza de Independencia, the center of town.

It was dark out. I had dinner with John and Jack at their lodging house in the suburban neighborhood of Bositoes along the splendid sandy beach. At the lodging house, I met several English boarders. Later we went to a cabaret. An orchestra played and there were many girls to dance with. John and Jack were popular and seemed to know them all. After one drink, some pleasant conversation, I excused myself and turned in. I was very tired.

My first day in Montevideo was a Saturday. I hated to roll out of bed. It was very dark inside the room. It looked like early morning. I overslept and failed to visit the U.S. consul before noon. The day was very windy and cold.

I must have wandered up toward the waterfront because the dress of the people wasn't too pleasant. They looked poor, shabby, and dark. I bought a magazine on the history of Uruguay, then went to a movie.

Montevideo is the capital and chief city of Uruguay. It is located on the north shore of the Rio Plata estuary. Today it is a great tourist attraction and is noted for its lovely beaches. Other points of interest are the Statue of Jose Artigas in the Plaza Independencia. He was Uruguay's first dictator. The Salis Theater is named after Juan Dias de Salis, who discovered the Rio de La Plata in 1515. The Municipal Palace, the Atheneum, the University, the Cathedral, the Legislative Palace, and the new hospital erected for the "workers" (general public). Montevideo's chief industry is meat-packing.

Montevideo has been the scene of many battles. With the aid of Argentina, her ally, she has been able to throw back the Bra-

zilians, the Spanish, the English, and the ambitious Paraguay-
ans.

The present republic dates from 1830. For a short time,
there was peace but in 1832, civil war broke out between rival political factions. These continued off and on for many years. Only
since 1910 has Uruguay been fairly free from political instability
and civil strife.

Uruguay was first visited by white men in 1516. The country
then was known as Banda Oriental. Juan de Solas was the first
white man to visit it, but the native Indians resisted his attempts to establish a settlement. Nearly a hundred years later,
another effort, with a large company of soldiers, was likewise a
failure. Not until 1726 was the first permanent Spanish settlement established.

Uruguay is the smallest independent country in South
America. It is located on the southeastern coast of the continent.
It is bounded by Brazil on the north, the Atlantic Ocean on the
east, and the Atlantic and river estuary, Rio de La Plata, on the
south.

The greater part of Uruguay consists of rolling green plains.
In the northwestern part are the wooded slopes and these range
to 2000 feet. The chief industry is animal husbandry. Cattle,
sheep and swine are most abundant.

Sunday found me sleeping till noon, then cussing the dark
cold room. It seemed like the early hour of the morning at every
hour of the day, then there was no place to read; the entire hotel
was dark and uncomfortable, yet one of the best in the city.

I cussed again. I asked the dark-complexioned maid if she
could press my shirt and clean a few spots on my trousers.

"Oh, yes indeed," she said. Later when I examined the shirt,
I found the collar burned and the trousers still retained the dirty
spots. I complained to the girl. She said the burn was there and
the trousers had to go to the cleaners. *What's the use,* I thought.
Later I cleaned the spots myself.

Such is the Latin way; they promise to do a job, but never
seem to do as they say and still collect the price.

Monday was my third day in Montevideo. Darn that room, I
slept till noon again. I walked up 18 de Julio several blocks and

catty-cornered to the U.S. consulate. No mail whatsoever, darn it. I catty-cornered back to 18 de Julio to the Brazilian consulate to obtain a visa for that country.

At the consulate I was given a bad time. First my passport photos were a little too small. I carried a sufficient supply of various sizes, but no, they gave me an address to a Brazilian photographer to obtain others. Then my health card was

a few weeks old. I got another address to go to a Brazilian doctor. He never examined or gave me a shot. He checked my old health card, wrote out a new one, and charged me $1.75 U.S. At the consulate I was told to return three days later for my visa and passport.

At the photo shop, I met a Swiss fellow whom I had met at the tourist hotel in Cuzco. He had difficulty getting a visa for Argentina. He said, "All over Europe is propaganda to visit South America. I come as a tourist and they treat me and all Europeans like criminals."

He had worked several months in Lima, Peru. He said he had enough of South America, up to his neck, the drowning point. He lifted his chin with the back of his hand to demonstrate. When I said I liked Lima, he said, "Oh, don't say that." He really didn't like it. "To like Lima," he continued, "it depends on where one lives."

He had a date with a Uruguayan girl whom he met at the Swiss Consulate. She was an office worker. He wanted me to join them to a movie. "Okay by me," I said. The girl was tiny, but very pretty. After the movie we had tea, then strolled many blocks to a brightly illuminated 18 de Julio. The night air was invigorating. When we reached my corner, I said good night and they walked on.

On Tuesday morning John and Jack called for me. We were going to school. The building did not look much like a school. In one of the rooms, I met the Spanish teacher. John and Jack took lessons from him. He could not speak a word of English. We sat about a great table. John and Jack were the only two students present. I sat at the table and listened in. The subject turned to girls.

Lessons were two hours a day, from ten to twelve. At eleven

a girl from another class joined us. We promptly took our books and went a block or so to a restaurant. There we had coffee and the lessons resumed. The male teacher and the young lady talked on. How to and how not to ask a girl for a dance, what to say if she accepts, and what to say if she refuses. With a little bit of acting, the lesson was interesting and funny.

The lady was learning some English also and once she remarked, "Stop pulling my leg." With her accent, it sounded like a lyric tune. The lesson continued a bit after twelve.

I had planned on spending the afternoon with John and Jack, but on entering the hotel, I met Swiss. He wanted to see me, so John and Jack said they would see me in the evening.

After lunch, topped off with a bottle of wine as usual, Swiss and I went past the docks. What a terrible odor there was! I had to hold my nose in a handkerchief for several blocks, regardless of the glares I received from folks living or standing by. We walked the pier well out into the stream and took pictures of the men fishing with rods and nets from huge breakwater blocks.

We walked to town, holding my nose again, and stopped at the French steamship company. Swiss wanted to buy a ticket to return home. He spoke French with the clerk. The clerk was elderly, bald-headed, squat, and Jewish. It was the first time I ever heard French spoken. I could hardly repress from laughing. The clerk made such funny beeps and burps.

Swiss and I went to the Brazilian consulate. The clerk said, "You were told to come at 5:30 and not 3:30." I grinned and said, "Okay." He smiled back as I left. Such are the Latin's ways, never come early or before time, better to come late or next day. When I did return at 5:30, I had to wait another hour as I expected.

Swiss had an important engagement for the evening and asked if I could meet his girl friend and take her to a movie. I said, "I'd be delighted."

Jack called for me at 7:30. I was surprised to learn he taught English at night. We drove to a public building that served as a school. There were many students and many classes. Jack had ten students in their fifth year of English. They spoke very well. They read *Time* magazine, then held discussions on the topics of interest. Later Jack had me telling them about my trip. "I came to listen in," I said, "not to lecture." But the students were curious about my opinions of their northern neighbors.

One new word they learned that evening was "hitchhiker." There is no Spanish word for it. The nearest word is *"andarin,"* which means "walker." The lesson lasted two hours. Jack was pleased, then we drove to 18 de Julio, had tea and listened to an all-girl orchestra. They played from an elevated floor, ten feet high, and gave the boys plenty of legs to look at.

We soon left and I still had time. Jack and I waited five minutes by the theater, then she came. She was as pretty as a picture in slightly wind-blown, dark, curly hair, pretty face, and dressed keenly in a green coat and a white scarf about her neck.

I explained, "Swiss asked me to keep his date, okay?"

"Sure," she answered.

Jack grinned, nodded his approval, and departed. Viola and I took in a double feature. Afterwards we had tea and sandwiches. Boy were they thin, not more than a quarter of an inch thick. Outside again in the cool air, Viola asked, "Where to now?"

"Sleep," I said. "Want to join me?" I expected to get my face slapped. But the pretty thing said, "Sure, why not?" After an hour, feeling satisfied, I thought I'd sleep better alone and sent her home.

A visit to Uruguay is not complete without making a tour of the capital city. So Jack and John called for me next day at noon. First on the list was the beautiful monument of oxen pulling a cart. It is a great work of art, the straining muscles of the oxen are outstanding. Beside the oxen is a prodder on horseback. The team of oxen, cart, and rider is mounted on a small grassy slope. It is most impressive. Surrounding it are beautiful lawns, and in the foreground is a small pond full of fishes. The statuettes of the dogs were stolen. It is a monument and a tribute to the early pioneers. A picture of this great work is found on the Uruguayan five-peso note.

Next on the list was the new hospital. It is a great big beautiful white structure with many windows. It has nineteen stories in all. It is equipped with the latest medical equipment science has produced. It is called the Obreros (workers) hospital. Money for the construction came from deductions in the people's pay.

Many people were visiting, and a nurse and a hospital attendant took us on a tour of the hospital. It was very modern. There were a score of elevators. We got off at various floors. There were new beds; a number could be cranked into various angles for people suffering with broken bones or cut limbs. There were modern bathrooms, great windows, air conditioning, operating tables, and huge telescopes. Student doctors sat in a room without windows. On the wall was a circular screen; watching this they were able to see the operations performed by doctors. Actually the screen was a telescope. In this way they could only see the doctors' hands at work and a close-up of the operation. Then we visited the cold storage room used for the corpses, the sanitary wash machines, and the kitchen. From the top floor, we got a wonderful view of the white city, the white sandy beaches, the blue sea, a football stadium, etc. The hospital is in the heart of the city. Looking from the hospital, it was a clean white city indeed.

We visited the yacht club. Surrounding it were hundreds of gay-colored canoes and yachts in the quiet bay. We stopped at a roadside restaurant. We had some peculiar toasted tomato and pepper sandwiches. They were good. We asked the waiter the name of them. Five minutes later we forgot it. Then we paid a visit to some Uruguayan folks they knew. The home was beautiful. John and Jack speak Spanish very well after only four months of intense study.

There are many coffee houses in Montevideo, specializing in Brazilian coffee, but nowhere could I find a soda fountain. Montevideo needs only one ice-cream soda fountain and it will be like hometown, U.S.A.

The following day I decided to present myself at the immigration office in Montevideo. When I entered the country at the city of Colonia, the officials there told me I would have to check with the authorities in Montevideo. The office opened at noon, 1:30 to be exact. A large line was waiting for the doors to open. I got in line also. Soon others came and it was a block long. Then more foreigners came and crowded about the doorway. An uproar started in the line. A lady shouted, a la cola, a la cola" (to the end of the line). The group gathered about the doorway refused to budge. When the door finally opened, there was a terrible pushing and shoving. I was pushed along.

The heavy-set fellow in front of me, upon nearing the doorway, swung a blow at one of the group. I got the back slap of his elbow in my nose. It was a hard blow and I expected the nose would bleed, but it did not. The shoving continued to the second floor. I was first at the teller's window, but hasty Latins from behind jammed their hands and documents under my arms, over my head and all sides to the easy-going receptionist.

He noted my hopeless, disgusted look and attended to me, but not before three or four loud- shouting men or women behind me got waited on first. He then told me, as an American tourist, I did not have to present myself at the immigration office or the police.

Such are the Spanish ways; at one place they tell you to present yourself, at another they say it's unnecessary.

It seemed unfair also, as a tourist that one would just about have to get himself killed to clear customs red tape.

Soon afterwards I met Swiss at the Cathedral Café. He was happy. He finally succeeded in getting a tourist visa to visit Argentina, but only because he had bought a ticket to return to Europe within two weeks.

It is a beautiful sunny day for a change and no strong wind blowing. We go strolling and buy a couple of Spanish berets. Most every fellow wears them in Argentina, Chile, and Uruguay, but I'm told only workers and low class people wear them. A business or society fellow never wears it.

Six days I spent in Montevideo, on my last I had to go to the Officina de Correos (post office). There they had a statue of a man, nude and sculptured, to the point of embarrassing the women as they walked past. It's not the only one in the city, there are many more. They are the object of much criticism and many jokes from newcomers and the residents.

I went to class with Jack again; the two hours went swiftly. I had dinner with John, Jack, and several Spanish businessmen in Bositoes. Conversation and wine lasted till midnight, as I was leaving, John was putting a tangerine on Jack's seat, forever a practical joker.

At the hotel, the night watchman gave me my bill and I paid him. Later in my room, I checked it. I found I was charged eight days instead of seven and a half days. It was agreed, when I checked in, that I would pay only a half a day the first day because I had missed all my meals. I was also charged 1 peso 60 centésimos instead of 1 peso 20 centésimos for wine. I had four bottles. I was overcharged about $3.

The watchman called at 5:30. Later downstairs I told him about the mistake. I told him to wake up the owner and have it corrected. The manager said, "Sorry, it's correct."

I said, "Okay, forget it."

As I walked out of Hotel Vascongado, the night watchman who was also the assistant manager, shook his head from side to side and sighed, "Sh, sh, sh." At the door he shook my hand and said, *Que le vaya bien, felicidades.* (Have a good journey, happiness).

Such are the ways of Spanish hotels throughout South America. An American traveler does not like to argue or call the police for a dollar or two, but take a loss at every hotel for five or six months and it adds up to a lot of money. It brings the day's cost of living to parallel with the U.S. high cost.

Once outside it was still dark and chilly. The streets were nearly deserted. I walked up 18 de Julio, looking for an open café. There were dozens of policemen in dark blue uniforms scattered about. *Gosh,* I thought, *this city doesn't need all that protection or does it?* One of them directed me to an open café. I had black coffee and once again those very thin quarter-inch sandwiches. I had to have six to make up for two.

I waited for bus number 103 or trolley number 24 to take me to the end of town. I flagged a bus, but it failed to stop. Next came the trolley, and I hopped on. I asked the conductor to let me out at the end of the line. The ride lasted forty-five minutes. It became crowded with newsboys and workers in dark, drabby clothes. It looked like any U.S. trolley in the early hours of the morning.

I became the object of many stares. I sat in the last seat at the rear entrance. When talking to the conductor at intervals, naturally, at the sound of my voice, they had to rotate their heads, listen, and stare. This Latin habit is annoying, but one must get used to it and ignore the curious.

It was pitch dark when I got out at the end of the line. Many "Pando" buses passed me by on the cement highway. Ten kilometers I walked before I got a lift to Punto de Rieles, three kilometers farther away.

I walked again. I didn't mind. It was cool. The countryside was rolling green and dotted with grazing cows. Four and a half hours out of Montevideo, I stopped for lunch at a tiny gas station. The man sliced up about a pound and a half of cheese and sausage into bite-size bits and with some lemonade, it filled me up swell.

Soon afterwards a 1948 Packard convertible stopped. The man and wife spoke English. They had been to the States and said at once, "You must be American." Where else in the world would there be hitchhikers?

The man was in the lumber business and had spent some time in Europe also. He pointed out a huge Christ statue on a small hilltop, near the beach. It is called Pan de Azucar (sugar loaf). The statue has winding stairs within, and one can get a view of the countryside.

Soon after passing Pan de Azucar, he suggested we have dinner. I said that I just had mine. He said, "Well, have it again." We drove off the main road towards the beach to a huge log cabin restaurant amidst a grove of trees. It was a lovely spot with the pounding sea only a dozen feet away. It was interesting inside also. It reminded me of Santa Claus Lodge in Alaska. Only the huge bear skins were missing. We had a splendid dinner of chicken and wine. It was his treat.

We drove on again along a fine road. The wife was very pretty, and both were dressed handsomely. We talked politics. His opinion was, "The world needs a master. Rather than to see the Russians or Germans be masters, I'd like to see the Americans be." After some time the ride came to an end. We separated at a junction. They were going to Punta del Este, and I had five kilometers to walk to San Carlos.

It was about 4:00 P.M. I walked along, hoping for another long lift, but none came. Some came in forms of horse-drawn wagons, loaded with hay or wood. Drivers offered a lift, but I said, "No thanks." It would mean telling them a story. I walked slowly and finally entered San Carlos. It was still broad daylight.

I started looking for a hotel. No rooms at one place, nor another. I asked the lady if I could deposit my pack while I scoured other hotels. "No," she said, "impossible."

What harm could there be in checking my pack for a half an hour, but such are the ways of the Latins. I then crossed the main plaza. Hundreds of eyes were upon me. I came to another hotel. No luck, but I could deposit my pack. I felt like camping out but it started raining and getting colder.

The Hotel America is about seven blocks away from the plaza. I got quarters there. It was simple but very clean, like the tourist camps in the U.S.A. Along the way I received many a shy, pretty smile from girls standing in doorways, patios, or windows. The town was nice and full of them. It was a shame I couldn't afford to be a spendthrift.

My first day out of Montevideo I averaged 137 kilometers (85 miles). It was not very good.

I started the second day by getting up a little late. Nine o'clock found me hiking out of town along a dirt road. It was a nice day for tramping, even if it was a Sunday. Three hours I walked. Two cars went by—taxis. Well out into the country, I saw a man digging up his garden. I asked if he could be kind enough to give me some water. "Sure," he said, "come on in and rest awhile."

We sat under the porch roof of his large mud house. I drank several glasses of water. He suggested I try drinking "maté." He handed me a pear-shaped gourd filled with grain. It looked like dry grass seeds. He then poured hot water into the gourd, and I sucked up the liquid through a silver tube called a "bombilla." It is supposed to contain much vitamin. It tasted bitter and I handed it back.

Everywhere one sees people drinking maté, in Argentina, Chile, Uruguay, and Brazil. They drink it at home, in the offices, and walking down the streets.

I was surprised when his wife called us to dinner. They were very hospitable. We sat on boxes and benches at the crude table.

431

We had noodles with bits of pork and ground cheese. It was supplementary and good. About the table were three lovely children. They were white and blond. The parents were healthy and handsome also. She believed a black man was the same as a white man.

I asked the man how long it took to build the home. "Three days," he said, "with the help of three or four men." It was painted pink on the outside. The inside was whitewashed. The floor was dry mud, so unlike the damp Indians' huts of the Andes. The roof was thatched, the walls of compressed mud.

They wanted me to linger, but I had "itchy feet," commonly known as "roaditis." I shouldered my pack and moved on. From a hilltop I waved back and soon they were out of sight. I plodded on and on along the dusty road. Two hours later an ancient Ford came along. It had no windows or windshield. The young driver wore a woolen "helmet" that covered his ears and mouth. He drove very fast. We talked not at all. One could not hear with all the noise that the car made.

Several hours later he turned off the main road and left me out. He was going to a mine. I was only two kilometers from Rocha. Hiking into Rocha I passed a strange cemetery. Like the people of Peru, the Uruguayans do not believe in burying their dead. Instead the bodies are placed in cement vaults, similar to a morgue. The vaults are five or six rows high. Many Latins think it's much nicer this way, but if the rentals of the vaults are not paid, the bodies of the ancestors will be removed.

I avoided the principal street going through town; I followed one block east of it, heading north. Even so a lot of people stared after me. One bold young lady called out, "Where do you come from, Caballero?" "North America," I answered and continued walking. One question after another followed till I was out of earshot. At the end of town, it started to pour. I dodged into a pool room. Many fellows were there playing pool. They merely asked where I came from. They usually think I'm *Aleman* (German) till I advise them different.

A soft drink I had cost about a penny. It stopped raining, so I started hiking again. I walked till it was almost dark. I was well out in the country. No traffic went by. It looked like I'd be camping out in the pasture with cows for companions. But as I walked, contemplating my predicament, a large bus came rolling over a slight ridge. I "flagged" and it stopped. I rode it for 56 kilometers into Castillos. The fare was expensive because gasoline was high priced. ($1.25 for 35 miles). It was another bad day. I went only 124 kilometers (77 1/2 miles).

In Castillos, it was no easy matter to find a room. I went to three hotels. What joints! Each had a bar at the entrance, crowded with drinking, bearded gentry. I didn't like entering with a full pack on my back, but I had to. The bartender said, "Yes, we have rooms," then asked the *dueno* (manager). Each time the *dueno* said, "No," at every hotel. I was beginning to imagine that foreigners or white men without mustaches were not welcome.

At long last I wandered up to the Uruguay-Brazil Hotel. The lady said, "Sorry, no rooms." I told her I'd been to the other three, the bartenders said, "Yes," the owners said, "No." What goes? She then said to wait; she could fix me up a cot in her son's room. "Okay," I said.

I ate supper alone at the hotel. A pretty blond waited on me. An elderly woman at the next table asked me many questions, then she jerked her thumb towards the girl. I looked beyond, out the window, saw nothing. They laughed. They meant if I liked the girl I said, "Yes, she is pretty, but too young for me." The girl pouted, saying, "I'm seventeen years, going on eighteen."

Later in the evening, I stood in the doorway, looking out into the starry night. She came and stood beside me, but not for long. A couple of drunks, in bad shape, came and sat on a bench near the doorway. One was very sick and moaned in such a way that I thought he would die. The girls' mother came and pushed her inside. She did not return again.

I undressed and lay down; suddenly, "crash," the cot caved in. I reset the legs and soon fell asleep. I turned over and "crash," the cot went again. I noticed the lady's son's bed was unoccupied. He probably would not be in, so I rolled into his bed.

I rolled out of bed early, had breakfast as usual, black coffee and bread. I strolled about town a bit. It was about 5,000 population and not a paved street in it. I must say they were wide enough, though. All the buildings were Spanish, Portuguese adobe design. All the cobblers were too busy to fix my shoes. I decided not to linger an longer in that friendly city. I paid my bill and as I walked out, the pretty girl said, "Oh, you leave me." I said, "Yes," hugged her in Latin style, and said "Adios."

I was told Americans almost never come to Castillos. Therefore at the hotel, once they knew my nationality, they were most friendly.

After several hours walking and no traffic, I stopped to lunch on chocolates and oranges that I had bought on my way out of Castillos. I sat on a grassy knoll and read *Time*.

After a period, I walked again and found myself walking alongside a large lake called Lago Negro de las Difuntos, on my left and the Atlantic Ocean on the right, only I could not see the Atlantic waters. It started to rain, and again luck was with me. A sand truck came along. It took me twenty kilometers. The driver said I would only have ten kilometers more to Santa Theresa Fortress, near the Brazilian border. He was wrong. I walked from Kil. 291, where they stopped to work on the road, to Kil. 299. There I found another marker saying eight kilometers more to the fortress. That made a total of sixteen kilometers.

I walked on and came to a few stray houses and a store. I was tired with about twenty-five kilometers (15 miles) in my legs. It would be dark in another hour. It started raining again. At the store I supped on cheese, cookies, and lemonade. I was told a bus would come by at 5:30. I had ten minutes to eat, and sure enough, it came on time.

I rode the primitive bus past the fortress. I had given up hopes of "catching" a ride on that lonely highway. The fortress loomed big and red through the downpour. Surrounding it was a great lawn and a park. It had been built in 1764 and was said to contain a museum. It was one of the tourist attractions of Uruguay.

I figured I might as well sleep in Brazil. The bus was going to Victoria. So I bought a ticket to that city. It was raining hard when we came to Chuy (chew-ee) on the border. There was an *aduana* (customs) sign, but no border officials came aboard to check the passengers or the cargo. I changed currency there at a fair rate; one Uruguayan peso equaled 12.5 Brazilian cruzeiros.

It was hailing ice as we rolled into Brazil. It became pitch dark. The road underneath was rolling, pitching, slicking, and bumpy. We couldn't see anything, and I wondered what kind of country I was getting into. The ride lasted two hours. We came to a stop at the principal pension in Victoria. I was charged $1.50 for supper and lodging. We were rushed into dinner. The table-cloths were filthy. The silverware was placed in tripod shape on the table, like rifles. The silverware was tin alloy. The food was abundant, but a Brazilian mystery.

I didn't get very far that day, a mere 86 kilometers (48 miles). Hitchhiking was a lot worse there than in the States.

49
Along the Beach of Brazil

I awoke to a bright sunny day. It was my first day in Brazil. But alas, it was a disappointment at the start. I learned that I was thirty-odd miles into the interior of Brazil and not on the coast highway. This meant I would have to return to Chuy on the border and get on the coast highway going north. A "dead" highway confronted me to the border. I would, no doubt, have to spend the day walking to reach it.

I met the Uruguayan consul, and he advised me not to worry about the immigration at the border, but to present myself to the police at Rio Grande do Sul or in Rio de Janeiro. I lunched on black coffee and cakes and bought a supply of chocolates to carry me over. The wide streets were six inches deep in mud, and my twelve-inch boots came in handy. Several horse-drawn carriages went by, but the women driving evidently were afraid to give me a "lift." The muddy road stretched ahead, full of rolling ridges and mud puddles. On either side were green farmlands and heavy timber. I hiked along for an hour and a half. It looked like a hard day's tramp ahead of me. I heard the sound of a motor and looked back. I was most pleased and surprised to see a dump truck coming my way out of the isolated wilderness of Victoria.

Sure enough it stopped, like motorists do in all isolated parts of the continent. The barefooted, low-class driver could not speak Spanish, and I could not speak Portuguese. Therefore we rode in silence till we reached the outskirts of Chuy, where I got out on the coast highway. The ride took about an hour.

The coast highway did not look much like a road. Nothing but sand ruts, water and mud, but it had all the signs of recent travel. I started hiking again. I came to a cabin and decided to inquire if I was on the right road. Here, the road is the beach of the Atlantic Ocean. Around the corner, a huge dog startled me. He jumped at me viciously, but luckily he was chained and missed me by inches. The owner silenced it and said, "Yes, you're on the right road." I thanked him and continued walking on grassy ridges and banks, avoiding the mud and water on the road. An hour went by, then a loaded truck passed me. Then another came and stopped for me. The cab was full. The driver asked to see my *documentos* (documents). Satisfied, he said to climb aboard. I did and settled down on a tarpaulin covering a load of dry sheep skins.

Four a half hour, I hung on while the truck rolled, swayed, bumped, and splashed on the sandy road. Soon a towering light house came into view. Moments later we were entering the village of Baileneario. The truck stopped at a Hotel Silva, and several officials came forth to register and check his cargo. I was then invited to a cup of coffee and paõ (bread). We crossed a field to a crude mud house where we lingered a half an hour over our lunch.

Baileneario is along the beach. We drove out and the driver headed the truck toward the pounding waves of the mighty Atlantic. I did not know the reason at first. I thought he had gone crazy. Just as we reached the water's edge, the driver turned sharply left and headed north on the hard, water-packed sand. So that was the reason.

It was a wonderful view; as far as the eye could see was the broad, clean white sands. It stretched ahead for miles and miles. I never knew such a lovely beach lined the coast of southern Brazil. We drove along at forty miles per hour more or less. I'd seldom seen a speedometer running on South American trucks. They disconnect them because of the difference in miles and kilometers. I was riding in the cab. One of the passengers got out at Baileneario.

My driver said, "When the moon comes out, one cannot drive along the beach." Meaning that when the tide comes in the beach is dangerous. We had several hours of wonderful driving on the hard water-packed sand. We passed the remains of three wrecked ships. Two were Argentine and one was American. It was late afternoon, and I was beginning to wonder if we would reach the lighthouse where my driver said we would sleep. The waves rolled up closer to the soft sands and washed deep ridges (ruts) that were difficult to drive over. Some were so deep that we had to head into deeper water to avoid them, and then there was a sickening sensation that there might be a deeper rut underwater and we might stall and a huge wave could turn us over.

Soon we spotted the circling beacon light, and my driver said we would make it. We drove on a ways over smooth water-packed sand, then ran into ruts again. It was hard driving, over ruts and through salt water. My driver said, it took a lot of experience to drive along the beach, and I believed him.

It was 5:30 and only a half-hour before sunset when we pulled off the beach, up a soft sandy lane to the Faro Barton (Lighthouse Barton). It was a lonely outpost. I met the chief of the lighthouse, his wife, and life guard crew. We entered his shack. It became pitch dark, and by candlelight, they talked in Portuguese. My driver spoke Spanish and did the interpreting for me.

Out of the darkness came several youths. One of them spoke English. He had shipped to New York, New Orleans, and Florida a lot while on board Panamanian ships. While we talked, everyone was silent, listening to this strange language, for seldom do visitors of a strange land end up at a lonely lighthouse on a dismal windswept, bleak beach.

We were there several hours without a word being said about food or coffee. I had an empty sensation that we would spend the night sitting up talking and hungry. Then all at once, out of the kitchen came macaroni, cheese, bread, and coffee.

Not long after the dinner, we were guided through a sandy field, sparse with dry brush. The cold night wind was biting cold. About a hundred yards away, we came to a three-room shack. The lady fixed up the beds, and we undressed and turned in. All was quiet except for the howling of the night wind and the ceaseless circling of the beacon lights.

We were awakened before daylight by the driver. It was mighty cold climbing into my trousers. We hurried across the cold windswept field to the chief's house. We had several cups of hot black coffee and bread. It was still dark when we drove out to the beach and turned north. The tide was out.

For an hour the beach was smooth. It was raining hard, and a strong cold wind blew some of it through the canvas flags covering the windows. The sea was very rough, then the beach became bad. Streams flowing to the sea from the distant mountains to the east washed the sand away, and deep ruts and channels were formed. Some of them were a foot to two feet deep, and it was impossible to drive over them. We could not go farther ashore because of the soft sand. We had to drive into the water and play games with the mountainous waves. Even in water a foot or two deep, there were sudden unseen ridges and we dropped roughly into them and with a lot of luck, out again. Many times we caught our breaths, and many were the tense grins of success as we plowed through. Why the engine never stalled or became flooded, I'll never know, and surely this salt water had to be hard on the metal parts of the truck. Two-and-a-half hours of dodging the waves and high ridges had tired my driver. He drove off the beach to a dismal shack on shore. He said we might have to lay over another night if the waves didn't subside. Sometimes, he said, trucks or cars were laid up for four and five days in bad weather.

It was still raining. We entered the dreary, weatherbeaten, one-room shack. Two young women prepared black beans and rice, fried in lard, for us. They were dressed in shabby, dirty clothes. They were fat jowled and the baby likewise from a diet of rice and beans, I imagined. A solitary porker grunted about the doorway on the outside. *Some day*, I thought, *it would make their meals more tasty*.

After two hours we were ready to start again. The rain had slowed down. The starter locked and the driver's helper crawled under the truck in the bitter cold. He pulled down the fly wheel case and disengaged the locked gears. Twenty minutes later he crawled out again. His fingers were frozen. We then drove out to fight the waves and ridges again. It was a miserable day, rainy, cold, and gray. We came upon a stranded bus with a flat tire. They were far up on the beach in the soft sand. They had been stuck all night, and the passengers looked weary and red-eyed from a sleepless cold night.

We were stuck in the sand ourselves, but by placing six or

439

eight foot planks under the wheels, we were able to get out again. We had offered to help, but the bus driver said we weren't needed. We drove on for an hour, then ahead of us, stuck on the beach was an abandoned U.S. landing barge. The Brazilian navy was salvaging it. One of their crew hailed us. My driver was afraid to stop for fear of getting stuck in the sand. But true to custom, we came to a stop.

We were invited aboard for coffee and cookies. What a filthy mess the quarters were in, toilets busted, floor wet, dirty clothes everywhere, and a dozen crewmen unshaven and dirty were sitting or lying in their filthy bunks. One of the crew wanted a lift to Casino, the next town. He was busy shaving, and cussing at a busted mirror. He was heavy set, and it was a tight fit in the cab. Now there were five of us. We got moving again only by placing planks under the wheels.

The driver carried a vacuum bottle full of hot water. Every so often his assistant brought out a gourd, filled it with maté (grain), and poured the hot water in next. Then they each took turns sipping the hot liquid through the silver bombilla (tube). The gourd went around and around like a peace pipe.

It was an exciting trip along the beach. In the late afternoon, we left the town of Casino. The entire trip along the beach covered a distance of 144 miles (238 kilometers). It was raining heavily in Casino. It was a nice little town. A modern Spanish hotel was the most outstanding building. There were gardens, trees, and paved streets. We stopped at a gas station to fill up the tanks and the extra hundred-gallon drums.

The gas station was a store and a restaurant all in one. We entered a back room for dinner. At the doorway loafed fellows in slippers and drinking maté. The lady proprietor was letting off firecrackers inside the room. She was drunk and didn't give a hoot about the annoyed looks of her customers. The firecrackers were loud and deafening. She threw them everywhere, and small children were in danger of getting their eyes burned from the sparks. The room was full of smoke. The fellows in the doorway looked in and laughed. When we drove off, she was still letting them off. I was under the impression that she was a lunatic, till my driver said she was from Portugal and celebrating a Portuguese holiday.

We drove along a macadam highway, then turned off on to a side road. It was muddy and became so bad that we nearly got stuck. We reached a little town called Quinta. It was late afternoon, and my driver decided we should stay overnight. There were only a handful of one-story weather-beaten buildings. We entered one of them. It looked like a backwoods country store. There were sacks of grain, barrels, and boxes littered about. There were a half-dozen men or more, sitting or walking to and fro. While they talked, they drank maté incessantly. The gourd seemed to go around and around like a peace pipe. Some of the fellows wore long black cloaks, as in the sixteenth century. They all wore slippers. My driver removed his shoes and donned slippers also. The soles were of wood and the straps of leather.

We were called to the back room for supper. Now there are a lot Negroes in Brazil and there seems to be no discrimination against them. I've seen black and white children playing together and black fellows and white girls riding together on horseback and wagons. So even at the table this evening were mixed white and black. They talked and talked till no end.

After supper, I asked for my room. I don't believe there was a better inn in this town. I was directed through a dark alley to my room. I still had to share it with a roommate, but he seemed pleasant, quite young, and had no more gusto (likes) for his surroundings than I had. The mattress was one-inch thick, made of straw, and laid on boards. There were no toilets; one had to use the back alley.

I slept quite well and awoke as my roommate was leaving the room. I found a water pump and a basin behind the shack. I was able to clean up a bit. My driver talked so much I believed he wanted to stay another day. I read a book to pass the time away. My driver was a tall, thin elderly fellow and had paid all my expenses this far. He took me for an *andarin* and was disappointed when I said I did not carry a book for autographs.

Finally we pulled out of Quinta after a lot of handshaking and farewells We went about three miles along a muddy road, full of mud puddles. Then we came to a slim gate, closing the road. A man on duty said the road was flooded ahead and no traffic was to go through. We drove back to Quinta. The truck would have to wait till the road opened, but I could still take a train over the bad stretch to Pelotas. The train was due in one hour. I had dinner again and said "so long" to my driver and friends.

The train came at 12:30. First-class fare cost thirteen cruzeiros (50¢). It took an hour to cross over the flooded fields, swamps, and a huge bridge into Pelotas. The train was going northward, but I got off here. I was amazed to find it a large city, about 100,000 population. I had a little difficulty making the Brazilians understand me.

I asked a fellow at a store, "How do I get on the road, going north to Porto Alegre?" He answered, "Yes, you're on the right road, just follow this street out." I walked on a few blocks and decided to check again at a gas station. I soon learned the first chap had given me a "bum steer." I always believe in asking three or four fellows and getting the benefit of a doubt.

This reminds me of a buddy of mine back home who got lost in the big city of Philadelphia. He did not want to ask questions because he feared people would think him a "hick." So he walked and walked all day in "Philly" till he found his own street again.

The directions I received called for taking a taxi or walking four blocks down, six blocks right, then six blocks left, then right again, and follow to the end of town. The town was jammed with dusky people. The sidewalks were quite narrow. The stares of the people didn't annoy me that day. I walked on. I left the crowded streets behind; then a pretty blond stared at me. I caught her eye and held her gaze till she smiled. I waved for her to come along. She was on the opposite side of the street. She started to follow, and for a while I thought she would follow me for the rest of the day, but it only went for two blocks.

It took another hour to clear the long row of adobe houses that make up the suburb. A number of horse-drawn carts passed me by. The cement road turned to cobblestone. Along the road was an irrigation ditch. Here were many beautiful white children playing in the water with Negro children.

Soon a bus came along. I "flagged" it. It stopped and I asked the driver if he was going to Porto Alegre. "No, but get in," the driver said. He took me about fifteen kilometers (ten miles) to a junction. "How much do I owe?" I asked.

"You are an *andarin* (walker)," he said. "You don't owe anything."

"Thanks," I said. I'd heard a lot of good stories about Brazilian kindness. Seems like it may be true. The road was now sandy and dirt. Darkness was falling and I was well out in the country. A half-hour went by, then another bus came along. I "flagged" and it skidded to a stop. It was battered and beat up. There were a half-dozen dusky farmers. I took a seat. The ticket collector charged me eight cruzeiros (40¢). We rolled and bumped over a number of miles. I somehow dozed off and awoke when we came to the end of the line. We were out in the country, and the bus stopped at a lonely inn. There we would have food and lodging for the night.

It was a tiny place. The proprietor was Brazilian of German descent. He had several husky boys. We entered a room that served as a store and a barroom. There was only kerosene lamps to light up the room. The little ticket collector ordered drinks of strong sugar cane whiskey for himself, the driver, and me. The way I took it down made even the bartender's eyes open wide. Thanks to my training in Alaska. After several rounds, we had a splendid dinner of chicken and wine. The driver refused to let me pay for my dinner. Back to the bar we went. The little fellow was ordering drinks and refusing to let me pay. After about a dozen drinks, he puts his arms around me, said how much he liked North Americans, and wished he could go there some day.

Then when he asks me, *"Polli Vou France"* over and over a dozen times, everyone agrees he is pretty drunk. he could speak some French and seemed proud of it. He spoke Spanish very well. He did most of the talking and was quite funny.

Only one ugly low-class, half-breed (Negro and Indian) didn't like my presence. He was standing near me and mumbled and grumbled something about Americans. I had only to look at him and he slunk cowardly away. When I finally turned in, I felt sure that these people had a lot of respect for Americans.

I spent the night on a thin straw mattress and planks for springs. It was like a dormitory, and I had four or five fellows for roommates. My breakfast and lodging cost nine cruzeiros (45¢). My friends had returned to Pelotas before I awoke. It was a cool, pleasant morning. I waved back to the German-Brazilian proprietor and wife standing in the doorway, then I continued down the damp dirt road.

The inn and school house faded out of sight. Only the clanging of a school bell could be heard, calling the children to class. Nothing but green farmland and pine trees lay ahead. A truck came along and took me a dozen kilometers. Then an old Ford took me two dozen more kilometers. Some of the rolling hills were very steep, but always very picturesque.

I was left at a junction, out in the country. I walked along for an hour. A truck came towards me, headed south, and chasing it were a couple of huge dogs, barking their heads off. I got into their path, and they turned on me with sudden fury. Before I could say "Jack Robinson" and turn around once, they had torn into my boots a dozen times and put long gashes into them with their sharp fangs. Then both dogs ran off with their tails between their legs and looking backwards. It happened so suddenly that I could hardly move. I was in such a spot that there were no sticks or stones about, only sand and grass. If I had a gun, I would have killed them. Yet where the dogs came from was a mystery, for there were no houses in sight for miles.

Upon examining my boots, I found deep cuts and indentations. About an inch above the twelve-inch boots, I found a gash about an inch long but deep only to the bleeding point on my leg. Iodine I carry at all times. I used it as a disinfectant. If it wasn't for the protection of the boots, my legs would have been torn to shreds.

I had always believed in a theory and it worked many times, in the States and on this trip. It is to walk along slowly without fear, and dogs will leave you alone. I read that theory in a newspaper column, now I was not so sure any more.

I walked along for several hours. The road was "dead." I was anxious to get into a town to have my leg treated by a doctor. After endless hours a dump truck came along. It stopped for me. The driver and assistant were a couple of barefooted peons (low-class laborers). They were beginners in driving. An hour

444

later we came to a river crossing. There were no bridges. The crossing was made on a barge towed by a motor boat. There was a long line of heavily loaded trucks waiting to go across. It meant several hours of waiting, but we were lucky. Our truck was empty, so we were able to go across first because the barge had a lot of leaks and the pumps were out of order to drain the water.

After a fifteen-mile crossing, we continued on for twenty kilometers (13 miles) more. Then they turned off the road to a lonely ranchhouse. Dusk was falling. I continued onward, hoping for one of the heavy trucks to come along. They never came. It became pitch dark. My flashlight wouldn't work.

I could barely see the gray gravel road as I trampled along. The night was very still. There were not even the sound of a cricket. Occasionally, the barking of a dog broke the silence. The next town was twenty kilometers away. I was tired but I had to push onward. I passed the dark shadow of a house. Then suddenly a beam of light from it played on me. Somebody was curious as to whom was passing by, and that somebody got mighty scared when I walked up to him. He backed inside the house. Then I saw it was a country store. He was visibly nervous when I entered the store. He probably never expected to see a foreigner in field clothes and a full pack. He probably took me for a spy or an escaped prisoner of war and that I had to do my traveling by night.

I then asked him, "Do you have lodging here?"

"No," he answered, "there is not room enough in my house, but down the road about three kilometers on the right-hand side is a big white house that has rooms for rent." I figured it may be a "bum steer" just to get rid of me, but I had no alternative. I then had him cut up some sausages and cheese, and with cookies and soda pop, I had a dinner.

The three-kilometer hike I made in forty-five minutes. It was very dark, and I could not buy batteries for my flashlight at the store. I walked in the middle of the road. Once or twice a shadow of a man shuffled past me, walking along the edge of the road. Then I saw a white house, but it was on the left side of the road. Dogs at the gate kept me from entering the yard. I whistled a couple of times, but no answer came from the house. It must be the wrong house, so I moved on again. Then out of the shadows stood a very large white house, on the left side of the street. I must say, "No bum steer from that Brazilian."

I was told by the lady of the house, "Yes, there is one room left, but you will have to share it with a companion." "It's okay by me," I said. It was a simple adobe room. A bed of straw and boards for springs. My roommate was middle-aged, small and dirty. He looked mean and every bit like a thief. My bed was parallel to his with about a foot of clearance between them. I certainly wouldn't feel at ease sleeping that close to him. So I pulled my bed to the far end of the room. Boy did he "squack," but I said, "Shadup, shadup (shut up)."

I settled down to sleep at once. He went out and came back an hour later. The heavy scraping of the door was enough to wake the dead. I slept quite well, but nerves set to awake at slightest noise or touch. I had my valuables under cover.

I awoke again at dawn by the scraping of the door. The blasted so-and-so had left the door wide open, and the cold wind and air blew in. After a few minutes, it was cold enough to make anyone get up. I closed the door and started dressing. My roommate reentered and left again, leaving the door wide open. A blasted shout from me brought him back to close the door. Later the landlady served me coffee and bread, then asked where was my roommate. "Hell, I don't know," I said. "He probably made off without paying for lodging."

I hiked down the damp, dirt road. It was a cool morning, ideal for hiking. The farms and countryside was very picturesque, like Pennsylvania in the springtime. I got only two rides all day. I did a lot of walking. I covered a distance of about sixty miles altogether. Along in the afternoon, two Brazilians, of German descent, gave me a lift to Talpa. It was still two hours before sundown, and I tried to put a few more miles behind me. I did not walk far out of town. I merely strolled and lingered on the outskirts. Several cars and trucks went by, but evidently they did not understand the sign of the "thumb" signal. I hated to change over to the traffic cop signal, but I would have to if I wanted to catch a ride. A truck or two stopped, but they were going only a few miles into the country. Darkness fell, so I strolled the half-mile back to town and asked for lodging at a pension.

The manager was a little "high" and happy as could be. I asked what the rates were for lodging and dinner. "Twenty-five cruzeiros," he said.

"Too much," I said. One has to bargain for everything in South America. He then smiled again broadly and said, "Fifteen cruzeiros." "That's better," I answered.

After a full-course dinner, I turned in. My bed was of straw and boards again. It was very stiff and uncomfortable, but a tired body sleeps anywhere. I could not turn the light off. There was only one switch for the entire pension (hotel). Nevertheless, I fell asleep at once. A couple of hours later, I was awakened by a blaring radio in the next room. I arose out of bed and went to the next room. A young fellow had the radio apart and was experimenting. There was music, whistles and static. It was nerve wracking. I asked the fellow to kindly turn off the radio, as I wanted to sleep. He turned it off, and I soon fell asleep again. A half hour later, I awoke again to the loud noise. The thin plank wall could not keep the racket out. I got out of bed again, this time angry and half naked.

"Look, fellow," I said, "it's 10:30 and the entire town is in bed. It's time you turn that damn thing off." He checked his watch and said it was 11:30. Mine had stopped.

"11:30," I said, "my God if you don't turn that thing off, I'll brain you," and I meant it. There was no more music that night, bu the lights never went out. I risked breaking my neck climbing atop a wobbly table to twist the bulb. I couldn't sleep any more after that.

I was awake at daybreak. I had coffee and then walked five or six muddy streets to the highway. A big fat Negro lady stopped, stared at me, then outstretched her hand for a handout. I still felt mean and said, "Sorry, lady." I thought to myself, with all that fat, she's probably better fed than I.

On the highway, luck was with me. A big 1948 truck came to a stop. There were so many new trucks in the region that I couldn't help thinking, how does Brazil rate to have so many and how's the trucking situation back home in the U.S.? The driver was small, middle-aged. He said he was going to Porto Alegre. "Gee, that's swell," I said. The truck fairly bounced along the road, and we bounced on the new spring seats. Once I hit the roof. We ran into some rain. Some of the steep hills were in bad shape. They were muddy and slick. For a while it looked like the truck would not make it over. We burned some rubber and with luck we were successful.

At mid-noon we drove out on a dock, onto a large steamer, and were ferried across the bay to Porto Alegre. There were many large steamers and ferry boats playing the water. The crossing took about a half an hour. On the steamer beside us were a lot of passengers, horses, carts, autos, and a few trucks. Upon disembarking we still had a dozen miles to drive to reach the city. We drove rapidly along a fine cement highway, then we followed streetcar tracks to the heart of the city. I was surprised to see how big Porto Alegre really is. It is like any city in the U.S. aside from the colonial homes of the Portuguese.

In the center of town, I told my driver I was looking for a moderate-priced hotel. Some of the hotels he recommended, but upon visiting, I said, "No." The cheapness was beyond description. I told him I'd find a better place, pay more, and feel cleaner and safer from thieves.

At one of these, the manager made me fill out duplicate questionnaires, then countersign. Then he checked and re-checked my *passaporte,* my tourist card signature, and entry cards. All this red tape just to get a room put me on edge. Then he said 45 cruzeiros and a large placard on the wall, staring me in the face, said 28 cruzeiros a day. He knew I was an American and took me for a sucker. "Never mind," I said, "I'll go elsewhere."

I did , but he sent out a bellhop to help me find a place. We had a bit of difficulty, but the first thing the big bellhop said was, "El is Americano." (He is an American). I could have socked him, for it's the Latin way for doubling the rates. The lady said it would be 22 cruzeiros for the room. I then had dinner at an outside restaurant. It was double what I expected.

It is Sunday in Porto Alegre and the people wear their best clothes. I changed also into loafer shoes, tan trousers, T-shirt, blue sweater, and a light jacket. Because of the T-shirt, I looked like an American seaman. Many American ships come into Porto Alegre. I strolled about the crowded business district, came to a park, sat down and waited for the theater to open at 7:30.

The picture playing starred Joan Crawford and Henry Fonda. The theater was very crowded. Many of the men, Army and civilian, failed to remove their hats throughout the picture.

The movie lets out and the sidewalks are crowded with thousands of girls. Many are lovely and many wear the latest long-style skirts called the "new look." They promenade up and down the sidewalks. I never expected to find so many white girls in Brazil and what's more, blondes. A few of the blondes were bleached, I couldn't help but notice. The majority of the whites are sons and daughters of German settlers. The states of Rio Grande do Sul and Santa Catharina are said to have the largest German colonies. While the girls promenade on the sidewalks, the fellows stand in the gutter (street). They are dressed in their best Sunday suits, ties and white shirts. They stand in an endless line for blocks and watch the parade of passing lassies. A few of the men move to and fro, but the majority, thousands of them, stand, watch make remarks, smile, or pass compliments or jests.

I had been walking on the sidewalk, then felt silly with all those girls. I moved to the gutter. It's a nice Latin custom, but still I believe meeting a girl at a dance in nicer. Back at the hotel, I have a dark-complexioned fellow for a roommate. We share some bananas, then turn out the light.

My roommate and I awoke at the same time. He tells me he had paid 10 cruzeiros for lodging. I paid 22. I then call at U.S. Consul. No mail. Usually they do not change money at the consulate, but a secretary there gave me 23 cruzeiros to a dollar. I changed forty dollars. I got a 120 cruzeiros extra on the high rate of exchange, about six dollars. The lady was American and nice to talk to.

I felt like leaving town, but it was cold and gray with a slight drizzle. I decided to rest up. I did some shopping, then had dinner. Back at the hotel, the greedy looking landlady said I had to pay 35 cruzeiros a day whether I eat or not. Fine, I thought, after missing several dinners. I let her know about my roommate paying 10 to my 22 for lodging. She got very angry and beat her chest. She said, "I should know. I collected 15 from him."

My goodness, I thought, *what is it that can make a woman so mean and nasty?*

I spent the afternoon indoors, writing and resting up. I had been on the road eight and one-half days and one night without a day's layover since I left Montevideo, Uruguay, and I covered merely 800 kilometers (500 miles) more or less in all that time. It was poor indeed.

I had supper at the hotel. There were approximately thirty boarders, all Latins. I was the only gringo present. We got plenty to eat—soup, roast beef, Polish sausage, scrambled eggs, rice, beans, lettuce, potatoes, pudding, and coffee. We couldn't complain about that. There were two to four people at each table.

I took in a movie again. Even there I was overcharged. The price list said eight cruzeiros, I got only two cruzeiros change from a twenty-cruzeiro note. There was a large crowd behind me and while buying my ticket, hasty always hasty, Latins pushed their money forward and gave reason for the lady clerk to short-change me.

The seats were mostly filled, and the color picture was in motion. The people just kept coming in, way on into the middle of the picture and obstructing the view. I could understand the English words spoken, but the Portuguese writing under the film was also obstructed by the passing customers and seated Brazilians never knew what was said, so their anger was much greater. Why the management couldn't hold the showing till all the seats were filled, I don't know.

Tyrone Power played in *Cortez*. It was the beginning night, and thousands were outside waiting for the next performance. I headed for the water front nearby. I had a beer at a cabaret. Some old sailors were there drinking beer also. They spoke English with a European accent, yet they were Americans. One of them bought me a beer, but I didn't join their table. I just wanted to have peace and quiet and enjoyed it. I had a couple of sandwiches also. What was I charged? Double for everything. Yet in the interior of Brazil, everything is cheaper, to the south.

I turned in early and had no roommate. The bed as usual

was straw and boards, yet it cost a dollar for lodging. One gets used to it and I slept quite well.

I was up at 5:30. By 6:00 o'clock, I was ready to leave. I was told breakfast was served from 6 to 8. At the hour of 6:15, the dining room was still closed. Rather than ask the mean *duena* (landlady) for coffee, I took it at a street corner café. I also had some heavy pastry cakes that gave me a stomach ache later on.

I succeeded in getting on the right trolley to the end of the line. I had many more blocks to walk before I'd be out of town. It was still dark, and I was lucky to have a fellow guide me to the highway. There were so many turns to the left and to the right, I would have found it difficult to find my way alone to the highway.

I walked for a long time. I was far out in the country. The sun was beginning to get hot, and I was getting hungry and thirsty. Then I got a ride to Gravatá, then another truck took me as far as Santo Antonio, eighty kilometers (fifty miles) from Potro Alegre. It was mid-noon, the sun hot and bright. I was going to have dinner and refreshment, but I chanced to pass a third truck filling up at a gas station. I asked the driver if he was going to São Paulo. He said, "No." Then I noticed an American flag, about six inches square, tied to his radiator cap. I said to the driver, "That's my country." He was so surprised. He asked me a few questions concerning it, the meaning of the stars and stripes, then said to climb aboard. They would be driving day and night to within eighty kilometers (fifty miles) of Florianopolis. "Swell," I said. they were leaving at once, and I didn't even have time to get a dinner or a glass of water for my dry throat.

The cab was full, so I rode on top a load of wood with a half a dozen Brazilian fellows. We held on for dear life as the truck bounced over the uneven dirt road. The sun was hot, but there was a strong cold wind. After about 60 kilometers, we left rolling green hills behind and turned to the great white sandy beach at Tramandai. We then follow the Atlantic waters for 150 kilometers (95 miles) to Araranguá. The sand was smooth and hard as a surf board. We hit but three or four bumps caused by rivulets flowing down to the sea from the distant hills. Only the black

451

shadows in the distance reminded us that it was no mirage. The beach in reality is a great white desert.

We stopped at a tiny village called Teresina to unload some wood. It was like a tiny oasis on the vast white plain. We rolled over the holes in the sand, for what purpose I do not know, except to hold fresh water perhaps. These natives lived a meager life on the fish they caught, and even these were in danger of being eaten by the few pigs that followed them about. Yet where these natives lived we did not know. There was no sign of habitation anywhere, and there was bleak, open desert as far as the eye could see. Where did these few scattered natives and pigs come from? How did they get there? Where did they live? These were the questions that mystified me, and my companions were at a loss to answer. They didn't know either.

Dusk was already falling. Another hour on the beach and we would be swamped by the incoming tide. We already were up to the soft sands and riding in deep water. Luck was with us, and we pulled up on shore at Araranguá. There was a restaurant and we stopped to lunch.

The fellows bought whiskey and gave me a few shots. It made me feel fine after the cold, open-air ride. We then had a large supper with three types of meat, chicken, pork, and beef, and rice, beans, salad, potatoes, etc. My driver refused to let me pay my own.

We drove over special wooden driveways to get over the sandy fields, but the driveway didn't go far. We got stuck in the sand as soon as we got off. Then there was a scurry to place long six to eight-foot planks (that each truck carries for this purpose) under the spinning wheels for traction. We got out almost at once.

There were four fellows and fourteen-year-old blond boy riding behind with me. They huddled up in blankets and ponchos. I covered up as best I could with the canvas covers. But they had large holes. The wind drafts blew in there, then in there, and all night, there was always one little spot of my body cold.

The road became bumpy, winding, twisting, up and down grades, letting us know we were no longer on the smooth beach, but in the hills.

Till then, I don't know how I ever managed to fall asleep. I was awakened in the middle of the night. "Don't you want some coffee?" "Sure," I answered. "Aren't you coming with me?" when I noticed the fellows were not moving toward the restaurant with me. They laughed and said, "We already had ours." The little boy joined me; after drinking the hot black coffee, he reached into his pocket to pay. I wouldn't let a boy as young as he pay for me, but it was an interesting gesture. Most Latin boys I'd met his age, always tried their best to get a coin from me. This lad was Brazilian and perhaps there lay the difference.

The stars and the half moon had disappeared behind heavy fog and clouds. There wasn't anything more to do but cover up, hang on, and while the night away. Only at river crossing, the driver blew the high-toned horn to wake up the barge man. The horn echoed and re-echoed in the dead stillness of the night. The sleepy barge man came forth in about ten minutes. We drove onto the barge.

A taut steel cable stretched across the river. The barge moved along this cable. The barge man alone worked a handle, attached to the cable, and slowly pulled us across. It was a primitive method and very laborious. During the long night, we made several of these crossings. It was daylight when we came to the end of my ride. It was still no-man's land. There was a fork in the road. The truck would be going left, and I would be going to the right. It was mountain country, full of jungle foliage and huge trees.

There was a house on the left fork. I would be able to have lunch there. The keeper and the wife were German settlers. The children were full grown, born in Brazil. While they prepared hot coffee and black bread, I washed up in a river nearby. The settlers were pleasant, but they could not speak English.

Nine o'clock found me walking up steep mountain roads. In the shade it was cold; in the sun it was fine. Two hours later I came to a stop on a high knoll overlooking the valley and the road below. There was not a single moving object in sight. I opened up *Time* and read for another hour. Occasionally I glanced to the valley, trying to spot an oncoming car. Sure enough, one was coming. I picked up my pack and started walking again. A horn sounded around a curve, the next minute the car was beside me and stopping.

It was a 1946 Ford. Inside were two young businessmen and a champion cock fighter. I had all I could do to hang on to the back seat. The fellow drove fast and the bumps sent me toward the ceiling. I had long ago learned to double up on a bump and chances are I wouldn't hit the roof with my head.

We didn't go far before the driver stopped for dinner. We had whiskey, chicken, and Churrasco (beef) dinner. Again these Brazilians insisted on paying for me. We arrived at San Jose at 1:30. We parted there. They took a barge to the island of Florianopolis, which is a seaport and a large city. I had only to walk out of the the village of San Jose on the dusty road going north. The villagers were as curious as ever. They stopped working to watch me go by.

A large Red Cross ambulance stopped for me. I did not even "flag" it. The driver was a sailor with the Brazilian Navy hospital. I rode with him for 51 kilometers (32 miles). We went through Biguaçu and Tjucas. He was a nice chap. He didn't talk much and seemed to be the understanding kind. We shook hands and he said, *"Vaya bien"* (good going). It was still two and one-half hours before sundown, and I wanted to put some more mileage behind me. I was unfortunate. My last ride left me at the south end of town. I spent a half hour going through it, heading north. Several vehicles passed me, none stopped. I walked far out into the country. There were banana trees on all sides. I passed many peons (low class workers). Some wore flimsy woody sandals; others went barefoot. Their clothes were light and simple. All of them were dark featured. Some had fierce expressions and many carried machetes (long knives used for cutting cane or brush).

If I said hello, they answered. Most of the time, I kept quiet. It was late afternoon. A bus went by. I "flagged" it, and it kept on going. I finally came to a tiny settlement. Two or three of the houses were modern Portuguese design. The others were weatherbeaten plank houses and shacks. I stopped at a tiny store. The clerk said, "No hotels here, but large house yonder has rooms at times."

454

"No rooms," said the lady there, but she seemed hesitant, probably afraid of strange travelers. I could only move on, thinking I'd be sleeping under banana trees. Two more cars went by and refused to stop. I came to another settlement. Darkness was falling rapidly. At a store, I asked for lodging. "All filled up," the man and lady said.

"Okay," I said, "I'll sit on yonder bank and wait for a bus, truck, or anything going to the next town." I then walked over and sat on a bank alongside of the road. I had done a lot of walking and was tired. Presently the owner of the store, his sons, and a couple of natives came and sat beside me. They asked where I came from and I said, "You guess." First they said:

Aleman (which means German)

Second	Frances (French)
Third	Italiano (Italian)
Fourth	Ingles (English)
Fifth	Polacko (Polish)

To someone's remark I said, "No, I speak Spanish." Right away they all laughed and said, "You're from Spain." I decided to let it go at that; now I was a Spaniard.

To some of their questions about Spain, I answered well and fair enough. For my history and geography knowledge was broader than these people who probably never saw the inside of a school house or studied world affairs. They are brought up to live and die where they are born.

Two trucks came by. They stopped but were overloaded. Soon I was invited to enter the store, sit down, have coffee and cookies. Then the conversation went on by kerosene lamp. I was glad when it left me out. The lady of the house was plump, white, and considerate. She thought I was very young and asked if my folks were still living.

By eight o'clock, she had cleaned up a tiny room and invited me to stay overnight. This surprised me. I thanked her and rolled in at once. The talking continued outside my door, but then it lulled me to sleep.

I was up at dawn. I had slept wonderfully well. The lady had hot water in a basin for me to wash up, then hot black sweet coffee. The owner and his sons were up also. They asked if I slept well. I said, "Yes." The lady was frying bananas as I arose to leave. She asked me to stay for breakfast and wait for a bus. "No, thanks," I said. But I did stuff some bananas into my pockets. The lady refused money for the food, and the lodging I had. I shook hands with them and left.

From their tiny plank store, they watched me go down the dusty dirt road and disappear out of sight. I wondered what these good, courteous people thought about me. To them I was still a Spaniard.

The day was sunny and warm. A bus went by. I did not "flag" it. I was sorry later. I had to walk for about five hours before another vehicle came along. It was a truck. I climbed behind amidst loose boards and household furniture. I had all I could do to hang on. The fellow drove fast. The truck had stiff springs, and we took a beating. I sat on a straw mat on the floor. We hit many bumps, and I bounced terribly hard on my rump. Sometimes I bounced eight to ten inches in the air in rapid succession. It was enough to make the most timid person bitch.

We stopped at Itajaí for dinner. We got plenty to eat. One thing about the truck drivers is that they know the best places to eat and cheaply. We each paid ten cruzeiros (50¢). We rode on, picking up and dropping off various passengers. I succeeded in getting into the front seat as some passengers got out. The driver charged them regular bus fare. One fellow jumped out and ran away without paying. Boy, did the driver get mad! We crossed two rivers on barges. We were lucky; we did not have to wait long. The driver was going to Joinville, but he stopped about forty kilometers from there for a load of wood. It would take at least an hour or two to load up, and I would have to help. I asked the driver how much I owed. I knew he was a bit on the selfish side. He said to wait awhile. It would take only fifteen minutes to load up, but I knew what fifteen minutes was in South America. I asked again how much I owed. He said, "Pay how much you think is fair." "No," I answered, "you name the price." So then he said twenty cruzeiros. I paid him. It was a fair price.

I continued walking. I honestly didn't expect to catch another ride, because there was almost no traffic all day. But sure enough a truck came along and stopped. There were two big husky Brazilians, the sons of German settlers. We rode along for awhile, then stopped at a country roadhouse for beer. Conversation flowed freely, with my knowledge of Spanish, the Brazilians understood me very well. They each bought a round. Then I bought one so as not to be a piker.

We arrived in Joinville presently. We stopped at a café again. We had beer, lunch, and more beer again. Now they refused to let me pay. They were very courteous and hospitable and finally drove me to the best hotel in town and introduced me to the Yugoslav proprietor. We shook hands, then they drove off to their farm nearby.

The hotel had ran out of meals, so they served me sandwiches and coffee. The proprietor was very friendly. He spoke Spanish, English, Portuguese, and Yugoslav. The hotel was clean and nicely painted; only the toilets were a mess and my bed wasn't worth a nickel. The mattress had seen so much service that a pillow was placed in the center of it to level the depression.

I hardly slept. When the night clerk called me at 5:30, I was fully awake. I walked out of Joinville a half hour later. Early morning risers greeted me as I passed by. They went on foot, horseback, and bicycles. I walked about four hours. The sun became very warm. Then a truck came along and stopped. The driver was a brawny, surly fellow. He was going to Curitiba, a hundred and forty kilometers away (88 miles). I thought we would make it in three hours, but the driver said it would take seven or eight hours because there were two mountain ranges to cross over. The bad stretch was only forty kilometers (25 miles) but would take four hours to cross over.

Along the way we met a girl. She was waiting for a ride outside her mud house. She wanted passage for herself and three children. The driver said he could only take her and one child. She agreed and sat between the driver and me. After about fifteen kilometers, the driver propositioned her. She refused his desires. He then smiled, stopped the truck, and left her out in "no-man's land." She could either walk back home or wait for another ride.

We stopped at Palmital for dinner. It was nice, neat, and

clean. The proprietor was a German settler. After a hearty meal, the driver refused to let me pay my own. We rolled on again. Up ahead workmen were clearing a landslide. One of the workmen was wearing his best clothes, a clean white linen suit. He wanted passage to Curitiba. The driver asked, "How much will you pay?" The boy did not have much to offer. The driver said, "Sorry," and drove on. He did not go far; he stopped and called the boy. I guess he was a good "Joe" at heart.

On the outskirts of Curitiba, he asked us to get out. The law prohibited trucks to carry passengers, and he feared the police might catch him. The young boy paid twenty cruzeiros, but the driver refused my money. To him I was an *andarin extranjero* (foreign walker) and *andarino extranjeros* do not have to pay.

It was late afternoon, but still sunny bright. I decided to look for lodging. It was a big town; the main street was cobblestone. There were many people, and they watched me as I walked past. I was unfortunate at several pensions, then I succeeded in getting a room. I'd have to share it with three roommates, but they looked clean cut, small and timid. I deposited my pack and went looking for a cobbler to fix my worn boots. I located a German cobbler, and in forty-five minutes he did a swell job, just before quitting time. I also located a doctor and had my leg treated.

At supper I talked with the fellows and the manager in broken Spanish, English, and Portuguese. I told them I had been out of the States twenty-one months. They thought I had been walking all that time. Finding it difficult to explain "hitchhiking," I decided to let them believe I walked. They said, walking all that time is *muy forsado* (very forceful) and *muy fuerte* (very strong).

I didn't trust the filthy sheets, so I slept in my clothes, atop the blanket. One of the fellows wore pajamas. They were in shreds and full of large holes. I couldn't see why he wore them. They were so ragged.

I slept quite well. The manager called me at 5:30. I believe in getting an early start. I had coffee and bread. I expected to be overcharged, but the manager liked me and charged very little. It was still dark. I walked a dozen blocks to the heart of town. The streets were wide. The sidewalks were strikingly beautiful in the mosaic designs. There were many large modern buildings, and it was a big town. Dawn was breaking. Many people hurried about the moist streets and sidewalks. I asked a fellow standing beside a car, what street to follow out of town. He said he would be glad to drive me out. It was a fifteen-minute ride. We passed many beautiful new homes. The town was very clean.

I walked several hours again. The morning was cool, misty, and cloudy till about ten o'clock. Then the sun broke through and warmed the green countryside. Several loaded trucks passed me by. Most of them were '47 and '48 models. I wondered again how Brazil rated to have so many. Finally a '47 truck stopped for me. The young driver said he was going to Saõ Paulo (pronounced San Paulo). *Swell,* I thought, *we would be there to spend the Sunday.* But the driver was in no hurry; he made many stops for coffee, refreshment, dinners, and to chat with other truck drivers.

We drove all day. By midnight we had gone 206 kilometers (130 miles). We stopped at a little town called Guapiara. The driver was tired and wanted to sleep there. He pointed to a trucker's hotel. There were many trucks lined up in front of it. There was not a sound. It was a late hour. The streets were dark. He awakened the sleepy night watchman and told him to give me a bed. He would sleep in the cab and asked me to awake him at six o'clock. There were many cots in the large room and the hallways. There were sleeping forms on each. The watchman directed me to a cot. I was surprised at the cleanliness and feel of clean sheets.

I slept well and at six I was up. It was still dark and misty. I let the driver oversleep an extra hour, then I awoke him. We had coffee and bread. The night's lodging cost ten cruzeiros (50¢). It was heavy for those drivers. We then drove on into Capão Bonito. Then the driver took another route. I could no longer follow my map. The route he took was considerably shorter. We entered the state of Saõ Paulo. At the border the police checked us for cargo. They had a strange law also. All truck drivers must wear a driver's cap on penalty of a fine. It seemed strange. My driver would drive all day without the hat, but once entering a town or stopping at a gas station, he hurriedly put his driver's cap on. All the drivers wear the same kind.

We rode all day over slightly rolling hills. In the state of Saõ Paulo, the trees are different. The wood is very hard, and the leaves are ordinary. In the southern states of Santa Catharina and Rio Grande do Sul, the trees are soft pine called "Pino." The Pino is a curious tree. The trunk and limbs are bare. It is tall and slim like a palm tree. The curious feature is the ball-shaped leaves and twigs on the end of the long protruding limbs. Each ball varies in size, like a balloon. Some are as large as three feet in diameter. Other Pino trees are like tall mushrooms. The bells and "mushroom tops" are a rich green in color.

The state of Saõ Paulo is also noted for producing Brazil's chief export. That is coffee. Brazil produces more than 60 percent of the world's coffee and most of it comes from the state of Saõ Paulo alone.

The driver stopped numerous times along the highway. We got out of the truck and sat on the road bank. Other trucks pulled up behind us. The fellows fell into conversation, then we lunched on oranges. It looked as if they take it easy on Sundays. We stopped other times for coffee, dinners, and refreshment. The driver and I paid alternately. We arrived in Saõ Paulo in the early part of the evening. My driver let me out near the business district, across from the carnival show and on the main street leading to Rio de Janiero, the capital and principal city of Brazil.

It was a very large city and brightly illuminated. The avenues were very wide and crowded with pedestrians and vehicles. Hotel rooms were scarce and expensive. After five or six tries and numerous phone calls, I succeeded in getting a room. At first I was dissatisfied. The manager said, "You better take it or somebody else will before long." I tried elsewhere and finally had to return.

It was a bed, placed in a closet under a stairway. How they ever got the bed inside, I don't know. Yet I had to take it or spend the night looking for better. Still it was expensive. It cost a whole dollar. Then it cost fifteen cents for a towel to take a shower. The manager said, "Yes, always hot water." But there wasn't, either at night or the next day.

460

I was awakened by people walking up and down the wooden stairs. I had breakfast at one of those "stand up and eat" counter cafés popular in Brazil. Then I went to the heart of town. It was a city of contrasts. The modern buildings stand side by side with colonial Portuguese. There are many churches, great public squares, ancient traffic lights, cobblestone streets and paved streets. The center of town is jammed with crowds. Most of them are a dark brown or Negro. Many of the modern buildings are very impressive. Not far distant is the Parque do Estado (state park). Here the tired people come to rest on the lawn or on the benches. There are many tiny lagoons.

After taking some pictures, I inquired what bus to take to Insituto Butantan. This institution is famous for its large collection of Brazilian snakes. I succeeded well enough. A modern bus went to the institution. It seemed to be located on the outskirts of town. There was a large campus, with green lawns and stately trees, but I did not see the building. A lovely girl on the campus answered my inquiry, then she asked me in good English, "How did you know I could speak English?" To me almost every beautiful Latin girl of the big cities speaks some English, but I didn't say that.

I came to a large cream-colored building. In front of it was a huge, rectangular pit, surrounded by a three-foot well. Within the pit were hundreds of snakes and cobras. They ranged in size from a few inches to a dozen feet. There were mounds made of red clay. These served as shelter for the snakes. A large sign in seven or eight different languages stated, "Poisonous Snakes." I was alone walking about the huge pit when suddenly two truck loads of Japanese students drove up and several cars of loud, happy Latinos. The Japanese kids ran about, here and there, very noisy, excited, and interested.

Presently the snake doctors came out of the building, dressed in white coats and wearing knee-length rubber boots. First we followed them to the non-poisonous snake pits on the opposite side of the building. There was the largest cobra I had ever seen. It was approximately fifteen or twenty feet long and a foot in diameter. It was within a steel cage. The doctors entered the pit and with harpoon-shaped sticks, they carried this big,

461

live, snapping fellow out of the cage into the center of the pit. Then from the trees, mounds, and various parts of the pit, they gathered more snakes together. Some of the larger ones they wrapped about their necks and shoulders to prove them non-poisonous. They lifted the snakes to the high walls for the students to do likewise. A few had barely enough nerve to touch them.

Then the doctors went into the poisonous pits by ladder. At once rattlers were heard. Large and tiny snakes snapped at their boots, some snapped very high. The doctors picked up the snakes with harpoons and placed them on a pile. Then one of the doctors caught a snake with his harpoon. He placed the V-shaped stick at the snake's head, then caught it from behind with his fingers at the neck, and forced the jaws to open. The doctor climbed out of the pit, and everyone circled about him for the demonstration. The doctor pulled out the two tiny white pieces of bone with tweezers. These, I understand, contain the poison.

One girl asked if it takes long for new replacement. The doctor said, "No, it grows back very rapidly." It was a most interesting exhibition. I only wished I could have understood the Portuguese language better.

Tuesday came along and I was out of bed at 5:30. I had a hell of a time dressing in that tiny room under the stairs. I stood on the bed to put on my clothes, opening the door to put my boots on. No hot water, ice cold. I had coffee and bun at a "stand up and eat café." It's funny how one gets into the habit of only bread and coffee for breakfast and feels satisfied.

I never thought I'd ride one of those ancient trolley cars, but that morning I did. I just stood on the running board and hung onto the handlebars. The long eight-passenger seats were all taken. One can enter or get off at either side of the trolley. I got a seat after a while and rode the trolley to the end of the line. Then for a nickel, a bus took me well out into the country. The morning was cool and cloudy. Luck was with me, and a truck took me to São Miguel. Then a '37 Chevrolet took me rapidly to Mogy Das Cruces, 52 kilometers (33 miles) from São Paulo.

It was nearly ten o'clock when the sun broke through the mist and clouds on time to warm up the green pasturelands. I left Mogy Das Cruces and walked far out into the country. Then a truck came along. The cab was crowded, so I rode behind. We bounced and bumped over the dirt road. I had all I could do to hang onto the braces. I wore only a T-shirt and field jacket, but the wind and air no longer were bitter cold.

We stopped at a flour mill for a load of flour. I took the advantage to walk a few blocks to town to get something to eat. I returned in twenty minutes. The truck was loaded to the top with sacks of flour. I climbed on top the load and became snowy white. An hour later we arrived at Guaratinquetá, the end of the "lift." I did not like the town. It looked poverty stricken and unclean.

I walked out of the old village, and almost at once I got another lift in a truck. It went as far as Lorena, 221 kilometers (140 miles) north of Saõ Paulo. That was good time and mileage. As I walked through Lorena, I looked for a hotel or pension. I saw one but did not like it. Most of the houses were adobe and painted in blue, white, green, or tan. Many were in bad shape. Finally I came to the end of town without seeing another hotel. It was two hours before sundown. I hoped to catch another ride. On the outskirts of town, I passed a large, modern army base. I passed many soldiers and officers. Some said hello, others saluted. At the end of the camp were posted many soldiers. They were spaced about fifty yards apart in groups of four or five, sometimes six and eight. They guarded the entrance to town for about two miles. Alongside the road were deep ditches. From them smells and odors conveyed unsanitary personal habits to the very doorstep of the up-to-date quarters.

The Brazilian soldier wears a smart, snappy uniform in light and dark shades of green. The blouse looks like a U.S. Army blouse but is a light green in color and ordinary broadcloth. The trousers are a dark green and heavy woolen material. The hats are light green and typical of the U.S. overseas hats. Some of the blouses worn are like U.S. Navy peacoats and dark green in color. The officer's uniform is similar except for garrison hats, braids, and occasionally a long cape. The Brazilian Army has good equipment and a large supply. The army also had gained valuable battle experience in Italy with the U.S. troops.

I hadn't been stopped once to present my credentials. When

463

darkness fell, the base was far behind me. Several cars, trucks, and even a bus passed me. Four hours after leaving Lorena, I gave up. I was tired and sleepy. My eyes refused to stay open, and my knees kept buckling under. I rolled into a field under a barbed-wire fence, spread my hammock on the ground, and crawled inside of it. It was a warm evening. I put on an extra sweater, felt comfortable, and soon fell asleep.

I awoke to the heavy rumbling of trucks going by. It was 5:30 by my watch. I soon started walking. Not till the break of dawn, an hour later, did I catch a ride and then it was good. The fellow said he was going all the way to Rio de Janiero. "Swell," I said, "I guess this is my last ride in South America."

The driver was a young fellow. Soon he took another road, and I could not follow the map that I had obtained at the Argentine automobile club. This new route was shorter, newly constructed and paved. It was very wide. Many huge, deep cuts were being made along the road, but to all appearances, it was sandy earth, easily worked. There were hundreds of laborers with picks and shovels, cutting the mountain sides and hauling the dirt away in mule carts. There were no bulldozers, scrapers, or trucks. South America was still destined to use many primitive methods.

My driver said he had lost two brothers in the war in Italy. From the government insurance, he received enough money to buy the truck, which was a new 1947 model, and go into business for himself. He showed me pictures of his wife and baby and was very proud of them. He stopped occasionally while I took pictures of scenic houses and ribbon fields on a mountainside. We had dinner twice and he insisted on paying.

We arrived in Rio de Janiero late in the evening. On a high hilltop, a lighted statue of Jesus Christ lit up the dark sky. We rode through many busy sections. The driver said, "This is only the suburbs of Rio." Later we arrived in the heart of the city. He recommended a Hotel Bandeirantes. It was not a nice neighborhood, but the hotel was fine, clean, and not very expensive. It was only lacking hot water. I had to catch and hold my breath as I went under the cold shower.

So Rio de Janiero at last after seventy-nine days and three

nights on the road from Macuto, Venezuela, 14,698 kilometers or 9,186 miles and an average of 112 miles per day.

From Montevideo to Rio de Janiero, it took seventeen days. From Buenos Aires to Rio de Janiero eighteen days.

Cost of my trip for buses, taxis, trains, horses and guides to Rio:

Venuezula	$3.00	1,175 kms.
Colombia	2.25	1,740 kms.
Ecuador	18.55	1,273 kms.
Peru	13.00	3,748 kms.
Bolivia	6.00	740 kms.
Chile	3.55	2,000 kms.
Argentina	10.60	1,094 kms.
Uruguay	4.00	524 kms.
Brazil	.65	2,407 kms.
	61.60	14,698 kms. or 9

50
The City of Rio de Janeiro

Rio de Janeiro, the capital of Brazil, is located in the southeastern part of the country in the Bay of Guanabara. It is one of the most beautiful land-locked harbors in the world. The entrance to it is through a narrow channel, less than a mile wide. It is guarded by the very famous pointed rock, called the Paõ de Acucar (Sugarloaf). Rising in the background is famous Corcovado (hunchback) Mountain. On its summit, 2,800 feet above sea level, stands a huge statue of Christ the Redeemer. Rio de Janeiro is the leading commercial city of the country. It receives more imports than any other port on Brazil and is second in exports to Santos, the great coffee port. The population is bordering on 2 (two) million.

The city is built on a small plain, several feet above sea level. It surrounds the harbor on three sides. The Avenida Rio Branco is the principal thoroughfare. It runs for about two miles through the heart of the business district. The Avenida Rua Flamengo curves around the bay for fifteen miles, ending at Rio de Janeiro's splendid beach, Praia de Copacabana. At night, looking down on the lights on this avenida from "Sugarloaf" or a plane, it has been well named the "String of Pearls." Along this beautiful boulevard, the promenade sidewalks are paved with colored tiles arranged in striking patterns.

Along Avenida Rio Branco are some of the city's finest buildings, the Monroe Palace, named after the father of the Monroe Doctrine, National Library, Municipal Building, Municipal Theater, the Academy of Fine Arts. An entire hill was leveled to make a peninsular airbase for Rio's international airlines. It is named Alberto Santa Dumont, after the dirigible designer, a Brazilian by birth.

Rio de Janeiro was founded in 1565 by Estácio de Sá. It owes its name, however, to an earlier Portuguese explorer, Martin Affonso de Souza, who believed that when he sailed into the Bay of Guanabara, on January 1, 1541, he had entered a river. He named it Rio de Janeiro, which means river of January.

Brazil has the distinction of being the only independent country of South America where Spanish is not the official language. In accordance with the line of demarcation drawn by Pope Alexander VI in 1493 and confirmed by the Treaty of Tordesillas between Spain and Portugal. This part of the continent became Portuguese America, and Portuguese has continued to be the language ever since.

The people of Brazil are descendants of the early Portuguese settlers, and later immigrants. The other whites are mostly Italians, Spanish, and German. About a third of the population are mixed bloods (*mestizos*) and the others are descendants of Negro slaves and Indians.

Brazil occupies three-sevenths of the continent of South America. It has a coast line of 4,106 miles. Brazil is bounded on the north by Colombia, Venezuela, and the three Guianas, the Atlantic Ocean on the east, Uruguay and Argentina on the south, and Peru, Paraguay, and Bolivia on the west. Only Chile and Ecuador fail to touch her borders.

In other respects than coffee and size is Brazil notable. It has the world's greatest river, the Amazon. It has more unexplored land than any other country in the world. Junglelike forests, called "silvas," extend thousands of miles into the northern interior. The parts that have been penetrated along the riverbanks yield valuable timber, rubber, Brazil nuts, and yerba mate. Such deadly forms of animal life as the boa, cougar, jaguar, and the sloth have given that jungle region the name "Green Hell." The Amazon and its affluents make it possible to penetrate by boat into that wild interior.

The Brazilian Republic came into existence on the overthrow of Dom Pedro II, the youthful emperor in 1889. It got its name from its dyewoods that looked like burning coals and called "Braza."

For thirteen days I remained in Rio de Janeiro. Some were interesting and exciting, others were a bit trying. But one thing

I'm certain of, and that's the eternal sunshine. Every day was bright and sunny. The sunny days are pleasant when there is only play but when there is work to be done, the hot, sunny days wear one out.

The first thing I wanted to do was to visit the American Consulate, for no matter where I go, I'm always anxious to receive a letter from home. That always comes first. I inquired from a policeman, standing on a street corner.

"How do I get to Avenida President Wilson?" I asked.

"It is very far," he said. "It is difficult to direct. It is better you take a taxi. The taxi," he added, "cost no more than ten cruzeiros (50¢)."

The cab driver took me some fifteen complicating squares. I gave him a twenty-cruzeiro note and expected ten cruzeiros change. Instead the driver asked for five more. I was feeling good-natured and said, "Police told me not to pay more than ten, what more do you want?" He understood my poor Portuguese, grinned, and drove off. Twenty cruzeiros is a dollar; even Stateside, taxi fare isn't that high.

At the consulate I had only three letters; I had expected about ten. I realized at once that the consular section did not hold my mail long and returned it "unclaimed."

My sister wrote that $200 would be waiting for me at a bank, but what bank in Rio she did not say. The bank at home was to send a note to the embassy, letting me know where to go. There was no note at the embassy. In the phone book were half a dozen pages listing all the banks in Rio de Janeiro. There had to be at least two hundred listed. I didn't know where to start looking.

I got pretty tired walking to various banks and was about to send a telegram home—"What bank is the money in?"—when luck smiled at me. It was the Bank of Brazil, number five on my list. "Yes, we have a money order for you, Mr. Nanko," the clerk said.

But luck and disappointment go hand in hand. The bank refused to pay me in dollars, as was stated on the order. They insisted on giving me cruzeiros at the official rate of 18.5 to a dollar. They likewise refused to make out travelers checks for $200. I explained that I was traveling and wouldn't need so

468

many cruzeiros. At any street *"cambio"* (exchange house), dollars and checks sold at 24 and 25 cruzeiros to a dollar. On $200 I lost 1,000 cruzeiros ($50), more or less.

I took my complaints to the president, but the no-good son of Israel refused to listen, dropped his eyes to a manuscript, and thus dismissed me. It would have done my heart good to punch him in the nose, but that would make matters worse.

Bank orders or cables pay 18.5 to a dollar; if possible the best way out is to have a draft check sent out registered and insured. American Express Agency is another way, but they only allow $100 the maximum to be sent out.

I refused to take the money; I sent a cable home. It cost me $6.00. It never got there. At week's end I was compelled to take the heavy loss regardless. That's black market in South America.

Next thing I did in Rio was to look up a lady named Cris Cotton. She was staying at the Young Women's Christian Association. She had transferred from one building to another, and that meant more blocks to walk. Luck was with me, and I found her in. She was much taller than I, rather thin, blond, young and pleasant. After telling her I had met her girl friend Anne Laurie in Bogotá, Colombia, her wishes, regards, etc., we had tea at her tenth-floor studio. I was introduced to several more ladies. All of them spoke English, some with a heavy Portuguese accent. I was surprised that Cris Cotton was Brazilian. She was married to an Englishman named Dennis Cotton. She had studied in a college in upstate New York. Her English was faultless. She and Anne Laurie were classmates.

She invited me to have dinner, I said, "No." I wasn't dressed properly. But she insisted. We rode a bus to a section of town, then waited at a gas station for her husband. Now there I met my first Brazilian lady mechanic. She was the boss and proprietor of the efficient garage and gas station. Cris said she had studied in the States, she knew her work and handled her employees nicely. An employee came up to her with a cut finger. It was bleeding slowly. The fellow was jokingly crying. The chief mechanic in this case had to act as a nurse also.

Cris's English husband came along in a '41 Chevrolet coupe with a young girl. He was a handsome fellow, blond and pleasant. He owned a paint factory and was a successful businessman. We drove out to the suburbs to his pleasant home. We had a fine dinner, followed by delicious ice cream. We talked about various things. The English conversation, about times in New York, etc., was wonderful to hear after weeks of only Portuguese conversation.

Chris and her husband helped to make my stay in Rio most pleasant. They drove me here and there on sightseeing trips, had more dinner dates, and went to a house party.

I was on my own one day. I called Cris and said I would be out to her place in an hour. I then took a Lotaci. It is a station wagon; sometimes it is a car. It picks up passengers here and there along a route. It charges less than a cab and more than a bus. I asked the driver if he was going my way. "Yes," he said. "Step in." I was a lone passenger, but not for long. He picked up one passenger after another. Business was good. He no sooner dropped one, two, or three passengers, than he picked up another group. Soon I began to realize we were going in a circle, around and around the blocks. I got to see some of the beautiful sights at one end of the city. After an hour I was no closer to my destination than when I entered the Lataci . My patience was at an end. I told the driver this had gone on long enough and to let me out. He tried to make me stay, and in the Latin way, he said, "We will be there in a minute."

"Nuts," I said. "This is where I get out." The station wagon was full, and I let the driver know what I thought. It was a hell of a way to treat a foreigner. He did not ask for fare, but I gave him ten cruzeiros (50¢). His face was red with embarrassment, and it had a right to be.

I then asked a distinguished-looking gentlemen, standing on a corner, what bus to take, for one does get better directions from a bus driver. I was told to wait on that corner for bus number 11. I took it when it came along. Then the driver told me I was on the wrong bus. I would have to take number 11 going the opposite way into town and transfer to a trolley. Reading this will give you a headache just like asking for information gave me a headache.

I got off the bus. At the next corner were taxis. A driver said sixty cruzeiros to where I wanted to go. I said twenty and then we settled for forty ($2.00). One has to bargain for everything in South America.

I arrived at Cris's home. They were waiting for me. I was late. We spent some time playing records, had dinner, then to a house party. The hostess was Russian; the party was a Welcome Home for her daughter who was returning from New York. Most every one was Brazilian, except for Dennis, the Russians, a girl from Turkey, and me. Everyone was dressed nicely. The home was beautiful, surrounded by shrubs and flowers. We had a lunch, then cocktails. It was some time before I started to dance. I danced with Cris, Virginia (Dennis's secretary) the Russians, Brazilians, and the pretty girl from Turkey. I enjoyed dancing most with the girl from Turkey. I made a date with her for the following day, but her big husky brother probably had something to say about that, for she never came.

An American came in later. He wore one of those loud flashy ties. He was loud himself and jitterbugged a lot. He was at least thirty-five, but he carried on like a spoiled high school kid. There tonight we had two examples. Dennis was about the same age. He is English, but his manner was quiet, pleasant, his tie conservative, neither spoiled or conceited. Yet one was just as popular as the other. The party broke up long after midnight.

Every tourist, transient, businessman, traveler, or immigrant must go through a lot of red tape, banks, offices, police stations, etc., when traveling through foreign countries. A lot of time is wasted, and the business is a trying ordeal. Following is a typical day.

One must rise early if one wishes to accomplish something. First I go to the French consul. He was very nice, spoke politely and could only give me a transit visa for one day to French Guinea.

I could get a visa for a week from the French consul at the tourist agency as the consul there had more authority.

I went to National City Bank of New York and tried to get a two hundred dollar loan. They refused me.

To kill time I went for a walk along the waterfront. What a

terrible odor. Bits of fish meat were lying everywhere on the docks, rotting in the sun and millions of flies feasting on it.

Sat in a park nearby and the wind carried the stench with it. Had to move again. Wrote some notes. Decided to register myself at the police station as the law requested foreigners to do. They wondered and asked, "How the hell did I get into the country?" I told them there was no border customs at Chuay.

I was sent along with a guide to a health official so he could check my health papers. The stupid official who did not conceal his hatred of Americans checked and rechecked my passport. Evidently, the frontier of Uruguay didn't exist to his knowledge.

My guide and other officials explained to him that I entered the country by bus, and not by plane or boat.

Then he wanted to know why I was twice in Colombia, twice in Venezuela and twice in Chile. This questioning of where I'd been was unnecessary, and I wondered, *What's wrong with this fellow? He isn't at all polite.* I then pointed out that I was twice in Colombia, and only once in Venezuela and Chile. The other officials took him and my passport to a private room to spare themselves the embarrassment. The secretary said to me, "Have a seat and do not worry." I had no worries.

Presently they returned, humbly handed me my passport, and stamped the health card. The belligerent official neither apologized or said a word.

My guide and I returned to the police station, now five o'clock. They refused to stamp the passport. It was after hours. Now I had to return and go to two more investigation offices. I'd have to leave that for another day. All this running around, speaking a strange language, unnecessary obligations, and a big confusing city to find one's way around in is enough to temper a headache and fatigue.

Back at the travel agency, I relaxed in a soft leather chair. Later I asked the boy what I owed. He said, "Nothing," but I placed thirty cruzeiros in his palm as I said so long. He had helped me a lot all day.

Everywhere one must wait; the various banks set their own hours and one waits for them to open up. One waits in long lines

472

at bus stops, at consular offices, immigration and police stations. Always it is wait, wait, wait.

I had been in Rio only a few days and one bright sunny day as I was walking down the wide mosaic sidewalk along Avenida Rio Branco, whom should I see coming toward me but Bob, from the Alaska Jeepers. He wore a light blue shirt, a brush haircut, and wide grin. Both of us were pleased to see each other again. We strolled into the consulate, but being a Saturday, it was closed. We then met Dorothy at a souvenir shop. She was buying some diamonds and testing them on her forehead for validity. If it was cold, it was good; if not, it was worthless.

We exchanged experiences. Bob and Dot were alone in Rio, living at a very poor hotel. The girl, Jeanie, one of the jeepers, had flown back to the States, another fellow had gone back to get married, and George, Joe, and Pat were stuck in Buenos Aires without money. If they could have sold the jeeps, they would have been all right, but the law would not permit it. Bob had already loaned them $400 and could not afford to lend any more. Bob and Dorothy hoped to return to college in September. The boy's parents could not send them money, because they didn't have it. Bob had hitchhiked from Montevideo to Saõ Paulo, became tired, and then took a train to Rio. Dorothy had flown up to Rio from Buenos Aires with Jeanie. Dorothy did not have enough to fly all the way to the States.

We spent part of the afternoon at sidewalk cafés, lounging in comfortable straw chairs, drinking *guarana,* chatting, and watching the passing crowds. Along Avenida Rio Branco, everyone seemed well dressed. It seemed that everyone must have finances to stay in this colorful city. What we saw most of is long skirts on the graceful women and short haircuts on the men. Dot remarked, at first she thought they were bad haircuts, but then we saw so many that the conclusion is they are traditional Brazilian style. It reminded us of the early American Indians. They seemed to be scalped except for a brush cut atop the head. Even bank clerks had them. Most of the fellows wore white tropical suits, the women's clothes were strictly, the "new look."

We part long enough for me to have dinner at the busy modern railroad terminal, then a shower, cold to be sure, because very few Brazilians know what a hot bath is like.

Bob, Dot, and I spent the evening at the agreeable sidewalk cafés on Avenida Rio Branco. Bob, by some coincidence, had tested aviation engines at the Packard Motor Car Company in Detroit. I had held the same job for a time. We had much to talk about in that respect.

The street became jammed when the movie let out. A fellow was trying to attract a friend's attention across the wide busy street. He did not whistle or yell, "Hey, Joe," or "Hey, Mike," instead he hissed. He hissed a dozen times before he succeeded in catching his friend's attention, and a hundred others. To an American or a European, this is an annoying sound. I have never heard a Latin whistle, only hiss or clap. That's their motto.

Brazilians are always trying to invent new ways of committing suicide. In the daily paper, a fellow used a kerosene lamp. First thing he did was to swallow the wick. It tasted bad, but he still lived. Then he drank the oil. No, he didn't light a match, but the oil made him sick Finding himself still alive, he smashed the lamp glass to fine bits and swallowed that. Finding himself still alive, he decided to go to a hospital. The police asked him what the reason was for trying to commit suicide. He refused to say and added, "Maybe a woman is the cause of it."

After saying goodnight to Bob and Dot, I headed for the hotel and stopped at a popular U.S. Seaman's bar for a drink. A lady of about thirty, sitting at the next table, asked me if I was tired. I said "Yes," but I did not fall into conversation. A few moments later, the comments from waiters and customers confirmed my suspicions of what type of girl she was. I did not ask for the comments, but when a "gringo" comes in, Brazilians like to practice their few words of English in a merry way. I don't believe the girl was embarrassed much when the fellows said—"How much? Six cruzeiros;" Eight cruzeiros? Ten cruzeiros?"

A trip to Rio de Janeiro is not complete without going to the top of "Sugarloaf" and Corcovado Mountains, Copacabana Beach and Paquete Island. At least two days are required to see all. So on one bright Sunday morning, I hurried to the railroad terminal. I got in line and waited for bus number 13 to come along. A

Spaniard on the bus pointed out the points of interest as we rolled along Avenida Rio Branco, then along scenic Rua do Flamengo; he pointed out the palace of the former emperor, Dom Pedro II.

At the foot of the cable car station, there is a tiny restaurant. Here I found Dot and Bob waiting for me. We had a cake; then the cable car was ready to take us to the top of Pão de Acucar (Sugarloaf). There were eighteen passengers in all. I didn't believe the car could take so many. There were seats for all of us (benches), but in the excitement and thrill of rising above the city and toward the huge rock in the Bay of Guanabara, we stood up and looked out of the windows. Everybody seemed to be taking pictures of the red-roofed city, white buildings, palm-lined streets, and the long arm of Copacabana beach, stretching out into the deep blue sea. Directly below us the dense jungle trees blossomed up. There was much chattering, and Bob said, "The floor should be of glass." It wasn't a bad thought. The ride to the first rock took about fifteen minutes; the cable car did sway a bit. It was a helpless feeling, to be suspended so high up by a mere cable.

There were paths, benches, guard rails, and a restaurant on top of the huge rock. There was a place to dance also. The view was breathtaking. I have never seen a shoreline as picturesque as Rio. Lining it were huge white modern buildings, and they seemed to curve with the shore line. The white sandy beaches, the tiny green islands in the bay, and the blue sea were very picturesque.

Looking from this hill, "Sugarloaf," was just ahead of us. It stood out of the sea like a giant cone or a thumb. Connecting "Sugarloaf" and this hill (rock) was another cable car. Fifteen minutes later we bordered it and started on the dizzy accent to the top of the Sugarloaf. How these cables were stretched between these huge gaps, I'll never know.

The second ride seemed shorter. We had attained a total height of 1,200 feet above sea level. From the top of Sugarloaf, the view was even more impressive. Rio seemed to lie in a valley between high mountains, the shore line, is truly a "string of pearls," is never to be forgotten. The top of Sugarloaf is approximately eighty feet in diameter. We had Cokes at the restaurant situated there. To build and furnish it must have required many trips of the cable car.

The descent took only twenty minutes. We had spent two hours on the trip. They were the fastest I ever spent.

We then rode an open-air trolley car to the docks. There were many fellows and senoritas wearing only bathing suits, returning to town from the beach. No doubt they felt comfortable. The trolley cars were cleaner and fresher than the buses.

At the docks, we asked a girl at the gate entrance if the boat was going to Paquete Island. She said, "Yes." Forty minutes after leaving Rio, we found ourselves at Governor's Island and not Paquete Island. The boat was returning to Rio. Such are women employees, too tired to care about giving correct information. It must be the hot, sultry climate. We spent the afternoon at a café on peaceful Governors Island drinking beer. Dot fell asleep in her comfortable chair.

Paquete Island is well known for its beautiful parks and amusement centers. We never got to see it. We returned to Rio by ferry. The crossing was interesting, but getting off the boat, what a beating we took by the pushing, rushing crowd. The ride cost merely two cruzeiros (10¢).

The following day I hurried to the terminal station and took bus No. 45 to the front of Mount Corcovado. I was a bit early, so I drank *gaurana* while I waited. Presently, Bob and Dorothy came. She looked swell in a gray gabardine suit. Sometime later the cog-wheeled train came down the mountain, to pay homage to the Christ statue or merely to get a view of the valley.

The way the train came in, it looked more like a roller-coaster. There were two cars, with seats for about 120 people. There were eight passengers to a seat and they were set parallel, one to the other. The train went up at a crazy incline. The ones sitting in the front seats had to brace their legs to keep from sliding onto the persons in the back seat. The incline was very steep; the engine pounded heavily. It threw up sparks, flame and smoke. We passed jungle foliage and trees, and it seemed strange to find native huts located on the steep hillside. Strange enough there was a cobblestone highway winding its course to

476

the Christ statue. It was possible to drive up. The train ride was very interesting, but not as exciting as the cable car going to the "Sugarloaf."

At the top, a photographer had the disembarking crowd pose momentarily, then took our picture. Later this photo was a nice souvenir. It came in a folder marked, "Remembrance of Corcovado, Rio de Janeiro." It cost only ten cruzeiros (50¢).

From the tracks, we follow huge winding concrete stairways to the base of the Christ statue. It is the biggest I've ever seen. It is at least seventy-five-feet high and ten-feet thick, standing with outstretched arms, looking over the beautiful city of Rio de Janeiro. At night it is illuminated by floodlights and can be seen from a great distance. Located on top of Corcovado, it stands 710 *metroes* above sea level.

From the base of Christ, we get wonderful views of the surrounding hills, valleys, beaches, islands, the blue sea, the white city, racetracks and "Sugarloaf." Many great platforms have been erected with guard rails for this purpose.

There were a couple of newlyweds from New York. They were young and happy. With their moving camera, Bob took pictures of them as they kissed one another, with "Sugarloaf" behind them. Next to Rio, Peru is the nicest place to spend a honeymoon in South America.

One can spend an entire day there and enjoy it. We waited a long time for the train to come up. Many passengers were waiting, and it looked like we would not get a seat going down till very late. With luck we got on; station masters kept an orderly line. A little later we stopped at a large hotel, situated on the halfway mark. We had a twenty-minute rest period. We drank *guarana* and got a view of both the statue and the valley. We reached bottom in the late afternoon. The trip cost eight cruzeiros (40¢) for a round trip. The ride took approximately forty-five minutes.

From Corcovado we rode trolleys and buses to the suburb beach, Praia de Copacabana. We had a lot of fun, and the crowd stared at us happy Americans. We found the beach crowded. It was very colorful, the sun umbrellas, the gay swimming suits, blankets, balloon balls and sun-tanned fellows and senoritas swimming, lounging, playing volley ball, or Spanish football. The sidewalks were colorful and the sidewalk cafés were full of people in light robes and dresses. Copacabana is said to be the home of the wealthy; all along the beach are modern homes, apartments, hotels, restaurants, and department stores. There is where I spend many carefree hours, bathing in the sun and the sea while in Rio.

In Rio, I learned that a road went north to Salvador (Bahia). It is possible to drive. Salvador is along my route and 1,800 kilometers away. I would have liked to hitchhike there, but time was short and I was very tired of hitchhiking. No trains ran to Salvador, no buses. A boat would be going there in a few days, then on to the Amazon. I intended to be on that boat, so I didn't dare risk the chance of missing the boat at Salvador. I had long learned how desolate and isolated those thousand-kilometer stretches could be in Peru, Bolivia and Chile and the slim chances of getting a "lift."

At the steamship agency, Lloyd Brazilero, I had to be the patient one and persistent. The clerk, a lady, had little sympathy for non-speaking Portuguese. She gave me, "No, yes, no, yes, no." She wasn't the least bit interested in where I was going or giving correct data. But with quiet perseverance, I got my information to the pleasure and bewilderment of many understanding customers beside me. When they learned I wanted first-class passage to Manaus, I got better service and soon got my ticket. It cost 2,120 cruzeiros ($105.00).

On my last evening in Rio, I waited a half-hour within a huge crowd for bus No. 15 to Rio Cambrido. It was beat-up and full of gas fumes. I was glad when I got out. I had dinner with Dennis and his mother-in-law. Cris is a schoolteacher and has gone on an expedition to Saõ Paulo with her students. We looked at pictures, had cocktails, then moved the table and played records. Two girls came over, Marie and Virginia. We danced to American and Brazilian music. We really went to town.

The girl Marie was a good dancer, just the kind I like. She taught me the samba. She knew how to jitterbug. It was twelve o'clock when Dennis asked if I would walk the girls home. "With pleasure," I answered.

Dennis was a character; he had thieves in his house one night and fixed up a contraption to catch them. One night he tripped it himself.

I enjoyed walking the girls home. They gave me pictures for remembrance and asked me to write. The trolleys and buses were slow at night. I walked to the hotel, meant to pack my pack, lay down momentarily and fell asleep. The lights burned all night. It was the end of a pleasant stay in Rio, one of the fairest cities of South America.

51

Aboard the Brazilian Ship *Poconi*

The great day had come, the day that I would be sailing northward and homeward. I checked out of the hotel and hailed a cab. I entered and at once I got into the customary argument with the cab driver, asking the driver what the fare was to the docks. He pretended not to hear. I asked again, only louder.

"*De donde es?*" (Where are you from), he asked. "*No importa,*" (Not important) I answered. "Now, how much is the fare?"

"*Fifteen cruzeiros,*" he said.

"Nuts," I answered. "I'll get out here."

"Ten cruzeiros," he then said and still wanted to know where I came from. The fare was still expensive because we had not gone more than eight blocks to the docks.

I was truly surprised to see a large ocean-going steamer at the pier. It was a combination freighter and passenger ship. There were four holds for cargo and seventy-seven staterooms for first-class passengers. I was fortunate. I got into the last state room, number 77. There were four bunks and one couch. I had the strangest roommates, Brazilian navy officers, soldiers, civilians, then an Italian and an Arab.

I was an hour early and watched the coming of passengers and loading of cargo. The passengers were most interesting. Strolling the upper deck behind me was a group of American and Canadian women. I soon joined them in conversation. Only two of the group were going to sail. They were Elenore Paulson, of the American Embassy, and Margie Nelson of the Canadian Embassy. The others were on board, merely to see them off. One of the ladies remembered being introduced to me by Cris Cotton at the Young Women's Christian Association.

Coming on board was an English-looking gentleman. He

was tall, heavy set, and quite bald-headed. He made up for the lack of hair with a magnificent blond beard and an enormous mustache. When he yawned it reminded me of a huge sleepy lion. Later I was surprised to have him for a roommate. He was not English, but Italian.

Another interesting passenger was a fellow traveling third class. He wandered aimlessly on the main deck. He had long, black, shaggy hair that came to his shoulders and whiskers on his face touched his second shirt button. His clothes were dirty and black and a beat-up hat covered his shaggy head.

At nine o'clock sharp, the boat pulled away from the harbor, punctually on time. There was a sounding of fog horns and whistles. There was much hand-waving, handkerchief-waving, and many tears. This continued till the tug boat drew us well out into the stream, circled us around, and headed north. Soon the crowd on shore was a blurred line of color.

It was sunny bright when we pulled away from the docks of Rio, but soon it became cool and gray. At eleven o'clock, we had dinner. Margie, Elenore, and I dined together at a small table in the dining room. We were the only American or English people on board. A few of the officers and passengers could speak some English. Margie and Elenore were glad to have me for company. They had been so afraid that they would be the only two English-speaking women on board. Yet they both were young and pretty and looked at me as a protector and a companion.

The sea became a little choppy and Elenore of Seattle, Washington, a tall lovely blonde, became a little sick, so she retired. Margie, of Ontario, Canada, a pretty brunette, kept me company. We leaned over the rail and talked till our throats were dry. This often happens when meeting our own kind of people and we regret it later, but it was nice leaning over the rail and watching the pitching waves.

Margie retired and I tried reading *Time*. The rolling of the sea and my trying to read did not coordinate. I felt I'd get sick. At two o'clock, they rang chimes and we had tea, coffee, cookies, bread and butter. At five o'clock we had dinner. It was pretty good, but the servants hurried us too much. In forty-five minutes, the room was empty. Margie, Elenore, and I were last to

481

leave the dining room. Elenore had remarked, "Joe, everyone is so quiet. Do we talk too loud?" I said, "Never mind them, just wait a day or two, you'll see how loud they become."

Sure enough in a day or two, the Brazilian ladies and gentlemen became used to our presence and the racket and chattering they made is hard to describe. Where they found so much to talk about, I'll never know.

After dinner we went into the tiny lounge. A dark-complexioned Brazilian lady was playing the piano. After a number or two, she stopped playing. Our presence had made her self-conscious. We ask her to play more, but she shyly refused. Like many Latins throughout South America, she seems to have an inferiority complex. Even the officers on board this ship, I've heard them say, "We are a backward people." Yet there is little reason for it. They have many fine characteristics. I believe they see too many U.S. movies.

In the evening we sit on wooden deck chairs. Elenore brings a bottle of wine and the white-uniformed officers gather around us. Margie and Elenore find themselves very popular with the boys.

We sail on through the night, and next day at six o'clock the chimes are sounded to announce breakfast is ready. On land or on sea, the Latins follow the simple course of only "pan" (bread) and coffee or tea for breakfast.

The day is cold and gray. I put on warmer clothes and make myself comfortable in a wooden deck chair. I read a book called *Vagabonding Down the Andes,* by Harry Frank. I found it very dull and felt like throwing it overboard. I found it hard to believe, and he is from my home state, I learned later on my trip (Harry Frank, that is). The girls rise late and bundle up, they sit in chairs beside me. They write notes and letters. I got into a friendly argument with Margie. She said her hometown, Toronto, was on the St. Lawrence River. I had once hitchhiked to Toronto from Windsor, Canada (across the river from Detroit), and I felt sure that Toronto was on the Atlantic Coast. Margie insisted that Toronto was inland. We made a bet. If I lose, I take the girls to the movies at Victoria, our first stop. If I'm right, they would take me. We checked a map, and I was wrong.

We have dinner at eleven o'clock, and while dining, our ship drifted toward the docks at Victoria. Margie and Elenore had things to do, so I went ashore alone. On land it was sunny bright. The town was large indeed, population about 25,000, and most interesting. It was slightly busy commercially. Near the center of town was a lovely park with tiny ponds, wooden rainbow bridges, benches, gardens, flowers, trees, and whistling senoritas (wolf bait).

Victoria is in the state of Spirto Santo, and a huge Governor's Palace stands on a hillside, overlooking the bay. Dizzy heights of winding stone stairs lead up to it. At one of the numerous restaurants, I stopped for a beer; the price was up two cruzeiros from Rio. Rio was four cruzeiros.

I stopped momentarily to watch bronze-colored natives unloading trucks. They were naked, except for tiny shorts. Their teamwork and speed was surprising. Two fellows would toss a hundred-pound sack of coffee beans into the air, one would walk under it and catch the load on his head, and run off to the warehouse; soon as he left, another sack went into the air and another fellow took off, etc.

I wandered farther up the street, a *trambeo* or bondy (streetcar) lumbered up the grade. It was loaded with dark-featured townsfolk. As it passed, necks turned backwards. I was no longer in boots and field jacket, yet the sight of a white stranger and a camera bring curious glances. "A tourist, no doubt?"

At the movies, a picture was playing called *Alexander's Ragtime Band.* It was at least ten years old. Upon returning aboard the *Poconi,* I told Elenore and Margie about it. I said, "The theater is not ultra modern!" Margie and Elenore said, "It should be fun to see an old, popular picture; we'll go."

Soon after five o'clock dinner, we went on the third-class deck. (There is no second-class on Brazilian ships.) We listened to the dark-complexioned deck hands and passengers singing in Portuguese. They clapped their hands, played a guitar, used spoons, tin plates, and cans full of pebbles to make music. It was a lively tune, and the outcome was wonderful. Some of the fellows were flushed with wine, beer, or whiskey, and they danced the samba very well. They were tipsy and funny. Margie made a

483

request, and the fellows played the song. An old lady who looked like a wrinkled old witch asked the girls and me to dance. She was smoking a pipe, and we all laughed.

Sitting on the rail was a slim girl, no longer in her twenties. She watched the performance. We had heard rumors that an American woman was on board, traveling third-class. She looked like she might be American. Margie said, "She must be lonely, Joe. Why don't you talk to her?" I was just about to walk over when she dropped to the deck and came over to us.

She said her name was Janie, and she was from "Frisco," California. She had started on this trip from Alaska, had gone through Central and South America, and hoped to journey all around the world to write a book. She was traveling alone; she had always planned to travel with her husband, but when he returned from the war in the South Pacific, he was tired and did not wish to travel anymore. Janie obtained a divorce and took off alone.

Janie had a lot of courage, but I did not envy her after she said she never spent more than two dollars a day on her entire trip. I couldn't help thinking about the many cheap hotels I'd stayed in at two dollars a day, so unfit for a lady. How could she say, "It was a lot of fun," when truthfully it was misery and hell.

In the days that followed, we found Janie to be a spirited, independent, friendly, and a nice girl to talk to. She was not the least bit discouraged or unhappy about her third-class quarters and food. She was plenty strong; she had studied jujitsu from a Japanese in Hawaii. She was very outspoken.

We visited her quarters; she had an upper bunk, and a fat old Negro lady slept beside her. There were about thirty women in that section of the boat. Many of them were filthy and dirty, all colors, all ages, some smoking pipes; the young girls smoked just like the old native women. Janie had two huge suitcases and expensive clothes. She had collected a lot of jewelry on her trip and feared having everything stolen. Each time we pulled into a port, she had to stand guard so some of the departing passengers wouldn't depart with her possessions.

Janie's breakfast consisted of coffee and bread, at five o'clock, at ten o'clock, rice and beans for dinner, and supper likewise. A few times they got smelly stew. Janie, in order to offset this diet, had dinner on shore every time the ship docked. In order to take a bath, she had to use a wash tub and a "spicket" (faucet). She kept herself very neat at all times.

Margie, Elenore, and I set off for the movies. Janie did not wish to go. At the movies, Elenore peeked in behind the drab yellow curtain. She was undecided about entering. She peeked in again, and again, evidently annoying the people watching the show. Finally she said, "No." It looked rough with probably dirty seats and rats. It was no place to take two well-dressed women from the embassy, but I had previously warned them that it was not ultra modern. They apologized and returned to the ship. I went to the movie, promising to tell them all about it.

As old as the picture was, I still enjoyed it. The customers sat on long wooden benches. Many men smoked and had their hats on. Overhead were the steel girders and unpainted roof. Soon as the picture ended, everyone got up in unison, and what a racket those flimsy benches made.

We left Victoria at noon the next day. The morning was cool and cloudy; at noon the sun came out. The girls were becoming most popular with the Brazilian officers. They had breakfast in bed and extra rations—poached eggs.

Out at sea, Elenore gets sick again and turns in. Margie and I read on deck. In the evening we walk along the deck, then go to the bridge. A lovely tropical moon is out, and we sail the sea of reflection. She has had a boy friend and lost him. I have had a girl and lost her, too. She looked just like Deanna Durbin and it's a temptation to take her in my arms. It was pretty late when we descended.

The following day is spent at sea. Sometimes we wish we would never dock. We simply enjoy sailing along over the wide expanse of sea with nary a sight of land. It is a bit rough, and the day is gray and cool. Nothing exciting happens all day, not a sail or a ship is seen on the horizon to break the monotony. In the evening, Margie, Elenore, and I broke the stillness by running around and around the deck. Their high-heeled shoes and my leather ones sounded like galloping horses on the wooden deck.

All the officers stared in amazement. "Have the three gringos gone mad?"

Elenore is a lovely blonde, with the sweetest purring voice. It is a shame she is so tall. She is so considerate, she excuses herself and retires to her room. Margie and I lean over the rail. staring into the dark night as our mighty "galleon" rises and falls and plows its course through the dark seas. We get a bath from the mist, and so ends another day.

Not every day do I awaken at the same time. Today I awaken at nine, take a shower, find no hot water on this coal-burning tub. About 10:30, Saõ Salvador (Bahia) is sighted. Across our bow a steamer is forging ahead to dock at the port first. After dinner I return to my deck chair. It took us exactly forty-seven hours from Victoria to reach Salvador (Bahia). I was in no particular hurry to go ashore. We would be docked for twenty-four hours.

Suddenly, visitors. I was surprised to have visitors at that outlandish place. It was Bob from the steamer that had crossed our bows and made port first. I hadn't expected his ship to catch up with us. We went ashore and joined Dot. She looked swell in a clean blue-white dress. We rode an elevator to the top of the hill amidst many pushing, shoving laborers and town folk. A small fee was charged for the ride.

The town is very old, full of adobe homes and cobblestone streets. Nowhere have I ever seen steeper streets, except for La Paz, Bolivia. It is noted chiefly for the large number of churches. There are eighty-four in all. The population is roughly about 25,000. It is a quaint city, but not one desirable to live in.

There were sights that were not so nice. A fellow sauntered down a crowded sidewalk, carrying two slaughtered pigs across his shoulders. His shirt and trousers were a black and red greasy mess from the blood and slime. His pigs were bloody and covered with dirt. Dot remarked, "That's probably our dinner on the *Itaquice.*" Bob and Dorothy were traveling third-class and their dinners were pretty grim.

Looking down on the bay from the hill top, we saw a circular fortress in the center of it. No doubt, it carried a beautiful historical background, but even if someone had explained to us, it would be hard to understand in Portuguese.

We stopped at a busy modern restaurant; fans circled overhead, but still the day was hot, moist and clammy. We did not feel like walking anymore. Bob and Dorothy had a large dinner (for a change). Bob and I then drank twelve bottles of beer, Dot drank five Cokes. We had a pleasant afternoon. Beer was up now four cruzeiros more than Rio. When we returned to our ships, we staggered like drunken sailors.

The girls were still ashore, so I had dinner alone. Then I took a two-hour nap. Bob and Dot came on board, then Marge and Elenore came loaded down with souvenirs. They had souvenirs of beautiful ships and birds, made and carved out of bone. They required much patient work and were sold ridiculously cheap by the natives. Elenore and Marge had more interesting stories to tell about the churches and black magic.

At ten o'clock next day, we pulled away from the docks of Saõ Salvador (Bahia). We had taken on some cargo and deposited some. We dropped the bearded Italian and picked up an Arab. He became my roommate. We had stayed exactly twenty-two hours at Bahia.

At dinner Elenore asked me, "What do you think about having two pretty girls to dine with you every day?" "It's better than eating alone," I remarked. They sat up straight and drew deep breaths. I thought they would blow their "tops." "Is that all you can say?" they asked. "Well, we like that!" I could only grin in amusement. They went "topside" to get a tan. I remained on deck to write a letter.

After supper we strolled the decks, the girls stopping here and there to speak Portuguese to some officer or passenger. I could only stand by. We went into the lounge. Elenore played some music on the piano to the great pleasure of the uniformed officers who gathered about them. Then a Brazilian lady played some nice tunes. It was a peaceful and friendly gathering till a loud, blond, Brazilian girl dropped in, threw open the windows to a strong night wind, banged the piano, and talked at the top of her voice. Soon the lounge emptied and by ten o'clock everyone was in bed.

We sail on through the night and morning finds us pushing ever northward on rolling seas. I rise early and go "topside"

487

again. Marge joins me and we lay on a blanket on the deck, but keep our clothes on.

It was nice there on the rolling seas. We watched the rise and fall of the bow. It was peaceful and quiet. Our ship played "tag" with the *Itaquice* all morning and at noon. One would pass the other, and there was loud cheering on deck, sometimes the pilots sounded whistles and fog horns to make it a merry affair.

One of the officers came up to check the hearing on a gyro, then another came. Soon they sat on Margie's side and babbled in Portuguese. She could understand it pretty well. Her country had sent her to Rio with the embassy for three-and-a-half years. She had spent two years there already. The officers never said a word to me. I could not ask them to leave. I just had to lie patiently and listen to their chatter. I did not wish to offend anyone by leaving. This kept on for several hours. At three o'clock the Port of Maceio was sighed. Both the steamers *Poconi* and *Itaquice* moved toward land. It was anyone's guess which ship would dock first. At four o'clock, both ships docked simultaneously.

Soon we saw Bob and Dot on the dock. Marge, Elenore, and I joined them. We took a cab into town; there were five of us and we pitched in six cruzeiros each to pay for the ride. A long rainbow causeway, similar to the "pike" of Los Angeles, separated the docks from the town.

The town was old and picturesque, but not dirty like Saõ Salvador (Bahia). It was quiet and clean, with beautiful sandy benches surrounding it. We strolled together, five abreast. Townsfolk looked after us from the sidewalks, doorways, and windows. We took some pictures by an old church, then strolled lazily along the beach, lined with palm trees. It was warm and we became thirsty. We saw a large cement building, stained and dirty. We asked a fellow in the doorway if they sold Coca-Cola here.

"Yes, certainly," he said; "this is a private club, but you all are welcome." He no doubt knew that we were American tourists from the boat. We were indeed surprised upon entering to find a lovely, up-to-date club, beautifully designed. There was a polished tile floor, a promenade, and large rectangular windows opening up to get a healthy sea breeze and a view of the beach, the rainbow causeway, the three ships at dock, and the sea beyond.

Our host took us on a tour of the club; there were several floors, dance halls, and modern bathroom facilities. We then sat at a table by one of the large windows and ordered *chopp* (beer). We were surprised when our host started bringing us large crabs. He cracked the shells and gave us the meat. There were five of us, and we each had three or four crabs apiece and then more *chopp* (beer). We spent several hours there, enjoying ourselves immensely. Elenore had struck up some music on the brand-new piano to help entertain.

Our Brazilian host only let us pay for the first round, which cost each of us a dollar apiece. He insisted on paying the rest. Then he ordered a cab and took us to another club. Dot was wearing slacks, and he feared we might not get in, but we did. That club was not much to write about. A simple Spanish garden in the center and a promenade about it with chairs and tables. No music, no dancing, we only drank more *chopp* (beer).

Five hours after coming ashore, our host had a cab waiting to take us back to the ship. At the causeway gate, we were stopped by a guard. He demanded a fee and a terrible argument ensued between cab driver, our host, and the guard. It was embarrassing to the girls, Bob, and me. Finally our host and driver paid the fee. It seemed like the guard saw we were American passengers and had to collect a dollar for himself. His .45 revolver and uniform stood for authority.

We invited our Brazilian host aboard for a drink since he had been so kind to us. We ordered more *chopp,* then I got Janie from her third-class quarters to join us. She already was in bed but joined us in pigtails and nightgown. It gave everyone a laugh. Only one thing spoiled our host's enjoyment. A couple of his friends, big husky thugs, followed us aboard, and sat at the next table beside us. They asked Marge and Elenore in whispers for a drink. Our host was a bit drunk, and we decided to get him ashore. I took him to his waiting cab. He hugged and patted me in affectionate Latin style. Then he decided he must go back on board. I could not stop him with words and did not wish to rely on force. He ran up the gangplank to the girls leaning on the rails. They had been watching us on the dock.

Imagine my surprise when he took each of their hands and kissed them. Then he went into the dining room and came out a moment later with the two thugs. They nodded as they passed us again, returned to the cab, and drove away.

Bob and Dot returned to their ship, the *Itaquice.* I joined them for a minute. Bob and Dot changed into heavy slacks, clothes, and slept on the deck, covered with blankets. All about them were trucks, cars, lumber, dogs, and more natives. Lucky for them they were strong and healthy, but it was embarrassing to them to have to travel in that manner. The fare was ridiculously cheap, yet as Americans they couldn't afford it. First-class cost $100 for three weeks; third class about $25.

I said "Good night" to Bob and Dot, then returned to the *Poconi.* Marge and Elenore were holding a Portuguese conversation with the purser and several mates. I asked the girls if they cared to polish off the remaining beer in the dining room. "Sure," they said. "I'll bet the officers are mad at me for taking you away from them," I said. But the girls said they liked me and would join me. We "polished off" the remaining beer. We agreed that our host had been a swell guy.

We docked at Maceió only eight hours. We pulled out at midnight. The *Itaquice* had left an hour earlier. When I turned in, I found all my roommates in bed except for the Arab. He walked the deck till it was deserted of all females.

We sail on and on through the tropical night and another day breaks, the beginning of the second week aboard the *Poconi.* I had a lousy taste in my mouth after all the chopp I had last night. Brushing my teeth and gargling didn't help much. The rolling and pitching of the sea don't help matters any. I succeed in getting into the bathroom. Every morning there is a long line waiting to get into it. The days are becoming much hotter, and at noon and evening, there is a continuous line. One limits one's shower bath to five or ten minutes. Usually there is a steady banging on the door to hurry the bather on. They all come out with fierce angry looks. Trying to take a shower on a tossing sea is quite an ordeal, as I found this morning.

490

Went "topside" to get a tan, but showers kept me on the deck chair most of the morning. Had dinner with Margie and Elenore. We have a terrific appetite, but once we sit down, we can't eat; we barely nibble. It has been this way right along on the ship. There are about twenty Brazilians in that dining room. They hurry through their meals and talk loudly. We find ourselves last to leave each day. We spend the afternoon playing "tag" with the *Itaquice* on the green bounding waves. Land is sighted and soon we are coming in to dock at Recife, sixteen hours after leaving Maceió.

Both ships came into dock at four o'clock. The shore was lined with huge German cranes, flat cars, warehouses, and waiting, hand-waving crowds. Certainly I never expected to find such a large city on the coast of Brazil, so isolated from Rio de Janeiro and the rest of the world. A good road connecting these towns would break that isolation, but evidently the jungle and forests are almost impenetrable.

Elenore and Marge were leaning against the rail, waving and calling to an English acquaintance on shore. I leaned and talked to an English-speaking Brazilian girl named Mary Frances. She was brown colored, I should say, like their famous coffee. She was dainty, rather quiet, long black hair, sparkling eyes, and the prettiest smile ever, revealing even white teeth.

She had spent two years in Africa with an American outfit from 1945 to 1947. She learned to speak English very well. She asked me if I would care to come to her home for dinner. I said I'd be delighted. Marge and Elenore had made engagements with the English fellow. There was no sense in spending an evening alone.

The gangplank went down, and native porters rushed aboard, carrying bags, trunks, and boxes atop their heads; others started going off the ship. The gangplank became jammed and unsafe. Laundry women came on board and the ship's officers said it was safe to trust them to do our laundry. Peddlers, men and women, came on board selling blouses, tablecloths, fruit, fish, and beautiful pocketbooks, belts, ships, and combs made out of bone. An electrician came on board and installed a telephone to connect with the shore.

Dot and Bob came aboard to visit. Janie came up from below decks. Dot and Janie decided to stay on board. I went ashore with Bob, Elenore, and Margie. We walked through large iron gates, ignored the cries of taxi drivers, and strolled to a tiny park. From there we were undecided which street to follow. We were at the hub and five or six streets stretched out like spokes or sun rays ahead of us.

"Where do we go?" they all asked.

A little fellow walked up to us and settled our problem. He was very small, but he had a strong driving voice. He was dressed in a white tropical suit and spoke English fluently. We thought he was from New York because of his accent, but he had only visited New York. He was a Swiss, working many years in Brazil.

"Where is the British Consul's office?" Marge asked. The Swiss pointed off to the right and numbered the blocks.

"Where is the American Consul's office," Elenore asked. The Swiss pointed off to the left and counted off the number of blocks. I said, "This is no joke, but where is the French Consul's office?" They all laughed and the Swiss said, "That's all right," and he pointed straight ahead and counted off two blocks. "I can take you where you wish to go."

"To the nearest bar," I said, and everyone agreed. He drove us about the town, pointing out the points of interest. "Recife," he said "is the Venice of South America because of it's many channels and boats." He suggested the best restaurants and hotels, and he said there were no night clubs or dance halls in Recife.

We went to the modern Gran Hotel. It was very lovely, especially the lounge. The benches and chairs were covered with spotted black, white, brown calfskin fur. There we had beer, breaded chicken leg, and various types of tasty fish concoctions. The Swiss did most of the talking; he had a gift of speech and certainly was not a boring fellow. He soon had to leave; his wife had supper waiting. He said, if he had time, he would take us around tomorrow. He insisted upon paying, saying, we would be on our own after that.

Certainly, never had I met fellows like that in other Latin countries or the U.S. for that matter, who come up a perfect stranger, offering information and service and paying for the privilege.

Soon afterwards we went strolling through brightly illuminated streets, then to a dimmer section of town. We came to a market place. Sitting on a curb were men and women roasting corn over large cans of live coals. Marge, Elenore, Bob, and I stopped to buy some. Only butter and salt was missing. The roasted black breads were good. We continued strolling and munching on the corn cob. It seemed perfectly natural to do so in that environment. We passed a shop; a one-armed youth shouted his head off like a radio announcer (Walter Winchell). Lots of people laughed heartily and applauded at his remarks, but his wares did not cross over the counter. Many listened, then moved on. We walked on and came to a Catholic church. Its large doors were fully open. The beautiful interior was visible. My companions were not Catholic, but they were set upon entering. I followed suit. I went through my customary sign of the cross and prayer—while they respectfully sat. Ten minutes later we were outside again. The church was beautiful, but not very large. People came in for a few minutes, prayed, and left.

Back to the hotel, Bob and I escorted the girls. There engagement was at seven o'clock. We hated to part; we had had a nice afternoon. "Where to now?" I asked Bob.

"Back to the ship," he said.

"Not me," I said. "I have a Brazilian baby to visit. Want to come along? She may have a girlfriend."

"Okay," he said.

In Portuguese, we inquired what bus to take to Boa Viaja (Beautiful Way). After four tries, a policeman directed us to the proper street and corner. There were several long lines of people waiting for a bus. Ten minutes later Bob said, "I don't think I will go. Dot may be alone on the ship." So he left and I decided to check again if I were in the proper line. I was not; even policemen make mistakes; around the corner was another bus. I stepped into it and was off at once.

The ride seemed long through town, then along a beautiful sandy beach and modern residential section. The bus driver let me out at the right street. It was very dark. I came to a house

493

with burning porch lights. The number was 799. I asked a lady on the porch, "Where is 757?"

"*Muto longe,*" (very far) she answered and pointed down the dark street. According to the number, I couldn't be far away. Just two houses down, about sixty feet, I heard Marie's voice call, "Over here, Joey." I've had the Indians of the high Andes in Ecuador give me "bum steers," but why in hell in this civilized city, I'll never know.

At Marie's home I met her mom, sister, brother, a cousin, and the doctor from the *Poconi.* The dinner was of spaghetti, Spam, sauerkraut, soup, and dessert. They asked if I liked wine. "Sure," I answered. Later they apologized, saying, "the store is closed." I felt like a piker, I did not mean for them to go and buy some. But such are the Brazilian people; they are nice and wish to please. Marie's home was nice and well furnished. She had many souvenirs of her stay in Africa "Too many black people," is all she said about it.

We looked at photographs, and she autographed two large ones to me with the nicest comments. Her mom, sister, brother, and cousin went to the movies. The doctor returned to the ship. After a while, Marie and I went walking along the beach. The night was dark, but still it was a beautiful place to live, along this lovely beach. Soon our shoes were full of the clear white sand; we didn't mind. Hand in hand we walked in the deep sand, then along the hard-packed water's edge for a mile or so. Here and there were shelter houses of thatched roofs and strange fishing rafts. They were odd and flimsy. They had crude wooden benches and locks for the oars. The sails were taken down at night and stored away safely. To go fishing on them, one had to be an expert swimmer. The chances of mishap were very great.

A strange girl was Marie, aside from her Brazilian color. She was about the closest I'd come to meeting a girl with American way of thinking. At ten o'clock, she had to be in. At 10:30, there was no stopping her. Her parents in Recife were strict. In Rio de Janeiro, where she worked, she had more liberty. She had come home for a ten-day visit after working a year in Rio. At the dock, her reception was heart-warming. In the evening at home, it was very quiet. It seemed like she had never been away.

The bus ride to town took twenty minutes. The driver drove beyond limits. At a modern soda fountain, I stopped, picked up a menu, and ordered a sundae; a few minutes later I received an ice-cream soda. *Good enough,* I thought. *Maybe they don't know the difference.*

Walking along beautiful mosaic sidewalks, I returned to the *Poconi.* I found Marge, Elenore, and the Englishman on deck, drinking highballs. I joined them and had one also.

Our first morning in Recife, I was supposed to go to town with Marge and Elenore. They were not up for breakfast. At 8:30 I banged on their stateroom door. They had paid the price of four, so they could have the stateroom private. At 9:30, Marge appeared on deck, bright as a "morning glory," dressed in light blue and white. We sat on deck chairs and waited for Elenore. The phone rang, it's only a dozen feet from where we were sitting. No one could be more surprised; it was a call for me. It was Marie. Marge couldn't help overhearing and wondered, *What goes on here?* She didn't say anything. I told Marie I'd see her at six as Marge told me they had another engagement for the evening. Bob and Dot came aboard. It was 10:30 and Elenore still had not come out. Marge excused me to go ashore with them.

We went to the French consul; we found Janie there. I was the only one entitled to a visa for French Guiana because the consul in Rio sent them a letter to give me one. If Bob, Dot, and Janie had called at the consul in Rio, they would have been able to obtain visas also. It is confusing and seems silly, but that's how it is worked.

This was a surprise and a shock to my friends. It was the first time they had ever been refused a tourist or transient visa. Only a short while, previous, Bob had stated proudly, "With this good old U.S. passport, we can go anywhere." I was charged 500 francs for my visa ($2.50). We then go calling on British and the Dutch consuls concerning entry to their respective Guianas. No visa is required for Americans to British Guiana; for the Dutch, yes. After these visits, it's time for a large dinner, but we do not eat in peace; peddlers annoy us, selling tablecloths, clothes, etc.

We go sightseeing, of all places, to a market place. It's like bordertown, Mexico. Vendors come at us like flies to buy their wares. Bob and Dot had them display trousers, jackets, shoes, etc. The men talked and talked, wearing themselves out in the heat of the day; then neither Bob or Dot bought anything. I became tired and drowsy, excused myself, and returned to the ship. Instead of lying down, I ran into Margie. She asked if I would walk her ashore to meet Elenore at the Gran Hotel. I couldn't refuse a lady, and we walked the dozen blocks to the hotel.

We found Elenore and ran into Bob, Dot, and Janie also. We all started for the second-floor lounge. Marge and Elenore, our fair, dainty lassies, stopped halfway across the lobby to settle a suggestion, with the lot of cooing, apologies, and more cooing; they wasted a lot of time being so considerate and polite that it became trying to men or women who had an aptness for quickness. Once upstairs we had sandwiches, Cokes, and highballs. The girls were good sports and insisted upon paying their share of the checks.

Elenore had her hair done at a hairdresser's this morning. It looked swell. She said the hairdresser was a man and made such a fuss over her, telling her, "You're not from Rio or America; you're from Heaven," etc. etc.

Outside the hotel, we separated again, Janie going her way, a lonely, undiscouraged traveler, Bob and Dot going their way. Elenore, Marge, and I got to call on our Swiss friend. He is very busy and cannot drive; he got his foot badly infected. His apologies are good. We run into a Brazilian fellow from the ship. He orders a cab, and we go to a popular soda fountain parlor. There we see Dot and Bob again. How we keep running into each other is a mystery. It's getting late and I'm worried about missing my date; then at five we start back for the ship. I feel bad because I can't change a thousand-cruzeiro note and the fellow pays for everything, a typical good-natured Brazilian.

Marge and Elenore have a date at 7:00. I keep mine with Marie at 6:00. Just outside the huge steel dock gates, I waited five minutes for sweet Marie. She came in bright clothes. We went strolling through town, stopping for milk and hot dogs. It was a bun all right but filled only with hamburger sauce. We took in a movie, *Golden Earrings,* and I promised Marie, if ever I got rich, I'd send her a pair. We then went to her neighborhood;

along the beach we strolled. It was a lovely evening; we stopped at a hut and a fellow trimmed coconuts with a machete for us. We drank the sweet milk like natives do. We continued strolling and suddenly a heavy rain fell. We dashed to a shelter house. When the rain stopped, we moved on and came to a stop under a palm tree.

I took sweet Marie into my arms, she reminded me of slim, lovely, South Sea Island girls and she truly was just that. Marie was passionate and warm. Why couldn't I miss the boat or come back to Rio and work? She said she would even get me a job. Why did I want to return home? We leaned against the tree together; suddenly there was a sickening "thud." What was that? Then we saw it; a coconut had fallen from the tree and missed striking our heads by inches. That was a close call; a shiver went down my spine. That brought up the question, "Could a coconut kill a man?" I believe it could from the height it fell, thirty or forty feet. We start for her home, because she is wonderful pleasant company, I promise to see her in the morning.

Back on the ship, passengers have strung up hammocks all over the deck. Many sleep out all night because of the stifling heat in the rooms. The mosquitos are becoming annoying. It is near midnight, and I call on Janie in her third-class quarters. She is awake and we talk a while. A steward shouts at me that men are not allowed in women's quarters after ten o'clock. Janie has an interesting tale to tell me. "Elenore and Marge," she told me "did not have a date with an Englishman, but with the dashing Brazilian hairdresser. They were stood up. They then met the American consul and went to his home for dinner."

I rise early in the morning; it is raining heavily and it looks as if I'll have to break my date. It stops in time for me to walk to the appointed place, the movie near the canal. Marie is not there. I wait and some interesting sights go by. Porters carry heavy trunks atop their heads, hands swaying freely. I fear their heads will crush. Then a friar (priest) goes by in the traditional haircut, long brown frock, and a big black umbrella to ward off the hot sun; Negro women carry huge bundles of laundry atop their heads; then the well-dressed go by also.

Marie comes fifteen minutes late. She looks very pretty in a polkadot blouse, blue skirt, and a bright kerchief. Near the Justice Palace, a huge colonial building, we wait for a bus. It leaves at ten o'clock for Duis Irmanos Parque (Two Brothers Park).

We roll out of the business and residential sections onto a rough, bumpy, dirt road. The old bus and this terrible road pushing through a solid jungle does not let me forget the many hours and days I've spent bumping south on the Pan-American Highway. The half hour's ride wears me out more than if I had never made the long journey.

We pay a small fee to enter the park. It really is a forest. We stroll casually by many rectangular man-made pools. In them are various species of Brazilian fish; then past cages of parrots and birds in glorious color. The tiny ones were prettiest. They had red breasts, black wings, and a few had red heads; a couple of the owls were funny looking; the mere sight would make anyone laugh. Others were mean looking. Black and white hawks, then past monkey cages, African beasts, and crocodiles lay by dozing in the sun and shallow water. Farther on were gardens of bright flowers, names I'd never learn and likewise I've never heard before nor seen before.

We come to a small lake; nearby is a restaurant. Marie bought some bread and then threw bits of it into the lake. At once big fish seemed to burst out of the water, making a frightening noise and showering water into the air as they caught and swallowed the bread. They were most interesting to watch. They were as big as sharks.

We lunched on sandwiches and Cokes, then went strolling in the nearby forest. In Marie I found a likable companion. I always loved hiking in the forests. We found them deep and cool. After a long walk, we found a bench to rest on. It was a lovely way to spend an afternoon.

Sometime later it started raining and we raced back to the restaurant. It was time for sandwiches and beer again. There was good music on the radio and I asked Marie if she cared to dance. She in turn asked the proprietor if we were allowed to. He said, "Yes." There were about a dozen people. They all smiled pleasantly at us dancing together, the Samba, the waltz, Mexican La Raspa, and U.S. jitterbugging. Marie was surprised that I could do the Samba, but then it's easy, but to do it the way the natives do on the boat is another story. It was wonderful dancing with the rain pouring down off the thatched roof; there were no walls. The floor was tile and smooth. We spent several hours dancing and drinking. It looked like I might miss the boat if the rain did not subside.

At six o'clock it did; the park gates were closed and a guard let us out. We had just missed the bus. It looked like I would miss the boat for sure. It sailed at eight. Then another bus came and we got in. Near town it had to make several detours because the road was flooded from the heavy rain. I thought surely I would miss the boat. Marie hoped I would, but luck was with me and not Marie. We had a half-hour to spare. Marie came to my room; she stayed just long enough to say farewell in the nicest way. She was crying when she left.

I went on deck hoping to see her one more time, but she was gone. She was gone, and I saw her no more. I went up on deck. The worried purser crying asked, "Where are the girls?"

"I don't know," I answered. Fifteen minutes before sailing time, they came on board, much to the relief of the officers.

"So you deserted us this morning. Where have you been?" I only grinned. I hoped to catch sight of Marie again on shore, but she was not there to wave good-bye.

I was a little bit dizzy after all the beer that I had, when Elenore and Marge fell into another of those long Portuguese conversations with the officers, I walked off, over to the rail. I did not expect Marge to join me, but she did, telling how she had spent the day, how tired Elenore was of struggling with the Portuguese language, and how she almost changed boats to go on a more elaborate, expensive American boat to Manaus. They quarreled and nearly separated. I told Marge I was weary of Portuguese also. Marge was all right; her knowledge of the language was great. Comes along nine-thirty, we all turn in, after seventy-six hours of Recife, we say farewell and sail on through the night.

Eleven days out of Rio, the day breaks clear and fair weather is forecast. After typical Latin breakfast (coffee and bread), I go

499

topside for a tan; an hour later Marge comes up and she brings the rain. We dash down again.

After dinner, we three go topside for a tan. Elenore and I lie on a blanket together; Marge is lying on another near our feet.

"Hope you don't mind lying at our feet?" I remarked good-naturedly. She laughed and said, "I don't mind."

Soon a Brazilian officer comes up and starts talking Portuguese to Margie, then he sits down beside her. Elenore and I move slowly forward and away, to get out of earshot. We prefer silence. Marge notices our reactions, complains, and moves forward after us.

After a bit, I said "I wish my feet did smell." The remark was timely and Elenore laughed and couldn't stop for a long time, when she did, it came again. Marge heard the remark, laughed, and moaned. She had a hard time explaining to the officer what we were laughing about.

Soon Elenore said, "Joe, I'm going down. If you want to stay and use the blanket, it's okay." I was going to, but on second thought said "No." I didn't wish to listen to Portuguese either. As we started down the ladder, Marge moaned and came running after us. She did not wish to be left alone.

After supper I was introduced to a Mr. and Mrs. Don Williams, young Baptist American missionaries. "Well, we got rid of a priest who had everyone praying every morning; now we got you," I said. They all laughed good-naturedly, and Myra Williams said, "Well, we like that." They were assigned to the hot northern parts of Brazil for three years. They had a lovely little girl.

We were all seated on deck chairs, Marge, Elenore, the Williamses, and I, drinking Coca-Cola. The night air was hot and sultry, but we enjoyed pleasant conversation on the lighted deck. We were suddenly interrupted by a sixteen-year-old boy who had gone berserk from the heat. He moaned a strange sound continuously and went chasing all the ladies and girls on deck. The women scattered. He started for Margie. I blocked his way, I felt like knocking him out, but I feared I might get myself into trouble; I was a foreigner on this boat. I then caught and held him around the arms and chest while Marge, Elenore, Mrs. Williams, and all the women ran for their rooms.

Soon the officers came and I released him; he went running about the deck, opening cabin doors. A fellow said, "He won't harm the women; he only wants to touch their breasts." One officer caught him, but no one else offered a hand. There were at least a dozen officers about in their smart white uniforms. The lad broke away and the officers went after him. Then the big husky 260-pound "Commissario" came; the boy pushed him aside also. Down below decks they went; they would hold him momentarily, then let him get away. All this went on for a half hour. Then a fellow came (his father, I believe) with a hypodermic needle, and the shot knocked him out.

Certainly, on an American ship, a person wouldn't run berserk for five minutes before he was subdued.

Back on deck, we all met again, except for Margie. She seemed to enjoy the company of the officer of our afternoon session. Marge was the type of girl who feels sorry for people. Elenore and I made a few rounds on the deck and turned in.

All night we sailed on; up and down our galleon rolled over the waves; at daybreak we dropped anchor at Fortaleza. To go ashore, we had to go by *jungadas* (large, picturesque sailboats). There were many taking passengers and cargo to and from shore. At noon several passengers and I board a tipsy *jungada*. The huge white sails caught the wind and we glided swiftly and silently toward shore. It took several minutes, and a 25-cent charge was made (5 cruzeiros.).

Once ashore, I learned it was six or seven miles to the center of town. The beach was dry, barren and hot. While waiting for a bus, I decided to hitchhike. I "caught" a ride in an ancient truck. I sat beside the driver in a tiny cab. My knees almost touched my chin. The road was bumpy and dusty. All along the beach were strewn bamboo and reed houses. Poverty was everywhere; children ran naked, women wore torn, ragged, dirty dresses, men in undershirts and trousers; a few were drunk. Everyone seemed thirsty; animals and poultry ran rampant. Pots, clothes, and debris lay everywhere.

Coming into town, I was surprised to be entering a modern

city. The residential suburbs were full of lovely, colonial and modern homes. I had never expected to find a display of wealth in that part of the country. My driver left me out ten blocks from the center of town. I waited for a bus. Whom do I meet on it but the Arab and a boy and girl from third class? They pay my fare on leaving the bus.

In town we strolled along, the Arab and boy decided to go to a movie; the girl wished to go with me, but I preferred her not to. She was too fat for me! She was good for the Arab; he liked all girls, any shape.

I stopped for a "Coke"; the waitress's expression seemed to say—"He don't savvy Portuguese; I'll pretend I don't understand." It irritated me because Coca-Cola was pronounced the same in all languages. After five tries, it sank into her head, then she said. *"No ha"* (No have). On a menu card, I pointed out mineral water and received soda water.

While drinking it, I saw Bob passing the doorway; his ship came in also. I ran and called him back. He was glad to see me. He said Elenore and Marge were ashore with Dorothy. Bob and I went sightseeing about town, but there wasn't much to see except a lot of men in white tropical suits, seated or standing about the clock in the plaza.

We strolled toward the beach; the day was hot and sultry. We became tired and thirsty. We stopped for a beer at a thatch-roofed restaurant. It had no walls. We started for a table and were called by four Brazilians. They asked us to join them and have a drink. All of them spoke English; two were exceptionally good. One looked just like our Harry Truman. He cocked his head this way, and that way for us to observe his features. He was a radio telegraph operator. Another was a huge strapping fellow, of Swedish origin. He was a former seaman and now a well-to-do import-export man. Another looked like a Yugoslav friend of mine; he did not like the remark and said, "But I'm not a Red."

We had stopped for only one beer, but our Brazilian neighbors just kept setting them up, and by the time we left, we each had two gallons under our belts. Again our neighbors refused to let us pay at least part; their generosity amazed us. Bob and I agreed that the Brazilians were the best of our Latin neighbors.

Bob's ship was leaving at six; we decided to return to our ships. Along the poverty-stricken beaches, the fishermen were returning; there were hundreds of *jungada* (sailboats) on the sea and on shore, in the sunset they were very picturesque. Never have I seen the likes of these primitive, but attractive boats. Fortaleza should be famous on their account.

I had supper alone, turned in early; our ship, the *Poconi,* lifted anchor at midnight and steamed through the night ever northward.

The thirteenth day out of Rio breaks clear. I spent the morning "topside," getting a tan. But the sad part was that a few days away from the sun and I sweated the tan away in this tropical humidity. At noon the girls displayed the lovely hammocks they had bought at Fortaleza for only ten dollars. They had spent their visit at the U.S. consul's home. At dinner there was a lot of joking. Afterwards they went "topside" for a tan; I stayed on deck. I preferred silence; I knew the officers would be topside also. The girls didn't stay up long and came on deck to sit beside me; I could not read in peace; the officers followed the girls there again. The day moved on and night fell black. We sailed on through the night and daybreak found us still out at sea.

I go topside for the morning sun and Marge soon joins me. We lie flat on our stomachs, and I read *Time* to her. She likes that, but then more and more, we disagree on various subjects. At dinner we take turns buying beer, mineral water, or wine. Today it's Elenore's and she insists upon signing the check.

They go topside; I decline. Soon they return on deck, saying, "It's too hot." Elenore writes notes on her lap; I occasionally read a joke to them. The Arab comes, sits at Elenore's feet, and talks to them in Portuguese. We all get a big laugh out of him.

This morning at breakfast, one of the passengers had bought some cookies for herself.

"What have you got there?" the Arab asked her.

"Cookies," the girl answers.

"Well, put them on the table," he said.

She refused and handed him two. He wouldn't take them

503

and told her again to place the bag of cookies on the table. Everyone laughed. The girl refused and he got mad. She placed three on a dish for him, but he refused to take them. Everyone laughed again.

In the evening some soldiers made fun of him. They wrapped white sheets about their bodies and head, leaving only the faces bare, and sat in the deck chairs. As passengers strolled by, they cocked their heads and mimic.

The Arab was a nosy fellow, asking personal questions, such as "What do you have in your bag?" What I had in my pack was my own business. Aside from his faults, he was an interesting passenger. Soldiers loved me to ask him, "How do you like the Jews?" I never asked.

I went to my quarters. A little later, Janie and Elenore knocked on my door. Janie said, "There is a cute Brazilian girl who is dying to meet you. Come on down; the girl is all dressed up, nice and pretty to see you."

"No, thanks," I said. "Where is she going?"

"Manaus," answered Jane. "She's really cute, like a South Sea Island girl, nice, long black hair and pretty teeth."

"If she is going to Manaus, I'll have plenty of time to see her later," I said. Elenore tried to make me go, but I still said, "No."

They come inside to look at my quarters. "Where does the Arab sleep?" they asked. "The upper bunk," I said. "I have the lower."

At supper we have wine; we drink to the king, president, health and bon voyage on the Mighty Amazon. We hoped to enter the mouth of the Amazon in the early morning. We were quite excited about being so close.

Marge asks me to go for a walk. We walk around and around the deck a few times. A loud bawdy girl sings at the top of her voice. We pass her by twice, then go topside. The night is black and starry. We lean against the rail. A soft wind blows. I place my arms around her waist, and she squeezes my hand.

Soon we hear Elenore's voice, and she joins us. A few minutes later, we hear Janie's voice, and she comes up also, followed by the South Sea Island girl. Janie introduces her to all of us. She

504

couldn't speak English and in the darkness, she stood out darkest, smallest, and stoutest.

"Could you imagine four girls going after Joey?" Elenore ribs me. "I haven't noticed," I answer.

A few minutes later, Elenore said, "Coming down, Marge?" Marge weakly answered, "Yes."

Down on deck, Marge and Elenore brought out their hammocks. We strung them up. They had never slept in a Brazilian hammock. The Williams demonstrated. They lay catty-corner in each. Each hammock is eight to ten feet wide when stretched out. Marge was afraid to sit in it; I tested it, then she sat beside me. I became sleepy; Elenore rolled me out and I fell on deck. I got in again, feeling truly sleepy. I got rolled out again. Everyone laughed. I excused myself to go to bed at eight.

The day breaks clear and sunny. I take the usual morning sun bath. We are steaming into the mouth of the Toscantins River to reach the important port of Belém. There are shorelines on either side of us. There is a heavy jungle growth and the river becomes muddy.

We drift into the dock at eleven just as we are having dinner. Soon afterwards I go ashore with Janie. It is very hot, damp, and sultry. We had to check on boats going north to the Guianas. We tried several agencies; a few had boats running.

"When?" we asked, very interested.

"When we have cargo," they answered.

"But that may be weeks," we complained.

"Sorry," they said, "there is not any cargo at present."

We checked the air lines; there were several, PAA, Cruzero del Sul, and Taca. They had planes going to Guianas daily from Belém, but there were not any flights from Manaus to the Guianas. We did not wish to go up the Amazon to Manaus and then return to Belém to fly.

We stopped at the American consul's to check on mail. I was surprised when he walked over to us and said to me, "Are you the hitchhiker?" I was caught off guard and became slightly embarrassed.

"Yes," I said. "How did you find out?"

"The girls, Miss Paulson and Miss Nelson, had been here

505

earlier and informed us about you, and you must be Miss Janie Hallager, the writer," he said, looking at Janie.

"Well, I hope to write," Janie said. He became very interested; I always feared the American consul would try to put a stop to my hitchhiking in South America. Instead he wanted to know how I would continue on to Georgetown, British Guiana, from Manaus. Evidently, Elenore and Marge must have done some nice talking for me. He then told me it was possible to continue northward from Manaus by river boat and cattle trail to Georgetown on the Atlantic Coast on the northeastern shoulder of South America. He then gave me the name and address of an engineer who had been working in that region. Mr. Coleman, the consul, then asked, "Won't you two come to dinner tonight? The girls will be present also."

We said, "We'd be delighted."

Janie and I called on the engineer. He was an American. He looked Spanish and was merely five feet tall. He had installed the water system in a little town called Boa Vista. It was north of Manaus, approximately six hundred miles. It would take seven to ten days to reach it by small boat. From there a cattle trail led to Georgetown. One would have to walk it and it takes only nine days. Later when I got into that "neck of the woods," I learned it took at least nineteen days. There was not any need to fear the Indians, but the country was full of black desperate Negro cutthroats. Then the engineer said he wouldn't trust the Indians either.

"Do you carry a gun?" he asked. I said, "No." "Well, you should," he said. "The native boats are not pleasant to ride, but you can live through it, I guess; the road is bad. Boa Vista has about two thousand people and someday may become a dude ranch because of cool, pleasant climate."

I asked Janie if she cared to go on that trip. "Hell, no, that's too rough for me," she said.

We thanked him, then went sightseeing. Belém in itself is a nice city with beautiful parks, palm trees, wide streets, some nice homes, a modern hotel, and street car and bus service. We visited a museum; a Swiss lady was sketching a few pottery vases that were found along the Amazon. They are so different from the vases found in Indian excavations in Peru. We visited the zoo and ran into Elenore and Marge. The zoo had mostly birds and animals found along the Amazon.

At seven o'clock, Janie and I called at the consul's home. Elenore came sailing in, a little under the weather. But she was in the best of spirits. After a little while; Mr. Coleman made highballs for us. We had several; each was different; the liquor had been made at Obidos, a town along the Amazon River. It tasted almost like wine. After three or four, all of us were gay and spirited, except for the consul's wife; she doesn't drink.

We had dinner, Mr. Coleman saying the prayer. We ate by candlelight. Mr. Coleman warned us frankly to eat plenty because there was only one choice and not six. The Latins usually have five or six courses of food, and much is wasted. The dinner was excellent.

Mrs. Coleman, a pleasant, heavy-set woman, took us on a tour of the house. There were many rooms and beautiful patios. She had a wonderful collection of baskets, hats, robes, native statuettes, a ragged doll, full of pins, that was supposed to carry a curse, butterfly fans, leathers, furs, and various sizes of crocodiles. She had a stick called *guarana*. It was made by squeezing the juice out of a lot of berries by hand, forming the seeds and skin into a stick, and letting it dry and harden. A fish bone was then used to scrape the stick and the powder, mixed with water, made a delicious drink called *guarana*. I tried to get Mrs. Coleman to make some, but she only smiled and dropped the subject.

We then looked at picture albums, seated comfortably in the living room. Janie told her story about traveling third class; she said it was a lot of fun. As she continued, Mrs. Coleman listened and seemed to have a shocked expression on her face. Elenore—I'd never seen her thus—looked plainly bored. Later Mrs. Coleman offered Janie some money. She refused it. Mrs. Coleman did not insist; it was only a gesture.

Mr. Coleman, a busy, thin, gray-headed fellow, had been working in his office. He joined us. We had more highballs, then he displayed his collection of whips, blow pipes, and arrows. Elenore and I took turns shooting at one another. We had to blow

quite hard. Later I fanned her, saying, "I'll be your slave for life."
Smiling she said, "Will you, honest?" We had more fun and a
pleasant evening.

In Brazil, eleven o'clock is a late hour, so Mr. Coleman drove
us back to the ship. We all agreed that he and his wife were very
nice.

We stayed in Belém another day; hammocks were strung up
here and there, and passengers swayed back and forth. Margie
regretted she did not have dinner with us at the consul's. She
had a headache and stayed on board ship. I called on the consul
again. He gave me wonderful ideas. I could not understand why,
but I guess he liked me. Last night he had all of us sign a book for
him, with comments. He wished me luck.

I rode a bus to a Rodriques Park. It was closed, but I told the
man on duty I was off the ship and could not return another day.
He let me enter. I strolled along the lanes. There were pedestals
spaced apart every twenty feet or so. On each was a lovely parrot
in the gayest colors of green, red, blue, etc. Groves of large palm
trees and shrubs lined the way, and the mosquitoes played havoc
with me. Then on to a lagoon, reflecting the trees, floating ducks,
and a white rainbow bridge, then into a huge cave within a rock
formation. I did not go far; huge white bats whipped over my
head and scared me back out. I climbed the rock formation for a
view of the park, then returned for the exit. Small animals, looking like a cross between a pig and a rabbit, raced across my path
in a frightening manner.

It seems that when the ship is in port, they bring out the best
food. At supper we had pork chops. I had dinner alone. I have another dinner engagement with Marge and Elenore at seven. My
appetite couldn't wait. We would dine at the Gran Hotel. The
girls made it known that it must be a "Dutch" treat; everyone
pays for his own.

I meet them in the lobby. There were many Americans
seated about. Some of them are pilots in transit. We go into the
bar room. It is air-conditioned and very cold. After a bit we get
used to it. The place is very modern, the lights are low; we occupy
a table, have several whiskey sours and chat. When we leave the
lounge, the lobby seems sticky hot. We enter the dining room and

have chicken dinner; my stomach becomes nice and round. An orchestra is playing; soon we are the only ones left. The orchestra quits; it is ten o'clock. The lights grow dimmer, and we have to leave.

Back on ship, Marge says she will join me on deck. When she does she says, "The officers offered me a drink; I must join them." It annoyed me. She says the fellows treat her so nice and want me to have a drink also.

I join them in the first mate's cabin. Elenore brings up a bottle. She seems shocked when I say I'm surprised; I never expected girls of her position to be traveling with a bottle as "baggage." "Joe, you don't think I'm terrible, do you?" she asked.

"I'm the understanding type," I say, "it's okay."

The mate pours the drinks, never saying, "Here's to health or anything." They have fun, never a word said to me by the two officers. After the second "shot" and no word spoken to me, I excuse myself. They ask me then to have another drink. "No thanks," I say.

Down on deck again, the girls joined me almost at once. I hadn't expected that. I told them I was sorry, I didn't mean to break up their party, but there was no sense in my sitting in, listening to their crude English and Portuguese, while I stupidly sat by.

Our ship pulled out at midnight. Because of shallow water, our ship could follow the inside straight to meet the water of the Amazon, we steamed out toward the Atlantic and around the Island of Marajó, which lies at the mouth of the Amazon. On its northern shore, we entered deep water and the mouth of the Amazon. At this point, we were only a few miles south of the equator.

The ships pilots were changed. Only men who knew the river could steer an ocean-going vessel through the shallow, narrow, and bad curves of the river.

Morning finds us well on the river, looking out the port holes; we have shores on either side of us. They are a solid jungle. The river is muddy. We are going westward, and Manaus is a thousand miles away. That is as far as ocean-going vessels can go. The river then continues westward for another 2,850 miles to its head in the Peruvian Andes.

Native grass huts are visible on the shore. Soon we see naked Indians; they paddle out in crude dugouts and call for bread. Large loaves are thrown overboard, one at a time; the Indians paddle and retrieve them. Sometimes clothes are thrown overboard for them. All morning we pass some isolated Indian huts, and the Indians come paddling toward us yelling for bread. The bread floats on the water till it is picked up. We wonder how hungry some of these Indians may be.

On passing a sawmill, our ship blows three blasts on its horn, then the sawmill sounds three; the ship sounds a single and the sawmill answers. It is a way of greeting. The sound of our ship's mighty horns echoes and reechoes through the jungle. It brings a feeling of exultation to the passengers.

In the afternoon a huge water boa was sighted. From all appearances it looked like a floating log, but upon seeing it coordinating with the waves, we realized a log could not do that. Soon the rail was full of passengers taking pictures of it. It was at least twenty feet long and a foot thick.

Then Manuel, our table servant, tells us some stories. The water is supposed to be full of man-eating fish called *piranjas.* They are like sardines and not larger than six inches long. They travel in schools. "One day," Manuel said, "a lady scolded her servant for some misdemeanor or another. The servant became frustrated; the intense heat of the Amazon had its effects on her. She grabbed the lady's child and jumped overboard from this very ship." Many peculiar things happen in the tropics, and Manuel said, "Many people have jumped overboard from other ships due to the heat."

We had picked up a lot more passengers in Belém; they had paid first-class fare, but there were not enough bunks, so they slept on the floor in the lounge, in hammocks on decks, and the passageways of the first-class sections.

We spent the following day steaming up the river. It was too hot to take a tan. The girls had risen so early this morning that everyone wiped their eyes in disbelief, even the officers. We spent the day on deck, watching the shore or swinging in our hammocks.

After supper we watched the lovely sunset; we were very close to the shore and could hear the chattering of monkeys and parrots. Many colorful birds flew about the trees, and here and there we spotted colorful parrots called *parpagados,* sitting on a branch. Most of the passengers were crowded on the boat to watch the splendid sunset. We were going straight westward, and it disappeared just ahead of us.

I spent most of the evening swinging in my hammock. I had to put on my field jacket, the mosquitos were biting terribly.

Morning of the eighteenth day finds us anchored out in the stream. We are at the river port of Santarém. Marge and Elenore are ashore; Janie asks me to go; I don't feel well and decide to sit on the deck chair. A couple of Brazilian girls sit on either side of me, touching and annoying me. I go topside for an hour. It's terribly hot. I keep a towel over my head, come down, and take a shower.

I spent afternoon on deck. A clipper was taking off the water into the air. It was a surprise to me that seaplanes land on the Amazon at these little towns carved out of the jungle. A two-tower church was the most prominent building standing out on shore. A cluster of tan-and-white houses surrounded it, then stretched out along the shore. The green land and blue skies with drifting clouds gave it a very picturesque touch.

Dugouts and canoes, plied back and forth, from ship to shore. The natives use the strangest type of paddles. The bottom is oval-shaped, like a Ping-Pong paddle and the handle is unshapely, like a broomstick. Many of the paddles have pretty pictures painted on them.

Marge and Elenore came aboard with an American nurse, stationed at Santarém. We had dinner together, then they dressed up pretty and went ashore. Jane and I stayed on board. Janie has a boyfriend now. He is dark-complexioned, handsome, and quiet. He is the ship's nurse.

We had lifted anchor during the night, and looking out the port hole at dawn, I saw the shore, covered with a tangle of jungle trees and foliage. We were very close. The river seemed swift and muddy.

At dinner the girls told me how their rowboat got forced by others to pass under a drain of bilge water. They got wet. Later in town, Marge kept sniffing after Elenore to see if she smelled—such remarks from girls of the embassy.

I told them about the one where a fellow told a girl, "You must have passion with me." What the fellow meant to say was, "You must have patience with me." His English was very limited. I had heard the story a few days ago. I didn't recall who told it to me. Then it turned out that one of the officers had said it to Elenore. Her face turned pink and she said I shouldn't tell anyone, for it would embarrass the officer, who was a nice lad.

In the afternoon I was swinging in my hammock; from the commotion I knew we were coming into another port. It was the port of Obidos. We could not steam to the dock, for another steamer was tied up there. Rowboats came to our ship to take passengers ashore for twenty-five cents. Marge and Elenore asked me to go ashore. I felt lazy and wanted to return to my hammock. Janie didn't go either. She wanted to save a few stops for her return trip to Belém.

I spent an afternoon in the hammock; the girls returned later with armfuls of beautiful red flowers. We had them on our dinner table. Suddenly, at dinner, there was excitement on deck. The loud bawdy girl had taken a fit. The heat had gotten her down. She was yelling and screaming as several officers carried her past the dining-room window. It seemed so common to the other passengers that they hardly took notice.

After supper I lay down in my hammock again. Marge sat on a deck chair. She watched me enviously. I asked her if she wanted me to put hers up.

"Oh, will you, Joe?" she cried and hurried off to get it. I had to string it up on the opposite deck. There was no room on the starboard side. She did not wish to be alone, so I lay catty-corner from her in the large hammock. We swung back and forth. We both enjoyed it.

Then one of the officers came, rudely broke our conversation, and fell into Portuguese chatter with Marge. Marge did not ask him to leave, so I swung the hammock higher and higher, striking and pushing him back, but he didn't take the hint and leave. A few minutes later, I couldn't stand the chatter; if she wanted his chatter, she could have it. I'd rather be peacefully alone in my hammock. She got angry as I silently walked off. "Joe," she cried, but I walked on. I've had all I could stand of these inconsiderate officers. Never do I have peace when I'm with the girls; sun-bathing, sitting, eating, deck walking, or swinging in the hammock. On opposite decks, a Brazilian girl stops to talk and flirt with me, but a moment later, an officer comes along and they talk and talk. My goodness, don't these fellows ever get tired of talking so much? I turned in disgusted before midnight.

We had pulled up to the dock; laborers wearing only shorts were unloading grain. When the other ship left, there was the customary sounding of horns, three and one. It made the night air echo, and reecho.

The Arab had left the ship at Belém, but I still had four strange Brazilian roommates. Two of them were brothers; they would be going to the diamond mines in northern Brazil. My roommates watched me continuously, changing clothes, combing my hair, shaving or brushing my teeth. I always found their eyes on me. What was so strange about me, I'll never know. Maybe it's because I am an American.

Morning finds me swaying in my hammock on deck. Marge and Elenore are writing nearby. While swaying I sing and Elenore wants me to keep it up while she tries to doze off. She is wearing white shorts and a pretty blouse and looks nice.

At three in the afternoon, we are steaming into the river port of Parintins. Some of the trees on shore have bright colors, just like autumn in Pennsylvania. We drop anchor and go ashore in a rowboat. We have been warned to be seated and keep our hands out of the water.

Parintins is a peaceful town; it has been carved out of the jungle also. There are no paved streets, only dusty lanes. It reminds both Janie and I of towns along the Yukon River in Alaska. So very much alike, except for the houses and trees. The people look very much the same, short, squat, and mostly Indian.

513

Marge, Elenore, Janie, and I stroll through a tiny mercado. We find a number of slaughtered beef hanging and flies buzzing around them. We continue on past grass houses with naked children all about, then to the cemetery. There are many more dead in the cemetery than there are alive in the whole town. A large number of the graves are infants; some of the inscriptions are very touching. At the foot of the graves are wooden benches. Several natives sit and stare at the graves, apparently in mourning.

I suggest we leave; there is something about cemeteries that wears me out. I was full of pep upon leaving the ship, and now I felt tired and lazy. A number of children followed us and asked us to take their pictures. Then like in all Latin countries, they wondered why we didn't give them a copy of it at once.

We sit along the bank of the river. We had not seen Dot or Bob after leaving Fortaleza; we wished they were with us. Small boys throw us large cuias from the tree tops. They are green and not good to eat. They are as large as a bowling ball. We plan to bowl with them on deck and use beer bottles for ten pins.

While we wait for a rowboat, we can't help seeing naked children swimming. Among them are some fully grown boys, totally naked. Elenore's face turns pink. She said later that mine did too. She didn't have the nerve to take their picture.

We returned to the ship; near the gangway we saw large schools of squirming fish. They were no longer than sardines. We had heard so many stories about the man-eating fish that Elenore took these to be them. On deck she remarked to one of the officers, "You should see how many piranhas there are."

"Piranhas, in your head," remarked a lady in Portuguese from behind Elenore. Elenore hadn't been talking to her and became terribly embarrassed. Later in her room, she cried. Before she came to dinner, I had to change seats with her as she wouldn't want to face those impudent ladies. Her eyes were red and swollen.

After a year in Rio, she had yet to learn that there are many people who don't like the American ways. Right after supper she went to here room.

Marge and I walked about the deck, then leaned over the rail and stared into the starry night. It seemed strange that the river should be full of dangerous fish and yet we see the natives swimming in it.

On turning in, I passed a group of elderly and young Brazilian women. The "crazy" girl, who had taken fit, mimicked as I went by. "How are you, Speakie English?" I kept on going, saying nothing. No loud laughter followed the remark, only a snicker or two. To me, there is still plenty of Latin in some Brazilians. I'm glad that I haven't talked to many and those were a few soldiers, headed for the Colombian border for duty.

It was five o'clock when I awoke to the racket of my roommate. We were still two hours from Manaus. They were busy packing and chattering. I turned over and slept till we docked. It was the end of three weeks aboard the *Poconi*.

52

My Flower of the Amazon

I awoke again to the quiet stillness of my room. My noisy room-mates had departed. There was not a sound on the ship. I dressed and packed my "gear." Then I went on deck. We were tied up to the harbor at Manaus. So finally the officers, through understanding and expert direction, were able to bring the ship through the treacherous Amazon and Negro rivers to Manaus.

The river was named Amazon. A Spanish explorer named Francisco de Orellana named it. He made the descent from the Andes to the sea in 1541. He found that in some tribes, the women assisted the men in battle and applied the name of the women of a Greek legend to the river and the territory around it, which is still called "Amazonas," in western Brazil. Manaus is in the heart of this region.

The *Poconi* was deserted of passengers except for Marge and Elenore, who had some packing to do. Marge and I sat on deck; then a chap named Gleason came on board and presented himself to the girls. He was English and had read about the girls coming through.

We went ashore together to make our own discoveries. We were most surprised to find buses, streetcars, and taxicabs. We never expected to find a large town full of vehicles, lovely parks, churches, beaches, and girls in modern dress. Many of them were beautiful and graceful. These were not savages. I must confess that that is what Marge, Elenore, and I had expected to find, nothing but black peering faces. Instead we found many whites and tan-colored people. Old Francisco de Orellana came four hundred years too soon. Manaus today is a paradise.

We had dinner together, then called on a Mr. Brown, at the Astoria Agency. We sat in his office, and he listened to our stories, principally the girls. He had a pleasant gift of speech. I was thankful for him because through his office clerks, he had made rapid and positive inquiries as to planes, boats, dates, and fares on our outgoing journey. It saved us a lot of time and walking.

He said he had an extra apartment, and the girls were welcome to it. He had no accommodations for me. He would be only too glad to be rid of me, for seldom do lovely English girls come visiting this way.

The girls and I then called on the British Consul. He was an elderly fellow who talked of his experiences. I liked him, but the girls thought he talked too much. He had no mail for me, and that was disappointing. I was very low on funds. I had sent a telegram from Belém for money to be sent to Manaus. They received the telegram, but the clerk failed to send the address. Every day I waited for a letter; it never came.

There was a boat leaving for Boa Vista that very night and another three days later. I decided to stay around for a few days. I checked at the Gran Hotel, the most noted in Manaus. They asked three dollars a day. It was worth only a dollar. I said I'd return later.

In the afternoon, the girls would be busy. I decided to call on Marie Lu, my Flower of the Amazon. She was a pretty girl whom I met on the *Poconi.* She had made the six-day trip from Belém. She had been traveling first class and dined with aristocratic snobs on the *Poconi.* From all appearances she was of a social and well-to-do family.

I had nothing to do, so I decided to pay a social call. I had promised her I would if I had time. At her hotel, the *duena* (landlady) gave her my name, then said for me to go right in. I was shocked to find her wrapped up only in a bed sheet. I started to back out the door; she took my hand, pulled me back in, and made me sit on the edge of the bed. It was a hot day, and it was hotter inside the room. The open windows didn't help much. If I was to stay another minute, I had to take my field jacket off and that is just what my flower of the Amazon wanted me to do, for she put her slim arm around my neck and kissed me. It became much warmer. It was some time later before we left to take in a movie.

After the movies, my flower of the Amazon went home. I

517

stopped at a sidewalk café for a *guarana,* spotted a couple of Americans at a table, walked over and joined them. They were seamen of the American ship *Moore Mackclark.* They drank beer and I had *guarana.* Beer in this hot climate gives one a headache and makes one sleepy. Bob, one of the seamen, had a Brazilian girl for company. He called her his "dusky princess;" he handled her roughly, but she liked it. Bob was only playing with her, but he had no intentions of sleeping with her. After some time she realized this and went away.

I told Bob about my embarrassing situation, my flower of the Amazon. "What would you do?" I asked, "if you paid a social call and found the girl in only a bed sheet?"

"What would I do?" he said. "Are you trying to be funny?" he asked me.

I was invited aboard ship for food and lodging. I ate and slept on it for four days till it left on the fifth. It cut my expenses. I hoped to receive mail from home by that time. When the girls learned I was staying on board, they were very envious. This was the boat that Elenore wanted to travel on from Recife.

Boy, what chow we had on that ship, hotcakes and eggs for breakfast. How I loved that. I had only recently talked with Marge and Elenore about how much I missed it. For dinner, pork chops, I couldn't believe it, but we did.

I called on my flower of the Amazon again, but she was not in. Her pretty girlfriend entertained me, she stripped to the nude, insisting I take her picture and send her a copy.

I returned to the ship plenty hot, keeping a handkerchief in hand all day long, sweating profusely. I had supper of frankfurters and cabbage. How good they are. Then a drunken Latin seaman of Puerto Rico complained about the food to the steward. The steward, an elderly, educated American, got angry and said, "What do you think I am, your son? I won't listen to your talk and if you don't like the food, you can get off the ship." He then walked off.

I felt like saying to the Puerto Rican, "You should be a sailor on a Brazilian ship or any other Latin one for that matter and see what kind of 'grub' the crewmen get; nothing but fish, beans, rice or soup daily and for breakfast only black coffee and bread." I knew it wise to be quiet. I was only a guest on the ship, but I hated his guts for that. All of the sailors were friendly and cheerful toward me. They asked many questions about my journey. They thought it was the best life.

I went ashore with the seamen; we sat about a table and swapped stories. Some of us drank beer, others guarana. It comes in the same size bottles. One is alcoholic, the other is a soft drink. It was a pleasing evening, about ten of us seated under the garden trees. Most of us returned to the ship before midnight.

About four in the morning, I awoke to loud voices. I heard Bob say, "Well, go ahead, but be careful," then silence. I thought a fight must be going on ashore. I turned over and went back to sleep. The night air was sticky hot; a fan was running all night.

At breakfast, I was told that one of the seamen had drowned in the river. It was "Chico," the Puerto Rican, about thirty-five years old. He had gotten very drunk and was returning to the ship a little after midnight. He had stepped into the rowboat to the rowed out to the ship tied up at the midstream wharf. He was standing in the bow; he should have sat down, another fellow sat in the stern and the third fellow sat in the middle rowing the boat.

Chico evidently had lost his balance and fell into the river; he went under the water and did not come up even once. The two fellows were too far apart to grab for him.

All night they searched for him, then all day in the hot sun. It is claimed that a five mile undercurrent lies under water, yet the surface is very calm. It was feared that his body had been washed down stream. A large crowd watched the dragging of the area. By 9:30, only a single boat remained. It was an American boat from the ship and two seamen. Their faces were strained and looked sickly. They rowed back and forth, and every now and then, the grappling hook caught hold of something or another. It was the thought of raising a torn shipmate that made the seamen look sick, but they had their orders.

Soon the crowd dispersed, except for a lone person who watched the dragging continue from a causeway. I went ashore, and I ran across Elenore and Marge at Mr. Brown's office. They asked if I would go to the airport with them. They were to fly at

519

10:00 for Puerto Vallo and then to Rio de Janeiro. I had nothing else to do and said, "Okay. It will be a pleasure." We hailed a taxi. It was quite a long ride to the airstrip. It had been built by American soldiers during the war, and a radio station likewise had been set up there.

We passed the poor, miserly, wooden shacks on the outskirts of town, then a dusty country road for a half-hour to the airport. There we met the British consul and various other prominent people. Among them was an American padre, called Father Van. He was dressed in a long white robe; around his waist he wore a black sash and the ends came down his sides to his ankle. I remarked after meeting him, "I couldn't tell if you were a bell hop or a Padre." They all laughed. "In this country, you see most everything," the young padre answered. "We wear the white robes because of the hot climate."

He had spent four years in and about the Amazon region. He was very young, not more than thirty. He had a year to go, and would be very glad when he got back to Oregon, his home state. He missed American cigarettes the most. Elenore had two cartons on hand and gave them to him.

The plane came in. Elenore and I shook hands; she thanked me for a nice time. Marge gripped my hand firmly and held it for some time; she said some things, but her eyes were questioning. She apologized for not being able to go to the movies with me, wished me luck, and wanted me to write to them.

Father Van and I watched and waved as they entered the "Catalina" plane. Then it taxied to the head of the runway, stopped, warmed up its engines. Then the throttle went forward, and they were off in a cloud of dust. We watched them drift into the horizon; then I said, "I hate to say this, but there they go. I'll probably never see them again." For after three weeks on the *Poconi,* having dinner together always had brought a feeling of close friendship and understanding.

Father Van said, "Yes, you meet them; then they must go." There was a note of great sadness in his voice, and no doubt he was melancholy and homesick for home. Five years out of a young man's life, preaching the gospel to the Indians in the wilds of the Amazon Basin is a great sacrifice in any man's life.

Father Van drove me back to the ship in his delivery truck. On Friday the thirteenth (August), a sailor had drowned; I hoped Marge and Elenore did not have bad luck.

At 6:00, two American Catholic priests came aboard. In the stern, the U.S. flag was at half-mast. The priest had come to say the last rite for the lost sailor. Everyone gathered aft, the captain, officers, crew, and I, everyone removed their hats, others who were shirtless put on shirts. The prayer was in Latin for the benefit of many Puerto Ricans on board; the memorable words were said in English. The church bells tolled solemnly at 6:00 and at 6:15. It was all over at 6:20. The flag was lowered, folded diagonally, military style, and put away. The crowd dispersed slowly and bewildered. They said Chico was a nice guy, never bothered nobody; he just liked to drink.

It wasn't till 4:00 the next day that a cry went up. The body of the seamen had come to the surface. It had been pulled out of the water and lay on the wooden causeway that stretches out into the stream. I had been on board reading a book in a bunk. Bob started to go with me, but was stopped by the chief mate. He had gotten a slight bump on his head and was confined to his bunk for three days. For coming out on deck, he would be penalized another day or lose a day's pay.

In a rowboat I go with several other seamen to the causeway. A large crowd surrounds the body. It is lying flat on its back, face upwards and uncovered. It has been under water nearly forty hours and already has a bad odor. The strangest thing is that its face, eyes, nose, lips, cheeks, and ears have been almost totally consumed by the little man-eating fish called piranhas. The fish stories I've heard are not a hoax. This was evidence enough. They are swift, dangerous, and bite like tiny sharks. The seaman's arms were not bitten, although his sleeves were rolled up above the elbows, but his ankles were bitten; deep gashes of flesh were missing. His body was bloated immensely. His teeth were clenched as if in agony or pain against being bitten. Someone said the fish go after the sparkling eyes, only empty sockets remained on this fellow. His trousers had a large gash; evidently they became caught and held him under so long.

For an hour he lay there, uncovered; the large crowd soon

521

backed away from it. A very old, yellow and black hearse rattled over the wooden causeway. Two men lifted the body into a crude coffin; strange, it seemed limber as if rigor mortis had not yet set into it. They put the coffin into the hearse and took it to a morgue, later buried it on a hillside; still later a telegram from his mom in Puerto Rico requested it be sent home, possibly by plane.

I had a talk with the chief mate; he was a big husky fellow from New Jersey. He asked what I was doing on the ship. I explained I was invited. He was not well liked by the crew. I kind of liked him. He was friendly. He and I had a long talk. I could have signed on the ship, in place of the lost seaman and return to the States in nine days; instead I decided not to. I probably should have my head examined, but I longed to make the journey into northern Brazil for the sake of adventure. Very few Americans get to make this trip.

I said, "So long" to the mate, Bob, Charlie, the boatswain, Johnny, the chief electrician, and many others. I went ashore about midnight; their ship would be pulling out at four in the morning with the hatches full of Brazil nuts for New York.

I walked about in the cool evening, sat in the park, reminiscing. A full moon floated overhead. I felt low; my boat, scheduled to leave today, had been canceled to the sixteenth or seventeenth; two or three more days to wait. I was very low on funds. I worried, why doesn't the money come?

Then about five in the morning, a drunken policeman sat beside me and asked for some money, of all times. I told him I didn't have any, then ignored him. After a while, I got tired of him and walked off. He blew his whistle. If I wouldn't have stopped, he would have blown it several more times and a flock of police would come running. He kept asking for forty cruzeiros ($2.00) in English and Portuguese. I moved on again. I became angry. If he tried to force me to stop again, I would have knocked him flat. At the gate entrance to the dock, he stopped and followed me no more. I sat on the dock and watched the sun rise. It rose up simply and unimpressively.

By nine o'clock, I became tired. I checked in at a hotel. It was simple, but clean, the usual straw mattress. The rates were low,

522

fifty cents per day. There I had a decent shower; in that respect it was better than the Gran. The heat woke me up at noon.

Now a British ship has come to port. It is the S.S. *Hilary*. I became acquainted with some of the sailors and have dinner aboard. I spend several evenings with them at the American sidewalk café. They all like Manaus, chiefly because of the many pretty girls. All one has to say is, "Come here, baby," and they do. Entertainment and drinks are very cheap.

I check at the British Consul daily, (there is no American consulate in Manaus). We had many pleasant talks. One day the young British consul from Belém came to Manaus. Mr. Turner introduced me to him. He was shocked at my proposed adventure up the Rio Branco then to British Guiana by river launch. They knew I was low on money. I feared the young consul might try to stop me, but Mr. Turner liked my idea, furnished more information, and said I wouldn't have any trouble. He reminded me of that great aging move star . . . (forgot his name, darn it)

I went to buy my ticket. A few days ago the clerk had said the fare is $359.20 cruzeiros; now he asked for $461.00 cruzeiros. I complained, then walked off. The plane flies to Boa Vista occasionally; it charges twice as much, but the trip only takes two hours, not ten to twelve days like the boats do. They called me back and gave me a ticket for $360.00 cruzeiros. The reason for my going by boat is to know the country and the ways of the people.

Day after day my boat canceled the sailing. I was almost beside myself with impatience and disgust. I could and did call at the consul's office again. I asked the Brazilian clerk if any mail came in for me. He said, "No."

I then asked, "Do you know what my name is?"

"No," he answered.

"Then how the hell do you know there is no mail for me," I said angrily. He was surprised to learn I was American. I had called daily and he thought I was a British subject.

I spend some of the time drinking cheap, but delicious *guarana* at the American café or sitting on a grassy bank leaning against a big shady hardwood tree, writing letters or reading a book. Occasionally, I look down on the sidewalk as pretty senoritas go by. Some smile and say, "How contented you look, sitting there, nothing to do but pass the time away."

A Brazilian reporter took me for an English seamen. He came up to me and inquired about the three English sailors who got into an auto accident the night previous. I told him two were in the ship's hospital, badly hurt; the other was walking about. He spoke English well and went to the ship to get the story. He said he worked hard and got little pay.

Two cars were involved in the crash in the early hours of the morning. A lovely girl was in the sailors' company. She could speak English fluently. She received a cut over the eyes, and doctors feared she would go blind. Their cab driver had a leg amputated and the drunken driver of the other car was killed.

I took time out to go sightseeing in Manaus. When the British ship left, I had little company. Strolling through the park facing the church, I saw two English sailors fast asleep on the ground. They had whiskey bottles beside them and evidently were very drunk. They had missed the boat. I continued walking up the steep streets, lined with trees. The branches of the trees were trimmed in squares, just as one would trim hedges. I came to the famous opera house, now almost abandoned. It was built during the rubber boom of 1899, then remodeled again in the second boom in 1905. It is a huge stone structure; there are great driveways and stairs leading up to it. It is crowned with a huge dome in diamond patterns. Tile bricks in colors of yellow, blue, and green are used on the dome, and it glistens in the sun continuously.

Great singers and players and stars were brought from Europe to perform for the rubber workers. There was great wealth in those days, yet it is so hard to imagine such refinery coming to the heart of the world's greatest equatorial forest. The natives were enslaved and worked in the forest. There was great profit for the white man.

Most of the doors and windows were closed and barred. I found a door open, and within were a few workers remodeling and repairing. One of them was nice enough to take me on a tour of the inside.

The interior was handsomely designed and decorated. There

were three balconies and private boxes. The main floor, the banisters, walls and seats, were covered with dark red woolly upholstery. The balconies and stage had beautiful ivory and marble carvings. On the walls and ceilings were greats paintings; truly great artists and craftsmen worked there. The main patio had a marble floor and great pillars. The second-floor patio had a floor of sixty different types of hardwood. There were many natural colors and patterns.

The priceless furniture, beautifully carved in figures of animals or humans, were borrowed one by one by visiting governors, till a lot of them disappeared, never to be returned. But enough still remained to be fully appreciated. Rest rooms had been installed, but were of the late twenties design. My guide told me the opera house was used occasionally for school plays and admission was charged.

After the opera house, a trip around the city is most interesting. One has only to board the open-air streetcar "Circular." It takes you all around the city. The city was much larger than I expected. We rambled up hills and around crowded adobe houses. Everywhere there was wealth and poverty, side by side. Then the track led us into the jungle. I wondered why in the world it went there and so far. Still people got on and off, here and there, to go to their miserly shacks set in the jungle. We continued bumping along; then we were coming back into the city again, only at another part of town. The trip lasted over an hour and was worthwhile.

From the central station, I took the street car, Fabrica de Cervaza (Factory of Beer) to visit the three American Catholic priests. All of them were ex-army chaplains. Father Van introduced me to Father Joseph and Father Nicholas. They were very glad that I called, for seldom do they have American visitors. Father Van got some beer, and we sat and talked. Their home was very simple, littered with books, paper, radio, records, electrical apparatus, and bottles. I said that it looked more like a clubhouse. They laughed. Father Van said at one time the house had contained pigs, and had a tree in the center of it. It took a lot of work to put it into shape.

Father Van told me interesting tales about slavery in the

Amazon basin. It was dissolved in 1888, but a lot still goes on. He knew of several families in Manaus that held slave house servants. He could not mention their names. He referred to an American who knew the whole story, including slavery in the interior, but dared not to publish it for fear of being blackmailed by wealthy families.

Father Joseph looked a lot like me. In town I had been stopped several times by people; they asked if I was the American Padre. He laughed at that. They showed me some splendid army maps of the Rio Branco and pointed out where a U.S. Army mission was wiped out by savages on a tributary to the Rio Branco. They were enthusiastic about furnishing information. They said it was a dangerous trip. They gave me a dozen pocket-size books to read on the boat. They wished me luck and said they would pray for my safety.

I wished to stay longer, they were so interesting and so nice, but my boat was to leave between four and six o'clock. It was four already. I walked rather than wait for a streetcar. I came to the dock an found the boat gone. A little boy directed me a dozen blocks or so to an inlet or tiny cove. There I saw my boat. There were several boats around it and many shacks on shore. I took a canoe to it. The captain told me they would lay over there till tomorrow. I became angry, dejected, and disgusted again. I had worked up a sweat, chasing and looking for the boat. I thought it had left and then I learned they wished to lay over again.

I stayed on board. I watched the sun go down. It was lovely, then the moon came up over the quiet, still inlet. It was full and golden in the soft evening. I tried to be patient and calm, but I had a terrific urge to go ashore to take a walk. I could not understand the chatter of Portuguese coming from the mess hall. The expectations of my coming trip would not permit me to be quiet. Everyone said it was so dangerous. I felt I must walk or go out of my head. No sane person would undertake the trip without weapons, more or less with only ten dollars left in my pocket and 350 miles of unknown country to traverse after leaving Boa Vista. After Boa Vista, there is not any plane service, boats or roads, to Georgetown, British Guiana, only a cattle trail after the border is reached. Lots of the information I have received is contradictory; one says it's mountainous, jungle country, another says it's flat dry plains. The American Padres only had maps of Brazil, none of British Guiana. I had sold a fine new gold watch to an American seaman for the ten dollars I had left.

Out of a nearby shack, a naked man dropped into the river for a bath, returning to the cries of women. I hailed a passing canoe and was rowed to shore. I walked toward town and felt better. I came upon the two English fellows who had missed their ship. They were quite sober, so I listened to their story.

They had missed the boat on purpose. There was too much work on it. From six in the morning till ten at night, there was no rest for them. They worked in the steward's department (kitchen). Mr. Turner, the British consul, had tried to make them take the plane to Belém and catch the ship there. But they refused to pay nineteen pounds for the plane fare. It was a month's wages to them (80 dollars). So the consul put them up with room and board at a cheap hotel till the next English ship came in. They were truly bums. I listened to them because I wanted to quiet my nerves, and English was all I needed to hear to quiet them. We stopped at the American sidewalk café. They didn't order anything; instead the younger fellow pulled out a bottle of liquor from his hip pocket. It was very sweet. We had a long pleasant chat for a while, then we went strolling. They stopped at coffee wagons, put their arms around the old woman, and said "Mommy," Mommy, coffee, coffee," in dearest tones, and they got it free as the old woman smiled and poured it out.

Likewise in bars, they got free drinks, they told the bartenders, "Tomorrow the consul pay us, we pay you back." Over and over, all evening I had to laugh; Old Mr. Turner would sure have a lot to pay tomorrow. Strangely enough, these Latins believed these fellows. What topped it off was one of the fellows carried a fifth in his hind pocket, covered by his protruding shirt tail. Those fellows certainly were not sad about missing the boat; they were happy.

One of them, the older one, at least thirty-eight, had bummed all over Australia. He had risked his life many times, hoped to write, but never knew the right people to publish his story. He had turned into a true hobo. The other fellow was no

527

more than twenty-five. He was husky and good looking. He had been a soldier and had a number of war experiences. He recited some sad war poems in a crowded bar room, then said disgustedly, "Hell, these people don't understand," then we left that place. He could be a nice, decent fellow if he laid off the booze and his hobo friend.

We went down dimly lit streets; there were girls in every doorway. They called to us. I didn't realize Manaus had a neighborhood of this type. The sailors stopped, talked, joked and laughed; the girls were friendly, but no money, no girl, and we moved on. Then they bummed free lunches at a wagon.

53
Through Green Hell on *Turtle* No. III

I spent the night at the sailors hotel, sleeping on a long wooden bench. Both of them were sprawled across the bed, fully clothed and fast asleep. I had quite a few that night and had a bad taste in my mouth. I felt a bit low-down.

I went to the park and watched the sun rise, went to the American Bar for breakfast, and said "So long" to Mr. Brown and several of his friendly, helpful office workers at the Astoria Agency.

I walked the dozen blocks to the tiny inlet. I had to go in a dugout to reach the launch called *Tartaruga* III which in English means *Turtle* number three, according to Mr. Brown. It was the best of the launches that ply the Rio Branco. I nearly fell into the river; I had to stand in the flimsy dugout. It was crowded with utensils, and I had no room to sit. As it tipped over, my knee touched water and I scared the oarsman and myself silly. I kneeled down, and the canoe righted itself.

It was twelve-twenty when *Turtle III* pulled out of the inlet. It vibrated and pounded its protest. Tied to our launch were two huge barges, one on either side, and tied to them were a lot of tiny house boats and dugouts, hitchhiking a ride. The *Turtle* was about forty feet long with two decks. One for the passengers, the other for the cargo, livestock and the crew. The *Turtle* carried a heavy load.

I had expected to have only half-breeds and Indians for company. I was surprised to see a lot of white people. Among them were the captain, purser, three pretty senoritas, four women, and several children. The others were dark-complexioned government agents or workers, headed for the diamond mines. The tension was gone, and I could look forward to pleasant company.

In the center of the deck was a large table; under it were

529

sacks of cargo. Lining the table were two long wooden benches. Suitcases, baggage, and trunks were lined against the rails. There were only four rooms; one for the captain and purser, another was the kitchen, another the shower room, and the fourth was the toilet, used by men and women alike. There are no state rooms, and at night everyone sleeps in private hammocks, strung from either side of the table to the eaves over the gunwales.

We drift away from the inlet and shacks of Manaus; soon they fade away in the distance. We are on the crystal-clear waters of the Rio Negro. The engine and propellers pound and shake the *Turtle* as it battles the strong, swift current.

Well out into the afternoon, we pass villages on the sandy shore. The banks have a copper color, then pink and white like marble stone. The houses are built on high wooden poles, and beyond lies the green dense jungle. We followed the shore line, but the opposite shore, on port side, could not be seen. So wide is the Rio Negro. It's like the expanse of an ocean.

For dinner and supper, we had rice, beans, and meat. The pork looked so delicious that I took several choice bits, but alas, as I bit into it, it smelled. I had to leave it alone and suffice on rice and beans. I said nothing as the others ate, for what I might say to a girl or a fellow sitting beside me on the long bench would be talked around later among themselves. I know the Latin ways and did not wish to spoil the trip by complaining.

At six, the sun sets. It's a beautiful setting and reflects itself on the clear waters. I lean against a rail, reading a book; the girls sitting at the bow, on deck, look up and smile at me. I continue reading and occasionally find them watching me. When it becomes too dark to continue reading, I sit on the deck beside them and watch the last rays of light disappear.

They ask where I'm from, my name, and then what songs I know. Their names are Juci and Edna. They sing a bit and ask me to sing the song "You'll Never Know." I sing it for them, then Edna sings it in Portuguese. It's the same tune, only the words are different. We sit at the bow for several hours, the moon is high and full, and it's a shame that they have to turn in at 8:30. Edna is really a lovely girl, but she seems a bit irritated when I

530

don't understand some of her lingo. The girls of the tropics see so much of the soft moon that they wouldn't possibly understand how wonderful it looks to a person from the far north.

Everyone strings up a hammock midship. The mosquitos are bad; everyone uses mosquito netting over their hammocks. Mine is an Army jungle hammock and ideal for the region. All night the engine pounds and shakes the *Turtle,* but one gets used to it and hardly notices it. Only a dim lantern is kept burning all night.

We are awakened at six in the morning by a terrible clanging of a cow bell. It is breakfast time. Everybody gets up; if one doesn't, others rock the hammock and make the nap miserable. We roll up the hammocks and put them away. Luckily, there is one clean, decent basin. Everyone has an opportunity to clean up.

We have, for breakfast, hard biscuits and black coffee; nothing else. The *Turtle* still has the "shakes," and dishes rattle and bounce on the table before us. The River Negro seems to have narrowed down; we have shores on either side of us. The water reflects the trees, clouds, and the sun. Part of the morning, I read; the hot sun forces me to go midship into the shade.

Dinner is served daily at 10:30. We have rice, beans and steak. The steak is good. I hate to think of eating rice and beans for a week. But I'm not the only one. I've heard some fellows complaining already. The girls are silent. I don't believe Edna and Juci were brought up on this, but one never knows. Somehow I feel sorry for them. We have only river water to drink. I hate to think, all the sewage goes into the river, then we drink the water. The drinking water is passed through a stone filter first, but I've seen the cook pull buckets of water out of the river to use it for cooking and washing dishes. Our shower baths are river water also, passing through a filter.

I spent part of the afternoon reading the books the American Padre gave me. Occasionally, the girls come by, little being said. Once we start talking, a half-dozen fellows stop to listen. We have our language faults. It's no laughing matter.

Supper is served at 5:00 daily. We have rice, beans, and ribs. There are about twenty of us seated, ten on each side of the table.

There are two set-ups, the captain, purser, wife, and several other passengers eat later because of lack of seats.

The sunset is bloody, but wonderful. It reflects a long, oblong shape on the water. It looks like red-hot steel axles rolled out of a blast furnace. The river seems quite placid now, but still reflecting the trees and tangible brush. No signs of life on shore all day. We come very close to it. I couldn't help wondering if some wild Indians weren't peering at us from that impenetrable "green hell."

It seemed strange that we were steering side to side, but I imagine that was to gain headway against the current. During the night, another launch had tied up behind us to give more power. We had been traveling too slow. I was sitting at the bow; there one gets a bird's-eye view of our advance up the river. One does not feel the vibration there at all. The moon came out; I sang to myself for a while. I got my blue jeans and started repairing them. The girls laughed, and Juci insisted upon sewing them for me. The radio played and when some English tunes came on, Edna started jitterbugging alone. I offered to help. Everyone laughed. There was so little room to dance.

As I turned into the hammock, the girls whistled and Edna sang, "You'll never know," in Portuguese, well into the night.

From my side of the boat, I could see the moon and the tree tops; yet they didn't look like trees but odd shapes endlessly drifting by. I still wondered about the trip from Boa Vista to Georgetown and fell asleep after that.

I awoke at daybreak; it was the cold that got me up. I was the first to get into the cold shower. It was the third day out. It was cloudy and cold. It seemed like we are in a tiny lake because of the dense jungle on all sides. The current was still noticeably strong.

When we had started on the trip, I noticed a huge side of beef hanging on the barge. Now it was gone, consumed by the passengers. A live steer had been standing beside it for several days, now I found it being quartered in plain view of everyone. It would be severed for our dinners.

Our dinner was rice, beans, ribs, and hash. The hash was bad; I left it alone. While we dined, one of the inspectors gave a boy an injection shot with a hypodermic needle at the foot of the table. He did not have sense enough to go elsewhere; yet he was one of the more educated fellows.

The sun came out at noon. In one of the tiny house boats, towed by the *Turtle,* an old lady smoked a pipe; she caught fish in the river and fried them on a tiny stove for herself. There was barely room enough for herself and her husband to sit or lie within the tiny boat. It was covered with a thatched roof. To pass the time away, I read Shakespeare's, *A Midsummer Night's Dream,* then I watched the sun set. It was white and dipped behind dark clouds. We did not see it touch the horizon, but a reflection remained on the Black River (Rio Negro).

Storm clouds passed over; the water became a bit choppy. I was alone for some time. I was enjoying this trip up the river. The radio played nice music (with a lot of static). I only wished I had some English company, boy, girl, man or woman to enjoy and share the trip through this wild, little known region as much as I did. In another hour the captain said, we would be entering the Rio Branco (White River). I was getting sleepy, so I strung up my hammock, said good night to the girls, watched the moon drifting by for a while, then fell asleep.

I awoke with a terrible start; there was a crashing of lightning and thunder. The wind and rain came with a fury. It soaked me in my hammock. It was in the middle of the night. The *Turtle* was rocking violently, and the engine was pounding. I felt sure that the barges that we were towing would sink; the waves went crashing over their low gunwales. Then the pumps were set up. Everyone, even the girls, were up, running about and moving suitcases and clothes away from the rails. Members of the crew lowered canvas sheets over the rails from the roof to help keep the wind and rain out. It was very dark. I had a hard time going back to sleep; the girls talked and sang, the lightning and thunder still cracked and rumbled.

I rolled out of the hammock at the sound of breakfast dishes being laid out. It rained all morning, and it was cold. Everyone had a sweater or jacket on. We had left the Rio Negro behind and were on the Rio Branco. Every so often, men checked the depth of the water with a twenty-foot bamboo pole for sand bars. They hadn't touched any yet.

At breakfast we had the usual black coffee and hard biscuits (hard tack). At dinner, beans, rice, macaroni, beef and spare ribs. After dinner I sorted out some pictures and threw them overboard. The girls complained. I gave them a few nice ones and autographed them. It was nice talking to them, but a call from their mother took them away from me.

Soon we came to a place called Malmate. There were only two houses on shore. They were made of sticks and straw and raised above the ground four or five feet on wooden poles. All about was a solid jungle. The only reason for the few people living there was to cut firewood for the boats that ply the river. There we deposited supplies and took on a load of firewood.

The girls and the captain asked me to go ashore and bring them some quaqui, a tropical fruit. I didn't know what kind it was, but I went anyway. It was raining and risky, walking on the narrow wet planks from the barge to the banks. I went to one of the crude shacks; they had no fruits on hand. Hanging on the rafters and the walls were jaguar and cougar skins. There were dozens of them. They sold for 50 cruzeiros each($2.00). In Manaus they asked 150 to 200 cruzeiros for them. This region abounds with wild deadly game that comes to their very doorstep. What risks these fellows take to live, work, and hunt here. I went through the wet grass jungle, grass came to my waist, brush and trees encircled me on all sides. I feared a snake in the grass, but I was going to bring something back. Everyone was clapping on board as I headed into the "green hell." In a minute I was out of sight. I went in for about a hundred yards before I spotted some large cuias. I knew they weren't any good, but I had to bring something back; there wasn't any sense in going farther without a gun and getting wet. I saw no other fruits. Surely if the South Pacific theater of war is like this, it's not to my liking.

I came back just as the planks were pulled in. I had my arms full of cuias, I had to jump aboard. I almost failed, thanks to an Indian who gave me a helpful shove on the rump. I almost went backwards as I lost my balance and nearly fell into the river. The crowd cheered and clapped again as I made it. But they laughed because I brought fruit that wasn't good to eat. The names were almost similar, so they excused me. Even the girl's mother gave me a winning smile.

The rain continued well into the afternoon. At two o'clock sharp, it's coffee time. Everyone gets a midget-size cup of sweet black coffee. One gets into the habit and looks forward to it. The captain says we average about ten kilometers per hour. He is a tall, lanky, friendly fellow, well up in his fifties. At all times he runs about barefooted. He is a white man, but he sure has native ways. When he isn't steering the boat, he is usually found reading a Christian Science book. The river is about a quarter mile wide at this point with shore lines on all sides. I spent some time studying Spanish. The rain stopped, the sun came out, and we watched a glorious sunset. I sat on the bow rail, sang, and talked with Edna. Soon a half a dozen fellows came and crowded about us. This broke Edna's mood for singing, and she left at once. These fellows all talk to me and are swell, but they cut in on my pleasure.

I spent the evening talking with them. Nice music came over the radio (Portuguese). A full moon out and the stars are reflected in the water. It's a nice night and I'm lonesome.

The fifth day out of Manaus breaks cloudy and gray. We are awakened by the clanging of the cow bell. The *Turtle* had stopped and tied up during the night because of heavy fog. Now the motors have started up again, and it seems like hell has broken loose.

Well, I'm not the only one who believes in taking a cold shower to wake up. There is a line waiting invariably. I no sooner get to the door when someone dashes ahead of me, usually a girl or a lady.

After coffee and "hardtack," I read a Portuguese funny book of Donald Duck. I hardly understand the words, but the pictures and expressions tell a story also, so that I laughed a lot and the Portuguese near me asked if I understood the words. I never paid much attention to expressions of comics before, but now I find that is an art in itself.

At dinner, I noticed two types of rice on the table. I took a helping of the one covered with cinnamon, then beans and steak.

I didn't realize till later that the sweet cinnamon-covered rice was the dessert. Everybody laughed and asked if I liked my dessert with beans. But I didn't feel so stupid; rice is rice and there was so much of it.

The *Turtle* moves close to the shore. We hear the racket of birds and monkeys, millions of butterflies flutter about, but few birds fly over the water. Fifteen minutes in the hot sun burns my arms badly. There are millions of tiny mosquitos; one hardly feels the bites, but arms become full of blood clots. The captain checks the depth of the water with a long rope and a half-pound weight. He winds up and twirls the weight like a cowboy twirls a lasso and throws it ahead of the barge; when the barge reaches the weight, it is many feet under water.

Just before sundown, it looked like a storm was coming. Just as I suspected, we ran into a terrible storm. The wind howled and the rain came in heavy sheets. The crew men lowered the rain flaps over the sides and rails. It became dark inside. We could only look out of the bow and stern. But the sheets of rain poured in there also. Lightning and thunder snapped, cracked, and rolled. The river became very choppy. The captain and his son had their hands full on the huge steering wheel. Both wore black rain capes and hats, but still remained barefooted. Some of the hitchhikers had a rough time in their open canoes or dugouts. They wore only shorts and bailed the water out with tin cans as fast as it filled up. The strange fact was, we were crossing the Equator at that point.

The storm lasted about two hours, then darkness fell. I leaned over the rail at the stern, thinking of Mom and Dad, thinking of my friends, my car, the girls I left behind, the dances, the soda fountains, roller skating, and the hamburger joints. I also thought and sang some songs, "A Long Long Trail A-winding," and I wondered how in the world I'd get over the trail from Boa Vista to Georgetown, for before I could get home, I had to go over it.

After two hours of reminiscing, I turn in. I'm the first to do so. I do not stop to talk to the girls. I had talked to them earlier in the day. They told me they were engaged. Edna seemed to be upset. For no reason at all she said she was engaged to a blond Eng-

536

lish fellow who had skin as white as mine. She pointed to her skin and said, "Mine is *morena* (brown)," and she seemed to think I held that against her. Actually, she had a very light brown complexion that was attractive, like a healthy tan. Many Latins have an inferiority complex in that respect. We talked only a few minutes, then her mom called her away.

All night the motors pound and shake the *Turtle*. We are awakened by the cow bell at six. It is a beautiful day: we have opportunity to see the sun rise. The shower is occupied, the toilet and wash basin also. Everyone is busy brushing their teeth and spitting over the rail. Others are rolling up the hammocks and putting them away and some are combing their hair. Then another bell rings to announce black coffee and "hardtack" is ready. When one is hungry, this is satisfying. Edna's mom has a box full of dry toasted bread and they dine on this. I don't see where the big difference is.

I spent the sixth day on the bridge of the second barge. It was not so noisy or bumpy from the engines. I read the pocket-size book, *Davy Crockett*. The sun set was lovely, but I alone seemed to enjoy it. In the evening we got some good music on the radio. It was enough to make one want to dance. I asked the girls. They laughed and said, "Sorry, we can't, Mom won't allow it, we're betrothed."

I helped a fellow study English for a while, then strung up my hammock. I was the first to do so. Swarming about the kerosene lamp, our only light, were millions of large and small bugs and mosquitos, on the long dirty tablecloths were other millions of bugs and mosquitos. As I was placing a half-hitch on the hammock cord, I felt a hot searing burning on my bare arm, I howled in pain, jumped a foot or two. I thought a red-hot poker fell on my arm, but it was only a large mosquito and it got away. A large bump swelled on my arm at once, I immediately put iodine on it. I then put on my field jacket, buttoned the sleeves and neck to work off the swarm of mosquitos. It was a battle with them to tie up my hammock, but I won. Everyone envied it, for it was easy and fast to put up, pull a zipper and roll in.

The nights are cold, and I have to cover up with my field jacket. I hate to roll out at dawn. It is our seventh day. We have been going day and night since we left except for one night that we tied up, due to heavy fog. We still have several days to go. A total of no more than 360 miles.

The day breaks beautiful and sunny. The Rio Branco (White) is muddy and brown. It widens and narrows, it curves left and then right, so that one would believe one was on a highway and not on a dark, little known river. The shore line looks like green hell; only palm trees are lacking, the trees are smaller, there are various shades of green and here and there a few tinted red and yellow trees. Occasionally, a loud racket of monkeys or parrots is heard.

Edna has a black eye; it is badly swollen. She said a "Bishu" bit her during the night. She meant a mosquito bit her. It seemed hardly possible that a mosquito could do that, but so it happened. I loaned her my dark glasses to relieve the strain on her eyes from the bright sun.

After usual breakfast, another book, *The Valley of the Sky*. Dinner is lousy. I feast on rice and beans after sorting out a few tiny bones. The tongue, I cannot eat; the sweet, fried bananas are delicious. Supper is lousy. Watch the sun go down; it's lovelier than ever. It goes over the horizon in painted gold, leaving brush strokes of golden-yellow behind. Five blue-white rays streak over the sky, the river reflects them, and the green shore line is reflected in a truer green, farther up the river. It reflects a purple cloud and still farther up, two pink clouds. The river is a double image of everything, including the *Turtle* and the people along the rails.

Soon afterwards I turn in; there are millions of mosquitos about the light. I put on my field jacket for protection. I keep slapping my face as they attack. Two got into my eye at once and I immediately swatted them, killed them both, and rubbed them out of my eye; but not before they left a stinging bite on the lip of my eyelid. It burned for several hours. I had to finish tying up my hammock with eyes closed. I no sooner turn in than everyone else does. It's the same at breakfast and dinner. They seem to wait for me to come and sit down first. I usually start the "ball" rolling.

Clang, clang, clang, goes the bell, and we all start rolling out of our hammocks. Another day has begun. It's a most beautiful day, the sun rising over the range of jungle in yellow and golden splendor, spotted with a few gray clouds.

There is a hurry for the shower, toilet, the extra sink and water container in the stern. Usually the women get there first, mainly through the courtesy of the men. After the usual breakfast, I start another book to while the hours away. It's titled *Mr. Glencannon Ignores the War*. It's a good jolly English comedy and I pass the hours pleasantly.

Clang, clang, clang, goes the bell again and it's dinnertime. Dinner of rice, beans, beef, and delicious fried bananas. Mind you, the way these bananas are made, the tastiness of them, I doubt if I'll ever be able to find them back in the U.S.A. They are tops.

We were approaching the village of Caracari. Just before we docked along its muddy banks, everyone, the fellows, girls, captain, and purser reminded me over and over, it was their friendly manner. *"Illgamos a Caracari, muy bonito, no?"* (We arrive in Caracari, very beautiful, No?) I said "Yes," but actually all I saw were mud and thatched-roof houses and a few weather-beaten planks and a crowd of barefooted natives on the high banks watching the *Turtle* pull in.

Upon going ashore, I found it to be a village of several hundred people. Edna, Juci, and a little girl were ahead of me. They stopped and waited for me to catch up. Again they said, "It's beautiful, isn't it?" "Yes," I agreed and its natural scenery was pretty. There were green meadows, with cows and horses grazing, as far as the eye could see. We followed a dusty lane to the end of the village. There were only two good substantial buildings; one was a large adobe building painted blue and white with a red-tile roof. It was the home of a prosperous farmer. The other was an enormous wooden building. It comprised the school, the theater, commercial store, hotel, post office, hospital, and radio station all in one. It was built of hewn planks and looked like a big barn.

Caracari was a quiet, peaceful place. Only a loudspeaker announced some news over the radio station. It was the community's public radio and was heard all over the village. It was

539

sunset and the land had a hot wind sweeping over it. At times it was suffocating. Only a cross wind from over the river seemed to bring cool relief.

We went back to the launch for supper. I was going to turn in, but I was invited to go to the movies. All the passengers, crewmen, captain, and the purser were going ashore. I walked along with Nilo, a chap of about thirty-four. He was interested in learning English. We chatted broken English and Portuguese. I was surprised to have Edna side up to me. Nilo dropped behind with the rest of the crowd. It was very dark. Edna sang, made remarks, and smiled up at me. She took my arm. I didn't understand her; one day she avoided me, next day she cuddled up. I guess women are fickle. She had rather short curly soft black hair and a divine figure eight.

We go into the public building. We enter an old-time class room. There are about twenty desks, and two people can sit in each. There is no charge, for it's only somebody's film being projected. It's about the Rio Branco and the launches. It must have been taken on a former trip because it showed the *Turtle,* our captain, sweating at the helm and the purser as they ride the rapids. As the picture continues, large bats fly overhead and across the screen. They zoom right over my head. There are no comments from anyone. I guess they are used to the bats, but they scare me. The lights go on and the girls asked if I liked it. "Yes," I said. It was a novelty.

The lights go off again and we have Mickey Mouse cartoons in black and white film. Boy, what a cheering he got.

After the movie, one of the chief engineers proudly displayed a new U.S. gas engine and a dynamo used to generate electricity for the community. On returning to the launch, I walked with Edna. It was very peaceful and quiet on the long walk back. One would never believe there was a troubled outside world.

Up at dawn, a beautiful day breaks. Our ninth out of Manaus. We are still docked at Caracari, but with no activity going on. I read a while, I wonder what is the delay, and why we don't move on. After dinner we are still there and no activity, no loading or unloading of cargo or anything. I feel I must go ashore. It's sunny, and bright. I walk along a dusty trail. I really enjoy it.

It would be much nicer with Edna along. I had a notion to ask her but decided not to. This trail goes to Boa Vista and trucks can drive it in four or five hours. Just now the roads are flooded because of heavy rains.

I do not go far before I get caught in a rainstorm. I return to the launch. The *Turtle* is due to leave in a few more hours. About suppertime we are off. I breathed a sigh of relief, but I breathed too soon. We did not run fifteen minutes when we pulled up to tie up again for the night. Now we could not even go ashore. I could only hold my impatience in silence and spend the evening listening to the radio by kerosene lamp, with millions of mosquitos for company.

We were awakened by the starting of the *Turtle's* engines. They started up with a terrific clanging and pounding. Then they slowed down to a steady beating and vibration. Most everyone lay in their hammocks till the loud breakfast bell was rung. When it did, there was a hurry-scurry to do morning duty.

Now we are off; we are not handicapped with the barges. We left them behind. We roll along at a terrific speed, skirting the trees along the shore. The river is wide, but we always follow the shore for some reason or another. Soon the river narrows, the current becomes rapids, huge rocks, whirlpools and brush appear everywhere. Everyone is at the bow, watching the steering and dangerous waters ahead. The *Turtle* speeds around many narrow curves and danger lurks at each. The bell rings continuously to slow down or full speed ahead. There are two men at the wheel and the barefooted captain sits on the gunwales, a foot higher than the deck and calls out directions.

Once we ran over a hidden rock. There was a terrific din of crushing timbers. It seemed like we were losing our bottom. We had no life belts or life boats, and it would be hell to have to swim in those rapids.

Another shock—I don't know how to account for it—we and the *Turtle* just seemed to drop, like hitting an air pocket in an airplane. We had to catch our breaths on that one. There was a solid creaking of timbers, a woman swore, and we were over again. We touched rocks a dozen times more, but they weren't worth mentioning. We had three hours of this tense, dynamic

541

cruise, then we were in quiet waters again, and the *Turtle* pulled up to tie up. I felt the steersmen needed a rest for a while, but I didn't imagine they would lay over for the rest of the day and night also as they did.

In the evening by lantern and mosquitos, I helped Nilo with his English lessons and listened to the radio. We had picked up a dozen more passengers at Caracari. Now we would be sleeping like cattle, side by side in hammocks. There were two rows, one on the port side, the other on the starboard side. In each row were about twenty-five hammocks. The long dining table was in the middle between the two rows. I fortunately had one on end, for air, so to speak. There was not more than two inches clearance between the hammocks. To get from one end of the launch to the other at night, one had to crawl under the rows of hammocks on hands and knees.

Ten days out of Manaus, it's a gray morning and we awaken to a tropical storm. It is Sunday. I spend the morning reading *David Copperfield.* I thank the American padres of Manaus for giving me these books. I didn't know how I'd spend the days otherwise.

At dinner, I was completely shocked at their table manners. Some of the fellows rinsed their mouths with water and spit over the rails or on the floor. They ate so terribly fast, their chins close to the plates. One would think a race or a contest was going on. I was swept along likewise; my food went down half-chewed, like I was sure theirs must be. I must or I'd probably look silly being last and eating alone. Believe me, rice, beans, and beef went down in exactly five minutes. Some of the fellows hadn't got the sense to ask for butter, sugar, or toothpicks, but stood up to reach over two or three persons to get it themselves. Then there was a five-minute wait for dessert. While they waited, every one of them, Edna and Juci also, picked his or her teeth. They covered their mouths with one hand while the other hand was picking away. Their faces made weird contortions. After the dessert of bananas or brown sugar, there was another ten-minute wait for black coffee. In the meantime everyone was wiping their mouths in the tablecloth. I wonder what they thought when I used my handkerchief. There were no napkins on the table. Coffee, they drank in a hurry, whereas I liked to linger and take it slow. I was usually last. They had a water filter, but there was only one glass; everyone used it.

Like most Latins in Latin America, they are right handed, but eat left handed. I have picked up their method of patting rice and beans on a fork with the knife and eating left handed.

The barges had been taken through the rapids by smaller boats and were again tied to the *Turtle's* side. That was the reason why we tied up after going through the rapids. We sailed along all day over quiet, muddy waters. Occasionally, we went around a curve. Toward evening a mountain stood over the flat green jungle.

I was told by Edna's mother that I would miss some lovely sights, the glistening mountainsides, waterfalls, etc. They would make wonderful pictures, she said, but it was my misfortune that we would pass by the mountain at night. It is near the heart of the diamond region.

This is our last evening aboard the *Turtle*. Everyone is at the bow talking excitedly in the darkness. Edna says Boa Vista is her home town, but she does not like it very much. She likes Manaus better. Nevertheless, she was quite excited about returning home as the rest of the passengers were.

54

American Missionaries Abroad

We were awakened by the cow bell at six for our last breakfast of black coffee and hardtack. We were expected to arrive at Boa Vista by ten o'clock. "Beyond that Sierra (Mountain)," my companion said, "lies Boa Vista."

Everyone was dressed in their best clothes and brown and white shoes. Edna, Juci, and several other girls had me take their picture on the boat, but it was a little too dark. I promised to take some on shore in the sunlight. Then we ran into a terrible rainstorm, and I thought, *This is a fine day to arrive in Boa Vista.*

But upon entering Boa Vista (Good View), the rain stopped and the sun came out. Everybody leaned over the rails. We could see the banks lined with waiting people. Evidently boat arrivals from Manaus are a big event there. The usual mud and thatched-roof houses stood out on the shores. I wondered if these pretty girls lived in them.

It was mid-noon when the *Turtle* pulled up to shore to end its eleven-day journey. It had made a gallant voyage and was none the worse for the beating it took over the rapids. Everyone was hungry, for we had missed the dinner served at 10:30. It wasn't served because they expected an early arrival. I expected to be the last one off the boat, for there was no reason for me to hurry. I was really surprised when the immigration officers in smart blue uniforms came aboard and asked at once for the "Americano." He checked my passport, then advised me to follow another official to the immigration office and wait. So I was the first to go ashore. I did not get to take the girls' picture again. They called "Joey!" as I got off, and I know they were disappointed. Photography is a novelty here and they seldom get to have their pictures taken.

I waited about ten minutes in the "Frontier" office. It was tiny, but artistic and one of the better buildings of Boa Vista. Comprising the town were two large churches, both Catholic; one was old, the other new. Then there was a large company of soldiers at wooden barracks, the guardians of the frontier, a modern playground, wide dirt streets, a handful of small commercial stores and restaurants, and a large number of mud houses. There was only a spattering of adobe or stone houses.

The *commandante* (commander) came after a bit, stamped and signed my passport. Then he told me there were two American missionaries there with their wives and children. I was so surprised, for no one on the boat told me there were American missionaries in Boa Vista and I would never have suspected. So I decided this was the best place to get information. I hardly understood Portuguese and their strange stories were so contradictory. It would be nice to hear English spoken again also. I located their home after the usual Brazilian custom of misdirection. It was a large unpainted adobe house. In one of the larger rooms, they had their church.

I found them all at home, and I presented myself. They likewise introduced themselves. They were Mr. and Mrs. Garner Trimble and two blond children, and Mr. and Mrs. Harry Babcock and two blond children likewise. Mr. Trimble was sick in bed. He had a touch of malaria. They were most happy to meet an American, and I was promptly invited to dinner. I told them about my trip, and they told me about their work. Mr. Trimble was very tall and thin, soft spoken. He has been in Brazil, chiefly about Boa Vista, for nine years. Mr. Babcock was short and stout. He had been there only three years. He was about thirty years old and Mr. Trimble was about thirty-six years old. Their wives are about the same ages respectfully, pleasant looking and friendly. They live in the same house; they all like their work and the people. They had their complaints also. They liked Boa Vista so much that they planned to remain there always but as Americans. The children were healthy. They could speak Portuguese and English fluently. They spoke the language better than their parents. They played with the Brazilian children and picked up the language. They refused to wear shoes and ran about native style, barefooted. The missionaries had started work to build a large Baptist church, and they wanted it to be a Brazilian church and wanted the Brazilians to know it.

Mr. Babcock is going to go up the river into the interior in a few days. He is trying to convert the Indians there with medicine and supplies. They really go into the wilderness, usually without guns. They take a gun sometimes when they wish to shoot some game. We have to hand it to the missionaries; they have guts.

We had a wonderful dinner of meatloaf, lettuce, and tomatoes from their own garden. It certainly was good after eleven days of rice, beans, and beef on the *Turtle*. In the afternoon, Messieurs Trimble, Babcock, and I went calling on various folks. But the folks desired were never at home and the information I needed on British Guiana, we never got. The amazing thing was how slow and unhurriedly the two missionaries walked. There was no haste. When we were told that folks weren't home, my friends expressions seemed to say, "Well, if not today, later maybe, or tomorrow or next week, No hurry, no hurry." The day was hot and sultry; it accounted for the slow lazy feeling. Even Americans fell into slow Latin habits if they stayed in the region long enough.

Wearing their white tropical helmets, we made a tour of the garden, the chicken coop. It was a lot better than many of the houses the natives of Boa Vista lived in. Mr. Trimble said they lost a chicken on an average of one a week to the thieving natives. Then we visited a store house; it was full of sacks of cement, tile and tools needed to build the new church. The cement came from the States to Belém, up the Amazon to Manaus, then up the Rio Negro and Rio Branco to Boa Vista by boat. It cost seven dollars a sack. It certainly would cost a lot of money to build that church.

I was invited to lodge and dine with the kind missionaries. They had no extra bed, but I was welcome to string up my hammock in the children's play room. This was "okay" by me, for at the only hotel in town, they had no beds and one had to pay to sleep in a hammock. That's the way it was in Boa Vista. The hotel had a lot of filth and garbage about the place, and for that reason, I accepted the missionaries' kind offer to stay with them.

546

Mr. Babcock and I strolled a dozen blocks to retrieve my gear from aboard the *Turtle.* I was able to present him with all the books I had read, and he was glad to have them. In the evening we strolled about the quiet, muddy main street. In all it was a peaceful, pleasant country town. We stopped at a tiny café to chat and drink guarana. In Manaus, a bottle cost three cruzeiros and in Boa Vista, eight cruzeiros (40 cents). Everything was expensive in this distant, isolated town. Baby food cost 25 to 40 cents per tiny can.

Before the water system was laid in, the missionaries had their troubles. They had to pay five cents for a five-gallon can of water, brought from the river on a boy's head. They had to do all their cooking and washing with river water and to take a bath; that ran into money. Still many times boys were hard to find and they had to go to the river themselves and bring it up in wheelbarrows.

People had remarked over and over, "The only time we will have a water system is when the Americans put it in." And so it came to pass.

I had met the engineer in Belém who had installed the system, but their telling me that Boa Vista was a dangerous community without a gun was nonsense.

I laid over in Boa Vista two days, waiting for a boat going north. Then we learned one would be going north on the morning of the third day. I was told by the missionaries that I was very fortunate. Sometimes they waited five, six to ten days for a boat going north and into the interior. So I guess I was lucky. On second day in Boa Vista, I took a shower and washed all my clothes in the missionaries' back yard. I had the children for company and they were teasing. After dinner, everyone took a siesta; this custom is popular, not only in Mexico, but all over South America also. In the evening we played cricket in the back yard, and after supper, we played a game, similar to Chinese chess, called "Sorry." We really had a lot of fun playing it, and the evening passed swiftly. It was an unusually late hour when we turned in.

An Indian maiden rang a bell at dawn to announce breakfast was ready. I joined the missionaries at breakfast, Mr. Trimble said the blessings and prayed to God to take care of me on my journey. This was unexpected and I had to thank him for his kindness and consideration. The boat was to leave at 8:30, but a heavy rain delayed it, my captain, or should I say my pilot, was not in any particular hurry to leave. He preferred to linger at a saloon in town till noon.

My captain asked for 150 cruzeiros ($7.50), and I would have to bring my own food for the three-day journey. This is a preposterous rate, but as the missionaries said, "Everyone is very independent here and they charge what they please." It was either pay or you don't go. I had to sell my second watch to Mr. Babcock to pay the heavy fee. I sold it ridiculously cheap for only ten dollars. I really valued it, the sentiment and good service it gave me. But I didn't feel bad about selling it to him because they were so nice. He needed a watch badly, he said.

Mrs. Trimble packed me a lunch to last me three days. She also gave me a prayer book and a lecture. As I left their home, she had a half-dozen Indians with cut and bruised hands and feet. Some of them were badly infected. She treated them all and did not charge them for service, medicine, or bandages.

They do a lot of good for the people, yet when their furniture came from the States, the Brazilian government charged them a high price; a heavy duty of $500 was placed on the furniture. They are cheated here and there by the people, yet when their money comes from the States, they willingly accept the official rate of exchange to keep honest face.

I said good-bye to Mrs. Trimble and Mrs. Babcock; they had work to do in their house. Mr. Babcock and Mr. Trimble and the children waited to see me off. They even brought extra bananas, oranges, and lemons for me to take along. All I can say is they were swell.

At twelve o'clock noon, my twelve-foot motorboat, *Uruguay,* pulled away from the muddy banks of Boa Vista; we drifted downstream toward the center, then turned around into the strong current and headed north. I waved back to the missionaries and children on shore; then they disappeared out of sight.

I thought about Edna and Juci. I regretted that I did not see them again. Now my attention turned to my fellow companions. There were five of us on the boat. There was the captain, the owner of the boat. This man was young, about twenty-five, and good looking. His assistant was younger, about nineteen, and good looking also. Both had discarded their clothing and wore only swimming trunks. Their copper skins fairly glistened and both had nice, developed bodies like husky athletes. The other two were passengers. They were fully clothed and headed for a ranch up the river. Both spoke Portuguese, but one was a British subject from British Guiana. There was little conversation. Everyone seemed to be busy with his own thoughts.

The *Uruguay* was actually a row boat with an outboard motor attached to it. It was unpainted and had seen a lot of service. It looked like a floating house because of the makeshift canvas roof and sides. The sides were rolled up to the overhead beams. It had stopped raining, and a hot sun beamed down.

All afternoon we chugged against the strong current. We passed women washing clothes in the river, then naked men swimming in it, and farther up were naked boys and girls swimming. They waved and cheered as we went by. Then not more than five hundred yards farther up the river, near the shore, we saw a big cobra swimming downstream, its head about fifteen inches above the water. The fellows in the boat shouted and yelled at it, trying to attract its attention, but we continued onward. I asked if it was a poisonous one; they said "No," but I didn't believe them and I worried about the people swimming below. And still I wondered why the people swim in water that is full of dangerous fish and snakes.

In Boa Vista I saw a fellow catch a fish two feet long; it had an orange back and a white belly. It was flat-shaped horizontally and had a huge vicious mouth full of sharp teeth. Then I heard more tales of men, horses and, cattle that had been bitten, went panic-stricken, and were lost in the river when driving across the herds. I had seen the effects of the drowned American in Manaus to believe the stories.

We passed other small boats. Some were heavily overloaded and overcrowded. If a sudden storm came along, they wouldn't have had a chance in rough water. The water at the moment was only a few inches from the gunwales.

The river was muddy, and at no time was it more than 200

yards wide. In the late afternoon, we caught up to another boat; we tied together and chugged along. Some conversation flowed between the two boats, then silence. We got a little rain, and the rain flaps were lowered.

The assistant pilot made coffee, using river water. He used a blow torch for fire. We drank it from tin cans. It was black and sweet but seemed to be full of dirt. It was satisfying and relieving to our tired bodies. We continued all evening to ply northward. About midnight we turned into the Rio Itakutu, and the other boat continued up the Rio Branco. We did not go very far; we hit shallow water, there was a clanging, snapping sound; it startled me. I had been dozing on a load of sugar. The propellers had struck ground and rock; something had busted. We pulled up to shore; the assistant jumped into the water and tied the boat to a tree. The shore looked very wild, I feared the kid would get his bare legs bitten, and later I wondered if savages would not attack from that solid jungle. All of us were very sleepy, and we decided to investigate the damage in the morning. We strung up our hammocks to the cross beams of the crude roof. There was barely room for five hammocks. We slept close together and managed okay.

We were up at the break of day. The coffee was made out of river water and made with the blow torch. We sufficed on hard-boiled eggs and hard biscuits I had. I lay in the hammock and read while the captain and assistant repaired a broken part of the propeller. After about two hours, they had it fixed and we were under way again.

I had to roll out of my hammock lest my swaying tip the boat over or cave in the weak poles supporting the roof. We putted along all day. The river seemed about 300 feet wide, with dense jungle on all sides. I read a book most of the time, then made lemonade with river water. The lemon helped to kill the germs.

The fellows had some canned beans; they mixed a lot of bread crumbs with it, and we dined on this. The people of this region used a lot of these crumbs with all their meals. We had a lot of it on board the *Turtle* also. They use it in soup, rice, and beans and over meat, etc.

The day was quiet and peaceful, the sunset was glorious; it

550

was a golden sky with a few streaks of dark clouds. When darkness fell, we traveled by lantern light. It was rather interesting. Everybody except the pilot was dozing off on the load of sugar. Only the pilot sat up, steering the boat and singing love songs in Portuguese. It sounded lousy.

When he got tired, we pulled up to shore, a solid jungle it was. We strung up our hammocks and went to sleep. The night became very cold.

We awoke with the dawn, pulled down our hammocks, and were off again. Four hours later we stopped at a tiny place called Paraiso. On the high bank was an adobe ranch house. In fact it was well built, comfortable, and had all the necessities of life. This was where the English lad and the other passengers lived. We were invited in for coffee and a chat. We met the rancher, his wife, and several full-grown sons. Paraiso was actually a large ranch. The land was level and seemed to be free of the jungle. Here and there could be seen cattle and horses grazing. The river, aside from the airplane, was the only way possible to reach the ranch. For this reason the house was built along the river bank.

We do not linger long at Paraiso, we unload some cargo, then continue up the river. Two hours later we are approaching Conception, on the south of the river Manu. (The natives called the river "Maoo.") Here we meet Sr. Figuero, a rancher who is well known throughout the region and a personal friend of the American missionaries. He was noted as a very wealthy rancher. We had coffee, met his large family, and chatted.

Soon we parted and left the river Itakutu behind and turned into the mouth of the river Maoo. This river looks like a channel or a great canal. It is evenly spaced and not over a hundred feet wide. On either shore, jungle trees and foliage covered the banks, but beyond lay the open range.

We had four long hours ahead of us to Nova Estrella (New Star). It was the end of the river journey. The river is dark, but clear and not very swift. My captain was wrong and the trip took four hours and forty-five minutes and as usual, upon approaching a village or passing a boat, our pilot (operator) blew three times on a hollow tube. It sounded like a fog horn. It was a way of

551

greeting or making an approach known. It was a popular custom throughout Brazil.

We arrived at Nova Estrella; it was on the Brazilian side of the river. The opposite shore was British Guiana. Nova Estrella was not a town but a name of a ranch. I asked the pilot to take me over to the British Guiana side since they told me it was only an hour's walk to the American Ranch. I was very surprised to learn there was an American in this region and especially a ranch. I learned this from the British Guiana lad and Sr. Figuero. It was still two hours before sundown, but my pilot and the rancher of Nova Estrella suggested I lay over till morning also. I'd be likely to lose the trail. The rivers and flooded lands I had to cross would recede in the morning.

I did not wish to listen to Portuguese another night, but I decided to be patient and lay over.

Underneath thatched roofs, and surrounded by mud walls, we had a splendid supper of beef, chicken, sausages, and milk by kerosene lamps. I watched the fellows play cards, then along dusty lanes, bothered by mosquitos, I strolled back to the boat, placed my hammock, rolled in and looked forward to entering a new land, the colony of British Guiana in the morning.

55
A Week on a Ranch in British Guiana

We awoke early. I rolled up my hammock while our pilot made coffee in a can and used the blow torch for fire. He had promised to take me across the river at 6:00 in the morning. But first, in a very independent manner, he had to take his motor apart, clean plugs, gas tanks, and what not. Then we were called to breakfast again at the Brazilian "New Star Ranch."

It was nine o'clock before we got to the British Guiana shore. The sun was high and hot. For this reason I disliked the delay. I did not wish to hike under a blazing tropical sun. We had gone downstream several hundred yards, then pulled up to the shore, and scampered up a bank. There were several trails. My friends were undecided which I should follow. Then they were kind enough to go along with me for an hour or so. They were barefooted, and one wore only shorts and his copper skin glistened in the sun. He reminded me of a savage Indian on the trail. Horses and cattle stopped eating and watched us go by. It was the great savannah, the Rupununi cattle region, the great, flat, green plains of British Guiana. Here and there were deep patches of water. We waded through and found the trail at the opposite end of it.

My naked guide climbed a sun-scorched tree and said he could see the windmill. I could not be sure. It looked like a palm tree to me. There we parted and they advised me to stay on the trail until I came to the ranch. It should only be a half hour hike.

I stayed on the trail for two hours. The sun was directly overhead. I was hot and perspiring. I decided to drop my pack under a tree, tie a handkerchief to a branch for a marker, and push onward. I came to bigger swamps. When it came to my waist, I became scared. I feared it might be quicksand, and I didn't want to get stuck. I had read terrible stories about quicksand in northern Brazil and British Guiana.

I circled around the swamp, found the trail again, and followed it till it petered out. I was on the wrong trail. I came back to the swamp, found another trail, followed it and it petered out. I decided to return to my pack for lunch. Now I couldn't find it. The sun was straight overhead and I couldn't tell if I was going north, east, west, or south. I was utterly lost.

I felt very tired. I sat under a tree, but the stifling heat was so acute, and the mosquitos such a nuisance that I could not rest a minute. When walking, there was a slight cool refreshing breeze. There was no rest (for the wicked), and I had to push my tired body on. I wandered on and it was a terrible feeling, no one in sight, nothing but a vast prairie full of swamp puddles and a few mute animals.

Then I saw the palm trees again. Each about a mile from the other. I couldn't be sure which might be the windmill. There were about a dozen, and one faintly looked a little odd. I guessed it might be the windmill. There was a mile of swamp ahead of me. There was no avoiding it. My boots, trousers, and feet were soaked already, so I plunged in and forward. The closer I came, the more distinct the trees became and sure enough, one of them was a windmill. I breathed a sigh and my senses relaxed under the hot sun.

The thatched roofs and walls blended with the land so that it was hard to distinguish the houses. Many trees grew out of the river, and I succeeded in crossing over by crossing fallen logs and rocks.

I arrived just as the Hart family was having dinner. So they asked me to join them, and being very hungry, I did. I perspired profusely and felt guilty eating with wet boots and pants on.

Mr. Hart asked where I came from.

"Pennsylvania," I answered.

"Like hell you are!" he answered, with a pleased smile.

Boy, what a wholesome dinner we had, of beef, rice, bananas, milk and pumpkin.

Mr. Hart was an American. He had come to South America thirty-five years ago. He had been an engineer working on the railroad in Brazil near the Bolivian border. He came and settled in British Guiana on this ranch. It was called "Good Luck Ranch." It was 250 miles from Georgetown, the seaport and market for his cattle. He had settled down there, hoping some day a highway would be built to his ranch. The prospect never came true, and his dreams of making a fortune collapsed. Discussions between Ford and the British had been held. Ford had volunteered to build a highway from Georgetown to the Brazilian border free of all cost as long as only U.S. cars could be permitted on the highway for ten years. The British government considered, then rejected the offer. Ford dropped the time request to five years. Still, the British refused. The highway was never built, and Mr. Hart has to drive his cattle overland to Georgetown on foot instead of in trucks. The trip takes about thirty days. The cattle then sold at $60 a head.

Mr. Hart had only been back to the States once in the last thirty years. It was last season. He spent three months in the U.S. and had a wonderful time.

He had four sons and a daughter here on the ranch and another boy and a daughter in the States. Two of the boys had served at Atkinson Field during the war. All of his children were registered as Americans. He was married to a British Guiana woman, who spoke Brazilian perfectly. She has never been out of the colony.

His two boys, Larry and Jimmy, showed me to my quarters, which was an army cot in an adobe house with a thatched roof. The floor was wooden and swept clean. It had simple necessities, table, chair, lights.

After resting several hours, I started walking to get my pack. Larry asked if I could ride a bicycle. "Sure," I said, so the three of us, Larry, Jimmy, and I went on English bicycles over the narrow cow trail, then over patches of grass under water. The wheels slipped and churned. Larry and Jimmy (shirtless) were in the lead. Evidently they rode bicycles over this prairie many times. I had all I could do to keep up. We crossed two rivers, one to our waists, the other to our heads. We had to strip and carry bikes overhead. The grueling ride over sods, sand, and water lasted another hour, then Jimmy spotted the handkerchief on a limb of a tree. The pack behind it was safe. Larry lifted it and said, "It must weigh at least 80 pounds." I said "No, it couldn't be over 50." Later we checked it on a scale. It was 45 pounds. We rested under the tree for a while, then started back. Larry was an ex-GI. He had been in the Infantry and insisted upon carrying the pack. The ride back was grueling. Larry swam across the river with the pack on his head. The water was muddy, and we had to take a shower and change clothes.

On the ranch, there is a wooden shed that serves for a shower room. In the morning we can have a cold shower; in the afternoon a hot one. The night cools the water; the sun heats it. Two and three times a day everyone takes a shower. The water is pumped into a tank from the river by a windmill. It came from Chicago. After passing through filters, the water is crystal clear and used for all purposes.

At suppertime I explained my desire to continue overland to Georgetown. They all advised me it was impossible at present because of the heavy rainfall. They said it would be best to wait for the plane that came twice a month. It would be due in a week. I was welcome to stay.

Next day a couple of Negro boys came to the ranch. They had come from Georgetown over the cattle trail. They described their trip to me. It had taken them nineteen days. This was by foot. The plains were flooded. Water came up to the knees, and on one stretch for four miles, the water came to their waists. The trail, they said, had eight or ten small tracks, all leading forward together. If in doubt of the trail, stop, cross over to the right, and check for four or five lanes. Return to where you stopped and cross over to the left for four or five lanes. If you can see red dirt, you are okay. If you see white sand, you are off the trail. Then around the mountains, the lanes go haphazard. Take the deepest rut and you'll be okay.

They asked if I had anything for snake bites. I said "No." Yet these fellows walked barefooted the long distance (250 miles). But they depended on their eyes and ears, and if a snake should dangle its head from a tree into their path, they would merely look it in the eye and stealthily dance away.

These boys spoke English, and there was no misunderstanding them. Along with the words, they acted a bit, so that their experience with snakes were not uncommon.

And if I should see a cat's paw, not to turn and look behind me, but to head for the nearest and highest tree. We all laughed at this. These fellows do not carry guns, but they do carry long knives for protection.

For the first three days one can sleep at a ranch house; after that along the trail are simple shelter houses. Three bars along the trail represent a corral gate, open it and string our hammock under the thatched roof of the shelter house. The shelter houses are placed ten to twenty-five miles apart. Then there is a seven-day stretch where you don't see shelter houses or anything. One must carry one's own grub for the trip.

Then there was a bridge covered with slippery muck. The high water had hidden the bridge, and one had to feel each step under water and rub the muck away for a solid footing. There were guide cables, but should not be depended on. They had too much slack. To fall off the bridge meant falling into the river.

Considering the dangers, the time, my run-down condition, my homesickness, no gun, no knife, no guide, no horses, I decided it was foolish to continue the hardship for the sake of adventure. Because of hoof-and-mouth disease I could not acquire a horse for the journey. The cattle drive started next month in October, the beginning of the dry season.

So now I would accept Mr. Hart's invitation to content myself for several more days on the Good Luck Ranch till the plane came in on Friday. Instead of nineteen days on the road plus maybe a week waiting for a boat from Ebini to New Amsterdam, then a train to Georgetown, I could content myself with a two-hour flight by plane over this wilderness.

The days passed very peacefully and quietly, too quietly. The day started at 6:00 A.M. and ended at 8:00 or 9:00 P.M. A clanging bell announced chow time at 7:00 A.M., and 12 noon, at 3:00 in the afternoon and 6:00 in the evening. Every day it sounded punctually on time.

At mealtime the conversation was one sided. I made effort at conversation, they listened, smiled, made courteous remarks

557

and silence again. I felt ill at ease several times. Mr. Hart had taken ill and I hadn't seen him till the day of my departure.

All of his children went barefoot at all times. Jimmy was always shirtless, even at dinner. One of the little children remarked to me one day, "Don't you feel funny wearing shoes?" All except Mr. Hart spoke Portuguese fluently, much better than English. Their nearest neighbors were the Portuguese across the river Maoo at Nueva Estrella. The next nearest neighbors were Orelas, seventeen miles away near Lethem, British Guiana.

Mr. Hart had a lot of Negro help. He paid them fifty cents a day, with room and board. The ranch house, barns, sheds were situated along a lovely creek. The entire setting of ranch house and buildings formed a beautiful panorama. All the buildings had thatched roofs. Huge palm trees and other species were clustered about and green fields were everywhere. Even the sky and clouds added hues to the picturesque ranch.

One thatched roof sheltered hundreds of sheep; many were a few days old and sucklings, which took butting around from older sheep. It was fun to watch them. Another thatched roof covered a pig sty. There were about ten in all. Other thatched roofs served for barns, storage rooms, blacksmith shops, and toilets. The chickens ran into the thousands scot-free.

After supper the conversation turned to cattle. Beef sold at nine cents a pound in Georgetown. A radio report stated beef selling at two dollars a pound in New York. What a comparison.

Brazilian travelers came by quite often; they stay overnight and were gone at dawn. Conversation flowed freely with them at the table. Sometimes we listened to the radio afterwards.

I spent most of my time resting on the cot, writing letters or notes, washing and pressing my clothes. Since I had left Venezuela seven months and two weeks ago, I had three shirts left out of eleven, two pair of trousers out of seven, and I'd drop from 152 pounds to 130 pounds.

I enjoyed the quiet rest for a week. I was glad when the day came to travel again. There was no dancing, no girls, no nothing. It seemed like a dull place to waste a lifetime, never any excitement. I'll bet the boys really let loose when they went to Georgetown.

I saw Mr. Hart on the last day. He was feeling much better. He looked only 53 but was actually 75. We had a long pleasant talk. He had been the first man to start cutting the cattle trail to Georgetown. He got as far as Harts Creek, which is named after him. He also knew Harry Frank, the Footloose Vagabond, who wrote a number of books. Harry Frank had stayed on his ranch for two weeks over thirty years ago. Mr. Hart paid him a visit last year in Pennsylvania. Old Harry hardly recognized him, but then it all came back to him.

After three o'clock tea, Larry and I started out on bicycles to the air strip at Lethem. It was about twenty-three miles south of the Good Luck Ranch. We followed the cattle trail. At three o'clock, the sun was still high and beat down heavily. Every five or ten minutes, I had to remove my dark glasses to wipe the sweat away. It blinded and burned the eyes terribly.

I could not stand up on the pedals, for my pack was tied between my legs to the bicycle bars. To stand up, I'd be bowlegged. The bike had no carrier, and it was impossible to strap the pack to the English-style handlebars. So for seventeen miles I peddled away, sitting down, legs bowlegged.

I had all I could do to stay on the six- to ten-inch cow trail, sometimes completely hidden by grass. Half the time I was bouncing over the sods. The path was sandy and that gave me trouble. We crossed I don't know how many flooded stretches. Larry went barefooted like a native and went through quite easily. My water-logged boots became a drag on me. They kept sticking to the soft mud and sand under water. Every step was an effort. The flooded stretches varied from ten feet to a quarter of a mile. The water at times came above the waist so that we had to carry the bikes to keep the packs from becoming wet and damaging the contents.

We were on the trail for three and a half hours, arriving at Orelas at sunset. We would sleep there and continue in the morning six miles farther to the air strip. We had ridden and walked seventeen miles. My rump was calloused and legs aching. I didn't believe I would last.

The Orelas had quite an orderly ranch with flowers and a neat lawn facing the ranch house. Nearby was a garden surrounded by a white picket fence. The house was large with a shiny galvanized roof. The furniture included a radio, home-made easy chairs, benches, tables, well-polished. There was a large modern refrigerator. I wondered and asked, "How in the world did that get here?" By ox cart, I believed. There were no roads for cars or trucks.

"It came by plane," Mrs. Orelas said. "It cost $500 freight from Georgetown." They had a tractor flown in by plane also.

Before supper we all went for a bath in the river. It was clear there. The river served all purposes. Boy, for supper we had breaded chicken dinner, what's more, butter, milk and U.S. peanut butter and jam. The Orelas had simple guest rooms for travelers. There we slept.

The morning was brightened by three little boys riding horseback. They were funny; one had a dead pan (blank face) and looked just like Butch Jenkins, our own movie star. He had an unsmiling face, sandy hair, and freckles. They all fought to ride on one horse. They rode alone, then double; one was good, the other held on for dear life. That was "Butch." He sure looked funny, then he grinned and we roared. Later he fell off the horse and started crying. He was not hurt. These three lads were on a visit here, with reservations to fly to Georgetown today.

The idea of riding bicycles was changed. We would go in an ox cart, taking baggage and the children along. The ox cart was a two-wheeler, covered with a roof of palmetto leaves to keep the hot sun off. It was towed by two brown oxen and guided by a barefooted Indian girl of twenty.

Everywhere on the plains could be seen huge ant hills of sand, ranging two to five feet in diameter and six to ten feet high. They were as common as corn-stalk bundles on a farm in October.

The Indian girl had her hands full trying to keep the oxen on the trail. She spoke only Portuguese, no English. We crossed several streams and once a river that flooded the floor of the ox cart. The Indian girl lifted her dress above her waist, revealing white bloomers as she waded and prodded the oxen across the high water. The oxen strained to pull up the opposite bank. They nearly fell backwards onto us in the cart as they climbed over. The trip to Lethem lasted several hours.

There were about a half-dozen thatched-roof buildings and one red-frame building. A British flag waved from it. I presented myself to dark-complexioned Mr. Young. He was on a fine horse, dressed in Khaki shorts, shirt, and a white jungle helmet. "Make yourself at home," he said, then rode off, making no effort to stamp or sign my passport. He was the chief official at this government station. He said he had to meet the plane when it landed. Cripes he knew I wanted to be flying on it.

The plane came in. It was a C-47, piloted by an American named Williams, an ex-army major. I presented myself to him. He was not friendly, as most Americans would be to a countryman in this neck of the woods. He took on a load of freshly slaughtered beef and twelve passengers.

Behold my surprise and disappointment when Williams said, "Sorry, I can't take you. I got a full load." The next flight would be in two weeks. "Christ," I said, "What am I supposed to do, walk?"

"I guess so," he replied. He wasn't the least bit friendly. Then he remarked. "I'll be back Sunday."

The day was Friday; that meant two more days of waiting on this quiet wilderness of the savannah plains. Oh, how that dismayed me, but that was better than waiting two weeks or walking the cattle trail north. I had gone over twenty-three miles of it south; it was no laughing matter.

A couple of horsemen had to ride down the runway to clear it of stray horses and cows. Then I watched the plane throttle up, race down the grassy field, take wing and disappear into the sky. The crowd dispersed. I walked slowly back to the few houses, dropped my pack at the general office, then went on the banks of the mighty Itakutu to brood over my predicament. I sat down in the grass beneath the shade of a large tree. It was a lovely spot, but I could not enjoy it long; swarms of mosquitos and bugs made me rise and leave.

Larry and the ox cart had returned homeward. I would have to stay at Lethem. George had no room for me, but he said I could string my hammock under the porch of his house.

561

At supper I met Harry, Ruth, and Mr. Sing. They were employed at the government station there at Lethem. We had Brazilian whiskey, then supper of beef, rice, beans, and black coffee. Then we sat in sun chairs outside the house under a thatched roof that served as a porch.

We watched the golden sunset over the vast green plains. An Amerindian strummed on a guitar. Over and over he sang, "Red River Valley." He was off tune on the guitar, but it didn't matter. After two days at this quiet place, I was humming it myself unconsciously.

One gets up early in this country. I spent my time reading *True Story* magazines that the police sergeant had loaned me. He came at noon the next day. He took my passport to Mr. Young. He came back, saying, "It's Saturday. Mr. Young has his office closed." The sergeant said I'd have it stamped before I left.

The dinner had been of rice and greasy intestines. Supper of rice, farina, and meat balls. It was beefy, like hash, and not good at all.

The evening was spent drinking high balls made of sugar-cane whiskey, lemon and water. Fellows strummed on guitars and a newcomer sang a lot of cowboy songs.

On Sunday the fellows have a day off; they all rise early just the same. Some of them like this quiet life. They all came from Georgetown. Mr. Sing had been most fortunate; he had been sent to London once. All those fellows have a dream of seeing London.

I packed my gear, for I hoped the plane would come in today. Everyone laughed, and said I was optimistic. But it's best to be prepared, for the plane only stays a few minutes.

One of the fellows liked my hammock. So I said I would sell it for the price of airplane passage to Georgetown, about $15.00. He said it was a bit high but okay. He wanted to help me out also. In Panama I got the hammock free of charge, from a friend working with U.S. Foreign Liquidations in Balboa.

I waited on Mr. Young to stamp my passport for two hours. His office had a large sign over the door: "Private." I believed he could not hurt me, only give me the devil, so I burst in. I was tired of waiting.

I found them drinking. One fellow, a large chubby person,

562

stood in the middle of the floor, a Pepsi-Cola bottle in hand and mouth agape at my intrusion. A white man immediately got up from behind the desk.

I said to him, "This is pretty damn good. You have time for drinking but no time to stamp my passport."

He was angry but said nothing and stamped the passport—angrily. I then left, worried that he might have me arrested or give me problems when I reached Georgetown.

About three o'clock I had already given up hope of the plane coming in. Just then the keen ears of the Indians heard the sound of engines. They looked up to the sky; a few minutes later, we saw it pop out of the clear sky. Down to the strip we went through field and swamp. The plane landed and pulled up to a stop.

There was one passenger, Major Williams, and his wife and co-pilot. The police sergeant came on his bicycle after me. He asked for the passport. I gave it to him. I was afraid he would try to keep me from going aboard without an "Entry" visa in my passport. He glanced through it thoughtfully, then handed it back (to my relief) and said "Good-bye and good luck."

I asked George what I owed for food and lodging. "One dollar," he said.

We soon took off; after three minutes I said, "Why are we flying so low?" to the lonely passenger. He said, "We are going to land and sleep at Orelas." I thought he was kidding. A few minutes later, we landed and Major Williams confirmed the passengers's reply. Could you imagine my surprise. In disgust I said, "Your plane service is as bad as the river boats; you stop at every village or house." Major Williams, his wife, and co-pilot got their packs and headed across the field to Orelas house. I got mine and followed suit. The Orelas were surprised to see me.

After bathing in the river, we had a wonderful supper of fried chicken and other good things. Mrs. Williams was a very plump woman who did a lot of talking. She was most friendly. She wanted to know all about me. They all laughed about the way I had sold one watch, then a flashy tie, then another watch, then my hammock to keep going. So tonight I had nothing to sleep in. Mrs. Williams had the guest room.

Mr. Williams had traveled all of South America. He preferred the high cold altitudes of Bogotá, Colombia, and La Paz, Bolivia. But I preferred the warmer air of Lima, Peru, or Rio de Janeiro, Brazil.

Mrs. Orelas's son fixed up an army cot for me, and I really slept well.

All of us were up at seven o'clock next morning and went to the river to clean up. I had a large breakfast and offered to pay Mrs. Orelas. She refused the money. I said, "I won't return anymore," and she laughed and said, "It's okay."

We got into the sky, and looking down on the savannah (plains), I wondered how I could possibly get through those flooded fields walking. I was now convinced more than ever of the impossibility of getting through alone. About a half hour later, we were coming down again. It was a rough landing on the bumpy plains. Mrs. Williams said, "We are going to sleep here again. We are out of gas." I said, "I don't believe it." I unbuckled my safety belt and said, "Guess we might get out and see what the town looks like." They all laughed. "Sure, let's go and see the town."

There was only one thatched roof shelter house on that vast plain. There were several Negroes and from what conversation I gathered, there was supposed to be a load of cargo and eight passengers for the plane. "When will it get here?" Mr. Williams inquired. "Several hours," the Negroes replied.

I wouldn't wait, I remarked in modest Negro accent and backed away, for I was sure Major Williams wasn't asking for my comments. Nevertheless, they all laughed and Mrs. Williams's high voice showed merriment. I dropped my head on my arms over a wing in tired resignation. Mrs. Williams had said, "We could go fishing in the river; it's only five miles away." "I'm tired," I replied.

She laughed and kidded me, but I said, "You can't cheer me up." For truly I was sick for news from home and I wanted to get to the consulate before it closed. Last I heard from home was in Rio de Janeiro, over two months ago.

I said "Doesn't this flat land remind you of Alabama?" She

laughed and said, "More like Monterey, California." I then lay flat on my back under shade of a wing and dozed off.

I awoke to see ox carts loaded with dry cow hides and the evilest bunch of Negroes I had ever seen pull up to the plane. Their clothes were in shreds. Some had rags tied about their heads and covered with battered dusty hats. All were barefooted, dirty, and the blackest I had ever seen.

If these are the picturesque cowboys of British Guiana, the writers should have their eyes and heads examined who wrote, "British Guiana."

Eight of these Negroes were passengers. Their belongings were a lot of junk. Suitcases were large, rusted, bent metal boxes, others of wood with the paint scratched and rubbed out. All had large metal padlocks on them. Still others were baskets made of roots, designed to be carried as knapsacks. Along with the baggage were tools, picks, shovels, lanterns, lumber, and what-not. The co-pilot's face seemed to have an embarrassed look because of the kind of cargo and people he flew.

An ox cart unloaded, would leave and disappear over the plains. It would return a half-hour later with more cow hides. He made about five trips. All the baggage and hides were carefully weighed on a large scale that the ox cart brought along. Only three of the passengers changed clothes for the plane ride. The plane smelled and I was glad when we took off again. I did not talk; for that matter, the Negroes were a bit too scared about flying to talk much. We flew over heavily wooded mountains. We could see the Essequibo River winding its course below, somewhere to our left were the famous Kaietuer Falls.

The Essequibo River separates, and farther on it joins into the main stream again. The flight lasted about forty-five minutes. We were coming into land at Americas' army base, Fort Atkinson.

From the air, it is another sign of American way of life. Carved out of the jungle, twenty-five miles from the coast, it is as neat and picturesque as can be. Long rows of barracks, tan colored, typical of Canal Zone, raised ten feet above the ground, green lawns, painted palm trees, fine paved roads and landing strips make up the scene.

We landed about noon. I could still make it to the consulate; instead Mr. Williams drove us in a pickup to the club house for dinner. Boy, what ham, eggs, and spuds, all for sixty cents. After dinner Williams had to go out on another flight. I had to wait for a truck going to town. I waited three hours while a heavy tropical rain fell.

56
The Land of Six People

At four o'clock, the truck was ready. I hated to ride with all those Negroes, but I had no alternative. They were so filthy and dirty. I imagine a fellow could stand it, but I'd feel sorry for women passengers. We rode along a fine paved highway. Even the black and white poles along the road were typical of American neatness. On either side of the road was thick impenetrable jungle.

The road was paved only to the limits of the base. Once we passed the sentry at the gates, the road became thin, muddy, and full of mud puddles. The dirt was a peculiar red color. Now on either side of this narrow road were the poor, dilapidated homes of the Negro population. Some were made of boards, others of reeds and thatched roofs, and still others of sticks and rusted galvanized tin. They looked so poor and ugly, and I felt sure that every roof had a bad leak.

We passed hundreds of colored schoolchildren. All of them were barefooted and cheerful.

A heavy rain came. The Negroes walked or ran with huge leaves overhead for umbrellas. Some Negroes just didn't give a hoot; they walked and got soaked. Some women walked with their wet dresses sticking to their breasts. There were many jests as we passed them. A fine spray of rain and mud swooped into the back of the canvas-roofed truck and sprayed us all a light red. It was a thirty-five mile drive to Georgetown from Atkinson Field. As we neared the city, the road was cluttered with pedestrians and others on bicycles. As I was soon to learn, the people of that city move about chiefly on bicycles. They are rented out at three dollars a week.

Nearing the city, here and there I spotted a decent house amidst the rows of ugly dilapidated houses. Outside of one nice home, I saw a white woman pushing a buggy with a white child in it and coming out of the house was a white man. They probably were English subjects, either government officials or missionaries. The Negroes were very friendly, but it was a sorry, pitiful neighborhood.

The truck stopped at the British Guiana Air Agency depot. We were approximately still two miles from town. The white passenger I flew with suggested we take a cab into town. We got into one of those small English Fords. The fare was one dollar each. We drove along the left side of the road. I found this very confusing and perplexing. British Guiana is the only country or colony in Central or South America where the people drive on the left-hand side of the road. The town seemed to be full of bicycles and tiny English Fords.

My driver dropped me off at the Hotel Victoria. The room alone cost $1.50. I felt that I was being cheated. At first the clerk said, "No rooms." When he learned I was not a soldier from Atkinson Field, he gave me the room. The best hotels in Georgetown are the Woodbine and the Towers. The rates were six to ten dollars a day, and that was too high for me.

In Georgetown there is a large and popular restaurant called "Chinatown." It is complete with a bar and a soda fountain, but the interior is not what one would call deluxe. It is very large and simply furnished in dark oak. I spent my first evening at the bar, drinking beer and dining on sandwiches. A couple of U.S. seamen tried to "rush" the waitress off her feet and asking for a date. She was pretty and well-designed. Having no luck, the seamen left. She came over and talked to me. Her name was Iris. She would wait on a customer and always return behind the counter and talk to me. She asked if I had just got in from the bush. I said "yes." She was so interested. We talked and became pretty fast friends. But they speak a strange English here. It's more of a sing-song, as some sailors put it, and one has to listen carefully to understand them. I had a pleasant evening talking to Iris. It was good to speak English. It sounded so sweet. I returned to the hotel almost broke and hoping I would have money waiting for me at the consulate's in the morning.

Next morning the waitress at the hotel brought me breakfast to my room. I barely had enough to pay for it (thirty-five cents). I then strolled up Victoria Alamedia (the main street) to the consulate's office. It was a pleasant walk in the cool morning along paved sidewalks lined with green trees, shrubs, and lawns. I was surprised to find the consulate open at such an early hour. The hours were most unusual from 7:00 to 4:00 P.M.

I had six letters, five from home and one from Mary Franca in Brazil. The best news was that $60 was waiting for me at the Bank of Canada. Dad had won a $100 prize, so I guess he sent me his prize money.

I called at the bank, picked up the money, then went to the tourist agency, got some reading material, returned to the hotel, sat in a chair, propped my feet out of a window, relaxed, drank Cokes, and read up on facts and points of interest concerning British Guiana.

British Guiana is a crown colony of Great Britain. It lies on the northern shoulder of South America. The Atlantic borders it on the north, Dutch Guiana (Surinam) on the east, Brazil on the south, and Venezuela on the west. The population is roughly 376,000 and ninety-percent of it live along the flat coastal part of the country. The majority of the population are Negroes, descendants of African slaves who had escaped into the impenetrable jungle of British Guiana. They could not be pursued, and so they came to make their home there. The others are East Indians who were imported as plantation laborers; Amerindians who the natives of British Guiana, and Portuguese, Chinese, and other Europeans. Because of these people, British Guiana has been called the "Land of Six People." All of them can be seen at the Starbroek Market in Georgetown.

There are three distinct types of country in British Guiana. There is the flat, junglelike coastal region, the sand-and-clay section in higher country, and then the mountains and plains (Savannah) of the far interior.

Her principal products are sugar cane, coffee, rice, coconut, rubber, gold, diamonds, and the world's hardest lumber called "greenheart."

Georgetown lies in the coastal belt. It is the capitol and "garden city" of British Guiana. The northeast trade winds keep the city fairly cool the year around.

The executive authority is a governor appointed by the British Crown. He is assisted by an executive consul and seven appointed and eight elected members to the legislative council and better known as the Court of Policy.

Great Britain obtained the colony after the Napoleonic War in 1815. For more than a century previous, it had been held by the Dutch.

Georgetown suffered a great disaster a few years ago, 1945 to be exact. A fire destroyed the priceless exhibits of the natural history section of the museum, the century-old Royal Agriculture and Commercial Society, the best curio shop, the Self-help Depot, the rooms of the Chamber of Commerce, and the B.G. tourist committee. A committee at present was studying to rebuild new buildings.

British Guiana has the highest waterfalls in the world. The Kukenaam is 2000 feet. The most popular is the Kaieteur, 741 feet and others are King George VII, 840 feet; and the Chamberlain, 200 feet. It is possible to reach these points by rail, ferry boat, lorry, horseback, and plane. The trip can take from one day to ten days, depending on mode of travel. The tourist agency plans trips and charters planes. The rates are very high. Jungle picnics and natural swimming holes entice the tourist.

There were five or six steamship agencies in Georgetown. I called them all on the telephone. I planned to go to Trinidad on my way home. The earliest boat leaving for that point would be in eight days. The fare was $48 first class, and $23 second class. The plane fare was $48 also, and it left every day. I tried to go cheaper, I went to the dock and talked to the captains on schooners. I was told to come "tomorrow." I believed a trip on a schooner on the high seas would be most exciting.

I spent part of the evening at the "Chinatown" restaurant talking to Iris and a Norwegian sailor. The Norwegian invited me to go visit some nightclubs. Along the main street, in the center of town, we walked up a flight of reeky wooden stairs to a huge room. There was a colored band playing, and in the center were dancing Negroes. Dancing with the Negro girls were a lot of white seamen. Along the bare walls were crude tables and chairs. We sat down and had a drink. The place disgusted me.

My Norwegian companion enjoyed it. The club was full of black Negro whores. I didn't know if any of the seamen were American or not, but they all spoke English fairly well. I did know that a number were Norwegian. It made me sick to see those drunken or half-drunken seamen hugging, kissing, and dancing with those black girls. There seemed to be no end to the cussing. Which was the better, girl or seaman, was hard to tell.

After leaving this place, I was ready to go home, but my Norwegian friend said he knew a nicer place. This nicer place was no better. We had rum and cokes again. My companion made no effort to pay, yet I was invited. He then said, "Sorry, I have no money." He was tall, thin, about forty-five and just another bum. He knew quite a few of the black girls. They put their arms about him and asked for a drink. He told them, "I have no money." He knew better than to ask me to buy them a drink. He asked me if I was enjoying myself. "Sure," I answered. I watched the disgraceful show. I wondered how many of these sailors were married or had sweethearts back home. I drank slowly, but not as slowly as my companion. I finished and said, "I'm shoving off, mate," and I do believe he was glad I left.

I walked the dark street back to the hotel. I passed a drunken seaman fighting with a colored girl. She was trying to run away, but he had other ideas. He wanted to spend the night with her or a "short time." I walked on. Then a car with several colored girls and fellows stopped beside me. "Do you care to go for a ride with us?" they asked. "No thanks," I said. I then wondered what kind of ride it would be. To be cheated at some joint or robbed or maybe pass a pleasant evening. All the people seem to be very friendly and courteous. I continued on and turned gingerly into bed.

I was up at seven. The room was nice and cool. The mosquitos had given me a bad time during the night. I went to the docks and met a Captain Clark. He was a small, pleasant, colored fellow. He said he would take me to Trinidad for $15 on Friday (two days later). He also said I would have to have at least $100 before the immigration officials would permit me to land at Trinidad. He would not take me otherwise. I advised him I would cable home for more money and have them send it to the bank in Trinidad. The agreement was settled after I showed him my receipt from the telegraph office.

I had a surprise visit from the immigration officer at the hotel. He was a big, heavy-set British officer in khaki uniform and a chest full of campaign ribbons. He wore tropical shorts, knee-length socks, and a full-length blouse. This unexpected visit made me slightly uneasy. He asked me for my documents. He checked them and asked me to report at the office at one o'clock.

At one o'clock, I presented myself at the office. Courteous officers in knee-length shorts directed me to the chief of immigration. He asked me why I didn't present myself sooner. I said that I didn't think there was need to hurry. He asked if Major Williams had advised me to present myself, and I said, "No, Major Williams said nothing about immigration." Then he wanted to know how in hell I got into the country. "Through the back door," I explained. This wasn't the first time I had mystified the immigration officials. Peru, Brazil, Costa Rica, and Guatemala were others. The officer was a serious chap. He was like an F.B.I. agent, and I felt like a criminal suspect. He became interested and pleasant. He got up from behind his desk, walked over to a huge map on the wall to see how I came in. Then he asked why I came in that way and the purpose.

"Adventure," I said, and I hoped it would not sound silly to him. It seemed to satisfy him. He had received a cable from Mr. Young at Lethem, telling him I was coming in by plane. He then placed a transient visa into my passport.

I then left and walked about town. It seemed so strange; the town seemed to move on bicycles and they kept to the left side of the road. Every time I crossed the street, I got confused by the flow of traffic. I spent the evening indoors studying a map. Then, tired, I fell asleep in my clothes, awoke sometime later, undressed, put out the light, and turned in under a mosquito netting.

I spent the following day doing some laundry to save on expenses, sent my boots out to be fixed, and took some pictures. I went through Stabroek Market. It seemed very different from Spanish markets. Negroes and Indians squatted on the cement floor, selling oranges, bananas, and other tropical fruits. In other sections everything from clothing to household furniture was being sold. Mingling in the crowd were the six people of the colony, but strangely enough, everyone seemed to speak English.

I stopped off at Chinatown after supper for ice cream. There they had honest-to-goodness Stateside ice cream. Well, it tasted the same anyway.

Iris, the light-complexioned waitress, asked me why I hadn't been around last night.

"Busy," I answered.

"I missed you," she said.

"Honest." I laughed.

This place reminded me of a bar in Panama where I spent many of my leisure hours. I would sit on a stool at the end of the bar and lean on the wall. I did likewise here, but Iris asked me to sit in the middle because my place was open to the passing public, and she didn't want her friend to see her talking so earnestly to me. She looked Spanish, was very pretty, and talked intelligently. At quitting time I was going to walk her home, but when I saw a coal-black girl friend waiting to go along, I changed my mind. I said I would see her next day and see the sights on bicycles.

I couldn't sleep well all night. At six-thirty I was awakened by Captain Clark. He told me the schooner would be leaving at three in the afternoon. He left and I went back to sleep. The waitress awoke me at eight for breakfast. I felt so sleepy. I had a date at nine with Iris. I didn't feel like going. I couldn't make up my mind if she looked Spanish or a Negress. Still I wanted to pass the day as enjoyably as I could without looking conspicuous.

At nine-twenty, I rented an English bicycle. A two-dollar deposit was required and cost twelve cents an hour to ride it. The law prohibits riding on the sidewalk. Riding long the left side of the road as traffic regulations require, confused me, especially at five corner intersections. I had to ride slowly and carefully till I got used to it.

I arrived at the Botanical Gardens at nine-thirty. I was a half-hour late for my date. I waited in the shade of a large tree at the main gate. Iris never came. I decided to ride within the gardens alone. The gardens are actually a huge park. There are wide red roads, and many species of palm trees, flowers, birds, numerous lagoons filled with lovely lotus and gigantic Victoria Regina lilies and pleasant lawns for tired cyclists.

The main road goes for a mile or so. On either side of it are lagoons covered with lilies, and beyond are dense palm trees. Leading off the main road are branches that go to the sugar, rice, and cattle experimental farms. These are one of the principal industries of Georgetown. I rode along these various trails and caused many strange birds to take wing. I had hopes of running into my date, but nowhere was she to be found. After two hours I returned to the main gate. Nearby is a tiny lake. Here are the much talked about sea cows called manatees. They are big, black, and uncomely, but very gentle. To bring these aquatic mammals to surface, one has to whistle. They were the slowest, laziest creatures that I ever saw. I had expected to see ferocious sea lions.

A Negro or two tore up grass, whistled, and handed the grass to the manatees. They slowly came to the surface, lazily opened their big mouths, and took a bite of the grass. What big teeth they had! Wow!

While the Negro or two fed the manatees in hopes of getting a tip, a few British tourists and officers, dressed in white tropical shorts, took pictures. It was such a lazy scene in contrast to a hot, sultry day. It made life seem slow, dull, and not worth living.

Once outside the park, I rode the bike first up, then down the macadam road, taking in the general outlook of the town. Along the road trooped many asses and carts; Negroes walked, some carried bundles atop their heads. There were many neat rows of white barrack houses. They looked somewhat similar to the Canal Zone quarter houses. I wondered what class of people occupied these neat, trim houses. They could not all belong to white people because the percentage of white people in Georgetown is very low. Then I rode past many shabby, dilapidated homes, but none were as bad as the ones along the road to Atkinson Field. I rode on past an old wooden schoolhouse. There were dozens of black children playing ring-around-the-rosy in front of it. I turned around and headed toward the bike shop. There are hundreds of cyclists all about and I enter the stream.

Everywhere I go it's "Hello, Joe, Hello, Joe," and nothing more. The hospitality of the people overwhelmed me. Very, very few of the negroes annoy or try to sell me something.

I turn in my bike and stop in at "Chinatown" for a Coke and who do I run into but Iris. She is wearing a bright red dress and one of those great big straw hats, customary to the Negro women. At the sight of that I was glad I was late for the date. She bawled me out. She had waited, become restless, and went into the gardens alone. It seemed strange that we did not cross one another's path. We talked awhile, then she said, "You're leaving today, aren't you?" She knew I was because I wore my traveling togs.

I went to the hotel, had dinner, packed my pack, and asked for my bill. The manager's son, a little smart brat said I owed 11, then 12, then 13 dollars. I knew he knew no better, but he tried to act as if he did. I told him to call his father and get the bill correct. While I waited a white man came over to me. He said, "I'm not drunk." But he sure looked stinko to me. He looked decent, so I listened. He had two stones with a grain or two of gold in them. He asked me if I were a mining engineer. I said, "No, I'm not." He then said he would sell the stones to me, each for $25.

I laughed and said, "Man, you don't have $5 of gold in both of them." I had seen quartz gold before and knew the price of it. My friend seemed to think I was a wise guy. I left him and went to the bar for a drink. I was making some notes when my friend came, stood beside me, then slowly pushing, elbowing, and whispering to me. I told him I was busy and to leave me alone. I then walked off to another part of the bar. He followed me and from behind, he put his arm around my shoulder. Now this had gone far enough, and I shoved it off. He then grabbed my arm and said, "What's the matter with you?"

"Nothing," I said. "Do I bother you?" He made no answer, but he looked me in the eye. "Then don't bother me," I said. Any further offense and I would have hit him. He may be a white, but he sure as hell acted like a native and I wasn't going to be laughed at or pushed around, for there were a number of fellows in the room watching us.

Someone shouted, "Take him away," and immediately three

colored fellows dragged him off. I then had another Coke and ignored him, as he glared at me from the other end of the bar.

The manager came and charged me $11.75. He was an educated man. He was very polite and courteous. I liked him from the start. My stay had been pleasant till his young brat and the drunk spoiled it. Now I left in silence, no word spoken, only a slight nod of farewell from each of us.

I took my pack and headed for the schooner. I walked through several crowded streets. Here and there a call rang out, "Hello, Joe. What are you, a Globe Trotter?" I didn't like these words much, but it was true. Evidently Globe Trotters are nothing new to this town, one of the crossroads of the world. I went on board the schooner over a load of oil drums. There were a dozen Negro crewmen to greet me.

Again I had company. Two British immigration officials came after me. They wanted to inspect my pack. I opened it, but they didn't go through it. They then stamped my passport again (leaving). They were friendly, shook my hand, and wished me a good trip. I felt I had put them to a lot of trouble. It was a long walk from the immigration office to the docks.

57

Aboard a West Indies Schooner

I was surprised to be shown to a bunk. I didn't know these schooners had any. I had expected to sleep on deck. There were only two bunks. The captain had the upper, and I had the lower one. The mattress was good, and clean sheets had been laid out. I was the only passenger and only white man on board. There were nine crew members. All of them were Negroes or dark Latins. They came from the island of Barbados. The schooner was from Barbados also.

After four days in Georgetown, I was glad when we started moving. We pulled away from the docks at three-fifteen. I was surprised to hear the putt-putt-putt of an engine. It was coming from within the schooner. Well, what do you know about that? Our ship had not only great, glistening sails for propulsion, but an engine also.

As the trip turned out, for three whole days, we were almost constantly dependent upon the engine for propulsion. We had calm weather and little breezes. The fellows were as nice and courteous as could be. After three days aboard the schooner, I could only form one opinion. They were poor fellows, but very kind.

In the evenings we had full, tropical moons. There is no need telling what runs through a man's head on these quiet nights with the great white sails reaching high into the sky, and the schooner dipping gracefully up and down, then over and under from side to side. There is a creaking of timber and masts, but our *Elene* is a sturdy ship and quietly plows onward. It is pleasant to sit on the gunwales or on a coil of rope. The cool breeze is very soothing. The moon casts a huge silver streak on the waters.

Once in a while, the silence is broken as our thoughts go. Everyone wishes they had a girlfriend to sail with them. All the fellows claim the best sailors in the West Indians come from the island of Barbados, their home. They stay away from home for six months. They make the run from Georgetown to Trinidad. They carry oil and gasoline to lonely outposts along the 1,754-square- mile island.

Only Captain Clark is married. He has six children, and it's on nights like this that he misses them most. The rest of the fellows are unmarried. Their ambition as one, then another, and then another told me, whenever we were alone, was to ship out on American ships.

I looked at some of these barefooted, ragged, husky fellows, and I can see what a big improvement that would make in their lives. Only one of these fellows had been to the States. He was the captain's son. He was a short, stocky, heavy-set lad. He was twenty-one-years old. He was much darker complexioned than his dad, but very polite also. He had been to New York, New Orleans, and Florida. He had spent about eight months on American ships and hoped to get on U.S. ships again some day.

It seemed odd as they steered the hundred and twenty foot schooner from the stern. There was no roof to offer protection from the wind, rain, or sun for the man at the wheel. The men rotated at two-hour shifts.

Breakfast came at six o'clock. We had only sweet tea and cookies. Dinner came at ten o'clock. We had corn meal smothered with fried fish. It was very oily and salty. The fish was caught daily from the sea. Then we had rice, sweet tea, and crackers.

The first two of these meals I enjoyed; the third became trying, the fourth became forceful, and the fifth and last meal I refused. The meals were the same every day. My system could not stand all that oil and salt. I only looked forward to tea and crackers. To me it seemed like my shipmates could eat it every day and enjoy it.

I had gotten a terrible headache, and it lasted the entire trip. I believe it was from the strong sun and the heat in the cabin. The 100-horsepower engine was right next to our bunks. I had spent most of the hours in my bunk, sleeping, tossing, sweating. I was amazed that I was not seasick, although the schooner pitched and wallowed continuously. My only regret was that I traveled alone. Never do I hope to undertake such a long journey alone again. My company is okay, but I feel bored when I have to talk about myself. Strangely enough we talked very little on the entire trip.

On Sunday morning, the third day out, we were passing the island of Tobago. It was off the starboard bow. It was a huge mass of green mountains protruding out of the sea. Straight ahead, a little off the port bow was a huge black shadow rising over the horizon. The man at the wheel said, "That is Trinidad, yonder. We should reach it by midnight." The water is supposed to be full of porpoises and barracudas. I hadn't seen any, although some of the sailors said they had.

We did not reach Trinidad till next day. We dropped anchor at seven-thirty. I came out of the cabin into the bright, warm sunlight. I was amazed to find a whole fleet of schooners, tankers, freighters, ferryboats, and speed boats all about and as far as the eye could see. There were flags from many nations. Venezuela, Canada, Netherlands, America, Norway, Greece, etc. The war was over, but this convoy of vessels made me believe it was still on. There were hundreds of schooners, similar to the *Elene,* anchored out and sails pulled down. Mr. Clark said they were waiting for cargo. How long would they wait? "Many weeks sometimes," said Mr. Clark.

Soon as we dropped anchor and had breakfast, I expected Captain Clark and I would go ashore. He was dressed in his best suit, but then he gave orders to drop, fasten, and corner the sails and spars. This took half an hour. Then he gave orders to spread a huge canvas as a roof over the deck. Then he strung up a hammock under the tarpaulin, lay in it and made himself comfortable. Now what were we waiting for? Two hours I waited. Two rowboats came alongside, and I was going to go ashore; but Captain Clark hollered, "Don't come alongside here, man," and they rowed away. I then asked, "What are we waiting for? I'm anxious to go ashore."

"We have to wait for a launch," the captain said. Ten minutes later a launch came toward us. I called his attention to it. Then he said, "We will go in the rowboat."

Into the rowboat went the whole lot of us. Two Negroes

rowed to an immigration control station in the middle of the stream. There we got out of the boat and climbed the ladder to the station house. A half hour later, the immigration officials came in a powerful police boat. They checked my passport and asked how much money I had. "Thirty dollars," I said, "but I have money in the bank." I had put a phone call to shore to the Bank of Canada and they assured me they had something for me. My telegram was answered by my folks, and I was more than grateful to them. Mr. Clark breathed a sigh of relief.

All the ship's crew were checked on a list by the officials, then we rowed back to the schooner for my pack, then we rowed to shore. A guard checked my passport, then we went through customs inspection. The officials only asked what I had in my pack. They gave me a huge questionnaire to fill out, then a kindly official filled it out in a hurry as I answered his questions. After this I was able to pass into the streets of Port of Spain, Trinidad. Mr. Clark then informed me the official expected a tip for his services. This surprised me. I felt like a piker. Since when has it been customary to tip customs officials?

58

On the Isle of Trinidad

Mr. Clark and I walked several blocks. They were not very nice. They were crowded with Negroes and East Indians in undershorts and torn clothes. Mr. Clark directed me to a Hotel Miranda. It was in the center of town along the main street. It looked like a flop house, but it was the best I could find and afford. The manager said he had no rooms, but after a good word from Mr. Clark, he directed me along a rickety porch, surrounding a foul patio to several rooms marked "Reserved." My spirit sank at the sight of it, but I decided it would have to do for a night or two. It cost $2.50 a day. I had always pictured Trinidad as a lovely place, but already I didn't like it and was anxious to leave it behind.

I went about inquiring about boats going north to Puerto Rico. There weren't any. The next boat would leave in two or three weeks if there was cargo. It cost $100 to fly there. I then decided to return to Venezuela and visit my friends. I was not very far from La Guaira. There was a boat leaving at night, an American Grace Line. I could not make it because I didn't have a visa for Venezuela as yet. It was late afternoon. The next boat would go a week later. I decided I would fly to save on expense.

Gathering information here and there, I occasionally dropped into a restaurant for a Coke to cool off. It was very warm in Trinidad. I could not drink in peace. Beggars and bums annoyed me for an offering. Everywhere I went, I was annoyed. I could only brush by and ignore them. Even returning to the hotel, they followed me up a few steps or tried to block my way, either begging or trying to sell me something.

A half-dozen Spanish-speaking Venezuelans stayed at this same hotel. We fell into conversation about Venezuela. One pretty Venezuelan girl dined with me at the same table. She was very sociable.

After dinner I sat on the *portico* (porch) and looked down on the busy street. Several girls stood beside me. They were in their late thirties. We then sat at a table and drank Cokes. A few more girls came and joined us. I listened to their conversation. Always you could hear them say, "Yes, man; no man; yes, man." They used "Man" incessantly, as the people in Georgetown do. Their language was bawdy. They weren't such nice girls as they pretended to be. They certainly lived a rough life. Their skirts came far above the knees, and to me they were common whores. They were part white and part Negro.

A white seaman came on the porch. He sat down beside us. He was about forty-five, slim, and looked British. He talked some, then ordered whiskey and Cokes. I refused his offer, but he insisted on buying me a drink. When it came, I hesitated, then drank it. I hardly paid any attention to his prattle. He raved about himself. "Don't tell me about any place; I've been in every port; I've been all over the world." He really thought he was somebody. I felt like telling him that all he knew about the world was the waterfront whorehouses and bars; beyond that, nothing. But I kept my silence; why talk to a fool? None of us thought he was wonderful. I looked out into the night and the street below. My thoughts drifted elsewhere.

The waiter asked for the money for the drinks. The seaman (a Trinidadian, I believe) looked at me to pay, but he knew better than to ask. My quiet look told him, "You ordered, you pay." He then told the waiter he had no money. An argument ensued and the seaman promised to pay next day.

Sometime later I took a walk along the main street. I stopped here and there to look at window displays. I was annoyed again by bums and Negro girls who put their arms around my waist and said, "Let's go to sleep, man, three dollars. What do you say, man?" I smiled and said, "Sorry, baby. I can't afford it." One reason was as good as another.

Lots of these girls had boyfriends called "sackers." The girls lure a man who has some money through dark alleys or to secluded houses. Then the "sackers" pounce on the victim, attacking and robbing him. Captain Clark and his crew told me many stories about the viciousness of these sackers. I did not stay on the street long nor does any decent, respectable person roam the streets after ten o'clock. The manager of the hotel pointed out to me that to go beyond several lighted street blocks, one is beyond police protection and on his own.

Certainly Georgetown, British Guiana, is very different in contrast to its nearby neighbor, Trinidad.

The first thing I did on my second day in Trinidad was to go to the office of Linea Aeropostal Venezalano to get information on plane rates and time of departure for La Guaira, Venezuela. Then I had to get a visa from the Venezuelan consulate. I was lucky. The Linea Aeropostal had a car drive me to the consulate. It was a long drive. We came to Queens Park. It was a beautiful neighborhood. In this neighborhood lived the well-to-do and prominent government officials. There was a large green field. It was the park. It reminded me of a baseball park. Street car tracks looped around it.

At the consulate, a plump lady in her late thirties received all applicants. She was a nasty, mistrusting woman. She seemed to look upon all present as criminals. She knew her work, the laws and regulations pertaining to visas, very well. She treated everyone with suspicion. She wanted to know why I wanted to return to Venezuela. "To visit my friends," I answered. She wanted to give me a transient visa good for only one or two days. "I hope to stay at least a week," I said. She refused to give me a tourist visa. She feared I might try to go to work again. Finally, she said they could give me a business visa.

She then took my passport, pictures, health certificate, and police record. While I waited, fellows from Cuba and Trinidadian Negroes got a bad time. Their requests for visas were refused. Venezuela, I am told, is trying to keep the country clean of Negroes. I was called into another office and fingerprinted. Few Latin countries require this system of identification. I then received my passport. The lady had said she could only give me a "business" visa, but they gave me "transient" visa good for thirty days. I was thankful, nevertheless.

I went to the park and waited for the open-air trolley car to come. A policemen came by. He was dressed in a clean, white blouse with a stiff, white collar that buttoned at the neck. He wore a spotless white "Jungle Jim" hat and navy blue trousers. He looked very trim and smart. Trinidad and British Guiana had the best dressed policemen of all Latin America. Ohter policemen wear dark blue shorts and short-sleeve shirts, garrison caps, and knee-length socks.

This policeman I chatted with spoke a soft English with a Trinidadian accent. I wondered how he managed to keep his white blouse and hat so clean. His face and neck were as black as coal. It's only true, I guess, that the Negroes are much cleaner than Indians.

We were near the Queens Hotel, the best in Trinidad, beautiful and modern. This young policeman told me that at ten o'clock at night it wasn't safe for the tenants to walk out of it because of the whores and sackers who walked in the neighborhood and prey on them.

The trolley came. It was ancient but cool. It whisked me back to the heart of town. We became stalled by a traffic jam. An old, ragged beggar was standing by a huge store window. He let the world know what he was thinking. A tall policeman came by, and the beggar let him know what his complaints were. The policeman walked on, and the beggar's rantings continued unabated. The jam lasted fifteen minutes. It was hot, congested, and irritating. Finally we moved on, and I made my way to Linea Aeropostal and purchased my ticket.

The fare was 43 U.S. dollars. I gave the clerk my last 42 U.S. dollar notes and asked her to take the rest in British Guiana dollars. She refused and I had to give her 10 dollars in U.S. Then she gave me change, not in U.S. dollars, but in British Guiana currency. In this way she made for herself a dollar or so on the rate of exchange. I decided not to complain; she probably needed the dollar more than I did.

Nothing more to do but return to the hotel, wash my shirts and socks, have them pressed and my suit. Then shine my boots and pack my pack for a presentable meeting with my friends in Venezuela next day. Thus I spent the evening in my shabby room. The management had a key for special guests to the clean toilets. I was one of them.

The great day had come, the one when I would surprise my friends in Venezuela. I talked with the manager. He was a pleasant fellow, big, husky, and almost white. He gave me letters, cards, and checks to advertise his hotel. As nice as he was, I could hardly recommend the place for pleasant lodgings.

I leaned over the porch railing and watched a beggar from India slowly walk to the small park, sit in the grass, cross his legs, then take some food out of a cloth sack, and a bright, shiny, brass kettle. Then he said his prayers, bowing back and forth. He was dressed in a mere, ragged, dirty sheet. He looked very old and tired. It seemed strange to see these fellows from across the sea bringing their strange dress and customs. About one-third of the people in Trinidad are East Indians, and they account for the many Hindu temples seen on the island.

A tenant from the hotel leaned beside me. He made a remark or two about the Hindu. He seemed respectable, then the next minute, he asked if I could spare a shilling. "Sorry," I said. *Just another moocher,* I thought.

At noon the car came for me. There were six of us in the car. It cost each of us one dollar to ride to the airport. It was worth it. It was a long drive. The road was good, paved in asphalt. (Trinidad is one of the world's greatest producers of asphalt. It supplies the U.S. with three-fourths of what we use.) The countryside was green and spotted, with many palm trees. I can't say anything derogatory about the scenery. It's very nice. A few ox carts and covered straw wagons went by.

At the airport the plane was late. The terminal was new and modern. Painters were busy painting the waiting room. Passengers had to walk carefully. I had lunch and Cokes at the modern restaurant. There I met an American lady. Her husband, she said, was working in Venezuela, but she lived in Port of Spain, Trinidad. I asked her how she liked it. She said she got used to it, and going to the movies that were full of colored people. I did not envy her, for Trinidad was the place I liked the least of all my Western hemisphere travels.

Trinidad, incidentally, was discovered by Columbus on his

third voyage in 1498. It was held by Spain until 1797. Then it was captured by the British and formally ceded to Great Britain in 1802, by the Treaty of Amiens. Trinidad receives its name from its three high hills emblematic of the Trinity. Trinidad has the same form of government as British Guiana.

59
Back to Venezuela

The plane came over two hours late. It was a twin-engine DC-3. Immigration checked and stamped our passports. They hardly checked my pack. Then we boarded the plane. There were about eight passengers. I had a young, white Trinidadian fellow for company. He had had several drinks too many at the airport. He became sick. The stewardess gave him a large paper container for the purpose. His stomach did flip flops.

We were high in the sky. I was thrilled and excited about returning to Venezuela. It would be swell to meet friends I know very well. We flew over the deep blue waters of the Gulf of Paria, then over dense jungles. Far below was the San Juan River. It seemed to cut a wide, brown trail through the jungles. Farther on we passed over flat, barren waste lands that had no signs of life at all. Then we were flying over the Caribbean Sea. Far below were a number of barren, desert islands. There was no vegetation or life of any kind. It would be a hell of a spot for a forced landing. Some of the islands were long, sandy strips; the others were odd, circular shapes. We made three ten-minute stops at oil camps or little cities. My companion got off at one of the oil camps. He hoped to get a job.

For the last half hour, I was very impatient as I watched the green mountain shore for glimpses of smoke that would mean La Guaira or Maiquetía was just ahead. The three-hour flight seemed endless to me.

Soon I saw what I was looking for. Glimpses of smoke told me we were nearing La Guaira; then the air strip came into view at Maiquetía. We circled around a lone sentinel of a mountain on the brink of the sea, made a left bank, and came in to land in the valley between the odd-shaped lone sentinel and the rain-washed mountainsides on the opposite side. We came in rapidly, and swift glances told me vast improvements and construction were going on. Hangars were being built and landing strips extended. The plane made a nice landing; at the end of the runway it turned about, then followed another runway, and came to a stop in front of the terminal.

Upon disembarking, I heard a customs official paging me. I was most surprised. When I said, "Yes," the official said, "Ten Bolívars, please, 10 Bolívars." "What for?" I asked. "Entrance fee," he said. I had exactly ten Bolívars. I had exchanged some currency at Trinidad. The official was considerate and said, "Pay sometime later if you like." I preferred to pay on the spot. Ten bolívars was equivalent to three U.S. dollars. It was nearly quitting time for them, and so they didn't even bother to check my gear, but passed me through "okay."

First thing I did was head for Taca where I used to work. It was a five-minute walk. I noticed the expansion of the field, the building materials, more planes and more personnel. The first fellow I met was Flores, my old friend from Quatemala. Boy, was he surprised to see me. We embraced in Latin custom and I was really excited. Then I met Barrios from Nicaragua and Guiterrez from Peru. How happy they were to see me. Then George Piegon, the Latin from Manhattan; when he saw me, he yelled, "Joe-ooooo." He came forward with a big happy smile on his face and said, "Goddammit, you done it." We shook hands; he seemed to have lost weight. Then Jimmy Frew, my former boss, came. He smiled and we shook hands. "How was the trip, Joe? You look good." Then Bearnie, the Polish paratrooper, said, "You son of a basket, Joe," in broken English. He was pleased and happy to see me. Then there was Tinto, the Venezuelan Negro, Moreno; Rodriguez; Layman, the American; the Santa Maria brothers from Costa Rica. With everyone it was handshaking, embracing, and back-slapping. I was happy to see them, and it pleased me to find their feelings mutual.

Then Gonzales, the machinist, came and Edward, the time keeper, and many others. Many of my friends were missing, but I learned they are on another shift or had gone to work for other companies up and down the field, with Avensa, PAA, Creole, or

Linea Aeropostal. Jimmy Frew introduced me to the new foremen.

Some asked what country I liked best? How much my trip cost? How long had it been? Would I go to work again here? You haven't lost weight! Hell, yes, I did!

I'm sure the new employees wondered, *Who is this lad who receives such a mighty reception and knows everybody?*

It was near quitting time. Jimmie the *Jefe* (boss) told me to go to the terminal, get my pack, and wait for the Taca bus as it came by. I did that and when I boarded the bus, a great shout went up. It was "Nanko, Nanko" all the way to Macuto for a good six or seven miles. They asked so many questions that I hardly noticed the improvements along the way. The long ride that used to wear me out went by like two minutes.

I did not know where to go. I was invited to stay at various pensions with my friends, but I decided to go where I used to stay, at the good old "Hencoop House." I came to the house, and knocked on the door. A new waitress answered. I asked her if "Stones still lived here." "Yes," she answered, "upstairs." I went up the stairs and ran into Rothel Stone, the big husky son of Mrs. Stone. He let out a cry, "Joe, Jesus Christ; hey, Mom, Joe's back." Mrs. Stone came out of her room and hugged me. She was just as glad and enthusiastic to see me as I was to see her.

When did I come back? How did I feel? How was the trip and hundreds of other questions. She then introduced me to several new tenants. There were two pretty girls, one from the U.S. and the other from Costa Rica. They said they had heard a lot about me. Buck was working late, and Mr. Wilder had returned to the States. David Graham had started on his tour of South America by plane and bus. He had gotten himself engaged to the Costa Rican girl at the Hencoop House. She was the only one he wrote to. He was last heard from in Chile. I had supper with them and I was last finishing because I was busy answering their questions.

After supper I went to the Plaza. I met Mack, my dear Portuguese friend, and Tony. Mack and I embraced in Latin style and made fun of it. We were very glad to see each other. Mack is one of my closest friends. He and Tony got a big kick out of the few Portuguese words I had picked up in Brazil. Mack had moved out of the Hencoop House since the landlady had raised the rent to 15 Bolívars a day ($4.50). I spent a very enjoyable evening with my various friends on the plaza. I also had my share of Cuba libras (rum and Coke).

I spent a pleasant, memorable week at the Hencoop House in Macuto. Mrs. Stone one morning told me about an incident that had occurred on the day I left on my jaunt of South America. I had given Mr. Wilder that day, money to pay the landlady when she returned from Caracas. Mr. Wilder forgot and went to work. The Venezuelan landlady returned, found I had gone, became excited, and started to call the police. There was some delay, and Mrs. Stone, Buck, and David worried that I'd be picked up by the police. They did not know that I had given Mr. Wilder money to pay my debt. Mr. Wilder returned from work, heard my name being mentioned, and said, "Holy Hell, I forgot; Joe gave me the money to pay you." Mrs. Stone said they all breathed a sigh of relief, and then there was peace and quiet again. The landlady had bawled out the cook about why she didn't collect from me, but I had felt I could trust Mr. Wilder rather than a low-class, underpaid cook.

The landlady and her husband were very nice and courteous. I never would have suspected their misunderstanding of me. They asked how long I planned on staying. A few days or a week, I advised them. "Supper is free tonight," they told me. "Thanks," I said.

I rode the Taca bus to the airport to see some of my other friends. I saw Benny Zayas. He was working for Creole. He was sitting down on the job as usual and working on a starter. When he saw me he shouted, "Joe oooo, God damn you, Joe; when did you get back?" He then went on to tell his buddy, "This crazy bastard works for 250 bucks a month, then he goes hitchhiking all over South America." It was his way of giving me credit, but I made a lot better than 250 bucks a month. I said, "So long, see you later, Benny," and went over to Linea Aeropostal.

I then saw Alfado of Peru. He was underneath the belly of a DC-3, inspecting the landing flaps. When he saw me, the first words he said and probably the first English words he had learned were, "Jesus Christ, Goddammit; how are you?" He was pretty excited about seeing me. We chatted a while, then I started for the terminal. I saw Herman going up a flight of stairs. He saw me at the same time. He came back down and towards me. He had a broad smile on his face from ear to ear. I didn't know what to expect. I beat the hell out of him the last time we met and he had warned me. "You're pretty proud of yourself, aren't you? But we'll meet again some day."

Now he advanced toward me. I stopped. He then said, "Boy, am I glad to see you. Jesus Christ, when did you get in? You're looking good!" He extended his hand so I shook hands with him. I noticed he lost a lot of weight, and he had a bad scar over his head. He had been in a jeep accident and had his head fractured, several ribs busted, and a broken leg. He was in good shape again.

"You lost a lot of weight," I said.

"Yes," he agreed. "Where are you going now?"

"To get a Coke at the terminal," I said.

"I'll join you in about ten minutes," he said.

When he did, he hardly had enough to pay for his own coffee. He showed me his empty wallet and said he was in debt again. He no longer lived in Macuto, but in Caracas, thirty-five miles away. No doubt the society gossip of Macuto drove him away. I asked if he still had any hard feelings about the fight.

"No," he said, "it was all my fault." So it seems Herman and I became friends again.

Now everyone tells me it is easy to hitchhike a ride in a plane back to the States. There are cargo planes that come from Miami, Florida. They dump their cargo at Maiquetía and return empty. I could probably catch a ride with them. But that means waiting around the terminal for days. The cargo planes have no definite schedule. It cost me six to seven dollars a day to lay around. Transocean Air Lines and Caribbean Air Lines come in almost every day. They bring in immigrants from Europe and fly back to the states empty.

I had a long chat with one of Transocean agents. He was afraid of the Venezuelan contract laws and the captains of the big planes could not take me. Even Ramrey agents tried to get a

591

ride for me but luck was against me. My hopes of catching a free plane ride sank.

Now a lot of Americans and Latins believe that if an American is destitute the American Consul will give him money and put him on a ship going to the states. I wish to inform these people how wrong they are. For devilment and a desire to learn the real truth, I went to the American consul in La Guaira. We had known each other for a long time.

I asked him if he could put me on an American ship as a workaway. I had my American passport and everything except seamen's papers. He said, "I can't help you, Nanko; it's against the Union Laws. If the captain of ship wants to take you, it's okay."

The American ship *Santa Theresa* was in port. I went on board and met the captain of the ship. He was nice and listened longer than most captains would. Captains of ships are an impatient, despicable lot. They look down upon a man who is on the beach as dirt and scum. He also said, "No, the union law forbids workaways and even forbids the captain to take a person as a guest." He suggested I try a passenger ship or try to reach Panama and try to get a ship from there.

There were no passenger ships in port, and it was foolish to go to Panama. I had worked in Panama for four months and had registered with the captain of the port as ready to ship out any time. In Panama they advised me that they had many fellows in quarantine who held seamen's papers. They would be the first ones to be called when a ship needed a man. When they were gone, I'd be called. But evidently someone was always in quarantine waiting for a ship. I was never called. I would enjoy going to Panama to visit my friends, but to wait for a ship was like waiting for kingdom come. I had money enough to reach there, but not enough to get to the States.

I thanked the skipper for his time, went below, and met some officers. They offered sympathies. On the main deck, I met some "AB" (able-bodied seamen). I knew these fellows because this ship comes to Venezuela every fifteen days or so from New York. I had a wonderful dinner on board, including ice cream and pie. The ABs were curious about the captain's reply. I gave them his answer, "No."

They could not understand it; here was an American, practically destitute and the American consul and the captain of an American ship refuse to take or send him home. They said there was only one thing left to do in my predicament and that was to stowaway.

Two of the fellows were willing to hide me at the risk of themselves getting caught and losing their seamen's papers for aiding a stowaway. For every stowaway a ship brings into the States, the company is fined $20,000.

After a few days at sea, I'd have to present myself to the captain. Then upon landing I'd be put into quarantine for a week or so while the F.B.I. and police checked my passport with my parents, causing them endless worry and embarrassment. I could have stowed away. It was easy enough and I had the nerve, but I could not stand having my family humiliated by the police and neighbors. My folks always said, "If ever you are desperate and need money, we'll send you money. That's what parents are for."

Still all Latins believe if an American is broke, the American consul will give him money. For once I decided to try it to see what happened. I called up the consul. I told him I could not get a plane or a ship home, and asked if he could kindly loan me one hundred dollars till I got home. I smiled yet as I heard his funny voice come over the phone. "I ain't got no money to lend, Nanko." Then he continued, "Lots of Americans think consuls give money away."

He knew me better and remembered how I came in every week for my mail and where I worked. He suggested I go to the American Aid Society in Caracas. They would then consider my case. If I was deserving, they would help me out financially or try to get me a job. If I wasn't deserving, I was out of luck, and happen what may, Americans who leave the States are not supposed to become destitute. I thanked the consul, but I had no intention of going to Caracas or getting a job. My Dutch friend at Hencoop House loaned me one hundred dollars for plane fare.

I had called Aura Romero up three times. She was my dear old girl friend in Caracas. Her mom had preferred a rich Venezuelan to a poor me (American). Now she told me she had broken her engagement to marry him. She asked if I was coming over to see her. I could only say "maybe." I was low on funds, and I hated the long torturous ride to Caracas. At the end of a week, I had to call apologies because I hadn't gone to see her. She was a lovely girl, and I shall always regret I failed to see her.

After visiting Yanelli, the photographer, Chez Earnest, the owner of a night club, Conners, Hogg, Hernandez, Chulito, and Garcia, I visited Mrs. Shubert, the wife of tall, handsome Franc Shubert. I had met her in Lima, Peru. Now she was surprised to see me again. She was mixing some dough when I called at her home, but still we embraced in affectionate Latin style. We had a long chat and I called again for a special dinner. Her husband was away in Cuidad Bolívar. Someone told me he was looking for me, meaning that he did not like my dating her while in Lima. But this was merely a joke because he himself had given me her address. I spent the evening with her over highballs, chatting and dancing. It amazed me to learn that she knew Mr. Brown in Manaus, deep in the heart of Brazil. She and Franc had lived in Manaus for over a year. Strange as it seems, South America is a big country, but people know one another though thousands of miles separate them.

Mrs. Shubert had her son in Venezuela. I only regretted that I did not see Franc.

60
Fly Away Home

Came the day of my departure, the 29th of September. I was going to fly P.A.A. to Miami, due to leave at twelve o'clock noon. The consul just happened to be using the P.A.A. phone as I came to the desk to purchase my ticket. He said hello and grinned as I purchased my ticket.

I lounged about the waiting room then went to the second floor restaurant. I sat at a counter, sipping a Coke and talking to a young American destined to spend a long time in Venezuela. There were a number of well-dressed air travelers seated at tables or watching the planes come in or take off from a grand stand balcony.

George Piegon came up in his work clothes to keep me company. He was grinning broadly, "I knew I'd find you here, you bastard." He was excited about me going home. He wished he was going also. The loudspeaker went on, announcing my plane. George and I went down to the plane. It was a great big silver four engine plane, a DC4.

It was twelve o'clock. It was quitting time for the Taca boys. Racing down the field I saw a dozen of my Latin buddies coming toward me to say farewell. It was very kind and considerate of them. I embraced with all of them and fat Barrios was perspiring so. *Vaya bien* (good journey), *felicedades* (happiness), *escribe pronto* (write soon), *saludé* (health), and *adios* (good-bye), they said. It was a pleasant sendoff and George Piegon said, "You'll probably never return, and yet you have us all worried about you."

I was last to board the plane. There were about a dozen passengers. I had a seat by myself and fastened my safety belt. It was warm inside the plane. The door closed, then the four engines kicked over. We taxied to the head of the runway and

595

turned about. The engines roared louder, and we were off. The runway seemed to slip away, and we were over the deep blue waters. The plane gained altitude; the hostess came by and said, "We will have dinner as soon as we level off."

At ten thousand feet, we had dinner of chicken, peas, carrots, potatoes, olives, soup, and coffee. We were flying over the Caribbean Sea. We made our first landing at Curacao, a Dutch possession. We had a twenty-minute period to stretch our legs while the plane gassed up. We had to pass through gates at the terminal while the customs called off our names.

We took off again; after several hours of flying, we landed at Cuidad Trujillo in the Dominican Republic. We had a twenty-minute rest period, then took to the sky again. We had supper at ten thousand feet. We had veal cutlets, peas, potatoes, carrots, pickles, soup, coffee. We had good flying weather, and there was hardly a bump. We had two stewardesses. Occasionally they would sit and keep us company.

In the evening I joined the stewardesses. They had the last two seats. It was much cooler there. Darkness had fallen and the twinkling stars could be seen. They were lonesome for company. They said they got very tired of flying. It was very monotonous. One of the girls knew the consul at Belém and promised to give him my regards. They told me how they let loose one night at a party that he gave and embarrassed him.

We came down to land in Cuba. We were thirty miles from Havana. We had another twenty- minute break. I had a yearning to visit that gay city, but I had a mere twenty dollars in my pocket. We took to the air again, and a half hour later, we were circling over Miami. Miami was all lit up, and it looked so big and beautiful. From the sky it looked like the biggest city in the world. To me it seemed like I was coming back to civilization and leaving a rough, backwoods country behind me. The long, bright landing lights went on, the landing gear went down, we banked to the left, the flaps went down, the plane slowed, and we hit the runway with hardly a jar. The trip took eight and one half hours. We pulled up to the station.

The stewardess made an announcement. "We will all go together. We have to pass health inspection first." The captain, co-pilot, and the stewardesses led the way. We, the passengers, trooped after them. We entered a room at the terminal and were asked to be seated. A nurse took our temperatures. None were sick. We entered another room and customs checked our bags; then we were at liberty to go to the streets.

I had carried some rum through the customs for the stewardess. Seemed like they were going to have a party. For this favor the captain offered me a ride into town. His wife was waiting for him in a brand new, flashy '48 station wagon. It was a beauty. The wife was a beauty also, a delicious blond. They asked what it felt like to be back in the States after two years. I said, "It feels like I just got out of the bush." They told me to be careful of the stewardesses, they were wolves, but then after two years, I should be the one.

Everywhere were bright lights, new cars, smooth roads, and bobby soxers. They left me out at the Y.M.C.A. They said I'd easily get a room. They knew about my hitchhiking, and the captain's wife called to me, "Don't forget to write a book." There were no vacancies at the "Y." They wouldn't even let me check my pack momentarily while I looked for a hotel. I then checked it at a bus station across the street.

I strolled about the bright, illuminated streets. It felt good to be back in the U.S. There were small crowds, all wearing smart or tricky summer clothes. I passed many window displays and traffic lights. After two dozen blocks, I returned to the bus station, had a milkshake, and a real hamburger.

I stopped in at some clubs. What surprised me was the large number of women at the bars. Many of them were drunk and mean and wore dresses that showed too much neckline and legs. Miami had never been like this before. I then went to the better clubs along Biscayne Boulevard. There I paid fifty cents for a Coke, and the girls at the bar or at the tables were, without a doubt, "Blue Mooners." I had seen the likes of them in Panama to recognize them. There were plenty of females, but very few males. I couldn't believe it, in this day of prosperity, to find women like that in the States.

I soon departed myself. Heavy rains fell outside. A few days previous, they had had a hurricane. The newspapers gave it a lot of publicity. I read about it in Venezuela. The people of Miami said it was nothing at all.

About two in the morning, I went to the bus station, changed my clothes, took my pack, and hit the road. I followed U.S. No. 1 homeward. The rain had stopped, and I caught a city bus to the end of the line. Then I started walking again. I imagined I was still in the tropics because I started to sweat at once.

It was a dark morning. I became tired and stopped under the arc of a street light so that cars going by could see me. Many went by, but none stopped. Then a police prowl car came and stopped. One of them asked for my identification. I showed him my passport and said that I just got in from South America. He checked it and said, "You really have been around, haven't you?" Then he said I should move along for about a mile. There I'd find a truck restaurant open and be able to catch a ride easier. I moved on. I walked several hours. I was well out in the country and saw no sign of an open restaurant. Many cars passed me by; then a fellow stopped and gave me a lift for thirty odd miles.

We parted on a lonely country cross road. Dawn was beginning to crackle. Ten the bright, smiling sun came out. It was a long, black, lonesome road ahead of me. More and more cars came with the dawn and swiftly passed me by. A good three hours later, a powerful yellow car stopped for me.

A beautiful blond girl was behind the wheel. She gave me a pleasant Good Morning smile. She wore a very light sunsuit. The shoulder straps hung low and as we rode along, the wind blew her skirt well above her knees. She had a small child, aged two years, sitting beside her. She was cute also. She had blond curly hair and pink cheeks.

For a while the trip was nice. It was a hot morning, and we became thirsty. We stopped in at a drive-in for some beer and lunch. Coming out of the diner, her dress unbuttoned behind and I helpfully buttoned her up. She laughed and said, "What's the difference? Nobody knows; you could be my husband."

We got into the car and drove on. The beer must have affected her. She told me about breaking up with her husband, who was nineteen years her senior, the night before. They just couldn't get along together; they had a quarrel. She packed all her clothes into the car and was headed for Jacksonville to see her father. Jacksonville was three hundred miles farther north along my route.

While she talked, she stepped on the gas, and before long we were doing eighty miles an hour. Now to one who had returned from a land where everything moved so damn slow and then to step into a car doing 80, it's enough to scare anybody. Not only that but she was visibly emotionally upset and had swelling tears in her eyes.

I also noticed that the oil pressure gauge registered low at this high speed. I told her to stop at the next station to get some oil. She listened and stopped at the next station. I was happy that I got her to stop. The oil gauge registered empty. The car took four quarts of oil.

The girl's name was Janice. When the car was ready to go I told her, "Janice, I know you're feeling bad, but your driving scares me and you have that child to worry about and unless I drive from now on, I'll just get out and walk."

"Do I scare you?" she asked.

"Yes," I said. Then without another word she moved from behind the wheel and I took over. I was doing about forty-five and getting the feel of the car. I had been driving about ten minutes when suddenly the car started pulling to one side. It could only mean one thing, a flat tire. I slowed down fast and pulled off the road. We didn't say anything but we both realized what might have happened at 80 miles an hour.

Would a hitchhiker leave a damsel in distress? Not me. I jacked the car up and pulled the wheel off. The spare was flat also. We had to flag a car to take one of the tires to a gas station to have it fixed. My lady had no pump, no repairs. She watched the car and child while I went to get it fixed. When I returned she was frustrated and undecided whether to continue to Jacksonville or return to Miami. I encouraged her to return to Miami, it was closer. The tires were in bad shape and she just had a silly argument with her husband. I would lose a 200 mile lift to Jacksonville, but I didn't care. She seemed relieved and promised to drive slowly on her return.

I had lunch at a roadside restaurant. It seemed very strange to hear waitresses ask for my order in English. I walked along the road all day. It hurt my feelings to see cars with Pennsylvania, New York, and New Jersey license plates pass me by. There were so many of them, and none would stop. There were one or two hitchhikers, but not a sign of a service man. Three years ago the highway had been full of them.

I am told motorists are afraid to pick up people because of crooks and murderers, but I draw another conclusion. It was not fear so much as a sense of superiority, selfishness, and desire not to be bothered. In Central or South America, cars or trucks never pass a disabled car and seldom pass a stranded individual along the road. Yet in Latin America, there is more danger of thieves and cutthroat bandits.

It was near sundown when I gave up hope of catching a ride. I then stopped a Greyhound bus and rode it to Jacksonville. I slept a little on it, and early morning found me walking through the large empty streets of Jacksonville. I used to think of it as a dirty city, but this morning it looked clean, neat and orderly.

Rides continued, slow, few and for short distances. I had to take a bus every so often to put miles behind me. Then out of Wilmington, North Carolina, a '48 Cadillac stopped for me. This ride took me all the way through Richmond, Virginia, Washington, D.C., Baltimore, Maryland, to Harrisburg, Pennsylvania. The driver was a few years older than I. He was a chauffeur for some millionaire in Miami. We stopped for dinner occasionally and to clean up at gas stations.

By the time we reached Harrisburg, I was in pain. My stomach was taking a beating from the change in food, climate, traveling, and a lack of rest. I hadn't slept but a few hours since I had left Venezuela four days ago.

The Cadillac had a phone, and we were able to call up my dear friend Jack Thornsley on it. He was very surprised to hear from me and agreed to meet me at the railroad station. Here I parted with my friend, and soon Jack came about in a '46 Ford. It was cold in Harrisburg, and I had to stay indoors. Jack had a big grin on his face. "Joe, you old son of a gun. How you doing?" he asked. We then drove to his home. His folks were just as glad to see me. We had dinner together, and they insisted I stay overnight and rest. They were very interested in where I'd been. It had been three years since I last saw the Thornsleys. They hadn't changed much. I had stayed at their home when I had worked in Harrisburg.

Jack is the same age as I and was due to be married in three weeks. He insisted that I be present.

I slept very well and next day after a huge breakfast, I said "so long" to Mom and Pop Thornsley, and Jack drove me to the railroad station. I decided to spend my last few dollars for train fare and ride home in style. We had a fifteen-minute wait, and Jack said, "Why don't you come back and try to get a job here?" "Maybe I will," I said cheerfully.

The prices on trains had really gone up, and soon I saw why. The interior was ultra-modern, and the engines were electrically driven and streamlined.

I enjoyed the scenery. The rolling hills in Pennsylvania are always beautiful. The trees were in full autumn glory. For company I had a young beauty, but she had her hands full; she had a baby boy.

I had placed my ticket inside my camera as an ideal place to hold it. Coming around the famous horseshoe curve at Altoona, I left my seat and opened the platform door to take a picture of it. I opened the camera case, and my ticket blew away. I didn't get the picture either. The conductor came along a minute later and asked for my ticket. I explained what had happened. "Sorry," he said, "$1.30 please." He charged me fare only from Altoona to Johnstown.

Coming into Johnstown, I saw the dirty, coal-black houses in the valley and on the hillsides. Then I said to myself, "No, no, no, this can't be it." But it was. It was Johnstown, Pennsylvania, my hometown.

How dirty it looked after coming from clean, white cities like Lima, Buenos Aires, Montevideo, Rio de Janeiro, Miami, etc. I was almost late getting off the train due to the shock.

I walked through the station to the street. Everyone seemed to be in dark, grimy work clothes and open collars. The first person I met that I knew was a lad called Tony. From him I received a strange hello. He did not even smile when we shook hands. He

601

looked white, thin, and tired. We had been schoolmates, he was always energetic and happy. Now there was a big change in him. The last time I saw him had been four years ago. Now he was a married man, had two children, and a goat farm, twenty miles out of Johnstown. I guess he had a lot of responsibilities. But whatever made him become a farmer, I don't know.

His younger brother, Alex, was with him, aged twenty and married also. The last time I had seen him he was just a little kid playing with marbles.

So we parted and I took a taxi home. Only my neighbor Rosie saw me coming. She let out a shout, "Joey." I went on to the house and knocked on the door. Dad opened it. He was surprised and cried "Joey." We embraced. We both had happy tears in our eyes. He asked how I was. "Fine," I said. "How are you?" I asked. "Okay," he said.

Then Bill, Alex, and Ann were home. How Bill and Alex had changed. Both were tall. Alex was lanky, always happy, and looked like Abe Lincoln. Bill was quiet, heavy-set, and strong. I called him "Little Jughead." Ann had turned into a real beauty. She looked a lot like my elder sister, Helen, who was married and lived a few blocks away.

Alex and Bill ran upstairs to tell Mom that I was home. She refused to come down. She thought they were playing pranks. I then went upstairs and found her making small rugs. She looked up in surprise. Then I kissed her. She said in Czech, "*O ti chudacu, Chudacu*" (rascal, rascal). Soon she had supper going and I was telling them stories.

Later I visited Jack and Helen. They were very happy to see me. I embraced Helen and kissed her. Jack and I shook hands; then he brought the "bottle" out.

It did my heart good. I wasn't forgotten by my friends. All my neighbors and friends brought me beer and whiskey one after another. They chauffeured me here and there. Little school kids asked me questions in Spanish.

After a few days, the generosity and friendship seemed to turn this dark, grimy, dirty city into a lighthearted city of paradise from which I have no desire to leave.